EXPERIENCING

MIS

FOURTH CANADIAN EDITION

DAVID M. KROENKE
University of Washington

ANDREW GEMINO
Simon Fraser University

PETER TINGLING
Simon Fraser University

PEARSON

Toronto

Editor-in-Chief: Claudine O'Donnell
Acquisitions Editor: Carolin Sweig
Marketing Manager: Jessica Saso
Program Manager: Karen Townsend
Project Manager: Jessica Hellen
Developmental Editor: Rebecca Ryoji
Media Editor: Kristina Joie
Media Producer: Kelli Cadet
Production Services: Cenveo® Publisher Services
Permissions Project Manager: Joanne Tang
Photo Permissions Research: Rebecca Ryoji and Caroline Mariya Vincent, PMG
Text Permissions Research: James Fortney, PMG
Interior and Cover Designer: Anthony Leung
Cover Image: Fotolia

Library and Archives Canada Cataloguing in Publication

Kroenke, David M., 1948-, author
    Experiencing MIS / David M. Kroenke, Andrew Gemino, Peter Tingling.—Fourth Canadian edition.

Includes index.
ISBN 978-0-13-376887-9 (pbk.)

    1. Management information systems—Textbooks. 2. Business—Data processing—Textbooks. I. Gemino, Andrew C. (Andrew Carlo), 1962-, author II. Tingling, Peter M. (Peter Maxwell), 1960-, author III. Title.

T58.6.K767 2015   658.4'038011   C2014-904910-2

ISBN 978-0-13-376887-9

To C.J., Carter, and Charlotte. DK

This book is dedicated to my wife Kathy, my children Christina and Matthew, and all of the students, teachers, reviewers, and colleagues who helped us make a better book. AG

This book is dedicated to those who continue to teach me great things. My partner, Susanne, our children, my parents, colleagues, and, of course, my students, who never fail to astound and inspire me. PT

About the Authors

David Kroenke

David Kroenke has many years of teaching experience at Colorado State University, Seattle University, and the University of Washington. He has led dozens of seminars to college professors on the teaching of information systems and technology; in 1991, the International Association of Information Systems named him Computer Educator of the Year.

David worked for the U.S. Air Force and Boeing Computer Services. He was a principal in the startup of three companies. He also was vice-president of product marketing and development for the Microrim Corporation and was chief of technologies for the database division of Wall Data, Inc. He is the father of the semantic object data model. David's consulting clients have included IBM, Microsoft, and Computer Sciences Corporations, as well as numerous smaller companies. Recently, David has focused on using information systems for teaching collaboration.

His text *Database Processing* was first published in 1977 and was released in its twelfth edition in 2011. He has published many other textbooks, including *Database Concepts*, fifth edition (2011), and *Using MIS*, fourth edition (2011). David lives in Seattle. He is married and has two children and three grandchildren. He enjoys woodworking, making both furniture and small sailboats.

Andrew Gemino

Andrew Gemino has taught at Simon Fraser University (SFU) for over 15 years. He is an accomplished teacher who received the SFU Teaching Excellence Award, the TD Canada Trust Distinguished Teaching Award with the Beedie School of Business, and the MBA Teaching Excellence Award at the University of British Columbia.

Andrew is a past President of the Special Interest Group on Systems Analysis and Design in the Association of Information Systems. He teaches and consults in IT project management and his research is featured at www.PMPerspectives.org. He co-founded a software company that specialized in professional sports scouting and scheduling/payroll systems for sports and entertainment companies.

Andrew's research, has been funded through grants from the National Sciences and Engineering Research Council (NSERC) and the Social Sciences and Humanities Research Council (SSHRC). His work has been published in *Communications of the ACM, Journal of MIS, European Journal of IS, Data and Knowledge Engineering, Requirements Engineering,* and *Data Mining and Knowledge Discovery.* He lives in Coquitlam, B.C., with his wife and two children.

Peter Tingling

Peter Tingling has worked in information-intensive industries for more than 30 years. He has held senior line and staff positions at a variety of top-tier firms, and has provided consultations to government, startup, and Fortune 500 companies across North America.

Peter's research interest is in decision process and analysis and his work has involved organizations that run the range from banks to professional sports organizations. Peter's research has been published in academic and practitioner journals and has often been referenced in the public media.

Joining academia because he was interested in "why," Peter considers himself an eclectic reader, although he prefers biographies. His favourite authors are Feynman, Halberstam, Lewis, and Ferguson. Peter is the founder and chief executive officer of Octothorpe Software Corporation and now lives in Vancouver with his wife and four children.

Letter to Students

Dear Student:

You have chosen to begin a career as a business professional by majoring in a business discipline. If your experience is anything like that of the authors of this Canadian edition, you will not regret your choice. Working in business leads to fulfilling, enjoyable experiences and relationships with interesting, quality people.

The overall purpose of this book is to help you prepare for success in your business career, and in today's business environment success will most likely come through your ability to innovate. Canadian businesses face increasing pressure to improve the effectiveness and efficiency with which products and services are delivered to global customers. This innovation will require a workforce with new skills and an improved understanding of the role of information systems in business. In writing the book, we kept in mind three goals:

1. To explain the impact of information systems on organizational issues and how you can apply it address problems and make better decisions in business
2. To show you how to increase your unique value (and marketability) in business by applying knowledge of information systems
3. To describe, in the context of management information systems (MIS), how you can become a better business professional

Note that the emphasis is on you. It is up to you to prepare yourself. No particular book, no course, no professor, no TA can do it for you. However, many people have worked hard to structure this book, so you can maximize the benefit from your study time.

To help you achieve your goals, we have updated the content to ensure that it is as current as possible. Beyond the new sections added to the third edition (Web 2.0, Social Media, Smartphones, etc.), we have updated specific technologies such as cloud computing, social trends such as showrooming, and the business environment such as Blackberry.

We have made minor updates to the opening cases for each chapter and the four rich running cases that run through each group of three chapters. In addition, at the end of every third chapter, there are questions to promote analysis of the running case and collaborative questions that can be used to solidify your understanding of the running case and the material presented in each chapter.

We have retained the five Application Extensions, one for database design and one each on MS Excel, MS Access, MS Visio, and MS Project. We believe that these application extensions provide some basic skills for personal productivity software that will be important for future business professionals. The introduction that each of these application extensions provides is intended to make you aware of the capabilities of each application and enable you to explore the further power these applications offer.

In addition to content changes, the book contains five unique features that provide interesting opportunities for learning. First, we have organized the material in every chapter around a set of questions. Use these questions to manage your study time. Read until you can answer the questions.

Second, Collaborative Exercises have been included at the end of every chapter. These new assignments are designed to be accomplished in groups and are meant to help to build your teamwork skills and provide a larger opportunity for developing your interpersonal communication skills. The abilities to communicate and work in a team are critical skills for business professionals.

Third, short MIS in Use cases are included in each chapter, and we have added a number of new cases to this edition. These cases provide real-life examples of how organizations deal with information systems issues. You will also find a Case Study near the end of each chapter for additional insight.

Fourth, we have included a profile of a young and successful business student who has gone on to a professional career in information systems at the beginning of each part. These profiles demonstrate how important knowledge of information systems can be in developing your own career.

Finally, the two-page What Do YOU Think? feature found at the end of each chapter provides stimulating ideas for class discussion and individual thinking. The exercises often include ethical issues and ask you to develop opinions about important issues in information systems. If possible, discuss the questions in these guides with other people. Such discussions will give you a chance to develop your own opinions about important topics in information systems.

Like all worthwhile endeavours, this course takes work. That is just the way it is. No sustainable competitive advantage can ever result from something that is quickly and easily learned and no one can succeed in business without sustained focus, attention, desire, effort, and hard work. It will not always be easy, and it will not always be fun. On the other hand, you will learn concepts, skills, and behaviours that will serve you well throughout your business career.

We wish you, as an emerging business professional, the very best success!

Sincerely,

David Kroenke
Seattle, Washington

Andrew Gemino
Peter Tingling
Vancouver, British Columbia

Brief Contents

Contents

Preface

We undertook the development of the fourth Canadian edition of *Experiencing MIS* because we believe that the skills inherent in the study of information systems are important to the innovation and productivity of every Canadian industry. We are not alone in this belief. The Canadian Coalition for Tomorrow's ICT Skills (www.ccict.ca), a collection of companies and educational institutions, has recognized the growing innovation gap and the challenge of developing the skills for tomorrow's workplace in students today. The foundations for these skills are firmly rooted in studies of both information technology and business. We view this course as a gateway to these topics for many students. Our hope in developing this edition is to interest students in furthering their knowledge in the combined study of business and technology.

In the coming years, technologies will radically change how people relate to one another. Organizations will become more virtual, and people will work with other people they may never meet face to face. Many jobs that are here today will be eliminated, and new jobs will take their place. All of this change will be driven by people who experience MIS. So, start your experience today!

Key Updates to This Edition

We have revised this edition of *Experiencing MIS* to include the latest innovations in the field of information systems. We have also added unique new features and application information to help students interact with and apply the material. Key updates to the fourth Canadian edition include the following:

- New and updated material on Database Design
- New thorough coverage on how to use Microsoft Access 2013
- New useful guide covering an Introduction to Microsoft Excel 2013
- New discussion regarding *Big Data* and the controversies about this new term
- Expanded coverage of ereaders and tablets and their influence on information sharing
- Expanded and up-to-date discussion on cloud computing

In addition, for those instructors looking for a more detailed discussion of enterprise systems, we have coordinated the material in this third Canadian edition to fit neatly with Chapters 7 and 8 from the book *Processes, Systems and Information: An Introduction to MIS.* These additional resources focus on procurement (Chapter 7) and sales (Chapter 8) as detailed in SAP enterprise application. These chapters are available on the MyMISLab platform.

The features in this book are designed to encourage students to take an active role in developing their own understanding of MIS and how it relates to their business career. We believe that when we experience MIS from our own personal perspective, we realize the important role that information systems play in our lives now and in our future careers.

Features

Experiencing MIS is the theme of this book and student engagement is the ultimate objective. We have designed the book to engage students through a variety of features and to provide opportunities for students to ground their knowledge in practical exercises and real-life examples.

Student Profiles

Profiles of young, successful students from across Canada that illustrate why they believe that having knowledge of MIS is important and how they have applied it toward their everyday and longer-term goals open each part.

Running Cases

The four parts in the book each begin with a Running Case Introduction to help introduce that section. Following this Running Case Introduction, the chapter opens with a Running Case providing rich examples that run through each group of three chapters. The running cases provide an example that can be used in class and that students can relate to. Each part ends with a Running Case Assignment to promote analysis and collaborative questions that can be used to solidify understanding of the running case and the material presented in each chapter.

Chapter Study Questions

We made a choice to organize all of our content around questions. Each chapter typically focuses on seven or eight questions that guide students through the content. Using questions helps engage students in a search for relevant knowledge and challenges students to think about the material rather than memorize sections and lists.

Active Review

The chapter study questions are supported by Active Review questions near the end of each chapter. These questions are more detailed and offer an opportunity for students to see how much they have learned. If students are unable to answer the Active Review questions, they can turn back and review the appropriate section earlier in the chapter. This section reinforces learning and provides feedback to students so they can better target their study.

MIS in Use and Case Studies

Each chapter includes an MIS in Use mini-case that provides a real-life example of the questions discussed in the chapter. Each MIS in Use mini-case also comes with a set of questions that can be used in the lecture or as hand-in assignments. The mini-cases and their questions provide an additional opportunity to highlight important issues and create student engagement with the material. A Case Study at the end of each chapter provides additional real-world examples. We have worked to provide a wide range of case studies so that students are aware of the differences in MIS across organizations.

Using Your Knowledge

At the end of each chapter, we have included a number of Using Your Knowledge questions. These questions provide opportunities for written assignments or discussion questions that often integrate the various issues raised in the chapter. The Using Your Knowledge questions provide another mechanism for engaging students in developing their own ideas about what MIS means to them.

What Do YOU Think?

These exercises are a unique feature of *Experiencing MIS* because they are designed to encourage students to develop their personal perspectives about issues in MIS. Several of the exercises (Chapters 3, 8, 9, and 10) focus on ethical issues, but a variety of issues is covered. These exercises can be used in class for discussion or outside the classroom as personal assignments. The answers to these exercises are not hard and fast—they require students to develop their own opinions. This forging of opinions creates further engagement with the material. We encourage instructors to find ways to incorporate these exercises in their classes so that students can experience MIS in a personal way.

Collaborative Exercises

Students often comment that they learn from group experiences. The Collaborative Exercises at the end of each chapter provide opportunities for students to interact and discuss topics related to chapter content. These assignments allow students to engage with the material in a group format designed to stimulate discussion and feedback that supports individual learning.

Application Extensions

We have included five Application Extensions that focus on practical introductory skills for MS Visio, MS Excel, Database Design, MS Access, and MS Project. The Application Extensions on MS Excel and MS Project reflect the personal productivity skills that are now expected of graduating students in any business career.

We believe that the key to creating an effective experience for students in this course is to provide opportunities for them to engage with the material and to develop their own personal perspective on MIS. The features provided in this book are designed to support this development, while providing a stimulating introduction to the world of MIS. We believe this book effectively presents information that students will need to be successful in their careers. We trust that this book demonstrates that the field of MIS remains as important today as it was in the past and that our success in developing students with knowledge of MIS will play a critical role in our future economic development.

Additional Chapters on SAP Enterprise Systems

Through Pearson Canada, we have the unique opportunity to coordinate the material in this fourth Canadian edition to fit neatly with Chapters 7 and 8 from the book *Processes, Systems, and Information: An Introduction to MIS* by Kroenke and McKinney. Instructors who would like to provide students with more in-depth knowledge of how SAP treats the procurement and sales processes are encouraged to consider these additional resources. We have adjusted Chapters 1 through 7 in the Canadian edition so that the definitions and business process approach provide a seamless transition to these additional resources. These additional chapters are available on MyMISLab.

Supplements

The fourth Canadian edition of *Experiencing MIS* is accompanied by a range of supplementary material available to both instructors and students.

Teaching Tools for Instructors

The following instructor supplements are available for downloading from a password-protected section of Pearson Canada's online catalogue (www.pearsoncanada.ca/highered). Navigate to your book's catalogue page to view a list of those supplements that are available. See your local sales representative for details and access.

Instructor's Resource Manual

This valuable resource features numerous teaching tools to help instructors make the most of the textbook in the classroom. Chapter objectives, chapter outlines, and answers to the questions are provided for each chapter.

Computerized Test Bank

Pearson's computerized test banks allow instructors to filter and select questions to create quizzes, tests or homework. Instructors can revise questions or add their own, and may be able to choose print or online options. These questions are also available in Microsoft Word format.

Test Item File

This test bank includes all the questions from the computerized test bank in Microsoft Word format.

PowerPoint® Presentations

These presentations combine lecture notes with images from the textbook. The lecture presentations for each chapter can be viewed electronically in the classroom or printed as black-and-white transparency masters.

Image Library

This library contains .gif or .jpg versions of figures from the textbook.

Learning Solutions Managers

Pearson's Learning Solutions Managers work with faculty and campus course designers to ensure that Pearson technology products, assessment tools, and online course materials are tailored to meet your specific needs. This highly qualified team is dedicated to helping schools take full advantage of a wide range of educational resources by assisting in the integration of a variety of instructional materials and media formats. Your local Pearson Canada sales representative can provide you with more details on this service program.

MyMISLab

MyMISLab for Kroenke/Gemino/Tingling's *Experiencing MIS*, Fourth Canadian Edition, is a state-of-the-art learning management system complete with diagnostic tests with customized study plans, student remediation, and media resources such as case studies, PowerPoints, simulations, videos, and an eText. MyMISLab is the most effective way to manage and deliver your course and help your students master the material.

MyMISLab delivers proven results in helping individual students succeed. It provides engaging experiences that personalize, stimulate, and measure learning for each student. And, it comes from a trusted partner with educational expertise and an eye on the future. MyMISLab can be used by itself or linked to any learning management system. To learn more about how MyMISLab combines proven learning applications with powerful assessment, visit www.pearsonmylabandmastering.com.

CourseSmart

CourseSmart for Instructors

CourseSmart goes beyond traditional expectations—providing instant, online access to the textbooks and course materials you need at a lower cost for students. And even as students save money, you can save time and hassle with a digital eTextbook that allows you to search for the most relevant content at the very moment you need it. Whether it is evaluating textbooks or creating lecture notes to help students with difficult concepts, CourseSmart can make life a little easier. See how when you visit www.coursesmart.com/instructors.

CourseSmart for Students

CourseSmart goes beyond traditional expectations—providing instant, online access to the textbooks and course materials you need at a significant savings over the printed book. With instant access from any computer and the ability to search your text, you will find the content you need quickly, no matter where you are. And with online tools, such as highlighting and note-taking, you can save time and study efficiently. See all the benefits at www.coursesmart.com/students.

Pearson Custom Library

For enrollments of at least 25 students, you can create your own textbook by choosing the chapters that best suit your own course needs. To begin building your custom text, visit www.pearsoncustomlibrary.com. You may also work with a dedicated Pearson Custom editor to create your ideal text—publishing your own original content or mixing and matching Pearson content. Contact your local Pearson Representative to get started.

Acknowledgments

We have many people to thank for their help in developing this textbook. Our first thanks go to David Kroenke, who sold us on his teaching approach when he visited Vancouver and gave us the material from which to develop this text. We would also like to acknowledge our colleagues at Simon Fraser University, and in particular Kamal Masri, for helping us develop our introductory MIS course. We would like to thank Zorana Svedic for her teaching and Canvas design and support. Of course, we recognize the input from the many students we have had the pleasure of teaching in our introductory courses. Their feedback played a big role in how the Canadian edition was developed and has evolved.

We would like to acknowledge the input from colleagues from other Canadian schools, who provided their comments and ideas while the book was being developed. These include Anita Beecroft, Ed Bosman, John Bryant, Richard Crothers, Nelson Eng, Debbie Gorval, David Horspool, Jai-Yeol Son, Peter Thesiger, Robert Wood, and Jock Wylie.

We express our appreciation to the following reviewers of the previous edition, whose comments on various chapters and aspects of the entire project helped us understand the needs of both instructors and students and improve the book.

Michael Khan, University of Toronto
Hang Lau, McGill University
Jennifer Percival, University of Ontario Institute of Technology
Jeff Ryan, Grant MacEwan College
Anteneh Ayanso, Brock University
Hossein Abolghasem, St. Francis Xavier University
Rose Minton, Southern Alberta Institute of Technology, Polytechnic
Raul Valverde, Concordia University
Hossam Ali-Hassan, Dalhousie University
Carlene Blackwood-Broan, Sheridan College
Elliott Currie, University of Guelph
Dale Foster, Memorial University
Brian Murray, University of Prince Edward Island
Nilesh Saraf, Simon Fraser University

Thanks to all of the talented and patient people at Pearson Canada who guided us through the process of revising this book. Our thanks go to Claudine O'Donnell, Editor-in-Chief; Carolin Sweig, Acquisitions Editor; Karen Townsend, Program Manager; Rebecca Ryoji, Freelance Developmental Editor; and Jessica Hellen, Project Manager. We would also like to say special thanks to Ewan French, who introduced us to Pearson and helped us meet other colleagues who teach the introductory MIS course.

Most importantly, we would like to thank our families for providing us with the love, patience, and time necessary to create this fourth Canadian edition.

Andrew Gemino
Peter Tingling

EXPERIENCING

MIS

PART 1

MIS and You

> " Great success is often realized only after you have walked through the bridge of risk and failure. "

In Claudia's Words

Shark fin soup is popularly served at wedding banquets for middle- to high-income Chinese families as a symbol of respect, status, and generosity. While holding to these values, Shark Truth changes the tradition by rebranding what is deemed "good" or "important" from our culture through our annual Happy Hearts Love Sharks wedding contest. Rather than eat sharks, we ask couples to pledge a Fin Free banquet for a chance to win a trip to swim with sharks. This simple change has diverted 22 000 bowls (and counting) of shark fin soup and saved the lives of 2200 sharks.

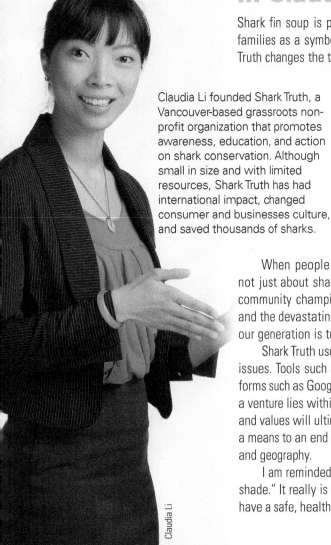

Claudia Li founded Shark Truth, a Vancouver-based grassroots non-profit organization that promotes awareness, education, and action on shark conservation. Although small in size and with limited resources, Shark Truth has had international impact, changed consumer and businesses culture, and saved thousands of sharks.

Whether starting a for-profit business, a nonprofit enterprise, or a social enterprise, entrepreneurs often face the same challenges: financial stability, finding the right people, and avoiding burn-out. Balancing perseverance and learning can be difficult. I often felt insecure about my skills, but I learned to ask for help by finding mentors and building a strong, diverse team.

When people ask me what Shark Truth does, I tell them we build community—it is not just about shark conservation. Our issue is shark finning, but our philosophy is to build community champions for long-term change. With species disappearing at alarming rates, and the devastating consequences of climate change and global inequality, the challenge for our generation is to empower leaders across all professions, ages, ethnicities, and genders.

Shark Truth uses social media to promote awareness and spread education on conservation issues. Tools such as Facebook and Twitter allow us to build a growing community, and platforms such as Google Apps enable us to virtually connect all our functions. Long-term success of a venture lies within its core values, which start with its people. Tools without the right people and values will ultimately fail. In spite (or because) of our limited budget, we use technology as a means to an end and connect with individuals and communities across cultures, generations, and geography.

I am reminded of the Chinese proverb: "One generation plants the trees; another gets the shade." It really is our responsibility to preserve these legacies so that future generations will have a safe, healthy planet.

Claudia Li

The effects of information systems have been so large and so widespread that it is difficult to imagine an industry or organization that has not been affected. Whether we consider the largest for-profit corporations, the smallest sole proprietorship business, any level of government, or nonprofit agencies, the accelerating rate of technology adoption has enabled changes that are difficult to believe. Entire industries, such as publishing and distribution, photography, music, and news, have either fallen or been radically restructured, and newer organizations, such as Google, AirBnB, Twitter, Pinterest, and Facebook, have displaced giants in relatively short periods.

With this in mind, we can say with some certainty that having a foundational understanding of management information systems (MIS) and the key concepts of information technology are essential not only for a career in business but also to be an informed and knowledgeable member of society. Regardless of whether you plan to concentrate in accounting, finance, marketing, human resources, or international business, and irrespective of whether your personal goal is to create significant wealth or make a positive impact on society (or perhaps both), the purpose of Part 1 of this textbook is to demonstrate why a basic understanding of MIS and technology are important to every professional today.

Running Case Introduction

At times, MIS can appear abstract and hard to understand. To help address this, we begin each section of the book with a case that runs for three chapters. We have also included a new feature, an integrative running case assignment, which is included at the end of every three chapters. The integrative case assignment helps tie together all the issues across the three chapters and provides a way to explore the issues raised in the chapters in more depth.

In developing the cases, we have selected situations that you are likely to be familiar with. We then use these concepts to encourage broader and deeper understanding of more complicated issues and ideas. Our first "running case" begins with Josie, a young student who has been asked by his grandparents to offer some advice about their coffee shop.

Started by Josie's grandfather in 1980, Café Italiano is located on Main Street and has had a small but steady following who want more than the traditional mass-market coffee. Josie grew up around Café Italiano, visiting his grandparents when he was younger and, as a teenager, working there during the summers and part time on weekends. He is familiar with almost all aspects of the business, including clean-up, serving customers, and roasting the shop's custom blend of flavours.

Café Italiano is being challenged by a franchise coffee shop that Josie's grandparents expect will soon open across the street. The case begins by considering how Josie can evaluate the effect of technology on the business and if there are opportunities that the family can consider. Josie has noticed that coffee shops have gotten much more sophisticated and that the business appears to be changing. More and more stores offer services such as internet access, have websites, and keep track of customers using computerized systems and social network likes. Last summer, while visiting a friend in another town, Josie was surprised to see a coffee shop on a few social networks. His friend had asked him if he wanted to like the shop on Facebook, sign up for the Twitter feed, and even if he wanted to check in on Foursquare.

This case will run throughout Part 1. Read more at the beginning of each chapter and then visit MyMISLab online to access the data files to complete the running case questions at the end of Part 1.

MyMISLab

1 Information Systems and You

Running Case: Café Italiano

Josie is quite familiar with Café Italiano. He has worked there for several years and helped out when his grandparents were on vacation. The café itself is set up in the European style with about half a dozen small tables and couches inside and four small tables outside. Most of the customers are regulars, who drop by in small groups to chat for 20 to 30 minutes. Café Italiano is aimed at the higher-quality coffee drinker who wants a coffee house experience rather than a quick cup. The café sells a wide variety of coffee and tea, and Josie's grandparents try to manage inventory carefully. The café also sells a variety of small snacks, such as biscotti, but has avoided donuts and other sweet treats. Besides his grandparents, the café has between six and eight employees (mainly students) and has very little technology aside from the grinding and espresso machines. The cash registers were new in 2012 and so are computer ready, but the café is not yet using all the features.

Getting ready for his weekly business class, Josie was thinking about the changes that the new coffee shop would bring. He knew that this situation would require careful consideration. Café Italiano may sell a good, but it also provides a service, a relaxing experience that could not be easily duplicated at home. He made a list of the things that Café Italiano *could* do, and then he wondered what things the café *ought to* do. Should the café start off small with a basic website, or was that even necessary? Should he register the domain "cafeitaliano.com" (or .ca) just in case? Did the café need to provide Wi-Fi access? Should he set up a page on Facebook and ask customers to like it? Should he start a Twitter feed?

Was Pinterest something that the café could use for marketing? His grandparents were supportive of making changes. What Josie needed was a strategy. He thought he should first estimate the benefits, costs, and effort required for each idea and then prioritize them. One thing for sure, having a plan would help him focus and increase the chances of success.

Sergey Nivens/Shutterstock

Study Questions

Q1 **What is an information system?**

Q2 **What is MIS?**

Q3 **How does an IS differ from IT?**

Q4 **How important are information systems to our economy?**

Q5 **How do successful business professionals use information systems?**

Q6 **What is the shape of things to come?**

Q7 **What is this course about?**

Go to MyMISLab to watch a video about what is an information system

Q1 What Is an Information System?

A *system* is a group of components that interact to achieve some purpose. As you might guess, an **information system (IS)** is a group of components that interact to produce information. However, while true, this definition raises some questions: Do all information systems involve technology, and what are the interacting components? As it turns out, these seemingly simple questions only remain simple if we have common or colloquial definitions for *information* and *technology*; for now, if we consider that most people think of technology as involving computers (at least when thinking about information systems and information technology) and consider information something that reduces uncertainty, then we can confidently say that not all information systems require computerization. For example, a public library organized with the Dewey Decimal System or a calendar posted outside a conference room that is used to organize bookings can both be considered information systems, even though they may not be computerized.

In this text, we will give much clearer definitions for *information* and provide a structure in which to discuss technology. But for now, if we accept the common definitions, we can then describe a computerized information system (which we will now simply call an *Information System*, since that is the focus of this course) as illustrated in Figure 1-1. In this figure, we show that all information systems, from the simplest (someone using a smartphone to find out when the next bus arrives) through to the most complicated (a high-technology Customer Relationship Management (CRM) system that uses algorithms and databases to predict customer behaviours), comprise a **five-component framework** of **computer hardware**, **software**, **data**, **procedures**, and **people**.

These five components are often linked together through networks that leverage the power of connectivity to tie software, hardware, and data together to make information more accessible and powerful. Social networks, such as Facebook and LinkedIn, and systems, such as Alibaba, Pinterest, and Groupon, use the internet to eliminate the effects of distance and to allow people to remain connected and interact in new ways.

You may already be familiar with the term *hardware.* Hardware has sometimes been used incorrectly to refer to all the tangible or physical aspects of a computer system. More correctly, hardware refers to the electronic components and associated gadgetry that constitute a computer system. CDs for example, do not technically qualify as hardware. *Software,* which has occasionally been used to refer to all the intangible or non-hardware components of a system, is nowadays more correctly used to refer only to programs (or **applications**) that run, or operate, on computer systems. That is how we use these terms throughout this book. *Data* are the basic building blocks of information, such as facts and observations. *Procedures* are the instructions or processes that you follow to achieve your desired objective; these can be formal and documented policies that are extensive and written down or less detailed, informal instructions. *People* are the actors who want to achieve a particular outcome by interacting with the system.

Let us look at what is hopefully a familiar example—the support system that your university or college uses to support active learning (perhaps even in this course), such as Moodle, Canvas, or Desire2Learn. Like all systems, it has all five components illustrated in Figure 1-1, and, like many, it makes extensive use of networking technology. The *hardware* of the system includes the tangible or physical devices used to access the system, such as personal computers or other devices (e.g., a tablet or smartphone). It is important to note that although most modern computer systems are designed to be used by multiple types of devices, there are still cases

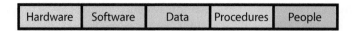

Figure 1-1

Five Components of an Information System

where specific types of hardware are required. The *software* of the system includes the stored set of instructions that run on your device, as well as the specific program that your university has licensed to provide the service. *Data* for the system may be stored on specialized computers called *servers*, which, through the power of networking, can be located almost anywhere in the world. Data for this system include such things as student identification numbers, enrollment dates, and answers to test questions. The system *procedures* are the steps that you follow to achieve your goal and include how you log on to, or access, the system and how you save or submit your work. You are one of the *people* in this system, but so are the IS professionals who built and maintain the site. An important point to learn in this course is that people are often the most critical part of an information system. Information systems are not just computers and data. Although we have not yet covered the communications aspects of modern information systems, in many cases, not only must systems be available to thousands, if not millions, of people at all hours of the day, but also they may use varying devices and be located in different places. Tying them all together is a network infrastructure.

Q2 What Is MIS?

Management information systems, or **MIS**, comprise the development and use of information systems that help organizations achieve their goals and objectives. The definition of MIS has three key elements: *development and use, information systems,* and *goals and objectives.* We have just discussed information systems. Now, let us consider development and use, followed by goals and objectives.

Development and Use of Information Systems

Information systems do not magically appear. Instead, they are designed and created by business analysts and systems designers at the request of senior managers or entrepreneurs in order to solve a particular problem or meet a perceived need. With this in mind, you might be thinking, "Wait a minute. I am a finance (or accounting, or marketing) major, not an information systems major. I do not need to know how to put together information systems" or (as we have been told by students in our classes), "I know what I want, I can get my staff to do it."

This could be a sign that you are headed for trouble. Consider, for example, that you are driving to work and you hear a strange noise from your car or you remember that it is due for some maintenance work. Imagine how an unscrupulous or perhaps mistaken person could talk you into a major engine repair, even if all you needed was air in your tires or an oil change. Think about how knowing even just a little about the basic operation of the car would enable you to have a much more insightful discussion with your mechanic, get better performance, and avoid being overcharged. If you really know nothing, then you are like a lamb headed for fleecing. Throughout your career, in whatever field you choose, you will need new information systems. To have an information system that meets your needs, you need to take an *active role* in that system's development. Without active involvement on your part, only good luck can enable the new system to meet your needs.

Throughout this book we will discuss your role in acquiring information systems. In addition, Chapter 10 is specifically focused on this important topic. As you

👁 Watch

Go to MyMISLab to watch a video about what is MIS?

read this text and think about information systems, you will learn how to ask critical questions, such as "Where did that information come from?" "How was that system constructed?" and "What roles did the actual people who will use it play in its development?" Important consequences depend on your answers so, if you start asking these questions now, you will be better prepared to answer them as you take your place in society.

In addition to helping choose and implement information systems, you will have important roles to play in the *use* of information systems. Of course, you will need to learn how to employ the system to accomplish your goals. But you will also have other important functions. For example, when using corporate information systems, you may be responsible for protecting the security of the system and its data; in managing your own computer and system usage, you may need to back up data to protect yourself from losing important information. When the system fails (and most do at some point), you will have tasks to perform while the system is down, as well as to help restore the system quickly and correctly.

Achieving Business Goals and Objectives

The last part of the definition of MIS is that information systems exist to help organizations achieve their *goals and objectives.* This statement has many important implications. First, because all businesses are organizations but not all organizations are businesses, information systems are found in almost every type of enterprise, social,

MIS in Use

Social Media: Changing the Relationship between Customers and Business

Social media connect people, and when people connect, they talk, share, and let friends know what they think about the world. When instant messaging (IM), web logs (blogs), wikis, video logs (Vlogs), podcasts, and social networking (SN) sites first became popular, many business organizations responded by simply ignoring them. From a pure accounting perspective, many SN sites did not, and may never, make positive cash flows; as a result, it seemed that there were few good business reasons to consider using social media. Some organizations, therefore, allowed only limited access to IM and SN sites because they did not want their employees wasting time on these sites while at work. Some organizations even created policies that restrained employees from responding to blogs about the company.

It was not too long before companies learned that ignoring social media could be bad for business. For example, when musician Dave Carroll discovered that his guitar was damaged on a United Airlines flight, he responded by writing a protest song "United Breaks Guitars" and posted it to YouTube and iTunes where it became an immediate hit and public relations embarrassment for the airline. United Airlines, of course, is not alone. Governments and large organizations have had to learn to deal with the influence that connected individuals can bring to bear on issues such as Kony 2012 or the Arab Spring.

Some Examples of Using Social Media

As social media mature, organizations are formulating strategies that incorporate blogs, wikis, and SN sites

and nonprofit organization, as well as governments of all levels. Indeed, we believe it is easier to find an organization without a marketing system than to find one without an information system. (Consider, for example, the penal system. Although prisons do not generally run advertising campaigns, they still have computerized systems for keeping track of inmates.) More importantly, you are probably aware that organizations themselves do not *do* anything. Although corporations are legally considered to have many of the characteristics of humans, they are not truly living beings and, thus, need people to think and act on their behalf. It is the people within an organization or business who sell, buy, design, produce, finance, market, account, and manage. Information systems exist to help organizational actors achieve the goals and objectives of that organization.

In most cases, information systems are not developed for the sheer joy of exploring technology. They are not created to make the company more modern or so the company can claim to be "new-economy." They are not created because the information systems department thinks they need to be created or because an executive thinks the company is "falling behind the technology curve."

This may seem so obvious that you wonder why we mention it, but every day organizations acquire and develop information systems for the wrong reasons. Right now, somewhere in the world, a company is creating a website simply because they think "every other business has one," rather than asking important questions such as "What is the purpose of the website?" "What is it going to do for us?" or "Are the costs of the website sufficiently offset by the benefits?"

into their business practices. For example, SCENE cards offered by Scotiabank and Cineplex have been used by Facebook (www.facebook.com/SCENE) to provide special offers and events that support the use of the cards. Another example is Molson in the Community (http://blog.molson.com/community), which provides a place for staff to share the work they do on behalf of Molson Canada in communities across the country. The site contains blogs and Vlogs about the staff's volunteer work. The Big Wild (www.thebigwild.org) was founded by the Canadian Parks and Wilderness Society (CPAWS) and Mountain Equipment Co-op to allow people to share pictures and videos of wild spaces and to connect with others who are interested in preserving these spaces.

What About Small Business?

The examples above are all large organizations, but perhaps the most exciting thing about social media has been its impact on small businesses. Mabel's Labels, a company based in Hamilton, Ontario, is a great example of how a small company can effectively use social media. Mabel's Labels has a blog called The Mabelhood (www.blog.mabel.ca), a podcast series on parenting, a Facebook fan page, a Twitter account (mabelhood),

a photostream on Flickr, and a YouTube account. All these social media channels help Mabel's Labels connect with customers and increase the size of the network familiar with their products. Social media are changing the way small businesses connect with their customers, and this is a message that businesses everywhere are listening to.

Questions

1. **Are the social media sites that Mabel's Labels uses information systems?**

2. **What are the benefits and costs of Mabel's Labels' participation in various social media sites?**

3. **Can larger companies do the same social media marketing and promotion that Mabel's Labels does? Do small businesses have an advantage in social media over larger organizations? Justify your answers.**

4. **What risks does Mabel's Labels face in its social networking strategy? That is, what are the downsides of using social media for small businesses?**

5. **Not all social media sites make money or make a direct and measurable financial contribution to organizations' bottom lines. Will this always be the case, and how will this fact affect management in planning social media initiatives?**

Even more seriously, somewhere right now, a business manager has been convinced by a technology vendor's sales team or by an article in a business magazine that his or her company must upgrade to the latest, greatest high-tech gadget or application. This manager is attempting to convince his or her manager that this expensive upgrade is a good idea. We hope that someone, somewhere, in the company (perhaps you) is asking questions, such as "What business goal or objective will be served by the investment in the gadget? Do we really need it, and does it add value for our customers?"

Throughout this book, we will consider many different information system types and underlying technologies. We will show the benefits of those systems and technologies, and we will illustrate successful implementations of each. The "MIS in Use" cases provided throughout the book discuss information systems in real-world organizations. As a future business professional and as a member of society, you need to learn to look at information systems and technologies only through the lens of *organizational need*. Learn to ask, "All this technology may be great in and of itself, but what will it do for us? What will it do for our business and our particular goals? Is it worth the investment?"

Again, MIS is the development and use of information systems that help organizations achieve their goals and objectives. Already you should be realizing that there is much more to this course than buying a tablet, writing a program, downloading an application for your smartphone, or working with a spreadsheet.

Q3 How Does an IS Differ from IT?

Information technology and *information system* are two closely related terms, and although they are often used interchangeably, they are different. **Information technology (IT)** refers to methods, inventions, standards, and products. As the term implies, IT refers to raw technology, and it concerns only the hardware, software, and data components of an information system and how these are networked together. In contrast, information system (IS) refers to a system of hardware, software, data, procedures, and people who produce information.

IT, by itself, will not help an organization achieve its goals and objectives. It is only when IT is embedded into an IS—that is, only when the technology within the hardware, software, and data is combined with the people and procedure components—that IT becomes useful.

Think about this from the standpoint of your college or university's IS. Do you care that the university network uses the latest, greatest technology to send messages or that the website uses the latest, fastest hardware to show you available classes? Probably not. Likely, it is only when people at the university (including you) use procedures to do something—to enroll in a class, for example—that IT becomes useful to you.

Consider Café Italiano and Josie's objective to increase profitability. He will use IT, but that is not his primary interest. His goal is to combine the hardware, software, data, and procedures with people to grow the business and keep it profitable. The people who will use the systems—customers, employees, suppliers, and his grandparents—are the most important part of the system for users like Josie.

So, the real difference between IT and IS is that IS includes people. And it turns out that if you include people and the way that they work in how you think about IS, it makes a *big* difference in how you design and implement systems. Successful business people understand this crucial difference between IT and IS, and they take advantage of it, as we show in this chapter.

Q4 How Important Are Information Systems to Our Economy?

Information systems are an increasingly important part of the Canadian economy. Industry Canada[1] is the federal government agency responsible for categorizing sectors and collecting information about them. The sector most closely related to the use of information systems in Canada is the **Information and Communications Technology (ICT) sector**.[2] This sector is special because it provides products and services that other industries, such as retail, manufacturing, insurance, and banking, rely on to get their work done. For many people, the ICT sector is a "hidden" industry. Would it surprise you to know that the ICT sector is nearly 3 percent of Canadian workers and generates $155 billion in revenue? The ICT sector includes companies involved in software and computer services, cable and other program distributors, telecommunication services, ICT manufacturing, and ICT wholesaling. Figure 1-2 shows the companies by ICT subsector and employee size.

In 2011, the Canadian ICT sector included over 33 300 companies. Most of these companies—more than 98 percent—had fewer than 100 employees. In 2011, only 75 companies in the ICT sector had more than 500 employees.[3]

In 2011, the ICT sector added $67.2 billion to the Canadian GDP, up 3.2 percent from 2010 (compared to a 2.6 percent increase in the rest of the economy). On average, annual growth in this sector has been 1.6 percent since 2007, a growth rate that is almost twice as high as the overall economy (0.9 percent). ICT is also the largest performer of research and development (R&D) in Canada, accounting for 30.6 percent of all private R&D in 2011. The latest data available show a 40 percent indexed growth in GDP Basic Prices from 2002–2011 compared to an overall rate of 1 percent for the Canadian economy. This growth is displayed in Figure 1-3.

So, what should all these numbers mean to you? In a word, *jobs*. The total number of workers in the ICT sector in 2011 was 521 702. So, where are the jobs? Most of the employment gains have occurred in the software and computer-services industries. These service industries include software publishers, business-communications services, data processing, computer system design, and related services. While ICT manufacturing jobs, reflecting overall structural change, have declined from 11.9 percent in 2007 to 9.1 percent in 2011, software and services increased from 54.4 percent to 58.2 percent during the same period.

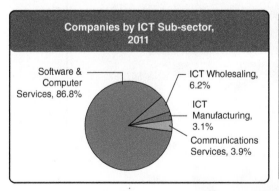

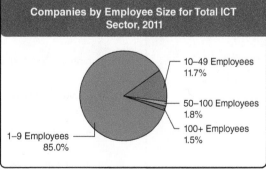

Figure 1-2

Companies by ICT Subsector, 2011

Source: Courtesy of Industry Canada. Reproduced with the permission of the Minister of Public Works and Government Services, 2014

http://www.ic.gc.ca/eic/ site/ict-tic.nsf/eng/h_ it07229.html

[1] www.ic.gc.ca

[2] http://strategis.ic.gc.ca/epic/site/ict-tic.nsf/en/Home

[3] The facts and graphs provided in this section come from the Canadian ICT Sector Profile, updated March 2013 and located at http://www.ic.gc.ca/eic/site/ict-tic.nsf/eng/h_it07229.html.

Figure 1-3

Indexed Growth in ICT
GDP 2002–2011

Source: Courtesy of Industry Canada.
Reproduced with the permission of
the Minister of Public Works and
Government Services

*http://www.ic.gc.ca/eic/site/ict-tic.nsf/
eng/h_it05864.html*

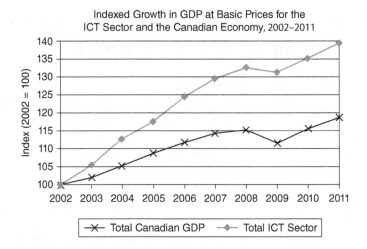

What we learn from these employment numbers is that there will likely be more jobs in the future in what are termed "service" industries. These are industries that supply services that improve business processes, rather than those that mainly produce products. These service companies help other companies, across almost every industry in Canada, more effectively use information systems. Even companies that make software are realizing that much of their revenue is based on services. In a recent study, Cusumano (2008) noted that many large software development companies (such as Oracle and Seibel) derive more than half of their revenues from the services they provide and not from the software products they produce.[4]

What all these numbers boil down to is that understanding how to choose and use IT effectively is an increasingly important skill to have. You might be asking yourself, "Who are these people getting jobs in this industry, and what do they earn?" Employment in the ICT sector is characterized by a high level of education. In 2011, 45.1 percent of all ICT workers had a university degree; the Canadian workforce average is 26 percent.

Figure 1-4 shows that employees in the ICT sector are relatively well paid. According to Industry Canada, workers in ICT industries earned, on average, $68 231

Figure 1-4

Average Annual Earnings
by Major ICT Industry, 2011

Source: Courtesy of Industry Canada.
Reproduced with the permission of the
Minister of Public Works and -Government
Services, 2014.

*http://www.ic.gc.ca/eic/site/ict-tic.nsf/
eng/h_it07229.html*

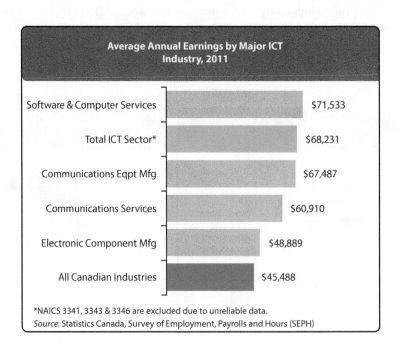

[4] M. A. Cusumano, "The Changing Software Business: Moving from Products to Services," *Computer* 41, no. 1 (January 2008): 20–27.

in 2011, which is well above the economy-wide average of $45 488. Employees in the software and computer services industries were the most highly paid, with average earnings of $71 533.

So, what does all this mean to you? The information presented in this section should help you understand that information systems are an increasingly important part of our economy. In particular, the delivery of services (where people serve other businesses) is a growing area of employment. This employment can be financially rewarding, with higher-than-average salaries, but it is a very knowledge-intensive industry, where more than half of all workers possess a university degree. Students in the Canadian economy who are working toward becoming business professionals cannot ignore the importance of understanding and working with information systems.

Q5   How Do Successful Business Professionals Use Information Systems?

Watch

Go to MyMISLab to watch a video about IS in the life of business professionals.

In today's world, it would be hard to find anyone who does not use or interact with a variety of information systems every day. In the industrialized world, almost everyone is able to use email, access webpages, use word processors and spreadsheets, create presentations, and use instant messaging and location-based services on their smartphones. Although the ability to use such basic information systems is essential, this level of knowledge and use does not give anyone a competitive advantage in the workplace. To be effective in today's economy, you have to know how to do more than the basics. Business professionals need to expand their knowledge of mobile devices and applications that include project management software (e.g., Microsoft Project, OpenProject), business graphics (e.g., MS Visio, SmartDraw), and collaborative systems, such as Google Docs (http://docs.google.com).

Knowing how to use mobile devices and applications is just the first step. The most important task is to understand the technologies and businesses well enough that you can identify opportunities for innovation through technology and understand the risks. And the really important question is, "What skills will be required for this?" Of course, a range of skills are necessary in any industry. Business majors with specializations in information systems, marketing, accounting, human resources, international business, and finance are developing core skills that will continue to be in high demand throughout the Canadian economy. However, you can do more to give yourself a competitive edge.

This fact is demonstrated in reports produced by the Information and Communications Technology Council (ICTC) of Canada (www.ictc-ctic.ca). In its 2010 report "ICT Labour Trends Outlook," the ICTC lays out the challenge ahead for Canadian employers in this high-tech sector.[5] The report signals the rather dramatic need for individuals with a core set of skills, including the following:

- Technical skills
- Specific technology and industry experience
- Satisfactory communication and other business skills

While the list of skills does begin with technological ones, do not underestimate how important communication and business skills are. Even in a high-tech sector, such as ICT, business skills are at the core of competitive advantage. So your business skills can take you farther than you might think, and it gets even better. The report

---

[5] The report can be found at www.ictc-ctic.ca.

also outlines the difference between ICT industries and ICT *user* industries. ICT user industries comprise companies, organizations, and public sector bodies that use ICT in their operations—in other words, all the industries other than those companies in the ICT sector.

For business majors, this is an important fact to keep in mind because it means that adding just a little bit of technical knowledge to your skills portfolio will increase your ability to work across a wide spectrum of industries.

You might ask, "What jobs will these skilled individuals do?" The report lists three occupations that the ICTC believes will have above-average growth rates:

- Manager, computer and information systems
- Information systems analysts and consultants
- User-support technicians

Managers, analysts, consultants—these look like business jobs and they are. Successful business professionals recognize that they can gain a competitive advantage and widen their opportunities by adding some technical knowledge to their business skills. The line between business and technology is rapidly blurring. Business professionals need to consider IT and IS when they think about the problems and opportunities that confront a department or organization.

To remain productive, organizations in the Canadian economy will have to innovate. Much of this innovation will be driven by IT. To take advantage of this trend and be a part of the changes that are coming, you do not have to be a software programmer, data administrator, or network guru. Rather, you need to develop your business skills and then learn to think creatively about the challenges and opportunities in your business and organization and how you can apply new technology and knowledge of information systems to address these business needs.

Q6 What Is the Shape of Things to Come?

Predictions of any kind can be difficult because innovation and human ingenuity rarely follow a straight line. Nevertheless, there are a few general underlying ideas that continue to affect IT. Having an understanding of these ideas is useful for understanding how we got where we are and where we may be headed. A few ideas are obvious. Technology keeps getting easier to use. Think of how intuitive tablets are for consuming media. Many phone systems now offer speech recognition, and Global Positioning System (GPS) receivers talk to us using text-to-speech technology while we are driving.

Much of the rise in ICT can be explained by a relatively short (four-page) article that Gordon Moore, co-founder of Intel, published in a 1965 edition of the magazine *Electronics*:[6]

> *The complexity for minimum component costs has increased at a rate of roughly a factor of two per year. . . . Certainly over the short term this rate can be expected to continue, if not to increase. . . . That means by 1975, the number of components per integrated circuit for minimum cost will be 65 000. I believe that such a large circuit can be built on a single wafer.*

This observation, which later became known as **Moore's Law**, noted that the density of circuits on an integrated chip was doubling approximately every two years or so.

---

[6] The report can be found at http://www.computerhistory.org/semiconductor/assets/media/classic-papers-pdfs/Moore_1965_Article.pdf.

Although this is not a real or natural law (like gravity), the prediction has proven to be surprisingly robust and generally accurate for almost five decades. The practical implication of this observation has been that the power of computers (as measured in transistor counts) has increased exponentially over the past 50 years. This trend has shown little sign of slowing suggesting that computing power will continue to increase at this rate. Indeed, just knowing that computer power is going to continue to increase has allowed entrepreneurs to plan new products and services that in the past would have been impractical from either a cost or size perspective.

A second major characteristic of IT has been what economists call network effects and lock-in of certain technologies, where the value that is received increases significantly as the number of users increases. Imagine, for example, how hard it would have been to sell the first fax machine. (In fact, the first sale probably was at least a pair of machines.) However, once a core group have fax machines, it is so much easier to get subsequent adoption because the number of people you can connect to is considerably higher. A similar situation exists with social networks, such as Facebook or Google+, where the most recent people to join have access to more connections compared with the first ones. Of course, an additional characteristic of this effect is that, once established, network effects and lock-in make it harder to switch. One of the most famous examples of this is the QWERTY keyboard. Although there is some ongoing debate about the veracity of the research, what is unarguable and true is that this keyboard layout was largely designed to slow down the rate of typing and by doing so reduce the mechanical sticking of keys. This, of course, has not been a problem for electronic devices for many years, and alternatives that speed up typing have been proposed. However, the sheer number of existing devices and the large investment required (what accountants and economists call *sunk costs*) tend to prohibit adoption.

The final factors affecting information systems today are the general shrinking of device size (which, of course, is tied to Moore's Law); the tendency for ubiquity, that is, existence everywhere (many people take their cellphones everywhere with them, for example); and the adoption of location-based services facilitated by GPS technology and mobile use.

So, why is the future of IT so difficult to predict? The primary reason is that IT is all about innovation, and this brings unexpected results. Few people, for example, would have predicted the popularity of the Apple iPad before it was introduced or that MP3 players would destroy the compact disc (CD) market (which had destroyed the cassette tape market earlier). Indeed, the ICT sector has enabled a lot of what famed economist Joseph Schumpeter termed creative destruction—the overturning of established industries, such as video stores, by new industries, such as video on demand (or the replacement of film-based cameras by digital cameras). The future is not always obvious. Before the smartphone was perfected, the Apple Newton and the Palm Pilot were both once prominent challengers that struggled initially. The history of the IT industry is full of "can't-miss" ideas that somehow found a way to miss and "best" technologies, even the first in a niche, that are not always successful.

Although IT certainly has a colourful history, in this book, we are more interested in the business of IT and IS. The question we pose is, "How will the changes in IT and IS affect the way we live and work?" Hal Varian, chief economist at Google, provides some perspective on this question.[7] He suggests that business is changing because of advances in IS and IT and that business people need a better understanding of how IT can be used to support innovation. For example, Varian suggests

[7] The full Hal Varian interview (on how the Web challenges managers) can be found at www.mckinseyquarterly.com/Strategy/Innovation/Hal_Varian_on_how_the_Web_challenges_managers_2286.

MIS in Use

Google Knows Best

Every day, millions of people worldwide log in to Gmail, Google's free web-based mail service. Launched 10 years ago, Gmail is supported entirely by advertising and can be considered a success by almost any standard. When email is sent or received, a fresh column of ads appears on the right-hand side of the screen. Type in the title of a book, and ads for online bookstores pop up. Mention a camping trip, and you will see ads for canoe rentals in the area. The ads are chosen to be relevant to the content of the email.

The ability to scan email, understand its content, and provide contextual advertising is what distinguishes Gmail from other web-based email providers. Yahoo! tracks what people view online and uses these data to customize ads, while Hotmail displays banner ads based on demographic information provided when users register, and the geographical decoding of their IP (Internet Protocol) addresses. But only Gmail attempts to understand what you are writing—the company calls it content extraction— to sell the data to advertisers. Google is tight lipped about the details, but content extraction involves sophisticated algorithms that examine all the information in a message, including the recipient's location, and links to webpages and attachments.

Privacy experts say that unlike the postal service, which does not read your letters, and telephone companies, which do not eavesdrop on your calls, Gmail is changing the role of the communication carrier and violating democratic principles. Commenting on this example in *Macleans,* Marc Rotenberg, executive director of the Electronic Privacy Information Center (EPIC) in Washington, said that "Gmail has broken a fundamental trust." Other commentators go even further, suggesting that Google does not have a great track record with regard to privacy. When you visit a Google site, your IP address is recorded, and all your searches are tracked. Because Google can track users across its various products, it has the potential to create complex profiles, combining search terms and email information.

Sarah Elton, a Toronto journalist, discovered recently just how relevant the ads were when she wrote an email (using Gmail) to a friend. Her message mentioned a pregnant woman whose husband had had an affair. The Google ads did not push baby gear and parenting books. Rather, Gmail understood that "pregnant" in this case was not a good thing because it was coupled with the word "affair." So, it offered the services of a private investigator and a marriage therapist.

Questions

1. **Do people who use free email systems understand the implications of the trade-offs that they have made? (***Hint:* **Do you?)**

2. **Is email different from the postal or telephone services? Is it more like a postcard, where privacy should not be assumed?**

3. **How complete a profile can Google assemble of a typical user? (***Hint:* **What Google services—Calendar, Google Maps, etc.—do you use?)**

4. **Is there a way you could use free email systems and still protect your messages from being contextually scanned?**

5. **Should these forms of communication service be regulated? If so, how, and by whom?**

6. **Is there a difference between what Google is doing and how spam filters work?**

7. **What are your privacy rights and expectations while using the internet?**

Source: Courtesy of Sarah Elton.

that mobile devices will change what it means to go to work. The work will come to you, wherever you are, and you will deal with your work at any time and in any place using the networks that have become so readily available. He notes that for business people, the ability to handle—that is, find, process, understand, visualize, and then communicate—data is going to be an important skill for decades to come. Varian also notes that industries are undergoing significant changes because of shifts in technology. For example, the traditional marketing industry (print, newspaper, television, and radio) has to come to grips with the prevalence and potential of the internet. This technological change affects how and where advertisers will spend their dollars. Traditional industries have to adapt to the changes at a pace that is faster than these industries are accustomed to. These topics are obviously important for business students, and we will cover them in more detail throughout the book.

A view of the future is also provided by David Ticoll in his report "ICTS Jobs 2.0," which was presented to the ICTC of Canada.[8] Ticoll suggests that within the next decade, unlimited storage will be almost free, that analytical software will reveal hidden information, and that the real world and the virtual world will collide as wide-area networks (WANs) become cheap, reliable, and widely available. He notes that these technology trends will enable deep, powerful, performance-enhancing innovations that will be felt in almost every industry.

So, what does all this talk about the future of IT mean to you? It means that our Canadian economy is undergoing some fundamental changes, but that shifts have occurred before and will occur again. When the world is shifting, the most important skill to develop is the ability to innovate and to adapt to the changes. So, rather than focusing on the learning of specific technical skills that may fade in importance over time, this book will focus on providing you with broad knowledge that will enable you to quickly understand and adapt to technological changes as they occur. Understanding the implications of technological changes will allow you to be a more effective business professional as well as a more flexible individual.

In many cases, the adaptations do not have to be dramatic. A sample innovation is shown in Case Study 1 at the end of this chapter. In this case, a small retail store, The Running Room, which sells jogging and walking equipment, uses the web to expand its business and increase its reach to customers. What this case demonstrates may not be rocket science, but it shows how organizations can adopt technology to make better products and services for their customers and employees.

The effects of innovation can be difficult to predict and can lead to unintended consequences that are both good and bad. For example, the MIS in Use case "Google Knows Best" described how Google ties advertising to email content. Although the idea is the result of significant innovation, the change has implications for privacy and security that our society has yet to fully understand.

Q7 | What Is This Course About?

Many students enter this course with an erroneous idea of what they will be studying. Often, students think of it as a computer class—or at least a class that has something to do with computers and business. Other students think that this course is about learning how to use Excel, Access, or some web development tool. Figure 1-5 lists a number of reasons students have given us when explaining why they do not need to take this course. As you can see, opinions vary on what the class is about.

---

[8] The report can be found at http://ccict.ca/reports/jobs-2-0

- "I already know how to use Excel and Word. I can build a website with FrontPage. Okay, it's a simple website, but I can do it. And when I need to learn more, I can. So, let me out of this course!"

- "We're going to learn how to work with information systems? That's like practising having the stomach flu. If and when the time comes, I'll know how to do it."

- "I'm terrified of computers. I'm a people person, and I don't do well with engineering-like things. I've put this course off until the last quarter of my final year. I hope it's not as bad as I fear; I just wish they didn't make me take it."

- "There's really no content in this course. I mean, I've been programming since high school, I can write in C++, though PERL is my favourite language. I know computer technology. This course is just a bunch of management babble mixed up with some computer terms. At least it's an easy class, though."

- "Well, I'm sure there is some merit to this course, but consider the opportunity cost. I really need to be taking more microeconomics and international business. The time I spend on this course could be better spent on those subjects."

- "The only thing I need to know is how to surf the Web and how to use email. I know how to do those, so I just don't need this course."

- "What, you mean this course is not about learning Excel and FrontPage? That's what I thought we were going to learn. That's what I need to know. Why all this information systems stuff? How do I make a website? That's what I need to know."

Figure 1-5

Student Thoughts About "Why I Don't Need This Course"

By now, you should have an idea that this course is about much more than learning how to use applications such as Excel or Access. You may, in fact, use those programs in this course, but the focus will not be on learning what keys to push to make the program work as you want it to. Instead, the focus will be on *learning to use those tools to accomplish organizational goals*.

Consider again the definition of MIS: the development and use of information systems that help organizations (and the people who work in them) achieve their goals and objectives. Thus, to understand MIS, you need to understand both business and technology, and you need to be able to relate one to the other.

This book's table of contents will give you an idea of how we will proceed. In the next two chapters, we discuss the relationship of business processes and information systems, and we show how information systems can be used to gain competitive advantages. Then, in Chapters 4 to 6, you will learn about hardware, software, content, and databases, along with network and communications technology. In Chapters 7 to 9, we will show how, with that foundation, technology can be used to gain a competitive advantage. Finally, in Chapters 10 to 12, you will learn how IT departments work, how the IT architecture is managed, about IS ethics and green IT, and about personal privacy and security. The exercise "Duller Than Dirt?" at the end of this chapter on pages 22–23 shares our opinion about why these chapters—and this book—matter to you.

Active Review

Use this Active Review to verify that you have understood the material in the chapter. You can read the entire chapter and then perform the tasks in this review, or you can read the material for just one question and perform the tasks for that question before moving on to the next one.

Q1 What is an information system?

List the components of an information system. Explain how knowledge of these components will guide Josie in his work at Cafe Italiano.

Q2 What is MIS?

List the three elements of MIS. Why does a nontechnical business professional need to understand all three? Why are information systems developed? Why is part of this definition misleading?

Q3 How does IS differ from IT?

Define *IS*. Define *IT*. Does IT include IS, or does IS include IT? Why does technology, by itself, not constitute an information system?

Q4 How important are information systems to our economy?

What does ICT stand for? How important is ICT to the economy? Is the ICT sector growing faster than the Canadian economy? Why are services of growing importance? How knowledge intensive is the ICT sector? What can an employee in the ICT sector expect to earn?

Q5 How do successful business professionals use information systems?

What new applications should a business professional be familiar with? What combination of skills is of growing importance in the economy? Can a business student work in the ICT sector?

Q6 What is the shape of things to come?

Describe Moore's Law and the fundamental change that technology can bring to an economy, an organization, and you.

Q7 What is this course about?

In your own words, state what this course is about. Look at this book's table of contents. What major themes does it address? How will those themes relate to you as a business professional? If you were (or are) employed and you had to justify the expense of this course to your boss, how would you do it?

MyMISLab is an online learning and testing environment that features the perfect study tools to help you master the concepts covered in this chapter. Log in to MyMISLab to test your knowledge of key chapter concepts and explore additional practice tools, including videos, flashcards, annotated text figures, and more!

Key Terms and Concepts

Applications 6

Computer hardware 6

Data 6

Five-component framework 6

Information and Communications Technology (ICT) sector 11

Information system (IS) 6

Information technology (IT) 10

Management information systems (MIS) 7

Moore's Law 14

People 6

Procedures 6

Software 6

Using Your Knowledge

1. "Outlook on Human Resources in the ICT Labour Market: 2008–2015" suggests that ICT workers need to have several core skills.
   a. What are these key skills?
   b. Identify ways that you can best obtain these skills.
   c. Do you believe a business student can work effectively in the ICT sector? Would a business student have a competitive advantage over a computer science student? Why, or why not?

2. The interview with Hal Varian, chief economist at Google, focuses on six themes: (i) flexible corporations, (ii) corporations and work, (iii) free goods and value, (iv) workers and managers, (v) computer monitoring and risks, and (vi) changes in industries. Choose one of these themes and discuss in more detail the implications of the change for you personally. Provide specific examples where possible. You can find the article at www.mckinseyquarterly.com/Strategy/Innovation/Hal_Varian_on_how_the_Web_challenges_managers_2286.

3. Consider the costs of a system in light of these five components: (i) the costs to buy and maintain the hardware; (ii) the costs to develop or acquire licences to the software programs and to maintain them; (iii) the costs to design databases and fill them with data; (iv) the costs to develop procedures and keep them current; and (v) finally, the human costs, both to develop and use the system.
   a. Over the lifetime of a system, many experts believe that the single most expensive component is people. Does this belief seem logical to you? Explain why you agree or disagree.
   b. Consider a poorly developed system that does not meet its defined requirements. The needs of the business do not go away, but they do not conform to the characteristics of the poorly built system. Therefore, something has got to give. Which component picks up the slack when hardware and software programs do not work correctly? What does this say about the cost of a poorly designed system? Consider both direct money costs as well as intangible personnel costs.
   c. What implications do you, as a future business manager, recognize after answering questions (a) and (b)? What does this say about the need for your involvement in requirements and other aspects of systems development? Who will eventually pay the costs of a poorly developed system? Against which budget will those costs accrue?

Collaborative Exercises

1. Watch the video "Did You Know? Shift Happens." There are many versions, an update is available at http://www.youtube.com/watch?v=PcZg51Il9no. Discuss this video with your group, and identify three specific impacts that you think the information in this video will have on your business career. Be as specific as possible, and link the ideas to your intended major, interests, and career aspirations.

2. Watch the video "A Vision of Students Today" (www.youtube.com/watch?v=dGCJ46vyR9o). Discuss this video with your group, and identify three ways that courses could be designed to improve the way students engage in the course. Be as specific as possible, and be prepared to share your ideas with the class.

Case Study 1

Watch

Go to MyMISLab to watch a video about IRS requirements.

Running at the Speed of the Web: The Running Room

The Running Room (www.runningroom.com) is North America's largest specialty retailer of sporting goods, apparel, and footwear for runners and walkers. The company operates over 90 corporately owned stores in Canada and the United States. The Running Room website was created in early 2000.

Questions

1. Do you think The Running Room would be as successful as it is if it did not have a website? In other words, is the company's website a critical component for success or simply a nice extra for its customers?
2. Could The Running Room provide the same customer experience without using its website? For example, could the company use more mailings and telephone calls to stay in touch with its customers?
3. Do you think The Running Room's website creates a barrier to entry for its potential competitors? Explain your answer.
4. Check out the goals that the company highlights in the About Us section of the Running Room's website. Does the website help the company meet these goals? Discuss why or why not.

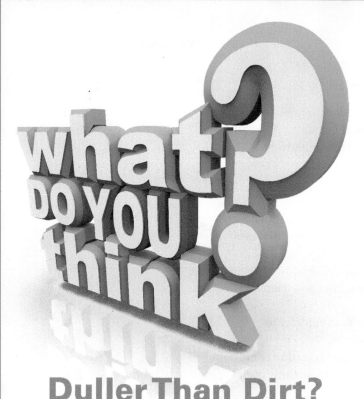

What Do You Think?

Duller Than Dirt?

Yes, you read that title correctly: This subject can seem duller than dirt. Take the phrase *development and use of IS in organizations.*

Read just that phrase and you start to yawn, wondering, "How am I going to absorb almost 400 pages of this stuff?" Do not worry. You are not alone. Take a few minutes and look at this video: "A Vision of Students Today." (www.youtube.com/watch?v=dGCJ46vyR9o).

Now stop and think: Why are you reading this book? Right now in the Sea of Cortez, Mexico, the water is clear and warm, and the swimming and diving are wonderful. You could be kayaking to Isla San Francisco this very minute. So, why are you here reading this book? Why are you not there?

Suppose you take an hour tonight to read your assigned chapter in this book. For a typical person, that is 4320 heartbeats (72 beats times 60 minutes) you have used to read this book—heartbeats you will never have again. For some reason, you chose to major in business. For some reason, you are taking this course. And, for some reason, you have been instructed to read this textbook.

Now, given that you made a good decision to major in business, the question becomes, "How can you maximize the return on the 4320 heartbeats you are investing each hour?" The secret is to personalize the material. At every page, ask yourself, "How does this pertain to me? How can I use this to further my goals?"

MIS is all-encompassing. To us, that is one of its beauties. Consider the components: hardware, software, data, procedures, and people. Do you want to be an engineer? Then, work the hardware component. Do you want to be a programmer? Write software. Do you like people? Become an IS trainer or a computer systems salesperson. Do you like business systems and sociology? Learn how to design effective organizational procedures. Do you enjoy management? Learn how to bring all those disparate elements together. We have worked in this industry for many years. The breadth of MIS and the rapid change of technology have kept us fascinated for every one of those years.

So, wake up. Why are you reading this? How can you make it relevant? Jump onto Google, and search for a career as a business analyst or in project management, or use some other phrase from this chapter as key search words and see what you get. Challenge yourself to find something that is important to you personally in every chapter.

You just invested 780 heartbeats in reading this editorial. Was it worth it? Keep asking!

Discussion
Questions

1. Are you awake to your life? How do you know? What can you do once a week to ensure that you are awake?

2. What are your professional goals? Are they yours, or are they someone else's? How do you know?

3. How is this course relevant to your professional goals?

4. How are you going to make the material in this course interesting?

Michaeljung/Shutterstock

2 Business Processes and Decision Making

Running Case

Josie is helping his grandparents with their coffee shop. His grandparents are worried about a franchise coffee shop opening across the street. Josie kept thinking, "What will Café Italiano's competitive advantage be?" The café had a loyal customer base developed over 30 years, but would that be enough?

One response might be for Café Italiano to remove the competitive advantages the franchise coffee shop might be counting on. For example, Josie noticed that all the franchise coffee stores offer wireless internet access, or Wi-Fi, as part of the customer experience. The idea of customers browsing the internet while drinking coffee seemed to fit well with the relaxed atmosphere at Café Italiano. While many of the older clients might not use the service, it seemed likely that many of the younger customers would.

Josie talked with his grandparents about wireless internet access for customers, but his grandparents were skeptical. They did not see why clients would want it. Josie's grandparents knew a lot about coffee but not so much about wireless access. Josie suggested that enjoying coffee was often viewed as a time to read and that the internet could provide much more reading material than the few daily papers available in the shop. Smartphones could also use the Wi-Fi instead of the cell network, and that would save customers money. His grandparents thought it would be very expensive to install such a network and argued that it would require someone with advanced computing skills. Josie said it was not that complicated. They agreed that if Josie could show them the benefits, and if it was not too expensive, then they would give the idea of installing the Wi-Fi network a try.

To learn more about these services, Josie started with his MIS textbook. He learned that building a Wi-Fi network required a high-speed internet connection, a router/access point/gateway device, and a computer to configure the device. Luckily, his grandparents already had a high-speed connection in their shop and a computer that they used to make orders for their coffee and other products. So, all they would need to buy would be a Wi-Fi router. Josie found that he could get a good router for about $70.

Reading more, he learned that the internet provider was really important. Some providers' end user licence agreements (EULA) allowed for sharing a broadband connection with customers. When he checked with the provider, he found that the current high-speed package his grandparents had bought would not support broadcasting to customers but that for an additional $40 per month, the shop could get even faster access that could be broadcast to their customers along with a 24-hour help line. The service provider would even supply the Wi-Fi router for a couple of dollars extra a month. His grandparents could then hook into the router using the wired connection while customers surfed wirelessly. Problem solved. It was almost too good to be true!

There was one last thing on Josie's mind. His grandparents wanted to know about the benefits of Wi-Fi. How could these be estimated? He thought a customer survey might provide some good information. Thinking about the survey also made Josie think about how customers would get access to the Wi-Fi. Usually, a password was needed. What would the process be for identifying customers and allowing them access? How would customers know what the password was? How often would it have to be changed, and who would do this? Not having password protection seemed risky, as it might encourage people to just drop by without making any purchase at the café. There was also the risk of people using the internet access inappropriately. The more Josie looked at it, the more he realized that providing wireless access was not so much a technical problem as it was a business problem.

Study Questions

Q1 "How did this stuff get here?"

Q2 What is a business process?

Q3 What are the components of a business process?

Q4 What is information?

Q5 What is the role of information in business processes?

Q6 How do information systems support business processes?

Q7 How do information systems support decision making?

Q8 What is your role?

Q1 "How Did This Stuff Get Here?"

Imagine you have graduated and, with a few years of hard work, you have achieved exactly the position you wanted. One April day, you find yourself in Toronto for a meeting at First Canadian Place. Like any responsible business professional, you arrived a bit early, so you decide to have a cup of coffee and a muffin at the Tim Hortons in the PATH underground walkway beneath First Canadian Place.

Sitting down with your coffee and muffin, your mind begins to wander. As you look around, you wonder, "How did this stuff get here—the milk, the coffee, the muffin? How did it all get here?"

You realize that somewhere, there must be a cow that produced the milk in your coffee. Where is that cow? Who owns it? Who decided to ship that particular milk to the Tim Hortons that morning? Who delivered the milk? How was the truck routed to customers?

For that matter, how did the coffee get here? Perhaps it was grown in Kenya, shipped to the United States, roasted in Rochester, New York, distributed through the head office in Oakville, Ontario, and delivered to the store. How did all that happen? And the muffin—who baked it? How many muffins were baked today? Who makes those decisions? How were all these decisions coordinated?

The more you think about it, the more you realize that just getting your cup of coffee was a near-miracle. Hundreds—if not thousands—of different processes successfully interacted just to bring together a muffin, coffee, and you. It is truly amazing. And those processes had to more than just barely work. They had to work in such a way that all the companies and people covered their costs and earned a profit. How did that occur? Who set the prices? Who determined how much nonfat milk had to be shipped to Toronto the night before? How does all this come about? The more you think about the process, the more amazing it becomes.

The reality is that all this activity comes through the interaction of business processes. Tim Hortons has processes for ordering, receiving, storing, and paying for ingredients such as milk and coffee. The coffee roaster has a process for assessing demand, ordering its raw materials, and making deliveries. All the other businesses have processes for conducting their affairs as well. Organizations make use of these processes to deliver goods and services to customers. So, business processes are central to what every organization does. That is why understanding business processes is critical to understanding how business works.

Q2 What Is a Business Process?

A **business process** is a series of activities, tasks, or steps designed to produce a product or service. A business process is best thought of as a system and is sometimes also referred to as a **business system**. In this book, we will use the term *business process*. In Chapter 7, we will introduce enterprise resource planning (ERP) systems that are used by many organizations to support their business processes.

We can start by considering an example. Examples of business processes include inventory management processes, manufacturing processes, sales processes, and customer support processes. Figure 2-1 shows a model of a sales and inventory-management business process that might be used at a Tim Hortons restaurant. These sales and inventory elements are often considered part of a "supply chain" for an organization. We will discuss the supply chain in more detail in Chapter 3 and also cover supply chain management systems later in Chapter 7.

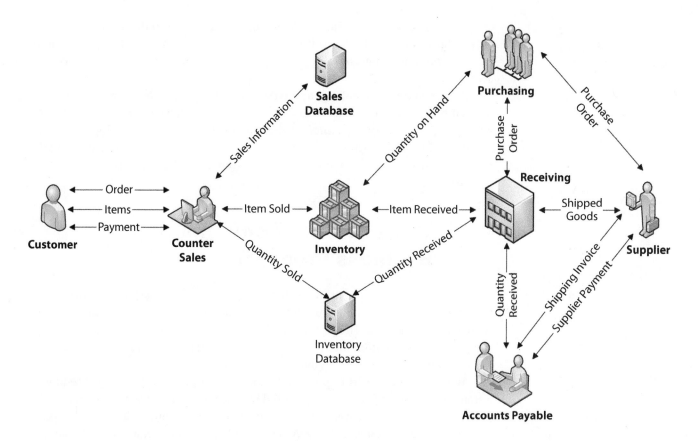

Inventory for a Tim Hortons restaurant includes all the goods (coffee, donuts, muffins, milk, etc.) that a Tim Hortons restaurant sells. Managing this inventory is a business process. The goal of this process is to ensure that there is enough inventory to fulfill customers' requests while making sure that there is not too much inventory (as otherwise the goods will spoil or profitability will suffer).

The inventory management process works to balance the demands of customers with the inventory purchased from suppliers. Purchasing, therefore, is an important activity in the inventory management process. But how can a manager at a Tim Hortons restaurant know how much coffee to purchase?

This is where the inventory management system comes in. The inventory management system supports the process by collecting information. An inventory database keeps track of what the customers have ordered (*quantity ordered*) and what is currently in inventory (*quantity on hand*). As customers make purchases, stock moves out of inventory. At some point, stock in inventory hits a critical point, often called the *reorder point*. When a good in stock hits this point, the system advises the manager that it is time to order new supplies. Since goods are bought and sold at different rates, each good can have its own reorder point.

To order new inventory, the manager creates a *purchase order (PO)*, which lists the items ordered and the quantity desired. This *purchase order* is sent to the supplier. The supplier receives the *purchase order* and then ships the appropriate goods along with the *shipping invoice* to the restaurant. The *shipped goods* are first checked to make sure the restaurant received what was ordered. The newly received goods are then placed in inventory and the inventory database is updated with the *quantity received*. The supplier is then paid for the goods the supplier has shipped.

The diagram in Figure 2-1 is a snapshot of the system. It does not show the logic behind it; that is, it does not show what causes what. It is just a picture of the elements of the business process and how they interact. There are many different

Figure 2-1

Model of an Inventory Management Business Process

ways of representing a business process. In the extension to this chapter, we provide a short tutorial on Microsoft Visio, a drawing program, which is often used to create a *dataflow diagram (DFD)*, one of the more common ways that processes are illustrated.

Understanding, modelling, and redesigning business processes are a big part of what business analysts do. In information systems, these modelling and design activities are called *systems analysis and design*. The goal is to develop an understanding of how an organization works. If you are interested in this type of work, you can learn more about business process analysis in a systems analysis and design course.

03 What Are the Components of a Business Process?

A business process consists of activities, resources, facilities, and information. Activities transform resources and information of one type into resources and information of another type. The payment activity transforms quantity received and shipping invoice information into a supplier payment (resource). The payment activity has rules and procedures that it follows for doing this.

Activities can consist of purely manual actions (people following procedures), automated or controlled procedures used by computers (hardware directed by software), or, as is often the case, a combination of manual and automated procedures.

Resources are items of value. A case of milk is a resource, a person working is a resource, and the customer's cash is a resource. In Figure 2-1, both suppliers and customers are considered resources because they have value in this process. They are not considered activities because they are external and, therefore, not under the restaurant's direction and control.

Facilities are structures used within the business process. Resources can be stored within facilities. Examples of facilities include factories, pieces of equipment, trucks, filing cabinets, and the like. In the case of digital resources, facilities might include inventories and databases (as in Figure 2-1).

Information is the fourth element of a business process. Activities use information to determine how to transform the inputs received into the outputs produced. Because this book is about information systems, and understanding the nature of information and ways of defining it are crucial, information created in processes will be our focus.

We have defined a business process in terms of activities, resources, facilities, and information. It should be noted that many other definitions are used by other authors, industry analysts, and software products. For example, IBM, a key leader in business process management, has a product called WebSphere Business Modeler that uses a different set of terms. It has activities and resources, but it uses the term *repository* for facility and the term *business item* for information. Other business modelling software products use other definitions and terms.

Accordingly, a software industry standards organization called the Object Management Group (OMG) created a standard set of terms and graphical notations for documenting business processes. The standard, called **Business Process Modeling Notation (BPMN)**, is documented at www.bpmn.org. BPMN provides four graphical elements that can be used to document a process. A complete description of BPMN is beyond the scope of this text. However, the basic symbols are relatively easy to understand, and they work naturally with our definition of business process in terms of activities, resources, facilities, and information.

Q4 What Is Information?

Information is one of those fundamental terms that we use every day but it turns out to be surprisingly difficult to define.

In this text, we will avoid the technical issues of defining *information* and will use common, intuitive definitions instead. The most common definition is that information is knowledge derived from data; the term *data* is defined as recorded facts or figures. Thus, the facts that employee James Smith earns $17.50 per hour and that Mary Jones earns $25 per hour are, of themselves, examples of data. The statement that the average hourly wage of all employees in the Garden Department is $22.37 per hour is information. Average wage is knowledge that is derived from the data of individual wages.

Another common definition is that information is data presented in a meaningful context. The fact that Jeff Parks earns $10 per hour is data. The statement that Jeff Parks earns less than half the average hourly wage of the Garden Department, however, is information. This is data presented in a meaningful context.

Another definition of information is processed data; that is, information is processed by summing, ordering, averaging, grouping, comparing, or performing other similar operations. The fundamental idea of this definition is that we do something to data to produce information.

There is yet a fourth definition of information, suggested by psychologist Gregory Bateson, where information is defined as a difference that makes a difference. For example, if you get new information and it does not make a difference to your decision, is what you received really information?

For the purposes of this text, any of these definitions of information will do. Choose the one that makes sense to you. The important thing is to differentiate between data and information. You also may find that different definitions work better in different situations.

Characteristics of Good Information

All information is not equal: Some information is better than other information. Figure 2-2 lists the characteristics of good information.

Accurate

Good information is **accurate information**. Good information is based on correct and complete data that have been processed correctly and as expected. Accuracy is crucial; managers must be able to rely on the results of their information systems. The information system (IS) function can develop a bad reputation in the organization if the system is known to produce inaccurate information. In such a case, the IS becomes a waste of time and money as users develop workarounds to avoid the inaccurate data.

A corollary to this discussion is that you, a future user of information systems, ought not to rely on information just because it appears on a webpage, in a seemingly well-formatted report, or as part of a fancy query. It is sometimes hard to be skeptical about information that is delivered with beautiful, active graphics. Do not be misled. When you begin to use an IS, be skeptical. Cross-check the information you are receiving. When you are certain that it is accurate, you may be able to relax a little. Begin, however, with skepticism, and keep in mind that, over time, information may lose its level of accuracy. In fact, because this can often occur gradually, it can sometimes create serious problems.

- Accurate
- Timely
- Relevant
  - To context
  - To subject
- Just barely sufficient
- Worth its cost

Figure 2-2

Characteristics of Good Information

Timely

Good information is **timely information**—produced in time for its intended use. A monthly report that arrives six weeks late is most likely useless. An IS that tells you not to extend credit to a customer after you have shipped the goods is unhelpful and frustrating. Note that timeliness can be measured against a calendar (six weeks late) or against events (before we ship).

When you participate in the development of an IS, timeliness will be part of the requirements you will request. You need to give appropriate and realistic timeliness needs. In some cases, developing systems that provide information in near real-time is much more difficult and expensive than producing information a few hours later. If you can get by with information that is a few hours old, it is important to say so during the requirements specification phase.

Consider this example. Suppose you work in marketing and you need to be able to assess the effectiveness of new online ad programs. You want an IS that will not only deliver ads over the web but also enable you to determine how frequently customers click on those ads. Determining click ratios in near real-time can be very expensive; saving the data and processing them some hours later may be much easier, cheaper, and sufficient for your needs.

Relevant

Information should be **relevant** both to the context and to the subject. A chief executive officer (CEO) needs information that is summarized to an appropriate level for her position. A list of the hourly wage of every employee in the company is unlikely to be useful to a CEO. More likely, she will expect the average wage information by department or division. A list of all employee wages is irrelevant in the CEO's context.

Information should also be relevant to the subject at hand. If you want information about short-term interest rates for a possible line of credit, then a report that details 15-year mortgage interest rates is irrelevant. Similarly, a report that buries the information you need in pages and pages of results is also irrelevant to your purposes.

Just Barely Sufficient

Information needs to be **sufficient** for the purpose for which it is generated, but **just barely so**. We live in an information age; a critical decision that each of us must make is what information to ignore. The higher you rise in management, the more information you will be given and the more information you will need to ignore. So, information should be sufficient, but just barely so. Knowing what information to ignore is, of course, difficult. Studying, for example, would be so much easier and more efficient if your professors told you exactly which questions were going to be on their exams. But their input might not help you to learn or prepare you for your career.

Worth Its Cost

Information is not free. There are costs associated with an IS—the costs of developing, operating, and maintaining the system, and the costs of your time and salary for reading and processing the information the system produces. For information to be **worth its cost**, there must be an appropriate relationship between the cost of information and its value.

You need to ask, "What is the value of the information?" or "What is the cost?" or "Is there an appropriate relationship between value and cost?" For example, spending $10 to find out how to save $8 is not particularly useful. Information and information systems should be subject to the same financial analyses to which other assets are subjected.

Q5 What Is the Role of Information in Business Processes?

This discussion about information may seem overly theoretical. What does information have to do with real business processes that move actual goods and provide services to real people?

The first thing to realize is that any time a good is moved or a service is provided, data and information are always created. Moving something from one place to another place creates new information about the location of that thing. During the move, the thing may change ownership (data) or may itself be modified (data). Any time there is a physical flow, there is the potential to capture a flow of information. We do not always collect the information, but we have the potential to do so if we need to. The same is true of a service. Flows of a service are always accompanied by a potential flow of data and information.

Look again at the inventory management process in Figure 2-1. Consider the payment process, which compares the *quantity received* (from receiving and stocking) to the *shipping invoice* (from the supplier). If the goods received match the goods billed, then payment generates a *supplier payment*.

Now, let us apply some of the definitions from the last section. Is *quantity received* an example of data, or is it information? By itself, it is just data, a recorded fact or figure: "We received these items from that supplier on this date." Similarly, the *shipping invoice* could also be considered to be just data: "We, Supplier X, delivered these items on this date."

When we bring these two items together, however, we generate information. As noted earlier, Gregory Bateson's definition of information suggested, "Information is a difference that makes a difference." If the *quantity received* indicates we received five cases of milk, but the *shipping invoice* is billing us for eight cases, we have a difference that makes a difference. By comparing records of the amount we received to records of the amount we were billed, we are presenting data in a meaningful context, which is a definition of information. Thus, a business process generates information by bringing together important items of data in a context.

The information generated by a business process is important for several reasons. For example, it lets us know when we need to make payments for goods or services received. Information also helps us keep track of what we have delivered and what has not been delivered; it keeps our inventory up to date. But information can take us beyond just collecting facts. Information becomes even more useful when we start using information to manage business processes.

Business Process Management

George Box, a pioneer in quality control, noted that a byproduct of every business process is information about how the process can be improved. For example, we could use the information produced by the process in Figure 2-1 over a period of a few months to determine the cheapest, the fastest, or the most reliable suppliers. We could use the information in the inventory database to assess our inventory ordering strategy. We could also use the information to estimate how much the organization might be losing from waste and theft. This type of work is called **business process management (BPM)**.

BPM is a field of management that promotes the development of effective and efficient processes through continuous improvement and innovation. Often, innovations in business processes are developed by integrating information technology into a business process. There are many methods that organizations have developed to support their improvements in business processes, including **total quality management (TQM)**, **six sigma**, and **lean production**. If you are interested in finding out more about these methods, two collaborative exercises at the end of this chapter ask you to explore these methods and use business process simulation to better understand how to manage business processes.[1]

We will not go into detail about the different methods of BPM, but what is important for you to remember is that information about the process provides the ability to better manage the process itself. Well-run organizations constantly seek better ways of providing goods and services to their customers. These organizations use tools, such as lean value map streaming, and process mapping tools, such as MS Visio, to support their work on business processes. Information about the business process is always the starting point for understanding what can and should be changed. So, whether you work in marketing, human resources, finance, or accounting, remember that as a manager, you will need to understand how to collect and use the information that is generated by business processes within your organization. The more you are able to understand business processes, the better you will be able to successfully manage the process. Information is, therefore, an important part of effective management.

Q6 How Do Information Systems Support Business Processes?

👁‑Watch

Go to MyMISLab to watch a video about the most important component – YOU.

👁‑Watch

Go to MyMISLab to watch a video about business processes, information, and information systems.

Information systems are used by the activities in a business process, but the particular relationship varies among the processes. In some processes, several activities use one information system. In other processes, each activity has its own information system; in still other processes, some activities use several different information systems.

During systems analysis and design, the analysts and designers determine the relationship of activities to information systems. You will learn more about this topic in Chapter 10 and 11 and can read more about how information systems support business process in "MIS in Use" (page 38). The case describes how an information system, Edoc, was used in the tugboat industry to support several manual business processes.

What Does It Mean to Automate a Process Activity?

We will consider the role of information systems for several of the activities depicted in Figure 2-1, but before we do that, think about the five components of an IS that we introduced in Chapter 1. Note the symmetry of components in Figure 2-3. The outermost components, hardware and people, are both actors; they can take actions. The software and procedure components are both sets of instructions: Software is instructions for hardware, and procedures are instructions for people. Finally, data form the bridge between the computer side on the left and the human side on the right.

An activity in a business process being handled by an **automated system** means that work formerly done by people who followed procedures has been changed so that computers now do that work by following instructions in software. Thus, the automation of a process activity consists of moving work from the right side of Figure 2-3 to the left side.

---

[1] IBM created an interactive game called INNOV8 that supports learning about business process management using business process simulation. You can access the game at www-01.ibm.com/software/solutions/soa/innov8/index.html.

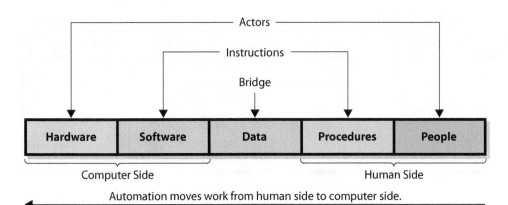

Figure 2-3

Characteristics of the Five Components

An Information System to Support Counter Sales

According to Figure 2-1, the counter sales activity at a Tim Hortons restaurant inter-acts with the customer. This activity receives the customer's order, takes the items from inventory, and receives the customer's payment. This is the familiar process of ordering coffee and a muffin at a restaurant.

Counter sales uses the IS shown in Figure 2-4. This system is, however, automated, and the cashiers may not even know they are using an IS. Each cash register contains a computer that communicates with another computer that hosts the inventory data-base. Programs in the cash register record sales and make appropriate changes to the inventory database whenever the cashier rings in a sale. The cashiers need to be trained only in how to use the cash register; they never need to work directly with the sales-recording programs on the computer.

The designers of this IS decided to fully automate the counter sales process because the cashier's job is seen as a low-skill-level position with high turnover. (Turnover refers to the rate at which new employees arrive and existing ones depart. Different jobs have different rates of turnover.) The designers wanted to reduce the amount of training time that cashiers required before they could productively use the cash registers.

An Information System to Support Payment

Now consider the payment activity in Figure 2-1. Payment receives the *quantity received* and the *shipping invoice*, and it produces the *supplier payment*. (In reality, payment does not generate a cheque to the supplier. Because of accounting controls, no single person should approve a payment and generate a cheque.) Instead, pay-ment generates an authorization, which is sent to someone else who produces the cheque. These details are omitted here for simplicity—they are important, however!

Hardware	Software	Data	Procedures	People
– Cash register computer – Database host computer	– Sales-recording program on cash register	– Sales data – Inventory database	– Operate cash register	– Cashier

Mostly an automated system.
Almost all work is done by computers and software.

Figure 2-4

Sales Recording Information System Used by Counter Sales in Figure 2-1

Figure 2-5
Payment System Used by Payment Activity in Figure 2-1

Hardware	Software	Data	Procedures	People
- Personal computer	- Adobe Acrobat Reader - Email	- Quantity Received - Shipping Invoice	- Reconcile receipt document with invoice. - Issue payment authorization, if appropriate. - Process exceptions	- Accounts payable

Mostly a manual system.
Little work is done by computers and software.
Most work is done by Accounts Payable clerk.

As you can see in Figure 2-5, the IS that supports the payment activity is a mostly **manual system**. The accounts payable clerk receives both the *quantity received* and the Shipping Invoice as Adobe Acrobat PDF files (the same sort of PDF files you receive over the internet). He or she then reads those documents, compares the quantities, and issues the payment authorization, as appropriate. If there is a discrepancy, the accounts payable clerk investigates and takes action, as appropriate.

The designers of this system chose to leave it as a manual system because processing exceptions is complicated: There are many different exceptions, and each requires a different response. The designers thought that programming all those exceptions would be expensive and probably not very effective, so they decided it would be better to let humans deal with the various situations. This means, by the way, that the accounts payable clerks will need much more training than the cashiers will.

An Information System to Support Purchasing

Now consider the information system that supports the purchasing activity depicted in Figure 2-1. This system, shown in Figure 2-6, balances the work between automation and manual activity. The person doing the purchasing has a personal computer that is connected to the computer that hosts the database. Her computer runs an inventory application program that queries the database and identifies items that are low in stock and need to be ordered. That application produces a report that she reads periodically.

Figure 2-6
Purchasing Information System Used by Purchasing Activity in Figure 2-1

Hardware	Software	Data	Procedures	People
- Personal computer - Database host computer	- Inventory application program - Purchasing program	- Inventory database	- Issue Purchase Order according to inventory management practices and guidelines	- Purchasing clerk

Balance between computer and human work.

The purchasing clerk then decides which items to order and from which suppliers. In making this decision, she is guided by the inventory management practices. When she decides to order, she uses the purchasing program on her computer. It is that program that generates the *purchase order* shown in Figure 2-1.

The designers of this IS decided to balance the work between the computer and the human. Searching the inventory database for items that are low in stock is a perfect application for a computer. It is a repetitive process that humans find tedious. However, selecting which supplier to use is a process that requires human judgment. The clerk needs to balance a number of factors: the quality of the supplier, recent supplier experience, the need to have a variety of suppliers, and so forth. Such complicated balancing is better done by a human. Again, this means that the purchasing clerks will need much more training than the cashiers.

The three different information systems at the restaurant support the needs of users in the company's various business processes—counter sales, payments, and purchasing.

Before we leave this discussion, it is important to understand how *you* will relate to information systems. One of the most important tasks a business manager has is making decisions, and information is often a critical part of any decision-making process. Therefore, we consider how information systems support business decisions next.

Q7 How Do Information Systems Support Decision Making?

Making decisions is central to managing organizations. We found earlier in this chapter that data are an important part of any IS and that data can be transformed into information. Information is an important starting point for decision making in most organizations. So, the first point we can make is that information systems support decision making by providing the information—the raw material—for many decisions.

Decision making in organizations is varied and complex, and before discussing the role of information systems in supporting decision making, we need to investigate the characteristics and dimensions of decision making itself.

Decisions Vary by Level

As shown in Figure 2-7, decisions occur at three levels in organizations: operational, managerial, and strategic. The types of decisions vary, depending on the level. **Operational decisions** concern day-to-day activities. Typical operational decisions include the following, for example: How many widgets should we order from vendor A? Should we extend credit to vendor B? Which invoices should we pay today? Information systems that support operational decision making are called **transaction processing systems (TPS)**.

Managerial decisions concern the allocation and utilization of resources. Examples of typical managerial decisions include the following: How much should we budget for computer hardware and programs for department A next year? How many engineers should we assign to project B? How many square metres of warehouse space do we need for the coming year? Information systems that support managerial decision making are called **management information systems (MIS)**. (Note that the term can be used in two ways: broadly, to mean the subjects in this entire book, and narrowly, to mean information systems that support managerial-level decision making. The context will make the meaning of the term clear.)

Watch

Go to MyMISLab to watch a video about how decisions vary by level?

- Decision level
  - Operational
  - Managerial
  - Strategic
- Decision process
  - Structured
  - Unstructured

Figure 2-7

Decision-Making Dimensions

Strategic decisions concern broader organizational issues. Examples of typical decisions at the strategic level include the following: Should we start a new product line? Should we open a centralized warehouse in Calgary? Should we acquire company A?

Note that, in general, the decision time frame increases as we move from operational to managerial to strategic decisions. Operational decisions normally involve actions in the short term: What should we do today or this week? Managerial decisions involve longer time frames: What is an appropriate goal for the next quarter or year? Strategic decisions involve the long term; their consequences may not be realized for years.

Decisions Vary by Structure

Figure 2-8 shows levels of information systems with two decision processes: *structured* and *unstructured*. These terms refer to the method by which the decision is to be made, not to the nature of the underlying problem. A **structured decision** is one for which there is an understood and accepted method for making the decision. A formula for computing the reorder quantity of an item in inventory is an example of a structured decision process. A standard method for allocating furniture and equipment to employees is another structured decision process.

An **unstructured decision** process is one for which there is no agreed-upon decision-making method. Predicting the future direction of the economy or the stock market is a common example. The prediction method varies from person to person; it is neither standardized nor broadly accepted. (As one pundit put it, "If you laid all the economists in the world end to end, they still would not reach a conclusion.") Another example of an unstructured decision-making process is assessing how well suited an employee is for performing a particular job. Managers vary in the manner in which they make such assessments.

Again, keep in mind that the terms *structured* and *unstructured* refer to the decision-making process, not to the underlying subject. Weather forecasting is a structured decision because the process used to make the decision is standardized among forecasters. Weather itself, however, is an unstructured phenomenon, as tornadoes and hurricanes demonstrate every year.

Supporting Decision Making

The decision type and decision-making process are loosely related. As shown by the oval in Figure 2-8, decisions at the operational level tend to be structured and

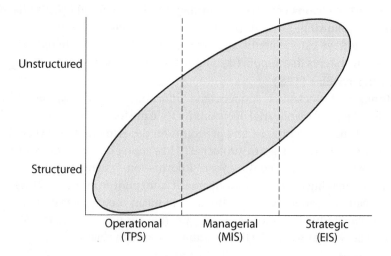

Figure 2-8

Relationship of Decision Level and Decision-Making Process

Decision Step	Description	Examples of Possible Information Systems
Intelligence gathering	• What is to be decided? • What are the decision criteria? • Obtain relevant data.	• Communications applications (email, video-conferencing, word processing, presentation) • Query and reporting systems • Data analysis applications
Alternatives formulation	• What are the choices?	• Communications applications
Choice	• Analyze choices against criteria using data. • Select alternative.	• Spreadsheets • Financial modelling • Other modelling
Implementation	• Make it so!	• Communications applications
Review	• Evaluate results of decision; if necessary, repeat process to correct and adapt.	• Communications applications • Query and reporting Systems • Spreadsheets and other analysis

Figure 2-9

Decision-Making Steps

decisions at the strategic level tend to be unstructured. Managerial decisions tend to be both structured and unstructured.

We say "tend to be" because there are exceptions to the relationship illustrated in Figure 2-8. Some operational decisions are unstructured (e.g., "How many taxicab drivers do we need on the night before the homecoming game?"), and some strategic decisions can be structured (e.g., "How should we assign sales quotas for a new product?"). In general, however, the relationship shown in Figure 2-8 holds.

Another way to examine the relationship between information systems and decision making is to consider how an IS is used during the steps of the decision-making process. The first two columns of Figure 2-9 show the typical steps in the decision-making process: intelligence gathering, formulation of alternatives, choice, implementation, and review. During **intelligence gathering**, the decision makers determine what is to be decided, what the criteria for the decision will be, and what data are available. **Alternatives formulation** is the stage in which decision makers lay out various alternatives. They analyze the alternatives and select one during the **choice** step, and then they implement the decision in the **implementation** step. Finally, the organization reviews the results of the decision. The **review** step may lead to another decision—and another iteration through the decision process.

As summarized in the right column of Figure 2-9, each of these decision-making steps needs a different type of IS. During intelligence gathering, email and videoconferencing facilitate communication among the decision makers. As well, during the first phase, decision makers use query and reporting systems as well as other types of data analysis applications to obtain relevant data. They use email and videoconferencing systems for communication during the alternatives formulation step. During the choice step, analysis applications, such as spreadsheets, and financial and other modelling applications, help the decision makers to analyze alternatives. The implementation stage again involves the use of communications applications, and all types of information systems can be used during review.

Q8   What Is Your Role?

You are part of every IS you use. When you look at the five components of an IS, you can see that the last component—people—includes you. Your mind and your thinking are not merely components of the information systems you use, they are the most important components.

Consider this example. Suppose you have the perfect IS, one that can predict the future. (No such IS exists, but, for this example, assume that it does.) Now, suppose that on December 14, 1966, your perfect IS tells you that the next day Walt Disney, the founder of Disney empire, will die. Say you have $50 000 to invest; you can either buy Disney stock or you can "short" it (an investment technique that will net you a positive return if the stock value decreases). Given that your IS is perfect, how would you invest?

Before you read on, think carefully about this question. If Walt Disney is going to die the next day, will Disney stock go up or down? Most students assume that the stock will go down, so they short it, on the basis of the theory that the loss of a company's founder will mean a dramatic drop in the share price.

In fact, the day after Walt Disney died, the value of Disney stock increased substantially. Why? There are several possible reasons, but one that many analysts agree on is that the market saw Walt Disney as an artist; once he died, it would no longer be

Helm: Software Making Waves

Tugboats might seem like the last place to look for innovative information technology. But Edoc Systems Group (www.helmoperations.com), a company with headquarters in Victoria, B.C., recognized the potential of information technology to automate business processes in this industry.

Tugboat companies are often family businesses that have been running for more than 100 years using paper-based systems. Things do not change quickly in this industry. For example, a Helm employee visiting an Oregon company found that the dispatch log sheet the company was currently using had been in use in the same format since 1952! How can information technology help this industry?

The first step is to understand the challenges the tugboat companies face. Each company has a fleet of vessels, a set of crews that run the vessels, and a list of jobs from various customers that need to be done. The dispatcher is the person at the centre of the business process that matches jobs with crews and vessels. It is a complicated process in which new jobs come in daily, vessels and crews have different capabilities, and customers have different priorities. Tugboats are also expensive (a tugboat can cost upward of $5 million and require thousands of dollars per day to run). Dispatchers require years of experience before they are ready to balance these factors and make efficient scheduling decisions.

Paper-based systems worked for decades, but they were relatively inefficient and prone to error. Why? To understand this, you need a more detailed view of the process: It began with a customer order (usually via phone or fax). An employee at the tug company wrote down the work that needed to be done; that description would then be rewritten and handed to tug captains as a job to do; dispatchers would copy it again onto the dispatch log sheet. When the job was completed, the captains handed their log sheets back to the dispatchers. Dispatchers reviewed the sheets and sent a delivery notice to their customer. The log sheets would then get passed to accounting staff, who rewrote (or retyped) the entire job into an invoice and sent it out. Finally, the

possible for more art to be created. Thus, the value of the existing art would increase because of scarcity, and the value of the corporation that owned that art would increase as well (another possible reason was that Disney would now be run by more professional management).

So what is the point? The point is that even if you have the perfect IS, if you do not know what to do with the information that it produces, you are simply wasting your time and money. The quality of your thinking is a large part of the quality of the IS. Substantial cognitive research has shown that, although you cannot increase your basic IQ (intelligence quotient), you can dramatically improve the quality of your thinking. You cannot change the computer in your brain, so to speak, but you can change the way you have programmed it to work. This course should help you think differently about information technology and its use in organizations. After reading this chapter, you should realize the central importance of information systems in supporting business processes and managerial decision making.

Figure 2-10
Edoc Logo

accountant would have to re-enter all the invoicing details into the accounting system.

Each job, therefore, was handwritten seven different times by at least four different people. Each written entry not only took a good deal of time but also was prone to copying errors.

Several years of work with tugboat companies resulted in developing HELM Marine Operations software. HELM supports the dispatch process first by equipping each vessel with a computer that runs HELM software. The software is used to keep track of the jobs assigned to the tugboat, details about each job, and

information about when the job is completed. This information from each of the boats is linked, through a computer network, with a central computer at the company's main office. This electronic linkage reduces the reliance on dispatch sheets and automates the job-completion notices that dispatchers need to send to their customers. The software also automatically produces invoices and links with the accounting system, thereby reducing even more data entry. HELM, therefore, provides more accurate and timely information. The hardware and software are used to save time for the dispatchers, captains, and accounting staff. HELM software has eliminated up to 60 percent of the steps involved in the invoicing process and saved companies tens of thousands of dollars each year by reducing errors. Reporting times have also been decreased by up to 90 percent—from 7 hours to 30 minutes in some cases. Helm now has customers around the world.

Questions

1. **What are the primary benefits realized by the use of HELM software?**
2. **Could HELM also result in increased revenue? Explain your answer.**
3. **Can you think of other benefits that might arise from the use of the software? For example, it is hard to find experienced dispatchers in the industry. Could the system help meet this challenge?**

Source: Edoc Systems Group Ltd.

Active   Review

Use this Active Review to verify that you have understood the material in the chapter. You can read the entire chapter and then perform the tasks in this review, or you can read the material for just one question and perform the tasks for that question before moving on to the next one.

Q1 "How did this stuff get here?"

Imagine yourself at a hockey or football game, or at a concert. What business processes are involved in producing that event? How did you buy a ticket? What processes were involved in that activity? What processes are needed to print the ticket? Who cleaned the stadium? What processes are involved in hiring, managing, and paying the cleaning staff?

Q2 What is a business process?

What is the definition of a business process? Consider one of the processes in your answer to Q1, and make a diagram similar to the one in Figure 2-1.

Q3 What are the components of a business process?

List the components of a business process. Define each component. Identify each type of component on your diagram from your answer to Q2.

Q4 What is information?

Give four definitions of *information*. Rank those definitions in the order of usefulness in business. Justify your ranking.

Q5 What is the role of information in business processes?

Explain how information is created in the payment activity in Figure 2-1. Describe three different types of information that could be produced from the data in the inventory database. Describe business process management and how it is related to information in business processes.

Q6 How do information systems support business processes?

Explain the meaning of each cell in Figures 2-4, 2-5, and 2-6. Explain the differences in the balance between automated and manual systems in these three information systems. Summarize the justification that the systems' designers used for constructing systems with the balance shown.

Q7 How do information systems support decision making?

Describe the differences among operational, managerial, and strategic decision making. What are the steps in a decision-making process? Explain how information systems can support these steps.

Q8 What is your role?

Explain why the quality of your thinking has a lot to do with the quality of the information system.

Key Terms and Concepts

Accurate information 29

Activities 28

Alternatives formulation 37

Automated system 32

Business process 26

Business process management (BPM) 31

Business Process Modeling Notation (BPMN) 28

Business system 26

Choice 37

Facilities 28

Implementation 37

Information 28

Intelligence gathering 37

Just barely so (information) 30

Lean production 32

Management information systems (MIS) 35

Managerial decisions 35

Manual system 34

Operational decisions 35

Relevant (information) 30

Resources 28

Review 37

Six sigma 32

Strategic decisions 36

Structured decision 36

Sufficient (information) 30

Timely information 30

Total quality management (TQM) 32

Transaction processing system (TPS) 35

Unstructured decision 36

Worth its cost (information) 30

Using Your Knowledge

1. Consider the four definitions of information presented in this chapter. The problem with the first definition, "knowledge derived from data," is that it merely substitutes one word whose meaning we do not know (*information*) for a second word whose meaning we do not know (*knowledge*). The problem with the second definition, "data presented in a meaningful context," is that it is too subjective. Whose context does it refer to? What makes a context meaningful? The third definition, "data processed by summing, ordering, averaging, etc." is too mechanical. It tells us what to do, but it does not tell us what information is. The fourth definition, "a difference that makes a difference," is vague and unhelpful.

   As well, none of these definitions helps us quantify the amount of information we receive. What is the information content of the statement that every human being has a navel? Zero—you already know that. However, the statement that someone has just deposited $50 000 into your chequing account is chock-full of information. So, good information has an element of surprise.

   Considering all these points, answer the following questions:
   a. What is information made of?
   b. If you have more information, do you weigh your decisions more? Why or why not?
   c. If you give a copy of your transcript to a prospective employer, is that information? If you show that same transcript to your dog, is it still information? Where is the information?
   d. Give your own best definition of *information*.
   e. Explain how you think it is possible that we have an industry called the information technology industry, but we have great difficulty defining the word *information*.

2. Reread the "MIS in Use" case to refresh your memory of the HELM system.
   a. Using Figure 2-1 as a guide, draw the paper-based process described in the case.
   b. Now draw the process after HELM was introduced.
   c. What are the major differences between the two processes?
   d. What are the improvements that have been made through the introduction of HELM? (*Hint*: Consider tangible and intangible benefits.)

3. The text states that information should be worth its cost. Both cost and value can be broken into tangible and intangible factors. Tangible factors can be directly measured; intangible ones arise indirectly and are difficult to measure. For example, a tangible cost is the cost of a computer monitor, while an intangible cost is the lost productivity related to a poorly trained employee.

   Give five important tangible and five important intangible costs of an IS. If it helps to focus your thinking, use the class scheduling system at your university or some other university IS to come up with your answer. When determining whether an IS is worth its cost, how do you think the tangible and intangible factors should be considered?

4. Singing Valley Resort is a top-end (rooms cost from $400 to $2500 per night), 50-unit resort located high in the Alberta Rockies. Singing Valley prides itself on its beautiful location, its relaxing setting, and its superb service. The resort's restaurant is highly rated and has an extensive list of exceptional wines. The affluent clients are accustomed to the highest levels of service.
   a. Give an example of three different operational decisions that Singing Valley personnel might make each day. Describe an IS that could be used to facilitate those decisions.

b. Give an example of three different managerial decisions that Singing Valley managers might make each week. Describe an IS that could be used to facilitate those decisions.

c. Give an example of three different strategic decisions that Singing Valley's owners might make in a year. Describe an IS for each.

d. Which of the decisions in your answers to questions (a) through (c) are structured? Which, if any, are unstructured?

Collaborative Exercises

1. This chapter introduced the concept of business process management (BPM). In the discussion, three methods for improving business processes were listed: total quality management (TQM), six sigma, and lean production. Do the following with your team:

a. Choose one of the methods listed above. Create a definition of the method, elaborate on how it works, and indicate where and when it was developed. Discuss how this method differs from other BPM methods.

b. Using the internet, find an example of at least one company that has used this method.

c. Combine what you have discovered in parts (a) and (b), and create a two-page (maximum) description of the method, aimed at an audience that has never heard of BPM or your method. Focus on what a manager should know about this method, and provide a list of useful web resources where more information is available. Be prepared to present your findings to the class.

2. Business process simulation is a method used to simulate a process so that you can explore different ways of managing the business process. IBM's INNOV8 software provides a "serious game" environment where you can explore business process simulation. Complete the following with your team:

a. Run through the demonstration for INNOV8 2.0. (You can find it at www-01. ibm.com/software/solutions/soa/innov8/innov8game.jsp.)[2]

b. Try at least one of the simulations (supply chain, customer service, or traffic). Record your best score.

c. Describe what your group learned from the simulation. Did you have enough information to make the necessary decisions? What data would you like to have had to help you get better scores?

Case Study 2

High Touch, High Tech

Founded in 1945, Vancity (www.vancity.ca) is Canada's largest credit union, with more than $13 billion in assets and 350 000 customers. The company is different from many other financial institutions because it is owned by its member customers rather than shareholders. Vancity's 2500 employees pride themselves on providing outstanding service that is personal and professional, while at the same time demonstrating innovation and social responsibility.

Like most financial institutions, Vancity offers its customers traditional banking products, such as savings and chequing accounts, loans, and credit cards, as well as a growing number of mutual funds and other investment and financial planning

[2] Courtesy of International Business Machines Corporation © International Business Machines Corporation.

services. However, this increase in the number of products and services is not without its challenges, particularly when coupled with increased customer access. The days when customers could transact business only while in a branch are long gone. Although a branch visit is still a cornerstone of banking, modern customers are just as likely to connect and do business with Vancity over the telephone or via the internet. Banking now happens anywhere and anytime, and customers are supported by sophisticated computer systems that are safe and secure. However, it is not just high technology for its own sake. Instead, as Tony Fernandes, former vice-president of Technology Strategy, puts it, "High tech is used to create high touch."

Although many people still visit their local branch and have developed a relationship with the customer service representatives (CSRs), this is not always possible and is increasingly becoming the least frequent way that customers do business. Staff changes, growth in the number of customers, and the fact that people are increasingly mobile mean that the in-branch staff are less likely to recognize their customers, and even if they do recognize them, staff may simply not be aware of the complete relationship the customer has with Vancity.

To address this problem, Vancity has implemented Customer Information File (CIF) technology to keep track of all the various types of business a customer has. Now, when customers visit the branch and present their customer card to the CSR, the CIF searches all the system records, identifies the services used, and develops a profile of the complete consolidated relationship between the client and Vancity. As a result, each customer receives the same high level of personal service even if it is his or her first time inside a particular branch, and Vancity is able to tailor or customize the experience specifically for that customer. For example, rather than ask all customers if they would like information on one of the new credit cards that Vancity offers, the system can advise the customer service representative as to whether the customer already has the card or should be offered something else. Alternatively, if a CSR member sees that a customer has an investment plan already set up, the CSR could be prompted to ask the customer about a new retirement product being launched by Vancity's mutual fund department.

Source: Vancity. Used with permission.

Questions

1. What challenges are created when providing anywhere, anytime services? (*Hint:* How and when did you conduct your last banking transaction?)
2. What business and technology issues would be faced by an organization that wants to have a complete view of its customers? (*Hint:* What are the benefits and costs of cooperation, and are there any privacy issues?)
3. Can you think of any examples where a lack of information or failure to consider the information could affect the profitability of a business?
4. If a customer has more than one account at a particular organization, should he or she receive separate mailings or all documentation in the same envelope?
5. Does being a credit union rather than a share corporation affect Vancity's structure?

Your Personal Competitive Advantage

Consider the following possibility: You work hard, earn your degree in business, and finally graduate, only to discover that you cannot find a job in your area of study. You look for jobs for six weeks or so, but then you begin to run out of money. In desperation, you take a job waiting tables at a local restaurant. Two years go by, the economy picks up, and the jobs you had been looking for are now available. Unfortunately, your degree is now two years old, and you are competing with students who have just graduated with fresh degrees (and fresh knowledge). Two years of waiting tables, as great as you are at it, does not appear to be good experience for the job you want. You are stuck in a nightmare, one that will be hard to get out of—and one that you should not allow to happen.

Consider the elements of competitive advantage as they apply to you personally. What are the skills that set you apart from the competition? Create a list of these skills. As an employee, the skills and abilities you offer are your personal product. Examine the first three items on the list, and ask yourself, "How can I use my time in school—and in this MIS class, in particular—to create new skills, to enhance those I already have, and to differentiate my skills from the competition?" (By the way, you will enter a national market and an international market. Your competition is not just the students in your class—it is also students attending classes in New York, China, Florida, Finland, and everywhere else MIS is taught today.)

Suppose you are interested in a sales job. What skills can you learn from your MIS class that will make you more competitive as a future salesperson? Get on the internet, and find examples of the use of information systems in the industry you are interested in. What about buyers and suppliers? How can you interpret those elements in terms of your own personal competitive advantage?

To get a job, you first need to have a working relationship. Do you have a co-op position or an internship? If not, can you get one? And once you have that co-op job or internship, how can you use your knowledge of MIS to lock in your job so that you get a job offer?

Human resources personnel say that networking is one of the most effective ways of finding a job. How can you use this class to establish alliances with other students? Does your class have a website? Is there an email list server for the students in your class? How can you use those facilities to develop job-seeking alliances with other students? Who in your class already has a job or an internship? Can any of those people provide suggestions or opportunities for finding a job?

Do not restrict your job search to your local area. Are there regions of Canada where jobs that interest you are more plentiful? How can you find out about student organizations in those regions? Search the web for MIS classes in other cities, and make contact with students there. Find out what opportunities there are in other places.

Finally, as you study MIS, think about how the knowledge you gain can help you save money for your employer. Even more, see if you can build a case that an employer would actually save money by hiring you. The line of reasoning might be that because of your knowledge of IS, you will be able to facilitate cost savings that more than compensate for your salary.

In truth, few of the ideas you generate for a potential employer will be feasible or pragmatic. The fact that you are thinking creatively, however, will indicate to a potential employer that you have initiative and are grappling with the problems that real businesses have. Keep thinking about competitive advantage and strive to understand how the topics you study can help you accomplish, personally, one or more of the objectives you have set out for yourself.

Discussion Questions

1. Summarize the efforts you have taken thus far to build an employment record that will lead to job offers after graduation.

2. Describe one way in which you have a competitive advantage over your classmates. If you do not have such a competitive advantage, describe actions you can take to obtain one.

3. To build your network, you can use your status as a student to approach business professionals. That is, you can contact them for help with an assignment or for career guidance. For example, suppose you want to work in banking, and you know that your local bank has a customer information system. You could call the bank manager and ask him or her how that system creates a competitive advantage for the bank. Also, you could ask to interview other employees. Describe two specific ways in which you can use your status as a student to build your network in this way.

4. Describe two ways you can use student alliances to obtain a job. How can you use information systems to build, maintain, and operate such alliances?

Application Extension 2a

Introduction to Business Process Modelling with Microsoft Visio

This chapter extension covers basic skills in modelling business processes. We have already provided an introduction to business processes in the previous chapter, so this application extension will be used to introduce process modelling. We will use MS Visio in this chapter to create the process models using **data flow** diagramming technique. We justify this choice in the discussion related to Study Question Q2 above.

Study Questions

Q1 What is business process modelling, and why is it important?

Q2 What tools can be used to create business process models?

Q3 How do you create a data flow diagram in MS Visio?

Q1 What is Business Process Modelling, and Why is it Important?

There is an old story about six blind men and an elephant that will help us introduce this topic. The story goes that a king asks six blind men to touch an elephant and describe what it is they are touching. One man touches the leg and says, "It is a pillar." Another touches the trunk and says, "It is a rope," . . . and on it goes, with each man touching a different part of the elephant and each suggesting a different thing. The truth is that all the men described the parts they touched, but the elephant is a collection of all those features. Business processes, by analogy, are like the elephant, and people who work in an organization are like the blind men. Not that everyone is blind in organizations, but when you work in an organization, you are sometimes completely unaware of the work done in other parts of the organization

When different people come from different departments to talk about the same business process, you can expect that each of them might describe the process differently (depending on their point of view). What business process modelling is supposed to do is provide the bigger picture—the picture of the entire elephant—so that everyone involved in the process can view the process from a wider and more inclusive perspective.

Given this introduction, business process modelling can be seen as the creation of a diagram and/or text that provides an overview of the flow of events that occur in an organization as a result of an important stimulus. The primary goal of business process modelling is to create a description of a process that enables people from different parts of an organization to understand and communicate effectively about the entire business process. Other goals in business process modelling might also include creating documentation of the process, gaining a better personal understanding of the process, or identifying areas for potential improvements in a process.

Business process modelling is part of a larger area of modelling sometimes referred to as *conceptual modelling*. People who are interested in conceptual modelling are trying to understand how the complicated "real" world can be simplified into models that "facilitate our developing, implementing, using and maintaining more valuable information systems."[3] It is the linkage between modelling and creating value that is important to understand.

---

[3] Y. Wand and R. Weber, "Research Commentary: Information Systems and Conceptual Modeling: A Research Agenda," *Information Systems Research* 13, no. 4 (2002), p. 363.

To begin, we have to recognize that a model of a business process, by itself, creates little or no direct value for an organization. An organization cannot sell its business process model to a customer because customers do not want to buy a "model" of a business process. Instead, customers want to use an "actual" business process. Customers want an organization to provide a reliable service or product when, where, and how they want it, at an acceptable price. The question we have to answer is: "How do models help organizations provide better products or services?"

Are You Process Aware?

There are many ways models can help create value through improving products and services, but each of these different ways comes from the same basic idea: Creating new value requires improving process knowledge in people involved in the process. This is the notion of making individuals **process aware**.[4] When people are process aware, they view their actions in the light of the larger business process, and they think about ways to improve the processes they are involved in. Developing this awareness can be very difficult, particularly when the processes are complex. This is where the value of process modelling becomes realized. Process models create value when they help individuals develop an improved understanding of the process as a whole and become more process aware.

The benefits of being more aware of the processes you are involved in can be substantial. It provides you with a better understanding of how the organization currently operates. You can see the limitations (what cannot be done) because you have an understanding of what the capabilities are in each part of the process. With a little bit of thinking and innovation, you also might discover the potential improvements in a process or room for new products and services. Being process aware keeps you thinking about not only what happens in the physical world around you but also what happens within the systems that collect information about these processes. Understanding how to create process models is an important first step in developing an awareness of processes and realizing these potential benefits.

02 What Tools Can Be Used to Create Business Process Models?

There are many applications that support the development of business process models. These applications are often referred to as *modelling tools*. These include commercial applications, such as Visio (Microsoft), Rational Rose (IBM), and Together (Borland). Each of these applications provides diagramming features that include shapes and templates that support the development of a number of process models. Most of the applications now provide the ability to import and export the graphic models so that the models can be shared across different modelling applications and platforms.

In the land of software applications, the term *tool* can sometimes be difficult to understand. When you hear different information technology (IT) professionals talking about the same piece of software as a "program" or "application" or "technique" or "tool," it can get a bit confusing. We would like to add some clarity to these terms so that you can understand what is included in the process modelling software you might use. We will, therefore, also discuss process modelling techniques and process

---

[4] J. C. Recker and M. Rosemann, "Teaching Business Process Modelling: Experiences and Recommendations," *Communications of the Association for Information Systems* 25, no. 32 (2009). pp. 379–94.

modelling applications. Taken together, the process modelling technique and the application that is used to draw the diagrams will be referred to as the "tool" for process modelling.

Process Modelling Techniques

The first thing to learn is that there are many different diagramming techniques that could be used to create a business process model. Each technique describes a set of graphical elements and rules for combining these elements to create a readable diagram. Some of the most common business **process modelling techniques** include **data flow diagrams (DFDs)**, systems flowcharts, workflow diagrams, use cases from the Unified Modeling Language (UML), and business process diagrams from the Business Process Modeling Notation (BPMN). Some of these techniques, such as data flow diagramming, have been around since the 1970s. Other techniques, such as UML and BPMN, are more recent and have been in use since 2000. An important first question to consider is which techniques are used most often by practitioners.

A group of Australian researchers—Islay Davies, Peter Green, Michael Rosemann, Marta Indulska, and Stan Galo—published an article in 2006 on this subject.[5] They reported that among Australian practitioners, the four most commonly used techniques for process modelling were (1) data flow diagrams (60 percent), (2) systems flowcharts (55 percent), (3) workflow diagrams (46 percent), and (4) Unified Modeling Notation (35 percent). In a related 2009 study of German practitioners,[6] the author found that the most commonly used techniques were (1) Unified Modeling Notation (78 percent), (2) data flow diagrams (58 percent), (3) workflow diagrams (58 percent), and (4) systems flowcharts (42 percent). Although differences in the use of process modelling techniques across countries are to be expected, the fact that data flow diagrams were used by approximately 60 percent of all practitioners in both studies suggests that data flow diagramming remains a useful technique for process modelling. We encourage those interested in more recent techniques, such as UML and BPMN, to take a course in systems analysis and design, where these more recently developed techniques are likely to be discussed in more detail. In this chapter extension, we have the space to focus on only one technique, so we will focus on the more traditional data flow diagramming.

Process Modelling Applications

When there are many applications to accomplish the same basic task, it is important to consider the application in which you want to develop skills. For example, if you learn how to create process models with an application that only a few people use, then you risk not being able to transfer your skills when either you move to a different company that uses a different tool or the organization you work for changes the application it is using. When you invest in learning an application, it is usually a good idea to find the market leader and learn to use tools that other organizations are also using.

Fortunately, the studies we noted earlier also provide us with information about the **process modelling applications** that are most often used. The Fettke 2009 study reported that the five most used applications were (1) MS Visio (74 percent), (2) Rational Rose (40 percent), (3) ARIS Express (38 percent), (4) Oracle Developer (28 percent), and (5) Together (20 percent). The Davies et al. 2006 study reported

---

[5] I. Davies et al., "How Do Practitioners Use Conceptual Modeling in Practice?" *Data and Knowledge Engineering* 58 (2006): 358–80.
[6] P. Fettke, "How Conceptual Modeling Is Used," *Communications of the Association for Information Systems* 25 (2009): 1–25.

that the four most used applications were (1) MS Visio (61 percent), (2) Rational Rose (21 percent), (3) Oracle Developer (15 percent), and (4) iGrafx FlowCharter (18 percent). Both studies showed that MS Visio is a market leader with regard to the number of practitioners using the application for process modelling. Therefore, this application extension will focus on the use of MS Visio. Data flow diagrams drawn using MS Visio are our tool of choice to introduce business process modelling.

03 How Do You Create a Data Flow Diagram in MS Visio?

Microsoft Visio is an application that is built to help people create diagrams. It has a more sophisticated graphics engine compared with presentation software, such as MS PowerPoint, and it comes loaded with shapes and diagram templates to help you create diagrams quickly. One of the templates provided in Visio is the Data Flow Diagram (DFD) template. Figure AE2a-1 shows how you can find the DFD drawing template under the "Software and Database" category of diagram templates.

Double-click on the icon to open the DFD template. This will give you a new blank diagram and also provide you with the basic shapes for drawing a DFD on the left-hand side of the screen. Click on "File/Save," and give your new diagram a name.

Figure AE2a-1

Choosing a DFD Template in MS Visio

Source: Microsoft Visio

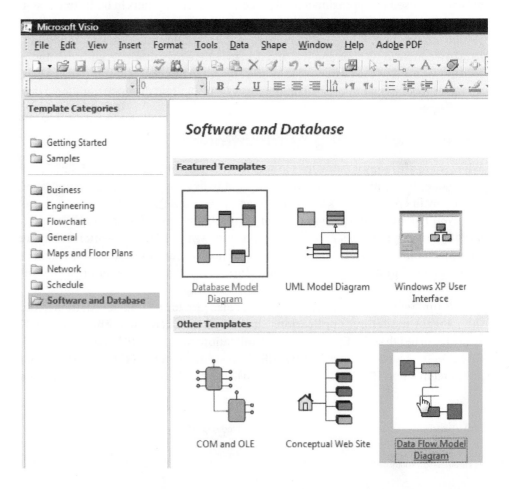

DFD Shapes

Take a look at the top left-hand side of the screen. You will see the title "Gane-Sarson" (Gane and Sarson are the original developers), which includes four simple shapes including (1) process, (2) interface (entity), (3) data store, and (4) connector (or data flow). The **process** symbolizes a set of related activities. The **interface** (often labelled "**external entity**") symbolizes a person or thing that exists outside of the process. The **data store** symbolizes a place where data are either stored or retrieved, and a data flow connector represents the data that flow between processes, entities, and data stores. One of the most appealing aspects of DFDs is the simple set of shapes used to draw a business process. It takes time and experience to translate a real system into a DFD, so do not get frustrated, as you should expect it to takes a bit of time to get used to.

Rules for Combining Shapes

Now that you are aware of the basic shapes, there are three basic rules you need to observe when drawing a DFD.

Rule 1: Every process should have at least one data flow connector coming into it and at least one data flow connector going out of it.

The second rule is that a data store should be secure, and, therefore, a data store cannot be directly connected to an external entity. It must be connected through a process.

Rule 2: An external entity cannot be directly connected to a data store.

The third rule recognizes that data stores do not work by themselves. Therefore, data stores cannot be directly connected to each other. Instead, data stores must be connected to a process that receives or sends data.

Rule 3: A data store cannot be directly connected to another data store. A data store must be connected to a process.

These three basic rules provide the constraints for how you can combine the different shapes. While the constraints might initially seem limiting, you will find that you can describe a wide array of business processes with the four simple shapes mentioned in the preceding section and these three simple rules.

Levelling

Business processes can be quite complex. The DFD model uses the concept of **levelling** to slowly reveal increasing amounts of detail. The least amount of detail is provided by what is called a **level-0 diagram** or a *top process*. Note that the label in the bottom left of the screen of the diagram in Figure AE2a-2 is "Top Process." This top process simply shows a large single process (often named the *business process*) and the external entities involved in the process. To show you a level-0 DFD, we will need an example of a business process. The example we will use is the process of organizing an entertainment event. In this process, we have two external entities—Promoter and Employee. We will provide more detail about this process in the coming pages, but for now, this is all we need to draw the level-0 DFD.

To draw the level-0 DFD, find the "Interface" shape at the top left of the screen, drag the shape, and drop it near the top left corner of the drawing area. Double-click on the shape, and you will be able to enter a label. Type the label "Promoter" into this entity. Next, drag another "Interface" shape to the bottom right corner of the drawing area. Label this entity "Employee." Now drag a "Process" shape into the middle of the drawing area. Grab onto the corners of the process shape once it has been dropped in

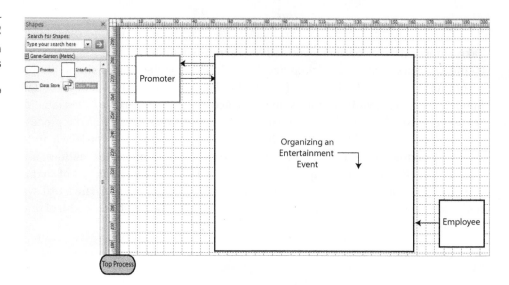

the drawing area, and you will be able to manipulate it to change its size. We are going to make only a single process in this top process diagram, so we will make the process shape larger. Once you have the right size, double-click on the process, and label it "Organizing an Entertainment Event." Refer to Figure AE2a-2 to see the size and location of the shapes.

Our next step is to connect the shapes with the data flow connectors. To make an automatic connection, click on the "Data Flow" connector shape, and drag it over the middle of the "Interface" shape on the drawing area labelled "Promoter." When you drag it over the middle of the shape, a red line will surround the shape. This red line means that an automatic connection will be made, as shown in Figure AE2a-2. When you release the mouse button, a connection will be made between the shape and the connector. Do not worry about the shape of the connection. This will be adjusted when we make our connection to the next shape.

Now we have to connect the data flow connector to the second shape, which is always the destination for the data flow. In this case, we want to connect the "Promoter" and the "Organizing an Entertainment Event" shapes. To do this, we have to find the unconnected "arrow" end of the connector we just dropped on the "Promoter" object. Click and drag the unconnected arrow end to the middle of the "Organizing an Entertainment Event" process shape and then drop the connector. What will happen is that a straight line will be drawn between the two shapes. If you want to delete a connector, you just need to click on it once and then hit the delete button. We often label these connectors; to place a label on a connector, double-click on the connector, and then type the label. One thing to note is that with an automatic connection, the connectors move and adjust as the shapes move, so it makes it easier to alter the diagram. Try adjusting or moving a shape and see what happens.

This is all we need for the top process diagram. Now save your DFD by selecting the "File/Save" option on the menu.

Creating a Level-1 DFD

The top process or level-0 diagram does not provide us with much detail about the process. Our next step is to create a **level-1 diagram**. To do this, we first have to insert a new diagram into the Visio file. We do this by selecting the "Insert/New Page" option on the Visio menu. When you make this selection, a pop-up window, such as the one shown in Figure AE2a-3, will appear, and you can name your new page "Level-1."

Figure AE2a-3

Adding and Naming a New Page in an Existing Visio File

Source: Microsoft Visio

An easy way to start your level-1 diagram is to copy and paste the shapes you made for the top process diagram into the page now labelled "Level-1." To do this, click on the tab at the bottom left-hand side of the screen labelled "Top Process." Next, click "Edit/Select All" to select all the shapes. Select "Edit/Copy" to copy the shapes to the clipboard. Next, click on the page tab labelled "Level-1," and then select "Edit/Paste." All the shapes have now been pasted from the "Top Process" to the "Level-1" page.

Our next step is to get rid of the big "Organizing an Entertainment Event" process, because we want to replace it with a more detailed one. To do this, just click on the big process, and then hit the "Delete" key. Now we want to add more detail. Below is a description of a set of activities related to creating an event application for holding an entertainment event:

To book an event, a promoter submits an event application that explains the type of event being promoted, the expected attendance, and a requested date and time for the event. After reviewing the promoter's application, the application is either accepted and placed in the program of events, or rejected. The promoter is contacted about the Reject/Accept decision.

How would we draw the process described above? Since the promoter submits an event application, we have a data flow (Submit Event Application) and a process (Review Event Application). The application submission is the input of the process and the "Accept/Reject Decision" is the output of the decision. Accepted applications get stored in the Program of Events, which sounds like a data store. You now have all the information you need to create this part of the diagram. Figure AE2a-4 shows how your diagram might look.

That takes care of the application process, but how are the employees involved? Organizing an entertainment event requires more than just reviewing the applications. You also have to provide staff for the event. The text below describes what happens after a successful application is placed in the program of events.

Figure AE2a-4

Drawing the Event Application Process

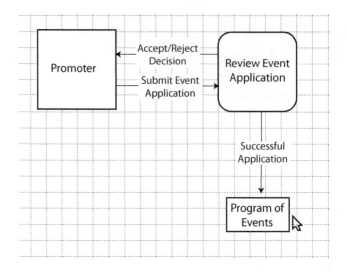

Events in the program of events must have a seating plan, and the appropriate number of security personnel, cleaners, and customer service representatives for the event must be decided. Once the staffing requirements are finalized, a deployment sheet is created. The deployment sheet lists the start time, end time, location, and skill requirements for every shift that will be required for the event. The empty deployment sheets are then passed to Human Resources, who schedule and contact employees who will work the event. Employees then confirm their work shifts.

How would we draw the process described here? Deciding the appropriate number and type of employees is a process (Determine Staffing Requirements). These requirements are placed in a data store (Staffing Requirements). A process (Create Deployment Sheets) then generates a data flow (Deployment Sheets), which is connected to a process (Schedule and Contact Employees) that results in employees being asked to work and provide a confirmation. We now have all the information we need to create the next part of the diagram. Figure AE2a-5 shows how your diagram

Figure AE2a-5

Drawing the Employee Scheduling Process

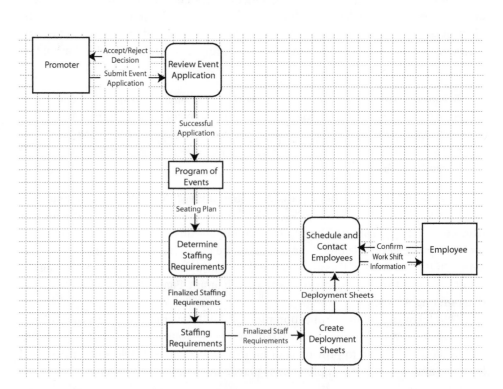

might look with these added shapes. Make sure to save your latest diagram using the "File/Save" menu option.

Level 2 Anyone?

Now that you have created a level-1 diagram, you are probably aware that you can go into even more detail in a level-2 diagram. Each of the processes in the level-1 diagram shown in Figure AE2a-5 could themselves be opened up and examined in more detail in a level-2 diagram. We will not do this in this short introduction. But the potential to go into ever-increasing detail does exist. Where does it stop? Here is where you have to go back to the objective of creating process models. The main goal is always to improve our knowledge of processes and provide a wider perspective. The need for detail will vary, depending on the experience of the people considering the process. Sometimes an overview is all that is needed, and sometimes you have to get into nitty-gritty details. Understanding what level of detail to provide is something that is usually learned through experience.

Summary

This material has introduced you to process modelling through data flow diagramming using Microsoft Visio. You have learned about process models, the importance of becoming process aware, the basic elements of a DFD, and how to create simple level-0 and level-1 DFDs by using MS Visio. We did not, however, show you the details with regard to numbering the various processes across DFD levels and how to document the linkages between DFD levels. Such tasks are part of a more advanced course on systems analysis and design. There are many other diagramming templates in MS Visio. The program has become a standard for many people working in the area of process modelling. Consider developing your skills in the area as your knowledge of the process will make you more valuable to an organization, and your awareness of the importance of business processes will also likely lead you to success, regardless of the business area you will be involved in.

Active ? Review

Use this Active Review to verify that you have understood the material in the chapter extension. You can read the entire chapter extension and then perform the tasks in this review, or you can read the material for just one question and perform the tasks in this review for that question before moving on to the next one.

01 What is business process modelling, and why is it important?

Explain what is meant by business process modelling. How does process modelling add value to an organization? What does it mean to be process aware? Describe how being process aware can make you more valuable to an organization.

02 What tools can be used to create business process models?

Define the term *process modelling technique*. Can you name three different process modelling techniques? Which techniques are most popular among practitioners? What process modelling applications are most popular?

03 How do you create a data flow diagram in MS Visio?

What are the four main shapes used in a DFD? What are the three rules for combining DFD shapes? What is meant by the term *levelling*? What does a level-0 diagram contain?

MyMISLab is an online learning and testing environment that features the perfect study tools to help you master the concepts covered in this chapter. Log in to MyMISLab to test your knowledge of key chapter concepts and explore additional practice tools, including videos, flashcards, annotated text figures, and more!

Key Terms and Concepts

Data flow 47

Data flow diagram (DFD) 49

Data store 51

External entity (Interface) 51

level-0 diagram 51

level-1 diagram 52

Levelling 51

Process 51

Process aware 48

Process modelling applications 49

Process modelling techniques 49

Using Your Knowledge

1. Draw level-0 and level-1 data flow diagrams that describe the registration process at your school. When creating the diagrams, keep in mind the objective—explaining the process to a student who will be entering your school next year. Provide as much detail as you think is sufficient to adequately explain the process to the entering student.

2. Draw level-0 and level-1 data flow diagrams for the following process descriptions:
   a. An Information Technology Infrastructure Library (ITIL) conference is an international conference centred on a topic of specific interest to one or more ITIL Working Groups. Participation in the conference is by invitation only. Two objectives of the conference organizers are to ensure that members of the involved Working Group(s) and Technical Committee(s) are invited and that attendance is sufficient for financial break-even without exceeding the capacity of the facilities available.
   b. Two committees are involved in organizing an ITIL conference: a Program Committee and an Organizing Committee. The Program Committee deals with the technical content of the conference, and the Organizing Committee handles financial and local arrangements, along with invitations and publicity. These committees work together closely and have a need for common information.
   c. When an ITIL conference is to be held, the Program Committee is responsible for several activities. These include preparing a mailing list of potential authors and sending a call for papers to each of these individuals. If the potential authors reply with a letter of intent indicating that they will submit a paper to the conference, the Program Committee registers the participant's intent to participate. After the paper is received, it is registered.
   d. After receiving the papers, the Program Committee assigns a set of reviewers for each paper and then sends the papers to the respective reviewers. Reviewers create a review report and send their reports to the committee. The committee then groups accepted papers into sessions and assigns session chairs. The list of accepted authors is forwarded to the organizing committee. This session information makes up the itinerary for the conference.

e. The Organizing Committee begins by preparing a list of people to invite to the conference. The committee issues priority invitations to National Representatives and to members of related Working Groups. The organizing committee also ensures that each of the contributing authors receives an invitation. Individuals who receive an invitation and who intend to come to the conference must indicate their intent to participate by sending an acceptance of invitation to the Organizing Committee. The final list of participants is then generated by the Program Committee, which makes an effort to avoid sending duplicate invitations to any individual.

3 Productivity, Innovation, and Strategy

Running Case

Josie worked through the issues with the wireless internet, and revenue at Café Italiano is up about 10 percent since implementing the network. Customers receive a wireless password on their receipt and must agree to a policy on appropriate use before using the network. There have been a few glitches, but, overall, the experiment has been a success. Josie's grandparents are delighted with the results.

Josie has been thinking about gaining an even greater competitive advantage before the franchise coffee shop opens. He has noticed that many customers are using their smartphones in the café and that they are often on social networking sites. Josie is thinking about setting up Facebook and Twitter pages to gather feedback and create more of a connection with customers. Good reviews will certainly help future business. He wonders though, who will monitor these sites, and what will keep them from getting outdated? Josie does not see his grandparents getting interested in Facebook anytime soon. Josie is also worried about the negative implications of some messages. It is impossible to control the flow of information and opinions on social networking sites, so Josie realizes that it is a big step and that Café Italiano should think about this carefully before joining these sites.

Josie is also investigating some group-buying discount services (e.g., Groupon). These come with a cost and require discounts to be successful, but they seem like good ideas. He has talked to other shop owners on the street, and they have said that group-buying discounts can be good advertising but that you have to be ready for the extra demand. Not every discount offer works, and other shop owners suggest that deep discounts are what people are really looking for. Josie and his

grandparents are concerned about the long-term implications of this strategy. Will people start to expect these discounts? Will the customers only come for coffee when the prices are deeply discounted? What signal does this send to their regular customers who enjoy their current experience?

Josie is realizing that participating in social networking sites and group-buying discounts requires an overall strategy. Does Café Italiano want to maintain its current customers, or does it want to grow? Is it looking to create a more upscale experience with higher prices and higher levels of customer service, or is the café looking to provide the best coffee value to a large number of customers? Making these decisions requires a firm understanding of the industry and the behaviour of competitors. Josie realizes that before he can make any decisions about using social networking, he has to get a better handle on the goals and objectives of his grandparents. In this way, he can better align his grandparents' overall strategy with the potential benefits of social networking. He has again realized that what looked like a decision to adopt some social networking *technology* is really an important *business decision*.

Study Questions

Q1 Why should I care about productivity and innovation?

Q2 What is business technology management (BTM), and how is it related to productivity and innovation?

Q3 How do information systems improve productivity?

Q4 How are organizational strategy and industry structure related?

Q5 What is the relationship between innovation and information technology?

Q6 How do information systems provide competitive advantage?

Q7 Can competitive advantage through information systems be sustained?

Q1 Why Should I Care About Productivity and Innovation?

Productivity, or, more precisely, labour productivity, is the ratio of the gross domestic product (GDP) of a country divided by the total paid hours worked by people in the country. Productivity is an important issue that we need to think about. The Conference Board of Canada has suggested that labour productivity is the primary indicator of our per capita income[1] and that increasing labour productivity is the best measure of Canada's future growth. Unfortunately, by all measures, Canada has not been doing well in increasing its labour productivity. Labour productivity in Canada measures the value that Canadian workers generate per hour, which, for the latest data available, was about $50 per hour (compared with $67 for the U.S. and $75 for Norway[2]).

It has not always been this way. Historically, Canada had a strong 4 percent average annual labour productivity growth from 1950 to 1975. This was followed by a weaker period of growth with an average of 1.6 percent from 1975 to 2000 and an even weaker period of growth since 2000. In 2008, Canada was ranked 14th among its peer countries on the level of labour productivity. Canada's level of productivity is much lower than that of the United States and has fallen to 80 percent of the U.S. level.[3]

Increasing productivity is not necessarily about working harder or spending more hours working. The fact is that even if Canadian employees worked more intensely, Canada would still not have addressed its productivity issues. Increasing productivity in our current global economy is all about working smarter. What will determine a country's level of productivity in the future is its ability to innovate and adapt to changing economic conditions.[4]

Canada has been trying to increase its productivity and innovative capacity for many years. Most experts agree that to enhance productivity, Canada must foster a culture of innovation, open its industries to more competition, and increase the amount of machinery and equipment (M&E) in the economy (particularly in the **Information and Communications Technology [ICT] sector**). Raising the economy's ICT capital intensity means increasing the amount of technology that supports people working. You may find it difficult to argue that computers do not have any impact on the productivity of our economy. But in 1989, that is precisely what economist Stephen Roach reported.[5]

Roach said that his analysis found no evidence of an increase in labour productivity associated with the massive increase in investment in information technology (IT). This result, along with those of other similar studies, led the Nobel Prize-winning economist Robert Solow to make the now-famous statement, "We see computers everywhere except in the productivity statistics." Thus, the **productivity paradox** was born. Although this issue is more than 25 years old, the question of how IT adds to **productivity**—that is, how IT can be used to create **business value**—remains important. Perhaps the most interesting fact about the productivity paradox is that it was never really viewed as a paradox by most organizations. Despite the widespread publicizing of the paradox, organizations continued to pour investment

---

[1] See discussion on "Economy" at www.conferenceboard.ca/hcp/Details/Economy.aspx

[2] Data accessed May 24, 2014, and quoted from http://en.wikipedia.org/wiki/List_of_countries_by_GDP_%28PPP%29_per_hour_worked

[3] There are many sources for these data, but an excellent one can be found at www.conferenceboard.ca/hcp/hot-topics/investProd.aspx.

[4] See discussion on "Innovation" at www.conferenceboard.ca/hcp/Details/Innovation.aspx.

[5] S. S. Roach, "America's White-Collar Productivity Dilemma," *Manufacturing Engineering* (August 1989): 104.

dollars into information technology. The majority of businesses seemed able to justify large investments in IT.

Over time, it has been recognized that measurement error may be a critical reason for the observed lack of productivity increase from IT investments;[6] this measurement difficulty may be more evident due to our increasingly service-based economy. The mismeasurement is also, in part, due to the often-invisible or intangible benefits associated with IT. (For example, you could complete your latest essay assignment without a computer and perhaps use a typewriter instead. You still have to type the words, so there is no typing time saved. What does a computer add to this process? Does the computer make you more productive? How much time does it save? How much does a computer improve your performance?)

One response to the productivity paradox is a careful consideration of the value that can be derived from IT investment.[7] Researchers have suggested three different ways in which the value of IT can be realized. The first is through productivity. IT allows a company to create more and/or better output from the same inputs and create them faster than before the technology was in place. For example, if you had a small accounting firm, investing in IT might allow you to add more customers, automate basic tasks (e.g., completing tax forms), and provide more up-to-date information for clients. This investment makes the firm more efficient and potentially more effective.

The second way to realize the investment value of IT is through the structure of competition. IT can alter the way corporations compete. For example, when one accounting firm invests in IT, often rival firms will follow suit to keep up with their competition. Accounting firms now compete with the software they offer and the technical support they can provide. The competitive structure changes because of IT. Another example is in the video rental industry. When IT enabled people to rent movies at home through Netflix, eliminating the need to get in the car and drive to the video rental store, the industry changed because the technology had changed the structure of competition.

The final way that IT investment value is realized is through benefits to the end customer. IT helps make processes more efficient and changes the nature of competition. With increased competition, the reduction of costs associated with new processes is often passed on to the final consumer. The consumer may, therefore, see cheaper and better goods and services as a result of IT. For example, competing accounting firms may be able to offer their clients more services or lower prices on services after investing in IT. Thus, the consumer, rather than the provider, often reaps the benefits of higher investment in IT.

Some controversy remains with regard to how productive IT investments are. In today's world, organizations cannot afford to invest in IT simply because "everybody else is doing it" and then hope for the best. We call that strategy "technology for technology's sake," and it simply does not work. Successful organizations need to understand specifically what business value they are seeking and how IT can help secure that value. Doing this consistently and successfully requires knowledge of both IT and business. It is for this reason that organizations value people who are able to understand both technology and business, leading to our next topic: Business Technology Management.

---

[6] See E. Brynjolfsson, "The Productivity Paradox of Information Technology: Review and Assessment," *Communications of the ACM* 36, no. 12 (December 1993): 67–77; and J. L. King, "IT Responsible for Most Productivity Gains," *Computing Research News* 15, no. 4 (September 2003): 1–6, http://archive.cra.org/CRN/articles/sept03/king.html.

[7] L. Hitt and E. Brynjolfsson, "Productivity, Profit and Consumer Welfare: Three Different Measures of Information Technology's Value," *MIS Quarterly* 20, no. 2 (June 1996): 121–42.

Q2 What Is Business Technology Management (BTM), and How Is It Related to Productivity and Innovation?

One of the responses to the challenge of low productivity has been to look more closely at the ICT industry sector in Canada. The ICT industry sector is considered an important industry for productivity and **innovation** because it includes technologies that can enhance individual and organizational productivity across many industries. It has sometimes been referred to as the "invisible" industry sector because it does not produce as much direct output as other industries, such as forestry, mining, or auto manufacturing. Instead, the ICT industry sector indirectly supports activities in other industries with tools that make these other industries more productive. Canadian policymakers, therefore, look to the ICT industry as a primary driver of innovation and increased productivity among all Canadian industries. In Canada, there are about a million workers in ICT-type jobs, which have grown by approximately 8 percent annually in the past decade.

The focus on innovation in ICT has influenced the set of skills that workers in this industry are expected to have to be successful. In the previous decades, success in the ICT industry was often directly related to a person's level of technical skill. The more highly technical the skills, the higher the salary, and the better the prospects in the job market. In the past 10 years, the types of skills demanded in the ICT industry have broadened; businesses are increasingly looking for people who can drive technological innovation within their organizations. These new skills combine both technology and more traditional business skills.[8]

On May 10, 2010, the Canadian government released a document titled "Improving Canada's Digital Advantage: Strategies for Sustainable Prosperity." This consultation paper contained a request for advice to shape the strategy for a multi-year digital economy for Canada. Between May 10 and July 13, 2010, more than 2000 Canadian individuals and organizations registered to share their ideas. The impact of this consultation has yet to be determined, but the future path seems clear. Jobs that combine business and technology will be in high demand in the future.

The need for students with combined technology and business skills has increased the need for educational programs that combine technology and business training. The **Canadian Coalition for Tomorrow's ICT Skills (CCICT)** was founded by Bell Canada in 2007 for just this purpose. The CCICT created an industry-led group of Canadian employers, educational institutions, and industries that could ensure the ability of Canadian organizations to hire ICT professionals for the twenty-first century workforce. In 2009, a working group of the CCICT designed a set of learning outcomes for a new program named **Business Technology Management (BTM)**. These learning outcomes drew on skills frameworks, such as the **Skills Framework for the Information Age (SFIA)**. The CCICT developed CareerMash (www.careermash.ca) to provide more specific information on jobs within the ICT industry. Many people are surprised to learn that the ICT sector has a wide variety of jobs and that not all jobs are highly technical in nature. The CCICT has now merged with the Information Technology Association of Canada (ITAC) to further the awareness and development of Business Technology Management skills.[9]

Now that these learning outcomes have been defined, universities across Canada are developing programs for BTM. They include a variety of course topics, such as

---

[8] A discussion of these skills can be found in a report titled "Jobs 2.0: How Canada Can Win in the 21st Century Global Marketplace for Information and Communications Technologies and Services (ICTS)," http://ccict.ca/reports/jobs-2-0.

[9] You can read more about this merger here: http://itac.ca/blog/ccict-merges-with-itac-to-form-itac-talent/.

business and technical training, financial accounting, system analysis and design, project management, IT infrastructure, marketing, international business management, writing and business communication, organizational behaviour, and teamwork skills. BTM programs are designed for students who are inspired to use technology to innovate and improve productivity.

⊙⊢Watch

Go to MyMISLab to watch a video about competitive strategy.

03 How Do Information Systems Improve Productivity?

We saw in Chapter 2 that companies organize work through business processes. Business processes use resources, facilities, and information to accomplish activities. Business processes are, therefore, an important consideration in productivity. Productivity for organizations can be increased either through increased efficiency or more effective business processes.

Increasing **efficiency** means that business processes can be accomplished either more quickly or with fewer resources and facilities (or both). Efficiency is usually relatively easy to measure once you have decided which measures are important. When organizations focus on efficiency, they are working toward "doing things right." Doing things right often means using just the right amount of resources, facilities, and information to complete the job satisfactorily.

When companies focus on increasing **effectiveness** rather than efficiency, they are interested in "doing the right things." Increased effectiveness means that the company considers offering either new or improved goods or services that the customer values. Doing the right things often requires companies to consider changing their business processes to deliver something new and improved.

Sometimes, "doing the right things" and "doing things right" can be in conflict in a company. For example, Company A could be so focused on increasing efficiency that it misses the fact that customers have changed and no longer value Company A's product. Company A might be doing things right, but it is not doing the right things.

In another example, Company B has a product that customer really value but Company B is so focused on changing its product to perfectly suit its customers that it does not spend enough time thinking about how efficient its processes are. Company B might be doing the right things, but it is not doing things right. Company B operates relatively inefficiently and would be at a cost disadvantage relative to other firms that are more efficient.

We might argue about whether "doing things right" or "doing the right things" is more important, but it is clear that companies with long-term success understand the importance of finding the balance between effectiveness and efficiency.

Business Processes and Value Chains

Business processes are closely related to the concept of a value chain. A **value chain** is a network of activities that improve the effectiveness (or value) of a good or service. A value chain is, therefore, made up of at least one and often many business processes.

Let us look at a specific example. A customer in Canada does not see much value in a large blob of natural rubber harvested at a rubber farm in Vietnam. What would you pay for something like this? Likely not much. But when a tire manufacturing company ships that blob of rubber to a factory, has engineers design a high-performance, all-season radial tire, and then sends the blob of rubber through the various processes required to make the tire, the blob of rubber has gained some value. How much would you pay for the rubber now? Even more value is gained when the tire is shipped to a tire store close to the customer, and more still is created when a mechanic at the store installs the tire.

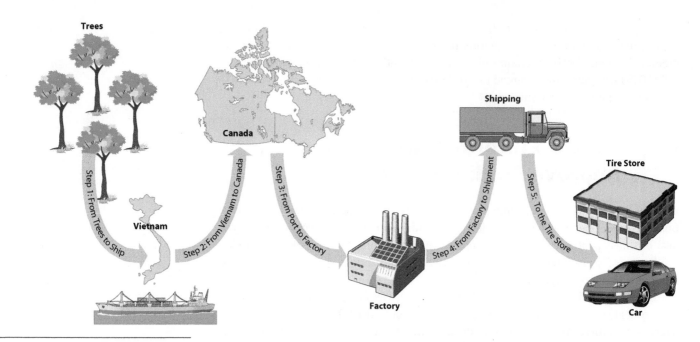

Figure 3-1

Business Process

Each of these steps in the chain—each of these business processes—adds some value, as shown in Figure 3-1. This is why we refer to this chain of events as a value chain.

Value chains have directions—upstream and downstream. Organizations that expand into activities related to the basic raw materials of a process—such as a tire company that decides to manufacture its own rubber or a coffee store that decides to grow its own coffee—are said to be undertaking backward integration or to be moving upstream in the value chain. Those that move closer to end customers—for example, a mining company that begins to cut and finish its own diamonds rather than sell raw stones wholesale—would be undertaking forward integration, or moving downstream in the value chain.

In general, the more value a company adds to a good or service in its value chain, the higher the price the company can charge for the final product. The difference between the price the customer is willing to pay and the cost the company incurs in moving the goods or services through the value chain is defined as the **margin**. Raw diamonds, for example, are sold at a much lower margin than finished diamonds. The greater the margin, the greater the profit (per unit) for the company.

The concept of a value chain was formalized by Michael Porter, a professor at Harvard University. He identified two types of activities that support value chains. **Primary activities** are activities in which value is added directly to the product. In our example above, shipping raw materials, designing the tires, manufacturing the tires, shipping the finished tires, and installing the tires are all primary activities. Each of these primary activities adds value for the customer.

But there is a whole range of activities in companies that do not add value directly to the product. For instance, who pays the workers in the factory? Who bought the machines at the factory that makes the tires? Who maintains the machines inside the factory and keeps the lights on and the heat working? Who schedules the shipping of the finished tires? Who keeps track of the mechanics' hours? These activities, and many more, are referred to as **support activities**, because they support the primary activities.

Support activities add value only indirectly. For example, nobody buys a tire because a company has a great payroll system. But a company could not run a factory without a payroll system. A great payroll system might make the company more efficient and allow it to offer a lower price than its competitors. The benefit of the payroll system may not directly add to the value as seen by the customer, but these

Primary Activity	Description
Inbound logistics	Receiving and storing inventory
Operations	Using inputs to create or generate the final product
Outbound logistics	Retrieving and distributing the product or service to the customers
Marketing and sales	Convincing the customer and enabling purchase of the good or service
Service	Supporting the customers use of the product or service

Figure 3-2

Task Descriptions for Primary Activities of the Value Chain

Source: Adapted with the permission of The Free Press, a Division of Simon & Schuster Adult Publishing Group, from *Competitive Advantage: Creating and Sustaining Superior Performance* by Michael E. Porter. Copyright © 1985, 1998 by Michael E. Porter. All rights reserved.

support activities are critical to the success of the organization. Figure 3-2 summarizes the concepts we have just discussed. The questions accompanying the "Winterbourne Bicycle Institute" in "MIS In Use" at the end of this chapter can be used to further explore the concept and ideas of the value chain.

Understanding the concept of the value chain helps us understand how information systems can increase productivity. One way is by enabling the development of more efficient or more effective supporting activities. These systems include such applications as financial accounting systems, human resources systems, production systems, and customer relationship management systems. Increasing the efficiency and effectiveness of these support systems increases the profit margin enjoyed by the company.

Information systems also increase productivity by offering new and improved services, primarily activities that would not be available without IT. These might include customer shopping through the web, 24-hour customer support through online discussion boards and frequently asked questions, online package tracking for the courier business, and online airline ticket and hotel reservations. Providing these new or improved services adds value for the customer and can contribute to the company's margin and its ability to compete.

Q4 How Are Organizational Strategy and Industry Structure Related?

 Watch

Go to MyMISLab to watch a video about five forces that determine industry structure.

You will learn in your strategy class that an organization's strategy reflects its goals and objectives. A company's strategy is influenced by the competitive structure of the company's industry. In theory, a company's information systems strategy should support, or be aligned with, the overall company strategy. In the real world, it is possible for the organizational strategy and information systems strategy to be somewhat out of alignment. We will address this alignment in Chapter 7.

Organizational strategy begins with an assessment of the fundamental characteristics and structure of an industry. One model used to assess an industry structure is Porter's **five forces model**[10]. According to this model, five competitive forces determine industry profitability: (1) bargaining power of customers, (2) threat of substitutions, (3) bargaining power of suppliers, (4) threat of new entrants, and (5) rivalry among existing firms. The intensity of each of the five forces determines the characteristics of the industry, how profitable it is, and how sustainable that profitability will be.

To understand this model, consider a particular industry—the soft drink industry. Let us look at each of the forces, beginning with the bargaining power of the customers.

[10] M. Porter, *Competitive Strategy: Techniques for Analyzing Industries and Competitors* (New York: Free Press, 1980).

Customers can switch pretty easily between competing soft drinks. So, the companies within the industry have to be ready to please customers because their tastes and desires are important forces. The threat of customers turning to substitutes, such as water (bottled or not), juice, or caffeine-laden energy drinks is ever present, so the soft drink companies must constantly respond to it, partly by expanding their product offerings to include these other choices.

Companies within this industry also have significant amounts of power over their suppliers because a contract with Coca-Cola or PepsiCo can often be very lucrative. Thus, soft drink companies get highly competitive prices for their ingredients. New entrants to the soft drink industry have a hard time because they are unable to obtain the same kinds of terms from their suppliers, so their costs are higher, placing them at a disadvantage. As well, the large firms that dominate the industry have made huge investments in the distribution network, so a new small firm will have a hard time gaining access to the stores and restaurants that sell established brands. This is a real uphill battle—many companies that want to compete choose not to because of these challenges. Finally, the competition within the industry—remember the Pepsi Challenge?—can be very intense. What is interesting is that the firms very rarely compete on price. Instead, they spend massive amounts of money on marketing their brand.

So, what does all of this mean? To make a profit in the soft drink industry, it helps if you are a large company that has access to the lowest-priced ingredients, an established network of distributors, and expertise in brand development and responding to changing consumer desires. The nature of the competitive forces in the soft drink industry suggests a certain competitive structure. Other industries will have different structures because competitive forces are different in each industry.

MIS in Use

Winterborne Bicycle Institute: Building the Biking Experience

Winterborne Bicycle Institute (www.winterbornebikes.com) was founded in 2001 by Jason Filer in picturesque Guelph, Ontario (Figure 3-4). Winterborne is a small company whose typical customer is a cycling enthusiast—a serious rider who knows a lot about bicycles and is ready to move up to a high-quality, custom-designed, hand-built bicycle.

The main parts of a custom bike are the frame and wheels, and the company offers a number of choices in each type, style, and price range. Extensive bike-fitting sessions are part of the design process. The customer can also specify the paint finish and component set that completes the bike build.

In conjunction with a local college, Winterborne has also begun to offer intensive bicycle-maintenance courses so that customers and current and aspiring bicycle mechanics can gain practical knowledge and experience with regard to all major bicycle components, including frames, bearings, wheels, drive trains, brakes, and shifting systems, on a variety of bicycle styles and vintages.

Many customers come to the shop looking to purchase a custom bike or wheels or to upgrade pieces for their current bike, such as forks, suspension, handlebars, pedals, gearing, shifting, brakes, saddles, and seatposts. The company offers a number of brands in a wide range of styles and sizes.

To be successful, organizations examine the five forces mentioned above and determine how they intend to respond to them. An organization responds to the structure of its industry by choosing a **competitive strategy**. Porter followed his five forces model with a model of four competitive strategies, as shown in Figure 3-3.[11] According to Porter, a firm can engage in any one of these four fundamental competitive strategies. An organization can focus on being the cost leader, or it can focus on differentiating its products from those of the competition. Further, the organization can employ the cost or differentiation strategy across an industry, or it can focus its strategy on a particular industry segment.

	Cost	Differentiation
Industry-wide	Lowest cost across the industry	Better product/service across the industry
Focus	Lowest cost within an industry segment	Better product/service within an industry segment

Figure 3-3

Porter's Four Competitive Strategies

Source: Adapted with the permission of The Free Press, a Division of Simon & Schuster Adult Publishing Group, from Competitive Advantage: Creating and Sustaining Superior Performance by Michael E. Porter. Copyright © 1985, 1998 by Michael E. Porter. All rights reserved.

[11]M. Porter, *Competitive Strategy* (New York: Free Press, 1985).

Figure 3-4

Winterborne Bicycle Institute

Source: Courtesy of Winterborne Bicycle Institute.

Filer and his business partner, retired information systems executive Alan Medcalf, both consider Winterborne more of a vocation than a business, and they help customers make the best possible choices for their cycling wants and needs. Both Filer and Medcalf are well-trained technicians, who set up each bike and offer such services as customization and bike repairs. Customers also rely on them for recommendations on a wide range of biking accessories, such as helmets, riding gear, lighting, gloves, and shoes.

The company's website provides customers with information about products and promotes events, such as weekend maintenance clinics, the advanced maintenance course, group rides and clubs, trail-maintenance days, and educational seminars.

Questions

1. Identify the value chain involved in obtaining a new bicycle from Winterborne Bicycle Institute. Can you identify the primary activities that create value for the customer when purchasing a new bike?

2. What information systems do you think could be used to support these primary activities?

3. Check out the company's website (www.winterbornebikes.com). Does the site fill the role of a primary activity, or is it more appropriately considered a support activity? Justify your answer.

Consider the car rental industry, for example. According to the first column of Figure 3-3, a car rental company can strive to provide the lowest-cost car rentals across the industry, or it can seek to provide the lowest-cost car rentals to an industry segment—say, domestic business travellers.

As indicated in the second column, a car rental company can seek to differentiate its products from the competition. It can do so in various ways—for example, by providing a wide range of high-quality cars, by providing the best reservations system, by having the cleanest cars or the fastest check-in, or even by bringing the cars to its customers' homes.

According to Porter, to be effective, the organization's goals, objectives, culture, and activities must be consistent with the organization's strategy. To those in the MIS field, this means that all information systems in the organization must facilitate and be aligned with the organization's competitive strategy. We will discuss the concept of alignment further in Chapter 11.

Q5 What Is the Relationship Between Innovation and Information Technology?

Changes to industry structure often occur through innovation. Over the last hundred years, technology has enabled much of the innovation we have seen in our economy. This technological innovation is all around us today. One hundred years ago, there was little electrical power. There were few telephones. Automobiles were just beginning to be produced. The world had just witnessed the first powered flight. Radio was still being developed, and television was just a dream. Now we take these innovations for granted and wonder how people ever lived without them.

When considering technological innovation, professors Bower and Christensen[12] described two general types of technological innovations. **Sustaining technologies** are changes in technology that maintain the rate of improvement in customer value. For example, the vulcanization of rubber allowed tire manufacturers to produce tires that facilitated faster and more comfortable rides. This innovation improved the experience of driving a car and helped sustain the original innovation.

In contrast, **disruptive technologies** introduce a very new package of attributes to accepted mainstream products. In the music industry, for example, the advent of the MP3 file format was a disruptive technology because it offered the ability to store and play music through digital devices. In less than a decade, people moved from buying CDs and tapes for their Sony Walkmans to downloading MP3s and listening to music through their Apple iPods.

IT has been an important part of technological innovations since the 1950s. From the first electronic computer in 1939 to the first personal computer in 1980 and the commercialization of the internet in the early 1990s, the rate of innovation in IT has been staggering. In some instances, IT acts as a sustaining technology. Improved size and speed of electronic memory help us store and retrieve data more quickly. Faster processors help us accomplish more with our computers in less time. Sustaining technologies help make processes more efficient (and often more effective) and thus create value for organizations.

In other cases, IT acts as a disruptive technology. For example, when the Royal Bank of Canada (RBC) first offered a national automated banking machine (ABM) network in Canada in 1980,[13] it presented customers with new choices. The other

---

[12] J. Bower and C. Christensen, "Disruptive Technologies: Catching the Wave," *Harvard Business Review* 73, no. 1 (January/February 1995): 43–53.

[13] See www.rbc.com/history/anytimeanywhere/self_service-detail.html#2

chartered banks in Canada quickly responded with machines of their own. Similarly, when the Waterloo, Ontario based company Blackberry (at that time called Research In Motion or RIM), launched the first BlackBerry in 1999, it provided worldwide customers with new communication options. Wireless companies around the globe had to respond to these new sets of choices.

Both RBC and RIM gained competitive advantage by employing IT. When a company gains competitive advantage using a disruptive technology, the potential to alter the structure of an industry is created. Competing companies must react to the new conditions or risk losing their profit margins and customers. Both large and small companies within the industry must react to these changes. You can learn more about how small companies react to a disruptive technology by reading Case Study 3, about ICS Courier, at the end of this chapter.

In some cases, the competitive advantage is so large that it leads to a new industry. Such was the case for the microcomputer. Its advent led to the development of the microcomputer industry and the creation of new companies, such as Microsoft, Intel, Apple, Oracle, and Dell. Amazon, eBay, and Google were born out of the commercialization of the internet. Wireless network technology innovation led to the development of such Canadian companies as RIM (www.rim.com) and Sierra Wireless (www.sierrawireless.com). More recently, innovations in networking services have created new industries in social networking and messaging, such as Facebook, Tumblr, Groupon, Foursquare, and Twitter.

One of the more important considerations when thinking about innovation is how quickly the innovation catches on in or diffuses through society. The theory of the **diffusion of innovation** was defined by Everett Rogers as "the process by which an innovation is communicated through certain channels over time among the members of a social system."[14] In his 1964 book, Rogers identified five stages through which the diffusion of an innovation occurs. The stages, or steps in the process, are, as shown in Figure 3-5, (1) knowledge, (2) persuasion, (3) decision, (4) implementation, and (5) confirmation. Since many innovations are not adopted, an individual or organization thinking about adoption does not necessarily have to go through all of these steps. It can drop the process at any point.

In Rogers's theory of diffusion of innovation, the *knowledge* stage occurs when you first hear about an innovation but lack specific information about it. For example, you may have heard about a particular Android phone, but you may not know much about

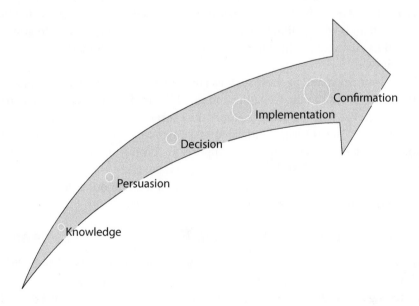

Figure 3-5

Roger's Theory of Diffusion of Innovation

Confirmation

Implementation

Decision

Persuasion

Knowledge

[14] E. M. Rogers, *Diffusion of Innovations* (Glencoe, IL: Free Press, 1964), p. 79.

it. The next stage is *persuasion*, when you become interested in the innovation and find out more about it. Once you have collected enough information, you move into the *decision* stage. Here, you consider the pros and cons of adopting the innovation, and make a decision to adopt or reject it. If you decide to pursue the innovation, you have reached the *implementation* stage. In this stage, you use the innovation and figure out whether to continue using it or look for an even better way. If you are happy, then you reach the peaceful state of *confirmation*, where you use the innovation to its full potential.

The theory of diffusion of innovation provides us with a way of thinking about the process of adoption of new technology. In Chapter 11, we will return to the concept of diffusion of innovation when we discuss why organizations invest in IT and what characteristics of the innovation are important to decision makers.

👁️⎾Watch

Go to MyMISLab to watch a video about how information systems provide competitive advantage.

👁️⎾Watch

Go to MyMISLab to watch a video about organizational strategy, information systems, and competitive advantage.

Q6 How Do Information Systems Provide Competitive Advantage?

If you take a business strategy class, you will study the Porter models in greater detail than we have discussed here. When you do so, you will learn numerous ways that organizations respond to the five competitive forces. For our purposes, we can summarize those ways in the list of principles shown in Figure 3-6. Keep in mind that we are applying these principles in the context of an organization's competitive strategy. (You can also apply these principles to a personal competitive advantage, as discussed in the exercise "The Digital Divide" at the end of this chapter on pages 78–79.)

Some of these competitive strategies are created via products and services, and others are enabled via the development of business processes. Each of these strategies is considered below.

Competitive Advantage via Products and Services

The first three principles in Figure 3-6 relate to products and services. Organizations gain a competitive advantage by creating new products or services, by enhancing existing products or services, and by differentiating their products and services from those of their competitors. As you think about these three principles, realize that an information system can be part of a product or it can provide support for a product or service. The MIS in Use box on pages 66–67 discusses how a company that builds bikes and offers bike-maintenance courses uses the internet to provide additional services to its customers. The company's use of the internet adds value to customer interactions with the company.

Consider a car rental agency, such as Hertz or Avis. An information system that generates data about the car's location and provides driving instructions to help drivers get to wherever they are going is part of the car rental package and, thus, is part of the product itself. In contrast, an information system that schedules car maintenance is not part of the product but, instead, supports the product. Either way, information systems can achieve the first three principles listed in Figure 3-6.

The remaining five principles listed in Figure 3-6 are about competitive advantage created by the implementation of business processes.

Competitive Advantage via Business Processes

Organizations can retain customers by making it difficult or expensive for them to switch to another product. This business strategy is sometimes referred to as adding **switching costs**. Organizations can also lock in suppliers by making it difficult for them to switch to another organization or, in a positive sense, by making it easy for

Product Implementations
1. Create a new product or service
2. Enhance products or services
3. Differentiate products or services

System Implementations
4. Lock in customers and buyers
5. Lock in suppliers
6. Raise barriers to market entry
7. Establish alliances
8. Reduce costs

Figure 3-6

Principles of Competitive Advantage

them to connect to and work with the organization. Finally, competitive advantage can be gained by creating entry barriers that make it difficult and expensive for new competition to enter the market.

Another way to gain competitive advantage is to establish alliances with other organizations. Such alliances create standards, promote product awareness and needs, develop market size, reduce purchasing costs, and provide other benefits. Finally, organizations can gain competitive advantage by reducing costs. Such reductions enable the organization to decrease prices and/or increase profitability. Increased profitability means not just greater shareholder value but also more cash, which can fund further infrastructure development for even greater competitive advantage.

Q7 Can Competitive Advantage Through Information Systems Be Sustained?

We have noted that IT can provide a competitive advantage for companies. But can these advantages be sustained? Competitors often react to innovations by replicating the technology. Since the effects of IT can often be readily seen, it may be hard to hide the innovation. Technology and software can be purchased or developed. It is, therefore, almost impossible to keep competitors from developing competing technology.

The credit unions that adopted the first bank machines were quickly copied by competitors. Although patents can provide some initial protection for technologies (such as the BlackBerry), patents are difficult and expensive to enforce, and they are not permanent. Does this mean that all IT innovations are doomed to offer only temporary advantage?

In his *Harvard Business Review* article "IT Doesn't Matter,"[15] Nicholas Carr suggested that the evolution of IT in business follows a pattern similar to earlier disruptive technologies, such as railway and electricity. As disruptive technologies are being developed, they open opportunities for companies to gain strong competitive advantages. But as the availability of the technologies increases and their cost decreases, these technologies become more like commodities. From a strategic standpoint, the technologies become invisible and no longer provide advantages. In other words, the more ubiquitous (i.e., existing everywhere) IT becomes, the less competitive advantage IT provides.

We have noted above that this is true to a certain degree. But it is important to understand clearly what we are talking about. If we are considering IT (hardware, software, and networks), then what Carr has said is largely true. Hardware and software have become readily accessible to almost all companies and, although not entirely a commodity, they have largely become commoditized. These investments are not a source of long-term competitive advantage.

However, if we consider information systems (which also include procedures and people along with hardware and software), then what Carr has stated is less convincing. The same IT installed in different organizations might result in very different outcomes. The machines and the software may be commodities, but organizational procedures and the people in the organizations are not standardized. Some companies (and some people) might be able to quickly adapt to new technology. Other companies (or people) may be less willing or able to do so.

It is important to recognize that long-term competitive advantage lies not with the technology but rather in how a company and its people adopt the technology. The most important thing you can learn from this chapter is that when it comes to IT, people make all the difference. So, while the IT itself may not provide a sustainable

---

[15] N. Carr, "IT Doesn't Matter," *Harvard Business Review* 81, no. 5 (May 2003): 41–49.

competitive advantage, the effective integration of people, procedures, and technology can certainly provide an organization with the potential for long-term advantages.

So, what is **sustained competitive advantage**? It requires companies to find a distinctive way to compete. This way of competing will change over time. The emphasis should be placed on developing increasingly sophisticated integration of IT and the people and procedures in the organization. Companies with sustainable competitive advantage work to integrate many activities: marketing, customer service, product design, and product delivery. When a company successfully integrates many technology systems with its people and procedures, competitors have to match the whole system. Although competitors might be able to purchase the technology component, it takes time for their people to gain the necessary experience and skill to really make the technology work for those organizations. Matching the entire set of information systems can be a steep hill to climb for companies that have less experience and success in integrating people and technology. So, sustained competitive advantage comes from developing people and procedures that are well supported by the underlying technology.

Active ? Review

Use this Active Review to verify that you have understood the material in the chapter. You can read the entire chapter and then perform the tasks in this review, or you can read the material for just one question and perform the tasks for that question before moving on to the next one.

Q1 Why should I care about productivity and innovation?

What is labour productivity? How does Canada compare globally with regard to labour productivity and innovation? Explain what is meant by the productivity paradox. Can you explain how using a computer makes you more productive than using a typewriter? List three ways in which information systems can create value.

Q2 What is business technology management (BTM), and how is it related to productivity and innovation?

Why is the ICT industry important to innovation in Canada? How are ICT skills changing? What organization was responsible for developing learning outcomes for BTM programs? How is the SFIA related to BTM? What is the CCICT, and what is its role? What is the name of the certification process for BTM?

Q3 How do information systems improve productivity?

Explain the relationship between business processes and value chains. What are the differences between primary and support activities? How does IT affect value chains?

Q4 How are organizational strategy and industry structure related?

Briefly describe Porter's five forces model. Can you analyze an industry based on the strengths of the different forces? What are the four main types of competitive strategy identified by Porter?

Q5 What is the relationship between innovation and information technology?

Explain the differences between sustaining and disruptive technologies. Provide examples in which IT is a sustaining technology and those in which IT is a disruptive technology. What is meant by diffusion of innovation? Describe the steps in the process of diffusion of innovation.

Q6 How do information systems provide competitive advantage?

List and briefly describe eight principles of competitive advantage. Consider the bookstore at your school, for example. List one application of IT that takes advantage of each of these principles.

Q7 Can competitive advantage through information systems be sustained?

Describe what is meant by sustained competitive advantage. Explain why IT does not generally provide sustained competitive advantage. Explain why information systems can provide sustained competitive advantage.

MyMISLab MyMISLab is an online learning and testing environment that features the perfect study tools to help you master the concepts covered in this chapter. Log in to MyMISLab to test your knowledge of key chapter concepts and explore additional practice tools, including videos, flashcards, annotated text figures, and more!

Key Terms and Concepts

Business Technology
  Management (BTM) 62

Business value 60

Canadian Coalition for
  Tomorrow's ICT Skills
  (CCICT) 62

Competitive strategy 67

Diffusion of innovation 69

Disruptive technology 68

Effectiveness 63

Efficiency 63

Five forces model 65

Information and Com-
  munications Technology
  (ICT) Industry 60

Innovation 62

Margin 64

Primary activities 64

Productivity 60

Productivity paradox 60

Skills Framework for
  the Information Age
  (SFIA) 62

Support activities 64

Sustained competitive
  advantage 72

Sustaining technologies 68

Switching costs 70

Value chain 63

Using Your Knowledge

1. Apply the value chain model to a video game developer, such as Electronic Arts (www.EA.com). What is its competitive strategy? Describe the tasks Electronic Arts must accomplish for each of the primary value chain activities. How does EA's competitive strategy and the nature of its business influence the general characteristics of EA's information systems?

2. Apply the value chain model to a video game retail company, such as EB Games (www.EBGames.com). What is its competitive strategy? Describe the tasks EB Games must accomplish for each of the primary value chain activities. How does EB Games' competitive strategy and the nature of its business influence the general characteristics of its information systems?

3. Suppose you decide to start a business that recruits students for summer jobs. You will match available students with available jobs. You need to learn what jobs are available and who is available to fill those positions. In starting your business, you know you will be competing with local newspapers, craigslist (www.craigslist.org), and your college or university. You will probably have other local competitors as well.
   a. Analyze the structure of this industry according to Porter's five forces model.
   b. Given your analysis in (a), recommend a competitive strategy.
   c. Describe the primary value chain activities as they apply to this business.
   d. Describe a business process for recruiting students.
   e. Describe information systems that could be used to support the business process in (d).
   f. Explain how the process you describe in (d) and the system you describe in (e) reflect your competitive strategy.

4. Samantha Green owns and operates Twigs Tree Trimming Service. Samantha graduated from the forestry program of a nearby university and worked for a large landscape design firm, doing tree trimming and removal. After several years at the company, she bought a truck, a stump grinder, and other equipment and opened her own business in Winnipeg.

Although many of her contracts are one-time operations (e.g., removing a tree or a stump), others are recurring ones (e.g., trimming a tree or group of trees every year or every other year). When business is slow, she calls former clients to remind them of her services and of the need to trim their trees on a regular basis.

Samantha has never heard of Michael Porter or his theories. She operates her business "by the seat of her pants."

a. Explain how an analysis of the five competitive forces could help Samantha.

b. Do you think Samantha has a competitive strategy? What competitive strategy would seem to make sense for her?

c. How would knowledge of her competitive strategy help her sales and marketing efforts?

d. Describe, in general terms, the kind of information system Samantha needs to support sales and marketing efforts.

5. FiredUp Inc. is a small business owned by Curt and Julie Robards. Based in Brisbane, Australia, FiredUp manufactures and sells a lightweight camping stove called FiredNow. Curt, who previously worked as an aerospace engineer, invented and patented a burning nozzle that enables the stove to stay lit in very high winds—up to 140 kilometres per hour. Julie, an industrial designer by training, developed an elegant folding design that is small, lightweight, easy to set up, and very stable. Curt and Julie manufacture the stove in their garage, and they sell it directly to their customers over the internet and on the phone.

a. Explain how an analysis of the five competitive forces could help FiredUp.

b. What does FiredUp's competitive strategy seem to be?

c. Briefly summarize how the primary value chain activities pertain to FiredUp. How should the company design these value chains to conform to its competitive strategy?

d. Describe business processes that FiredUp needs to implement its marketing and sales and also its service value chain activities.

e. Describe, in general terms, information systems to support your answer to question (d).

Collaborative Exercises

The High-Value Bike Rental Company rents bikes to business executives at conference resorts. A well-dressed rental agent greets each potential customer and has a discussion to determine his or her biking needs. When the customer is ready to rent a bike, the agent enters his or her information into the customer database and checks to see if a bike is available in the bike inventory database. When the customer returns the bike, he or she pays for the rental by providing the hotel room number. The bike is then cleaned and put back into the bike inventory database. This triggers an update to the database, which then bills the customer for the rental. A charge is sent from the database to the hotel billing system. Figure 3-7 shows the rental process and related information systems for the High-Value Bike Rental Company. Using this information, collaborate with your team to answer the following questions:

1. Explain the relationship of value and cost according to Porter's value chain model. When does it make sense to add cost to a business process?

2. Suppose you are told that the business process in Figure 3-7 has a negative margin. Explain what that means. Suppose the margin of some business process is negative $1 million. If costs are reduced by $1.2 million, will the margin necessarily be positive? Explain why or why not.

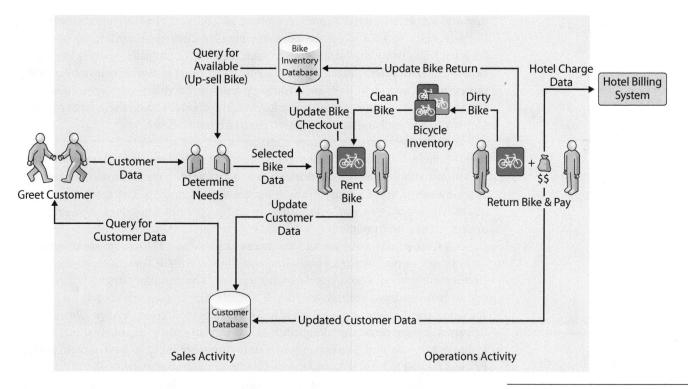

Figure 3-7
Rental Process for High-
Value Bike Rental

3. Consider alternatives for replacing the rental agent from the business process in Figure 3-7.

   a. Describe changes that will need to be made to the process documented in Figure 3-7.

   b. Would eliminating the rental agent change the competitive strategy of this company? Is it possible to be a high-value company with no rental personnel? Explain why or why not.

   c. Would eliminating the rental agent necessarily reduce costs? What costs would increase as a result of this change?

4. Consider the alternative of increasing the value delivered by the existing rental agent—for example, renting more kinds of equipment or selling items of use to guests who are renting bicycles. Consider other options as well.

   a. Describe four ways that you think the existing personnel could increase the value of this business process.

   b. For the four options you developed in part (a), name and describe criteria for selecting among them.

   c. Using the criteria developed in part (b), evaluate the options you identified in part (a) and select the best one. Explain your selection.

   d. Redraw Figure 3-7 using the option you selected in part (c).

Case Study 3

ICS Courier: Keeping Up with the Joneses

What happens to smaller companies when larger companies in the same industry invest heavily in information systems? How can smaller firms expect to "keep up with the Joneses"? A good example is provided by the courier industry. In Canada, this industry is large and competitive. It distributes more than 2.1 million packages every

👁—⟨Watch

Go to MyMISLab to watch a video about the BOSU Balance Trainer.

👁—⟨Watch

Go to MyMISLab to watch a video about how Dell leverages the internet directly.

day, and has an estimated annual revenue of $4.7 billion.[16] FedEx gained a competitive advantage in 1994 when the company enabled customers to view the status of their packages using the Internet. Dominant firms in the industry, such as Purolator Courier, DHL Courier, UPS, and Canada Post, responded to FedEx's move by providing customer access to their own tracking systems. Barcoded packages, handheld scanners, and a complex network of information systems enabled these large companies to provide package status to customers in a timely fashion.

But how could smaller courier companies respond to this technological investment? Smaller companies do not usually have the ability to pay for large and complex information systems. ICS Courier (www.icscourier.ca), for example, is a relatively small courier business, with annual revenues of $100 million. The company, headquartered in Toronto, was established in 1978, operates 35 offices, and employs approximately 1000 people.

ICS Courier did not have the resources in place in 1994 to provide customers with access to package tracking. How could it survive? ICS recognized that as a smaller company, it could specialize its services. The company began focusing on business-to-business courier services. ICS made sure that its drivers stopped at the same locations at the same time each day. This personalized service allowed ICS drivers to be the most knowledgeable in the industry; they became experts in the industries they served. The service consistency and reliability, as well as competitive pricing, helped to keep ICS growing in the Canadian marketplace.

By specializing, ICS Courier also bought some time before it had to make larger information systems investments. Its customers continued to demand package tracking, and the company made a significant investment in information systems. The company upgraded many of its support systems and successfully delivered an online package-tracking service. This was not an easy or inexpensive process for ICS Courier. Often, smaller companies risk losing the entire business if their investments in an IT project are not successful.

When large companies invest heavily in information systems, the bar is raised for the entire industry. Some companies cannot compete, and they end up leaving the industry. Other companies, however, do find a way to compete successfully. ICS Courier is an example of a smaller company that made a difficult transition in response to a change in IT. This successful transition required a strong commitment to a company strategy focused on specialization and a successful implementation of information systems to support the strategy.

Questions

1. ICS Courier focused on business-to-business customers, servicing insurance companies, financial services, and health care professionals. How did the fact that drivers arrived consistently at the same place and at the same time support the strategy of specialization?
2. Why would offering package tracking through its website support the specialization strategy for ICS? Given the companies that ICS serves, do you think ICS could survive long term without having made this technology investment?
3. Do you think package tracking through the web is a disruptive technology? Justify your answer.
4. Can you think of another disruptive technology for the courier industry?

---

[16] See Transport Canada, "Canadian Courier Market Size, Structure and Fleet Analysis Study," which has been archived at www.hrsdc.gc.ca/eng/labour/employment_standards/fls/research/research04/page39.shtml.

Running Case Assignment Part 1

Questions

1. Josie has decided that he wants to understand more about the customer experience at Café Italiano. He spent two days (a Tuesday [weekday] and a Saturday [weekend]) observing the number of customers who came into the café, how much they purchased, how long they waited in line for their purchase (wait time), and how long they stayed in the café (relax time). He collected these observations in an Excel spreadsheet labelled "Café Italiano Customer Observation.xls." You can find this spreadsheet in Chapter 3 of MyMISLab. Use the data in the spreadsheet to answer the following questions:
   a. How many customers were served on Tuesday? How did this compare with the number of customers served on Saturday?
   b. What was the average total time spent in the café (total time equals wait time plus relax time) on a weekday? How did this average compare with the total time spent on a weekend?
   c. What is the average wait time for a customer on a weekday between 7:30 and 9:30 a.m.? How does this compare to the wait time on a weekend between 7:30 and 9:30 a.m.?
   d. On average, across both days, what was the average relax time for the customers? What was the average relax time for a weekday? How did this average differ from the weekend?

2. The "Café Italiano Customer Observation.xls" spreadsheet is an example of information that can be collected and stored in an information system. These data can be valuable when considering changes in marketing. Use the results you found in Question 1 as well as some additional information from the spreadsheet to fill in the table below to create a full profile of weekday versus weekend customers at Café Italiano.

Customer Characteristic	Weekday	Weekend
Average number of customers between 7:30 and 9:30 a.m.		
Average number of customers between 11:30 a.m. and 1:30 p.m.		
Average purchase between 7:30 and 9:30 a.m.		
Average purchase between 11:30 a.m. and 1:30 p.m.		

Customer Characteristic	Weekday	Weekend
Average wait time between 7:30 and 9:30 a.m.		
Average wait time between 11:30 a.m. and 1:30 p.m.		
Average relax time between 7:30 and 9:30 a.m.		
Average relax time between 11:30 a.m. and 1:30 p.m.		
Average total time between 7:30 and 9:30 a.m.		
Average total time between 11:30 a.m. and 1:30 p.m.		

3. The profile completed in Question 2, provides a useful summary of the characteristics of customers on a weekend and weekday.
   a. Using the data in the table developed in Question 2, draw three conclusions about the differences between weekday and weekend customers.
   b. We learned in Chapter 2 that the validity of data is always an important consideration. The data above come from sampling of one Tuesday and one Saturday. Can you provide at least two reasons why the data may not be valid (i.e., they do not represent the true customer experience)?

Collaborative Question

4. Using the data from the profile table created in Question 2, make at least one suggestion for a change in the way that Café Italiano is currently serving its customers. For example, you might suggest that on weekends the café have some soft acoustic music in the early afternoon while customers are relaxing.
   a. Share your ideas on the discussion board with others in the classroom. Remember to justify your suggestions using the data provided above.
   b. In your opinion, what was the best idea suggested? Justify your answer.

MyMISLab Visit MyMISLab to access the data files to complete these questions.

The Digital Divide

An adage of investing is that it is easier for the rich to get richer. Someone who has $10 million invested at 5 percent earns $500 000 per year. Another investor with $10 000 invested at that same 5 percent earns $500 per year. Every year, the disparity increases as the first investor pulls further and further ahead of the second.

This same also applies to intellectual wealth. It is easier for those with considerable knowledge and expertise to gain even more knowledge and expertise. Someone who knows how to search the internet can gather information more readily than someone who does not. And every year, the person with greater knowledge pulls further and further ahead. Intellectual capital grows in the same way that financial capital grows.

Searching the internet is not just a matter of knowledge, however—it is also a matter of access. The increasing reliance on the web for information and commerce has created a digital divide between those who have internet access and those who do not. This divide continues to deepen as those who are connected pull further ahead of those who are not.

Various groups have addressed this problem by making internet access available in public places, such as libraries, community centres, and retirement homes. But not everyone can be served this way, and even with this kind of access, there is a big convenience difference between going to the library and walking across your bedroom to access the internet—and in your bedroom, you do not have to stand in line.

The advantages accrue to everyone with access, every day. Do you want directions to your friend's house? Need to know what movie is playing at a local theatre? Want to buy music, books, or tools? Need convenient access to your chequing account? Want help to decide whether to refinance your condo? Want to know what TCP/IP means? Use the internet.

All of this intellectual capital resides on the internet because businesses benefit by putting it there. It is much cheaper to provide product support information over the internet than in printed documents. The savings include not only the costs of printing but also the costs of warehousing and mailing. As well, when product specifications change, an organization just needs to update its website. There is no obsolete material to dispose of and there are no costs for printing and distributing the revised material. Those who have internet access gain current information faster than those who do not.

If you are taking MIS, you are already connected; you are already one of the haves, and you are already pulling ahead of the have-nots. The more you learn about information systems and their use in commerce, the faster you will pull ahead. And so the digital divide increases.

What happens to those who do not have internet access? They fall further and further behind. The digital divide segregates the haves from the have-nots, creating new class structures. Such segregation is subtle, but it is segregation, nonetheless.

Do organizations have a responsibility to address this matter? If 98 percent of our market segment has internet access, do we have a responsibility to provide non-internet materials to that other 2 percent? On what assumptions is that responsibility based? Does a government agency have the responsibility to provide equal information to those who have internet access and those who do not? When those who are connected can obtain information nearly instantaneously, 24/7, is it even possible to provide equal information to the connected and the unconnected?

This is a worldwide problem. Connected societies and countries pull further and further ahead. How can any economy that relies on traditional mail compete with an internet-based economy?

Discussion Questions

1. Do you see evidence of a digital divide on your campus? in your hometown? among your relatives? Describe personal experiences you have had with regard to the digital divide.

2. Do organizations have a legal responsibility to provide the same information for unconnected customers as they do for connected customers? If not, should laws be passed requiring organizations to do so?

3. Because it may be impossible to provide equal information, another approach for reducing the digital divide is for the government to enable unconnected citizens to acquire internet access via subsidies and tax incentives. Do you favour such a program? Why, or why not?

4. Suppose that nothing is done to reduce the digital divide and that it is allowed to grow wider and wider. What are the consequences? How will society change?

Andres Rodriguez/Fotolia

Chapter Extension 3a

Chapter 3 provides the background for this extension.

Introduction to Microsoft Excel 2013

Chapter 3 introduced business processes, innovation, and strategy. One of the most important resources we use to consider how to innovate and improve business processes is information about processes. Much of this analysis of business process information is accomplished through tools such as Microsoft Excel. This chapter extension teaches basic skills with Microsoft Excel, a product for creating and processing spreadsheets. If you already know how to use Excel, use this chapter extension for review. Otherwise, use this chapter extension to gain essential knowledge, which every businessperson needs today. "Running Case Assignment Part 1" on page 77 assumes that you have some basic Excel skills. This application extension can help you prepare to answer the questions in that assignment.

Q1 What Is a Spreadsheet?

A **spreadsheet** is a table of data having rows and columns. Long before the advent of the computer, accountants and financial planners used paper spreadsheets to make financial calculations. Today, the term *spreadsheet* almost always refers to an *electronic* spreadsheet, and most frequently to a spreadsheet that is processed by Microsoft Excel. Electronic spreadsheets provide incredible labour savings over paper spreadsheets and were a major factor in the early adoption of personal computers.

As shown in Figure AE3a-1, Excel spreadsheets have rows and columns. The rows are identified by numbers, and the columns are identified by letters. Because there are only 26 letters in the alphabet, the following scheme is used to label columns: The letters A through Z identify the first 26 columns; the letters AA through AZ identify the next 26; BA through BZ the next 26; and so forth.

In Excel, the term **worksheet** refers to a spreadsheet. One or more worksheets are combined to form a **workbook**.

In the lower left-hand corner of Figure AE3a-1, notice the tab called Sheet 1. Excel creates just one worksheet when you create a new workbook, but you can create more worksheets if needed.

Figure AE3a-1 shows a spreadsheet processed by Excel 2013, the current version of Excel. You can process spreadsheets in earlier versions of Excel, but the structure of commands and menu items will be different from that described here. If you are just starting to learn Excel, learn Excel 2013 rather than an earlier version.

The intersection of a row and a column is called a **cell**. Each cell is identified by the name of its row and column. In Figure AE3a-1, the cell named A1 is highlighted. The cell K5 is the cell in the K column, row number 5. The cell AB1207 (not visible in Figure AE3a-1) is the cell located in column AB and row 1207.

You may be asking, "Row 1207? How many rows and columns can I have?" Don't bother asking...you can have more than you will ever need or want. And if you should ever run out of rows and columns, you're using the wrong tool. In that case, you probably should be using Microsoft Access or another DBMS (see Chapter 5) instead.

Study Questions

Q1 What is a spreadsheet?

Q2 How do you get started with excel?

Q3 How can you enter data?

Q4 How can you insert and delete rows and columns and change their size?

Q5 How can you format data?

Q6 How can you create a (simple) formula?

Q7 How can you print results?

MyMISLab

Visit MyMISLab for simulations, tutorials, and end-of-chapter problems.

Figure AE3a-1

Excel Spreadsheet Showing
Rows and Columns

Source: Microsoft Excel 2013.

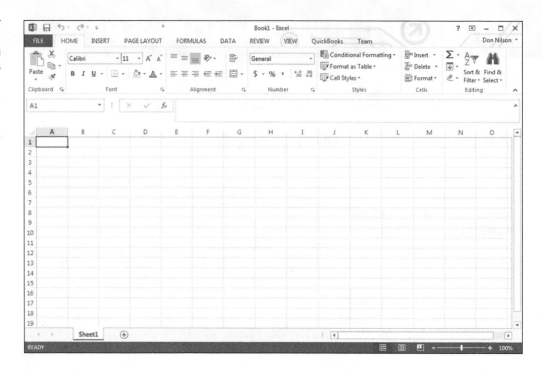

Figure AE3a-1

Excel Spreadsheet Showing
Rows and Columns

Source: Microsoft Excel 2013.

Q2 How Do You Get Started with Excel?

When you first start Excel 2013, it will create a workbook exactly like that in Figure AE3a-1. Even though you haven't done anything yet, your first task should be to save your workbook under an appropriate name. Life is uncertain; you never know when a computer might fail or power might be cut off or some other unplanned event might occur. Get in the habit of saving your work initially and then frequently after that.

To save your workbook, click *File* with your left mouse button (in the following text, unless otherwise specified, the term *click* means to click with the left mouse button), and click *Save As* as shown in Figure AE3a-2. The choices available to you will depend on the licence you have and your working environment. In this example, Excel displays a SharePoint site named *David Kroenke*, a Microsoft SkyDrive location, Computer, and *Add a Place* where you can define new locations for saving documents. For now, click Computer, then Browse as shown in Figure AE3a-2. Navigate to the location on your

Figure AE3a-2

Saving Your Workbook in Excel

Source: Microsoft Excel 2013.

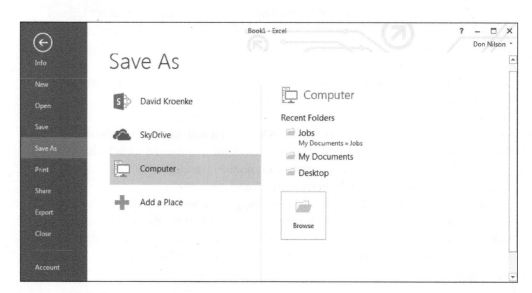

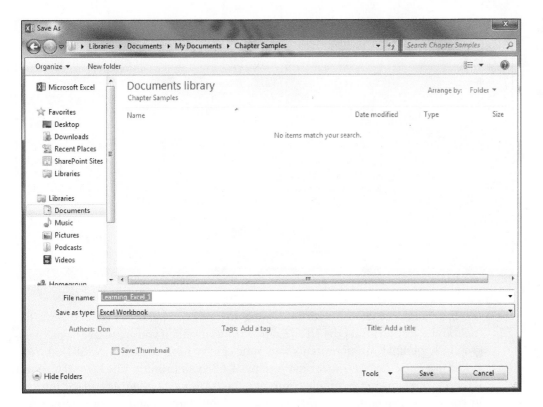

Figure AE3a-3

Entering a File Name in Excel

Source: Microsoft Excel 2013.

computer where you want to save your workbook. The display in Figure AE3a-3 will appear. In the lower center, find the label *File name:* and to the right of that label enter a name for this file. In Figure AE3a-3, I have entered the file name *Learning_Excel_1*. Your instructor may have given you instructions for creating file names; if so, follow them. Otherwise, follow this example or use some other scheme. Click the *Save* button to save your workbook. Once you have saved your workbook, you can perform subsequent saves by clicking the small disk icon located next to the Excel icon at the top left.

Figure AE3a-4 shows the workbook. A sequence of tabs appears in a horizontal line, just below the Excel icon. These tabs control the contents of the **ribbon**, which is the wide bar of tools and selections that appears just under the tabs. In Figure AE3a-4, the *HOME* tab has been selected, and the contents of the ribbon concern fonts, alignment, and so forth. Figure AE3a-5 shows the appearance of the ribbon when the *PAGE LAYOUT* tab is selected.

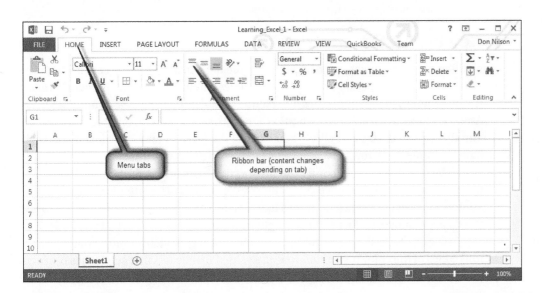

Figure AE3a-4

Excel Menu Tabs and Ribbon Bar

Source: Microsoft Excel 2013.

Figure AE3a-5

Ribbon with Page Layout
Tab Selected

Source: Microsoft Excel 2013.

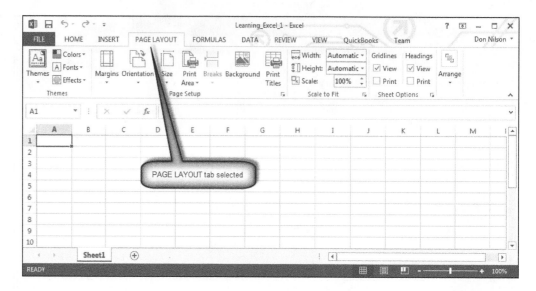

In general, you choose a tab depending on the task at hand. For general work, the tools and selection under the *HOME* tab are most useful. If you are inserting pictures, graphs, hyperlinks, or other items into your spreadsheet, click the *INSERT* tab. You would use *PAGE LAYOUT* to format your page, often for printing. The *FORMULAS* tab is used for creating more complex formulas, the *DATA* tab for filtering and sorting data in your spreadsheet, the *REVIEW* tab for tracking changes and making comments, and the *VIEW* tab for configuring the appearance of Excel.

At this point, don't worry about which tab to choose; just click around to see the tools and selections available. If in doubt, click on the *HOME* tab because it holds the most frequently used tools and selections.

Q3 How Can You Enter Data?

Data can be entered into an Excel worksheet in three ways:

- Key in the data.
- Let Excel add data based on a pattern.
- Import data from another program.

Here we will illustrate the first two options.

Key in the Data

Nothing very sophisticated is needed to key the data. Just click in the cell in which you want to add data, type the data, and press *Enter* when you're done. In Figure AE3a-6 the user has keyed names of cities into column E and is in the process of adding *Miami*. After typing the second *i*, she can press *Enter*. The value will be entered into the cell, and the focus will stay on cell E6. You can tell the focus is on E6 because Excel highlights column E and row 6.

If the user enters the second *i* and presses the down arrow, the value will be added to cell E6, and Excel will move the focus down to cell E7. The latter is useful if you are adding a vertical sequence of names like this. Also, you can press a left arrow to add the data and move the focus left or a right or up arrow to move right or up.

In Figure AE3a-6, notice the row just above the spreadsheet, immediately above the names of the columns. In that row, the value E6 indicates that cell E6 has the focus and further to the right the letters *Miam* indicate the current value of that cell.

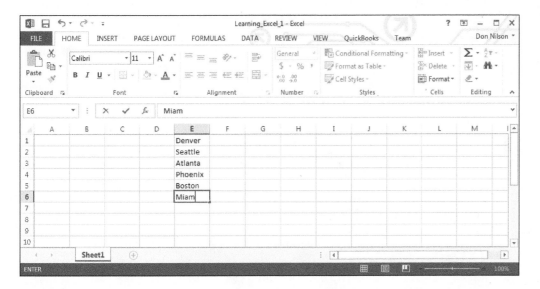

Figure AE3a-6

Entering City Names in Column E

Source: Microsoft Excel 2013.

Figure AE3a-7 shows a sequence of seven city names. But notice that the user never entered the second *i* in Miami. To correct this, she can go back to that cell and retype the entire word *Miami* or she can go to the cell and press the <F2> function key. In the latter case, she can just add the missing *i* to the word and press Enter (or down or up, etc.). Using the F2 key is recommended when you have a long value in a cell and you just want to fix a letter or two without retyping the whole entry. (If nothing happens when you press F2, press the F Lock key on your keyboard. Then press F2 again.)

Let Excel add the Data Using a Pattern

Suppose that for some reason for each of the cities we want to have the number 100 in column G of the spreadsheet in Figure AE3a-7. Another way of saying this is that we want the value 100 to be entered into cells G1 through G7. One way of proceeding is to type the value 100 in each of the seven rows. There's a better way, however.

If our user types the value 100 into cell G1, presses Enter, and then clicks cell G1, a rectangle will be drawn around the cell with a little black box in the lower right-hand corner, as shown in Figure AE3a-8. Now, if the user drags (left-click and hold the mouse button down as you move the mouse) that little black box down to cell G7, Excel will fill in the value 100 into all of those cells. Figure AE3a-9 shows the user dragging the cells, and Figure AE3a-10 shows the result.

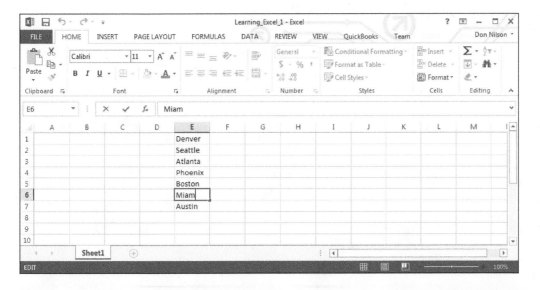

Figure AE3a-7

Using a Function Key to Make Entry Corrections

Source: Microsoft Excel 2013.

Figure AE3a-8

Entering Identical Data in
Multiple Cells, Step 1

Source: Microsoft Excel 2013.

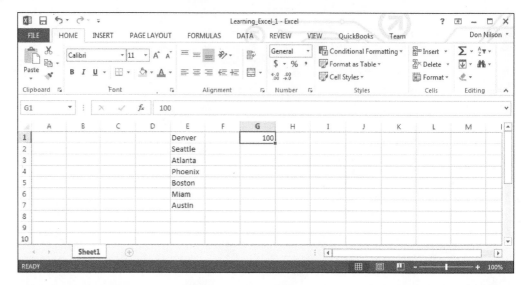

Figure AE3a-9

Entering Identical Data in
Multiple Cells, Step 2

Source: Microsoft Excel 2013.

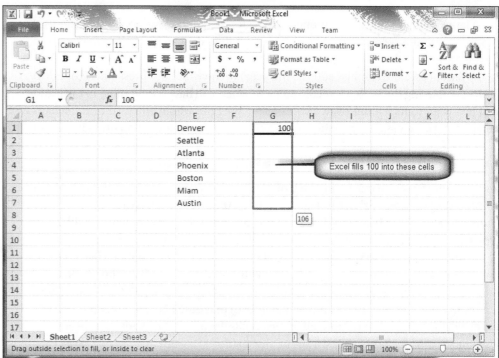

Figure AE3a-10

Identical Data Entered in
Multiple Cells

Source: Microsoft Excel 2013.

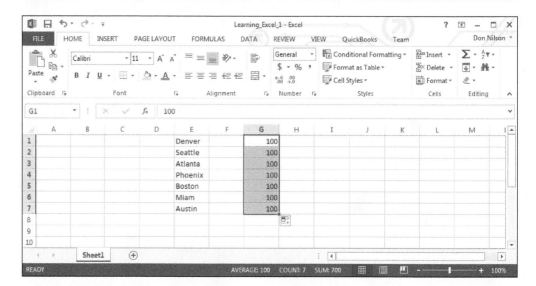

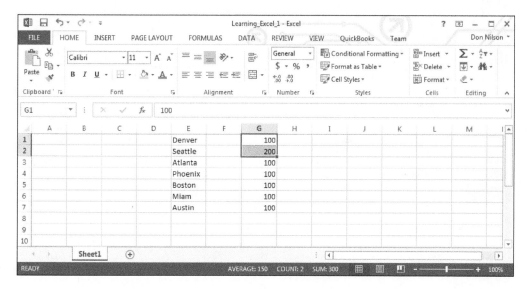

Figure AE3a-11

Entering Patterned Data in
Multiple Cells

Source: Microsoft Excel 2013.

But it gets much better! Suppose we want the numbers in column G to identify
the cities. Say we want the first city, Denver, to have the number 100, the second city,
Seattle, to have the number 200, the third city, Atlanta, to have the number 300, and
so forth.

Excel will fill in the values we want if we give it an indication of the pattern to follow. So, if our user types 100 in cell G1, 200 in cell G2, and then *selects both cells G1 and
G2*, Excel will draw a rectangle around the two cells and again show the small black
box, as shown in Figure AE3a-11. If the user drags the small black box, Excel will fill in
the numbers in a sequence, as shown in Figure AE3a-12.

Excel is sophisticated in its interpretation of the patterns. If you key *January* and
February into cells C1 and C2 and then select both cells and drag down, Excel will fill
in with March, April, May, and so on. Or, if in column A you key in the sequence *Q1,
Q2, Q3,* and *Q4* and then select all four values and drag the small black box, Excel will
repeat the sequence Q1 through Q4. Figure AE3a-13 shows the results of these last two
operations.

Excel will also find patterns within text values. In Figure AE3a-14, the user
entered *Figure 1-1* into cell J1 and 1-2 into cell J2. Selecting and dragging cells J1 and
J2 produced the sequence shown in Figure AE3a-14.

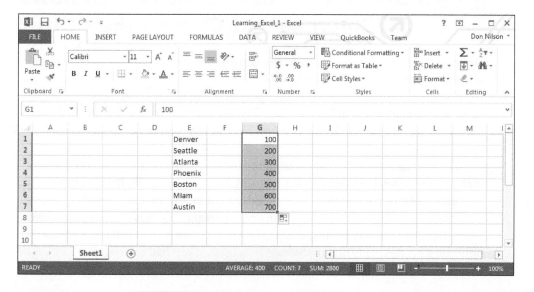

Figure AE3a-12

Patterned Data Entered in
Multiple Cells

Source: Microsoft Excel 2013.

Figure AE3a-13

Sophisticated Entry of
Patterned Data in
Multiple Cells

Source: Microsoft Excel 2013.

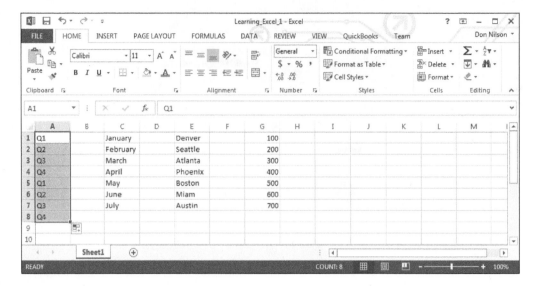

Figure AE3a-14

Patterned Data Within
Text Values

Source: Microsoft Excel 2013.

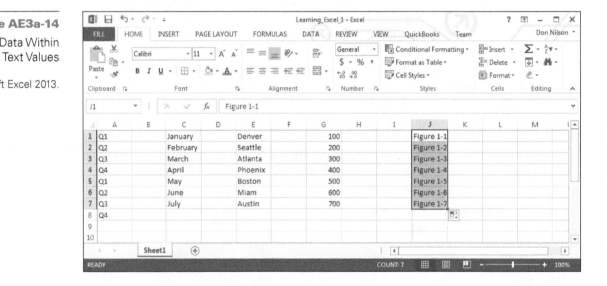

Q4 How Can You Insert and Delete Rows and Columns and Change their Size?

Suppose you are the manager of a sales team and you are recording this month's sales into the spreadsheet in Figure AE3a-15. You enter the data shown but then realize that you've forgotten to add column headings. You'd like column A to have the heading *Sales Rep* and column B to have the heading *Sales.* You don't want to retype all of the data; instead, you want to insert two new rows so that you can add the labels as well as a blank line.

To insert new rows, click the number of the row above which you want new rows, and select as many rows as you want to insert. In Figure AE3a-16, the user has clicked row 1 and selected two rows. Now, using the right mouse button, click the selection. The menu shown in Figure AE3a-16 will appear. Using your mouse, left-click the word *Insert* and two rows will be inserted, as shown in Figure AE3a-17. If you had selected only one row, then only one row would be added. If you had selected five rows, then five rows would be added.

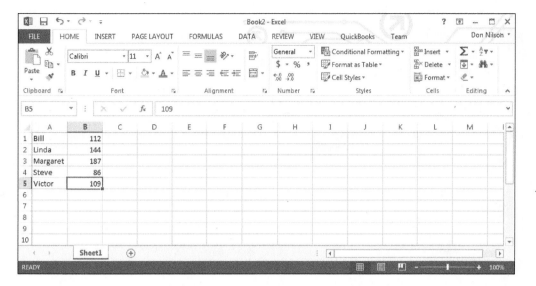

Figure AE3a-15

Spreadsheet to Which User Wants to Add New Rows for Column Headings

Source: Microsoft Excel 2013.

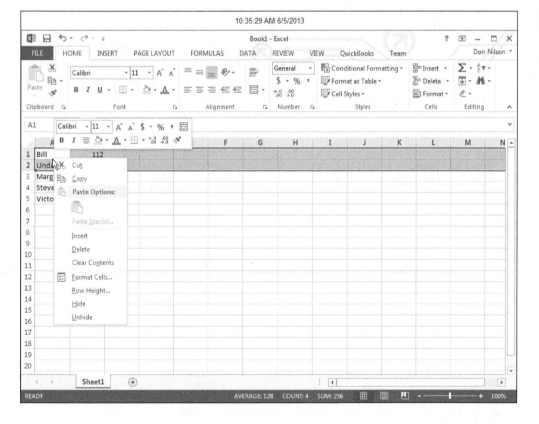

Figure AE3a-16

Menu for Adding Inserts Such as New Rows

Source: Microsoft Excel 2013.

Notice that when you click the name of a row (or column) you are selecting the *entire* row (or column). Thus, when you click the 1 of row 1, you are selecting the entire row, even if it has 1000 or more columns.

You can use a similar approach to delete rows. Click the name of the row (or rows) you want to delete and then right-click. Then left-click the word *Delete*. Those rows will be deleted and any remaining rows moved up.

Adding and deleting columns is similar. To add a column, click the name of the column before which you want to insert columns, select as many columns to the right of that as you want to add, right-click, and then select *Insert*. To delete, click the name of the columns you want to delete, right-click, and then select *Delete*.

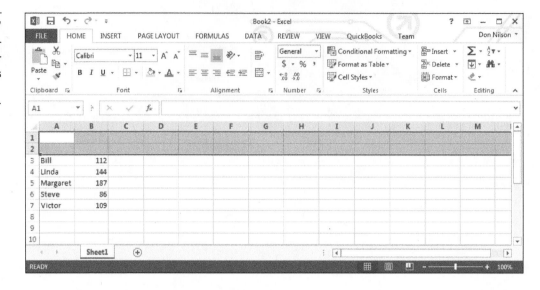

Changing the width of a column or the height of a row is easy. Suppose in Figure AE3a-17 that you want to include both first and last names in column A. At present, column A is not large enough to show both names. To make it larger, in the column headings click the line between the A and the B. Your cursor changes to a vertical bar with an arrow on each side, as shown in Figure AE3a-18. Move the cursor to the right to increase the size of the column and to the left to decrease it. Similarly, to increase or decrease the height of a row, click the line between the line numbers and drag up to decrease the row height and down to increase it.

Figure AE3a-19 shows the spreadsheet after column A has been made wider and row 1 has been increased in height. *Sales Rep* has been entered as the heading for column A, and *Sales* has been entered as the name for column B.

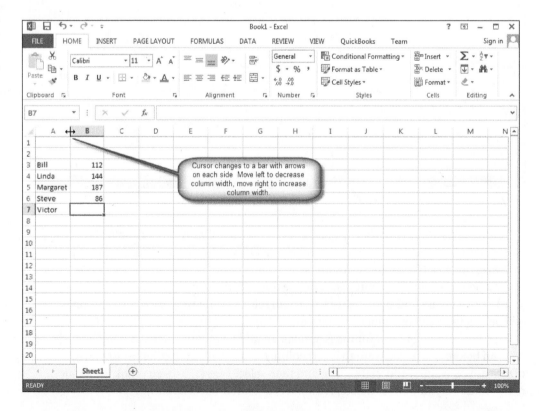

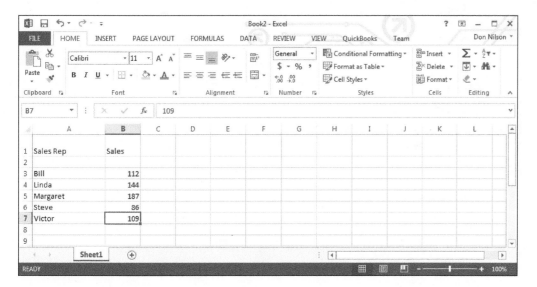

Figure AE3a-19
Spreadsheet with Rows Added and Sizes of Columns Changed

Source: Microsoft Excel 2013.

Q5 How Can You Format Data?

Excel has a powerful and complicated set of tools for formatting spreadsheets. Here we will just scratch the surface with a few of the hundreds of possibilities.

The spreadsheet in Figure AE3a-19 is boring and misleading. It would be better if the headings were centred over the columns and if they looked like headings. Also, are the sales in dollars or some other currency? If in dollars, they should have a dollar sign and maybe two decimal points.

To make the headings more interesting, highlight cells A1 and B1 (to do this, click A1 and hold the mouse button down as you move the mouse pointer to B1) and in the *Font* section of the ribbon select 16 rather than 11. This action increases the font size of the labels. In the same *Font* section of the ribbon, with A1 and B1 selected, click the bucket of paint. Select a medium blue. Now, still with cells A1 and B1 selected, in the *Alignment* section of the ribbon click the centre icons, as shown in Figure AE3a-20. Your labels will appear centred both horizontally and vertically in the cell.

The sales figures are actually in dollars, but they are formatted incorrectly. To place dollar signs in front of them, select cells B3 to B7 and in the *Number* section of the ribbon click the down arrow next to the dollar sign. Select $ English (United States), and your spreadsheet will be formatted like that in Figure AE3a-21.

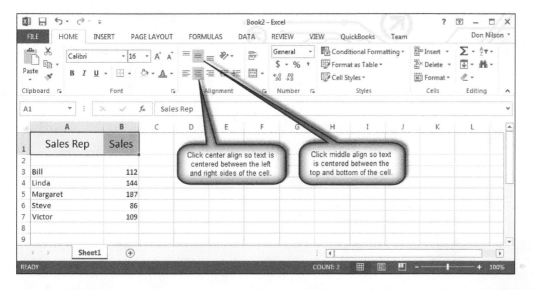

Figure AE3a-20
Centring Labels in Cells

Source: Microsoft Excel 2013.

Figure AE3a-21

Adding Dollar Signs in Cells

Source: Microsoft Excel 2013.

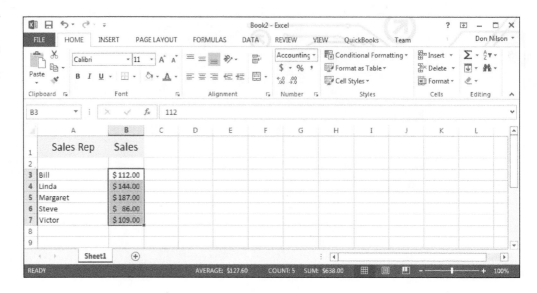

As stated, Excel provides hundreds of options for formatting your spreadsheet. You can add lines and borders, you can change the colour of font, and you can even add conditional formatting so that large sales numbers appear in bold, red type. There is insufficient room in this short introduction to explain such capabilities, but explore on your own using Excel Help (the question mark in the upper right-hand corner).

Q6 How Can You Create a (Simple) Formula?

In spite of how it might appear to you at this point, the power of Excel is not the ease with which you can enter data or change the form of the spreadsheet, nor is it in the flexible ways you can format your data. The real power of Excel lies in its amazing computational capability. In this section, we will introduce a few simple formulas.

Consider the spreadsheet in Figure AE3a-22. Suppose that we want to add Bill's sales numbers together to obtain his total sales for the months of March, April, and May. Those sales are located in cells C3, D3, and E3, respectively. A logical way to add the three together is with the following formula: *C3+D3+E3*.

Figure AE3a-22

Selecting Cells to Be Summed

Source: Microsoft Excel 2013.

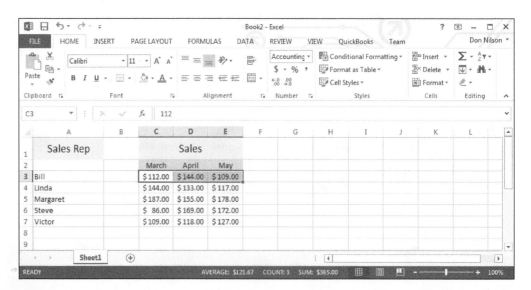

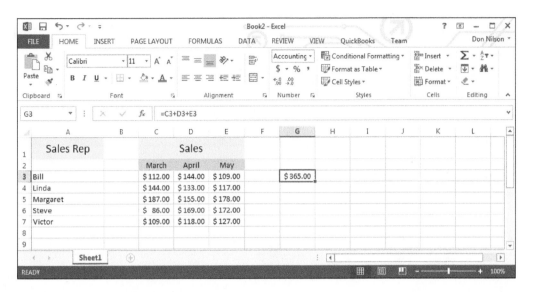

Figure AE3a-23

The Result of Applying a
Formula That Summed Cells
C3, D3, and E3

Source: Microsoft Excel 2013.

To enter this formula in Excel, first choose the cell into which you want to place the total. For the spreadsheet in Figure AE3a-22, suppose that is cell G3. Click that cell and enter the expression *=C3+D3+E3* and then press *Enter*. The result will appear as shown in Figure AE3a-23. (Be sure to start with an equal sign. If you omit the equal sign, Excel will think you're attempting to enter a label or text value and will just show the letters *C3+D3+E3* in the cell.)

Before you go on, select cell G3 and press the F2 function key, as shown in Figure AE3a-24. Notice the colour coding that Excel presents. The term *C3* is shown in blue ink, and the C3 cell is outlined in blue; *D3* and *E3* are shown in other colours. Whenever you have a problem with a calculation, press F2 to have Excel highlight the cells involved in that calculation.

The next operation is actually quite amazing. Suppose that you want to add the 3 months' sales data for all of the salespeople. To do that, right-click cell G3 and select *Copy*. Next, highlight cells G4 through G7, right-click, and select *Paste*. The formula will be copied into each of the cells. The correct totals will appear in each row.

Here's the amazing part: When Excel copied the formula, it did not do so blindly. Instead, it adjusted the terms of the formula so that each would refer to cells in the row to which it was copied. To verify this, highlight cell G5, for example, and press F2,

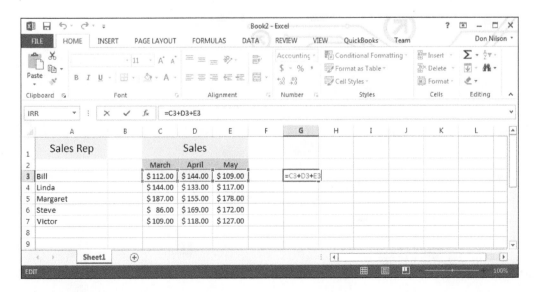

Figure AE3a-24

Using the F2 Function Key to
Show Colour Coding of Cells
Involved in a Calculation

Source: Microsoft Excel 2013.

Figure AE3a-25

Using the F2 Function Key to
Confirm That a Formula Was
Correctly Copied into Multiple
Cells

Source: Microsoft Excel 2013.

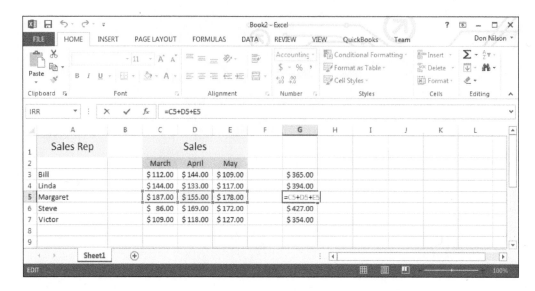

as shown in Figure AE3a-25. Notice that the formula in this cell is *=C5+D5+E5*. The formula you copied was *=C3+D3+E3*. Excel adjusted the row numbers when it copied the formula!

Suppose now we want to total the sales for each month. To obtain the total for March, for example, we want to total cells C3+C4+C5+C6+C7. To do so, we could go to an appropriate cell, say C9, and enter the formula *=C3+C4+C5+C6+C7*. This will work, but there is an easier way to proceed.

Highlight cell C9 and then select the *Formulas* tab at the top of the ribbon. At the top of the tab, click *Auto Sum*, as shown in Figure AE3a-26. Press *Enter*, and Excel will total the values in the column. If you click cell C9 and press F2, you will see that Excel entered the formula *=SUM(C3:C8)*. This is a shorthand way of summing the values in those cells using a built-in function called **SUM**. To finish this spreadsheet, copy the formula from cell C9 to cells D9, E9, and G9. The spreadsheet will appear as in Figure AE3a-27. Now all that remains to do is to add labels to the *total* row and *total* column.

You can use an Excel formula to create just about any algebraic expression. However, when you create a formula, remember the rules of high school algebra. For example, *=(B2+B3)/7* will add the contents of cell B2 to those of B3 and divide the sum

Figure AE3a-26

Auto Sum Function

Source: Microsoft Excel 2013.

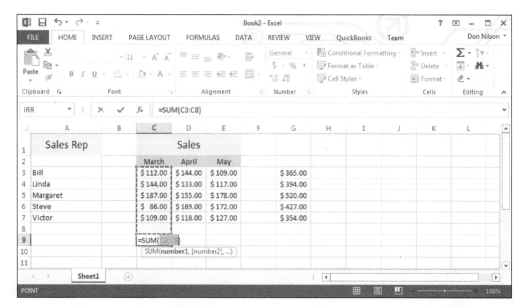

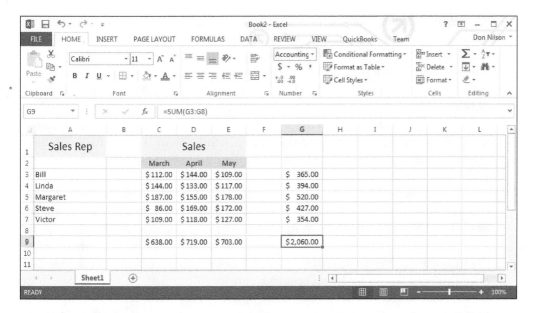

Figure AE3a-27

Summing Sales by Month

Source: Microsoft Excel 2013.

by 7. In contrast, *=B2+B3/7* will first divide B3 by 7 and then add the result to the contents of B2. When in doubt, just key in a formula you think might work and experiment until you get the results you want.

Q7 How Can You Print Results?

Excel provides a wide variety of tools and settings for printing worksheets. Here we will illustrate several features that will give you an idea of the possibilities. After you have read this section, you can experiment on your own.

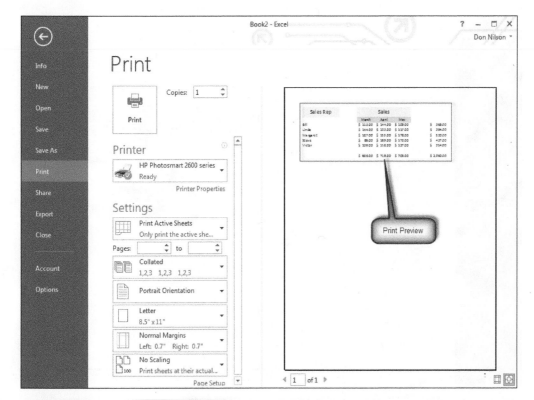

Figure AE3a-28

The Print Preview Screen in Excel

Source: Microsoft Excel 2013.

Before you start printing, you can save paper and ink if you make use of Excel's Print Preview feature. To do so, click *FILE* and then *Print*. The result is shown in Figure AE3a-28. Before you click the large *Print* button (next to Copies), examine the *Print Preview* thumbnail of your printout to see if you like it. If you do, press *Print*, and Excel will print your document. For now, however, select the *PAGE LAYOUT* tab in the Excel ribbon.

The tools and selections in the PAGE LAYOUT ribbon determine how the document will be arranged as a printed document. In this ribbon, the next to last group is *Sheet Options*; in that group, notice that you have the option of viewing and printing gridlines as well as column and row headings.

If you now select *Print* under *Gridlines* and *Headings*, and then select *Print Preview*, you can see that your worksheet will be printed with gridlines and headings, as shown in Figure AE3a-29. Most people prefer to see gridlines and headings in the screen display but not see them, or at least not see the headings, in the printed display. Click *Close Print Preview* to return to the spreadsheet view. For now, check *View* and *Print Gridlines*, but under *Headings* check only *View*.

As you can see, you have many other options in the PAGE LAYOUT ribbon. Use *Margins* to set the size of the page margins. *Orientation* refers to whether the worksheet is printed normally (upright) on the page (called *Portrait*) or sideways on the page (called *Landscape*). Try each and preview your print to see the impact each has.

You can use print area to specify the portion of the spreadsheet that you want to print. If for some reason you want to list only the name of the sales reps, you can highlight cells A1 through A7 and then click *Print Area* and then click *Set Print Area*. If you do this, your print preview will appear as in Figure AE3a-30.

These commands should be enough for you to print basic assignments. Of course, Excel offers many more options for you to explore. Experiment with them!

Figure AE3a-29

Using Print Preview to View the Spreadsheet with Gridlines and Headings

Source: Microsoft Excel 2013.

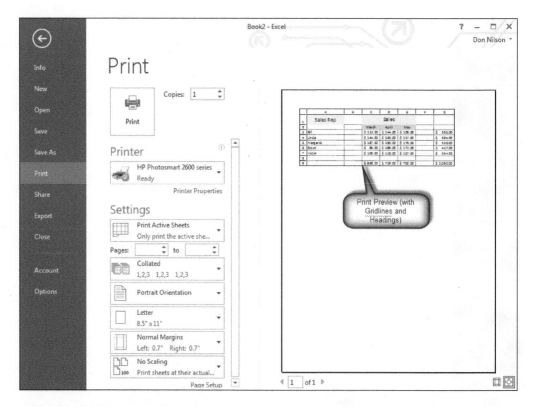

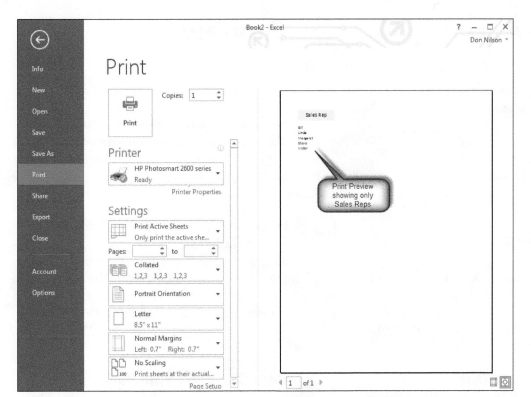

Figure AE3a-30

Using Print Preview to
Select Only a Portion of
the Spreadsheet

Source: Microsoft Excel 2013.

Active ? Review

Use this Active Review to verify that you understand the ideas and concepts that answer this chapter extension's study questions.

Q1 What is a Spreadsheet?

Explain how the following terms are related: *spreadsheet, electronic spreadsheet, Microsoft Excel, worksheet,* and *workbook.* Explain how spreadsheet cells are addressed. Where would you find cell Q54?

Q2 How do You Get Started with Excel?

Describe the first task you should do when creating a spreadsheet. Open a new workbook and give it the name *My_Sample_WB.* Explain the relationship of tabs and tools and selections. Which tab is the most likely one to have the tools and selections you need?

Q3 How Can You Enter Data?

List three ways of entering data into Excel. Describe the advantage of using the F2 key to edit data. Explain two ways that Excel uses a pattern to enter data.

Q4 How Can You Insert and Delete Rows and Columns and Change their Size?

Describe how to insert and delete rows. Describe a circumstance in which you would need to insert rows. Describe

how to make a row taller or shorter. Describe how to change the width of a column.

Q5 How Can You Format Data?

Open Excel and explain the purpose of each of the icons in the *Font* section of the *Home* tab of the ribbon. Explain the purpose of the *Alignment* and *Number* sections.

Q6 How Can You Create a (Simple) Formula?

Write the expression you would need to add the content of cell B2 to the content of cell B7. Write the expression to multiply the content of cell C4 by 7.3. Write the expression to find the average of the values in cells D7, D8, and D9. Use a built-in formula to total the values in cells E2, E3, E4, E5, E6, and E7.

Q7 How Can You Print Results?

Explain the purpose and use of *Print Preview.* Open Excel, go to the *PAGE LAYOUT* tab, and explain the purpose of the *Margins, Orientation,* and *Print Area* tools in the *Page Setup* section. Also, explain the function of the *View* and *Print* checkboxes in the *Gridlines* and *Headings* portion of the *Sheet Options* section.

MyMISLab MyMISLab is an online learning and testing environment that features the perfect study tools to help you master the concepts covered in this chapter. Log in to MyMISLab to test your knowledge of key chapter concepts and explore additional practice tools, including videos, flashcards, annotated text figures, and more!

Key Terms and Concepts

Cell 81	Spreadsheet 81	Workbook 81
Ribbon 83	SUM 94	Worksheet 81

Using Your Knowledge

AE4a-1. Open Excel and duplicate each of the actions in this chapter extension.

AE4a-2. Create a new workbook and take the following actions:
    a. Name and save your workbook using a name of your own choosing.
    b. Enter the value *This is the content of cell C7* into cell C7.

   c. Use F2 to change the value in cell C7 to *This is part of the content of cell C7.*

   d. Add the value *January* to cells B2 through B14. Only key the data once.

   e. Add the value *January* to cell C2 and the value *February* to cell C3. Highlight both cells C2 and C3 and drag the small black box down to cell C14. Explain what happens.

   f. Create a list of odd numbers from 1 to 11 in cells C3 through C8. Key only the values 1 and 3.

   g. Enter the value *MIS-1* in cell D2 and the value *MIS-2* in cell D3. Highlight cells D2 and D3 and drag the small black box down to cell D14. Explain what happens.

AE4a-3. Click the tab named *Sheet2* in the workbook you used for question 2.

   a. Place the labels *Part Description, Quantity on Hand, Cost,* and *Total Value* in cells B2, C2, D2, and E2, respectively. Centre each label in its cell and make the labels bold. (Do this by highlighting the labels and clicking the bold B in the *Font* section of the *Home* tab.) Make each column large enough to show the entire label after formatting.

   b. In cells B3, B4, B5, B6, and B7, respectively, enter the following values:
This is where one would type the description of Part 1
This is where one would type the description of Part 2
This is where one would type the description of Part 3
This is where one would type the description of Part 4
This is where one would type the description of Part 5
Enter these values using the fewest possible keystrokes.

   c. Enter the quantity-on-hand values *100, 150, 100, 175,* and *200* in cells C3 through C7, respectively. Enter these values using the fewest possible keystrokes.

   d. Enter the values *$100, $178, $87, $195,* and *$117* in cells D3 through D7, respectively. Do not enter the dollar signs. Instead, enter only the numbers and then reformat the cells so that Excel will place them.

   e. In cell E3, enter a formula that will multiply the quantity on hand (C3) by the cost (D3).

   f. Create the same formula in cells E4 through E7. Use select and copy operations.

   g. Explain what is magic about the operation in part f.

   h. Print the result of your activities in parts a–f. Print your document in landscape mode, showing cell boundaries and row and column names.

PART 2 Using Information Technology

> "The information systems program has the unique ability to connect graduates with jobs in their specific areas of interest."

In Sarah's Words

My degree in Information Systems has given me the opportunity to work anywhere, for any organization—and in positions that are in line with my values and my goal to empower people through technology.

Sarah Furey graduated in 2010 from St. Francis Xavier University with a Bachelor of Information Systems degree, majoring in Enterprise Resource Planning. As she studied, she put her skills into practice (and paid for her schooling) working as the vice-president of communications for the students' union.

After graduation, I accepted a CIDA (Canadian International Development Agency) placement in Botswana, Africa. As a technical assistant in Gaborone, I worked for a non-governmental organization (NGO) dedicated to promoting sexual health.

In Botswana, cultural differences made it difficult to figure out how I could be useful. My technical skills did not define my role; rather, my interest in people and my understanding of management information systems (MIS) did. Observing people using technology helped me appreciate the similarities of digital communication around the globe. People and organizations, from Botswana to Nova Scotia, use digital information daily and have the same needs: access and reliability. The skills I gained during my MIS classes taught me how the average person uses technology. Through open-mindedness and an understanding of MIS, I collaborated with local organizations to develop systems, file management tools, and mobile health tools that helped improve people's lives.

Working for the Botswana Family Welfare Association, I faced the same challenges I saw at the St. F.X. Students' Union—digital media management, file sharing, online presence, and software integration. The MIS skills I learned in school helped me in both cases, and I was able to develop and implement technically sound strategies and, most importantly, spend time explaining the new systems to employees. Empowering people through technology requires education.

My interest in health landed me a job as a developer on projects connected to the Botswana Ministry of Health. I was tasked with developing a remote diagnostic tool for use by dentists in the rural areas of southern Africa. To gain the technical and heath specs required, I interviewed many people, asked lots of questions, and persevered even when cultural barriers were overwhelming. Relating to people is the key to any successful project, including highly technical IT developments.

Sarah Furey

As a developer in Halifax for Bezanson's I.T. Solutions, I also work in areas of interest in line with my values. I develop custom modules to solve clients' business problems, essentially making their lives easier. I learn from my colleagues, share information, and continue to build strong relationships. Whether I am programming, planning, researching, or engaging with a client, I continue to hone my skills.

Our second "running case" begins with Marlo, a recent graduate who has just accepted a position at a bed-and-breakfast (B&B) hotel and started her career in the tourism and hospitality industry.

Tourism is an important part of the Canadian economy. In 2011, tourism accounted for $78.8 billion in revenues or approximately 2 percent of the gross domestic product (GDP) and 619 000 direct jobs. In addition, tourism also drives other key service industries, including accommodations (such as B&B hotels), food and beverage, passenger transportation, recreation, entertainment, and travel services for a combined total of 9.2 percent of all jobs in Canada.

Although you may not have previously stayed in a B&B, you are likely familiar with the overall concept. The fundamental premise is renting out rooms and some ancillary services, but, regular hotels, B&Bs tend to be smaller (usually having less than 20 rooms), focus on a high level of personal service, are often owner occupied, and consist of large, historic private homes that have been renovated and converted. While some are found in major cities, many B&Bs are located in smaller towns frequented by tourists. In the next three chapters, we will follow Marlo as she applies some of the ideas from her MIS course to her new career.

Running Case Introduction

Marlo Jenkins is a recent graduate with a joint major in Hospitality and Tourism, and Business. As an undergraduate, Marlo never really considered herself a "techie," but she decided to complete dual concentrations in Marketing and MIS (an excellent combination) because she recognized how important cellphones, computers, and social networks, such as Facebook, had become.

Following her convocation in 2014, Marlo attended a job fair. After a series of interviews, she was offered a position as a management trainee with The 1881, a medium-sized B&B hotel in Lunenburg, Nova Scotia. Although Marlo was originally from central Canada, she had visited eastern Canada with her family many times, and these trips had sparked an interest in hospitality and tourism.

As part of her degree, she had completed two co-op work terms. The first was with a large national hotel in Montreal, Quebec, and the second with a small motel in Niagara Falls, Ontario. Although Marlo had never stayed at a B&B, she was familiar with the concept. While there are many types of B&Bs, the majority tend to be medium to large family homes that have been converted to hotels in tourist areas. While some, such as The 1881, are large, many are quite small and have modest kitchens and dining facilities. Most B&Bs offer breakfast or brunch and have limited amenities (no swimming pools or exercise rooms).

Marlo was enthusiastic about starting her new job. Originally a private summer house built in 1881 (hence the name) for a wealthy family, The 1881 was converted to a B&B after the depression in 1939. Fully modernized to a five-star level in 2008, The 1881 included five basic rooms, nine luxurious rooms, and three full suites. It was definitely high end. The 1881 enjoyed an excellent reputation, and many guests returned year after year. Business included numerous corporate events, and the occupancy rate was very high. Off-season rates ranged from $149 to $279 a night, although additional discounts were sometimes available.

In 2014, The 1881 was purchased by a retired hedge fund manager and her spouse. Their vision for The 1881, which they shared with Marlo during the interview process, was to increase the number of high-end and affluent clients by offering more luxury and concierge-type services and to extend the season by catering to business needs for corporate executive retreats. Marlo believed that not only was this an excellent strategy but also that the new owners had the ability and resources to implement it. The owners were impressed by Marlo's positive attitude and willingness to learn. For them, The 1881 was a mix of a "hobby business" with an expectation of profit. They saw in Marlo an assistant manager they could trust, and someone who could one day run the entire operation when they were away or tied up with their other investments.

We meet Marlo as she begins her new position and is tackling her first major project, the revitalization of the computing resources. We continue to follow her adventure in Chapter 5, after she has modernized the technology and has decided to investigate a system to collect and manage information about the hotel's guests (a customer relationship management [CRM] system). In Chapter 6, Marlo deals with her first real crisis—a security breach of the hotel's computer information. While The 1881 and Marlo are fictitious, their experiences are based on facts, and these same experiences could happen to you!

Watch

This case will run throughout Part 2. Read more at the beginning of each chapter and then visit MyMISLab to access the data files to complete the running case questions at the end of Part 2.

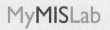

4 Hardware and Software

Running Case: The 1881 B&B

It had been eight hectic weeks but Marlo was quickly coming up to speed. Arriving in Lunenburg in September 2014, she managed to find an apartment that was just a short walk from The 1881, as well as a great roommate by using her Facebook connections. Talking to her parents on Skype, Marlo said that she was really enjoying herself and that it felt like every day was a great learning experience. Although the owners could be demanding and had very high standards, she found that they were also very supportive.

There were three other employees at the B&B—two cleaners who took care of laundry and housekeeping and a chef who came in every morning and worked from 6 a.m. to 2 p.m. Other services, such as maintenance and repair, were outsourced. Most mornings, Marlo met briefly with the owners, Cathy and Andre, to discuss immediate priorities and upcoming events. Marlo found these morning meetings quite informal, and the owners had made it clear to her that she was expected to ask insightful questions as well as to suggest ideas.

As the last guest departed at the end of the Thanksgiving holiday, The 1881 was closed for a week to repaint some rooms and perform routine maintenance on the freezer. Over coffee in the main breakfast room, the owners asked Marlo to investigate an upgrade of the computer technology and to recommend a strategy when they returned the next weekend.

Remembering her MIS courses, Marlo felt strongly that this strategy should begin with a hardware and software inventory. It was fairly obvious that computerization had not been important to the previous owners. The 1881 had only five computers, and the newest was close to five years old. Printing involved an inkjet printer that used hard-to-find cartridges, often jammed, and could not be connected to her new Ultrabook computer, which she had received as a graduation present. Hotel reservation and management used a popular and well-regarded software package that was fairly stable, but Marlo soon found out that the version that The 1881 used (2.0) was a far cry from the vendor's current offering of 12.0 and required new technology.

Marlo knew that the owners were much more aware of new technology and although they were willing to invest, she also knew that they would want more than a shopping list of shiny new gadgets. She needed to demonstrate a vision that was grounded in the business.

Knowing that the overall strategy was to attract more business clients, Marlo believed that The 1881 should portray the "right" image and appear to be on the leading edge. This would take investment that would have to be justified. Upgrading the computers made obvious sense and could be done for less than $7500, but the details were important. Should they all be desktops like the old ones were, or should she recommend tablets for portability? Updating the hotel software was also an obvious task, but would cost about $5000. Until now, The 1881 had been exclusively Microsoft but Marlo wondered if she should also include Apple technology.

Marlo wanted to be innovative. When guests arrived they were given paper information and photographs about The 1881 and Lunenburg history but what if there was an application instead that guests could load on their own devices or those loaned by The 1881. This would not only put The 1881 on the leading edge but could reduce overall costs.

Marlo was not too worried about the hotel's tablets being lost or stolen. She thought that in many ways, they would be treated just like any other hotel asset. But how should she sell her ideas to the owners? She knew that $25 000 had been set aside for computer infrastructure improvements, but the owners would still need to be convinced. Where should she start?

Study Questions

Q1 **Why do you need to know about information technology?**

Q2 **Where did all this information technology stuff come from?**

Q3 **What does a manager need to know about computer hardware?**

Q4 **What is the difference between a client and a server, and what is cloud computing?**

Q5 **What does a manager need to know about software?**

Q6 **What buying decisions does a manager need to make?**

Q7 **What are viruses, worms, and zombies?**

Nadino/Shutterstock

Watch
Go to MyMISLab to watch a video
about hardware and software.

Q1 Why Do You Need to Know About Information Technology?

At your next family gathering, ask your older relatives what life was like when they were younger. Consider the technologies that you now take for granted, and ask them which ones existed back then. You might be surprised by their answers. Depending on their ages, socioeconomic status, and where they grew up, their answers will vary. The technologies that you are thinking about may not have existed previously in any form. You might be comfortable with such technologies as smartphones, tablets, and internet-enabled services, such as YouTube, Facebook, Snapchat, and Google. Your grandparents grew up familiar with cars, the telephone, the television, and air travel. All of these technologies are only 100 years old (in 1903, the Ford Motor Company sold its first car and the Wright brothers had their first flight). The commercial telegraph system was developed in the 1830s, the radio was popularized in the 1920s, and black-and-white television was available in the late 1930s. Digital computers, which most people tend to think of when asked about high technology, first appeared in the 1940s, and the internet, which originated in the 1960s, evolved into the World Wide Web in the 1990s when many of you were just born.

There is a point to this short history. A true understanding of technology starts not only from the technology we have today but also the technology that our technology emerged from. You live in a very different world from the one your grandparents—or even your parents—lived in. However, technology cannot always distance itself from its past. Although using technology to improve commerce is probably as old as the abacus, knowing the basics of modern information technology (IT) (including hardware, software, and networking) will not only make you a more knowledgeable consumer of technology but will also help you consider how it can be used in business, recognize its positive and negative effects on society, and think about what its future could be. The central thesis of this book is that whether or not you want to change the world or make a lot of money, understanding and applying IT to everyday life is a fundamental building block for success.

Q2 Where Did All This Information Technology Stuff Come From?

The history of IT is recent and rich. The first digital computing devices were invented in the 1940s. The first commercial computers were available in the 1950s, and the first personal computers (PCs) came on the market in the early 1980s. The internet and cellular phones came into wide-spread use during the 1990s after the World Wide Web was invented, and mobile computing, texting, smartphones, and computerized social networking emerged in the early part of the twenty-first century. The sections below provide a brief history of the development of modern networked computing, a discussion that is also summarized on page 111.

Early Computers: 1939–1952

Like a lot of modern technology, early computers were financed by the United States military. Although there are several devices that can potentially claim to be the first computer, the consensus is that the ENIAC (Electronic Numerical Integrator and Computer) (Figure 4-1), originally designed in 1946 to calculate missile firing tables, was the first reprogrammable general-purpose computer. Like all early computers, it was large, complex, and expensive and only ran one program at a time. The term

H.Armstrong Roberts/ClassicStock/Alamy

Figure 4-1

The ENIAC Computer

Source: Collections of the University of Pennsylvania Archives.

"computer bug," or simply "bug," used to describe unexpected computer problems actually arose when a moth was caught between the mechanical relays of the Mark II Aiken Relay Calculator at Harvard University in 1947, and its removal led to the term "debugging," which is now commonly used to describe the process of fixing problems in computer programs. These early machines were slowly improved and commercialized. The FERUAT, the first digital computer in Canada (installed at the University of Toronto in 1952), was one of only a small number of digital computers in North America at the time.[1] The computer in your mobile phone is 1000 times smaller and 1 000 000 times faster than these early computers. Now that is progress!

Mainframes: 1952–Present

The first commercial digital computers, which were large, room-sized devices based on now-obsolete vacuum tube technology, were called **mainframes** and were mainly used by businesses and government. Costing between $200 000 and $400 000, they could add or subtract about 16 000 numbers per second. Second-generation mainframes introduced in the late 1950s used transistors, which made them smaller, easier to maintain, and more reliable. These early machines were often sold without software—the assumption was that companies themselves would develop the programs they wanted to use. Manulife Financial became the first insurance company in Canada to adopt this technology in 1956.

The third generation of mainframe machines, introduced in the mid-1960s, included operating systems and multiprocessing capability. This was a big step, and these computers cost millions of dollars. The multiprocessing allowed for time sharing or several programs to use the computer at the same time. Prior to multiprocessing, generally only one user could interact with the computer at a time. Time sharing eventually led to more sophisticated networking among computers (Figure 4-2).

Mainframes have been the mainstay of business computing since the early 1960s, and some models, such as the IBM Mainframe50, continue to be made even today. While small computer servers and cloud computing provide many services, some programs used in larger organizations still run on mainframe systems. Mainframes are designed for fast processing and massive storage, and, for this reason, they are likely to continue to be used far into the future as our need for information continues to grow.

[1] You can read more about the history of computing in Canada in the *IEEE Annals of the History of Computing* archive, Vol. 16, no. 2, June 1994.

Figure 4-2

The IBM 360

Source: Reprint Courtesy of International Business Machines Corporation.

Microcomputers: 1975–Present

Early mainframes were relatively large and often required to be housed in climate-controlled spaces. A typical second-generation mainframe would often include a central processing unit (CPU) (one closet-sized machine), short-term memory (another closet), and data storage such as disk or tape drives (multiple closets). But people wanted something smaller. The microprocessor was developed in the early 1970s by Texas Instruments and Intel. It incorporated a CPU and some short-term memory into a single silicon chip using integrated circuits (ICs). The microprocessors were small and originally used in such devices as handheld calculators. The microprocessors quickly became the critical piece in the development of the microcomputer.

The first **microcomputers**, such as the MITS Altair 8800 (Figure 4-3) and Datapoint 2200, were developed in 1975.[2] These early microcomputers often did not have a display screen or monitor and required their users to develop their own programs. As the hardware technology developed, companies such as Digital Research,

Figure 4-3

The Altair 8800

Source: Ron Wurzer/Getty Images.

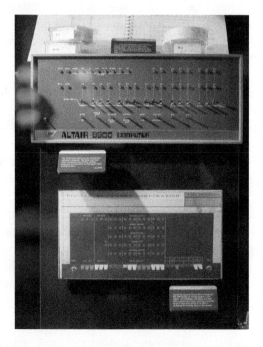

[2] For more information on the chronology of microprocessors, go to http://processortimeline.info.

THE FIRST VIDEO GAME

If you play any of the popular video or computer games, such as Farmville, Grand Theft Auto, or World of Warcraft, you may find it fascinating to know that the first video game, Spacewar, was developed in 1962 by a team of 25-year-old computer scientists inspired by science fiction novels. The game was created as a demonstration program for the PDP-1, a mainframe computer developed by Digital Equipment Company (DEC).

Although the program was based on real science (players had to consider the gravitational effects of the sun as they fired torpedoes at a space target), it had little to do with any practical application. However, it was still enormously popular and could apparently be found on almost all research computers in the United States throughout the 1960s.

Source: Based on The History of Spacewar, About.com, http://inventors.about.com/library/weekly/aa090198.htm.

Seattle Computer Products, and Microsoft created operating systems (QDOS) and programming languages (BASIC) that could be used by microcomputers. By 1981, the microcomputer had developed enough for some companies, such as IBM, Apple, Compaq, and Texas Instruments, to launch the personal computer (PC). These microcomputers had monitors, keyboards, portable floppy disks, and word processors, spreadsheets, and other software. Compared with mainframes, they were easier to use and were immediately popular with many users. The PC revolution was born.

Networking Personal Computers: 1985–Present

As microcomputers evolved and became more powerful, they also became easier to use. But like the mainframes before them, they were primarily designed to be used by one person at a time. Sharing data was a cumbersome process that required saving data on a floppy disk and then transferring it to another machine. This lack of networking capability also inhibited access to corporate or enterprise information that had been created and stored on mainframe systems. This problem was solved by the next computing development—local area network (LAN) technology.

Originally proposed by Robert Metcalfe at the Palo Alto Research Center (PARC) and later patented by Xerox, Ethernet was a set of rules, or protocols, enabling devices to communicate and share information. Although there were other network protocols, Ethernet's simplicity and popularity[3] provided the ability to connect many PCs together. By giving each device a specific address (see Chapter 6), LAN technology revolutionized business computing by providing shared access to data, printers, and other peripheral devices. Although LANs normally served relatively small groups of people within small areas, network technologies soon let users connect multiple LANs across a wide area.

This 1980s LAN revolution was followed by the commercialization of the wide area network (WAN) technology in the 1990s. WAN, exemplified by the internet, was originally developed in the late 1960s as a robust network of mainframe systems (stay tuned for more about WAN in Chapter 6). Building on email, the web browser, and access to a worldwide network of computers, networking became so firmly ensconced

---

[3] For more information on Ethernet, go to www.cisco.com/en/US/docs/internetworking/technology/handbook/Ethernet.html.

and is now taken for granted and has all of the characteristics of a utility. Like electricity, it is now noticed only in its absence during system failures or slowdowns (that is, long wait times for files to download).

Mobile and Tablet Computing: Late 1990s–Present

In addition to heralding the mainstreaming of the internet and fuelling the dot com bubble—a time when many new internet companies were funded by venture capitalists and which notoriously went bankrupt (e.g., WebVan, Pets.com, marchFirst)—the end of the twentieth century was an important period for two other technological reasons.

First, the high cost of early computer technology encouraged computer programmers to save resources by using only the last two digits of the year (e.g., 65 rather than 1965). Although this changed as time went by and costs decreased, a large number of these original programs were still in use many decades later and created a large problem because subtracting the earlier two-digit date from a later two- or four-digit date, say, 2000, yielded unexpected or invalid results (e.g., the age of someone who was born in 1960 could be calculated as –40). Although relatively few problems were actually encountered (either because they were properly fixed or the problem was exaggerated), the Y2K problem (K is a computer term for the number 1024 and is commonly but incorrectly used to mean one thousand) significantly raised the profile of computer technology and, coupled with the rising popularity of World Wide Web, ushered in a new age of technological change.

Second, the dramatic lowering of costs for cellular technology and mobile telephones meant that these technologies became commonplace and adopted by large groups of people across North America and Europe. Although early cellular phones were not very powerful and had very small displays, they were relatively small and many were carried by their owners at all times. Given this, it was perhaps predictable that cellular phones with larger screens and their own operating system that could run applications would be developed.

Although the early stage of personal computers was largely dominated by Microsoft, Apple's development of the easy-to-use MP3 iPod music player fuelled a resurgence of the company that was further leveraged into the 2007 release of the iPhone and the March 2010 launch of the iPad, a tablet-sized device that operated as an electronic book for reading, web surfing, email, and a variety of applications that included games, education, specialized professional programs, and office automation.

Technology, however, has shown that dominance is rarely unchallenged and frequently fleeting. Various companies, such as Google, RIM, Samsung, Sony, and Microsoft, have developed or announced similar devices, but it is too early to say which of these will achieve market success. While it is clear that small, lightweight, fast, powerful, and easy-to-use network devices have become important, what is not clear is which of these devices will survive over time. Which of these devices—computers, cellular phones or smartphones, and tablet computers—do you have, and which ones do you use most often?

Cloud Computing: 2010–Present

The rise of the internet and the use of websites such as Amazon and Flickr also brought in a movement away from privately owned technology toward shared or virtual storage and computing services commonly called cloud computing. Although a precise definition remains elusive (and will be discussed further in Chapter 6), cloud computing promises flexible, secure, and scalable low fixed cost computing that is available anywhere, anytime, and on any device.

Summary

What can we learn from this whirlwind tour of the history of technology? From the many things we discussed above, three important lessons can be extracted:

1. *Price and performance advances:* IT is continuously evolving. According to Moore's Law[4] (see Chapter 1), in 18 months the price of a given integrated circuit (IC) will be halved or, for the same amount of money, you will be able to buy a new IC with twice as many transistors. However, it is not just the price of processing power that has decreased. Data storage and network capacity have also improved dramatically, so inexpensive access to high-bandwidth resources, such as YouTube and Netflix, have quickly become a reality.

2. *Small is powerful:* The history of computing can be summarized as an ongoing effort to make IT smaller and more powerful, with the capability to be used almost anywhere. This trend is not likely to stop, as proven by the advancement of nanotechnology.[5] The three main components of a modern computer—the processor, the memory, and the storage—have all been getting smaller and costing less, and current technology is both small enough and powerful enough to be useful almost everywhere.

3. *The network is the thing:* The value of IT can be measured not only in the power of the processor but also in the power of the network that can be accessed through the machine. All computing machines have inevitably moved toward networks for communication and collaboration, and the bandwidth—the rate at which computers can communicate—has increased significantly. The pervasiveness of IT will continue to increase as networks become cheaper and easier to join. The interesting question to ponder is, after microcomputers, the internet, and social networking, what is next? As we will see in Chapters 6 and 9, the answer may be as close to you as your phone.

Q3 What Does a Manager Need to Know About Computer Hardware?

👁‑**Watch**

Go to MyMISLab to watch a video about what a manager needs to know about computer hardware?

As discussed in the five-component framework, **hardware** consists of the physical electronic components and related gadgetry that input, process, output, and store data according to instructions encoded in computer programs or software. Although technology is rapidly changing, all computers consist of four basic components: input, processing, output, and storage (as depicted in Figure 4-4).

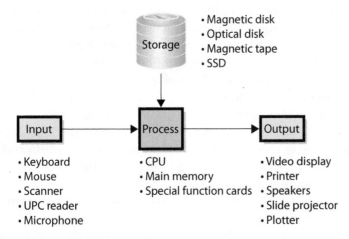

Figure 4-4

Input, Process, Output, and Storage Hardware

[4] For more information, see www.intel.com/technology/mooreslaw/index.htm.
[5] Learn more about nanotechnology at http://science.howstuffworks.com/nanotechnology.htm.

Input, Processing, Output, and Storage Hardware

Input devices may be one of the two most visible or familiar parts of the computer (output devices being the other). Most often, for PCs and tablets, the most common input device is a keyboard or touchscreen, but this does not have to be the case. For example, a barcode scanner is an input device to a cash register, and other special-purpose devices also capture input. Video games, for example, use cameras, controllers, and microphones, and many banks use specialized machines that read the magnetically and optically designed numbers that are printed on the bottom of cheques. Universities and other testing centres use scanners, such as the Scantron test scanner, to read and mark student assignments and exams.

Because input devices can vary greatly, they are often evaluated and compared on the basis of physical dimensions or according to how they will be used. Cameras, for example, can be selected on the basis of resolution and keyboards on the basis of size, layout of extra keys, and ease of use. Organizations that rely on or have a lot of specialized hardware will often conduct evaluations or compare input devices before choosing them to improve their productivity and reduce costs.

Processing devices include the **central processing unit (CPU)**, sometimes called the brain of the computer. Although the design of the CPU has nothing in common with the anatomy of real brains, this description is helpful because the CPU does contain the machine's smarts. The CPU selects instructions, processes them, performs arithmetic and logical comparisons, and stores results of operations in memory.

CPU performance is measured in **Hertz (Hz)** or cycles and counted in *gigahertz* (GHz), a measurement that is approximately a billion cycles per second. CPUs can vary in terms of speed, function, and cost, and the type that you need will often depend on the type of computing that you do. Financial risk modelling or video rendering, for example, may require the fastest and most sophisticated CPUs to boost performance. Ordinary word processing or simple email, however, may have far less taxing requirements that allow you to buy slightly older or less expensive technology. The investments required to be competitive as a computer chip designer or fabricator, such as Intel, Advanced Micro Devices (AMD), and National Semiconductor, can be significant. Estimates have put the cost of building a new laboratory in the United States at over 2 billion dollars. Manufacturers also continually invest large amounts in research and development to improve CPU speed and capabilities while reducing CPU costs (see Moore's Law in Chapter 1).

The CPU works in conjunction with the computer's **main memory**, often referred to as **random access memory (RAM)**. The CPU reads data and instructions from the RAM and then stores the results of its computations in the main memory. We will describe the relationship between the CPU and the main memory later in this chapter.

As noted earlier, **output hardware** also tends to be the more familiar or visible part of a computer, likely because it also has the most physical interaction with the computer user by producing or displaying the desired results of a computational task or request. Almost all devices have a display or monitor and, increasingly, microphones and speakers. As with input devices, there is a large variety, although the most common include video displays, printers, audio speakers, overhead projectors, and other special-purpose devices, such as large flatbed plotters. Evaluation of output devices will depend on the type; printers, for example, are often described not only in terms of resolution quality (typically dots per inch or DPI) but also by how many pages are printed per minute and how quickly the printing of the first page is completed.

Storage hardware saves data and programs. At the time of writing this book, magnetic disks are rapidly disappearing from portable computing devices but are still the most common storage devices on desktop computers. Optical disks, such as CDs and DVDs, are declining in popularity. Flash or solid state device (SSD) memory,

Figure 4-5

Special Function Card

such as the kind used in USB (Universal Serial Bus) memory, while more expensive is popular because it has no moving parts, requires less power, generates less heat, and is less susceptible to mechanical failure. USB or SSD storage is also faster in certain applications (because it does not have to wait for the moving parts) but has the disadvantage of tending to completely fail with no prior indication (mechanical disk drives will often provide indication of pending failure). As well, it does not yet have the utilities and software to partially recover data after failure (though this is changing). In large corporate data centres, data are often still stored on magnetic tapes because they remain a low-cost and easily stored backup medium.

Finally, personal computers may have **special function devices** (Figure 4-5) that can be added to augment each of its components. For example, video cards can be used to support an additional monitor for two or three screens, additional co-processors for analytical or high-end mathematics can be added, and extra storage can be added if required.

Computer Data

Before we can further describe hardware, we need to define several important terms. Let us begin with binary digits.

Binary Digits

Computers represent data using **binary digits**, called **bits**. A bit is either a 0 or a 1. Bits are used for computer data because they are easy to represent physically, as illustrated in Figure 4-6. A switch is either *closed* or *open*. A computer can be designed such that an open switch represents 0, and a closed switch represents 1. Or the orientation of a magnetic field can represent a bit—magnetism in one direction represents a 0, magnetism in the opposite direction represents a 1. Or for optical media, small pits are burned onto the surface of the disk so that they will reflect light. In a given spot, a reflection means a 1, while no reflection means a 0.

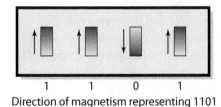

Direction of magnetism representing 1101

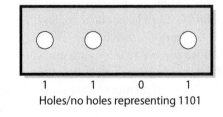

Holes/no holes representing 1101

Figure 4-6

Bits Are Easy to Represent Physically

Figure 4-7
Important Storage-Capacity
Terminology

Term	Definition	Abbreviation
Byte	Number of bits to represent one character	
Kilobyte	1024 bytes	K
Megabyte	1024K = 1 048 576 bytes	MB
Gigabyte	1024MB = 1 073 741 824 bytes	GB
Terabyte	1024GB = 1 099 511 627 776 bytes	TB
Petabyte	1024TB = 1×10^{15} bytes	PB

Sizing Computer Data

All computer data are represented by bits regardless as to whether it is numbers, characters, currency amounts, photos, recordings, or something else. All are simply a string of bits.

Bits are grouped into eight-bit chunks called **bytes**. Generally, the majority of data, such as the letters in a person's name, requires one byte for one character. Thus, when you read a specification that a computing device has 100 million bytes of memory, you know that the device could hold up to 100 million characters.

Bytes are used to measure sizes of non-character data as well. Someone might say, for example, that a given picture is 100 000 bytes in size. This means that the length of the bit string that represents the picture is 100 000 bytes, or 800 000 bits (because there are eight bits per byte). The specifications for the size of main memory, disk, and other computer devices are expressed in bytes. Figure 4-7 shows the set of abbreviations that are used to represent data-storage capacity. A **kilobyte (K)** is a collection of 1024 bytes. A **megabyte (MB)** is 1024K. A **gigabyte (GB)** is 1024MB, and a **terabyte (TB)** is 1024GB (for the true geeks among our readers the next units after this are petabytes, exabytes, zettabytes, and yottabytes).

Sometimes, these definitions are simplified: 1K equals 1000 bytes, and 1MB equals 1000K. Such simplifications make the math easy but, technically, not quite accurate. Also, disk and computer manufacturers have a motive to propagate this misconception. If a disk maker defines 1MB to be 1 million bytes—and not the correct 1024K—the manufacturer can use its own definition of MB when specifying drive capacities. A buyer may think that a disk advertised as 100MB has space for $100 \times 1024K$ bytes, whereas, in fact, the drive will have space for only $100 \times 1\,000\,000$ bytes. Normally, the distinction is not that important, but you should be aware of the two possible interpretations of these abbreviations.

In Less Than 300 Words, How Does a Computer Work?

Figure 4-8 shows a snapshot of a computer in use. The CPU is the major actor. To run a program or process data, the CPU must first transfer the program or data from storage to main memory. Then, to execute an instruction, it moves the instruction from the main memory into the CPU via the **data channel** or **bus**. The CPU has a small amount of very fast memory, called **cache**. The CPU keeps frequently used instructions in the cache. Having a large cache makes the computer faster, but more expensive.

In Figure 4-8, the computer's main memory contains program instructions for Excel, Acrobat, and even a browser. It also contains instructions for the **operating system (OS)**, which is a program that controls the computer's resources as well as a block of data.

The main memory is too small to hold all the programs and data that a user may want to process. For example, no personal computer has enough main memory to

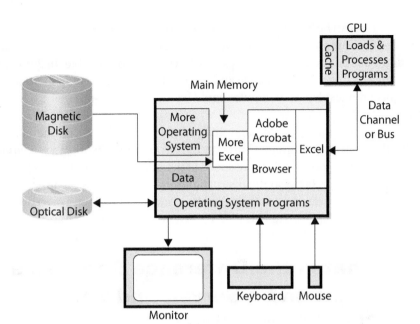

Figure 4-8
Computer Components

hold all the codes in Microsoft Word, Excel, and Access. Consequently, the CPU loads programs into the memory in sections. In Figure 4-8, one portion of Excel was loaded into the memory. When the user requests additional processing (say, to sort the spreadsheet), the CPU loads another piece of Excel.

If the user opens another program (Word, for example) or needs to load more data (a picture, perhaps), the operating system will direct the CPU to attempt to place the new program or data into unused memory. If there is not enough memory, the CPU will remove something, perhaps the block of memory labelled "More Excel," and then it will place the just-requested program or data into the vacated space. This process is called **memory swapping**.

Why Should a Manager Care How a Computer Works?

Computers can be bought with different amounts of memory. Someone who runs only one program at a time and who processes small amounts of data may require very little memory—2GB (gigs) would be just fine. However, a user who processes many programs at the same time (say, Word, Excel, Firefox, Access, Acrobat, and others) or a user who processes very large files (pictures, movies, or sound files) could benefit from more main memory, perhaps 8 or 16GB. If that person's computer has too little memory, then the computer will be constantly swapping memory, and it will run slowly. (This means, by the way, that if your computer is slow and you have many programs open, you can likely improve performance by closing a program or two.) Depending on your computer and the amount of memory it has, you might also be able to add more memory to it.

Two last comments about memory: First, the cache and the main memory are often described as **volatile**, that is, their contents are lost when power goes off. Solid-state devices, such as USB sticks, magnetic disks, and optical disks, are **nonvolatile**, that is, their contents survive even when power goes off. If you suddenly lose power, the contents of volatile memory—for example, documents that have been altered—could be lost. That is why it is a good idea to get into the habit of frequently saving documents or files that you are working on. Second, depending upon a variety of factors, it is important to realize that data may not be removed from hardware if information is deleted. Because information is stored as ones and zeros and magnetic information is not always erased, data may still exist even if you have deleted it and cannot access it yourself.

Computers can be bought with a number of different configurations. Not only can you choose from among different types (e.g., Apple or PC) and models (tablets, laptop, or desktop), but different types of chips and CPUs are also available. In 2014, a high-performance desktop PC could have an Intel i7 3.8GHz with 16GB of main memory, and a typical modest laptop computer could have a i5 2.2GHz processor with 4GB of memory.

When choosing a computer, one thing to keep in mind is that the ability and capacity of a particular computer to process a given amount of work in a set period will depend on more factors than just the speed of the processor. Not only can processors vary by manufacturer, but also the instruction set or basic operating instructions for each chip can vary, and some are optimized for certain applications. Direct one-to-one comparisons are not only extremely difficult, but in many cases, they are wrong.

Q4 What Is the Difference Between a Client and a Server, and What Is Cloud Computing?

Before we can discuss computer software, you need to understand the difference between a client and a server. Figure 4-9 shows the environment of the typical computer user. Users employ **client** computers for word processing, spreadsheets, database access, and so forth. Most client computers also have software that enables them to connect to a network. It could be a private network at their company or school, or it could be the internet, a public network. (We will discuss networks and related matters in Chapter 6. Just wait!)

Figure 4-9
Client and Server
Computers

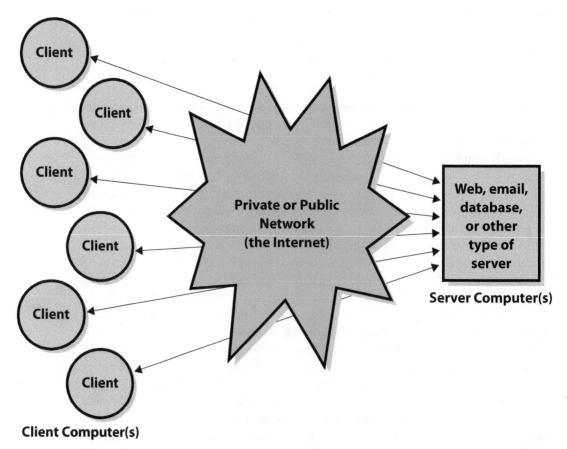

Client

Client

Client

Client

Client

Client

Private or Public Network (the Internet)

Web, email, database, or other type of server

Server Computer(s)

Client Computer(s)

Servers, as their name implies, provide services. Facebook, Google, Amazon, and YouTube all use servers that are accessed by other computers. Servers are used to publish websites, sell goods, host databases, support printing, and provide other functions.

As you might expect, server computers often need to be faster, larger, and more powerful than client computers. Servers usually have very simple video displays, and some servers have no display at all because they are accessed only from another computer via the network. For large commercial sites, such as Amazon.ca or Google.com, the server is actually a large collection of computers that coordinate all activities (called a **server farm**).

(By the way, the phrase *coordinate all activities* hides an incredibly sophisticated and fascinating technological dance—thousands, possibly millions, of transactions every minute, as well as dozens of computers handing off partially completed transactions to one another, keeping track of data that have been partially changed, picking up the pieces when one computer fails—all in the blink of an eye, with the user never needing to know any part of the miracle underway. This is absolutely incredible engineering!)

Although it can be difficult to provide a single common definition of **cloud computing**, it is similar to the concept of servers that supply applications and data. In cloud computing, customers do not necessarily own the computer infrastructure. Instead, hardware, software, and applications are provided as a service, usually through a web browser. The cloud is a metaphor for the internet, which makes software and data services available from any location at any time. The huge reductions in the cost per megabyte of storage and network bandwidth have made cloud computing a reality.

Examples of the use of cloud computing are web-based email systems, such as Hotmail or web-based document processing systems, such as Google Docs. Many people use these applications on a daily basis without thinking about where the data for these systems are being stored. These are an example of data stored in the cloud. A business perspective that students of MIS can relate to is provided in Salesforce.com (www.salesforce.com). Salesforce.com provides CRM services (see Chapter 7 for a description of CRM) to users entirely through the web. There is no installation or hardware required. All that is needed is a computer with a browser connected to the internet. Users of cloud computing rent the usage from a third-party provider and consume computing resources as a service. A user can access data, load applications, and store data using other people's servers. Cloud computing is theoretically more efficient because customers pay for what they use. Cloud computing adds on the ability to store and access data remotely and to pay for it as a service.

Cloud computing has become an increasingly popular way for companies to develop and deploy computer services. Cloud computing is still relatively new, and there are a number of technical and business considerations that managers need to be aware of. For example, what happens if a cloud provider becomes bankrupt? Where are the data actually stored, and who is responsible for ensuring that the information is secure and protected? Companies can choose private or public cloud services, and, in many cases, these services can be appropriate solutions that are financially attractive, especially for startup businesses that want to avoid large technology capital spending.

Q5 What Does a Manager Need to Know About Software?

Watch

Go to MyMISLab to watch a video about what types of applications exist, and how do organizations obtain them?

The essential knowledge that you need to have about computer software is summarized in Figure 4-10. If you already possess this knowledge, skip to Q6—What buying decisions does a manager need to make?

Category	Operating System (OS)	Instruction Set	Common Applications	Typical User
Client	Windows	Intel	Microsoft Office: Word, Excel, Access, PowerPoint, many other applications	Business Home
	Mac OS (pre-2006)	Power PC	Macintosh applications plus Word and Excel	Graphic artists Arts community
	Mac OS (post-2006)	Intel	Macintosh applications plus Word and Excel Can also run Windows on Macintosh hardware	Education Business Home Affluent users
	Unix	Sun and others	Engineering, computer-assisted design, architecture	Difficult for the typical client, but popular with some engineers and computer scientists
	Linux	Just about anything	Open Office (Microsoft Office look-alike)	Rare—used where budget is very limited
Server	Windows	Intel	Windows server applications	Business with commitment to Microsoft
	Unix	Sun and others	Unix server applications	Fading ... Linux taking its market
	Linux	Just about anything	Linux and Unix server applications	Very popular—promulgated by IBM

Figure 4-10

What a Manager Needs to Know About Software

Although there are a few exceptions, generally, computer software can be categorized into of one of two varieties: (1) operating systems, which tend to be large and complicated programs that control the computer's resources, and (2) application software, which are programs that perform specific user tasks. An example of an operating system for personal computers is Windows, and examples of computer applications are Microsoft Word and Oracle Customer Relationship Management.

There are two important software constraints. First, each version of an operating system is developed for a particular type of hardware. In some cases, such as Windows, there is mainly one commercially important version. Windows works only on processors from Intel and companies that make processors that conform to the Intel **instruction set**[6] (the commands that a CPU can process). In other cases, such as Linux, many versions exist for many different sets of instructions. In almost all cases, you cannot use an operating system that was designed for one environment in another environment.

Second, application programs are written to use a particular operating system. Microsoft Access, for example, will run only on the Windows operating system. Some applications come in multiple versions. There are, for example, Windows and Macintosh versions of Microsoft Word. But unless you have confirmed otherwise, it is safest to assume that a particular application runs on just one operating system.

---

[6] There are versions of Windows for other instruction sets, but, for our purposes, they are unimportant.

What Are the Four Major Operating Systems?

The four major operating systems (OS) listed in Figure 4-10—Windows, Mac OS, Unix, and Linux—are very important. At the time of publication, Internet Operating Systems (IOS) for such devices such as the Apple iPad, BlackBerry Playbook, and the Android family of cellular and tablet devices have also become important, as these devices have become more commonplace. However, there are very few enterprise or commercial types of applications, and these devices are mainly used for content consumption (reading and watching) rather than content creation although this is changing. The important thing to keep in mind is that both software constraints described above also apply to IOS. Android, for example, will not operate on an iPad or iPhone, and an application developed for the iPad will not run on an Android device.

Windows

For business computer users, the most important operating system is Microsoft **Windows** (the current version at the time of publication is Windows 10). Some version of Windows resides on more than 85 percent of the world's desktops, and among business users alone, the figure is closer to 95 percent. Among web browsers, however, and including tablets and smartphones, Microsoft dominance of the operating system is less obvious at 65%.

Mac OS

Apple Computer Inc. developed its own operating system for the Macintosh, **Mac OS**, whose current version is also known as *OS X*, or *Mavericks*. Unlike Microsoft, which focused on the software aspects of its business (rather than the physical and hardware components) by licensing its operating system across a broad array of manufacturers, Apple has tightly controlled all aspects of its computer systems, which are only available from Apple. This hindered Apple's growth initially and tended to keep the company's products within a core group of graphic and arts communities. However, Apple's decision in 2006 to move to Intel-based architecture allowed Apple computers to also run Windows, and an intense focus on design has led to a resurgence of the company. Apple still accounts for less than 1 of 10 computer purchases, but the average selling price of Apple computers is much higher than the average selling price of Windows-based computers, giving Apple an important, growing, and highly profitable business.

Unix

Developed at Bell Labs in the 1970s, the **Unix** operating system has been the workhorse of the scientific and engineering communities. Unix is generally regarded as being more difficult to use than either Windows or Macintosh. Many Unix users know and employ an arcane language for manipulating files and data. However, once they surmount the rather steep learning curve, Unix users often are die-hard enthusiasts. Sun Microsystems and other vendors of computers for scientific and engineering applications are the major proponents of Unix. In general, Unix is not used by the average business user.

Linux

Linux is a version of Unix that was developed by the **open-source community**. This community is a loose group of programmers, who mostly volunteer their time to contribute code to develop and maintain Linux. The open-source community owns Linux, and there is no fee to use it. Linux can run on client computers, but it is most frequently used for servers, particularly web servers.

IBM is the primary proponent of Linux. Although it does not own Linux, IBM has developed many business systems solutions that use Linux. By using Linux, IBM does not have to pay a licence fee to Microsoft or another vendor.

Owning versus Licensing

It is important to remember that even though many people talk about buying software, what is actually purchased is a **licence** to use that program. For example, when you buy Windows, Microsoft is selling you the right to use Windows. Microsoft continues to own the Windows program. This distinction, which prevents companies from reselling the right to use software that they no longer require, has been legally challenged in Europe and is something that businesses should continue to monitor.

In the case of Linux, no company can sell you a licence to use it. It is owned by the open-source community, which states that Linux has no licence fee (with certain reasonable restrictions). Some big companies, such as IBM, and smaller companies, such as Red Hat, can make money by supporting Linux, but because it is hard to charge for a product that is available for free, it is hard for any company to make money selling Linux licences.

What Types of Applications Exist, and How Do Organizations Obtain Them?

Although the operating system is very important, its primary role, as far as most users are concerned, is to create and support the environment for the other category of software, that is, application programs. **Application software** consists of programs that

MIS in Use

What Are You Looking At? Eye-Tracking Hardware and Software

Every year, billions of dollars are spent configuring displays and developing various goods and services. Yet, despite a few fairly simple heuristics, surprisingly little is known about how people actually interact with their environment and what really captures their attention.

To overcome this problem, researchers have typically resorted to such tools as surveys or observation. Although these methods can occasionally provide insight, they are often inaccurate. Participants are sometimes driven by subconscious desires or may feel social pressure to respond to questions in a way that is different from what they truly feel.

Entrepreneurs Colin Swindells, Mario Enriquez, and Ricardo Pedrosa believe that the solution to this problem lies in eye tracking. Although the concept—identifying what actually captures an individual's attention by tracking the movement of his or her eyes—is not new, their firm, Locarna (www.locarna. com), has developed what they call a real-world solution. Unlike primitive, bulky computer monitor technology or obtrusive field glasses developed by competing firms, Locarna's system consists of two complementary parts: (1) unobtrusive, lightweight

perform a business function. Some application programs are general purpose, such as Excel or Word. Other application programs are specific. QuickBooks, for example, is an application program that provides general ledger and other accounting functions. We begin by describing categories of application programs and then move on to describe sources for them.

What Categories of Application Programs Exist?

Horizontal market application software provides capabilities common across many organizations and industries. Word processors, graphics programs, spreadsheets, and presentation programs are all examples of horizontal market application software targeted at individual consumers.

Examples of such software are Microsoft Word, Excel, and PowerPoint. Examples from other vendors are Adobe Acrobat, Photoshop, and PageMaker and Corel's Paint Shop Pro. These applications are used in a wide variety of businesses, across all industries. They are purchased off the shelf, and little customization of features is necessary (or possible).

Vertical market application software serves the needs of a specific industry. Examples of such programs are those used by dental offices to schedule appointments and to bill patients, those used by auto mechanics to keep track of customer data and customers' automobile repairs, and those used by parts warehouses to track inventory, purchases, and sales.

Vertical applications can often be altered or customized. Typically, the company that sold the application software either provides customization services or offers referrals to qualified consultants who do.

camera glasses that can be calibrated in less than a minute and (2) sophisticated yet easy-to-use analytical programs.

The Locarna system requires little overhead and is a complete package that enables researchers and practitioners to immediately understand what captures participants' attention. Participants simply wear the glasses, plug the USB connector into a portable notebook, and interact normally in whatever situation or environment is being studied. Information about how they interact and what really requires or captures their attention is saved automatically on the computer for analysis or observation.

Within its first year of business, Locarna achieved international sales and received significant interest from security agencies, advertising firms, and cognitive scientists. Early applications have included retail environments, to improve the shopping experience; new-product development, to understand how people navigate websites using mobile devices; and comparative experiments, to determine the differences between novices and experts in such areas as security, medicine, and professional sport.

Questions

1. **Where are the main markets for Locarna's systems?**

2. **What problem does Locarna solve?**

3. **How important are systems such as Locarna's?**

4. **How have recent technological changes affected or enabled Locarna's business?**

5. **Are there groups or environments that might resist the type of analysis that Locarna provides?** (*Hint:* Who might feel threatened by Locarna's systems?)

6. **What do you think the future holds for Locarna?**

One-of-a-kind application software is developed for a specific, unique need. The Canada Revenue Agency develops such software, for example, because it has specific requirements that no other organization has (to audit tax returns).

Some types of application software do not neatly fit into the horizontal or vertical category. For example, customer relationship management (CRM) software is a horizontal application because every business has customers. But it usually needs to be customized to the requirements of businesses in a particular industry, and so it is also akin to vertical-market software.

You will learn about other examples of such dual-category software in Chapter 7, where we discuss materials requirements planning (MRP), enterprise resource planning (ERP), and other such applications. In this text, we will consider such applications to be vertical market applications, even though they do not fit perfectly into this category. We will discuss how organizations acquire information systems in more detail in Chapter 10. An organization can acquire application software in exactly the same ways that you can buy a new dress or suit. The quickest and least risky option is to buy your outfit off the rack or *prêt-à-porter*. By doing this, you get it immediately, and you know exactly what it will cost. You may not, however, get a perfect fit. Alternatively, you can buy your outfit off the rack and have it altered. This will take more time, it may cost more, and there is some risk that the alteration will result in a poor fit. Most likely, however, an altered outfit will fit better than an off-the-rack one, although an off-the-rack one may benefit from the fact that millions of others have already been made.

Finally, you can hire a tailor to make a custom outfit or *haute couture*, but you will have to describe what you want, be available for multiple fittings, and be willing to pay considerably more. Although there is an excellent chance of a great fit, there is also the possibility of a disaster. Still, if you want a yellow and orange polka-dot silk suit with an image of a hockey player on the back, tailor-made is the only way to go. You can buy computer software in exactly the same way: **off the shelf, off the shelf with alterations**, or **tailor made**. Tailor-made software is called **custom-developed software**.

Organizations develop custom application software themselves or hire a development vendor. Like buying the yellow and orange polka-dot suit, such development is done in situations in which the needs of the organization are so unique that no horizontal or vertical applications can meet those needs. By developing custom software, the organization can tailor its application to fit its requirements.

Custom development is difficult and risky. Staffing and managing teams of software developers is challenging. Managing software projects can be daunting. Many organizations have embarked on application development projects only to find that the projects take twice as long—or longer—to finish as planned. Cost overruns of 200 and 300 percent are common.

In addition, every application program needs to be adapted to changing needs and changing technologies. The adaptation costs of software are amortized or spread across all the users of that software, perhaps thousands or millions of customers. For custom software developed in-house, however, the developing company must pay all the adaptation costs itself. Over time, these costs can be a heavy burden.

Because of the risk and expense, in-house development is very often the last-choice alternative and is used only when there is no other option. Figure 4-11 summarizes software sources and types.

Over the course of your career, application software, hardware, and firmware will change, sometimes rapidly. The exercise "Keeping Up to Speed" at the end of this chapter, on pages 130–131, challenges you to choose a strategy for dealing with this change.

Software Source

Software Type	Off-the-shelf	Off-the-shelf and then customized	Custom-developed
Horizontal applications			
Vertical applications			
One-of-a-kind applications			

Figure 4-11
Software Sources and Types

Browsers

Although software can generally be grouped as operating software or application software, not everything fits into these two categories. There is an ongoing debate, for example, about whether web browsers are application software or operating software, since they often have characteristics of both. In fact, web browsers being part of operating systems was a key issue behind U.S. and European antitrust legislation, which questioned the extent to which Microsoft abused its dominant position, and this issue has been further complicated by the introduction of Chrome by Google, which has reconceptualized the browser as the primary element in the operating system.

What Are Firmware and Utility Software?

Firmware is computer software that is installed into devices such as printers, game controllers, and various types of communication devices. The coding of the software is similar to that of other software, but it is installed into the special, read-only memory (ROM) of the device. In this way, the program becomes part of the device's memory; it is as if the program's logic is designed into the device's circuitry. Users do not need to load firmware into the device's memory. Printers often require driver software that supports communication between the computer and the printer. These drivers are a type of software that does not fit into either operating software or application software. We might refer to this type of software as utility software. Other examples of utility software include disk optimization, data encryption, file and data recovery, disk image, security software, and uninstaller software.

The **Basic Input/Output System (BIOS)** is an important piece of firmware. The BIOS is used when a computer is initially started or booted up. It is required because all volatile memory is lost when the computer is shut down. The only way to get the computer running again is to provide a set of instructions in nonvolatile read-only memory (ROM). The first thing the computer does when starting up is to load the BIOS from ROM and run through the commands provided by the firmware. The BIOS checks to make sure that the memory and input devices are functional. Once these are working, the operating system will be loaded.

Firmware can be changed or upgraded, but this is normally a task for information systems (IS) professionals. The task is easy, but it requires knowledge of special programs and techniques that most business users choose not to learn.

What Is the Difference Between a Thin Client and a Thick Client?

When you use applications such as Word, Excel, or Acrobat, those programs run only on your computer. You do not have to be connected to the internet or any other network for them to run.

Other applications, however, may require code on both the client and the server. Email is a good example. When you send email, you run a client program, such as Microsoft Outlook, on your computer, and it connects over the internet or a private network to mail server software on a server. Similarly, when you access a website, you run a browser (client software), such as Internet Explorer, Firefox, or Chrome, on your computer that connects over a network to web server software on a server.

An application that requires nothing more than a browser is called a **thin client**. An application such as Microsoft Outlook that requires programs other than a browser on the user's computer is called a **thick client**. The terms *thin* and *thick* refer to the amount of code that must run on the client computer. All other things being equal, thin client applications are preferable to thick client applications because they do not require the installation and administration of client software.

However, the thick client application may provide features and functions that more than compensate for the expense and administration of its installation. In addition, a thick client does not need access to the network to run. So, if your network goes down, the thick client will still be available, whereas your thin client will be unable to run software.

Client and server computers can run different operating systems. Many organizations have standardized on Windows for their clients and Linux for their servers.

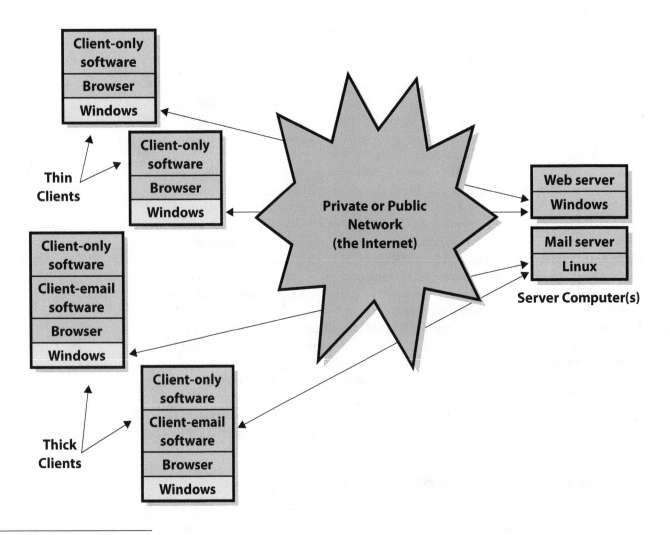

Figure 4-12

Thin and Thick Clients

Figure 4-12 shows an example. Two thin clients are connecting via browsers to a web server that is running Windows. Two thick clients are connecting via an email client to an email server that is running Linux. Those two clients are thick because they have client email software installed.

Q6 What Buying Decisions Does a Manager Need to Make?

In general, most business professionals have some role in the specification of the client hardware and software they use. Business managers also play a role in the specification of client hardware and software for employees whom they manage. The particular role depends on the policy manager's organization. Large organizations will have an IS department that is likely to set standards for client hardware and software. You will learn more about such standards in Chapter 11.

In medium to small organizations, policies are often less formal, and managers will need to take an active role in setting the specifications for their own and their employees' computers. Figure 4-13 lists the major criteria for both hardware and software.

Except in rare circumstances, medium to small organizations will usually standardize on a single client operating system because the costs of supporting more than one cannot be justified. Most organizations choose Windows clients. Some arts and design businesses standardize on the Macintosh, and some engineering firms standardize on Unix. Organizations that have limited budgets might choose to use Linux on the clients, but this is relatively rare.

Managers and their employees may have a role in specifying horizontal application software, such as Microsoft Office, or other software appropriate for their operating systems. They will also have an important role in specifying requirements for vertical market or custom applications. We will say more about this role in Chapter 10.

A business manager typically has no role in the specification of server hardware other than possibly approving the budget. Instead, the decision is made by a computer technician. A business manager and those who will be the clients of a

Category	Hardware	Software
Client	Specify: • CPU speed • Size of main memory • Size of magnetic disk • CD or DVD and type • Monitor type and size • Number of Monitors	Specify: • Windows, Mac, or Linux OS; may be dictated by organizational standard • PC applications such as Microsoft Office Adobe Acrobat, Photoshop, Paint Shop Pro; may be dictated by organizational standard • Browser such as Internet Explorer, FireFox, or Netscape Navigator • Requirements for the client side of client-server applications • Need for thin or thick client
Server	In most cases, a business manager has no role in the specification of server hardware (except possibly a budgetary one)	• Specify requirements for the server side of client-server applications • Work with technical personnel to test and accept software

Figure 4-13

A Business Manager's Role in Hardware and Software Specifications

client-server application specify the requirements for vertical and custom-server software. They will also work with technical personnel to test and accept that software.

In addition, business managers may be called on to provide unusual support involving IS, as "MIS in Use" on pages 118–119 describes.

Q7 What Are Viruses, Worms, and Zombies?

We conclude this chapter with a few notes about computer security (which will be explored in greater detail in Chapter 12). It is important for you to be aware of security when thinking about hardware and software. So, we will introduce some of the more serious threats that you may face in hardware and software security.

A **virus** is a computer program that replicates itself. Unchecked replication is like computer cancer; ultimately, the virus consumes the computer's resources. Furthermore, many viruses also take unwanted and harmful actions.

The program code that causes unwanted activity is called the **payload**. The payload can delete programs or data—or, even worse, modify data in undetectable ways. Imagine the impact of a virus that changed the credit rating of all customers. Some viruses publish data in harmful ways—for example, sending out files of credit card data to unauthorized sites.

Macro-viruses attach themselves to Word, Excel, and other types of documents. When the infected document is opened, the virus places itself in the startup files of the application. After that, the virus infects every file that the application creates or processes.

A **worm** is a virus that propagates using the internet or other computer network. Worms spread faster than other virus types because they are specifically programmed to spread. Unlike nonworm viruses, which must wait for the user to share a file with a second computer, worms actively use the network to spread. The subsequent computers that are infected with the worm or virus are often termed *zombie computers*, or **zombies**. Often, a compromised machine is only one of many in what is termed a **botnet**, which is a set of computers and applications that are coordinated through a network and used to perform malicious tasks. Most owners of zombie computers are unaware that their system is being used in this way. Because the owner is unaware, these computers are metaphorically described as zombies. Zombies have been used extensively to send email, allowing spammers to avoid detection.

You can take several measures to prevent viruses. First, most viruses take advantage of security holes in computer programs. As vendors find these holes, they create program modifications, called **patches**, to fix the problem. To keep from getting a virus, check Microsoft and other vendor sites for patches frequently and apply them immediately.

System vulnerabilities are typically weaknesses in system design that can be exploited by knowledgeable people. The Heartbleed security bug that affected the Secure Socket Layer (SSL) protocol of secure websites is one such example and a good illustration of why managers need to remain both aware and vigilant.

Viruses, worms, and bugs cause considerable damage and, thus, costs. To protect yourself and your organization, you should ensure that procedures are in place to install patches and updates as soon as possible. Also, every computer should have and use a copy of an **antivirus program**. We will discuss how to deal with these and other problematic programs, such as spyware, in more detail in Chapter 12.

Active ❓ Review

Use this Active Review to verify that you have understood the material in the chapter. You can read the entire chapter and then perform the tasks in this review, or you can read the material for just one question and perform the tasks for that question before moving on to the next one.

Q1 Why do you need to know about information technology?

How has IT changed the way you live? Think about what you would do if you did not have access to computers or the internet.

Q2 Where did all this information technology stuff come from?

Explain why you should be interested in advancements in IT. Explain some trends in computing technology that are likely to continue.

Q3 What does a manager need to know about computer hardware?

List the categories of hardware. Describe memory swapping. Explain situations in which more main memory is needed. Explain situations in which a faster CPU is needed. Define each of the hardware terms in Figure 4-4.

Q4 What is the difference between a client and a server, and what is cloud computing?

Explain the difference between a client and a server. Describe the differences in hardware requirements for clients and servers. Describe a server farm. What is meant by the term *cloud computing*?

Q5 What does a manager need to know about software?

Explain the difference between an operating system and an application system. Describe the constraints on an operating system imposed by a computer's instruction set. Describe the constraints on applications and an operating system. Describe the difference between a thin client and a thick client. When would you use one or the other? Explain the terms in Figure 4-11.

Q6 What buying decisions does a manager need to make?

Explain the terms in Figure 4-13.

Q7 What are viruses, worms, and zombies?

Define *virus* and *payload*. Explain the differences between macro-viruses and worms. Explain the importance of applying patches promptly. Describe other prevention steps. Explain the use of antivirus software. Describe actions you can take to eradicate a virus from a computer.

MyMISLab MyMISLab is an online learning and testing environment that features the perfect study tools to help you master the concepts covered in this chapter. Log in to MyMISLab to test your knowledge of key chapter concepts and explore additional practice tools, including videos, flashcards, annotated text figures, and more!

Key Terms and Concepts

Antivirus program 124

Application software 118

Basic Input/Output System (BIOS) 121

Binary digits 111

Bit 111

Botnet 124

Bus 112

Byte 112

Cache 112

Central processing unit (CPU) 110

Client 114

Cloud computing 115

Custom-developed software 120

Data channel 112

Firmware 121

Using Your Knowledge

1. Assume that you have been asked to prepare a budget for computer hardware (computers or tablets). Your company has identified three classes of computer user. Class A employees use the computer for email, web browsing, internet connectivity, and limited document writing. Class B employees use the computer for all the activities of Class A, and they need to be able to read and create complicated documents. They also need to be able to create and process large spreadsheets and small graphics files. Class C employees are data analysts who perform all the tasks that Class A and Class B employees do; they also analyze data using programs that make extensive computations and produce large and complicated graphics.
   a. Using the internet, determine two appropriate alternatives for each class of employee. Search www.dell.com, www.lenovo.com, www.hp.com, and any other sites you think appropriate.
   b. Justify each of the selections in your answer to part (a).
   c. Specify the cost of each of the selections in part (a).

2. Search the internet for the term *OpenOffice*. Explain what OpenOffice is. How do users obtain it? How much does it cost? Given this information, why do you think companies use Microsoft Office rather than OpenOffice? Why do you?

3. Describe the three categories of application software, and give an example of each. Explain the summary presented in Figure 4-11. Search the internet for an example of horizontal and vertical market software (other than those mentioned in this chapter). Search as well for the product QuickBooks. Briefly describe the functions of this product. What operating system(s) does it require? Suppose you wish to install and use QuickBooks, but you need some functions to be altered. Search the internet for vendors or consultants who could help you. List two or three such vendors or consultants.

Collaborative Exercises

Have your team choose one of the hardware or software topics in the list provided in Question 3. Use the internet and other resources to research the topic, and do the following:

1. Create a maximum two-page information sheet that summarizes the topic. The summary should include the following:
   a. An introduction to the topic (in English, not technobabble)
   b. The relevance of the topic to business managers (e.g., advantages and benefits versus costs, if they are known)
   c. Examples of products, vendors, or companies that use the particular technology topic
   d. Links to sites where you can find more information
   e. A statement about the future use of the technology: Are there any barriers to adoption? How prevalent will the technology become?

2. Now create a presentation (using PowerPoint, Keynote, or another presentation software) that can be used to present the topic to other students in the class. Be sure to include a title page, and be prepared to present to the class what you have found out about your topic.

3. Choose from one of the following topics (or check with your instructor to see whether you can create your own):
   a. Is open-source software here to stay?
   b. Who builds the best processor in your opinion—AMD or Intel?
   c. What is cloud computing, and why should you care about it?
   d. What is green IT, and does it really matter to you?
   e. What is the best operating system for computers for business applications, Macintosh or PC?
   f. Who will win the browser wars? Why should you care?
   g. What is the next important technology?
   h. What is the future for operating systems such as Windows, Linux, and OS X?
   i. Are e-books really the future of reading?
   j. What is Google Chrome best described as: a browser or an operating system?

Case Study 4

Network Effects, Increasing Returns, and Lock-In

How do the choices made by others affect your own options, and how should you evaluate new software? Those are two of the questions facing Brent North, managing partner of Stantec's Vancouver office, as he considers using a new three-dimensional drafting tool.

Founded in 1954, Stantec is an architecture and engineering firm that evolved from a single-person consultancy into a publicly traded corporation with more than 100 offices worldwide and 6500 employees through a combination of acquisitions and natural growth. The Vancouver office, which has recently been acquired by Stantec, has approximately 125 professional staff and is largely focused on architecture.

Architecture has changed a great deal in 50 years. While grounded in creativity and design, architects today are far more proficient in computer technology; although some of Stantec's senior architects still look fondly upon the slide rules and Mylar plastic that was used to create designs in the past, modern-day architects are far more likely to turn to their computers and use computer-assisted design (CAD), manufacturing, or engineering tools such as Computer Aided Manufacturing (CAM) and Computer Aided Engineering (CAE). There has been a large and growing market for these products, and numerous suppliers delivered a variety of tools. However, as in other software markets, it seemed that one or two suppliers developed to hold the majority market share, and the other products occupied niches that, although perhaps important, lacked widespread adoption. An example of a niche product is CATIA (Computer Aided Three-Dimensional Interactive Application), from Dassault Systems, widely used in manufacturing at Chrysler, General Electric, and Airbus (and had been used by Frank Gehry to design the Guggenheim Museum in Bilbao, Spain).

Several years ago, Stantec adopted AutoCAD by Autodesk. The de facto standard program, at that time AutoCAD had approximately 80 percent adoption among architectural firms. Virtually all new architects had been taught how to use it while in university and, provided they were using the same version, cooperating firms working on large projects could share and transfer files knowing that they were compatible and interchangeable.

Although Brent is generally satisfied with Stantec's existing software tools, he has recently become aware of a product with features and capabilities that he thinks can change the way Stantec competes. What concerns Brent, however, is the level of training required to make the change and the advantages of remaining with the industry standard. Not only will the new product require education and adjustment among the architects, but it is also incompatible with AutoCAD. While this new program can open files created by AutoCAD, files that it has created cannot be used by AutoCAD. This means that if Brent brought the new product in for a trial, he would no longer be able to easily cooperate with other firms on joint projects and, perhaps more importantly, it could reduce the level of cooperation and sharing within the firm. At the same time, he knows that, if pushed to the limit, this kind of conservative thinking will hold Stantec hostage and prevent positive change. Is it worth considering a new and incompatible product—and if he brings it in for a trial, how should he proceed?

Questions

1. How do the challenges faced by Stantec differ from those faced by other industries? (*Hint:* Think about sharing files among students for group projects.)
2. What are the implications of this case for companies that develop new software tools? How could adoption barriers be reduced? (*Hint:* Think of disruptive technologies.)
3. Are there any examples of inferior technologies that have achieved lock in and would therefore be hard to improve? (*Hint:* You probably have used one already today.)
4. How do the ideas of switching costs and of networks effects relate to high technology? Do they exist in other industries? (*Hint:* Consider the railway industry, for example.)
5. How should new software be evaluated? How important is market share? Are these factors more or less important to smaller firms?

Keeping Up to Speed

Have you ever been to a cafeteria where you put your lunch tray on a conveyor belt that carries the dirty dishes into the kitchen? That conveyor belt reminds us of technology. Like the conveyor belt, technology just moves along, and all of us jump on the technology conveyor belt, trying to keep up. We hope to keep pace with the relentless change of technology through an entire career without ending up in the techno-trash.

Technological change is a fact, and the only appropriate response to it is, "What am I going to do about it?" One strategy you can take is to bury your head in the sand: "Look, I'm not a technology person. I'll leave it to the pros. As long as I can send email and use the internet, I'm happy. If I have a problem, I'll call someone to fix it."

That strategy is fine, as far as it goes, and many business people use it. But following that strategy will not give you a competitive advantage over anyone—in fact, it will give someone else a competitive advantage over you. But as long as you develop your advantage elsewhere, you will be okay—at least on your own.

But what about your department? If an IS expert says, "Every computer needs a 2 TB disk," are you going to nod your head and say "Great. Sell 'em to me!" Or will you know enough to realize that it is a big disk (by 2014 standards, anyway) and ask the expert why everyone needs such a large amount of storage? Maybe you will be told, "Well, it's only another $75 per machine compared with the 1 TB disk." At that point, you can make a selection using your own decision-making skills, not by relying solely on the expert. The prudent business professional in the twenty-first century has a number of reasons not to bury his or her head in the sand as far as technology is concerned.

At the other end of the spectrum are those who love technology. You will find them everywhere—whether accountants, marketing professionals, or production-line supervisors, who not only are knowledgeable about their own field but also enjoy information technology. Maybe they were IS majors or had double majors that combined IS with another area of expertise (e.g., accounting). These people read *CNET News* and *ZDNet* most days, and they can tell you the latest on IPv6 addresses. Those people are sprinting along the technology conveyor belt; they will never end up in the techno-trash, and they will use their knowledge of IT to gain competitive advantage throughout their careers.

Many business professionals are in-between these extremes. They do not want to bury their heads, but they do not have the desire or interest to become technophiles (lovers of technology) either. So, what should you do? There are a couple of strategies. First, do not allow yourself to ignore technology. When you see a technology article in the newspaper, read it. Do not just skip it because it is about technology. And read the technology ads. Many vendors invest heavily in ads that subtly instruct their potential customers. Another option is to take a seminar or to pay attention to professional events that combine your specialty with technology. For example, when you go to the bankers' convention, attend a session or two on technology trends for bankers. There are always sessions like that at banking conventions, and you might make a contact in another company with similar problems and concerns.

Probably the best option, if you have the time, is to get involved as a user representative in technology committees within your organization. If your company is doing a review of its CRM (customer relationship management) system, for instance, see if you can get on the review committee. When there is a need for a representative from your department to discuss the need for the next-generation help-line system, sign up. Or, later in your career, become a member of the business practice technology committee, or whatever they call it at your organization.

Just working with such groups will add to your knowledge of technology. Presentations made to these groups, discussions about uses of technology, and ideas about using IT for competitive advantage will all add to your IT knowledge. You will gain important contacts and exposure to leaders in your organization as well.

It is up to you. You get to choose how you relate to technology. But be sure you choose: Do not let your head fall into the sand without thinking about it.

Discussion Questions

1. Do you agree that the pace of technology change is relentless? What do you think that means to most business professionals? to most organizations?

2. Think about the three stances with regard to technology presented here. Which camp will you join? Why?

3. Write a two-paragraph memo to yourself justifying your choice in Question 2. If you chose to ignore technology, explain how you will compensate for the loss of competitive advantage. If you are going to join one of the other two groups, explain why, and describe how you are going to accomplish your goal.

4. Given your answer to Question 2, assume that you are in a job interview and the interviewer asks about your knowledge of technology. Write a three-sentence response to the interviewer's question.

Justin Sullivan/Getty Images

5 Database and Content Management

Running Case

It had been more work than Marla thought, but she had finally finished upgrading the existing computers in The 1881 and initiated a tablet loaner program where guests could borrow an iPad to use during their stay. Fresh from this success, Marlo's next move was to get a better idea of the guests who were staying at The 1881. The old Hotel Reservation and Management System (version 2.0) was stable enough, but did not provide the ability to analyze guest information other than sorting the list by name, address, and telephone number. The updated version of the hotel reservation and management software had more advanced features, but the owners of The 1881 indicated that it was too expensive to purchase now.

Marlo was stuck. How could she get better information about the B&B hotel's clients? She decided to investigate and found that the current Hotel Reservation and Management System was built on a relational database, something she had learned about in her introductory MIS course. She had learned that the database could export names, vacation dates, room numbers, and even services that the guests enjoyed. She needed to get administrative access to the database. She argued successfully that since she was exporting information that was already stored in the system, there was no impact on the current system and no chance for her to delete or modify existing data.

The exported data were provided in a format that could be read by a Microsoft Excel spreadsheet. She was thrilled the first time she opened the spreadsheet and was able to see the guests' names and other information. However, after a few minutes of exhilaration, she realized that there may be some challenges. She needed to learn more about how data were stored before she could do much with the data.

After a few weeks of working on the data, Marlo had created an interesting set of spreadsheets. In one spreadsheet, she had carefully listed all of the rooms in the B&B hotel. In another spreadsheet, she had a list of the services provided by the hotel. In yet another spreadsheet, she had a list of all of the activities that guests had been billed for over the past three years, by date, along with the names of guests who purchased them. Another spreadsheet contained alphabetically listed names and the addresses of almost all of the guests who had stayed at The 1881. It was a lot of information spread over four different spreadsheets. Her problem now was finding a way to get all of this data to make sense.

Luckily, she had kept her introductory MIS textbook, which included a chapter on database design—and even a tutorial on using Microsoft Access (a program that helps create relational databases). She read through the chapter on designing relational tables, and within a week she was able to combine the four separate spreadsheets she had created into a single database. She now had the ability to consider such questions as "How many of our guests stay more than twice a year?" for which the database could provide answers within seconds.

To prepare for her next meeting with the owners, Marlo used the database to prepare answers to such questions as the following: "Who are The 1881's most frequent guests?" "Which guests buy the most services?" "Which guests have stopped coming to The 1881?" She went into the meeting with a great feeling, knowing she was not only learning more about the B&B but also that she had developed valuable skills in analyzing information that would be used throughout her career.

Study Questions

Q1	**What is content?**
Q2	**How can content be organized?**
Q3	**What is the purpose of a database?**
Q4	**What does a database contain?**
Q5	**What is a DBMS, and what does it do?**
Q6	**What is a database application?**
Q7	**What is the difference between an enterprise DBMS and a personal DBMS?**

Q1 What Is Content?

Content can be difficult to define. In the broadest sense, content is something of value and can be considered an asset just like other items of property. It is often closely related to **intellectual property**, which, in Canada, is defined as a form of creative endeavour that can be protected through a trademark, patent, copyright, industrial design, or integrated circuit topography.[1] Content varies by industry. In the advertising industry, content refers to the pictures, commercials, and text used to promote ideas about products and services. In the publishing industry, content refers to words. In the banking industry, content is account information.

Before the advent of computers, content was only available on physical assets such as paper, photographs, or film. But computers create digital content that can be stored, and networks, such as the internet, can distribute this content. Organizations have databases that store large amounts of data related to customers, employees, orders, and so on. Organizations also store a lot of other content. Word-processing documents (.doc, .txt, .pdf), spreadsheets (.xls), and presentations (.ppt) are a part of everyday work. Other content might include webpages (.htm, .html), text from blogs, Twitter, or discussion boards, graphics (.jpg, .gif, .bmp, .png, etc.), video files and video logs (.WMV, .AVI, and .MPG), audio files (.WAV, .MP3, .ACC, and .WMA), and even geographical information available through such applications as Google Earth. The expanding volume of content and the growing number of formats in which it is provided can make it difficult for individuals and corporations to effectively utilize that content. Managing content is, therefore, an important challenge for businesses to understand and appreciate.

The challenge today is not collecting and distributing content but also in presenting it appropriately for various stakeholders inside and outside of organizations. A company's website has become an important source of content for both customers and employees. Students who concentrate in marketing recognize that websites help to brand organizations. Websites have also become a critical part of customer support. It was hard enough to manage data and information when it was exclusively contained within a company and used only by employees—as information has become more available to other stakeholders, it has become increasingly difficult to manage the increased volume, format, and presentation choices for content.

Q2 How Can Content Be Organized?

The challenge in content management is indexing or cataloguing the right information, processing and storing it, and then getting it to the right person in the right format at the right time. One way of thinking about content management is to separate the *management* of content from the *presentation* of content. We learned in the previous chapter that all data in computing systems are represented by bytes. Content management focuses on how to efficiently and effectively store and process these bytes. Content presentation focuses on how best to present data to the person using the system.

The management of many types of content has traditionally been handled through organizational database management systems (DBMSs). DBMSs are central to the management of content data, and we will learn more about them later in the chapter. The presentation of content has gone through changes as company websites have matured. In the early days of the web, employees might have been

---

[1] You can read more about intellectual property at www.cipo.ic.gc.ca.

able to post content directly to a company's website. This practice did not provide a consistent look and feel and left the company at risk if incorrect data were posted. As organizational websites became more complex, employees could not be expected to keep up with all of the changes. The presentation of content in organizations today is increasingly handled through a series of steps supported by software. **Content management systems (CMSs)** have been developed to help companies organize this process.

When an employee wants to place some content on the organization's website, he or she will access the web CMS. The web CMS of a company is usually located on its website server. The employee typically loads the raw content into the web CMS. A copyeditor then reviews the document and makes any needed changes. He or she then passes the content on to layout artists, who prepare the content for presentation. The content and presentation are stored with the help of a DBMS. The manager in charge of the website will then review the content and presentation and publish the work to the public website. The web CMS helps manage each step of this process and enables a company to standardize the look and feel of a website and control the information available to customers and employees.

CMSs have also evolved. They have grown beyond their original role of simply organizing documents for corporate websites. These systems now actively seek out documents located across an organization and automatically manage access to this content. Media files, word-processing documents, html pages, and many other documents can all be categorized and searched by CMSs. This capability allows for the increased organization of a wider range of a corporation's data assets. Current CMSs also handle document archiving and the increased use of electronic files for document management. OpenText (see box below), a Canadian company located in Waterloo, Ontario (www.opentext.com), and EMC, a U.S. company (www.emc.com), are examples of these CMSs.

OPENTEXT: FROM SPINOFF TO MARKET LEADER

How does a small spinoff company from the University of Waterloo grow to become Canada's largest software company and the world leader in enterprise content management systems? It all started with a project to bring the *Oxford English Dictionary (OED)* into the computer age. The *OED* had become so large that it was unwieldy to update. Researchers at the University of Waterloo, with funding help from the Canadian government, worked to build full-text indexing and string-search technology for the *OED*. The project resulted in a product that was close to a web-based search engine—in 1989, years before web search engines were well known. OpenText was started in 1991. The company continued to develop increased functionality in the search engine through 1995. When management believed that the market for search engines no longer looked promising, the company turned to document management systems. (Astute students may note that Google, the current leader among internet search engines, was founded in 1998 and has a value almost 50 times greater than that of OpenText. In business, as in many areas, timing is everything.) Web-based document management systems proved to be a lucrative market, and OpenText grew from a company of 20 employees in 1995 to a company of more than 5000 employees with over $1.3 billion in sales supporting 100 million users in 114 countries by 2014. The company has continued its rapid growth and is recognized as the market leader in enterprise content management.

Source: You can find out more about the history of OpenText at www.opentext.com/corporate/our_history.html.

Watch

Go to MyMISLab to watch a video about the purpose of a database.

Watch

Go to MyMISLab to watch a video about database processing.

Q3 What Is the Purpose of a Database?

A database keeps track of things. When most people become aware of this, they wonder why we need a special technology for such a simple task. Why not just use a list? And if the list is long, can it just be put in a spreadsheet?

Many professionals do keep track of things using spreadsheets. If the structure of the list is simple enough, there is no need to use database technology. The list of student grades in Figure 5-1, for example, works perfectly well in a spreadsheet.

Suppose, however, that the professor wants to track more than just grades. He or she may want to record email messages as well. Or, perhaps, the professor wants to record both email messages and office visits. There is no place in a spreadsheet, such as the one in Figure 5-1, to record these additional data. Of course, the professor could set up a separate spreadsheet for email messages and another for office visits, but that awkward solution would be difficult to implement because it does not provide all the data in one place.

Instead, the professor may want a form similar to the one shown in Figure 5-2. With it, he or she can record student grades, emails, and office visits all in one place. Technically it might be possible to create a similar form like this in a spreadsheet, but with a database, it is much easier to develop and maintain.

The key distinction between Figures 5-1 and 5-2 is that the list in Figure 5-1 is about a single theme or concept—student grades. The list in Figure 5-2 has multiple themes—it shows student grades, emails, and office visits. We can create a general rule from these examples: Lists that involve a single theme can be stored in a spreadsheet; lists that involve multiple themes require a database. We will learn more about this general rule later in this chapter.

To summarize, the purpose of a database is to keep track of things that involve more than one theme.

Figure 5-1

A List of Student Grades

Source: Microsoft Excel

	A	B	C	D	E
1	Student Name	Student Number	HW1	HW2	MidTerm
2					
3	BAKER, ANDREA	1325	88	100	78
4	FISCHER, MAYAN	3007	95	100	74
5	LAU, SWEE	1644	75	90	90
6	NELSON, STUART	2881	100	90	98
7	ROGERS, SHELLY	8009	95	100	98
8	TAM, JEFFREY	3559		100	88
9	VALDEZ, MARIE	5265	80	90	85
10	VERBERRA, ADAM	4867	70	90	92

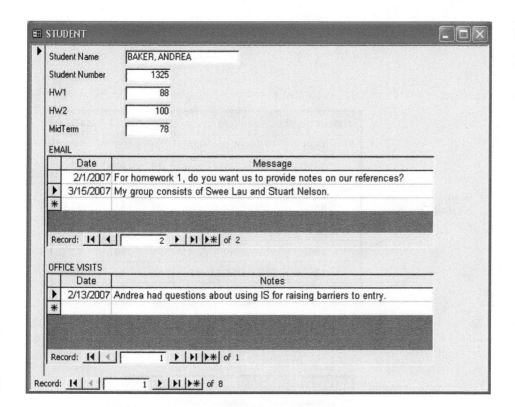

Figure 5-2

Student Data Shown in Form of a Database

Source: Microsoft Excel

Q4 What Does a Database Contain?

Database design is a specialized skill that everyone in the field of management information systems (MIS) should understand and any business student who plans to work with corporate data should be familiar with. You will learn the basics in this chapter. In addition, two extensions to this chapter, "Database Design" and "Using Microsoft Access," contain more in-depth information on this topic.

A **database** is a self-describing collection of integrated records. To understand this definition, you first need to understand the terms illustrated in Figure 5-3. As you learned in Chapter 4, a **byte** is a character of data. Bytes are grouped into **columns**, such as *Student Number* and *Student Name*. Columns are also called **fields**. Columns or fields, in turn, are grouped into **rows**, which are also called **records**. In Figure 5-3, the collection of data for all columns (*Student Number*, *Student Name*, *HW1*, *HW2*, and *MidTerm*) is called a *row* or a *record*. Finally, a group of similar rows or records is called a **table** or a **file**. From these definitions, you can see that there is a hierarchy of data elements, as shown in Figure 5-4.

It is tempting to continue this grouping process by saying that a database is a group of tables or files. This statement, although true, does not go far enough, however. As shown in Figure 5-5, a database is a collection of tables *plus* relationships among the rows in those tables, *plus* special data, called *metadata*, that describe the structure of the database. By the way, the cylindrical symbol represents a computer disk drive. It is used in diagrams, such as that in Figure 5-5, because databases are very often stored on magnetic disks.

Relationships Among Records

Consider the terms on the left side of Figure 5-5. You know what *tables* are. To understand what is meant by *relationships among rows in tables*, examine Figure 5-6. It shows

Figure 5-3

Student Table (also called a *file*)

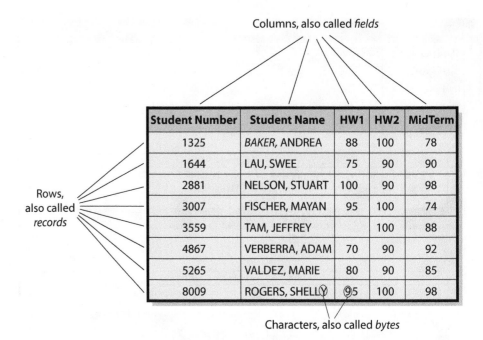

Columns, also called *fields*

Student Number	Student Name	HW1	HW2	MidTerm
1325	*BAKER*, ANDREA	88	100	78
1644	LAU, SWEE	75	90	90
2881	NELSON, STUART	100	90	98
3007	FISCHER, MAYAN	95	100	74
3559	TAM, JEFFREY		100	88
4867	VERBERRA, ADAM	70	90	92
5265	VALDEZ, MARIE	80	90	85
8009	ROGERS, SHELLY	95	100	98

Rows, also called *records*

Characters, also called *bytes*

Figure 5-4

Hierarchy of Data Elements

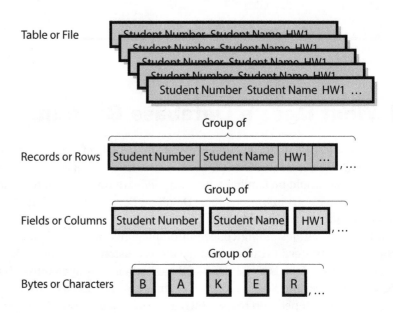

Table or File

Student Number Student Name HW1 ...

Group of

Records or Rows

| Student Number | Student Name | HW1 | ... |

, ...

Group of

Fields or Columns

| Student Number | Student Name | HW1 |

, ...

Group of

Bytes or Characters

B A K E R , ...

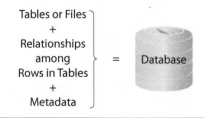

Tables or Files
+
Relationships among Rows in Tables
+
Metadata

= Database

Figure 5-5

Components of a Database

sample data from the three tables *Email, Student*, and *Office_Visit*. Note the column named *Student Number* in the *Email* table. That column indicates the row in the *Student* table to which a row of *the Email* table is connected. In the first row of the *Email* table, the *Student Number* value is 1325. This indicates that this particular email was received from the student whose *Student Number* is 1325. If you examine the *Student* table, you will see that the row for Andrea Baker contains this value. Thus, the first row of the *Email* table is related to Andrea Baker.

Now consider the last row of the *Office_Visit* table at the bottom of the figure. The value of *Student Number* in that row is 4867. This value indicates that the last row in *Office_Visit* belongs to Adam Verberra.

From these examples, you can see that values in one table relate rows of that table to rows in a second table. Several special terms are used to express these ideas. A **key** is a column or group of columns that identifies a unique row in a table. *Student Number* is the key of the *Student* table. Given a value of *Student Number*,

Email Table

EmailNum	Date	Message	Student Number
1	2/1/2007	For homework 1, do you want us to provide notes on our references?	1325
2	3/15/2007	My group consists of Swee Lau and Stuart Nelson.	1325
3	3/15/2007	Could you please assign me to a group?	1644

Student Table

Student Number	Student Name	HW1	HW2	MidTerm
1325	BAKER, ANDREA	88	100	78
1644	LAU, SWEE	75	90	90
2881	NELSON, STUART	100	90	98
3007	FISCHER, MAYAN	95	100	74
3559	TAM, JEFFREY		100	88
4867	VERBERRA, ADAM	70	90	92
5265	VALDEZ, MARIE	80	90	85
8009	ROGERS, SHELLY	95	100	98

Office_Visit Table

VisitID	Date	Notes	Student Number
2	2/13/2007	Andrea had questions about using IS for raising barriers to entry.	1325
3	2/17/2007	Jeffrey is considering an IS major. Wanted to talk about career opportunities.	3559
4	2/17/2007	Will miss class Friday due to job conflict.	4867

Figure 5-6

Example of Relationships among Rows

you can determine one and only one row in *the Student table*. Only one student has the number 1325, for example.

Every table must have a key. The key of the *Email* table is *EmailNum*, and the key of the *Office_Visit* table is *VisitID*. Sometimes more than one column is needed to form a unique identifier. In a table called *City*, for example, the key would consist of the combination of columns (*City, Province*) because a given city name can appear in more than one province.

Student Number is not the key of the *Email* or the *Office_Visit* tables. We know that about *the Email table* because there are two rows in *Email* that have the *Student Number* value 1325. The value 1325 does not identify a unique row; therefore, *Student Number* is not the key of the *Email* table.

Nor is *Student Number* a key of the *Office_Visit* table, although you cannot tell that from the data in Figure 5-6. If you think about it, however, there is nothing to prevent a student from visiting a professor more than once. If that were to happen, there would be two rows in the *Office_Visit* table with the same value of *Student Number*. It just happens that no student has visited twice in the limited data in Figure 5-6.

Columns that fulfill a role like that of *Student Number* in the *Email* and *Office_Visit* tables are called **foreign keys**. This term is used because such columns are keys, but they are keys of a different (foreign) table from the one in which they reside.

Before we go on, note that databases that carry their data in the form of tables and that represent relationships using foreign keys are called **relational databases**. (The term *relational* is used because another, more formal name for a table is **relation**.) In the past, databases existed that were not relational in format, but such databases

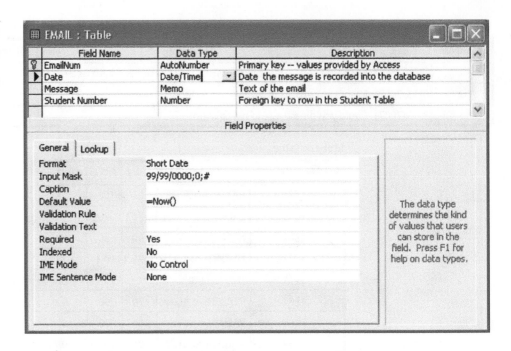

have nearly disappeared. Chances are you will never encounter one, and we will not consider them further.[2]

Metadata

Recall the definition of *database*—a self-describing collection of integrated records. The records are integrated because, as you have just learned, relationships among rows are represented in the database. But what does *self-describing* mean?

It means that a database contains, within itself, a description of its contents. Think of a library. A library is a self-describing collection of books and other materials. It is self-describing because the library contains a catalogue that describes its contents. The same idea also holds true for a database. They are self-describing because they contain not only data but also data about the data in the database.

Metadata are data that describe data. Figure 5-7 shows metadata for the *Email* table. The format of metadata depends on the software product that is processing the database. Figure 5-7 shows the metadata as they appear in Microsoft Access. Each row of the top part of this form describes a column of the *Email* table. The columns of these descriptions are *Field Name, Data Type*, and *Description. Field Name* contains the name of the column, *Data Type* shows the type of data the column may hold, and *Description* contains notes that explain the source or use of the column. As you can see, there is one row of metadata for each of the four columns of the *Email* table: *EmailNum, Date, Message*, and *Student Number.*

The bottom part of this form provides more metadata, which Access calls *Field Properties*, for each column. In Figure 5-7, the focus is on the *Date* column (note the filled-in right-face pointer next to its name, such as the one shown here ▶). Because the focus is on *Date* in the top pane, the details in the bottom pane pertain to the *Date* column. The *Field Properties* describe formats, a default value for Access to supply when a new row is created, and the constraint that a value is required for this column. It is not important for you to remember these details. Instead, just

---

[2] Another type of database, the object-relational database, is rarely used in commercial applications. Search the web if you are interested in learning more about object-relational databases. In this book, we will consider only relational databases.

understand that metadata are data about data and that such metadata are always a part of a database.

The presence of metadata makes databases much more useful than spreadsheets or data in other lists. Because of metadata, no one needs to guess, remember, or even record what is in the database. To find out what a database contains, we just look at the metadata inside the database. Metadata make databases easy to use—for both authorized and unauthorized purposes, as described in the exercise "Nobody Said I Shouldn't" at the end of this chapter on pages 154–155.

Q5 What Is a DBMS, and What Does It Do?

A database, all by itself, is not very useful. The tables in Figure 5-6 have all the data the professor wants, but the format is unwieldy. The professor wants to see the data in a form like that in Figure 5-2 and also as a formatted report. Pure database data are correct but in raw form, they are not pertinent or useful.

Figure 5-8 shows the components of a **database application system**. Such applications make database data more accessible and useful. Users employ a *database application* that consists of forms (such as the form in Figure 5-2), formatted reports, queries, and application programs. Each of these, in turn, calls on the DBMS to process the database tables. We will first describe DBMSs and then discuss database application components.

The Database Management System

A **database management system (DBMS)** is a program used to create, process, and administer a database. As is the case with operating systems, almost no organization develops its own DBMS. Instead, companies license DBMS products from vendors, such as IBM, Microsoft, and Oracle. Popular DBMS products are **DB2** from IBM, **Access** and **SQL Server** from Microsoft, and **Oracle** from Oracle Corporation. Another popular DBMS is **MySQL**, an open-source DBMS product that is free for most applications. Other DBMS products are available, but the five listed above account for the vast majority of databases on the market today.

Note that a DBMS and a database are two different things, even though many in the trade press, and even some books, confuse the two. A DBMS is a software program; a database is a collection of tables, relationships, and metadata. The two concepts are very different.

Creating the Database and Its Structures

Database developers use the DBMS to create tables, relationships, and other structures in the database. The form in Figure 5-7 can be used to define a new table or to modify an existing one. To create a new table, the developer just fills out a new form, such as the one in Figure 5-7.

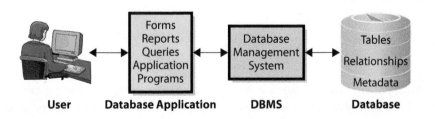

| User | Database Application | DBMS | Database |

Figure 5-8

Components of a Database Application System

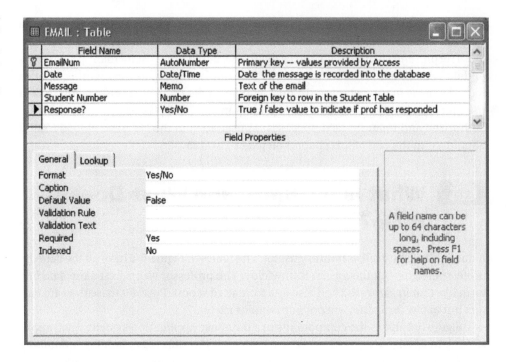

To modify an existing table—for example, to add a new column—the developer opens the metadata form for that table and adds a new row of metadata. For example, in Figure 5-9, the developer has added a new column called *Response?* This new column is created by adding the label "Response?" under the Field Name column. This new column has the Data Type *Yes/No*, which means that the column can contain only one of the values—yes or no. A professor will use this column to indicate whether he or she has responded to the student's email. Other database structures are defined in similar ways.

Processing the Database

The second function of the DBMS is to process the database. Applications use the DBMS for four operations: *read, insert, modify,* or *delete* data. The applications call upon the DBMS in different ways. For example, when the user enters new data or changes data on a form, a computer program processes the data provided on the form and then calls the DBMS to make the necessary database changes. At other times, an application program can call directly on the DBMS to make the change. No matter which way the database is called, there is only one language that relational databases use when communicating data from a database: **Structured Query Language (SQL)**, which is an international standard language for processing a database. A query can be thought of as a question. SQL (pronounced "see-quell") can then be thought of as a formal way of putting a question to a database. The answer to that query will be the data that is specified. All five of the DBMS products mentioned earlier accept and process SQL statements. As an example, the following SQL statement inserts a new row into the *Student* table:

```
INSERT INTO Student
 ([Student Number], [Student Name], HW1, HW2, MidTerm)
 VALUES
 (1000, 'Franklin, Benjamin', 90, 95, 100)
```

Such statements are issued behind the scenes by programs that process forms. Alternatively, they can also be issued directly to the DBMS by an application program.

You do not need to understand or remember SQL language syntax. Instead, just be aware that SQL is an international standard for processing a database. As well, SQL can be used to create databases and database structures. You will learn more about SQL if you take a database management course.

Administering the Database

A third DBMS function is to provide tools to assist in the administration of the database. Database administration involves a wide variety of activities. For example, the DBMS can be used to set up a security system involving user accounts, passwords, permissions, and limits for processing the database. To provide database security, a user must sign on using a valid user account before he or she can process the database.

Permissions can be limited in very specific ways. In the *Student* database example, it is possible to limit a particular user to reading only *Student Name* from the *Student* table. A different user could be given permission to read the entire *Student* table, but limited to update only the *HW1, HW2,* and *MidTerm* columns. Other users can be given still other permissions.

In addition to security, DBMS administrative functions include backing up database data, adding structures to improve the performance of database applications, removing data that are no longer wanted or needed, and similar tasks. One of these tasks involves setting up a system for dealing with database growth, as discussed in "MIS in Use," on page 144.

Q6 What Is a Database Application?

A **database application** is a collection of forms, reports, queries, and application programs that process a database. A database may have one or more applications, and each application may have one or more users. Figure 5-10 shows three applications; the top two have multiple users. These applications have different purposes, features, and functions, but they all process the same inventory data stored in a common database.

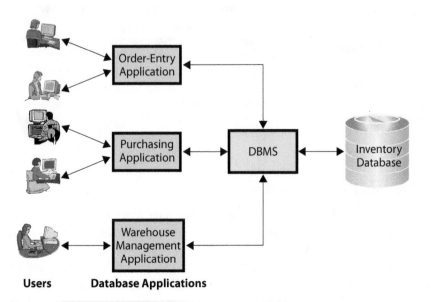

Figure 5-10

Use of Multiple Database Applications

Users   **Database Applications**

MIS in Use

The Many Names of One Customer

Founded in 1945, Vancouver-based Vancity is Canada's largest credit union, with more than $16 billion in assets. By a combination of organic (natural) and inorganic (acquisition) growth, Vancity now has 57 branches in Metro Vancouver, the Fraser Valley, Victoria, and Squamish and 501 000 individual and business customers.

The majority of Vancity's member customers did not have just a single product or service but, rather, a variety of products and services that could include savings and chequing accounts, loans, credit cards, and mutual funds and other investment products. Indeed, further complicating the relationship was that customers not only had multiple products/services but also had multiple instances of individual products/services. That is, a customer could have two savings accounts, multiple credit cards, and a number of mutual funds in a variety of ownerships (such as registered retirement savings programs [RRSPs], registered education savings plans [RESPs], and nonregistered investment plans), and these could be held or have been set up at different branches.

This diversity of products and services—although attractive to both Vancity and its member customers—created a major data-quality headache for Tony Fernandes. As the former vice-president of technology strategy, one of his responsibilities was the overall quality of information. His challenge was to ensure that the data in the customer information file (CIF), the database that held all customer data, were accurate and that the CIF identified customers uniquely and completely. As he put it, "My job is to manage similarities and differences. We need to know if the Jon Doe who lives on Victoria Street and has a savings account is the same Jonathan Doe who has a business account and a residence on Boundary Road."

The challenge was significant. In many cases, names were not unique and were complicated by short forms or by people having a variety of legal, given, and familiar names.

Vancity attempted to resolve many of these problems as customers activated each new product or service, but it was not always feasible. Something as relatively simple as spelling an address could result in duplicate entries that had to be reconciled. For example, the address "35 Westforest Trail" could also be entered as "35 Westforest Tr." At the lowest level, these types of entries caused inefficiencies, such as sending duplicate information. More troubling to Tony, of course, were problems of incomplete customer information or more complicated issues, such as misidentification of financial records.

Questions

1. How serious a problem is duplicate information to the financial services industry? Is it more serious for some industries than others? (*Hint:* How much of an issue is it for the health industry?)

2. Are there any other costs to Vancity when duplicate information is sent to customers? (*Hint:* What impression would you have if you received duplicate marketing information from various organizations?)

3. What are the various challenges in cleaning and grooming data? (*Hint:* Are there reasons why customers may have separate or changing information?)

4. Would the problem be solved by identifying customers numerically? How would customers perceive this? Are there legal issues?

Forms, Reports, and Queries

Figure 5-2 shows a typical database application data entry **form**, and Figure 5-11 shows a typical **report**. Data entry forms are used to read, insert, modify, and delete data. Reports show data in a structured context.

Some reports, like the one in Figure 5-11, also compute values as they present the data. An example is the computation of *Total weighted points* in Figure 5-11.

Figure 5-11

Example of a Student
Report

Student Report with Emails

Student Name	BAKER, ANDREA	HW1	88	
		HW2	100	
Student Number	1325	MidTerm	78	(53 homeworks)

Total weighted points: 422

Emails Received

Date	Message
2/1/2007	For homework 1, do you want us to provide notes on our references?
3/15/2007	My group consists of Swee Lau and Stuart Nelson.

Student Name	LAU, SWEE	HW1	75	
		HW2	90	
Student Number	1644	MidTerm	90	(53 homeworks)

Total weighted points: 435

Emails Received

Date	Message
3/15/2007	Could you please assign me to a group?

Recall from Chapter 2 that one of the definitions of information is "data presented in a meaningful context." The structure of this report creates information because it shows the student data in a context that will be meaningful to the professor.

DBMS programs provide comprehensive and robust features for querying database data. For example, suppose the professor who uses the *Student* database remembers that one of the students referred to the topic *barriers to entry* in an office visit, but he or she cannot remember which student or when. If there are hundreds of students and visits recorded in the database, it will take some effort and time for the professor to search through all office visit records to find that event. The DBMS, however, can find any such record quickly. Figure 5-12(a) shows a **query** form in which the professor types in the keyword for which he or she is looking. Figure 5-12(b) shows the results of the query.

Database Application Programs

Forms, reports, and queries work well for standard functions. However, most applications have unique requirements that a simple form, report, or query cannot meet.

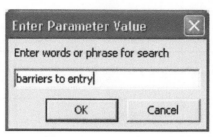

a. Form used to enter phrase for search

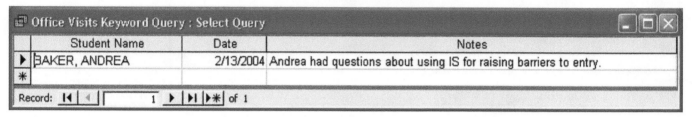

b. Results of query operation

For example, in the order entry application in Figure 5-10, what should be done if only a portion of a customer's request can be met? If someone wants 10 widgets and there are only 3 in stock, should a backorder for 7 more be generated automatically? Or should some other action be taken?

Application programs process logic that is specific to a given business need. In the *Student* database, an example application is one that assigns grades at the end of the term. If the professor grades on a curve, the application reads the breakpoints for each grade from a form and then processes each row in the *Student* table, allocating a grade based on the breakpoints and the total number of points earned.

Another important use of application programs is to enable database processing over the internet. For this use, the application program serves as an intermediary between the web server and the database. The application program responds to events, such as when a user presses a submit button; it also reads, inserts, modifies, and deletes database data.

Figure 5-13 shows four different database application programs running on a web server computer. Users with browsers connect to the web server via the internet. The web server directs user requests to the appropriate application program. Each program then processes the database, as necessary.

Figure 5-13

Four Application Programs on a Web Server Computer

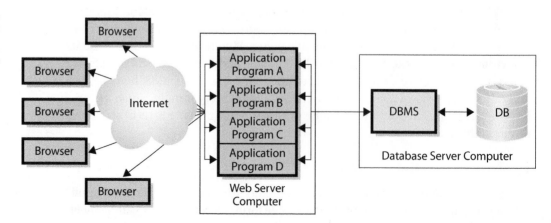

Multiuser Processing

Figures 5-10 and 5-13 show multiple users processing the database. Such **multiuser processing** is common, but it does pose unique problems that you, as a future manager, need to be aware of. To understand the nature of those problems, consider the following scenario:

Two users, Andrea and Jeffrey, are using the order entry application in Figure 5-10. Andrea is on the phone with her customer, who wants to purchase 5 widgets. At the same time, Jeffrey is talking with his customer, who wants to purchase 3 widgets. Andrea reads the database to determine how many widgets are in inventory. (She unknowingly invokes the order entry application when she types in her data entry form.) The DBMS returns a row showing 10 widgets in inventory.

Meanwhile, just after Andrea accesses the database, Jeffrey's customer says she wants widgets, and so he also reads the database (via the order entry application program) to determine how many widgets are in inventory. The DBMS returns the same row to him, indicating that 10 widgets are available.

Andrea's customer now says that he will take 5 widgets, and Andrea records this fact in her form. The application rewrites the widget row back to the database, indicating that there are 5 widgets in inventory.

Meanwhile, Jeffrey's customer says that he will take 3 widgets. Jeffrey records this fact in his form, and the application rewrites the widget row back to the database. However, Jeffrey's application knows nothing about Andrea's work and subtracts 3 from the original count of 10, thus storing an incorrect count of 7 widgets in inventory. Clearly, there is a problem. We began with 10 widgets, Andrea took 5 and Jeffrey took 3, but the database says there are 7 widgets in inventory. It should show 2, not 7.

This problem, known as the **lost-update problem**, exemplifies one of the special characteristics of multiuser database processing. To prevent this problem, some type of locking must be used to coordinate the activities of users who are unaware of each other. Locking brings its own complexity and problems that must be addressed, but these are beyond the scope of this chapter and text.

The purpose of this example is to illustrate that making a system usable by more than one person requires a lot more than simply enabling computer connections. The logic of the underlying application processing needs to be adjusted as well.

Be aware of possible data conflicts when you manage business activities that involve multiuser processing. If you find inaccurate results that seem not to have a cause, you may be experiencing multiuser data conflicts. Contact your MIS department for assistance.

Q7 What Is the Difference Between an Enterprise DBMS and a Personal DBMS?

DBMS products fall into two broad categories. **Enterprise DBMS** products process large organizational and workgroup databases. These products support many (perhaps thousands of) users and many different database applications. They also support 24/7 operations and can manage databases that span dozens of different magnetic disks with thousands of gigabytes or more of data. IBM's DB2, Microsoft's SQL Server, and Oracle's Oracle are examples of enterprise DBMS products.

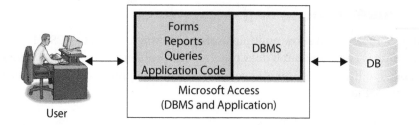

Figure 5-14
Personal Database System

User

Forms
Reports
Queries
Application Code

DBMS

Microsoft Access
(DBMS and Application)

DB

Personal DBMS products are designed for smaller, simpler database applications. Such products are used for personal or small workgroup applications that involve fewer than 100 users, and normally fewer than 15. In fact, the great bulk of databases in this category have only a single user. The professor's *Student* database is an example of a database that is processed by a personal DBMS product.

In the past, there were many personal DBMS products—Paradox, dBase, R:BASE, and FoxPro. Microsoft phased out these products when it developed Access and included it in the Microsoft Office suite. Today, the only remaining personal DBMS is Microsoft Access.

To avoid one point of confusion for you in the future, note that the separation of application programs and the DBMS shown in Figure 5-10 is true only for enterprise DBMS products. Microsoft Access includes features and functions for application processing along with the DBMS itself. For example, Access has a form generator and a report generator. Thus, as shown in Figure 5-14, Access is both a DBMS and an application development product.

Active <img> Review

Use this Active Review to verify that you have understood the material in the chapter. You can read the entire chapter and then perform the tasks in this review, or you can read the material for just one question and perform the tasks for that question before moving on to the next one.

Q1 What is content?
Describe what is meant by the term *content*. How has content changed with computers and access to the internet?

Q2 How can content be organized?
What is a web content management system? How have content management systems evolved over time?

Q3 What is the purpose of a database?
Describe the purpose of a database. Explain when you should use a spreadsheet and when you should use a database.

Q4 What does a database contain?
Explain the hierarchy of data from bytes to tables. Show how a database stores the relationships among rows. Define *key*

and *foreign key*. Define *metadata*, and explain how metadata makes databases more useful.

Q5 What is a DBMS, and what does it do?
Describe a database application system. Define *DBMS*. Name three prominent DBMS products. Describe the difference between a database and a DBMS. Explain the three major functions of a DBMS. What is SQL used for?

Q6 What is a database application?
Name and describe the components of a database application. Describe the circumstances that require a special logic for database applications. Describe the lost-update problem. Explain, in general terms, how this problem is prevented.

Q7 What is the difference between an enterprise DBMS and a personal DBMS?
Explain the function of an enterprise DBMS and describe its characteristics. Explain the function of a personal DBMS and describe its characteristics. Name the only surviving personal DBMS. Explain the differences between Figure 5-10 and Figure 5-14.

MyMISLab MyMISLab is an online learning and testing environment that features the perfect study tools to help you master the concepts covered in this chapter. Log in to MyMISLab to test your knowledge of key chapter concepts and explore additional practice tools, including videos, flashcards, annotated text figures, and more!

Key Terms and Concepts

Access 141

Byte 137

Columns 137

Content management systems (CMSs) 135

Database 137

Database application 143

Database application system 141

Database management system (DBMS) 141

DB2 141

Enterprise DBMS 147

Fields 137

File 137

Foreign keys 139

Form 144

Intellectual property 134

Key 138

Lost-update problem 147

Metadata 140

Multiuser processing 147

MySQL 141

Oracle 141

Personal DBMS 148

Query 145

Records 137

Relation 139

Relational databases 139

Report 144

Rows 137

SQL Server 141

Structured Query Language (SQL) 142

Table 137

Using Your Knowledge

1. Suppose you are a marketing assistant for a consumer electronics company and are in charge of setting up your company's booth at trade shows. Weeks before the shows, you meet with the marketing managers and determine what equipment they want to display. Then you identify each of the components that need to be shipped and schedule a shipper to deliver them to the trade-show site. You then supervise convention personnel as they set up the booths and equipment. Once the show is over, you supervise the packing of the booth and all equipment as well as schedule its shipment back to your home office. Once the equipment arrives, you check it in to your warehouse to ensure that all pieces of the booth and all equipment are returned. If there are problems because of shipping damage or loss, you handle those problems. Your job is important; at a typical show, you are responsible for more than $250 000 worth of equipment.

    a. You will need to track data about booth components, equipment, shippers, and shipments. List typical fields for each type of data.

    b. Could you use a spreadsheet to keep track of this data? What would be the advantages and disadvantages of doing so?

    c. Using your answer to question (a), give an example of two relationships that you need to track. Show the keys and foreign keys for each.

    d. Which of the following components of a database application are you likely to need: data entry forms, reports, queries, or application programs? Explain one use for each component you will need.

    e. Will your application be single-user or multiuser? Will you need a personal DBMS or an enterprise DBMS? If you need a personal DBMS, which product will you use?

2. Samantha Green owns and operates Twigs Tree Trimming Service. Recall from Chapter 3 that Samantha has a degree from a forestry program and recently opened her business in Winnipeg. Her business consists of many one-time operations (e.g., removing a tree or stump), as well as recurring services (e.g., trimming customers' trees every year or two). When business is slow, Samantha calls former clients to remind them of her services and of the need to trim their trees on a regular basis.

   a. Name and describe the tables of data that Samantha will need in order to run her business. Indicate possible fields for each table.

   b. Could Samantha use a spreadsheet to keep track of these data? What would be the advantages and disadvantages of doing so?

   c. Using your answer to question (a), give an example of two relationships that Samantha needs to track. Show the keys and foreign keys for each.

   d. Which of the following components of a database application is Samantha likely to need: data entry forms, reports, queries, or application programs? Explain one use for each component she needs.

   e. Will this application be single-user or multiuser? Will she need a personal DBMS or an enterprise DBMS? If she needs a personal DBMS, which product will she use?

3. FiredUp Inc. is a small business owned by Curt and Julie Robards. Based in Brisbane, Australia, FiredUp manufactures and sells FiredNow, a lightweight camping stove. Recall from Chapter 3 that Curt used his previous experience as an aerospace engineer to invent a burning nozzle that enables the stove to stay lit in very high winds. Using her industrial-design training, Julie designed the stove so that it is small, lightweight, easy to set up, and very stable. Curt and Julie sell the stove directly to their customers over the internet and via the phone. The warranty on the stove covers five years of cost-free repair for stoves that are used for recreational purposes.

   FiredUp wants to track every stove and the customer who purchased it. They want to know which customers own which stoves, in case they need to notify customers of safety problems or need to order a stove recall. Curt and Julie also want to keep track of any repairs they have performed.

   a. Name and describe tables of data that FiredUp will need. Indicate possible fields for each table.

   b. Could FiredUp use a spreadsheet to keep track of data? What would be the advantages and disadvantages of doing so?

   c. Using your answer to (a), give an example of two relationships FiredUp needs to track. Show the keys and foreign keys for each.

   d. Which of the following components of a database application is FiredUp likely to need: data entry forms, reports, queries, application programs? Explain one use for each needed component.

   e. Will this application be single-user or multiuser? Will FiredUp need a personal DBMS or an enterprise DBMS? If they need a personal DBMS, which product will it use? If they need an enterprise DBMS, which product can they obtain licence-free?

Collaborative Exercises

Collaborate with a group of students on the following exercises.

Figure 5-15 shows a spreadsheet that is used to track the assignment of sheet music to a choir—it could be a church choir, or school or community choir. The type

	A	B	C	D	E
1	Last Name	First Name	Email	Phone	Part
2	Ashley	Jane	JA@somewhere.com	703.555.1234	Soprano
3	Davidson	Kaye	KD@somewhere.com	703.555.2236	Soprano
4	Ching	Kam Hoong	KHC@overhere.com	703.555.2236	Soprano
5	Menstell	Lori Lee	LLM@somewhere.com	703.555.1237	Soprano
6	Corning	Sandra	SC2@overhere.com	703.555.1234	Soprano
7		B-minor mass	J.S. Bach	Soprano Copy 7	
8		Requiem	Mozart	Soprano Copy 17	
9		9th Symphony Chorus	Beethoven	Soprano Copy 9	
10	Wei	Guang	GW1@somewhere.com	703.555.9936	Soprano
11	Dixon	Eleanor	ED@thisplace.com	703.555.12379	Soprano
12		B-minor mass	J.S. Bach	Soprano Copy 11	
13	Duong	Linda	LD2@overhere.com	703.555.8736	Soprano
14		B-minor mass	J.S. Bach	Soprano Copy 7	
15		Requiem	J.S. Bach	Soprano Copy 19	
16	Lunden	Haley	HL@somewhere.com	703.555.0836	Soprano
17	Utran	Diem Thi	DTU@somewhere.com	703.555.1089	Soprano

Figure 5-15

Spreadsheet Used for Assignment of Sheet Music

Source: Microsoft Excel

of choir does not matter because the problem is a universal one. Sheet music is expensive, choir members need to be able to take sheet music away for practise at home, and not all of the music gets back to the inventory. (Sheet music can be purchased or rented, but either way, lost music is an expense.)

Look closely at these data, and you will see some data integrity problems—or at least some possible data integrity problems. For one, do Sandra Corning and Linda Duong really have the same copy of music checked out? Second, did Mozart and J. S. Bach both write a Requiem, or in row 15 should J. S. Bach actually be Mozart? Also, there is a problem with Eleanor Dixon's phone number and several phone numbers are the same, which seems suspicious.

Additionally, this spreadsheet is confusing and hard to use. The column labelled *First Name* includes both people names and the names of choruses. *Email* has both email addresses and composer names, and *Phone* has both phone numbers and copy identifiers. Furthermore, to record a checkout of music the user must first add a new row and then re-enter the name of the work, the composer's name, and the copy to be checked out. Finally, consider what happens when the user wants to find all copies of a particular work: The user will have to examine the rows in each of four spreadsheets for the four voice parts.

In fact, a spreadsheet is ill-suited for this application. A database would be a far better tool, and such situations are obvious candidates for innovation.

1. Analyze the spreadsheet shown in Figure 5-15 and list all of the problems that occur when trying to track the assignment of sheet music using this spreadsheet.

2. The following two tables could be used to store the data in Figure 5-15 in a database:

ChoirMember (*LastName, FirstName, Email, Phone, Part*)

MusicalWork (*NameOfWork, Composer, Part, CopyNumber*)

Note: This notation means there are two tables, one named *ChoirMember* and a second named *MusicalWork*. The *ChoirMember* table has five columns: *LastName, FirstName, Email, Phone,* and *Part*; *MusicalWork* has four columns: *NameOfWork, Composer, Part, CopyNumber*.

  a. Redraw the data in Figure 5-15 into this two-table format.
  b. Select primary keys for the *ChoirMember* and *MusicalWork* tables.

    c. The two tables are not integrated; they do not show who has checked out which music. Add foreign key columns to one of the tables to integrate the data.

    d. This two-table design does not eliminate the potential for data integrity problems that occur in the spreadsheet. Explain why not.

3. A three-table database design for the data in the spreadsheet in Figure 5-15 is as follows:

ChoirMember (*LastName, FirstName, Email, Phone, Part*)

MusicalWork (*NameOfWork*)

CheckOut (*LastName, FirstName, NameOfWork, Part, CopyNumber, DateOut, DateIn*)

    a. Redraw the data in Figure 5-15 into this three-table format.

    b. Identify which columns are primary keys for each of these tables.

    c. The foreign keys are already in place; identify which columns are foreign keys and which relationships they represent.

    d. Does this design eliminate the potential for data integrity problems that occur in the spreadsheet? Why or why not?

4. Assume that you manage the choir and you foresee two possibilities:

- Keep the spreadsheet, but create procedures to reduce the likelihood of data integrity problems.
- Create an Access database and database application for the three-table design.

Describe the advantages and disadvantages of each of these possibilities. Recommend one of these two possibilities and justify your recommendation.

Case Study 5

Behind the Race

For hundreds of thousands of athletes, competing in a marathon or triathlon is the culmination of years of dedicated training and endurance. Although largely invisible, a similar regimen can exist for the marathon's organizers, who must manage planning, donations, fundraising, creating custom websites, marketing, volunteer management, online registration, newsletters, and the publication of results. Although not directly related to the event itself, these activities can be individually and collectively overwhelming.

    The Active Network was originally formed by a small community of endurance race directors, league administrators, and enthusiastic volunteers. They realized that each time one of the hundreds of autonomous athletic organizations planned an event, they were in essence reinventing the wheel. So, the Active Network (www.active.com) was formed to harness the power of online technology and marketing solutions.

    Planning an event has now become vastly simplified. The Active Network provides tailored solutions for better experience and exposure for participants. Rather than one-off or ad hoc solutions cobbled together by part-time administrators—who, in many cases, were doing things for the first time—all organizations, regardless of their size, now have access to state-of-the-art systems.

The Active Network was a solution that had legs. By focusing on three areas—improving the site for the benefit of their technology customers, enhancing the athlete's overall experience, and providing heightened exposure for their clients—the Active Network now provides online technology and marketing solutions to thousands of business owners and organizers in more than 80 sports and recreational markets that serve millions of participants worldwide.

Building on its vision to enable and encourage every individual to learn about, share, register, and ultimately participate in any activity, Active.com has become the largest searchable worldwide directory of sports and recreational activities. By providing access to such tools as community message boards and specialized moderators and allowing members to post photographs and videos, Active.com has become a destination site for athletes and a trusted community among its members.

Questions

1. What problem does Active.com solve for event organizers?
2. Does Active.com have any other advantages other than economies of scale?
3. Are there are any network effects for Active.com? (*Hint:* What are the benefits to having a large number of events in one place?)
4. What kind of information does Active.com have about its members? How would this be useful and to whom? What is the value of this information?

Nobody Said I Shouldn't

"My name is Kelly, and I do systems support for our group. I configure the new computers, set up the network, make sure the servers are operating, and so forth. I also do all the database backups. I've always liked computers. After high school, I worked odd jobs to make some money, then I got an associate degree in information technology from our local community college.

"Anyway, as I said, I make backup copies of our databases. One weekend, I didn't have much going on, so I copied one of the database backups to a CD and took it home. I had taken a class on database processing as part of my associate degree, and we used an SQL Server (our database management system) in my class. In fact, I suppose that's part of the reason I got the job. Anyway, it was easy to restore the database on my computer at home, and I did.

"Of course, as they'll tell you in your database class, one of the big advantages of database processing is that databases have metadata, or data that describe the content of the database. So, although I didn't know what tables were in our database, I did know how to access the SQL server metadata. I just queried a table called sysTables to learn the names of our tables. From there it was easy to find out what columns each table had.

"I found tables with data about orders, customers, salespeople, and so forth, and just to amuse myself and to see how much of the query language SQL I could remember, I started playing around with the data. I was curious to know which order-entry clerk was the best, so I started querying each clerk's order data, the total number of orders, total order amounts, things like that. It was easy to do and fun.

"I know one of the order-entry clerks, Jason, pretty well, so I started looking at the data for his orders. I was just curious, and it was very simple SQL. I was just playing around with the data when I noticed something odd. All his biggest orders were with one company, Valley Appliances; even stranger, every one of its orders had a huge discount. I thought, *Well, maybe that's typical*. Out of curiosity, I started looking at data for the other clerks, and very few of them had an order with Valley Appliances. But when they did, Valley didn't get a big discount. Then I looked at the rest of Jason's orders, and none of them had much in the way of discounts, either.

"The next Friday, a bunch of us went out for beer after work. I happened to see Jason, so I asked him about Valley Appliances and made a joke about the discounts. He asked me what I meant, and then I told him that I'd been looking at the data for fun and that I saw this odd pattern. He laughed, said he 'just did his job,' and then changed the subject.

"Well, to make a long story short, when I got to work on Monday morning, my office was cleaned out. There was nothing there except a note telling me to go see my boss. The bottom line was, I was fired. The company also threatened that if I didn't return all of its data, I'd be in court for the next five years. .. things like that. I was so mad I didn't even tell them about Jason. Now my problem is that I'm out of a job, and I can't exactly use my last company for a reference."

Discussion Questions

1. Where did Kelly go wrong?

2. Do you think it was illegal, unethical, or neither for Kelly to take the database home and query the data?

3. Does the company share culpability with Kelly?

4. What do you think Kelly should have done upon discovering the odd pattern in Jason's orders?

5. What should the company have done before firing Kelly?

6. "Metadata make databases easy to use—for both authorized and unauthorized purposes." Explain what organizations should do in light of this fact.

Chapter Extension 5a

Chapter 5 provides the background for this extension.

Database Design

In this chapter extension, you will learn about data modelling and how data models are transformed into database designs. You'll also learn the important role that business professionals have in the development of a database application system.

Q1 Who Will Volunteer?

Suppose you are the manager of fund-raising for a local public television station. Twice a year you conduct fund drives during which the station runs commercials that ask viewers to donate. These drives are important; they provide nearly 40 percent of the station's operating budget.

One of your job functions is to find volunteers to staff the phones during these drives. You need 10 volunteers per night for six nights, or 60 people, twice per year. The volunteers' job is exhausting, and normally a volunteer will work only one night during a drive.

Finding volunteers for each drive is a perpetual headache. Two months before a drive begins, you and your staff start calling potential volunteers. You first call volunteers from prior drives, using a roster that your administrative assistant prepares for each drive. Some volunteers have been helping for years; you'd like to know that information before you call them so that you can tell them how much you appreciate their continuing support. Unfortunately, the roster does not have that data.

Additionally, some volunteers are more effective than others. Some have a particular knack for increasing the callers' donations. Although those data are available, the information is not in a format that you can use when calling for volunteers. You think you could better staff the fund-raising drives if you had that missing information.

You know that you can use a computer database to keep better track of prior volunteers' service and performance, but you are not sure how to proceed. By the end of this chapter extension, when we return to this fund-raising situation, you will know what to do.

Q2 How Are Database Application Systems Developed?

You learned in Chapter 5 that a database application system consists of a database, a DBMS, and one or more database applications. A database application, in turn, consists of forms, reports, queries, and possibly application programs. The question then becomes: How are such systems developed? And, even more important to you, what is the users' role? We will address these questions in this chapter extension.

Figure AE5a-1 summarizes the database application system development process. First, the developers interview users and develop the requirements for the new system. During this process, the developers analyze existing forms, reports, queries,

MyMISLab

Visit MyMISLab for simulations, tutorials, and end-of-chapter problems.

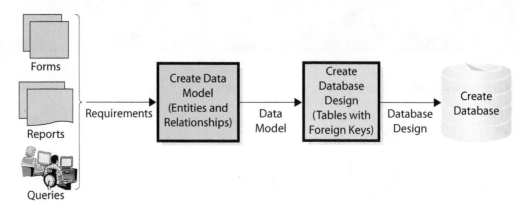

Figure AE5a-1

Database Development Process

and other user activities. They also determine the need for new forms, reports, and queries. The requirements for the database are then summarized in something called a **data model**, which is a logical representation of the structure of the data. The data model contains a description of both the data and the relationships among the data. It is akin to a blueprint. Just as building architects create a blueprint before they start construction, so, too, database developers create a data model before they start designing the database.

Once the users have validated and approved the data model, it is transformed into a database design. After that, the design is implemented in a database, and that database is then filled with user data.

You will learn much more about systems development in Chapter 10 and its related extensions. We discuss data modelling here because users have a crucial role in the success of any database development: They must validate and approve the data model. Only the users know what should be in the database.

Consider, for example, a database of students that an adviser uses for his or her advisees. What should be in it? Students? Classes? Records of emails from students? Records of meetings with students? Majors? Student organizations? Even when we know what themes should be in the database, we must ask, how detailed should the records be? Should the database include campus addresses? Home addresses? Billing addresses?

In fact, there are many possibilities, and the database developers do not and cannot know what to include. They do know, however, that a database must include all the data necessary for the users to perform their jobs. Ideally, it contains that amount of data and no more. So during database development, the developers must rely on the users to tell them what they need in the database. They will rely on the users to check the data model and to verify it for correctness, completeness, and appropriate level of detail. That verification will be your job. We begin with a discussion of the entity-relationship data model—the most common tool to use to construct data models.

Q3 What Are the Components of the Entity-Relationship Data Model?

The most popular technique for creating a data model is the **entity-relationship (E-R) data model**. With it, developers describe the content of a database by defining the things (*entities*) that will be stored in the database and the *relationships* among those entities. A second, less popular tool for data modelling is the **Unified Modelling Language (UML)**. We will not describe that tool here. However, if you learn how to interpret E-R models, with a bit of study you will be able to understand UML models as well.

Entities

An **entity** is something that the users want to track. Examples of entities are *Order, Customer, Salesperson*, and *Item*. Some entities represent a physical object, such as *Item* or *Salesperson*; others represent a logical construct or transaction, such as *Order* or *Contract*. For reasons beyond this discussion, entity names are always singular. We use *Order*, not *Orders*; *Salesperson*, not *Salespersons*.

Entities have **attributes** that describe characteristics of the entity. Example attributes of *Order* are *OrderNumber, OrderDate, SubTotal, Tax, Total*, and so forth. Example attributes of *Salesperson* are *SalespersonName, Email, Phone*, and so forth.

Entities have an **identifier**, which is an attribute (or group of attributes) whose value is associated with one and only one entity instance. For example, *OrderNumber* is an identifier of *Order* because only one *Order* instance has a given value of *OrderNumber*. For the same reason, *CustomerNumber* is an identifier of *Customer*. If each member of the sales staff has a unique name, then *SalespersonName* is an identifier of *Salesperson*.

Before we continue, consider that last sentence. Is the salesperson's name unique among the sales staff? Both now and in the future? Who decides the answer to such a question? Only the users know whether this is true; the database developers cannot know. This example underlines why it is important for you to be able to interpret data models because only users like yourself will know for sure.

Figure AE5a-2 shows examples of entities for the Student database. Each entity is shown in a rectangle. The name of the entity is just above the rectangle, and the identifier is shown in a section at the top of the entity. Entity attributes are shown in the remainder of the rectangle. In Figure AE5a-2, the *Adviser* entity has an identifier called *AdviserName* and the attributes *Phone, CampusAddress*, and *EmailAddress*.

Observe that the entities *Email* and *Office_Visit* do not have an identifier. Unlike *Student* or *Adviser*, the users do not have an attribute that identifies a particular email. In fact, *Email* and *Office_Visit* are identified, in part, by their relationship to Student. For now, we need not worry about that. The data model needs only to show how users view their world. When it comes to database design, the designer will deal with the missing identifiers by adding columns, possibly using hidden identifiers, to implement the users' view. You can learn about the modelling and representation of such entities if you enroll in a database class.

Relationships

Entities have **relationships** to each other. An *Order*, for example, has a relationship to a *Customer* entity and also to a *Salesperson* entity. In the Student database, a *Student* has a relationship to an *Adviser*, and an *Adviser* has a relationship to a *Department*.

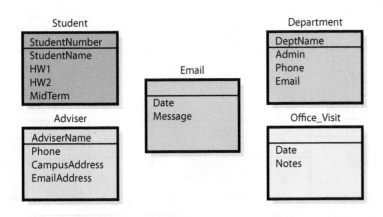

Figure AE5a-2

Student Data Model Entities

Figure AE5a-3

Example of *Department, Adviser,* and *Student* Entities and Relationships

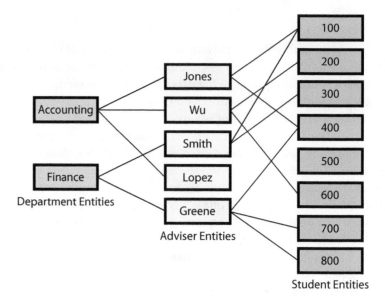

Figure AE5a-3

Example of *Department, Adviser,* and *Student* Entities and Relationships

Figure AE5a-3 shows sample *Department, Adviser,* and *Student* entities and their relationships. For simplicity, this figure shows just the identifier of the entities and not the other attributes. For this sample data, *Accounting* has three professors, Jones, Wu, and Lopez, and *Finance* has two professors, Smith and Greene.

The relationship between *Advisers* and *Students* is a bit more complicated because, in this example, an adviser is allowed to advise many students and a student is allowed to have many advisers. Perhaps this happens because students can have multiple majors. In any case, note that Professor Jones advises students 100 and 400 and that student 100 is advised by both Professors Jones and Smith.

Diagrams like the one in Figure AE5a-3 are too cumbersome for use in database design discussions. Instead, database designers use diagrams called **entity-relationship (E-R) diagrams**. Figure AE5a-4 shows an E-R diagram for the data in Figure AE5a-3. In this figure, all of the entities of one type are represented by a single rectangle. Thus, there are rectangles for the *Department, Adviser,* and *Student* entities. Attributes are shown as before in Figure AE5a-2.

Additionally, a line is used to represent a relationship between two entities. Notice the line between *Department* and *Adviser,* for example. The forked lines on the right side of that line signify that a department may have more than one adviser. The little lines, which are referred to as a **crow's foot**, are shorthand for the multiple lines between *Department* and *Adviser* in Figure AE5a-3. Relationships like this one are called **one-to-many (1:N) relationships** because one department can have many advisers.

Now examine the line between *Adviser* and *Student.* Here a crow's foot appears at each end of the line. This notation signifies that an adviser can be related to many students and that a student can be related to many advisers, which is the situation in Figure AE5a-3. Relationships like this one are called **many-to-many (N:M)**

Figure AE5a-4

Example Relationships— Version 1

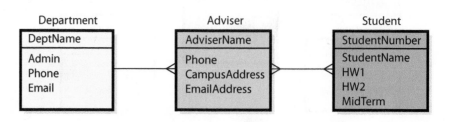

Figure AE5a-4

Example Relationships— Version 1

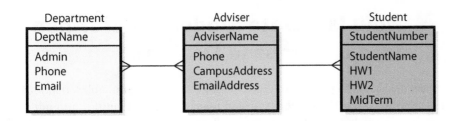

relationships because one adviser can have many students and one student can have many advisers.

Students sometimes find the notation N:M confusing. Interpret the *N* and *M* to mean that a variable number, greater than one, is allowed on each side of the relationship. Such a relationship is not written *N:N* because that notation would imply that there are the same number of entities on each side of the relationship, which is not necessarily true. *N:M* means that more than one entity is allowed on each side of the relationship and that the number of entities on each side can be different.

Figure AE5a-4 is an example of an entity-relationship diagram. Unfortunately, there are several different styles of entity-relationship diagrams. This one is called, not surprisingly, a **crow's-foot diagram** version. You may learn other versions if you take a database management class.

Figure AE5a-5 shows the same entities with different assumptions. Here advisers may advise in more than one department, but a student may have only one adviser, representing a policy that students may not have multiple majors.

Which, if either of these versions—Figure AE5a-4 or Figure AE5a-5—is correct? Only the users know. These alternatives illustrate the kinds of questions you will need to answer when a database designer asks you to check a data model for correctness.

The crow's-foot notation shows the maximum number of entities that can be involved in a relationship. Accordingly, they are called the relationship's **maximum cardinality**. Common examples of maximum cardinality are 1:N, N:M, and 1:1 (not shown).

Another important question is, "What is the minimum number of entities required in the relationship?" Must an adviser have a student to advise, and must a student have an adviser? Constraints on minimum requirements are called **minimum cardinalities**.

Figure AE5a-6 presents a third version of this E-R diagram that shows both maximum and minimum cardinalities. The vertical bar on a line means that at least one entity of that type is required. The small oval means that the entity is optional; the relationship need not have an entity of that type.

Thus, in Figure AE5a-6, a department is not required to have a relationship to any adviser, but an adviser is required to belong to a department. Similarly, an adviser is not required to have a relationship to a student, but a student is required to have a relationship to an adviser. Note, also, that the maximum cardinalities in Figure AE5a-6 have been changed so that both are 1:N.

Is the model in Figure AE5a-6 a good one? It depends on the rules of the university. Again, only the users know for sure.

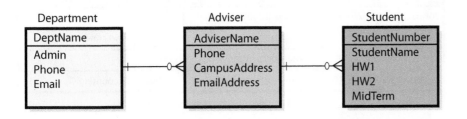

Q4 How Is a Data Model Transformed into a Database Design?

Database design is the process of converting a data model into tables, relationships, and data constraints. The database design team transforms entities into tables and expresses relationships by defining foreign keys. Database design is a complicated subject; as with data modelling, it occupies weeks in a database management class. In this section, however, we will introduce two important database design concepts: normalization and the representation of two kinds of relationships. The first concept is a foundation of database design, and the second will help you understand key considerations made during design.

Normalization

Normalization is the process of converting poorly structured tables into two or more well-structured tables. A table is such a simple construct that you may wonder how one could possibly be poorly structured. In truth, there are many ways that tables can be malformed—so many, in fact, that researchers have published hundreds of papers on this topic alone.

Consider the *Employee* table in Figure AE5a-7. It lists employee names, hire dates, email addresses, and the name and number of the department in which the employee works. This table seems innocent enough. But consider what happens when the Accounting department changes its name to Accounting and Finance. Because department names are duplicated in this table, every row that has a value of "Accounting" must be changed to "Accounting and Finance."

Data Integrity Problems

Suppose the Accounting name change is correctly made in two rows, but not in the third. The result is shown in Figure AE5a-7b. This table has what is called a **data integrity problem**: Two rows indicate that the name of Department 100 is Accounting and Finance, and another row indicates that the name of Department 100 is Accounting.

Figure AE5a-7

A Poorly Designed *Employee* Table

Employee

Name	HireDate	Email	DeptNo	DeptName
Jones	Feb 1, 2010	Jones@ourcompany.com	100	Accounting
Smith	Dec 3, 2007	Smith@ourcompany.com	200	Marketing
Chau	March 7, 2007	Chau@ourcompany.com	100	Accounting
Greene	July 17, 2010	Greene@ourcompany.com	100	Accounting

a. Table Before Update

Employee

Name	HireDate	Email	DeptNo	DeptName
Jones	Feb 1, 2010	Jones@ourcompany.com	100	Accounting and Finance
Smith	Dec 3, 2007	Smith@ourcompany.com	200	Marketing
Chau	March 7, 2007	Chau@ourcompany.com	100	Accounting and Finance
Greene	July 17, 2010	Greene@ourcompany.com	100	Accounting

b. Table with Incomplete Update

This problem is easy to spot in this small table. But consider a table in a large database that has more than 300 000 rows. Once a table that large develops serious data integrity problems, months of labour will be required to remove them.

Data integrity problems are serious. A table that has data integrity problems will produce incorrect and inconsistent information. Users will lose confidence in the information, and the system will develop a poor reputation. Information systems with poor reputations become heavy burdens to the organizations that use them.

Normalizing for Data Integrity

The data integrity problem can occur only if data are duplicated. Because of this, one easy way to eliminate the problem is to eliminate the duplicated data. We can do this by transforming the table design in Figure AE5a-7a into two tables, as shown in Figure AE5a-8. Here the name of the department is stored just once; therefore, no data inconsistencies can occur.

Of course, to produce an employee report that includes the department name, the two tables in Figure AE5a-8 will need to be joined back together. Because such joining of tables is common, DBMS products have been programmed to perform it efficiently, but it still requires work. From this example, you can see a trade-off in database design: Normalized tables eliminate data duplication, but they can be slower to process. Dealing with such trade-offs is an important consideration in database design.

The general goal of normalization is to construct tables such that every table has a *single* topic or theme. In good writing, every paragraph should have a single theme. This is true of databases as well; every table should have a single theme. The problem with the table design in Figure AE5a-7 is that it has two independent themes: employees and departments. The way to correct the problem is to split the table into two tables, each with its own theme. In this case, we create an *Employee* table and a *Department* table, as shown in Figure AE5a-8.

As mentioned, there are dozens of ways that tables can be poorly formed. Database practitioners classify tables into various **normal forms** according to the kinds of problems they have. Transforming a table into a normal form to remove duplicated data and other problems is called *normalizing* the table.[1] Thus, when you hear a database designer say, "Those tables are not normalized," she does not mean that the tables have irregular, not-normal data. Instead, she means that the tables have a format that could cause data integrity problems.

Employee

Name	HireDate	Email	DeptNo
Jones	Feb 1, 2010	Jones@ourcompany.com	100
Smith	Dec 3, 2011	Smith@ourcompany.com	200
Chau	March 7, 2007	Chau@ourcompany.com	100
Greene	July 17, 2010	Greene@ourcompany.com	100

Department

DeptNo	DeptName
100	Accounting
200	Marketing
300	Information Systems

Figure AE5a-8

Two Normalized Tables

---

[1] See David Kroenke and David Auer, *Database Concepts*, 6th ed. (Upper Saddle River, NJ: Pearson Education, 2013) for more information.

Summary of Normalization

As a future user of databases, you do not need to know the details of normalization. Instead, understand the general principle that every normalized (well-formed) table has one and only one theme. Further, tables that are not normalized are subject to data integrity problems.

Be aware, too, that normalization is just one criterion for evaluating database designs. Because normalized designs can be slower to process, database designers sometimes choose to accept non-normalized tables. The best design depends on the users' requirements.

Representing Relationships

Figure AE5a-9 shows the steps involved in transforming a data model into a relational database design. First, the database designer creates a table for each entity. The identifier of the entity becomes the key of the table. Each attribute of the entity becomes a column of the table. Next, the resulting tables are normalized so that each table has a single theme. Once that has been done, the next step is to represent the relationship among those tables.

For example, consider the E-R diagram in Figure AE5a-10a. The *Adviser* entity has a 1:N relationship to the *Student* entity. To create the database design, we construct a table for *Adviser* and a second table for *Student*, as shown in Figure AE5a-10b. The key of the *Adviser* table is *AdviserName*, and the key of the *Student* table is *StudentNumber*.

Further, the *EmailAddress* attribute of the *Adviser* entity becomes the *EmailAddress* column of the *Adviser* table, and the *StudentName* and *MidTerm* attributes of the *Student* entity become the *StudentName* and *MidTerm* columns of the *Student* table.

The next task is to represent the relationship. Because we are using the relational model, we know that we must add a foreign key to one of the two tables. The possibilities are: (1) place the foreign key *StudentNumber* in the *Adviser* table or (2) place the foreign key *AdviserName* in the *Student* table.

The correct choice is to place *AdviserName* in the *Student* table, as shown in Figure AE5a-10c. To determine a student's adviser, we just look into the *AdviserName* column of that student's row. To determine the adviser's students, we search the *AdviserName* column in the *Student* table to determine which rows have that adviser's name. If a student changes advisers, we simply change the value in the *AdviserName* column. Changing *Jackson* to *Jones* in the first row, for example, will assign student 100 to Professor Jones.

For this data model, placing *StudentNumber* in *Adviser* would be incorrect. If we were to do that, we could assign only one student to an adviser. There is no place to assign a second adviser.

This strategy for placing foreign keys will not work for N:M relationships, however. Consider the data model in Figure AE5a-11a (page 166); here there is an N:M relationship between advisers and students. An adviser may have many students,

Figure AE5a-9

Transforming a Data Model into a Database Design

- Represent each entity with a table
  - Entity identifier becomes table key
  - Entity attributes become table columns
- Normalize tables as necessary
- Represent relationships
  - Use foreign keys
  - Add additional tables for N:M relationships

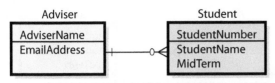

a. 1: N Relationship Between Adviser and Student Entities

Adviser Table—Key is AdviserName

AdviserName	EmailAddress
Jones	Jones@myuniv.edu
Choi	Choi@myuniv.edu
Jackson	Jackson@myuniv.edu

Student Table—Key is StudentNumber

StudentNumber	StudentName	MidTerm
100	Lisa	90
200	Jennie	85
300	Jason	82
400	Terry	95

b. Creating a Table for Each Entity

Adviser Table—Key is AdviserName

AdviserName	EmailAddress
Jones	Jones@myuniv.edu
Choi	Choi@myuniv.edu
Jackson	Jackson@myuniv.edu

Foreign Key Column Represents Relationship

Student—Key is StudentNumber

StudentNumber	StudentName	MidTerm	AdviserName
100	Lisa	90	Jackson
200	Jennie	85	Jackson
300	Jason	82	Choi
400	Terry	95	Jackson

c. Using the AdviserName Foreign Key to Represent the 1:N Relationship

Figure AE5a-10

Representing a 1:N Relationship

and a student may have multiple advisers (for multiple majors). The strategy we used for the 1:N data model will not work here. To see why, examine Figure AE5a-11b. If student 100 has more than one adviser, there is no place to record second or subsequent advisers.

It turns out that to represent an N:M relationship, we need to create a third table, as shown in Figure AE5a-11c. The third table has two columns, *AdviserName* and *StudentNumber*. Each row of the table means that the given adviser advises the student with the given number.

As you can imagine, there is a great deal more to database design than we have presented here. Still, this section should give you an idea of the tasks that need to be accomplished to create a database. You should also realize that the database design is a direct consequence of decisions made in the data model. If the data model is wrong, the database design will be wrong as well.

Figure AE5a-11

Representing an N:M Relationship

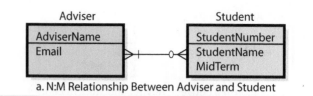

a. N:M Relationship Between Adviser and Student

Adviser—Key is AdviserName

AdviserName	Email
Jones	Jones@myuniv.edu
Choi	Choi@myuniv.edu
Jackson	Jackson@myuniv.edu

No room to place second or third AdviserName

Student—Key is StudentNumber

StudentNumber	StudentName	MidTerm	AdviserName
100	Lisa	90	Jackson
200	Jennie	85	Jackson
300	Jason	82	Choi
400	Terry	95	Jackson

b. Incorrect Representation of N:M Relationship

Adviser—Key is AdviserName

AdviserName	Email
Jones	Jones@myuniv.edu
Choi	Choi@myuniv.edu
Jackson	Jackson@myuniv.edu

Student—Key is StudentNumber

StudentNumber	StudentName	MidTerm
100	Lisa	90
200	Jennie	85
300	Jason	82
400	Terry	95

Adviser_Student_Intersection

AdviserName	StudentNumber
Jackson	100
Jackson	200
Choi	300
Jackson	400
Choi	100
Jones	100

Student 100 has three advisers.

c. Adviser_Student_Intersection Table Represents the N:M Relationship

Q5 What Is the Users' Role?

As stated, a database is a model of how the users view their business world. This means that the users are the final judges of what data the database should contain and how the records in that database should be related to one another.

The easiest time to change the database structure is during the data modelling stage. Changing a relationship from 1:N to N:M in a data model is simply a matter of changing the 1:N notation to N:M. However, once the database has been constructed, and loaded with data and application forms, reports, queries, and application programs have been created, changing a 1:N relationship to N:M means weeks of work.

You can glean some idea of why this might be true by contrasting Figure AE5a-10c with Figure AE5a-11c. Suppose that instead of having just a few rows, each table has thousands of rows; in that case, transforming the database from one format to the other involves considerable work. Even worse, however, is that application components will need to be changed as well. For example, if students have at most one adviser, then a single text box can be used to enter *AdviserName*. If students can have multiple advisers, then a multiple-row table will need to be used to enter *AdviserName*, and a program will need to be written to store the values of *AdviserName* into the *Adviser_Student_Intersection* table. There are dozens of other consequences as well, consequences that will translate into wasted labour and wasted expense.

The conclusion from this discussion is that user review of a data model is crucial. When a database is developed for your use, you must carefully review the data model. If you do not understand any aspect of it, you should ask for clarification until you do. The data model must accurately reflect your view of the business. If it does not, the database will be designed incorrectly, and the applications will be difficult to use, if not worthless. Do not proceed unless the data model is accurate.

As a corollary, when asked to review a data model, take that review seriously. Devote the time necessary to perform a thorough review. Any mistakes you miss will come back to haunt you, and by then the cost of correction may be very high with regard to both time and expense. This brief introduction to data modelling shows why databases can be more difficult to develop than spreadsheets.

Q6 Who Will Volunteer? (Continued)

Knowing what you know now, if you were the manager of fund-raising at the TV station, you would hire a consultant and expect the consultant to interview all of the key users. From those interviews, the consultant would then construct a data model.

You now know that the structure of the database must reflect the way the users think about their activities. If the consultant did not take the time to interview you and your staff or did not construct a data model and ask you to review it, you would know that you are not receiving good service and would take corrective action.

Suppose you found a consultant who interviewed your staff for several hours and then constructed the data model shown in Figure AE5a-12. This data model has an

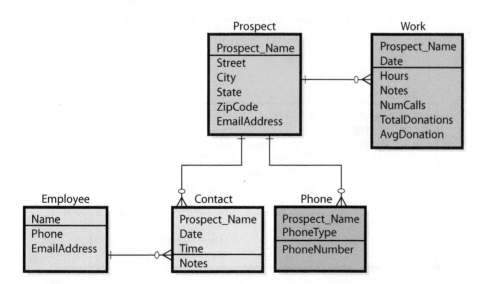

Figure AE5a-12

Data Model for Volunteer Database

Prospect (<u>Name</u>, Street, City, Province, Postal Code, EmailAddress)
Phone (<u>*Name*</u>, <u>PhoneType</u>, PhoneNumber)
Contact (<u>*Name*</u>, <u>Date</u>, <u>Time</u>, Notes, *EmployeeName*)
Work (<u>*Name*</u>, <u>Date</u>, Notes, NumCalls, TotalDonations)
Employee (<u>EmployeeName</u>, Phone, EmailAddress)

Note:
Underline means table key.
Italics means foreign key.
Underline and italics mean both table and foreign key.

entity for *Prospect*, an entity for *Employee*, and three additional entities for *Contact, Phone,* and *Work*. The *Contact* entity records contacts that you or other employees have made with the prospective volunteer. This record is necessary so that you know what has been said to whom. The *Phone* entity is used to record multiple phone numbers for each prospective volunteer, and the *Work* entity records work that the prospect has performed for the station.

After you reviewed and approved this data model, the consultant constructed the database design shown in Figure AE5a-13. In this design, table keys are underlined, foreign keys are shown in italics, and columns that are both table and foreign keys are underlined and italicized. Observe that the *Name* column is the table key of *Prospect*, and it is both part of the table key and a foreign key in *Phone, Contact,* and *Work*.

The consultant did not like having the *Name* column used as a key or as part of a key in so many tables. Based on her interviews, she suspected that prospect names are fluid—and that sometimes the same prospect name is recorded in different ways (e.g., sometimes with a middle initial and sometimes without). If that were to happen, phone, contact, and work data could be misallocated to prospect names. Accordingly, the consultant added a new column, *ProspectID*, to the prospect table and created the design shown in Figure AE5a-14. Values of this ID will have no meaning to the users, but the ID will be used to ensure that each prospect obtains a unique record in the Volunteer database. Because this ID has no meaning to the users, the consultant will hide it on forms and reports that users see.

There is one difference between the data model and the table designs. In the data model, the *Work* entity has an attribute, *AvgDonation*, but there is no corresponding *AvgDonation* column in the *Work* table. The consultant decided that there was no need to store this value in the database because it could readily be computed on forms and reports using the values in the *NumCalls* and *TotalDonations* columns.

Prospect (<u>*ProspectID*</u>, Name, Street, City, Province, Postal Code, EmailAddress)
Phone (<u>*ProspectID*</u>, <u>PhoneType</u>, PhoneNumber)
Contact (<u>*ProspectID*</u>, <u>Date</u>, <u>Time</u>, Notes, *EmployeeName*)
Work (<u>*ProspectID*</u>, <u>Date</u>, Notes, NumCalls, TotalDonations)
Employee (<u>EmployeeName</u>, Phone, EmailAddress)

Note:
Underline means table key.
Italics means foreign key.
Underline and italics mean both table and foreign key.

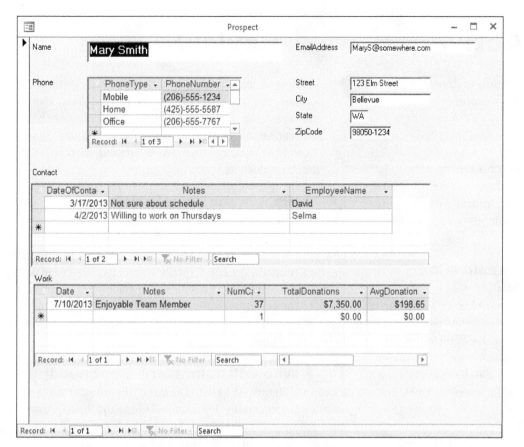

Figure AE5a-15

Volunteer Prospect Data
Entry Form

Source: Microsoft Access 2013.

Once the tables had been designed, the consultant created a Microsoft Access 2013 database. She defined the tables in Access, created relationships among the tables, and constructed forms and reports. Figure AE5a-15 shows the primary data entry form used for the Volunteer database. The top portion of the form has contact data, including multiple phone numbers. It is important to know the type of the phone number so that you and your staff know if you're calling someone at work or another setting. The middle and bottom sections of this form have contact and prior work data. Observe that *AvgDonation* has been computed from the *NumCalls* and *TotalDonations* columns.

You were quite pleased with this database application, and you're certain that it helped you to improve the volunteer staffing at the station. Of course, over time, you thought of several new requirements, and you already have changes in mind for next year.

Active ? Review

Use this Active Review to verify that you understand the ideas and concepts that answer this chapter extension's study questions.

Q1 Who will volunteer?

Summarize the problem that the fund-raising manager must solve. Explain how a database can help solve this problem. Describe the missing information. In your own words, what data must be available to construct the missing information?

Q2 How are database application systems developed?

Name and briefly describe the components of a database application system. Explain the difference between a database application system and a database application program. Using Figure AE5a-1 as a guide, describe the major steps in the process of developing a database application system. Explain what role is crucial for users and why that role is so important.

Q3 What are the components of the entity-relationship data model?

Define the terms *entity, attributes*, and *relationship.* Give an example of two entities (other than those in this book) that have a 1:N relationship. Give an example of two entities that have an N:M relationship. Explain the difference between maximum and minimum cardinality. Show two entities having a 1:N relationship in which one is required and one is optional.

Q4 How is a data model transformed into a database design?

Give an example of a data integrity problem. Describe, in general terms, the process of normalization. Explain how normalizing data prevents data integrity problems. Explain the disadvantage of normalized data. Using your examples from Q3, show how 1:N relationships are expressed in relational database designs. Show how N:M relationships are expressed in relational database designs.

Q5 What is the users' role?

Describe the major role for users in the development of a database application system. Explain what is required to change a 1:N relationship to an N:M relationship during the data modelling stage. Explain what is required to make that same change after the database application system has been constructed. Describe how this knowledge impacts your behaviour when a database application system is being constructed for your use.

Q6 Who will volunteer? (Continued)

Examine Figure AE5a-12. Describe the maximum and minimum cardinality for each relationship. Justify these cardinalities. Change the relationship between *Prospect* and *Phone* to N:M, and explain what this means. Change the relationship between *Prospect* and *Work* to 1:1, and explain what this means. Explain how each relationship is represented in the design in Figure AE5a-14. Show examples of both primary keys and foreign keys in this figure. In *Contact*, determine whether *EmployeeName* is part of a primary key or part of a foreign key.

Explain what problem the consultant foresaw in the use of the *Name* attribute. Explain how that problem was avoided. The consultant added an attribute to the data model that was not part of the users' world. Explain why that attribute will not add unnecessary complication to the users' work experiences.

MyMISLab MyMISLab is an online learning and testing environment that features the perfect study tools to help you master the concepts covered in this chapter. Log in to MyMISLab to test your knowledge of key chapter concepts and explore additional practice tools, including videos, flashcards, annotated text figures, and more!

Key Terms and Concepts

Attribute 159

Crow's foot 160

Crow's-foot diagram 161

Data integrity problem 162

Data model 158

Entity 159

Entity-relationship (E-R)
  data model 158

Entity-relationship (E-R)
  diagram 160

Identifier 159

Many-to-many (N:M)
  relationship 160

Maximum cardinality 161

Minimum cardinality 161

Normal form 163

Normalization 162

One-to-many (1:N)
  relationship 160

Relationship 159

Unified Modelling
  Language (UML) 158

Using Your Knowledge

AE5a-1. Explain how you could use a spreadsheet to solve the volunteer problem at the television station. What data would you place in each column and row of your spreadsheet? Name each column and row of your spreadsheet. What advantages does a database have over a spreadsheet for this problem? Compare and contrast your spreadsheet solution to the database solution shown in the design in Figure AE5a-14 and the data entry form in Figure AE5a-15.

AE5a-2. Suppose you are asked to build a database application for a sports league. Assume that your application is to keep track of teams and equipment that is checked out to teams. Explain the steps that need to be taken to develop this application. Specify entities and their relationships. Build an E-R diagram. Ensure your diagram shows both minimum and maximum cardinalities. Transform your E-R diagram into a relational design.

AE5a-3. Suppose you are asked to build a database application for a bicycle rental shop. Assume your database is to track customers, bicycles, and rentals. Explain the steps that need to be taken to develop this application. Specify entities and their relationships. Build an E-R diagram. Ensure your diagram shows both minimum and maximum cardinalities. Transform your E-R diagram into a relational design.

MyMISLab

Go to MyMISLab for auto-graded writing questions as well as the following assisted-graded writing questions:

AE5a-4. Assume you work at the television station and are asked to evaluate the data model in Figure AE5a-12. Suppose that you want to differentiate between prospects who have worked in the past and those who have never worked, but who are prospects for future work. Say that one of the data modelers tells you, "No problem. We'll know that because any *Prospect* entity that has no relationship to a *Work* entity is a prospect who has never worked." Restate the data modeler's response in your own words. Does this seem like a satisfactory solution? What if you want to keep *Prospect* data that pertains only to prospects who have worked? (No such attributes are shown in *Prospect* in Figure AE5a-12, but say there is an attribute such as *YearFirstVolunteered* or some other attribute that pertains to prospects who have worked in the past.) Show an alternative E-R diagram that would differentiate between prospects who have worked in the past and those who have not. Compare and contrast your alternative to the one shown in Figure AE5a-12.

AE5a-5. Suppose you manage a department that is developing a database application. The IT professionals who are developing the system ask you to identify two employees to evaluate data models. What criteria would you use in selecting those employees? What instructions would you give them? Suppose one of the employees says to you, "I go to those meetings, but I just don't understand what they're talking about." How would you respond? Suppose that you go to one of those meetings and don't understand what they're talking about. What would you do? Describe a role for a prototype in this situation. How would you justify the request for a prototype?

AE5a-6. MyMISLab Only – comprehensive writing assignment for this chapter.

Chapter Extension 5b

Chapter 5 provides the background for this extension.

Using Microsoft Access 2013

In this chapter extension, you will learn fundamental techniques for creating a database and forms, queries, and reports with Microsoft Access.

Q1 How Do You Create Tables?

Before using Access or any other DBMS, you should have created a data model from the users' requirements, and you must transform that data model into a database design. For the purpose of this chapter extension, we will use a portion of the database design created in Chapter Extension 5a. Specifically, we will create a database with the following two tables:

```
PROSPECT (ProspectID, Name, Street, City, Province,
Postal Code, Email Address)
```

and

```
WORK (ProspectID, Date, Hour, NumCalls, TotalDonations)
```

As in Chapter Extension 5a, an underlined attribute is the primary key and an italicized attribute is a foreign key. Thus, ProspectID is the primary key of PROSPECT, and the combination (ProspectID, Date, Hour) is the primary key of WORK. *ProspectID* is also a foreign key in WORK; hence it is shown both underlined and in italics. The data model and database design in Chapter Extension 5a specified that the key of WORK is the combination (*ProspectID*, Date). Upon review, the users stated that prospects will sometimes work more than one time during the day. For scheduling and other purposes, the users want to record both the date and the hour that someone worked. Accordingly, the database designer added the Hour attribute and made it part of the key of WORK.

The assumption in this design is that each row of WORK represents an hour's work. If a prospect works for consecutive hours, say from 7 to 9 p.m., then he or she would have two rows, one with an Hour value of 1900 and a second with an Hour value of 2000. Figure AE5b-1 further documents the attributes of the design. Sample data for this table are shown in Figure AE5b-2 on page 175.

Note the ambiguity in the name *PROSPECT*. Before someone has become a volunteer, he is a prospect, and the term is fine. However, once that person has actually done work, he is no longer merely a prospect. This ambiguity occurs because the database is used both for finding volunteers and for recording their experiences once they have joined. We could rename PROSPECT as VOLUNTEER, but then we'd still have a problem. The person is not a volunteer until he has actually agreed to become one. So, for now, just assume that a PROSPECT who has one or more WORK records is no longer a prospect but has become a volunteer.

Starting Access

Figure AE5b-3 shows the opening screen for Microsoft Access 2013. (If you use another version of Access, your screen will appear differently, but the essentials will be the same.) To create a new database, select Blank desktop database in the templates

Study Questions

Q1 How do you create tables?

Q2 How do you create relationships?

Q3 How do you create a data entry form?

Q4 How do you create queries using the query design tool?

Q5 How do you create a report?

MyMISLab

Visit MyMISLab for simulations, tutorials, and end-of-chapter problems.

Table	Attribute (Column)	Remarks	Data Type	Example Value
PROSPECT	ProspectID	An identifying number provided by Access when a row is created. The value has no meaning to the user.	AutoNumber	55
PROSPECT	Name	A prospect's name.	Text (50)	Emily Jones
PROSPECT	Street	Prospect's contact street address.	Text (50)	123 West Elm
PROSPECT	City	Prospect's contact city.	Text (40)	Miami
PROSPECT	State	Prospect's contact state.	Text (2)	FL
PROSPECT	Zip	Prospect's contact zip code.	Text (10)	30210-4567 or 30210
PROSPECT	EmailAddress	Prospect's contact email address.	Text (65)	ExamplePerson@somewhere.com
WORK	ProspectID	Foreign key to PROSPECT. Value provided when relationship is created.	Number (Long Integer)	55
WORK	Work Date	The date of work.	Date	9/15/2014
WORK	Hour	The hour at which work is started.	Number (Integer)	0800 or 1900 (7 PM)
WORK	NumCalls	The number of calls taken.	Number (Integer)	25
WORK	TotalDonations	The total of donations generated.	Currency	$10 575
WORK	AvgDonations	The average donation.	Currency	To be computed in queries and reports

Figure AE5b-1
Attributes of the Database

displayed in the centre of the screen, as shown in Figure AE5b-4. Then type the name of your new database under *File Name* (here we use *Volunteer*). Access will suggest a directory; change it if you want to use another one, and then click *Create*. You will see the screen shown in Figure AE5b-5 on page 176.

Creating Tables

Access opens the new database by creating a default table named Table. We want to modify the design of this table, so in the upper left-hand corner, where you see a pencil and a right angle square, click *View* and select *Design View*. Access will ask you to name your table. Enter *PROSPECT* and click *OK*. Your screen will appear as in Figure AE5b-6 on page 177.

The screen shown in Figure AE5b-6 has three parts. The left-hand pane lists all of the tables in your database. At this point, you should see only the PROSPECT table in this list. We will use the upper part of the right-hand pane to enter the name of each attribute (which Access calls *Fields*) and its *Data Type*. We can optionally enter a *Description* of that field. The Description is used for documentation; as you will see, Access displays any text you enter as help text on forms. In the bottom part of the screen, we set the properties of each field (or attribute, using our term). To start

Example of PROSPECT Data

Prospect ID	Name	Street	City	State	Zip	EmailAddress
1	Carson Wu	123 Elm	Los Angeles	CA	98007	Carson@somewhere.com
2	Emily Jackson	2234 17th	Pasadena	CA	97005	JacksonE@elsewhere.com
3	Peter Lopez	331 Moses Drive	Fullerton	CA	97330	PeterL@ourcompany.com
4	Lynda Dennison	54 Strand	Manhattan Beach	CA	97881	Lynda@somewhere.com
5	Carter Fillmore III	Restricted	Brentwood	CA	98220	Carter@BigBucks.com
6	CJ Greene	77 Sunset Strip	Hollywood	CA	97330	CJ@HollywoodProducers.com
7	Jolisa Jackson	2234 17th	Pasadena	CA	97005	JacksonJ@elsewhere.com

Example of WORK Data

ProspectID	Work Date	Hour	NumCalls	TotalDonations
3	9/15/2014	1600	17	8755
3	9/15/2014	1700	28	11578
5	9/15/2014	1700	25	15588
5	9/20/2014	1800	37	29887
5	9/10/2015	1700	30	21440
5	9/10/2015	1800	39	37050
6	9/15/2014	1700	33	21445
6	9/16/2014	1700	27	17558
6	9/10/2015	1700	31	22550
6	9/10/2015	1800	37	36700

Figure AE5b-2
Sample Data

designing the table, replace the *Field Name* ID with *ProspectID*. Access has already set its type to *AutoNumber*, so you can leave that alone.

To create the rest of the table, enter the *Field Names* and *Data Types* according to our design.[1] Figure AE5b-7 shows how to set the length of a Short Text Data Type. In this figure, the user has set City to *Text* and then has moved down into the bottom part of this form and entered 40 under *Field Size.* You will do the same thing to set the length of all of the Short Text Field Names. The complete table is shown in Figure AE5b-8.

---

[1] When you enter the Name field, Access will give you an error message. Ignore the message and click OK. The fact that you are using a reserved word for this example will not be a problem. If you want to be safe, you could enter *PName* or *ProspectName* (rather than *Name*) and avoid this issue. Many people, including me, believe that Access is poorly designed in this respect. You ought to be able to enter any value for Field Name the way you want. Access should stay out of your way; you shouldn't have to stay out of its way!

Figure AE5b-3

Opening Screen for Microsoft
Access 2013

Source: Microsoft Access 2013.

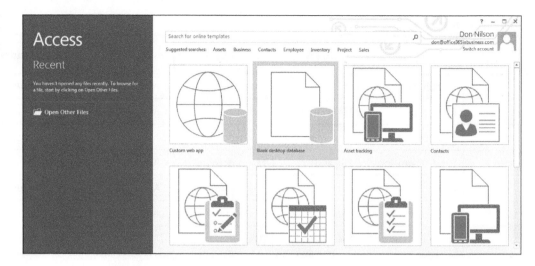

Figure AE5b-4

Naming a Desktop Database

Source: Microsoft Access 2013.

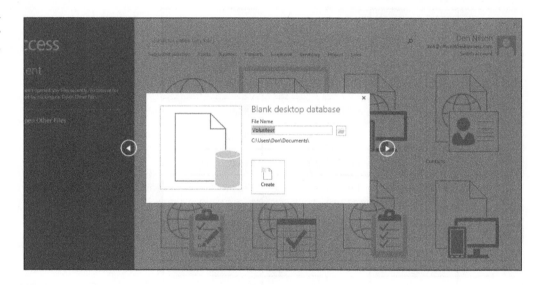

Figure AE5b-5

Access Opens with an Initial
Table Definition

Source: Microsoft Access 2013.

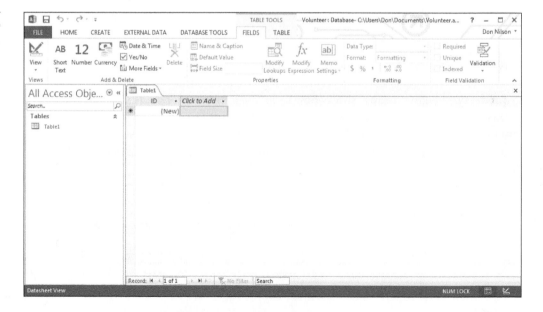

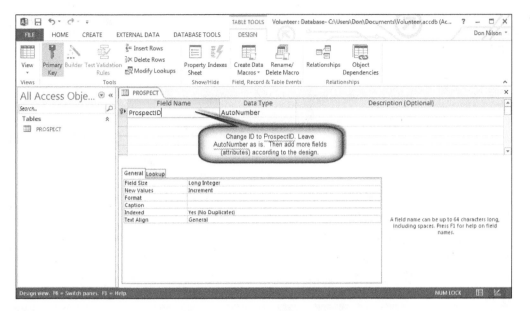

Figure AE5b-6

Creating Tables in Access, Step 1

Source: Microsoft Access 2013.

ProspectID is the primary key of this table, and the little key icon next to the ProspectID *Field Name* means Access has already made it so. If we wanted to make another field the primary key, we would highlight that field and then click the *Primary Key* icon in the left-hand portion of the *DESIGN* ribbon.

Follow similar steps to create the WORK table. The only difference is that you will need to create a key of the three columns (ProspectID, WorkDate, Hour). To create that key, highlight all three rows by dragging over the three squares to the left of the names of ProspectID, WorkDate, and Hour. Then click the *Key* icon in the *DESIGN* ribbon. Also, change the *Required Field Property* for each of these columns to *Yes.* The finished WORK table is shown in Figure AE5b-9. This figure also shows that the user selected *Number* for the *Data Type* of *NumCalls* and then set its *Field Size* (lower pane) to *Integer.* This same technique was used to set the *Data Type* of ProspectID (in WORK) to *Number* (*Field Size* of *Long Integer*) and that of *Hour* to *Number* (*Field Size* of *Integer*).

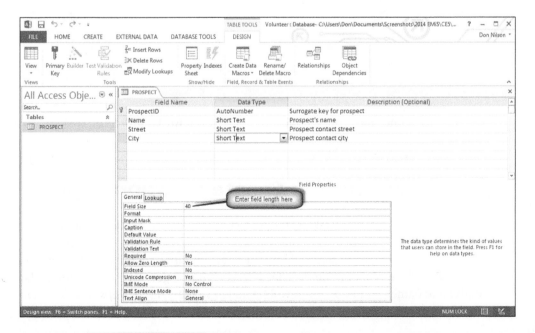

Figure AE5b-7

Creating Tables in Access, Step 2

Source: Microsoft Access 2013.

Figure AE5b-8

Complete Sample
PROSPECT Table

Source: Microsoft Access 2013.

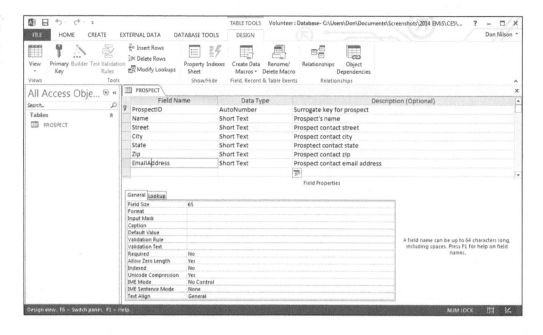

Figure AE5b-9

Finished WORK Table

Source: Microsoft Access 2013.

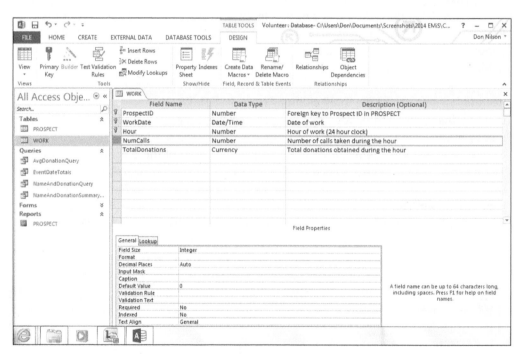

At this point, close both tables and save your work. You have created your first database!

02 How Do You Create Relationships?

After you have created the tables, the next step is to define relationships. To do so, click the *DATABASE TOOLS* tab in the ribbon and then click the *Relationships* icon near the left-hand side of that ribbon. The *Relationships* window will open and the *Show Table* dialog box will be displayed, as shown in Figure AE5b-10. Double-click both table names and both tables will be added to the *Relationships* window. Close the *Show Table* dialog box.

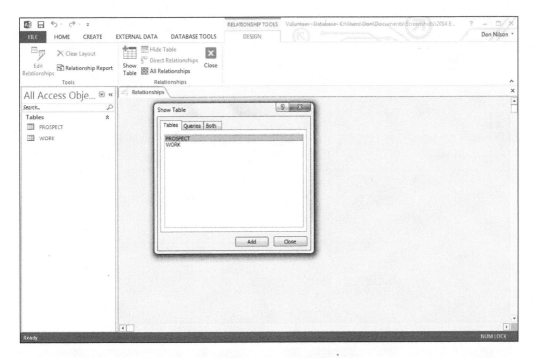

Figure AE5b-10

The Show Table Dialog Box in Access

Source: Microsoft Access 2013.

To create the relationship between these two tables, click on the attribute *ProspectID* in PROSPECT and drag that attribute on top of the *ProspectID* in WORK. (It is important to drag *ProspectID* from PROSPECT to WORK and not the reverse.) When you do this, the screen shown in Figure AE5b-11 will appear.

In the dialog box, click *Enforce Referential Integrity*, click *Cascade Update Related Fields*, and then click *Cascade Delete Related Records.* The specifics of these actions are beyond the scope of our discussion. Just understand that clicking these options will cause Access to make sure that ProspectID values in WORK also exist in PROSPECT. The completed relationship is shown in Figure AE5b-12. The notation *1...* ∞ at the end of the relationship line means that one row of PROSPECT can be related to an unlimited number (*N*) of rows in WORK. Close the *Relationships* window and save the changes when requested to do so. You now have a database with two tables and a relationship.

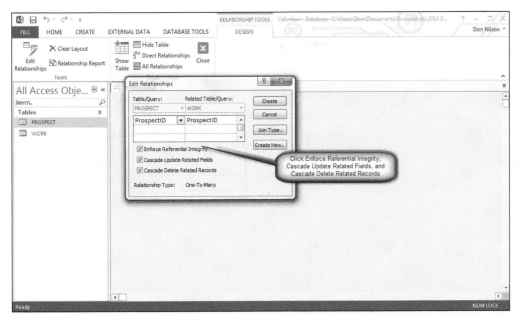

Figure AE5b-11

Creating a Relationship Between Two Tables

Source: Microsoft Access 2013.

Figure AE5b-12

Completed Relationship
Between PROSPECT and
WORK Tables

Source: Microsoft Access 2013.

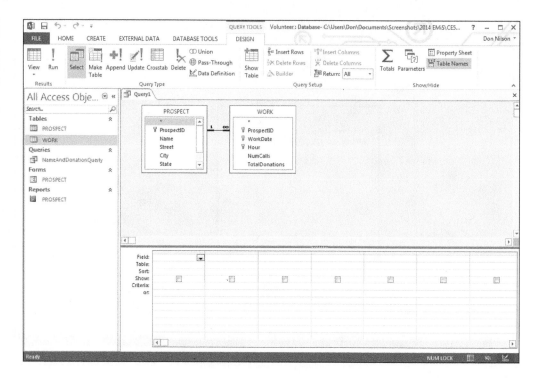

The next step is to enter data. To enter data, double-click the table name in the *left hand* pane. The table will appear, and you can enter values into each cell. You cannot and need not enter values for the *ProspectID* field. Access will create those values for you.

Enter the data in Figure AE5b-2 for both PROSPECT and WORK, and you will see a display like that in Figures AE5b-13a and AE5b-13b. Examine the lower left-hand corner of Figure AE5b-13b. The text *Foreign key to ProspectID in PROSPECT* is the Description that you provided when you defined the ProspectID column when the WORK table was created. (You can see this in the ProspectID column in Figure AE5b-9.) Access displays this text because the focus is on the ProspectID column in the active table window (WORK). Move your cursor from field to field and watch this text change.

Figure AE5b-13a

Tables with Data Entered for
PROSPECT

Source: Microsoft Access 2013.

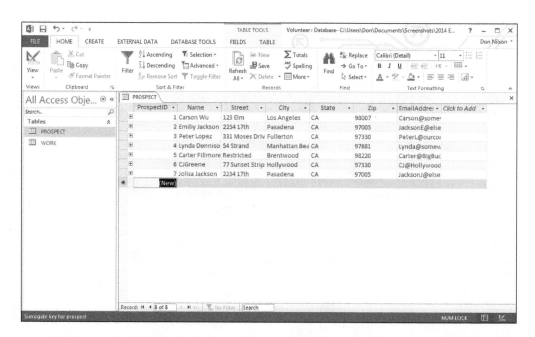

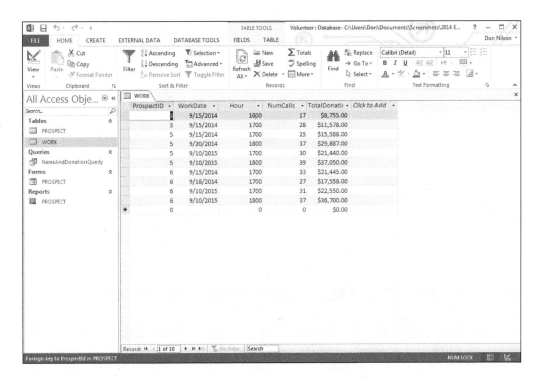

Figure AE5b-13b

Tables with Data Entered for WORK

Source: Microsoft Access 2013.

Q3 How Do You Create a Data Entry Form?

Access provides several alternatives for creating a data entry form. The first is to use the default table display, as you did when you entered the data shown in Figure AE5b-13. In the PROSPECT table, notice the plus sign on the left. If you click those plus signs, you will see the PROSPECT rows with their related WORK rows, as shown in Figure AE5b-14. This display, although convenient, is limited in its

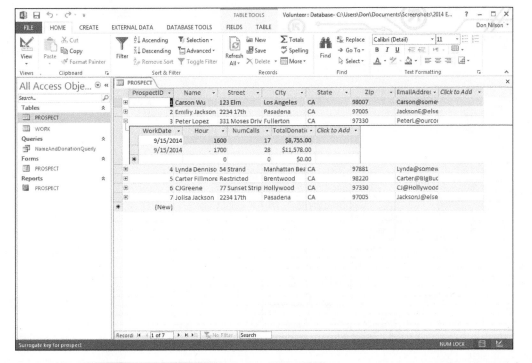

Figure AE5b-14

Default Table Display

Source: Microsoft Access 2013.

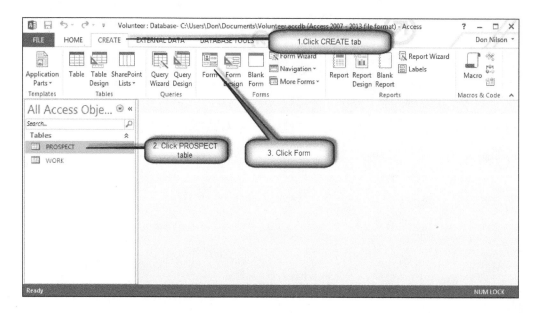

capability. It also does not provide a very pleasing user interface. For more generality and better design, you can use the Access form generator.

Access can generate a data entry form that is more pleasing to view and easier to use than that in Figure AE5b-14. The process is shown in Figure AE5b-15. First, click the *CREATE* tab to open the *CREATE* ribbon. Next, click the PROSPECT table (this causes Access to create a form for PROSPECT). Finally, click *Form.* Access uses metadata about the tables and their relationship to create the data entry form in Figure AE5b-16.

You can use this form to modify data; just type over any data that you wish to change. You can also add data. To add work data, just click in the last row of the work grid; in this case that would be the first row of this grid. To delete a record, click the *HOME* tab, and then in the *Records* section click the down arrow next to *Delete* and select *Delete Record.* This action will delete the prospect data and all related work data (not shown in Figure AE5b-16).

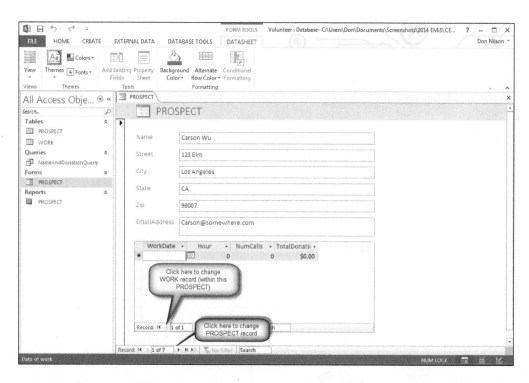

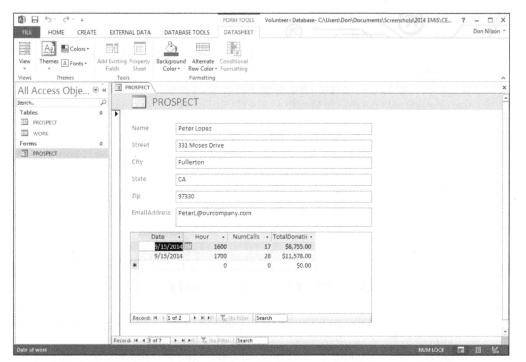

Figure AE5b-17

Reformatted Data Entry Form

Source: Microsoft Access 2013.

This form is fine, but we can make it better. For one, ProspectID is a surrogate key and has no meaning to the user. Access uses that key to keep track of each PROSPECT row. Because it has no meaning to the user (in fact, the user cannot change or otherwise modify its value), we should remove it from the form. Also, we might like to reduce the size of the fields as well as reduce the size of the work area and centre it on the form. Figure AE5b-17 shows the form after these changes. It is smaller and cleaner, and it will be easier to use.

The data about a prospect is shown in the top portion of this form, and data about that person's work sessions is shown in the bottom portion. The user of this form has clicked the arrow at the bottom of the form to bring up the third Prospect record, the one for Peter Lopez. Notice that he has two work sessions. If you click the arrow in the next-to-last row of this form, you will change the focus of the work record. To make the changes shown, see the steps illustrated in Figure AE5b-18. First, right-click

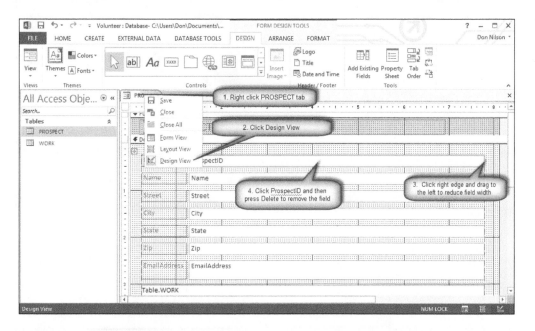

Figure AE5b-18

Process for Reformatting Data Entry Form

Source: Microsoft Access 2013.

the PROSPECT tab and then select *Design View.* The form will open in Design mode; click the right edge of the rightmost rectangle and, holding your mouse down, drag to the left. Access will reduce the width of each of these fields as well as the table.

Finally, click *ProspectID*, as shown in step 4. Press the *Delete* key, and the ProspectID field will be removed from the form. Click *View/Form View*, and your form should look like that in Figure AE5b-17. You can go back to *Design View* to make more adjustments, if necessary.

To save your form, either close it and Access will give you the chance to save it or click *FILE* and select *Save.* Save with an informative file name, such as PROSPECT Data Entry Form.

There are many options for customizing Access forms. You can learn about them if you take a database processing class after you complete this MIS class.

Q4 How Do You Create Queries Using the Query Design Tool?

Like all relational DBMS products, Access can process the SQL query language. Learning that language, however, is beyond the scope of this textbook. However, Access does provide a graphical interface that we can use to create and process queries, and that graphical interface will generate SQL statements for us, behind the scenes.

To begin, first clean up your screen by closing the PROSPECT Data Entry Form. Click the *CREATE* tab in the ribbon, and in the *Queries* section click the *Query Design* button. You should see the display shown in Figure AE5b-19. Double-click the names of both the PROSPECT and WORK tables, and close the *Show Table* window. Access will have placed both tables into the query design form, as shown in Figure AE5b-20. Notice that Access remembers the relationship between the two tables (shown by the line connecting ProspectID in PROSPECT to the same attribute in WORK).

To create a query, drag columns out of the PROSPECT and WORK tables into the grid in the lower part of the query definition form. In Figure AE5b-21, the *Name, EmailAddress, NumCalls,* and *TotalDonations* columns have been placed into that

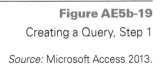

Figure AE5b-19

Creating a Query, Step 1

Source: Microsoft Access 2013.

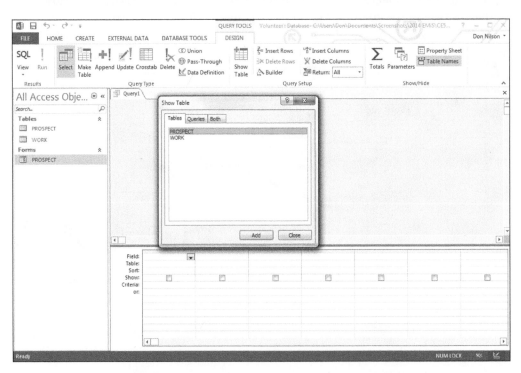

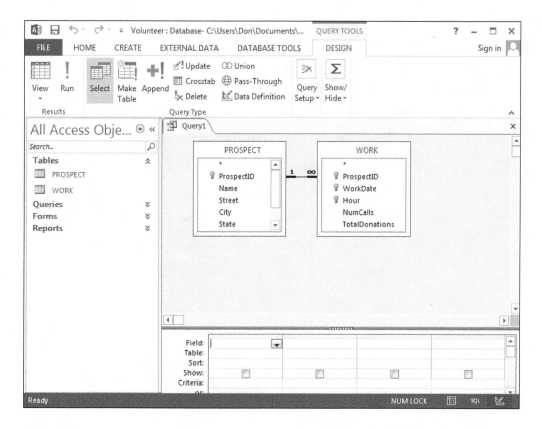

Figure AE5b-20

Creating a Query, Step 2

Source: Microsoft Access 2013.

grid. Note, too, that the *Ascending* keyword has been selected for the *Name* column. That selection tells Access to present the data in alphabetical order by name.

If you now click the red exclamation point labeled *Run* in the *Results* section of the ribbon, the result shown in Figure AE5b-22 will appear. Notice that only PROSPECT rows that have at least one WORK row are shown. By default, for queries of two or

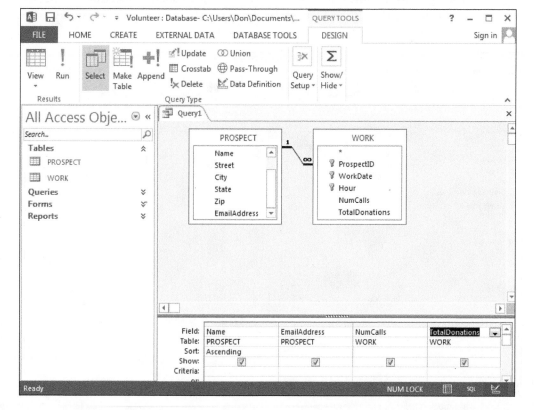

Figure AE5b-21

Creating a Query, Step 3

Source: Microsoft Access 2013.

Figure AE5b-22

Results of *TotalDonations Query*

Source: Microsoft Access 2013.

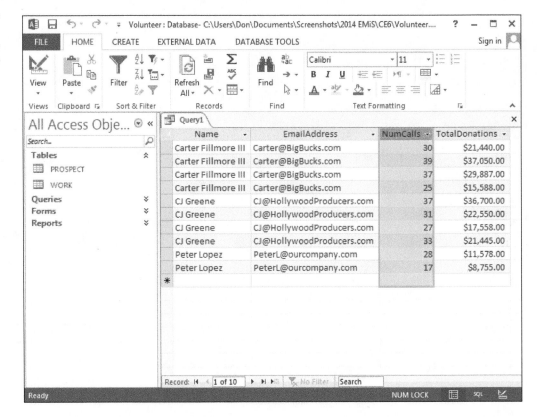

more tables Access (and SQL) shows only those rows that have value matches in both tables. Save the query under the name *NameAndDonationQuery*.

Queries have many useful purposes. For example, suppose we want to see the average dollar value of donations generated per hour of work. This query, which is just slightly beyond the scope of this chapter extension, can readily be created using either the Access graphical tool or SQL. The results of such a query are shown in Figure AE5b-23. This query processes the *NameAndDonationQuery* query just

Figure AE5b-23

Result of More Advanced Query

Source: Microsoft Access 2013.

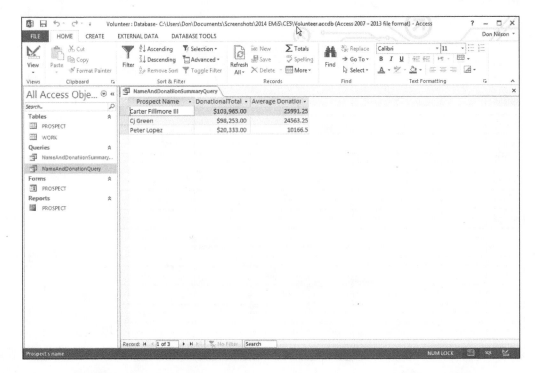

created. Again, if you take a database class, you will learn how to create queries like this and others of even greater complexity (and utility).

Q5 How Do You Create a Report?

You can create a report using a process similar to that for forms, but the report won't include the WORK data. To create a report with data from two or more tables, we must use the Report Wizard. Click the *CREATE* tab, and then in the Reports section click *Report Wizard.*

Now, click *Table: PROSPECT* in the *Table/Queries* combo box, highlight *Name* in the *Available Fields* list, and click the single chevron (>) to add *Name* to the report. You will see the display shown in Figure AE5b-24.

Using a similar process, add *EmailAddress.* Then select *Table: WORK* in the *Table/ Queries* combo box and add *WorkDate, Hour, NumCalls,* and *TotalDonations.* Click *Finish,* and you will see the report shown in Figure AE5b-25. (By the way, we are skipping numerous options that Access provides in creating reports.)

We will consider just one of those options now. Suppose we want to show the total donations that a prospect has obtained, for all hours of his or her work. To do that, right-click the *PROSPECT* tab, and then click *Design View.* Your report will appear as shown in Figure AE5b-26. (If it does not appear like this, click *View, Design View* in the ribbon.)

In the ribbon, click *Group & Sort* in the *Grouping & Totals* section. In the bottom of the form, under Group, Sort, and Total click *More,* and then click the down arrow next to the phrase *with no totals.* Next, select *TotalDonations* from the *Total On* box, and then check *Show Grand Total* and *Show subtotal in group footer,* as illustrated in Figure AE5b-27.

Click the *Report* icon in the *View* section of the ribbon, and you will see the report shown in Figure AE5b-28. The only remaining problem is that the label *NumCalls* is

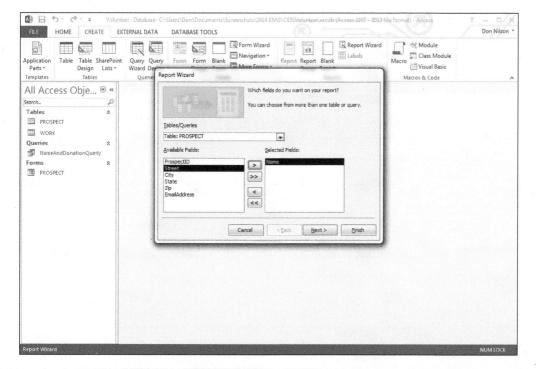

Figure AE5b-24

Selecting Data to Show in a Report

Source: Microsoft Access 2013.

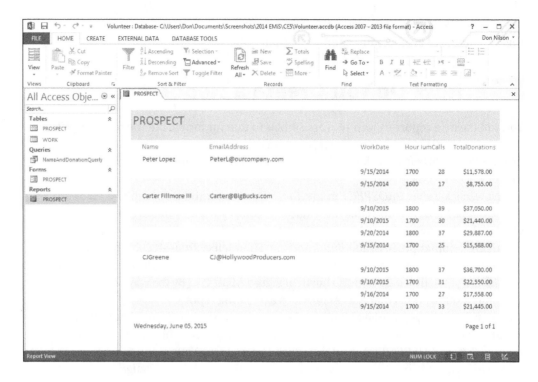

cut off. We need to expand the box that contains this value. To do so, select *Layout View* from *View* in the ribbon, click *Date*, and then slide it slightly to the left. Do the same with *Hour*. Then expand *NumCalls* until you can see all of the label, as shown in Figure AE5b-29. Click *Report View* in *View*, and your report should appear as shown in Figure AE5b-30.

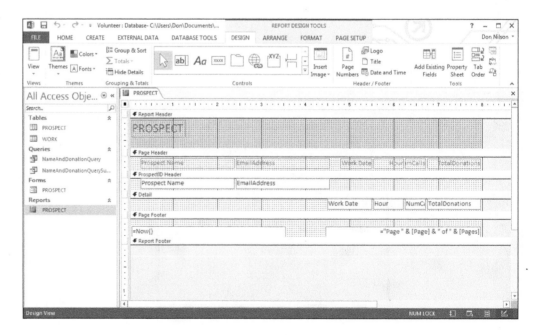

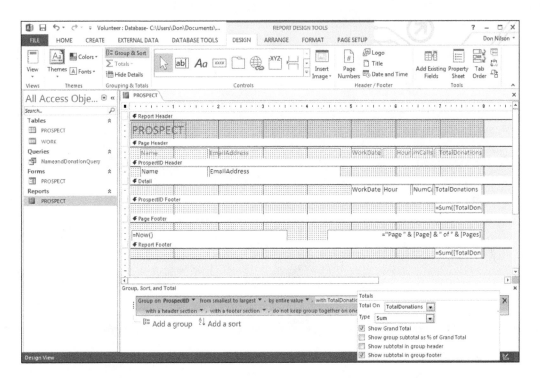

Figure AE5b-27

Creating a Sum of *TotalDonations* for Each Prospect

Source: Microsoft Access 2013.

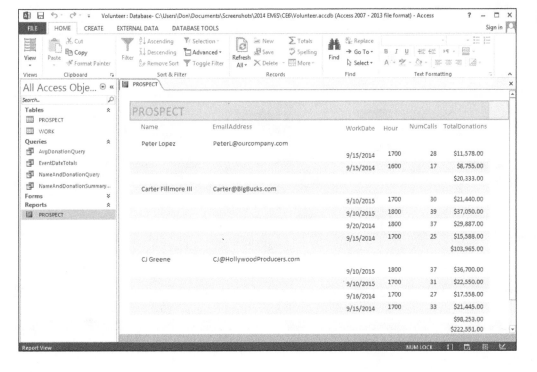

Figure AE5b-28

Report with Sum of *TotalDonations*

Source: Microsoft Access 2013.

Figure AE5b-29

Increasing the Size of the *NumCalls* Field

Source: Microsoft Access 2013.

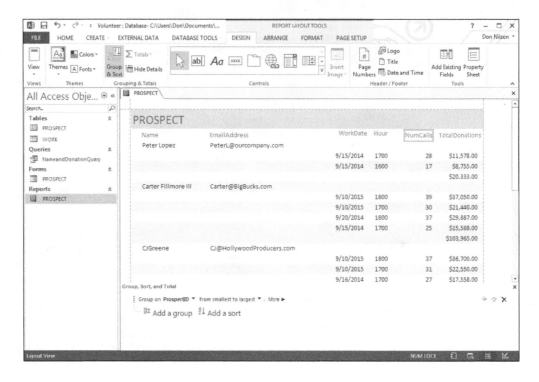

Figure AE5b-30

Final Version of Report

Source: Microsoft Access 2013.

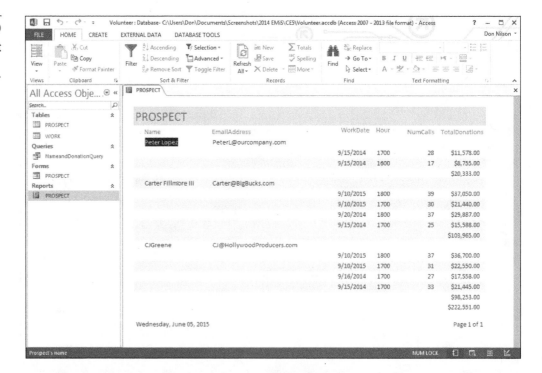

Active Review

Use this Active Review to verify that you understand the ideas and concepts in this chapter extension's study questions.

For this Active Review, assume that you are creating a database application with the following two tables:

CUSTOMER (*CustomerID*, Name, Email)

CONTACT (*CustomerID*, *Date*, Subject)

Q1 How do you create tables?

Open Access and create a new database with a name of your choosing. Create the CUSTOMER and CONTACT tables. Assume the following data types:

Attribute (Field)	Data Type
CustomerID (in CUSTOMER)	AutoNumber
Name	Text (50)
Email	Text (75)
CustomerID (in CONTACT)	Number (long integer)
Date	Date
Subject	Text (200)

Add Description entries to the Field definitions that you think are appropriate.

Q2 How do you create relationships?

Open the *Relationships* window and create a relationship from CUSTOMER to CONTACT using the CustomerID attribute. Click all of the check boxes. Enter sample data. Add at least five rows to CUSTOMER and at least seven rows to CONTACT. Ensure that some CUSTOMER rows have no matching CONTACT rows.

Q3 How do you create a data entry form?

Open the default data entry form for the CUSTOMER table. Click the CUSTOMER rows to display the related CONTACT data. Now use the *Form* tool to create a data entry form. Navigate through that form to see that the CONTACT rows are correctly connected to the CUSTOMER rows. Adjust spacing as you deem appropriate while removing the CustomerID field from the CUSTOMER section.

Q4 How do you create queries using the query design tool?

Create a query that displays Name, Email, Date, and Subject. Sort the results of Name in alphabetical order.

Q5 How do you create a report?

Use the Report Wizard to create a report that has Name, Email, Date, and Subject. View that report. Add a group total for each CUSTOMER that counts the number of contacts for each customer. Follow the procedure shown, except instead of selecting Sum for Type choose *Count Records* instead.

MyMISLab   MyMISLab is an online learning and testing environment that features the perfect study tools to help you master the concepts covered in this chapter. Log in to MyMISLab to test your knowledge of key chapter concepts and explore additional practice tools, including videos, flashcards, annotated text figures, and more!

Using Your Knowledge

AE5b-1. Answer question AE5a-2 at the end of Chapter Extension 5a (page 171). Use Access to implement your database design. Create the tables and add sample data. Create a data entry form that shows teams and the equipment they have checked out. Verify that the form correctly processes new checkouts, changes to checkouts, and equipment returns. Create a report that shows each team, the items they have checked out, and the number of items they have checked out. (Use *Count Records* as explained in Active Review Q5.)

AE5b-2. Answer question AE5a-3 at the end of Chapter Extension 5a (page 171). Create an Access database for the CUSTOMER and RENTAL tables only. Create the tables and add sample data. Create a data entry form that shows customers and all of their rentals (assume customers rent bicycles more than once). Verify that the form correctly processes new rentals, changes to rentals, and rental returns. Create a report that shows each customer, the rentals they have made, and the total rental fee for all of their rentals.

There are no Assisted-graded writing questions in this chapter extension.

6 Networks and Collaboration

Running Case

"This is definitely not good, but I guess it could be a lot worse" was just one of the things that Marlo was thinking as she tried to stay calm and decide what to do next. The day had started off normally enough—she had checked in with the staff and been given a thumbs up that the biggest technical issue was a low toner light on one of the printers (her initial thought had been to take it out and give it a shake—something that she had learned could usually save money by yielding 50 more pages). But, then, as she made herself a cappuccino, she ran into one of the guests, and her day darkened. The guest, head of human resources at a global fast food company, mentioned that when she was browsing the hotel's intranet page to reserve a couple of bicycles, she had noticed that she could access what looked like a complete list of The 1881 files! Marlo quickly assured the guest that this was definitely not normal and that she would immediately take action and get back to her.

So many thoughts were running through her head. Marlo knew that this was a new problem because at the beginning of the season, a group of computer science students from the local university had audited the configuration as part of a class project, and everything had been set up correctly. Security was something that the owners took very seriously, likely because of their backgrounds in investment banking. Marlo would have to quickly alert them, but first she wanted to size up the situation. She thought back to one of her MIS classes and wished she had paid more attention to the lecture on security and that she had developed a checklist. Marlo was not the sort to panic—working at a hotel was definitely not a place to be if you could not handle any sort of change—and so as she walked back to her desk she began to

identify her next steps. She knew some of the questions that the owners would ask: What is the impact? How long has it been going
on? How do we fix and prevent other similar problems? What
do we tell our guests? First things first, she thought.

Study Questions

Q1 Why should I care about networks?

Q2 What is a computer network?

Q3 What are the components of a LAN?

Q4 Why is mobile computing important?

Q5 What do I need to know about connecting to the internet?

Q6 How does email actually work?

Q7 What are firewalls, encryption, and VPNs?

Q8 How does a search engine work?

👁‑[Watch

Go to MyMISLab to watch a video about data communications.

👁‑[Watch

Go to MyMISLab to watch a video about alternatives for a WAN.

Q1 **Why Should I Care About Networks?**

Picture this: You have flown in to St. John's, Newfoundland, for a business trip. It is your first time in the city. The night is young, and you find yourself sitting in the Cabot Club in the Fairmont Newfoundland. You have just finished savouring your porcini-crusted sea scallops, and you are relaxing and taking in the harbour view. Suddenly, your smartphone rings. It is your friend (who was supposed to meet you there for dinner). You can barely hear your friend's voice over the music in the background. "You've got to get down here," he says. "The Barenaked Ladies are playing here at O'Reilly's on George Street . . . I'm calling from a public phone . . . I've only got 50 cents and—." Your cellphone drops the call. You use your credit card to pay the bill at your table and then make your way to your hotel room. You open the door with an electronic key. Along the way you think, "Where is George Street? Is there a cover charge at O'Reilly's?"

Once in your room, you connect your tablet to the wireless network. There is a slight delay, which seems like forever. You find 15 updates to your Twitter feed and what looks like an entire page of Facebook updates and snapchats just while you were at dinner. They can wait, however. You start up your browser and type "O'Reilly's George Street St. John's" into your favourite search engine. A few seconds roll by, and you wonder why the system seems so slow. The search comes back with information about the pub, and you think about using Street View to get a look at the building but think that it will be too slow and that it is only a short ride away. In the lobby, you use your debit card to get some cash from the automated banking machine (ABM). You use Halo to order a taxi and follow its progress. Once you get in you wait impatiently as the driver programs the destination into the global positioning system (GPS) receiver. Along the way, the navigation system tracks your progress and tells him where to turn. You get to the pub and take a selfie with the band. You send the picture, along with a text message, to your friends back in Montreal. When you get back to your hotel, you download a song just released by the Barenaked Ladies and sync up your iPod so that you can listen to the song on the flight home.

Let us think about this scenario. How many networks did you use? There was (1) the public switched telephone network (PSTN), which is tied to the cellphone network so that your friend could reach you; (2) the financial networks used for your ABM and credit card transactions (this could be a chapter in itself); (3) the local area network (LAN), which handles electronic key access in the hotel; (4) the wireless network (802.11) operating over a LAN (802.3), which provides wireless internet access in the hotel; (5) the wide area network (WAN), which provides internet access for email and web browsing; (6) the cellphone network using short message service (SMS) for the text message and multimedia messaging service (MMS) for the picture; and, finally, (7) the GPS in the automated navigation system, which is a satellite network service. That is a lot of networks!

Our brief history of electronic computing in Chapter 4 showed that computers become more useful to people when computing devices are connected to networks because they enable collaboration. You will learn in this chapter that when you are connected to the internet, you are actually part of a network of networks comprising millions of computers and other devices. This network allows you to send and receive email, browse webpages stored across the globe, download audio and video files, and even talk to friends using the telephone.

The technology behind computer networks is complex and can be intimidating to those who are unfamiliar with its terminology. And because a large number of electronic networks exist, it can become overwhelming. We will focus on only a few electronic networks that are related to computers. The goal of this chapter is not to turn you into a networking guru but to improve your understanding of the basic terminology of computer networks. Knowing these terms and understanding the basics of how networks work will make you a more informed user of network technology and help you realize the potential and limitations of computer networks in business.

Networks and Collaboration

Collaboration occurs when two or more people work together to achieve a common goal, result, or product. When collaboration is effective, the results of the group are greater than those that could be produced by any of the individuals working alone. Collaboration involves coordination and communication and often makes use of computer networks.

The effectiveness of a collaborative effort is driven by four critical factors (Figure 6-1):

- Communication skills and culture
- Communication systems
- Content management
- Workflow control

Communication skills and culture are often the key to effective collaborative effort. The ability to be a part of a group and to give and receive critical feedback is particularly important for employers. Surveys of companies frequently list communication as the most important skill they look for in employees. The reason for this is that the product of any group effort can improve only when group members believe that they can openly share and contribute ideas. This means that group members need to be able to constructively criticize each other's work without creating bad feelings and resentment and then improve their contributions based on that criticism. This can be difficult for many people, but it is essential to working well in groups.

The second important element is the availability of effective **communication systems**. Today, few collaborative meetings are conducted solely in-person. Group members may be travelling, be geographically distributed, or simply be unable to meet at the same time. In such cases, the availability of email, virtual private networks, instant messaging, video conferences, and more sophisticated communications systems is crucial. These communication systems depend on an organization's network technology, which is the focus of this chapter.

Another driver of effective collaboration is content management (the focus of the previous chapter). When multiple users are contributing and changing documents, schedules, task lists, assignments, and so forth, one user's work might interfere with another's, and keeping track of and synchronizing and integrating the

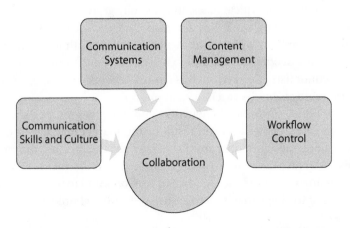

Figure 6-1

Critical Factors in Collaboration

various versions is critically important. Users need to manage content so that conflicts do not occur. Databases and content management systems help ensure that conflicts are handled correctly. It is also important to know why the changes were made, when, and by whom. Content management systems track and report these data. Finally, in some collaborations, members have different rights and privileges. Some team members have full permission to create, edit, and delete content, others are restricted to editing that content, and still others are restricted to a read-only status. Information systems and database management systems play a key role in enforcing such restrictions.

Workflow control is the final driver of effective collaboration. A **workflow** is a process or procedure by which content is created, edited, used, and discarded. The concept of workflow is very close to the concept of a business process, which we discussed in Chapter 2. The difference is that a business process focuses on delivering a good or a service *externally* to a customer, whereas a workflow focuses on the *internal* delivery of a good or a service to other employees in the organization. For a team that supports a website, for example, a workflow design might specify that certain members create webpages, other members review those pages, and still others post the reviewed and approved pages to the site. The workflow specifies a particular ordering of tasks and includes processes for handling rejected changes as well as for dealing with exceptions.

It is important to recognize that effective collaboration requires support for all four of these collaboration drivers, even if all the drivers are not equally important. For one-time, ad hoc workgroups (for example, group projects in this course), it might not be necessary to create and formalize workflows. However, for a team of engineers designing a new model of smartphone, a formally defined workflow is crucial. In this chapter, our focus is on understanding, at a high level, the network technologies that provide the foundation for communication systems. This understanding will allow you to make more effective choices for communication systems in your organizations.

Network Externalities

There is one fundamental fact about networks that is important to understand: In general, the larger the number of people using a network, the more valuable that network becomes. This phenomenon is called the network effect, or **network externality**. For example, consider YouTube (www.YouTube.com), which is a video-sharing website. The first person to join as a member gets almost no benefit—that person can only see the videos that he or she already has. The second user gets a little more benefit. As more and more people are added, the benefits get larger for everyone in the network.

When networks are first started, people often look for the critical mass. This is the point at which the value of being part of the network is larger than the cost of being on it. Once networks hit critical mass, they usually grow at a faster rate. That is why people who start these networks are interested in the critical mass. An example that you may be familiar with is Facebook versus Google+. Both may offer similar functionality, but most people will want to join and stay on the one where more of their friends are. Economists often refer to this type of network—where one can support all users and switching is hard—as a natural monopoly.

There are limits, of course, to networks and network growth. As a network continues to gain users, congestion can result or the market may become saturated or change (does anyone remember myspace?). When this occurs, the rate of growth diminishes and then either flattens or becomes negative. Therefore, as a business user it is important to understand the life cycle of networks and to recognize the value and costs rather than the hype that is often associated with technology.

WHAT IS THE GLOBAL POSITIONING SYSTEM (GPS)?

The **global positioning system (GPS)** uses a collection of dozens of satellites that orbit Earth and transmit precise microwave signals. A GPS receiver (perhaps you have one in your car) can calculate its position by measuring the distance between itself and several of the satellites. Believe it or not, with microwave signals from at least three satellites (triangulation), you can compute a GPS receiver's position. The GPS can even calculate the direction and speed of a

Neo Edmund/Shutterstock

Source: Courtesy of Neo Edmund/ Shutterstock Images.

GPS receiver. Combining the GPS with a map database has enabled the development of navigation systems that now sell for less than a few hundred dollars. GPS type of functionality has also been incorporated into cellphones although in many cases cellular towers rather than satellites are used for triangulation.

Q2 What Is a Computer Network?

A computer **network** is a collection of computers that transmit and/or receive electronic signals through transmission media. The **transmission media** might be physical media, such as copper cable and optical fibre (glass fibre) cable, or wireless media transmitting light or radio frequencies (including cellular and satellite systems). As shown in Figure 6-2, the three major types of networks are local area networks, wide area networks, and internets.

The **local area network (LAN)** connects devices within a relatively small, single geographical location. The number of connections can range from two to several hundred. The distinguishing characteristic of a LAN is that it is in *a single location*. **Wide area networks (WANs)** connect devices at different geographical locations.

This distinction between a single site and multiple sites is important. With a LAN, an organization can usually place communications lines wherever it wants because all lines reside on its premises. The same is not true for a WAN, however. A company with offices in Vancouver and Toronto cannot run fiber to connect the computers in the two cities. Instead, it must contract with a communications vendor that is licensed by the government and already has capacity or the authority to install more connections between the two cities.

An **internet** is a network of networks. Internets connect LANs, WANs, and other internets. The most famous internet is **the Internet**, the collection of networks that

Type	Characteristic
Local area network (LAN)	Computers connected at a single physical site
Wide area network (WAN)	Computers connected between two or more separated sites
The Internet and internets	Networks of networks

Figure 6-2

Major Network Types

you use when you send email or access a website. In addition to the internet, private networks of networks, called intranets, also exist.

The networks that comprise an internet use a large variety of communication methods and conventions, and data must flow seamlessly across them. To provide seamless flow, an elaborate scheme called a *layered protocol* is used. A **protocol** is a set of rules that communicating devices follow. There are many different protocols; some are used for LANs, some are used for WANs, some are used for internets and the internet, and some are used for all of these. The important point is that for devices to communicate, they must use the same protocol.

Q3 What Are the Components of a LAN?

A LAN is a group of computers connected together on a single site. Usually, the computers are located within a kilometre or so of each other, although longer distances are possible. The key distinction, however, is that all the computers are located on property owned or controlled by the company that operates the LAN.

Consider the LAN in Figure 6-3. Here, five computers and two printers connect via a **switch**, which is a special-purpose computer that receives and transmits messages on the LAN. In Figure 6-3, when Computer 1 accesses Printer 2, it does so by sending the print job to the switch, which then redirects that data to Printer 2.

Each device on a LAN (computer, printer, etc.) has a hardware component called a **network interface card (NIC)** that connects the device's circuitry to the network cable. The NIC works with programs in each device to implement the protocols necessary for communication. Newer machines have an integrated NIC, which is a NIC that is built into the computer. Many of the latest laptop computers go one step further and only include support for wireless networks. If you want to connect to a wired network, you must use a special adapter.

Figure 6-4 shows a typical NIC device. Each NIC has a unique identifier, which is called the **MAC (media access control) address**. The computers, printers, switches, and other devices on a LAN are connected using one of two media. Most connections are made using **unshielded twisted pair (UTP) cable**. Figure 6-5 shows a section of UTP cable that contains four pairs of twisted wire. (By the way, wires are twisted for reasons beyond aesthetics and style. Twisting the wires substantially reduces signal interference, which occurs when wires run over long distances.)

Figure 6-3
Local Area Network (LAN)

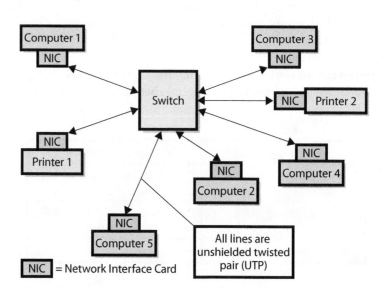

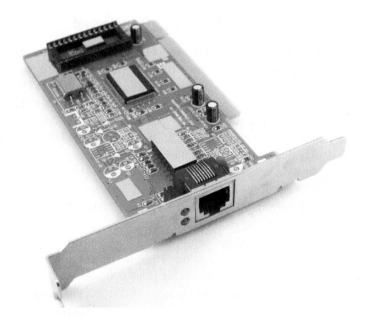

Figure 6-4
Network Interface Card (NIC)

Source: Sergei Devyatkin/Shutterstock.

Some LANs, usually those larger than the one in Figure 6-3, use more than one switch. Typically, in a building with several floors, a switch is placed on each floor, and the computers on that floor are connected to the switch with UTP cable. The switches on each floor are connected by a centrally located main switch, which is often located in a communications room.

The connections between switches can use UTP cable, but if they carry a lot of traffic or are far apart, UTP cable may be replaced by **optical fibre cables**. Optical cables have several advantages over other media beyond increased capacity. Although fragile (they are actually made of glass), fibre optics are resistant to signal interference, have greater transmission distance (which makes them ideal for undersea cables), and are more secure because the signals are optical pulses rather than electrical signals. Optical cables are wrapped in protective covers and use special connectors, which are shown as blue plugs in Figure 6-6.

Figure 6-5
Unshielded Twisted Pair (UTP) Cable

Source: deepspacedave/Shutterstock.

Figure 6-6
Optical Fibre Cable

Sources: (left) Lawrence Lawry/Getty Images; (right) Michael Smith/Getty Images.

The IEEE 802.3, or Ethernet, Protocol

For a LAN to work, all devices on the LAN must use the same protocol. The Institute for Electrical and Electronics Engineers (IEEE, pronounced "I triple E") sponsors committees that create and publish protocols and other standards. The committee that addresses LAN standards is called the *IEEE 802 Committee*. Thus, IEEE LAN protocols always start with the numbers 802.

The world's most popular protocol for LANs is based on the **IEEE 802.3 protocol**. This standard, also called **Ethernet**, specifies how messages are to be packaged and processed for transmission over the LAN.

Most personal computers today are equipped with an **onboard NIC** that supports **10/100/1000 Ethernet**. These products conform to the 802.3 specification and allow for transmission at a rate of 10, 100, or 1000 Mbps (megabits per second). By the way, the abbreviations used for communication speeds differ from those used for computer memory. For communications equipment, *k* stands for 1000, not 1024 as it does for memory. Similarly, *M* stands for 1 000 000, not 1024 1024; *G* stands for 1 000 000 000, not 1024 1024 1024. Thus, 100 Mbps is 100 000 000 bits per second. Note as well that communications speeds are expressed in *bits*, whereas memory sizes are expressed in *bytes*.

Wireless LANs

A wireless LAN is a computer network that allows users to connect to a network without using a network cable. Figure 6-7 shows a LAN in which two of the computers and one printer have wireless connections. A laptop, tablet, or **smartphone** equipped with a **wireless NIC (WNIC)** lets a user stay connected to his or her network without needing to plug in with a cable. Although many systems use the 802.11g wireless protocol, the faster 802.11n protocol, which allows speeds of up to 248 Mbps, is becoming increasingly popular. Other names for wireless LANs are "802.11," or "Wi-Fi."

Wireless LANs require one or more **access points (APs)** that wireless devices connect to. The AP then connects users to the wired network. The coverage of a wireless access point can range from 40 to 100 metres. But this depends on a variety of factors, including whether the location is indoors or outdoors (outdoors has longer range), the

Figure 6-7

Wireless Local Area Network

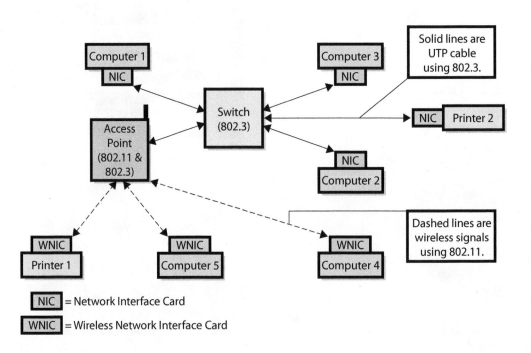

Type	Topology	Transmission Line	Transmission Speed	Equipment Used	Protocol Commonly Used	Remarks
Local Area Network	Local area network	UTP or optical fibre	10, 100, or 1000 Mbps, or 10 Gbps	Switch NIC UTP or optical	IEEE 802.3 (Ethernet)	Switches connect devices, multiple switches on all but small LANs.
	Local area network with wireless	UTP or optical for non-wireless connections	Up to 300 Mbps	Wireless access point Wireless NIC	IEEE 802.11n	Access point transforms wired LAN (802.3) to wireless LAN (802.11).
Wide Area Network	Dial-up modem to internet service provider (ISP)	Regular telephone	Up to 56 Kbps	Modem Telephone line	Modulation standards (V.32, V.90, V.92), PPP	Modulation required for first part of telephone line. Computer use blocks telephone use.
	DSL modem to ISP	DSL telephone	Personal: Upstream to 768 Kbps, downstream to 3 Mbps Business: to 7 Mbps	DSL modem DSL-capable telephone line	DSL	Can have computer and phone use simultaneously. Always connected.
	Cable modem to ISP	Cable TV lines to optical cable	Upstream to 768 Kbps Downstream 1–6 Mbps (30 Mbps in theory)	Cable modem Cable TV cable	Cable	Capacity is shared with other sites; performance varies depending on others' use.
	Point to point lines	Network of leased lines	T1–1.5 Mbps T3–44.7 Mbps OC48–2.5 Gbps OC768–40 Gbps	Access devices Optical cable Satellite	PPP	Span geographically distributed sites using lines provided by licensed communications vendors. Expensive to set up and manage.
	PSDN	Lease usage of private network	56 Kbps–40 Mbps+	Leased line to PSDN POP	Frame-relay ATM 10 Gbps and 40 Gbps Ethernet	Lease time on a public switched data network– operated by independent party. Ineffective for inter-company communication.
	Virtual private network (VPN)	Use the internet to provide private network	Varies with speed of connection to internet	VPN client software VPN server hardware and software	PPTP IPSec	Secure, private connection provides a tunnel through the internet. Can support inter-company communication.

Figure 6-8

Summary of LANs and WANs

weather, such obstructions as steel-reinforced concrete pillars, other devices that broadcast on a similar frequency, and the power output of devices. Devices called *repeaters* and *reflectors* are sometimes used to amplify and reflect signals to extend the range.

Figure 6-7 showed one of the computers and a printer in the LAN using both the 802.3 and 802.11 protocols. The WNICs operate according to the 802.11 protocol and connect to an AP. The NICs operate according to the 802.3 protocol and connect directly to the switch, which also operates on the 802.3 standard. The AP must be able to process messages according to both the 802.3 and 802.11 standards because it sends and receives wireless traffic using the 802.11 protocol and then communicates with the switch using the 802.3 protocol. If you understood this paragraph, then you are doing pretty well with network jargon! But there is always more to learn. The characteristics of LANs are summarized in the top part of Figure 6-8.

Knowledge of local area networks and wireless technology helped one student start a successful and profitable business while still in college. Read *Case Study 6* at the end of this chapter to find out how it was done.

Q4 Why Is Mobile Computing Important?

How do you access the internet? If you are like many people, you still use a personal computer for such things as writing reports and analysis. However, two trends have now become well established: (1) Your computer is more likely to be a portable laptop than a desktop; and (2) your new smartphone or other highly portable device (such as a tablet) is being used more often, especially when you are "on the go." Although there is no real agreement about what exactly a "smart" phone is, it is clear that cellular phones are no longer just phones but, rather, mobile devices that provide a wide variety of services. They are devices built for communication and collaboration and are, at the core of their designs, networking machines. Examples are Apple's iPhone (shown in Figure 6-9) or the latest Samsung Galaxy S5, which combine a powerful processor with sophisticated operating systems and cellular network technology to provide a host of applications, such as voice, text, email, web browsing, and much more, to their users. With these mobile devices, users can access email, instant message, respond via voice or text messaging, and browse the internet anytime and anywhere. These devices are already changing the way that people work, and the changes are likely to continue for some time.

Smartphones are also enabling new applications, which are often labelled **m-commerce** (mobile commerce), to allow users to conduct new kinds of transactions. Mobile banking and mobile ticket purchases at movie theatres and sporting events are examples of m-commerce, although this really is just the beginning. There are applications that allow you to track the delivery of your pizza, deposit a cheque using just a photograph, or see if a cheaper price can be obtained while you are shopping in a mall. Mobile coupons are also a fast growing service in m-commerce. Mobile coupons are replacing paper coupons with electronic versions, which are delivered to your phone and can be context sensitive. Imagine getting a coupon for $2 off a meal at 11:30 a.m. as you pass by a fast food outlet. Beyond mobility, m-commerce can also include aspects of collaboration. In a restaurant, for example, new applications that allow groups to allocate the cost among the members and pay electronically or even vote on choices are being developed. In many classes, perhaps even this one, students can interact among themselves, vote on choices, and even ask professors questions using their phones.

As a business student, you should consider how these changes will affect you. Traditionally, most people have thought about "work" as a place they go to, with an office, a phone, and a computer hooked into an organization's network. With the advent of notebook computers, workers are able to take their computing power with them when they leave the office. Mobile phones have done the same so now many people do not have a traditional (wired) telephone. Now smartphones and tablets enable you to access your organization's network and all the data and services available on WANs, such as the internet. And people are also storing their own personal information on these devices. With a smartphone, your office *is* your phone. The upside is that you now have access to all of the resources you need to work effectively. The downside is that now you have your office in your pocket, and so it can become very hard to leave the office behind (or deal with the consequences if it is stolen or

Figure 6-9
Touch Screen Smartphone

Source: istock.

scyther5/Shutterstock

lost). Balancing personal and professional lives is an increasingly important concern for business professionals.

Smartphone Basics

Smartphones are designed to be easy to use so that users do not have to know the intricacies of mobile device networks to get their work done. Although telecommunications companies are constantly upgrading their networks, not all smartphones use the same technology or offer the same level of geographical coverage. If you travel outside of Canada, particularly to Europe, your phone may not be compatible with the systems there (and you may get a large bill if you use it). The speed or bandwidth of the network is also an important factor. Most smartphones operate on a 3G (third-generation) network (standards are defined by the International Telecommunication Union). As you might expect, 3G provides higher data transfer rates compared with 2G and allows for simultaneous use of voice and data transfer, but faster 4G networks have already been deployed in some areas.

Finally, a person considering buying a cellular phone should understand the operating system at the foundation of each phone. The two main operating systems are Google's Android and Apple's iOS although others exist, including BlackBerry OS and Windows Mobile from Microsoft. An application built for an iPhone that runs the iPhone OS will not be compatible with a phone running a different operating system.

Critical issues emerge from the differences in operating systems, and this is where the differences between smartphones become more significant. For example, Apple is able to benefit from a high level of interoperability among its three types of devices (phone, tablet, and computer), and this is evident in how such applications as iTunes synchronize across platforms. Microsoft and Google have announced a similar direction for their operating systems (Windows 8 and Android, respectively), but it unclear how that will be accomplished. Blackberry has less opportunity for interoperability than the other operating systems and hence will have more difficulty leveraging interoperability between devices.

eReaders and Tablets

As the name implies, eReaders, such as the Amazon Kindle or Barnes and Noble Nook, were originally designed for reading books and magazines and, while many have expanded to support internet access, for the most part they are still used and optimized for reading. eReaders tend to use electronic ink, which functions well even in bright sunlight, thus reducing eyestrain, whereas tablets use traditional backlit LCDs (liquid crystal displays). Tablets however, in just a few short years, have gone from being a novelty device mainly used for the consumption of information (reading email or web browsing) to legitimate enterprise data collection and analytic devices. Besides support and security issues (which are risks when the devices are lost or stolen), two other big issues are (1) complexity in synchronization (e.g., email sent from one device being accessible on another) and (2) ownership. Many organizations are adopting what is sometimes called a **Bring Your Own Device (BYOD)** approach, whereby employees are encouraged to simply use their own devices for work rather than being provided with additional company-issued devices. Of course, this strategy means that companies have to deal with a wide variety of new issues, and the line between personal and professional use is further blurred. In one case, for example, a person found that their personal device had been wiped clean by the former employer the day after they left and they lost what they believed to be personal email and photographs.

Q5 What Do I Need to Know About Connecting to the Internet?

The internet is a WAN. A WAN connects computers located at physically separated sites. A company with offices in Regina and Toronto, for example, must use a WAN to connect its computers because the sites are geographically separated. Today, in most cases the company would use the internet to make this connection.

An important component in any WAN is a **router**. Routers are special-purpose devices that implement the protocol for WANs. When you connect your personal computer to the internet, you are working with a router to use the internet. The router normally connects your computer to computers owned and operated by your **internet service provider (ISP)**. If you are like the majority of Canadians, you likely have a router at home and it is similar to those used in other organizations.

An ISP has three important functions. First, it provides your computer, or router, with an internet address (see "Obtaining an IP Address," below). Second, it serves as your gateway to the internet. The ISP receives the communications from your router and passes them on to the internet. The ISP also receives communications from the internet and passes them back to your router and then on to you. Finally, ISPs help pay for the internet. They collect money from their customers and pay access fees and other charges on your behalf.

It is important to note that the web and the internet are often incorrectly used interchangeably but are *not* the same thing. The web, conceived in 1989 by Tim Berners-Lee, is a subset of the internet and consists of sites and users that process the **hypertext transfer protocol (HTTP)**. Programs that implement the HTTP protocol are called **browsers**. Three common browsers are Mozilla Firefox, Google Chrome, and Microsoft Internet Explorer. When you type the address "www.google.com" into your browser, you will notice that your browser adds the notation *http://* (try this, if you have never noticed this before). By filling in these characters, your browser is indicating that it will use the HTTP to communicate with the Google website.

The internet, which grew out of a US Department of Defence project in 1969, is the communications infrastructure that supports *all* application-layer protocols, including the HTTP, the simple mail transfer protocol (SMTP), and the file transfer protocol (FTP). When you send email, you generally use the SMTP. When you view webpages, you use the HTTP, and when you transfer files between computers on the internet you generally use the FTP. These are all part of the internet.

Names and Addresses

There are some rules for how sites are named on the internet. The last letters in any domain name are referred to as the top-level domain (TLD). For example, in the domain name "www.canada.ca," the TLD is .ca. This indicates that the site is a Canadian site. TLDs include .com, .org, and .biz, and many more have been proposed. If you want to register a domain name, the first step is to determine the appropriate TLD. You can then visit the website for the Internet Corporation for Assigned Names and Numbers (ICANN) at http://icann.org and determine which agencies ICANN has licensed to register domains for that TLD. You then follow the registration process as required by one of those agencies. If the domain name you want is already in use, your registration will be disallowed.

The letters "www.canada.ca" are an example of a **uniform resource locator (URL)**. The URL is an address on the internet that is stated in a way humans can remember. But this is not the actual address on the network. In every electronic network, each machine has a numbered address. For the internet, the address is given by four numbers, each separated by a period. This is called the IP address (we will talk about IP later). An IP address is a logical address (i.e., it is assigned through software) and not a physical address (such as a MAC on a NIC). For example, the site www.canada.ca is actually located at the following IP address: 198.103.238.30. If you type this number into your web browser, you will go to the same site as if you typed "www.canada.ca." (Try it—it works!)

Obtaining an IP Address

In practice, two kinds of **IP addresses** exist. Public IP addresses are used on the internet. Such IP addresses are assigned to ISPs and major institutions in blocks by ICANN. Each IP address is unique across all computers on the internet. In contrast, private IP addresses are used within private networks and internets. They are controlled only by the organization that operates the private network or internet.

Today, in most cases, when you plug in your computer to a LAN (or sign on to a wireless network), a program in your operating system will search the network for a DHCP server. This is a computer or router that hosts a program called Dynamic Host Configuration Protocol (DHCP). When the program finds such a device, your computer will request a temporary IP address from the DHCP server. That IP address is loaned to you while you are connected to the LAN. When you disconnect, that IP address becomes available again, and the DHCP server will reuse it, when needed.

Finding Domain Names

Once you have an IP address, you can access the network. You might, for example, open a browser and type "www.canada.ca." We learned earlier that when we type "www.canada.ca" the computer actually connects with the IP address "198.103.238.30." The question is, how does the computer figure out the IP address when we type in only the URL? This service is provided by the **Domain Name System (DNS)**. The purpose of DNS is to convert human-friendly URLs into computer-friendly IP addresses. You can think of it as a giant index that links human names for sites with IP addresses.

The process of converting a domain name into a public IP address is called *domain name resolution*. In the very early days of the internet, a human being was in charge of keeping the domain name index up to date. That did not last for long because the rate at which new sites were added created too much work for people to manually keep it updated.

Domain name resolution is now done by computers called *domain name resolvers*. The resolvers reside at ISPs, academic institutions, large companies, and government organizations. The resolvers keep track of domain name requests and store locations for future use. When a resolver cannot find a domain name, it searches for the IP address at a resolver that is at a higher level in the network. Although the highest-level resolvers are always up to date, it can take some time for lower-level resolvers to acquire accurate information. This is why it can take some time if an organization adds a new domain name or if the location hosting it changes.

Home and small-business computers are commonly connected to an ISP by either a special type of telephone line called a *DSL line*, or through a cable TV line (very few people in Canada use dial-up connections any longer). Both methods require that the digital data in the computer be converted to an **analog**, or wavy, signal before being sent. When receiving data, the analog signal must be converted to a digital signal before the computer can read it. A device called a *modulator/ demodulator*, or **modem**, performs these conversions. Figure 6-10 shows one way of

Figure 6-10

Analog versus Digital Signals

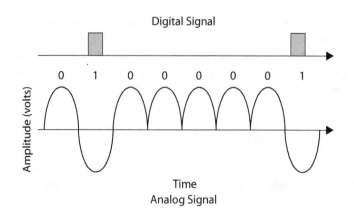

converting the digital byte 01000001 to an analog signal. Different modems use different protocols and speeds. When two devices connected by modems use the same protocols but different speeds, the slower speed is the one at which they operate. As shown in Figure 6-11, once the modem converts your computer's digital data to analog, that analog signal is then sent over the telephone line or TV cable. Generally speaking, digital signals are better and preferred over analog signals because they can be reproduced exactly with no distortion or loss, while analog signals must be amplified (unless digitized) which introduces noise and distortion.

A **digital subscriber line (DSL) modem** operates on the same lines as voice telephones, but it operates in such a way that its signals do not interfere with voice telephone service. Because DSL signals do not interfere with telephone signals, DSL data transmission and telephone conversations can occur simultaneously. Additionally, DSL modems always maintain a connection, so there is no need to dial in; the internet connection is available immediately.

There are various levels of DSL service and speed. Most home DSL lines can download data at speeds ranging from 1.5 M per second (Mbps) to 20 Mbps and can upload data at slower speeds—for example 1.5 Mbps. DSL lines that have different upload and download speeds are called **asymmetric digital subscriber lines (ADSL)**. Most homes and small businesses can use ADSL because they receive more data than they transmit and hence do not need to transmit as fast as they receive data. Some users and larger businesses, however, need DSL lines that have the same receiving and transmitting speeds. They also need performance-level guarantees.

Figure 6-11

Personal Computer (PC) Internet Access

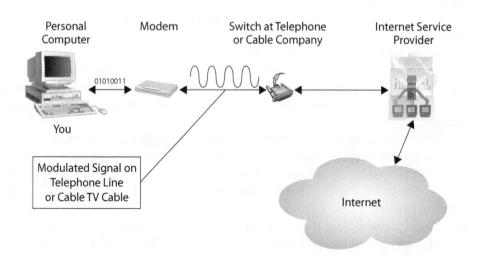

Line Type	Use	Maximum Speed
Telephone line (twisted pair copper lines)	Dial-up modem	56 Kbps
	DSL modem	3 Mbps
	WAN—T1—using a pair of telephone lines	1.544 Mbps
Coaxial cable	Cable modem	Upstream to 768 Kbps Downstream 1–6 Mbps (usually much less, however)
Unshielded twisted pair (UTP)	LAN	10 Gbps
Optical fibre cable	LAN and WAN—T3, OC-768, etc.	40 Gbps or more
Satellite	WAN—OC-768, etc.	40 Gbps or more

Figure 6-12

Transmission Line Types, Uses, and Speeds

Symmetric digital subscriber lines (SDSL) meet this need by offering the same fast speed in both directions. As much as 5 megabits per second (Mbps) can be guaranteed.

A **cable modem** provides high-speed data transmission using cable television lines. The cable company installs a fast, high-capacity optical fibre cable to a distribution centre in each neighbourhood it serves. At the distribution centre, the optical fibre cable connects to regular cable-television cables that run to subscribers' homes or businesses. Cable modems modulate in such a way that their signals do not interfere with TV signals. Like DSL lines, they are always on.

Because up to 500 user sites can share the distribution centre, performance can vary depending on how many other users are sending and receiving data. Depending on the configuration, users can download data from 5 to 25 Mbps and can upload data at 1.5 to 10 Mbps. Typically, however, performance is lower than this. In most cases, the speed of cable modems and DSL modems is about the same.

If you are curious about your network's performance, the website www.speedtest .net will measure the bandwidth of your connection. Figure 6-12 provides a summary of the lines and speeds used to connect to various networks.

What About Wireless WAN?

A wireless WAN (WWAN) differs from a wireless LAN in two ways. A WWAN covers a larger area than wireless LANs, and WWANs use cellular networks to transfer data. Cellular network coverage is generally offered on a nationwide level and provided by a wireless service carrier for a monthly usage fee, much like a cellphone subscription. For someone travelling across the country, access to a WWAN would allow access to the internet from anywhere a cellular phone receives a signal.

How does it work? It works just like a cellphone. A portable computer with a wireless WAN modem connects to a base station on the wireless networks via radio waves. The radio tower then carries the signal to a mobile switching centre, where the data are passed on to the appropriate network. The wireless service provider then provides the connection to the internet—and that is it, you are connected. Since WWANs use existing cellular phone networks, it is possible to make voice calls over a WWAN. Some cellular phones and all WWAN cards have the ability to make voice calls as well as pass data traffic on WWAN networks.

Watch

Go to MyMISLab to watch a video about how e-mail travels.

Q6 How Does Email Actually Work?

We now have just about enough information to talk about the technological miracle that occurs when you send an email. As an example, imagine you are sending a message from your hotel room in Niagara Falls to a friend who works in Ottawa for Service Canada. The email begins with an address for your friend (for example, somebody@canada.ca). We noted earlier that communication protocols coordinate activity between the computer sending the message and the computer receiving the message. There is quite a bit of complicated work to do when sending an email message. To handle the complexity, communication protocols are broken down into a four-layer scheme that balances simplicity and flexibility.

Network Layers

Definition and specification of the layers is done by the Internet Engineering Task Force (IETF). Although other schemes exist and the original model was recently expanded into five layers, we will use the simpler four-layer **transmission control program/internet protocol (TCP/IP)** as an illustration.

Figure 6-13 shows the four layers. As shown in the right-most column, the bottom layer, Layer 1, is used to transmit data within a single network. This is itself a highly technical function but largely beyond the scope of this text. The next two layers are used for data transmission across an internet (a network of networks, including the internet). The top layer, Layer 4, provides protocols that help different applications interact with each other and the person using the computer.

Step 1: Getting Internet Access and Pressing "Send/Receive"

Consider Figure 6-14, which shows the LAN operated by your hotel in Niagara Falls. You occupy a suite and plug your computer into the network as Computer C3.

Layer	Name	Specific Function	Broad Function
4	Application Layer	Data are passed between programs (such as email application, web browser, and file transfer programs) and the transport layer.	Programs for mail, web browsing, file transfer
3	Transport Layer	This layer deals with opening connections and maintaining them. It uses the Transmission Control Program (TCP). TCP works to ensure packets are received with correct content.	Transmission across an internet (TCP/IP)
2	Internet Layer	This layer works with IP addresses. There are many ways to navigate packets from one IP address to another. The internet layer standards also control packet organization and timing constraints.	
1	Network Access Layer	This layer describes the equipment that is used for communications (UTP, fibre-optic) the signalling used (analog, digital), and the protocols that will be used to communicate between machines.	Transmission within a single network (local area network)

Figure 6-13

IETF Network Levels

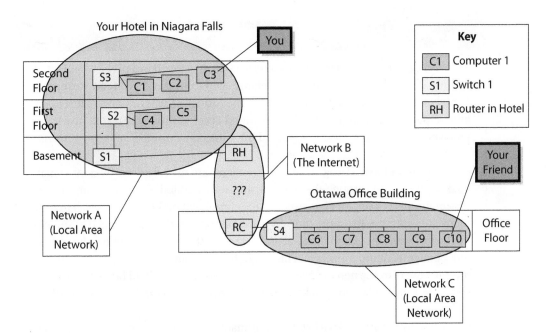

Figure 6-14
Example of Networks

When you do so, a program in your operating system will search the LAN at the hotel for a DHCP server; you are operating at Layer 1 on the LAN. The router labelled RH is this kind of server. Your computer asks RH for an IP address, and RH assigns one.

Your email program operates at Layer 4. It generates and receives email and attachments according to one of the standard email protocols, most likely a protocol called simple mail transfer protocol (SMTP). Let us say you have created an email message to a friend and have attached a picture of yourself at Niagara Falls. When you press "Send/Receive," you start the process described in detail below.

Step 2: Break Apart Message and Get Ready for Transport

The next step is to get ready to transport the message. This is the job of the Transmission Control Program (TCP) that operates at Layer 3. TCP performs many important tasks. The most important job TCP does is to examine the email (and any attached files) you are sending and break apart large messages (like an attached photograph) into pieces called *segments*. When it does this, TCP also places identifying data at the front of each segment so that the segments can be correctly ordered, content of the segment can be validated, and segments do not get lost. TCP also works to translate segments between operating systems. If you send an email from an Apple computer to a person working on a PC, TCP will help format the message correctly so that your friend using a PC will be able to see the segments in the correct format.

Step 3: Send and Receive Packets

TCP interacts with protocols that operate at Layer 2. The Layer 2 protocol is the internet protocol (IP). The chief purpose of IP is to route messages across an internet. In the case of your email, the IP program on your computer does not know how to reach your friend's mail server, but it does know how to start; that is, it knows to send all the pieces or segments of your email to a device on the network called a *router*.

WHY DOES THE INTERNET USE PACKETS?

As noted earlier, the basis for today's internet was developed in a project completed in 1969 for the U.S. Department of Defense as part of the **Advanced Research Projects Agency Network (ARPANET)**. The ARPANET was the world's first operational packet switching network. It provided access to many research investigators who were geographically separated from the small number of large, powerful research computers available at the time.

In a **packet switching network**, messages are first disassembled into small packets, then sent through the network and reassembled at the destination. The reason for this is twofold. First, expensive communication lines could be shared by many computers at the same time. In packet switching, there is no need to reserve the line to send messages. The second reason is that each packet can be routed independently of other packets. This might be important for the military. If one of the computers in the network was not working well (e.g., if it had been damaged in some way), the packets in a packet switching network could independently find their own way to the destination.

These two features of packet switching made the internet both efficient and resilient and have helped support its dramatic growth since 1989 when the World Wide Web was first proposed by Sir Tim Berners-Lee and the first popular web browser was developed by Netscape Communications in 1994.

To send a segment to the router, the IP layer program first packages each segment into a *packet*. The internet protocol places IP data at the front of the packet, which is in front of the TCP segment data. Adding the IP information to the segment is like wrapping an envelope that already contains a letter inside another envelope, and then placing additional To/From data on the outer envelope (see the box above).

The router examines the destination of each packet, one at a time, and uses the rules defined in the IP to decide where to send each packet. The router does not know how to get the messages all the way to their destination, but it knows how to get them started. The router bounces the packet to another router. When the packet arrives, it "asks" the new router, "Are you my destination?" If not, the receiving router bounces the packet to yet another router. The packets bounce through the internet, from router to router, looking for the proper destination. Each packet from the same message can take a different path. Dozens of routers on the internet may eventually be involved in sending each packet associated with your message to the proper destination.

Step 4: Reassemble Packets and Display Message

Once the email packets arrive at the correct destination router, they are sent off to a mail server. TCP waits for all the packets to arrive and then unpacks the packets back into segments. TCP also works to ensure that the content of the message is correct by validating the content and checking to make sure all segments were received. If all the segments are not received, TCP will resend the missing segment (using the same process). It then assembles the segments in sequential order as indicated by the data that the TCP originally provided with each segment. The email message now rests on the mail server in Ottawa waiting for your friend to open her email program and receive and read the email.

What is truly amazing about this process is that it happens millions of times per second all across the world, 24 hours a day, 7 days a week, in a network that includes hundreds of millions of computing devices. Instead of wondering why we have to wait a few seconds to receive an email as you walk across your campus, with all those packets bouncing around we should be marvelling that we receive any email at all!

Q7 What Are Firewalls, Encryption, and VPNs?

What Is a Firewall?

A **firewall** is a computing device that prevents unauthorized network access and gets its name from the way that forest fires are often contained by open spaces. A firewall can be a special-purpose computer, or it can be a program on a general-purpose computer or on a router. To understand how firewalls work, you need to understand what a port is.

A **port** is a number that is used to uniquely identify a transaction over a network. The port number specifies the service provided. For example, a person could have a network server running web service (HTTP), mail service (SMTP), and file transfer (FTP). When another computer connects to the server, it needs to indicate the correct IP address for that server as well as what service it wants to communicate with. The port number identifies that service.

For example, assume that the default port number for HTTP in your server is 80. If a packet requests the host "www.canada.ca" and port 80, then the data in the packet is transferred to the HTTP web server. The default for SMTP is 25. If the packet requests port 25, the data are transferred to the SMTP mail server.

Port numbers can be used to create firewalls. For example, if you do not want anyone outside of your intranet to access your web server, you could set up a firewall that would prohibit packets destined to port 80 (the port assigned to your HTTP server) from passing through your routers. A firewall also often has an **access control list (ACL)**, which keeps track of which IP addresses are to be allowed access and which are to be prohibited. As a future manager, if you have particular sites with which you do not want your employees to communicate, you can ask your IS department to enforce that limit via the ACL in one or more routers. Your IS organization will likely have a procedure for making such requests.

Packet-filtering firewalls are the simplest type of firewall. A packet-filtering firewall examines each part of a message and determines whether it should let that part pass. To make this decision, it examines the source address, the destination address(es), and other data. Packet-filtering firewalls can prohibit outsiders from starting a session with any user behind the firewall. They can disallow traffic from particular sites, such as known hacker addresses. They can also prohibit traffic from legitimate but unwanted addresses, such as competitors' computers. Firewalls can filter outbound traffic as well. They can keep employees from accessing specific sites, such as competitors' sites, sites with offensive material, or popular news or file-sharing sites, such as Vimeo. Other firewalls filter on a more sophisticated basis. (If you take a data communications class, you will learn about those.) For now, all that you need to know is that firewalls help protect computers from unauthorized network access.

Many ISPs provide firewalls for their customers. By design, these firewalls are generic and have the ability to limit access to ports and IP addresses. Large organizations supplement such generic firewalls with their own. Most home routers include firewalls. Third parties also license firewall products. The bottom line is that no computer should connect to the internet without some form of firewall protection. It is a minimum standard for access to the internet. You will learn more about firewalls and security issues in Chapter 12.

Encryption

Encryption is the process of transforming clear text into coded, unintelligible text for secure storage or communication. Considerable research has gone into developing encryption algorithms that are difficult to break. Most of these methods are based on the idea of encryption keys. A key is a number used to encrypt data. The encryption algorithm applies the key to the original message to produce the coded message. Decoding (decrypting) a message is a similar process; a key is applied to the coded message to recover the original text. In symmetric encryption, the same key is used to encode and to decode. With asymmetric encryption, different keys are used; one key encodes the message, and the other key decodes the message. Symmetric encryption is simpler and much faster than asymmetric encryption.

Most secure communication over the internet uses a protocol called *HTTPS*. With HTTPS, data are encrypted using a protocol called the *Secure Socket Layer (SSL)*, also known as *Transport Layer Security (TLS)*. SSL/TLS uses a combination of public key/ private key and symmetric encryption. The basic idea is this: Symmetric encryption is fast and is preferred. The two parties, however (say, you and a website), do not share a symmetric key. So, how can one be generated and shared? One of the parties must generate a symmetric key and use public/private key encryption to send it securely to the other party. The flow works as follows:

1. Your computer obtains the public key of the website to which it will connect.
2. Your computer generates a key for symmetric encryption.
3. Your computer encodes that key using the website's public key. It sends the encrypted symmetric key to the website.
4. The website then decodes the symmetric key using its private key.
5. From that point forward, your computer and the website communicate using symmetric encryption.

At the end of the session, your computer and the secure site discard the keys. Using this strategy, the bulk of the secure communication occurs using the faster symmetric encryption. And, because keys are used for short intervals, there is less likelihood they can be discovered.

The use of SSL/TLS makes it relatively safe to send sensitive data such as credit card numbers and bank balances. Just be certain that you see *https://* in your browser and not just *http://*. **Warning:** Under normal circumstances, neither email nor instant messaging (IM) uses encryption. It would be quite easy for one of your classmates or your professor to read any email or IM that you send over a wireless network in your classroom, in the student lounge, at a coffee shop, or in any other wireless setting. In much the same way that most locks can be broken or are vulnerable to attack, the same is true of encryption. Although the average person with a single computer may not be able to easily break typical or common encryption mechanisms, the 2014 discovery of a design flaw in Open SSL cryptography (known as the Heartbleed problem) in use at the time by more than two thirds of computer servers world-wide shook public confidence in computer security and reminded us that nothing can be totally secure. Moore's law, coupled with the ability to have multiple computers simultaneously work on a single problem, means that it is easier and easier to circumvent security. Communicators beware!

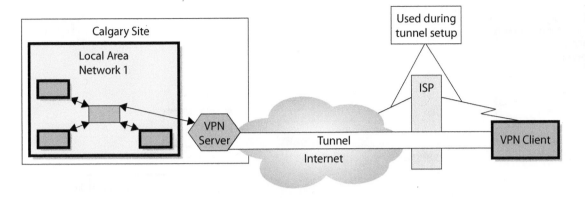

Figure 6-15

Remote Access
Using VPN: Actual
Connections

Virtual Private Network (VPN)

The **virtual private network (VPN)** is another communications alternative shown in Figure 6-8 (page 201). A VPN uses the internet or a private internet to create what appears to be private point-to-point connections (in the IT world, the term *virtual* means something that appears to exist but does not, in fact, exist).

Figure 6-15 shows one way to create a VPN to connect a remote computer, perhaps that of an employee working at a hotel in Montreal, to a LAN at the company's Calgary site. The remote user is the VPN client. That client first establishes a connection to the internet. The connection can be obtained by accessing either a local ISP, as shown in the figure, or a direct internet connection that some hotels provide.

In either case, once the internet connection is made, VPN software on the remote user's computer establishes a connection with the VPN server in Calgary. The VPN client and VPN server then have a point-to-point connection. That connection, called a **tunnel**, is a virtual, private pathway over a public or shared network from the VPN client to the VPN server. Figure 6-16 illustrates the connection as it appears to the remote user.

VPN communications are secure, even though they are transmitted over the public internet. To ensure security, VPN client software *encrypts* the original message so that its contents are hidden. Then the VPN client appends the internet address of the VPN server to the message and sends that package over the internet to the VPN server. When the VPN server receives the message, it strips its address off the front of the message, *decrypts* the coded message, and sends the plain text message to the original address on the LAN. In this way, secure private messages are delivered over the public internet.

VPNs offer the benefit of point-to-point leased lines, and they enable secure remote access, both by employees and by any others who have been registered with the VPN server. For example, if customers or vendors are registered with the VPN

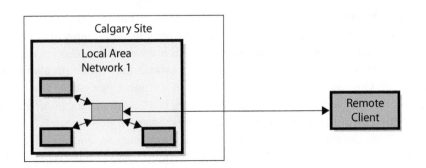

Figure 6-16

Remote Access Using VPN:
Apparent Connections

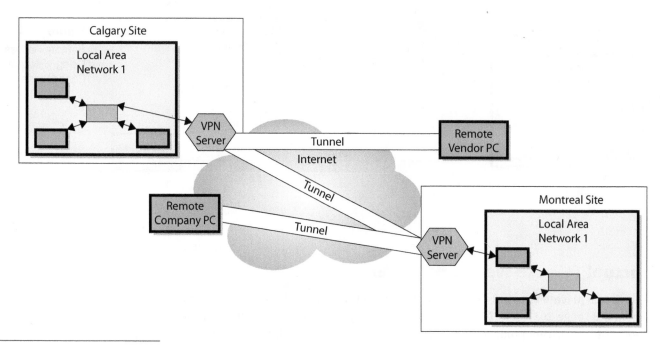

Figure 6-17

WAN Using VPN

server, they can use the VPN from their own sites. Figure 6-17 shows three tunnels: one supports a point-to-point connection between the Montreal and Calgary sites, and the other two support remote connections.

Q8 How Does a Search Engine Work?

Have you ever wondered where those search results on the web come from? Search engines are a tool used to search for information on the internet. The first tool created for searching the internet, called Archie, was developed in 1990 by Alan Emtage, a student at McGill University in Montreal. Archie stood for "archive" without the "v." The program created a searchable database of file names by downloading and storing directory listings of files located on public anonymous FTP sites. Search engines have grown tremendously since that time, but the technology behind them remains similar.

Web search engines require two things: (1) a way to collect URLs and (2) a method for storing/accessing the URLs so that they can be searched. Finding URLs is usually the job of a *web crawler*. A **web crawler** (sometimes referred to as a *web spider*) is a software program that browses the web in a very methodical way. The crawler starts with a list of seed URLs. It then visits the URLs and identifies, for example, hyperlinks in the page. Some crawlers harvest specific things, such as email addresses, which can then be used for spam. If you have your email address listed on webpages, one of these web crawlers may find it. This is why you will see some people list their email addresses on a webpage as "somebody at Canada dot ca" (as opposed to somebody@canada.ca, which is easier for a web crawler to harvest). Other crawlers might collect not only hyperlinks and email but also full text and images. Crawlers are even used to maintain corporate websites. The crawlers can make sure links are still active and validate HTML code on the site. The list of URLs created by the crawler can be referred to as the *crawl frontier*.

URLs from the frontier are just the start for a search engine. Once a URL is identified, it is necessary to organize the information retrieved. This process is called *search engine indexing.* It is accomplished by different programs that are organized by a set of rules. These programs work to create indexes for the results from the web crawling. These indexes then provide the ability to make fast searches from a vast amount of information. The specifics of search engine technology are important business secrets, and search engine companies do not normally publish information about the techniques they use to crawl through and index the web.

Two important considerations in understanding search engines are the breadth of coverage (what percentage of the web is covered by search engines) and the ordering of the results from a search. There are no official numbers on the breadth of coverage of search engines, but a study by Lawrence and Giles[1] showed that search engines do not index sites equally, that they may not index new pages for months, and that no engine indexes more than about 16 percent of the web. Although these numbers have likely changed, it is important to recognize that if a page is on the web, it does not mean the page has been indexed by, and is accessible through, search engines.

This brings us to our final point: How does a search engine choose to display results from a search? Commonly used search engines focus on indexing full-text documents; however, there are other searchable media types, such as graphics, audio, and video. When a person enters a query into a search engine, the engine first examines its index. It then provides a listing of the webpages that best match the query. The match depends on the criteria used. Search engines differ in how they assign relevance. There can be millions of webpages that are somewhat relevant, and the same search on two different search engines may provide different results.

It is important to recognize that search engines are normally operated by private companies that make money primarily through advertising revenue. Certain search engines may, therefore, employ the practice of allowing advertisers to pay to have their listings ranked higher in search results. Search engines that do not accept money for their results have to make their money through advertising. These engines might place related ads alongside the regular search engine results or might provide increased information for companies (such as pictures or maps) when displaying the results. Every time someone clicks on one of the ads, the search engine company makes a little bit of money (a few cents). With millions of users every day, it can be quite a lucrative business.

As an example of potential value, Google's initial public offering (IPO) on August 19, 2004, raised $1.67 billion—pretty good for a business started only six years earlier and another good reason why you should care about computer networks.

"MIS in Use," on page 216, outlines how some students have found business opportunities using networks. However, it is important to remember that although computer networks are important, human networks are even more important. Take some time to read the exercise "Human Networks Matter More" at the end of this chapter on pages 224–225 to gain insight into the importance of the human network you are building.

A Word of Caution

Despite the explosive growth in communication technologies and the benefits of networking, astute students are reminded that all change has both positive and negative consequences and the reality of technology can sometimes be a fraction of its promise. As the tragic cases of Amanda Todd and Rehtaeh Parsons illustrate,

---

[1] S. Lawrence and C. L. Giles, "Accessibility of Information on the Web," *Nature* 400, no. 6740 (1999): 107–109.

social networks can amplify bullying and enable criminal activity to take place over great distance. Furthermore, as the 2014 loss of the unfound (at time of publishing) Malaysian Airlines flight MH370 shows, networks require expensive and hard to change infrastructure that tends to favour dense population over remote geography. This means that while bandwidth in urban centres is fueled by the demands of Netflix and YouTube, significant gaps and intermittent connections can exist and that being always connected regardless of location remains much more of an idea than a reality.

MIS in Use

"Never Miss Your Bus"

Students John Boxall and Igor Faletski have not added up how many hours they have spent waiting for the bus, nor have they counted the number of buses they have missed. But during their four years at Simon Fraser University's Burnaby campus, they spent a lot of time commuting. They knew there had to be a better way. The problem was that to know when a bus was coming, you had to know the location of every bus stop and either have a copy of every bus schedule or be connected to the internet—neither of which was very practical.

Not content to simply complain, John and Igor decided to take matters into their own hands. Although they realized that they could quickly assemble a Java-based application that would enable them to browse the transit website, they also knew that the number of students with a compatible unlocked handset and a low-cost data plan was below 1 percent. Instead, they realized that text messaging covered the majority of cellphone users and did not require any special configuration. More importantly, the population that sent the most number of text messages, teenagers and young adults, was also one of the biggest users of public transit.

Connecting with TransLink, the Greater Vancouver Transportation Authority's website, and using each bus stop's unique five-digit numerical ID, they built a system they named MyBus. Using the university's existing access to a text messaging application programming interface (API), MyBus parses text messages, retrieves bus information, and sends the results back in a properly formatted text message. Of course, this requires that riders first know the bus stop number, but even this was solved through the use of aliases created for the most popular stops and posted on the website.

The system worked well. With minimal advertising, it received more than 200 requests during the first three-week trial, and some students began to use it on a regular basis. MyBus received coverage in the local media, and John and Igor were soon invited to present it to the transit authority, which had been developing its own version.

Keeping in mind Alfred Sloan's admonishment that there is no resting place for competition, Igor and John are continuing to refine, improve, and extend the system. Working with Peter McLachlan, a Ph.D. student at the University of British Columbia, they have recently developed a Facebook version of the application, and with input from a few faculty members and advisers, they have formed a corporation to commercialize the technology.

Questions

1. **What problem does MyBus solve?**
2. **How important was access to the Translink website and the text messaging API?**
3. **Does this system cooperate or compete with Translink?**
4. **What technological changes could affect John and Igor's efforts to commercialize MyBus?**
5. **What advice would you give John and Igor?**

Active ? Review

Use this Active Review to verify that you have understood the material in the chapter. You can read the entire chapter and then perform the tasks in this review, or you can read the material for just one question and perform the tasks for that question before moving on to the next one.

Q1 Why should I care about networks?

Think about and identify all the computer networks you have used today. Did you buy gas? take out money? search the web? Consider how your day might have changed if you did not have access to these networks. Now, think about networks you used to collaborate. Did you check email? text someone on your cellphone? instant message anyone? Does the ability to use these network technologies make you a more effective, and valuable, employee?

Q2 What is a computer network?

Define *computer network*. Explain the differences among LANs, WANs, internets, and the internet. Describe the purpose of a protocol.

Q3 What are the components of a LAN?

Explain the key components of a LAN. Describe the purpose of each of the components as shown in Figure 6-3. Define *MAC address* and *UTP*. Describe the placement of switches in a building with many floors. Explain when optical fibre cables are used for a LAN. Define *Ethernet*. Describe the purpose of each of the wireless components in Figure 6-7.

Q4 Why is mobile computing important?

What are the important trends in computing and the three different types of devices? What is BYOD, and what organizational issues does it create?

Q5 What do I need to know about connecting to the internet?

Explain what a router does. Explain what an IP address is and what the difference is between a public and private IP address. Describe the purpose of DHCP and how it helps you get connected to the internet. Explain what a domain name is and what DNS does. Describe what a modem does. What is the difference between a **dial-up modem** and DSL? How do DSL and cable modems differ? How does a wireless WAN work?

Q6 How does email actually work?

Describe the process of sending an email. What are network layers, and why are they necessary? What is a packet? What is TCP/IP? What was the first packet switching network?

Q7 What are firewalls, encryption, and VPNs?

What is a firewall, and how does it work? Why should any computer connected to the internet have a firewall? Describe the problem that a VPN solves. Use Figure 6-15 to explain one way that a VPN is set up and used. Define *tunnel*. Describe how encryption is used in a VPN.

Q8 How does a search engine work?

What is a web crawler and how is it related to the crawl frontier? What is a search engine, and why is search engine indexing important? How do search engine companies make money?

MyMISLab MyMISLab is an online learning and testing environment that features the perfect study tools to help you master the concepts covered in this chapter. Log in to MyMISLab to test your knowledge of key chapter concepts and explore additional practice tools, including videos, flashcards, annotated text figures, and more!

Key Terms and Concepts

10/100/1000 Ethernet 200

Access control list (ACL) 211

Access points (APs) 200

Advanced Research Projects Agency Network (ARPANET) 210

Analog 205

Asymmetric digital sub-scriber line (ADSL) 206

Bring Your Own Device (BYOD) 203

Browser 204

Cable modem 207

Collaboration 195

Communication systems 195

Dial-up modem 217

Digital subscriber line (DSL) modem 206

Domain name system (DNS) 205

Encryption 212

Ethernet 200

Firewall 211

Global Positioning System (GPS) 197

Hypertext transfer protocol (HTTP) 204

IEEE 802.3 protocol 200

Internet 197

Internet service provider (ISP) 204

IP address 205

Local area network (LAN) 197

MAC (media access control) address 198

M-commerce 202

Modem 205

Network 197

Network externality 196

Network interface card (NIC) 198

Onboard NIC 200

Optical fibre cable 199

Packet-filtering firewall 211

Packet switching network 210

Port 211

Protocol 198

Router 204

Smartphone 200

Switch 198

Symmetric digital subscriber lines (SDSL) 207

Transmission control program/Internet protocol (TCP/IP) 208

Transmission media 197

Tunnel 213

Uniform resource locator (URL) 204

Unshielded twisted pair (UTP) cable 198

Virtual private network (VPN) 213

Web crawler 214

Wide area network (WAN) 197

Wireless NIC (WNIC) 200

Workflow 196

Using Your Knowledge

1. Suppose you manage a group of seven employees in a small business. Each of your employees wants to be connected to the internet. Consider two alternatives:
   - Alternative A: Each employee has a modem and connects individually to the internet.
   - Alternative B: The employees' computers are connected using a LAN, and the network uses a single modem to connect.
   a. Sketch the equipment and lines required for each alternative.
   b. Explain the actions you need to take to create each alternative.
   c. Compare the alternatives using the criteria in Figure 6-14.
   d. Which of these two alternatives would you recommend?

2. You have decided to start up a web-based business and are considering what you need to make it happen.
   a. Explain the steps you would take in assigning a domain name for your website.
   b. Use the web to find the options available for ISPs to host your website. Find at least three different options and explore the differences among them. Explain why choosing a reliable ISP is important to your site.

c. You have also decided to set up a small office network for your company. Provide an example of a setup for your company that includes everything you need to connect to the internet.

d. Create an estimate for how much it would cost you to start up your business (including computer equipment, domain registration, ISP charges, and software). Did you consider web designer charges? Explain why or why not.

3. You have decided to set up a web-based business. You have investigated the costs, chosen an ISP, and are ready to get working on your site. You have heard that a quick way to get your site up and running is to use a website template. Some examples are provided at www.templatemonster.com or www.websitetemplates.com.

a. Choose an example of a web business and look for a template that you think fits that business.

b. Describe the changes you would have to make to the template to fit your business.

c. Determine the cost of the template and estimate the cost for the work needed to modify the template to fit your business.

d. Discuss the advantages and disadvantages of using a template for your website.

Collaborative Exercises

Collaborate with a group of students on the following exercises. Have your team choose one of the hardware/software topics listed in question 2. Use the internet and other resources to research the topic and do the following:

1. Create a maximum two-page information sheet that summarizes the topic. The summary should include the following:

a. An introduction to the topic (in English, not technobabble)

b. The relevance of the topic to business managers (e.g., advantages and benefits versus costs, if they are known)

c. Examples of products, vendors, or companies that use the particular technology

d. Links to sites that contain further information

e. A statement about the future use of the technology: Are there any barriers to adoption? How prevalent will the technology become?

2. Now create a presentation (using PowerPoint, Keynote, or other presentation software) that could be used to present the topic to other students in the class. Make sure to include a title page and be prepared to present what you have found about your topic to the class. Choose one of the following topics (or ask if you can create your own):

a. How does a global positioning system work, and what is the value of having one?

b. What benefits will Google's Android bring to the smartphone industry?

c. Which phone works best for business—iPhone or BlackBerry Q10?

d. What is WiMAX, and what advantages does it have over Wi-FI?

e. What is Google Wave, and how does it support collaboration?

f. What is Voice over Internet Protocol (VoIP), and how is it related to Skype?

g. What is packet switching, and how has it changed the use of networks?

h. Who will win the smartphone operating systems war? What will this mean to the mobile phone industry?

Case Study 6

Keeping Up with Wireless

Data communications technology is one of the fastest changing technologies, if not *the* fastest changing, in all of IT.

Consider the example of wireless technology. Craig McCaw built one of the world's first cellular networks in the early 1980s, making cellphone communication available to the masses. In the 1990s, he sold his company to AT&T for $11.5 billion. In 2003, McCaw started a new venture, Clearwire, which uses an emerging technology called *WiMAX* to address what is often referred to as the last-mile problem. When someone with McCaw's knowledge, experience, and wealth starts a new venture based on new technology, we should pay attention.

To begin, what is the last-mile problem? The bottleneck on data communications into homes and smaller businesses is the last mile. Fast optical fibre transmission lines lie in the street in front of your apartment or office. The problem is getting that capacity into the building and to your computer or TV. Digging up the street and backyard of every residence and small business to install optical fibre lines is not an affordable proposition. Even if it could be done, such infrastructure is not mobile. You cannot watch a downloaded movie on a commuter train using an optical fibre line.

Existing wireless technology does not solve the problem either. Cellphones do not have the capacity to transmit video, and wireless technology based on the IEEE 802.11 standard is limited to devices that are within a few hundred metres of each other. WiMAX, the technology chosen by Clearwire, solves both of these problems—it is fast, and its range is measured in kilometres.

According to the WiMAX Forum, WiMAX is a standards-based technology that enables the delivery of last-kilometre wireless broadband access as an alternative to wired broadband, such as cable and DSL. WiMAX provides fixed, nomadic, portable, and mobile wireless broadband connectivity without the need for direct line-of-sight with a base station. In a typical cell radius deployment of 3 to 10 km, WiMAX Forum Certified systems can be expected to deliver capacity of up to 40 Mbps per channel, for fixed and portable access applications.[2]

What do the terms *fixed*, *nomadic*, *portable*, and *mobile* mean? The WiMAX Forum published a white paper with the table shown in Figure 16-18.

Figure 6-18

Types of Access to a WiMAX Network

Source: Table 1, "Types of Access to a WiMax Network," from Fixed, Nomadic, Portable, and Mobile Applications for 802.16–2004 and 802.16e WiMax Networks, prepared by Senza Fili Consulting on behalf of the WiMAX Forum. © 2005 WiMAX Forum, www.wimaxforum.org/technology/downloads (accessed June 2008).

Definition	Devices	Locations/Speed	Handoffs	802.16–2004	802.16e
Fixed access	Outdoor and indoor CPEs	Single/stationary	No	Yes	Yes
Nomadic access	Indoor CPEs, PCMCIA cards	Multiple/stationary	No	Yes	Yes
Portability	Laptop PCMCIA or mini cards	Multiple/walking speed	Hard handoffs	No	Yes
Simple mobility	Laptop PCMCIA or mini cards, PDAs or smartphones	Multiple/low vehicular speed	Hard handoffs	No	Yes
Full mobility	Laptop PCMCIA or mini cards, PDAs or smartphones	Multiple/high vehicular speed	Soft handoffs	No	Yes

---

[2] www.wimaxforum.org/technology, accessed August, 2007.

Using knowledge from this chapter, you can guess the meaning of the last two columns. They must refer to IEEE standards: 802.3 is Ethernet, and 802.11 is standard wireless, so 802.16 is a new IEEE WiMAX standard. *CPE* stands for *customer premises equipment* (i.e., a device, such as a computer chip or an access device). PCMCIA cards are older technology. Think instead of onboard devices that Intel will make for new-generation laptops.

With these definitions, you can interpret this table. *Nomadic use* allows a user to sign in from sites at home and at work, but not to be connected in transit. *Portability* allows the user to walk to work while connected. *Simple mobility* supports connection while driving on city streets, and *full mobility* allows access on the freeway or a commuter train.

Now, bring this back to Craig McCaw. He made cellphones accessible to the public in the 1980s, and he made portable, wireless broadband accessible with WiMAX.

With McCaw's track record, and with recent investors such as Comcast and Intel, something is clearly afoot. The question is: What opportunities does this create for you? That is the upside of all this change. It continually creates new opportunities for those who look for them.

Questions

1. What implications does WiMAX have for existing established traditional telephone companies? (*Hint:* Twenty percent of North American households use mobile phones in place of fixed wire [wireline] telephones).
2. Beyond television, what other new capabilities could be enabled by this technological innovation?
3. What are the differences, if any, between the implications of this technology for Canada versus other industrialized countries? (*Hint:* Canada's population tends to be less evenly distributed and is generally located within 250 kilometres of the United States–Canada border).
4. How much more would you be willing to pay for the capabilities enabled by this technology?

Running Case Assignment Part 2

Questions

1. Marlo has decided to understand more about her customers at the hotel. She collected information about clients in the last two years in an Excel spreadsheet labelled "The 1881 Customer Information.xls." You can find this spreadsheet on MyMISLab in Chapter 6. Use the data in the spreadsheet to answer the following questions:

   a. How many different customers did The 1881 have over the past two years?

   b. What were names of the five customers who spent the most money at the hotel over the past two years?

   c. What were the names of the five customers who had the highest frequency (number) of visits over the two-year period?

2. An RFM analysis looks at a customer database and rates each customer in relation to three categories: (a) recency (how recently they did business with you), (b) frequency (how often they do business with you), and (c) monetary value (how much they spend). The idea behind RFM is to help you identify your customers. Perform an RFM analysis on The 1881's customers by using the categories below, and then answer the questions that follow.

Customer Characteristic	High = 3	Medium = 2	Low = 1
Recency	1 order within last 4 months	1 order within last year	No orders within last year
Frequency	3 or more orders in a year	2 orders in a year	1 or fewer orders in a year
Monetary Value	Orders of more than $3000 per year	Orders between $500 and $3000 per year	

   a. What percentage of The 1881's customers had a high frequency of visits?

   b. What percentage of The 1881's customers were rated as having a high monetary value?

Collaborative Question

3. The "The 1881 Customer Information.xls" spreadsheet is an example of data that can be collected and stored in an information system. These data can be valuable when considering changes in marketing. One change in marketing being considered is contacting customers directly about staying at The 1881 and offering discounts for special customers. On the basis of your RFM analysis above, answer the following questions:

   a. Do you believe there are customers that The 1881 should be contacting directly? Identify three example customers from the RFM analysis.

   b. For each customer, suggest a special incentive or discount that you think would appeal to the customer. Provide a short (one or two sentence) justification for why the discount or incentive would be attractive to the customer.

   c. Are there any potential drawbacks from contacting customers directly? Justify your answer.

   d. Assume that you are Marlo and you have access to the spreadsheet information. What advice would you give to the owners of The 1881 about a marketing campaign for the company?

MyMISLab   Visit MyMISLab to access the data files to complete these questions.

Human Networks Matter More

Six Degrees of Separation is a play by John Guare that was made into a movie starring Stockard Channing, Donald Sutherland, and Will Smith. The title is related to the idea, originated by the Hungarian writer Frigyes Karinthy, that everyone on Earth is connected to everyone else by five (Karinthy) or six (Guare) people.* For example, according to this theory, you are connected to, say, Eminem by no more than five or six people because you know someone who knows someone, who knows someone . . . and so on. By the same theory, you are also connected to a Siberian seal hunter. Today, in fact, with the internet, the number may be closer to three people than five or six, but in any case, the theory points out the importance of human networks.

Suppose you want to meet your university's president. The president has a secretary who acts as a gatekeeper. If you walk up to that secretary and say, "I'd like a half-hour with President Jones," you're likely to be palmed off on some other university administrator. What else can you do?

If you are connected to everyone on the planet by no more than six degrees, then surely you are connected to your president in fewer steps. Perhaps you play on the tennis team, and you know that the president plays tennis. In that case, it is likely that the tennis coach knows the president. So, arrange a tennis match with your coach and the president. Voilà! You have your meeting. It may even be better to have the meeting on the tennis court than in the president's office.

The problem with the six-degree theory, as Stockard Channing said so eloquently, is that even though those six people do exist, we do not know who they are. Even worse, we often do not know who the person is with whom we want to connect. For example, there is someone right now who knows someone who has a job for which you are perfectly suited. Unfortunately, you don't know the name of that person.

It does not stop when you get your job, either. When you have a problem at work, for example, setting up a blog within the corporate network, there is someone who knows exactly how to help you. You, however, do not know who that person is.

Accordingly, most successful professionals consistently build personal human networks. They keep building them because they know that somewhere there is someone whom they need to know or will need to know. They meet people in professional and social situations, collect and pass out cards, and engage in pleasant conversation (all part of a social protocol) to expand their networks.

You can apply some of the ideas about computer networks to make this process more efficient. Consider it as a type of network diagram. Assume that each line represents a relationship between two people. Note that the people in your department tend to know each other and that the people in the accounting department also tend to know each other. That is typical.

Now, suppose you are at the weekly employee after-hours party and you have an opportunity to introduce yourself either to Linda or Eileen. Setting aside personal considerations and thinking just about network building, which person should you meet?

If you introduce yourself to Linda, you shorten your pathway to her from two steps to one and your pathway to Shawna from three to two. You do not open up any new channels because you already have channels to the people on your floor.

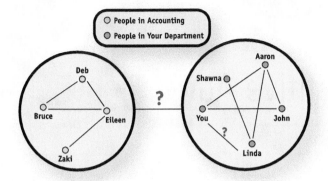

However, if you introduce yourself to Eileen, you open up an entirely new network of acquaintances. So, considering just network building, you use your time better by meeting Eileen and other people who are not part of your current circle. It opens up many more possibilities.

The connection from you to Eileen is called a weak tie in social network theory,[**] and such links are crucial in connecting you to everyone in six degrees. *In general, the people you know the least contribute the most to your network.*

This concept is simple, but you would be surprised by how few people pay attention to it. At most company events, everyone talks with the people they know—and if the purpose of the function is to have fun, then that behaviour makes sense. In truth, however, no business social function exists solely for having fun, regardless of what people say. Business functions exist for business reasons, and you can use them to create and expand networks. Given that time is always limited, you may as well use such functions efficiently.

[*] See "The third link" in Albert Laszlo Barabasi's book *Linked* (New York: Perseus Publishing, 2002), for background on this theory.
[**] See T. Granovetter, "The Strength of Weak Ties," *American Journal of Sociology*, May 1973, for more information.

Discussion Questions

1. Determine the shortest path from you to your university's president. How many links does it have?

2. Give an example of a network to which you belong and sketch a diagram of who knows whom for six or so members of that group.

3. Recall a recent social situation and identify two people, one of whom could have played the role of Linda (someone in your group whom you do not know) and one of whom could have played the role of Eileen (someone in a different group whom you do not know). How could you have introduced yourself to each person?

4. Does it seem too contrived and calculating to think about your social relationships in this way? Even if you do not approach relationships like this, are you surprised to think that others do? Under what circumstances does this kind of analysis seem appropriate, and when does it seem inappropriate? Are you using people?

5. Consider the phrase "It's not what you know, it's who you know that matters." Relate this phrase to a network diagram. Under what circumstances is this likely to be true? When is it false? When is it ethical?

6. Describe how you can apply the principle "the people you know the least contribute the most to your network" to the process of a job search. Are you abusing your relationships for personal advancement?

PART 3 Achieving Competitive Advantage

"Do what you're passionate about—the rest will follow. My passion is bridging technology and business."

In Tyler's Words

I spend most of my time with internal clients, gathering their business requirements and understanding their future business needs. I then use this information in an environmental scan for solutions that match their needs. Governments today face new challenges with respect to an aging population and fiscal constraints. If I can help them to adapt and to build a better province by applying my knowledge, then I think I will have a long and interesting career.

Tyler Stark graduated with a degree in Business Administration concentrating on Information Systems from Brock University in 2011. Upon graduating, he spent the first year of his career as an information technology (IT) business analyst for the Government of Ontario. What drew Tyler to the public sector was the range of opportunities. As he says, "Within one organization, I can develop in a number of areas and still leverage my knowledge and network."

Information systems/information technology (IS/IT) is a career where you bridge technology and business. A career in IS is not limited to service support, network administration, or software development. The many other important roles include procurement experts who manage vendor relationships and contractual obligations or systems analysts who map and document complex information systems.

I started developing my technical skill sets at an early age, building websites and developing computer applications in a variety of languages. As my knowledge grew, so did my understanding of the impact that technology has. I knew early on that a challenging and rewarding career would be working between the technological environment and the business world—a career in IS.

How would I advise someone to prepare for a career in IS? Do what you're passionate about—the rest will follow. My passion is bridging technology and business. Once I started working for the government, this approach quickly became my competitive advantage as most of my colleagues only had technology-related skills sets or only understood the business-side of solution delivery. As a result of this duality, I am able to actively participate in many conversations and am often invited to a variety of working groups to help translate and share my dual perspective.

IT has become a necessity for businesses of all sizes, and this is not going to change. It is one of those fields where it is not too late to join because the environment is constantly changing. Advancements in computer hardware and software that enable new business creation and opportunities occur constantly. For example, in the field of business intelligence, information systems that used to be costly and bulky to maintain are now more affordable than ever as a result of advancements in cloud computing.

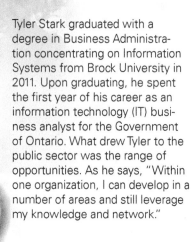

Tyler Stark

A career in IS is not necessarily based only on technical skills. They are great to have and will help you along the way—but the nature of the job requires communication and collaboration skills for you to be successful. Projects quickly become complex and require project management methodologies to stay on track. Communication with your peers and consulting with subject matter experts on a regular basis are key in IS. Some may find this a challenge. My advice? Get comfortable asking for information that you do not have in order to do your job effectively, and be prepared to regularly report on your progress.

Our third "running case" involves Carrie, a university student who started a custom fashion t-shirt and accessory business, Carrie's Custom Clothing, while working at her high school clothing store. Now in her second year at university, Carrie has studied the clothing industry and knows that it is generally considered to be made up of three key areas: (1) the textile industry, which takes raw materials and produces fabrics; (2) the apparel industry, which designs, creates, and distributes finished goods (clothes) to wholesalers; and (3) the retail industry, which is responsible for end customer distribution and sales.

Carrie knows first-hand that the Canadian clothing industry, which tends to have a high labour component, has been hit hard by globalization, improved technology, and the movement of labour to low-cost countries. Between 2007 and 2011, for example, Canadian manufactured clothing GDP shrank from $1947 million to $1363 million (equal to a Compound Annual Growth Rate of − 8.5%) and employment declined from 54 500 to 35 700 (−10% CAGR). Carrie, however, remains optimistic, largely because she knows that her customers buy clothes for fashion, rather than just to keep dry and stay warm, and some Canadian clothing firms that cater to the fitness and yoga segments have done well. Carrie hopes that by continuing to focus on customer service, remaining agile and responsive, and using ideas appropriately, all of which she is learning in this course, she will be able to continue to grow her business.

Running Case Introduction

In her high school, Carrie ran the school's clothing store. She learned about materials, suppliers, and printing/embroidering on all sorts of textiles. Even more important, she learned about how to sell school fashions. When she came to university, she decided to keep her focus on embroidery, printing, and fashion design for outerwear by becoming an entrepreneur and starting her own company.

Starting Carrie's Custom Clothing was not easy. She was busy with her school work and she had to find time not only to make sales but also to print t-shirts and hoodies and deliver them on time to her customers. Once she graduated, she decided to continue to grow her business. She has now expanded her line significantly and provides custom printing and embroidery solutions for teams, clubs, schools, and numerous events. She now takes t-shirts, hoodies, outerwear, accessories (such as scarves), pens, and mugs and adapts them to the needs of her customers.

One of Carrie's advantages has been her wide network of friends and acquaintances who have given her lots of repeat business. Carrie likes to say that once people deal with her, they never look anywhere else. She does personal delivery and backs her quality up with a seven-day return policy if people are not satisfied with the look of the product. Her excellent customer service has paid off as she has lost very few clients and continues to grow her list of happy clients. The problem is that her list is growing longer than she can keep in her head. The volume of orders is too much to keep track of, and Carrie feels that the business is simply outgrowing her ability to keep up with her customers. Unfortunately, as her customers grow, so does the amount of information that she needs to store. She has always kept excellent paper records, but

now it takes her longer at the end of each month to do her accounting and pay off her bills. She is starting to think about some systems to help her company grow.

Another consideration for Carrie is how she produces her t-shirts and outwear for her clients. There are two basic methods. One is buying machinery so that she can do it herself. This works well for small orders and allows Carrie to respond to rush orders. However, for larger orders, Carrie needs to rely on third-party vendors who have larger capacity. She makes less on every t-shirt when she uses third-party vendors. Moreover, often there is a longer delay in production, which makes it harder to ensure that the outwear will be delivered on time to customers. The question Carrie needs to answer is when to buy new machinery and when to send an order out to third-party vendors.

It is clear that selling customized clothing and accessories is a growing industry. T-shirts and print designs are available in any style imaginable. Many people have started their own t-shirt business. The low barriers to entry make the industry fiercely competitive. Carrie is well aware of the competition and has survived her first few years. She is looking for a way to give her company a competitive edge. The next three chapters provide information that can help Carrie with these decisions.

◉ Watch

This case will run throughout Part 3. Read more at the beginning of each chapter, and then visit MyMISLab to access the data files to complete the running case questions at the end of Part 3.

MyMISLab

7 Competitive Advantage and Business Processes

Running Case: Carrie's Custom Clothing

As her customer list grows, Carrie has been thinking about finding a way to manage her customers more effectively. She has found that customers' addresses and phone numbers often change and that she uses a variety of ways to store these numbers, including her personal phone, her purse, a paper calendar she keeps in her car, and even some sticky notes. "It gets a little frustrating when data are stored in so many places and I can't get access to them when I need them the most," Carrie noted. She added, "That is one of my main frustrations."

Another source of frustration is the accessibility of information about her previous sales. Carrie notes, "Sometimes, I have to remember what discount I gave to one of my customers, but I just don't have access to that information at my fingertips. I have my phone with me all the time, but I don't have access to the sales information on my phone." When she is in her office, she can look up her Excel spreadsheet for the information. She is very careful with the spreadsheet, as it includes her customers' names and personal information, so she does not bring it with her on the road.

Once she gets started, Carrie provides a larger list of her frustrations, "I'm also getting frustrated with entering stuff all over the place. My customer names go in the spreadsheet, but then they have to get re-entered in the accounting system. I then place the new numbers in my phone. That's three points of entry. Then I have to create invoices and collect payments that come in through a whole bunch of channels. It gets difficult to keep up with all of that data entry. And don't even mention how I interact with my suppliers. That is a whole different story. The prices change every day, and delivery times are key. You have to be on it to make sure you can deliver the orders on time. Ugh!"

Carrie's issues are very similar to many issues in smaller businesses. The question you should consider as you read through this chapter is this: How can Carrie address her frustration and add value to her company by investing in technology? It is an important question and one of central importance in understanding how to achieve competitive advantage.

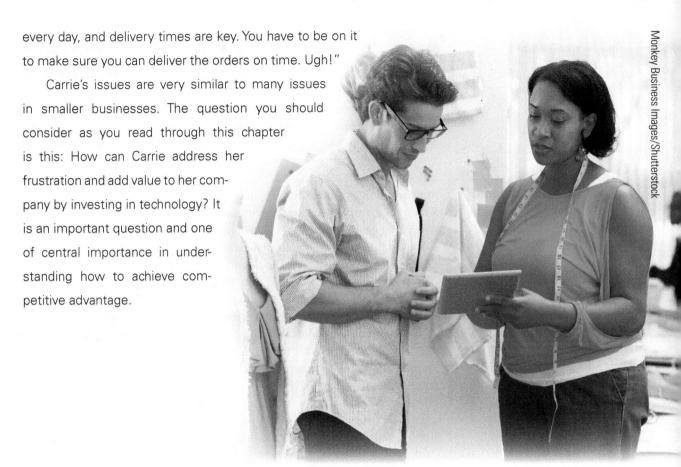

Study Questions

Q1 What are the fundamental ways of achieving competitive advantage?

Q2 What are business functions and functional systems?

Q3 How can business processes be improved?

Q4 What are the challenges of implementing business process changes?

Q5 What is the importance of industry standard processes?

Q6 What are ERP systems?

Q7 What are CRM systems?

Q8 What are SCM systems?

👁–⌐Watch

Go to MyMISLab to watch a video about three fundamental types of information systems within organizations.

Q1 What Are the Fundamental Ways of Achieving Competitive Advantage?

In Chapter 3, we looked at the ways in which organizations achieve a competitive advantage. We found that there are two basic ways to develop competitive advantage through systems. One way is to enhance the product or service through information systems. These changes enable organizations to differentiate themselves. An example of this kind of change is provided by Zipcar (www.zipcar.com), a car-sharing service available in over 100 university campuses and in downtown Toronto and Vancouver. Car sharing is a new service that provides an alternative to buying or renting a car. Unlike traditional car rental agencies, Zipcar uses the web and electronic card-reading technology to provide customers with access to short-term car rentals at a reasonable price. Customers do not visit a Zipcar agency. Instead, they go to a parking garage, use their card to open the car, and then return the car to the garage. These services would not be reasonably priced without the information systems that support them. Zipcar, therefore, is a good example of a company that uses IS to introduce a new or enhanced service.

The second way of developing competitive advantage is through business processes. Organizations look to technology to help retain customers, reduce costs, and create entry barriers for competitors in the market. For example, Grand & Toy, Canada's largest commercial office-supply company (www.grandandtoy.com), has traditionally sold office supplies to organizations. In the last decade, however, the company has aggressively grown the list of services it offers through the web. Website design and hosting, human resource management, and purchasing management are just a few of the professional services that Grand & Toy now offers. The information systems supporting these services help the company lock in their customers and create entry barriers for other office-supply companies.

The examples above demonstrate that information systems can affect competitive advantage by making the primary and support activities in an organization more productive than those of competitors. Increased productivity is realized when business processes within the organization become more effective, more efficient, or both. This is true for commercial companies as well as for nonprofit organizations and government. In this chapter, we look at the types of information systems that can be used to make organizations of all types more productive.

If you were to walk into any organization (say, your first employer), you would find a maze of different information systems. Some of the systems are designed to improve your personal productivity, such as Microsoft Office applications. Other systems, such as an accounts payable system, are designed to support business activities that relate to more than one person. The knowledge you derive from this chapter will help you to make sense out of that maze, to take a critical approach in identifying different kinds of information systems and what they do, and to understand how to help an organization achieve its competitive strategy.

Choosing the right information system may not be as easy as you think. Consider, for example, Bag Borrow or Steal Inc. (www.bagborroworsteal.com). This company uses web systems to provide an online borrowing experience that gives its customers access to fashion accessories, such as handbags, jewellery, watches, and sunglasses, through rental agreements. To make a consistent profit, the company has to balance the resources it invests in marketing and customer relationship development, website applications, and online transaction processing, as well as purchasing, payroll, and operations. With a limited budget, which of these information systems would you invest more in, and which of these systems would contribute the most to the company's competitive advantage? These are the types of questions business professionals need to answer.

Q2 What Are Business Functions and Functional Systems?

We can use Porter's value chain model (introduced in Chapter 3) to explain the scope and purpose of different types of business functions within the organization. For our purposes, the value chain model will be more useful if we redraw it as shown in Figure 7-1. The value chain consists of two types of activities. **Primary activities** that, as the name implies, deal with the main or core parts of the good or service that the organization produces or provides and **support activities**, which are secondary or ancillary to the good or service that is produced. Note that the question as to if an activity is primary or support will depend upon the organization and what it produces. The value chain starts with marketing and sales activities which are followed by inbound logistics, operations or manufacturing, outbound logistics, and, finally, service and support.

Organizational processes involve both primary and support activities, although for most organizations greater attention is paid to primary activities because these most often directly impact the customer. For example, a university may be more focused on its inbound logistics—how it manages student registration—than the human resource system used to manage the faculty and staff. The primary activities are facilitated by support activities: human resources, accounting and infrastructure, procurement, and technology. The primary activities of the value chain occur in the order shown in Figure 7-1. These primary and support activities are often referred to as *business functions*. No matter what industry or organization you work in, these basic business functions (accounting, finance, human resources, marketing and sales, operations, procurement, etc.) are almost always present.

These activities are often supported by what are called functional systems. **Functional systems** facilitate the work of a single department or business function. In each functional area, companies often add features and capabilities to information systems to support more functional-area activity. Figure 7-2 shows five functional systems and their relationship to the value chain. As you would expect, each functional system is closely allied with the activities it supports, and there is little cross-over among activities.

Functional Silos and Cross-Functional Systems

The problem with functional applications is their isolation. In fact, these systems are sometimes called **functional silos** because they are designed to work independently of one another. For example, the marketing department would do its work using the marketing and sales system. The accounting department would use the general ledger and other accounting systems, and the operations department would work with

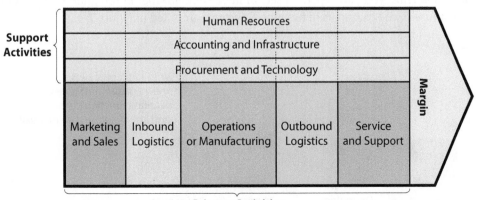

Figure 7-1

Reorganized Porter Value Chain Model

Source: Based on Michael E. Porter, *Competitive Advantage: Creating and Sustaining Superior Performance* (The Free Press, a Division of Simon & Schuster), Copyright © 1985, 1998.

Figure 7-2

Reorganized Porter Value Chain Model and Its Relationship to Functional Systems

Source: Based on Michael E. Porter, *Competitive Advantage: Creating and Sustaining Superior Performance* (The Free Press, a Division of Simon & Schuster) Copyright © 1985, 1998.

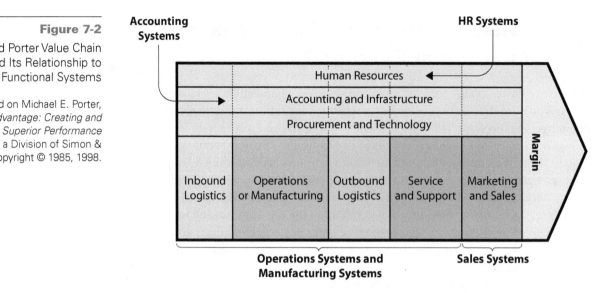

a number of operational systems. The separation between systems makes it seem as if various departments in the same company could work separately, almost independently of each other. An example of functional silos is shown in Figure 7-3.

The truth is that all of these functional systems are interrelated. When you make a sale to a customer, the rest of the company has to know what and when to deliver to the customer and for what price. Purchasing influences inventory, which influences production, which influences customer satisfaction, which, in turn, influences future sales. All of these different functions are linked. Decisions that are appropriate when considering only a single business function, such as purchasing, may create inefficiencies when considering the entire business process. Business processes are cross-functional, that is, they are processes that cut across functional areas.

The isolation problems of functional systems led to the development of **cross-departmental** or **cross-functional systems**. These systems integrate data and business processes across different departments and systems. As cross-functional systems have become more sophisticated, some information systems have begun to cross not only functional boundaries but also organizational boundaries. These systems that are used by two or more related companies are referred to as **interorganizational systems**. The most common of these include supply chain management systems and some e-commerce applications. We will talk about supply chain management systems later in this chapter and in Chapter 8.

Most organizations today have a mixture of functional and integrated systems. In the future, to successfully compete internationally organizations must eventually achieve the efficiencies of integrated, cross-departmental, business process based systems. Thus, you can expect to see an increasing number of integrated systems in the future. Some examples of functional systems are listed in Figure 7-4.

Figure 7-3

Separate Functional Systems

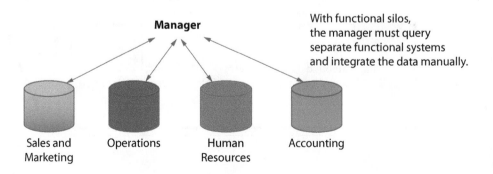

Function	Examples of Information Systems
Marketing and sales	Product management Lead tracking Sales forecasting Customer management
Operations	Order entry Order management Inventory management Customer service
Manufacturing	Inventory Planning Scheduling Manufacturing operations
Human resources	Payroll and compensation Recruiting Assessment Development and training Human resources planning
Accounting and finance	General ledger Financial reporting Accounts receivable Accounts payable Cost accounting Budgeting Cash management Treasury management

Figure 7-4

Typical Functional Systems

Why Are Functional Systems Changing?

Functional systems provide tremendous benefits to the departments that use them, but these benefits are limited because the systems operate in isolation. Figure 7-5 lists the problems encountered with isolated functional systems. First, data are duplicated because each application has its own database. For example, customer data may be

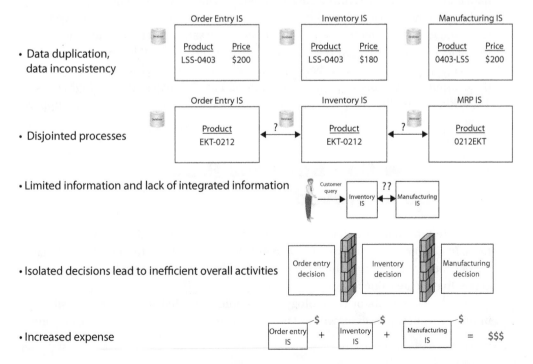

Figure 7-5

Major Problems of Isolated Functional Systems

- Data duplication, data inconsistency
- Disjointed processes
- Limited information and lack of integrated information
- Isolated decisions lead to inefficient overall activities
- Increased expense

Figure 7-6

Example of System
Integration Problem

- Order Entry System Product Number:
    Format: ccc–nnnn
    Example: COM–3344
- Manufacturing System Product Number:
    Format: nnnnccc
    Example: 3344COM

duplicated and possibly inconsistent when accounting and sales/marketing applications are separated. The principal problem of duplicated data is a potential lack of data integrity. Changes to product data made in one system may take days or weeks to reach the other systems. And during that period, inconsistent data will cause inconsistent application results.

Additionally, when systems are isolated, business processes become disjointed. There is no easy way for the sales/marketing system to integrate activity with the accounting system, for example. Just sending the data from one system to the other can be problematic.

Consider the example in Figure 7-6. Suppose the order entry and inventory systems define a product number as three characters, a dash, and four numeric digits. The manufacturing system in the same company, however, defines a product as four digits followed by three characters. Every time parts data are exported from order entry and imported into manufacturing (or vice versa), the data must be converted from one scheme to the other. Multiply this conversion process by several hundred data items, and possibly dozens of other systems, and you can see why processing is disjointed across functional applications.

A consequence of such disjointed systems is the lack of integrated enterprise information. When a customer asks about an order, several systems may need to be queried. For example, some order information is in the order entry system, some in the finished-goods inventory system, and some in the manufacturing system. Obtaining a consolidated statement about the customer's order will require processing each of these systems, with possibly inconsistent data.

A fourth consequence of isolated systems is inefficiency. When using isolated functional systems, a department can make decisions based only on the isolated data that it has. So, for example, raw materials inventory systems will make inventory replenishment decisions based only on costs and benefits in that single inventory. However, it may be that the overall efficiency of the sales, order entry, and manufacturing activities, considered together across the enterprise, will be improved by carrying a less-than-optimal number of products in raw materials inventory. Duplicated data, disjointed systems, limited information, and inefficiencies all mean higher costs. These kinds of inefficiencies led people to wonder if there were better ways to support business processes.

Q3 How Can Business Processes Be Improved?

We learned in Chapter 2 that business processes are supported by information systems. In Chapter 3, we saw that IT often enables organizations to innovate and make significant change. In this chapter, we consider how IT can be used to improve processes that create value for organizations.

Before talking about technology, we should note that it is always possible to improve business processes without technological change. For example, we can often get more done in a process by (1) adding resources (such as adding more workers); or (2) adding increased specialization (such as adding more skilled workers); and (3) changing/eliminating unproductive activities. Adding resources, such as (1) and (2) above, often costs more money but enables more production. This approach might be called doing more with more. However, many organizations often attempt to do more with less—in which case, they very often turn to IT.

The first step in considering how IT can improve a business process is to understand where the improvements might take place. The key to process improvement is to consider the underlying activities and/or resources. If you can change the activities so that you get more done with the same resources or you can accomplish the same activities with less resource cost, then you have made a productive change. This is what business process management, which we introduced earlier in Chapter 2, is all about. When organizations have functional silos, the organization is not as productive as it could be. There are opportunities to improve processes by integrating activities and resources across the functional areas, but it often takes changes in technology to make these improvements possible.

For example, as advanced networks became prevalent in the 1990s, systems developers realized that these networks provided a way to do more than simply automate functional systems. Developers began to wonder how they could create systems that would integrate many different functional areas in an entire value chain. This thinking became the foundation of enterprise data architecture and resulted in the idea of **business process design** (or, sometimes, *business process redesign*). The central idea is that organizations should not simply automate or improve existing functional systems. The process of making efficient what already exists is sometimes referred to as paving the cowpath because, while it makes things easier, it does not fundamentally change the way things are done. Business process design was not about paving the cowpath. Instead, it was about making significant changes by integrating functional systems.

The basic approach would be to establish more efficient business processes that integrate the activities of many functional departments involved in a value chain. So, in the early 1990s, some organizations began to design new cross-functional business processes that integrated functional systems with the hopes of making data accessible to the entire enterprise (and not just one functional area). The goal was to take advantage of as many activity linkages as possible. For example, a cross-functional customer management process could integrate all interactions with the customer, from prospect through initial order through repeat orders, including customer support, outbound logistics, credit, and accounts receivable.

Integrating Functional Systems: EAI and ERP

Integrating functional systems can be very complex; it requires careful thinking and a consistent design approach. We will talk briefly about two approaches to integration.

Enterprise application integration (EAI) is an approach to combining functional systems, which uses layers of software as a bridge to connect different functional systems together. The main design principle for EAI is that it leaves the functional systems basically intact. The data for each functional system stay within the functional system. A customized EAI interface is then created for each functional system. These customized interfaces allow a central EAI server to pull whatever data are necessary from each of the functional systems. The EAI server, thus, acts to centrally integrate the necessary enterprise information from the functional system. Users of the system see only the data that are integrated on the EAI server. To them, it looks like one giant integrated database. Users are not aware of all the complex linkages within each of the EAI interfaces. EAI provides the integrated data that users are looking for while minimizing changes to the functional systems. Figure 7-7 demonstrates this EAI design principle.

Figure 7-7
Enterprise Application Integration

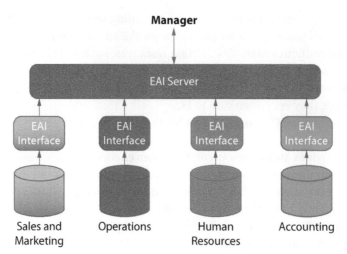

With enterprise application integration, the data stay in the functional system. The manager accesses the data through the EAI interface. The manager sees a single database.

The EAI interface sends data to the EAI Server.

The functional systems still exist separately and store actual data.

Figure 7-8
Enterprise Resource Planning

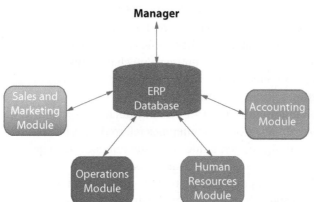

With enterprise resource planning, there is a single central database. The manager accesses data through this database.

People in the functional areas use ERP to send and receive data directly from the central database.

No functional systems exist. They were replaced by the ERP modules.

A second approach to combining functional systems is through enterprise resource planning (ERP). We will learn more about ERP later in this chapter, but, for now, it is important to understand the main design principle behind it. One central database is combined with a set of standard business processes built on top of the database to ensure integration between functional areas. The standard processes ensure that the organization integrates data into a single database that can distribute accurate data throughout the organization. The ERP approach uses prebuilt software so that an organization adopting an ERP system must remove its existing functional systems before adopting the ERP system. This also means that the current business processes must be changed to fit into the structure of the ERP system. Figure 7-8 demonstrates the central importance of a single enterprise-level database in an ERP system.

Q4 What Are the Challenges of Implementing Business Process Changes?

Unfortunately, process design projects are expensive and difficult to implement. There are three reasons for this. The first is that departmental managers very often focus mainly on their aspects of the value chain and are willing to implement changes that may not integrate across the entire organization. There is a lot of detailed work to be done to determine what to change, and many experts from different parts of the organization are needed to make an effective decision. Instead, managers may purchase point solutions that simply address their specific problem rather than take the time and effort to provide a complete solution.

Let us assume that the organization can work through this complexity. The next big challenge is to convince the organization that the changes are worth the effort. For some process changes, this can be easy. For other changes, the reasons are not so obvious. Understanding and estimating the business value that will emerge from business process changes is a risky business. If you underestimate the benefits of the changes (i.e., you undersell the impact of the changes), the organization might not be convinced to undertake them. If you overestimate the benefits of the changes (i.e., you oversell the impact of the changes), then the organization will be disappointed in the outcome and will grow more reluctant to make further changes.

Finally, once these first two challenges have been overcome and the new integrated processes are designed and approved, a new, even greater challenge arises. Many people like change but do not want to change. People often do not want to work in new ways, they do not want to see their department reorganized or abolished, and they do not want to work for someone new. Even if the process changes can be implemented in spite of this resistance, some workers will continue to resist the changes.

All these difficulties translate into more hours of labour, which translate into higher costs and increased risk of underperformance. Thus, business process design is very expensive, and the outcomes are often uncertain.

Q5 What Is the Importance of Industry Standard Processes?

👁‑[Watch]
Go to MyMISLab to watch a video about business process management.

Many early business process design projects failed because they were tailor-made. They were customized to suit a particular organization, so just one company bore the cost of the design effort. In the mid-1990s, a number of successful software vendors began to market pre-made integrated applications, with built-in industry standard processes. Such processes saved hundreds of hours of design work.

When an organization acquires, for example, a business application from large system companies, such as Oracle, Salesforce.com, Microsoft, or SAP, the processes for using the software are built-in or **industry standard processes**. In most cases, the organization must conform its activities to those processes. If the software is designed well, the industry standard process will effectively integrate activities across departments. These pre-built processes can save the organization the substantial, sometimes staggering, costs of designing new processes itself.

Figure 7-9 shows an example of an industry standard process in a software product called **SAP R/3**, a product licensed by SAP (www.sap.com). When an organization licenses this product, SAP provides hundreds of diagrams just like this one. The diagram shows the business processes that must be followed to effectively use the software and the flow and logic of one set of processes. In the top lines, if the purchase requisition does not exist and if the request for quotation (RFQ) is to be created, then the purchasing department creates an RFQ and sends it to potential vendors. You can study the rest of this sample diagram to get the general idea of this process illustration.

To some people, when an organization licenses cross-functional software, the primary benefit is not the software but the inherent processes in the software. Licensing an integrated application not only saves the organization the time, expense, and agony of process design, but also enables the organization to benefit immediately from tried and tested cross-departmental processes.

There are, of course, disadvantages too. The industry standard processes may be very different from existing processes and, thus, require the organization to change

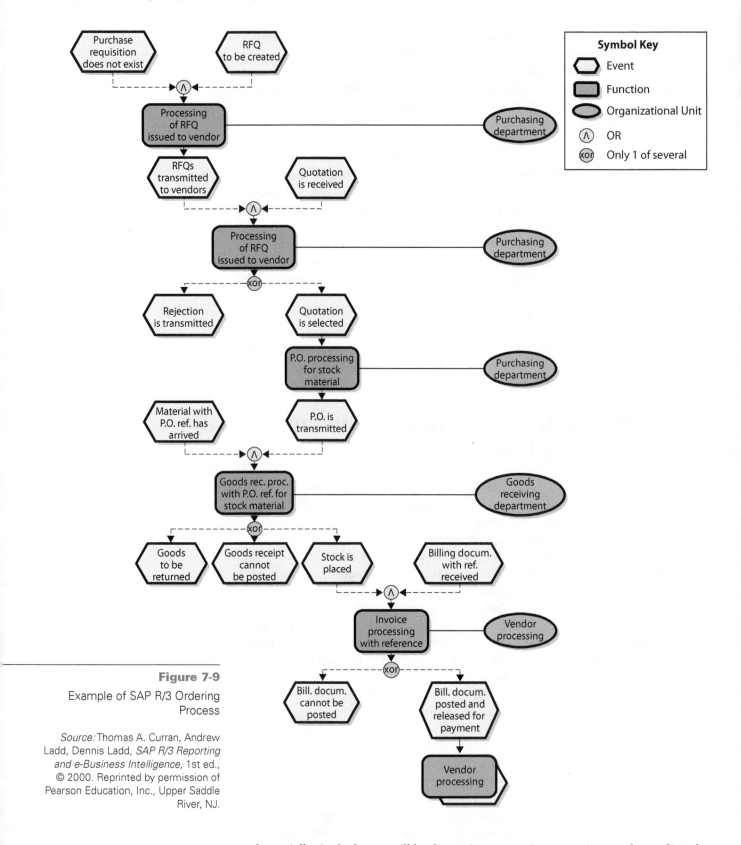

Figure 7-9

Example of SAP R/3 Ordering Process

Source: Thomas A. Curran, Andrew Ladd, Dennis Ladd, *SAP R/3 Reporting and e-Business Intelligence*, 1st ed., © 2000. Reprinted by permission of Pearson Education, Inc., Upper Saddle River, NJ.

substantially. Such change will be disruptive to ongoing operations and very disturbing to many employees. An example of this is provided in the "MIS in Use" on pages 246–247. Similarly, using enterprise systems can make it difficult for organizations to differentiate themselves so that they can radically alter the basis for competition. The exercise "Available Only in Vanilla" at the end of this chapter on pages 252–253 discusses the effects of organizational change in more detail.

Q6 What Are ERP Systems?

Enterprise resource planning (ERP) systems support many or all of the primary business processes as well as the human resources and accounting support processes. ERP is an outgrowth of materials resource planning (MRP), and the primary ERP users are manufacturing companies. One of the first vendors of ERP software for large organizations was a German company, SAP. Other large vendors include Oracle (www.oracle.com) and Infor (www.infor.com/). For medium-sized businesses, Microsoft provides a number of solutions (NAV, AX, GP, and Solomon), and a large number of smaller vendors provide integrated enterprise solutions for smaller firms.

ERP represents the ultimate in cross-departmental process systems. The system can integrate sales, order, inventory, manufacturing, customer service, human resources, accounting, and other activities. ERP systems provide software, predesigned databases, industry standard procedures, and job descriptions for organization-wide process integration.

ERP Characteristics

Figure 7-10 lists the major ERP characteristics. First, as stated earlier, ERP takes a cross-functional, process view of the entire organization. With ERP, the entire organization is considered a collection of interrelated activities. There is a single central database for collecting enterprise information.

Second, true ERP is a formal approach that is based on documented, tested business models. ERP applications include a comprehensive set of inherent processes for all organizational activities. SAP defines this set as the **process blueprint**, and documents each process with diagrams that use a set of standardized symbols.

Because ERP is based on formally defined procedures, organizations must adapt their processing to the ERP blueprint. If they do not, the system cannot operate effectively, or even correctly. In some cases, it is possible to adapt ERP software to procedures that are different from the blueprint, but such adaptation is expensive and often problematic.

- Provides cross-functional, process view of the organization

- Has a formal approach based on formal business models

- Maintains data in centralized database

- Offers large benefits but is difficult, fraught with challenges, and can be slow to implement

- Is often VERY expensive
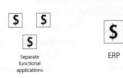

Figure 7-10

Characteristics of ERP

Once an organization has implemented an ERP system, it can achieve large benefits. However, as shown in Figure 7-10, the process of moving from separated, functional applications to an ERP system can be slow and is difficult and fraught with challenges. In particular, changing organizational procedures has proven to be a great challenge for many organizations and, in some cases, was even a pitfall that prevented successful ERP implementation. Finally, the switch to an ERP system is very costly (in some cases more than $50 000 000)—not only because of the need for new hardware and software but also because of the costs of developing new procedures, training employees, converting data, and other developmental expenses.

Benefits of ERP

Figure 7-11 summarizes the major benefits of ERP. First, the processes in the business blueprint have been tried and tested over hundreds of organizations. The processes are effective and often very efficient. Organizations that convert to ERP do not need to reinvent business processes. Rather, they gain the benefit of processes that have already been proved successful.

By taking an organization-wide view, many companies find that they can reduce their inventory, sometimes dramatically. With better planning, it is not necessary to maintain large buffer stocks. Additionally, items remain in inventory for shorter periods, sometimes no longer than a few hours or a day.

As discussed earlier, data inconsistency problems are not an issue because all ERP data are stored in an integrated database. Further, because all data about a customer, order, part, or other entity reside in one place, the data are readily accessible. This means that organizations can provide better information about orders, products, and customer status to their customers. All of this results in not only better customer service but also less costly customer service. Integrated databases also make company-wide data readily accessible and result in greater, real-time visibility, thus allowing a peek into the status of the organization.

Finally, ERP-based organizations often find that they can produce and sell the same products at lower costs because of smaller inventories, reduced lead times, and less expensive customer support. The bottom-line result is higher profitability. The trick, however, is getting there. Despite the clear benefits of inherent processes and ERP, there may be unintended consequences.

For example, it is reasonable to ask what the competitive advantage of ERP systems are if all competitors use the same "industry standard" processes. Although each firm might become more productive, the competitive advantage of ERP systems erodes as more and more competitors implement ERP products. This suggests that all companies within an industry that install ERP will receive the same benefits. We learned in Chapter 3 that this is not the case, however. Software and hardware do not necessarily provide a sustained advantage. It is the combination of people, procedures, hardware, software, and data that creates sustainable advantage. Installing ERP, therefore, creates an initial hurdle for competitors. Learning to effectively use the information provided by the ERP will be the key source of advantage to those companies that are best able to use the system.

Figure 7-11

Potential Benefits of ERP

- Efficient business processes
- Inventory reduction
- Lead-time reduction
- Improved customer service
- Greater, real-time insight into organization
- Higher profitability

Q7 What Are CRM Systems?

Cross-functional systems were developed to overcome the problems of functional silos. Not all cross-functional systems go as far as ERP in integrating enterprise information. One type of cross-functional system in use today is customer relationship management (CRM). **Customer relationship management (CRM) systems** support the business processes of attracting, selling, managing, delivering, and supporting customers. CRM systems support all the direct value chain activities that involve the customer. There are many software vendors who provide a wide variety of CRM software. Maximizer Software (www.maximizer.com) is a Canadian company focused on contact management for small- and medium-sized businesses. Larger CRM vendors include Oracle/Siebel Systems, CDC/Pivotal Corp, and Salesforce.com.

The difference between CRM systems and traditional functional applications is that CRM systems address all activities and events that touch the customer and provide a single repository for data about all customer interactions. With functional systems, data about customers are sprinkled in databases all over the organization. Some customer data exist in customer management databases, some in order entry databases, some in customer service databases, and so forth. CRM systems store all customer data in one place and make it possible to easily access all data about the customer.

Figure 7-12 shows four phases of the **customer life cycle**: (1) marketing, (2) customer acquisition, (3) relationship management, and (4) loss/churn. Marketing sends messages to the target market to attract customer prospects. When prospects order, they become customers who need to be supported. Additionally, resell processes increase the value of existing customers. Inevitably, over time, the organization loses customers. When this occurs, win-back processes categorize customers according to value and attempt to win back high-value customers.

The organizational website is an increasingly important tool. Web addresses are easy to promote (and remember), and once a target prospect is on the site, product

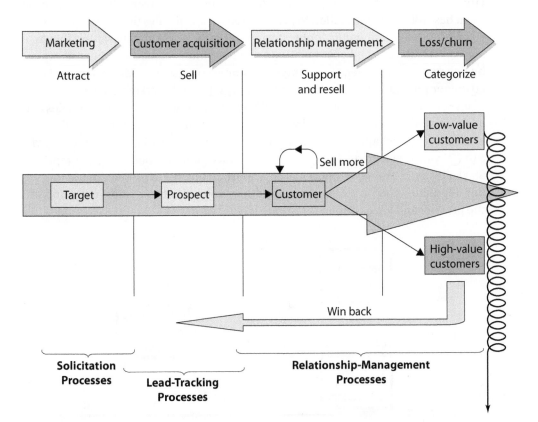

Figure 7-12

The Customer Life Cycle

Source: Douglas MacLachlan, University of Washington.

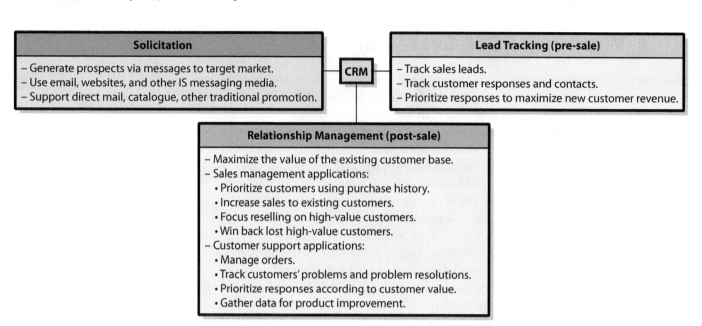

Figure 7-13

CRM Components

descriptions, use cases, success stories, and other solicitation materials can be provided easily. Further, the cost of distributing these materials via the web is substantially lower than the cost of creating and distributing printed materials. Many websites require customer name and contact information before releasing high-value promotional materials. That contact information then feeds lead-tracking applications.

The purpose of relationship management applications is to maximize the value of the existing customer base. As Figure 7-13 shows, two types of applications are used. *Sales management applications* support sales to existing customers. They have features that prioritize customers according to their purchase history. Salespeople can increase sales to existing customers by focusing on customers who have already made large purchases, by focusing on large organizations that have the potential to make large purchases, or both. The goal of such applications is to ensure that sales management has sufficient information to prioritize and allocate sales time and effort.

Integrated CRM applications store data in a single database, as shown in Figure 7-14. Because all customer data reside in one location, CRM processes can be linked to one another. For example, customer service activities can be linked to customer purchase records. In this way, both sales and marketing know the status of customer satisfaction, both on an individual customer basis for future sales calls and also collectively for analyzing customers' overall satisfaction. As well, many customer support applications prioritize customers to avoid, for example, giving $10 000 worth of support to a customer who has a lifetime value to the company of $500. Finally, customer support has an important linkage to product marketing and development—it knows, more than any other group, what customers are doing with the product and what problems they are having with it.

Figure 7-14

CRM Centred on Integrated
Customer Database

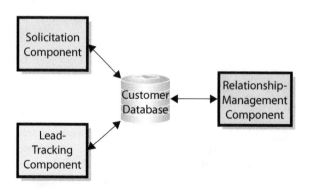

Q8 What Are SCM Systems?

Supply chain management (SCM) systems are interorganizational systems that enable companies to efficiently handle the flow of goods from suppliers to customers. A **supply chain** is a network of organizations and facilities that transforms raw materials into products delivered to customers. Figure 7-15 shows a generic supply chain. Customers order from retailers, who, in turn, order from distributors, who, in turn, order from manufacturers, who, in turn, order from suppliers. In addition to the organizations shown here, the supply chain includes transportation companies, warehouses, inventories, and some means for transmitting messages and information among the organizations involved.

Because of **disintermediation**, not every supply chain has all these organizations. Dell, for example, sells directly to the customer and seeks to begin manufacturing after the order is received (build to order) rather than before (build for the shelf). Both the distributor and retailer organizations are omitted from its supply chain. In other supply chains, manufacturers sell directly to retailers and omit the distribution level.

The term *chain* is misleading. *Chain* implies that each organization is connected to just one item up (toward the supplier) and down (toward the customer) the chain. However, this may not always be the case. Instead, at each level, an organization could work with many organizations both up and down the supply chain. Thus, a supply chain is most likely a supply network even though we used the term "chain."

To understand the operation of a supply chain, look at Figure 7-16. Suppose you decide to take up cross-country skiing. You go to REI.com (a company that sells

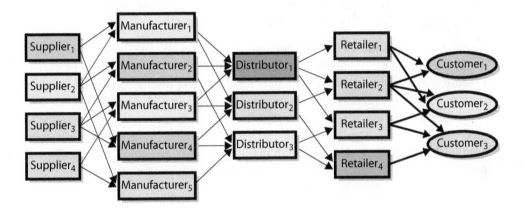

Figure 7-15

Supply Chain Relationships

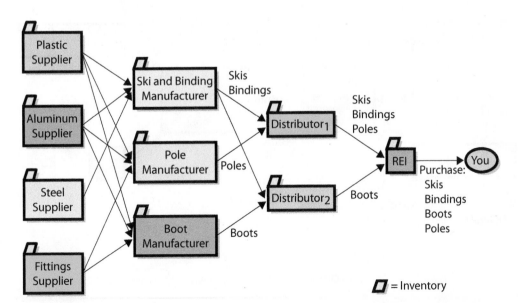

Figure 7-16

Supply Chain Example

outdoor sporting equipment and supplies) and purchase skis, bindings, boots, and poles. After filling your order, REI removes those items from its inventory of goods.

Those goods have been purchased, in turn, from distributors. According to Figure 7-16, REI purchases skis, bindings, and poles from one distributor and boots from a second. The distributors, in turn, purchase the required items from the manufacturers, who, in turn, buy raw materials from their suppliers.

The only source of revenue in a supply chain is the customer. In the REI example, you spend your money on the ski equipment. From that point, all the way back up the supply chain to the raw material suppliers, there is no further injection of cash. The money you spend on the ski equipment is passed back up the supply chain as payment for goods or raw materials. Again, the customer is the only source of revenue.

Four major factors, or *drivers*, affect supply chain performance: facilities, inventory, transportation, and information.[1] We will focus our attention on the fourth factor, information. (You can learn in detail about the first three factors in operations management classes.)

Information influences supply chain performance by affecting the ways in which organizations in the supply chain request from, respond to, and inform one another. There are three factors of information: (1) purpose, (2) availability, and (3) means. The *purpose* of the information can be transactional, such as orders and order returns, or it can be informational, such as the sharing of inventory and customer order data. *Availability* refers to the ways in which organizations share their information—that is, which organizations have access to which information and when. Finally, *means* refers to the methods by which the information is transmitted.

Supplier Relationship Management

Figure 7-17 shows the three fundamental information systems involved in **supply chain management**: (1) supplier relationship management (SRM), (2) inventory, and (3) customer relationship management (CRM). We have discussed all these applications except supplier relationship management, which we will now discuss.

Supplier relationship management (SRM) is a business process for managing all contacts between an organization and its suppliers. The term *supplier* in *supplier relationship management* is broader than the use of the term *supplier* in Figures 7-15 and 7-16. In those figures, the term refers to the supplier of raw materials and

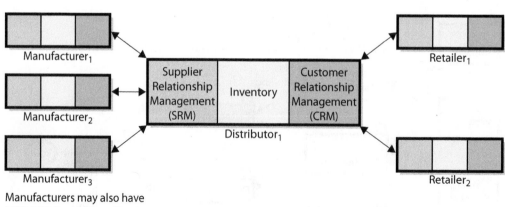

Figure 7-17

B2B in One Section of the Supply Chain

[1] S. Chopra and P. Meindl, *Supply Chain Management* (Upper Saddle River, NJ: Prentice Hall, 2004), pp. 51–53.

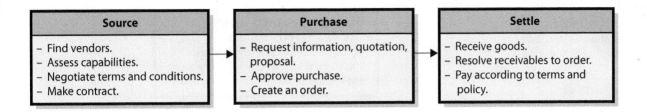

Source	Purchase	Settle
– Find vendors. – Assess capabilities. – Negotiate terms and conditions. – Make contract.	– Request information, quotation, proposal. – Approve purchase. – Create an order.	– Receive goods. – Resolve receivables to order. – Pay according to terms and policy.

Figure 7-18

Summary of SRM Processes

assemblies to a manufacturer. *Supplier* in SRM is used generically—it refers to *any organization* that sells something to the organization that has the SRM application. Thus, in this generic sense, a manufacturer is a supplier to a distributor.

SRM is an integrated system in the same way that CRM and MRP are. With regard to Porter's model, an SRM supports both the inbound logistics primary activity and the procurement support activity. Considering business processes, SRM applications support three basic processes: (1) source, (2) purchase, and (3) settle, as summarized in Figure 7-18.

With regard to sourcing, the organization needs to find possible vendors of needed supplies, materials, or services; to assess the vendors that it does find; to negotiate terms and conditions; and to formalize those terms and conditions in a procurement contract. SRM software is especially relevant to finding and assessing vendors. Some SRM applications have features that let users search for product sources and find evaluations of vendors and products. You see something similar to this functionality when you search for electronics products on a website, such as www.cnet.com. There, you can readily determine which vendors provide which products, and you can also obtain evaluations of products and vendors. Similar capabilities are built into SRM packages.

Once the company has identified vendors and has the appropriate contracts in place, the next stage is to procure the goods. The SRM application requests information, quotations, and proposals from would-be suppliers. The company can then use the SRM to manage the approval workflow in order to approve the purchase and issue the order.

The third major SRM activity is settlement. Here, the accounting department reconciles the receipt of the goods or services against the purchase documents and schedules the vendor payment. The payment portion of the SRM typically connects to the cash management subsystem in the financial management application.

Information systems have had an exceedingly positive impact on supply chain performance (see Figure 7-19). CRM, SRM, and less integrated functional systems, such as e-commerce sales systems, have dramatically reduced the costs of buying and selling. Sourcing, buying, and settling have all become faster, easier, more effective, and less costly.

Furthermore, the presence of information systems has expanded supply chain speed (the dollar value of goods exchanged in a given period). Without information systems, Amazon.com would not have been able to process an average of 158 items per second for 24 hours, as it did on November 29, 2010, that year's peak day. And, without information systems, it would not have been able to deliver 99 percent of those items on time.

As shown in Figure 7-19, a third factor is that information systems have also enabled both suppliers and customers to reduce the size of their inventories and thus reduce their inventory costs. These reductions have been possible because the speed and efficiency provided by information systems enable processing of small orders, quickly.

Figure 7-19

Benefits of Information Systems on
Supply Chain Performance

- Reduce costs of buying and selling.
- Increase supply chain speed.
- Reduce size and cost of inventories.
- Improve delivery scheduling—enable
  just-in-time inventory.

MIS in Use

Yes We Can: Lessons Learned in ERP Implementation at DPT

Implementing enterprise resource planning (ERP) software can be one of the most challenging projects for an organization of any size. "It takes a coordinated team effort," notes Eric Dang, systems administrator for Digital Payment Technologies in Burnaby, British Columbia, "and requires time upfront to understand what you want to accomplish before anything gets installed." Digital Payment Technologies (DPT) is a leader in the design, manufacture, and distribution of parking management technologies for the North American parking industry (www.digitalpaytech.com). DPT learned about implementing ERP the hard way, with an initial project that did not deliver expected results, but which eventually led to a second successful implementation.

In 2005, DPT was a medium-sized company that was growing quickly, averaging 29 percent annual growth, with 95 percent of its sales in the United States. With rapid growth came the challenge to quickly adjust to new sales and manufacturing targets. DPT felt the need for ERP software, but the core team at the company had little time and few resources to make it happen. The company was surviving on a combination of Excel spreadsheets and sales reports that were difficult, if not impossible, to integrate and share. So, after some investigation of ERP solutions and site visits with industry partners, DPT licensed Navision, a Microsoft product.

"Since our core people were busy just getting product out the door, we gave the task of installing the software to someone who had a little bit of time they could spare. We thought we could just install the program and run with it," noted Mark Gemino, VP of manufacturing. "But it didn't work the way we thought it would," he noted. "After a few months, nothing was working, and we couldn't balance our accounts or get simple BOM [bills of materials] working. We thought we had bought bad software. Later, we learned that it wasn't the software that was causing the problems. It was the way we had set the software up. We weren't aware that what seemed like small choices in the software setup could have really big implications on how the system as a whole operated. We also had to spend more time in getting our initial data correct. We hadn't invested enough time in understanding how we were going to really use the system."

Information systems also improve delivery scheduling. Using these systems, suppliers can deliver materials and components at the time and in the sequence needed. Such delivery enables just-in-time inventory and allows manufacturers to reduce the size of raw materials inventory as well as the handling of raw materials.

Employees quickly lost faith in the information provided by Navision, and DPT was spending time trying to fix the errors the system was creating. The bad news for DPT was that Navision had not provided the expected benefits and had stalled their attempts to improve efficiency. The good news was that the challenge led the company to find someone who could get Navision working for DPT. "Everything changed quickly when we brought Eric on board," noted Gemino. "He was able to explain the system in a way we could understand."

Eric Dang was hired in 2006 and spent the first six months getting back to basics with the Navision product. It took a lot of effort, not only from Eric but also from a team of people from different departments at DPT, but eventually the Navision system was stabilized and started providing useful and accurate information. "People took this work seriously," noted Eric, "because they understood what would happen if we didn't get things right."

By 2007, the Navision ERP system was running smoothly—so smoothly, in fact, that people at DPT felt they were able to take on an additional task of implementing the warehouse module. "A consulting firm told us that they had seen several companies try to implement the warehouse module, but none of them had been successful," noted Eric, "but that didn't stop us. We thought, yes we can." DPT's previous experience provided the team with the confidence to do things right. They started the project with detailed process mapping, created a prototype, and involved important

people in different departments in making the decisions about the new implementation before the system was rolled out. "When we rolled it out six months later, it went ahead with very few issues." DPT had learned an expensive and powerful lesson about teamwork, involving users, and detailed pre-planning for project success. When asked about the secret to their success, Eric noted, "It is summed up in a book my two-year old daughter got out of the library, called *Yes We Can*. It is a simple picture book story about a group of animals with different strengths which, when they work together as a team, get things done. As far as I am concerned, it should be required reading for anyone doing ERP implementation."

Questions

1. Consider the five components of an information system provided in Figure 1-1 in Chapter 1. Which of these components was the reason for the lack of success in the first round of ERP implementation at DPT?

2. What do you think is the most important component in the success of DPT's ERP in the second implementation?

3. What role did Eric Dang play in the ERP implementation? What skills do you think were most important for Eric's success?

4. Do you think that DPT had to fail in its initial ERP implementation before it succeeded? That is, do you think it is necessary for companies to understand clearly what can go wrong before they fully commit to the project? Justify your answer.

Active ? Review

Use this Active Review to verify that you have understood the material in the chapter. You can read the entire chapter and then perform the tasks in this review, or you can read the material for just one question and perform the tasks for that question before moving on to the next one.

Q1 What are the fundamental ways of achieving competitive advantage?

Define *competitive strategy*. Explain the relationships among competitive strategy, business processes, and information systems using technology.

Q2 What are business functions and functional systems?

Name five categories of functional systems. Name three problems of functional silos, and describe each. Give an example of a data integration problem. Describe what is meant by a cross-functional system. What are the consequences of a lack of data integration?

Q3 How can business processes be improved?

Name three ways of improving processes without technology. What is business process design? Describe the differences between EAI and ERP.

Q4 What is the importance of industry standard processes?

Describe what is meant by the term *industry standard practices*. What are the advantages of standard processes? What are the disadvantages? Can an organization develop competitive advantage with industry standard processes? Explain your answer.

Q5 What are ERP systems?

What are ERP systems? Name three ERP vendors. Explain why ERP systems are difficult to implement. How does an ERP system help address the problems that arise from functional systems?

Q6 What are CRM systems?

Define the term *customer relationship management*. Describe the customer life cycle. How is it related to CRM? How can a CRM system create competitive advantage?

Q7 What are SCM systems?

Describe what is meant by SCM. Why can there be conflict between companies using SCM systems? What is supplier relationship management? How does this differ from CRM? Justify your answer.

Key Terms and Concepts

Business process design 235

Cross-departmental systems 232

Cross-functional systems 232

Customer life cycle 241

Customer relationship management (CRM) system 241

Disintermediation 243

Enterprise application integration (EAI) 235

Enterprise resource planning (ERP) system 239

Functional silos 231

Functional systems 231

Industry standard processes 237

Interorganizational systems 232

Primary activities 231

Process blueprint 239

SAP R/3 237

Supplier relationship management (SRM) 244

Supply chain 243

Supply chain management 244

Support activities 231

Using Your Knowledge

1. Choose one of the following basic business processes: inventory management, operations, manufacturing, human resources management, or accounting/ financial management. Use the internet to identify three vendors that license a product to support that process. Compare offerings from the three vendors as follows: .
   a. Determine differences in terminology, especially differences in the ways vendors use the same terms.
   b. Compare the features and functions of each product offering.
   c. For each vendor, specify the characteristics of a company for which that vendor's offering would be ideal.

2. Consider Carrie's Custom Clothing company described at the start of this chapter. Assume that Carrie uses one system to collect information about her customers, an Excel spreadsheet to collect information about her suppliers, a Word document to create her invoices, and some accounting software to record her revenues and expenses.
   a. Give an example of some of the problems that Carrie faces by having these systems act as functional silos.
   b. Then, provide some suggestions for how these systems could be combined to add value to her company.

3. Distance learning could be considered an application of interorganizational information systems.
   a. Draw a process diagram of a regular, non-distance learning class. Label the activities and the flows among the activities.
   b. Draw a second process diagram of a distance learning class. In what ways are the two diagrams similar? In what ways are they different?
   c. What is the competitive strategy of your university? How do distance learning classes contribute to that competitive strategy?
   d. Assuming that no face-to-face meeting is required to successfully teach a distance learning class, neither students nor professors need live near campus. In fact, they do not even need to reside in the same continent. What opportunities does that fact present to your university? What new educational products might your university develop?

Collaborative Exercises

This chapter provides several examples of companies that use information systems to gain a competitive advantage. These include Zipcar, Grand & Toy, Bag Borrow or Steal, Amazon, Dell, REI, and DPT. In this collaborative exercise, your group has to take a more critical and in-depth look at the companies and their offerings. Using the web as a resource, collaborate with your team to answer the following questions:

1. Create a maximum two-page information sheet that summarizes the company, the idea, and the system it uses. The summary should include the following:
   a. Prepare an introduction to the company (example companies are listed above, but you are welcome to use another company).
   b. Identify, as clearly you can, the strategy of the company. (*Note:* You can use Porter's five forces to understand the company's industry.)
   c. Outline how the company uses technology for competitive **advantage**.

d. Identify the information systems you think will be most critical to support the strategy.

e. Provide suggestions on how the company should consider investing in information systems to support its business. Justify your suggestions.

2. Choose one of the following companies (or ask your professor if you can choose a different company):
   a. Zipcar (www.zipcar.com)
   b. Bag Borrow or Steal (www.bagborroworsteal.com)
   c. Grand & Toy (www.grandandtoy.com)
   d. Dell (www.dell.ca)
   e. My Virtual Model (www.MVM.com).
   f. The Running Room (www.runningroom.com)
   g. Ritchie Bros. Auctioneers (www.rbauction.com)

   Create a presentation (using PowerPoint, Keynote, or another presentation software) on the topic to the students in your class. Be sure to include a title page.

Case Study 7

Moving Like a Deere: Deere's Innovative Revolution

Looking at cotton growing on a farm, one could be forgiven for thinking that other than fertilizers, pesticides, and the practical deployment of the modern cotton picker in the 1950s, the picture seems frozen in time. However, at Deere & Company (www.johndeere.com), a second revolution is brewing, and this one is definitely adding cutting-edge technology to an old-economy business.

Founded in 1837 as a one-man blacksmith operation, John Deere is now a $22.1-billion corporation that employs more than 47 000 people worldwide and is one of the oldest publicly traded industrial companies in the United States. But rather than the brutality and razor-thin margins that usually accompany price competition, market leader Deere has staked out a bold differentiation strategy that incorporates technology to compete on innovation.

John Deere's machines still pluck cotton fibres with hundreds of finger-like spindles and then vacuum the cotton into a huge bin, but this is where the similarities with its old machines end. The company has used advanced computer-aided design (CAD) to reshape the intake ducts, allowing the cotton to travel 20 percent faster and reducing horsepower requirements by 5 percent, thus saving on fuel consumption while maintaining speed. Inside the new cotton pickers is the computing power of eight personal computers and a communications system that beams wireless information to a base station, which can automatically monitor and signal when service is needed. At the same time, microwave sensors and the global positioning system (GPS) technology allow the farmer to map the field's exact yield while harvesting the cotton. And by overlaying this information with other enabled systems, fertilizers, pesticides, and water can be applied with precision instead of indiscriminately distributing them across the entire field. Finally, in an industry first, Deere's latest generation of picker spools the cotton into cylindrical bales that are wrapped and gently placed on the field without the machine having to stop every 10 to 15 minutes.

The cost of the new technology has still to be determined, but the two-storey harvester has replaced four to six pieces of support equipment and has enabled a single operator to harvest nonstop until the 1100-litre fuel tank is sucked dry.

Questions

1. What are the advantages of the new technology used by Deere?
2. How does this technology allow Deere to compete against lower-cost manufacturers and producers?
3. Are there any other advantages to using this technology? What adaptation and extensions would increase the advantage? (*Hint*: Radio-frequency tags can be inserted into each bundle to track harvesting information and pinpoint where the cotton came from, identifying, for example, whether the cotton qualifies as organic.)

Available Only in Vanilla?

Designing business processes is difficult, time consuming, and very expensive. Highly trained experts conduct seemingly countless interviews with users and domain experts to determine business requirements. Then, even more experts join those people, and the team invests thousands of hours in designing, developing, and implementing effective business processes that meet those requirements. All of this amounts to a very high-risk activity that is prone to failure. And it must be done before information systems development can even begin.

ERP vendors, such as SAP, have invested millions of labour hours into the business blueprints that underlie their ERP solutions. These blueprints consist of hundreds or thousands of different business processes. Examples include processes for hiring employees, acquiring fixed assets, acquiring consumable goods, and for custom one-off (a unique product with a unique design) manufacturing, to name just a few. Additionally, since ERP vendors implement their business processes in hundreds of organizations, they are forced to customize their standard blueprint for use in particular industries.

For example, SAP has a distribution business blueprint that is customized for the auto parts industry, the electronics industry, and the aircraft industry. Hundreds of other customized solutions exist as well. Even better, the ERP vendors have developed software solutions that fit their business process blueprints. In theory, no software development is required at all if the organization can adapt to the standard blueprint of the ERP vendor.

As described in this chapter, when an organization implements an ERP solution, it first determines any differences that exist between its business processes and the standard blueprint. Then the organization must remove that difference, which can be done in one of two ways: (1) It can change business processes to fit the standard blueprint, or (2) the ERP vendor or a consultant can modify the standard blueprint (and software solution that matches the blueprint) to fit the unique requirements. In practice, such variations from the standard blueprint are rare. They are difficult and expensive to implement, and they require the using organization to maintain the variations from the standard as new versions of the ERP software are developed.

Consequently, most organizations choose to modify their processes to match the blueprint, rather than the other way around. This is often referred to as installing the software *vanilla* (the basic software with no custom features). Although such process changes are also difficult to implement, once the organization has converted to the standard blueprint, it no longer needs to support a variation. So, from the standpoint of cost, effort, risk, and avoidance of future problems, there is a huge incentive for organizations to adapt to the standard ERP blueprint. Initially, SAP was the only true ERP vendor, but other companies have since developed and acquired ERP solutions as well. And given the competitive pressure across the software industry, these products are beginning to have the same sets of features and functions. ERP solutions are becoming a commodity.

This is all fine, as far as it goes, but it does introduce a nagging question: If, over time, every organization tends to implement the standard ERP blueprint and if, over time, every software company develops essentially the same ERP features and functions, then won't every business come to look just like every other business? How will organizations gain a competitive advantage if they all use the same business processes?

If every auto parts distributor uses the same business processes, based on the same software, are they not all merely clones of one another? How will a company distinguish itself? How will innovation occur? Even if one parts distributor does successfully innovate a business process that gives it a competitive advantage, will the ERP vendors be conduits to transfer that innovation to competitors? Does the use of commoditized standard blueprints mean that no company can sustain a competitive advantage?

Discussion Questions

1. In your own words, explain why an organization might choose to change its processes to fit the standard blueprint. What advantages does it accrue by doing so?

2. Explain how competitive pressure among software vendors will cause the ERP solutions to become commodities. What does this mean to the ERP software industry?

3. If two businesses use exactly the same processes and exactly the same software, can they be different in any way at all? Explain why or why not.

4. Explain the statement that an ERP software vendor can be a conduit to transfer innovation. What are the consequences to the innovating company? to the software company? to the industry? to the economy?

5. Such standardization might be possible in theory, but since worldwide there are so many different business models, cultures, people, values, and competitive pressures, can any two businesses ever be exactly alike?

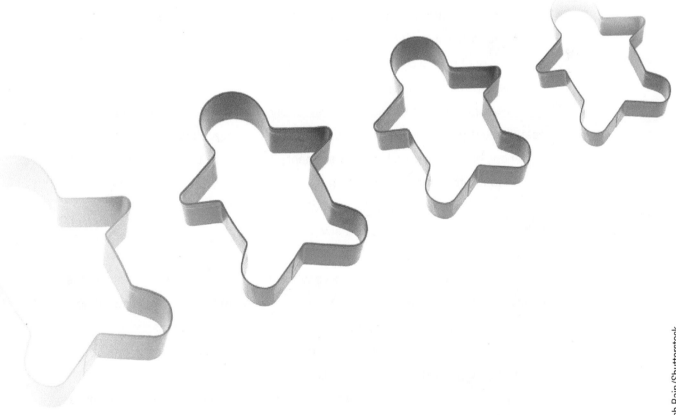

Kitch Bain/Shutterstock

8 Decision Making and Business Intelligence

Running Case

Carrie's Custom Clothing continues to grow and the average size of the t-shirt orders has steadily increased. The customized t-shirt market is very competitive, and one of the most important decisions Carrie must now make is whether to invest in new textile printing machinery. Carrie knows she will need to make a decision about this soon. In her industry, there are two basic approaches used to print t-shirts: (1) screen printing and (2) drop-on-demand inkjet printing. Both have advantages and disadvantages.

Screen printing is the traditional way of printing t-shirts and remains the most cost-effective method for very large orders. It can reliably produce 400 to 500 t-shirts in an hour, but it requires a bigger investment, larger machinery, and an experienced person to run the process. Only large textile printers use this method, and Carrie's business has not reached this level yet. When she needs to print a large volume of t-shirts, Carrie knows that she can always contract with the screen printers to get the job done.

Drop-on-demand inkjet printing uses what looks like an inkjet printer to print the design directly on the t-shirt. This is how Carrie does most of her printing. Almost any type of textile can be used (cotton, polyester, rayon). The t-shirts can be printed within 1 to 2 minutes for less than $1 for ink, and very little training is required to become quite good at producing a quality shirt.

Carrie is thinking about adding a second drop-on-demand printer for her business, but she is not sure if her business is ready. Adding another drop-on-demand printer will enable her to print two orders at the same time as well as increase her capacity

Glamour/Shutterstock

to fill larger orders without having to turn to screen-printing shops or other suppliers.

She has the choice of three different machines, but she believes that the Anajet Sprint will work best. She can either lease the printer over a five-year period for $320 per month or buy the printer for $16 500. Sometimes a used model may be available, which would be less expensive. The ink cartridges cost $250, and each t-shirt uses up less than a dollar of ink to print.

In this chapter, we will learn about decision-making and business intelligence systems. Looking at Carrie, it is obvious that her company has reached a decision point. She now needs to find answers for some important questions. Should she invest in a new screen-printing technology or work with what she currently has? Will the increase in t-shirt printing capacity create real value for the business? Should she lease or buy the printer? These are all important questions that a business owner needs to be able to answer. Decisions like these would make a difference in developing competitive advantage in Carrie's business.

Study Questions

Q1 What challenges do managers face when making decisions?

Q2 What is OLTP, and how does it support decision making?

Q3 What are OLAP and the data resource challenge?

Q4 What are BI systems, and how do they provide competitive advantage?

Q5 What are the purpose and components of a data warehouse?

Q6 What is a data mart, and how does it differ from a data warehouse?

Q7 What are typical data-mining applications?

Q1 What Challenges Do Managers Face When Making Decisions?

For business managers, decision making or choosing from a range of alternatives is the essence of management. Indeed, decision making, in some cases, is such a natural act that we often seem to do it without thinking. As you read this chapter, for example, you have made a decision about how to allocate some of the 168 hours that exist in each week and decided how to prioritize the various things that you could be doing (of course, some students have decided NOT to read this part of the text, but, for now, we will ignore them).

For most people, decision making is a rational act in which individuals or groups consider the possible choices and the likely consequences and choose what they think is the best alternative. This process, however, is much more complicated than it may appear for three reasons. First, the concept of rationality can be frustratingly hard to define. In most cases, processes are considered rational if they result in outcomes that are deemed good or are likely to lead to good outcomes, a definition that is often considered tautological or circular. Second, good outcomes may occasionally result from irrational processes, and bad outcomes can result from good processes. For example, it may not be rational to skip university and buy lottery tickets, but try telling that to someone who has successfully used such a strategy. Finally, and most importantly for this chapter, as Nobel prize winning economist Herbert Simon pointed out, humans intend to be rational, but there are limits to our cognitive capabilities—a process that he identified as "bounded rationality." For a variety of reasons, we are simply not capable of thinking through all the various options and permutations that are available to us. Instead of seeking the optimal solution, Simon suggested that we *satisfice*, or choose the most reasonable and available solution rather than the perfect choice. As an example, imagine that you are shopping for a used car. Besides the practical considerations (how far are you willing to go to see a potential option), it is unlikely that you can keep track of more than five to seven options. Moreover, how do you make trade-offs for a car that is better mechanically but not quite the colour that you want?

Human beings are not what economists call "economic automatons" or "lightning-fast calculators" who can compute the "perfect choice"; instead, we tend to settle, or satisfice, with an alternative that is generally good enough across a range of criteria. In this chapter, our main focus is on data-driven decision making in such areas as data mining and analytical systems. However, it is important to note that, on occasion, managers have been known to make decisions first and then construct evidence to support their positions[1] and that the processes used to make group decisions can be quite different from those used to make individual decisions. For now, it is enough to note that an important aspect of decision making is to consider as broad a range of choices as possible and consider the effects of each alternative.

Because computers deal with large amounts of information, it should be no surprise that applying computers to improve decision making has been popular for a long time. In fact, many of the early computer systems (such as the SAGE system in the 1950s) were originally designed to solve military problems. As mainframe computers became more popular in the 1960s, Russell Ackoff, in his article titled "Management Misinformation Systems,"[2] suggested that designers of management information systems (MIS) make several erroneous assumptions about managerial decision making and that computers might not necessarily provide good solutions. Although written over 40 years ago, many of the points Ackoff made remain relevant today.

👁—Watch

Go to MyMISLab to watch a video about how big an exabyte is, and why it matters.

---

[1] P. Tingling and M. Brydon, "Is Decision-Based Evidence Making Necessarily Bad?" *Sloan Management Review* 51, no. 4 (Summer 2010): 71–76.
[2] R. Ackoff, "Management Misinformation Systems," *Management Science* 14, no. 4 (December 1967): B147–156.

Kilobyte (KB)	*1000 bytes OR 10³ bytes* 2 Kilobytes: A typewritten page 100 Kilobytes: A low-resolution photograph
Megabyte (MB)	*1 000 000 bytes OR 10⁶ bytes* 1 Megabyte: A small novel OR a 3.5-inch floppy disk 2 Megabytes: A high-resolution photograph 5 Megabytes: The complete works of Shakespeare 10 Megabytes: A minute of high-fidelity sound 100 Megabytes: 1 meter of shelved books 500 Megabytes: A CD-ROM
Gigabyte (GB)	*1 000 000 000 bytes OR 10⁹ bytes* 1 Gigabyte: A pickup truck filled with paper 20 Gigabytes: A good collection of the works of Beethoven 100 Gigabytes: A library floor of academic journals
Terabyte (TB)	*1 000 000 000 000 bytes OR 10¹² bytes* 1 Terabyte: 50 000 trees made into paper and printed 2 Terabytes: An academic research library 10 Terabytes: The printed collection of the U.S. Library of Congress 400 Terabytes: National Climactic Data Center (NOAA) database
Petabyte (PB)	*1 000 000 000 000 000 bytes OR 10¹⁵ bytes* 1 Petabyte: Three years of EOS data (2001) 2 Petabytes: All U.S. academic research libraries 20 Petabytes: Production of hard-disk drives in 1995 200 Petabytes: All printed material
Exabyte (EB)	*1 000 000 000 000 000 000 bytes OR 10¹⁸ bytes* 2 Exabytes: Total volume of information generated worldwide [in 1999] 5 Exabytes: All words ever spoken by human beings

Figure 8-1

How Big Is an Exabyte?

Source: www2.sims.berkeley.edu/research/projects/how-much-info/data-powers.html. Used with the permission of Peter Lyman and Hal R. Varian, University of California at Berkeley.

We will look at three of Ackoff's assumptions. The first assumption is that managers will have no problem making decisions if they get the data they need. Ackoff countered that for most managers, too many possibilities exist; they should not expect to make better decisions even with perfect data. The uncertainty and complexity surrounding decisions make them challenging.

A second assumption is that poor decisions are made because managers lack relevant information. On the contrary, Ackoff argued, managers suffer more from an overabundance of irrelevant data. Today, we refer to this overabundance as **information overload**.

A third erroneous assumption is that managers know what data they need. Ackoff argued that in reality, managers are often not sure just what data they do require. And because they are unsure, the tendency is to ask for as much data as they can get, thus promoting information overload.

Information Overload

It seems clear that managers today are facing information overload. One interesting question to consider is just how much of an overload exists. According to a study done by the US multinational EMC, with analysis from International Data Corporation (IDC), the digital universe is doubling in size every two years, and by 2020 the data created and copied annually will reach 44 zettabytes, or 44 trillion gigabytes. Think about that number. As shown in Figure 8-1, 200 petabytes is roughly the amount of all the printed material ever written. The study also found that data is growing at the rate of 40 percent a year which suggests the challenge of information overload will continue for quite some time.[3]

Why does this exponential growth in data matter to us? First, we must understand that it occurs inside organizations just as much as outside of them. Every time Ford builds another car, its information systems generate megabytes of data about designs, bills of materials, supplier performance, production costs, employee productivity, customer payment patterns, market and product trends, and so forth.

Buried in all these data is information that, if found and made available to the right people at the right time, can improve the decisions Ford makes. For example, when negotiating with a supplier, how flexible does the company want to be? The decision to reduce price must be based, in part, on past experience. What was the quality of the supplier's products compared with Ford's requirements and the capabilities of its competitors? How many items were defective or late? How much service and support has the supplier needed?

The challenge for managers in a world overloaded with information is to find the appropriate data and incorporate them into their decision-making processes. Information systems can both help and hinder this process.

Data Quality

A final challenge in decision making is the quality of data. Up to this point, we have assumed that the data stored in systems are clean and accurate. But this is the exception rather than the rule in most systems. It is hard enough to make decisions when you have good-quality data. But what if the data are of low quality? How would this affect your decisions?

Data from operational systems can be processed to create basic reports with few issues. If we want to know, for example, current sales and how those sales relate to sales projections, we simply process data in the order-entry database.

However, raw operational data are seldom suitable for more sophisticated reporting or data mining. Figure 8-2 lists the major problem categories. First, the data may be problematic or what is commonly termed **dirty data**. Examples include using values such as *B* for customer gender; *213* for customer age; *999-999-9999* for a phone number; *gren* for a part colour; and WhyMe@GuessWhoIAM.org for an email address. All these values can be problematic for data-mining purposes.

Missing values are a second problem. A nonprofit organization can process a donation without knowing the donor's gender or age, but a data-mining application is impaired if many such values are missing.

Inconsistent data, the third problem shown in Figure 8-2, are particularly common in data that have been gathered over time. When an area code changes, for example, the phone number for a given customer before the change will not match the customer's number after the change. Likewise, part codes can change, as can sales territories. Before such data can be used, they must be recoded for consistency over the period of the study.

Figure 8-2

Problems with Using Operational Data for Business Intelligence Systems

- Dirty data
- Missing values
- Inconsistent data
- Data not integrated
- Wrong granularity
  - Too fine
  - Not fine enough
- Too much data
  - Too many attributes
  - Too many data points

[3] "EMC Digital Universe Study with Research and Analysis by IDC," www.emc.com/leadership/digital-universe/index.htm.

Data not integrated, the fourth problem, can occur if the data reside in different sources or are incompatible with the intended purpose. Because data that are critical for successful operations must be complete and accurate, data that are only marginally necessary or were not designed and collected with the specific purpose in mind may not be. In the case of the National Hockey League, for example, information about where each player was on the ice when a goal was scored has only recently been collected and matching it up with the timing of each player's shift for analytic purposes is difficult.

Data can also be too fine or too coarse. Data **granularity** refers to the degree of summarization or detail. *Coarse data* are highly summarized; *fine data* express details that are too precise. For example, suppose we want to analyze the placement of graphics and controls on an order-entry webpage. It is possible to capture the customers' clicking behaviour in what is termed **clickstream data**. Those data are very fine; they include everything the customer does at the website. In the middle of the order stream are data for clicks on the news, email, instant chat, and a weather check. Although all those data are needed for the study of consumer computer behaviour, such data will be overwhelming if all we want to know is how customers respond to advertisement locations. Because the data are too fine, the data analysts often throw away millions and millions of clicks to avoid the problem of having too much data and too many attributes to work with.

Generally, it is better to have granularity that is too fine than too coarse. If the granularity is too fine, the data can be made coarser by summing and combining. Google Analytics (www.google.com/analytics) provides a good example of the power of summing and combining data. Only analysts' labour and computer processing are required. If the granularity is too coarse, however, there is no way to separate the data into constituent parts.

This section has suggested that a number of factors, including complexity, uncertainty, information overload, and data quality, make management decision making challenging. Information from information systems has the potential to meet some of these challenges. In this chapter, we outline categories of systems that support the decision-making process.

Q2 What Is OLTP, and How Does It Support Decision Making?

In Chapter 7, we noted that functional systems, such as general ledger systems, human resources systems, and operational systems, are used to capture details about business transactions and then create updated information by processing these transaction details. There are many types of business transactions. Purchasing a product or service, receiving a shipment from a supplier, creating a purchase order for a new printer, making a customer service call, and returning defective items to a store are all examples of transactions. Information systems are a critical component for capturing and processing the details about these transactions because they are very efficient and accurate.

Using computers to capture information electronically is often referred to as being online. When a bank's customer service representative accepts your deposit, he or she enters the transaction online so that he or she does not have to write down information on paper and then copy it into the system at a later time. Most web-based applications are examples of online systems.

If you are collecting data electronically and processing the transactions online, then you are using an **online transaction processing (OLTP)** system. There are two basic ways that transactions can be processed. (1) If transactions are entered and processed immediately on entry, then the system is operating in real time because there is little or no delay in updating the system with new data. (2) The other option is to wait for many transactions to pile up before you process them. For example, at a gas station, you might collect all the transactions that occurred during the day and then send them at the end of the day to the central office for processing. This is an example of batch processing because the system waits until it has a batch of transactions before the data are processed and the information is updated.

The choice of whether to use real-time processing or batch processing depends on the nature of the transactions, the cost of the system, and the needs of the organization. Real-time systems tend to be more complex and cost more to implement. However, real-time systems provide the most up-to-date information, and that is often important. For example, Ticketmaster (www.ticketmaster.ca), a company that sells concert and event tickets over the phone and online, would find it difficult to use a batch-processing system. Why? The most important thing for Ticketmaster is to make sure it does not sell more than one ticket for the same seat. A real-time system will ensure that only one ticket is sold per seat because the system is updated after every transaction. A batch-processing system, however, might register two tickets for one seat if the sales occur within a single batch.

OLTP systems are the backbone of all functional, cross-functional, and interorganizational systems in a company. They are designed to efficiently enter, process, and store data. OLTP systems combine large databases with efficient input devices, such as grocery store scanners, automated cash registers, and debit and credit card readers, to process transactions quickly and accurately. Large OLTP systems, such as airline reservation systems and banking systems, are capable of reliably processing thousands of transactions per second over a long period. Whether large or small, OLTPs support decision making by providing the raw information about transactions and status for an organization.

Q3 What Are OLAP and the Data Resource Challenge?

Using OLTP to collect data is important. We have all heard that information is a competitive weapon and can be a source of competitive advantage for a company. But data alone are not enough. They do not create value if they are not used. It is important to realize that the competitive advantage of information is realized when organizations *use* the data they have collected to make better decisions.

Not all organizations use their data effectively. For example, Thomas Davenport[4] noted that a major grocery chain used less than 2 percent of the scanner data it had collected over the years. So, although data may be collected in OLTP, they may not be used to improve decision making. We refer to this idea as the **data resource challenge**.

The quickest way to explain the data resource challenge is to consider whether a company views its data as an asset. An *asset* can be defined as a resource from which future economic benefits may be obtained. When you think about it in depth, data are particularly good assets. They do not take up much space, are easy to store, do not depreciate in the same way physical assets depreciate, and can provide input for improved decision making.

---

[4] T. H. Davenport et al., "Data to Knowledge to Results: Building an Analytic Capability," *California Management Review* 43, no. 2 (2001): 117–38.

	A	B	C	D	E	F	G
1							
2							
3	Store Sales Net	Store Type ▼					
4	Product Family ▼	Deluxe Supermarket	Gourmet Supermarket	Mid-Size Grocery	Small Grocery	Supermarket	Grand Total
5	Drink	$8 119.05	$2 392.83	$1 409.50	$685.89	$16 751.71	$29 358.98
6	Food	$70 276.11	$20 026.18	$10 392.19	$6 109.72	$138 960.67	$245 764.87
7	Nonconsumable	$18 884.24	$5 064.79	$2 813.73	$1 534.90	$36 189.40	$64 487.05
8	Grand Total	$97 279.40	$27 483.80	$14 615.42	$8 330.51	$191 901.77	$339 610.90

Figure 8-3

OLAP Product Family by Store Type

Source: Microsoft Excel

But here is the challenge. If data, as a whole, is an asset, like money and real estate, who in the company is in charge of managing the data? What are the generally accepted accounting principles associated with valuing data as an asset? Where do data show up on a balance sheet? Who is in charge of extracting as much value as possible out of the data? You will find that most companies have a hard time answering these questions. What this means is that although we like to think of data as an asset, we are not really treating data as an important resource.

Systems that focus on making OLTP-collected data useful for decision making are often referred to as **decision support systems (DSSs)** or, more generally, as **online analytic processing (OLAP)** systems. OLAP provides the ability to sum, count, average, and perform other simple arithmetic operations on groups of data. The remarkable characteristic of OLAP reports is that their format is dynamic. The viewer of the report can change the report's structure—hence the term *online*.

An OLAP report has measures, or facts, and dimensions. A measure is the data item of interest. It is the item that is to be summed or averaged or otherwise processed in the OLAP report. Total sales, average sales, and average cost are examples of measures. A dimension is a characteristic of a measure. Purchase date, customer type, customer location, and sales region are all examples of dimensions.

Figure 8-3 shows a typical OLAP report. Here, the measure is Store Sales Net, and the dimensions are Product Family and Store Type. This report shows how net store sales vary by product family and store type. Stores of type Supermarket, for example, sold a net of $36 189 in nonconsumable goods.

The presentation of a measure with associated dimensions, as in Figure 8-3, is often called an *OLAP cube*, or simply a *cube*. The reason for this term is that some products show these displays using three axes, like a cube in geometry. The origin of the term is unimportant here, however. You should just know that an OLAP cube and an OLAP report are the same thing.

The OLAP report in Figure 8-3 was generated by SQL Server Analysis Services and is displayed in an Excel pivot table. The data were taken from a sample instructional database, called FoodMart, that is provided with SQL Server. It is possible to display OLAP cubes in many ways other than Excel. Some third-party vendors provide more extensive graphical displays. For more information about such products, check for OLAP vendors and products at the Data Warehousing Review website at www.dwreview.com/OLAP. Note, too, that OLAP reports can be delivered just like any of the other reports described for report management systems.

As stated earlier, the distinguishing characteristic of an OLAP report is that the user can alter the format of the report. Figure 8-4 shows such an alteration. Here, the user added another dimension, store country and state, to the horizontal display. Product Family sales are now broken out by the location of the stores. Observe that the sample data include only stores in the United States and only in the western states of California, Oregon, and Washington. With an OLAP report, it is possible to **drill down** into the data. This term means to further divide the data into more detail.

Product Family	Store	Store State	Deluxe Supermarket	Gourmet Supermarket	Mid-Size Grocery	Small Grocery	Supermarket	Grand Total
Store Sales Net								
Drink	USA	CA		$2392.83		$227.38	$5 920.76	$8 540.97
		OR	$4 438.49				$2 862.45	$7 300.94
		WA	$3 680.56		$1 409.50	$458.51	$7 968.50	$13 517.07
	USA Total		$8 119.05	$2 392.83	$1 409.50	$685.89	$16 751.71	$29 358.98
Drink Total			$8 119.05	$2 392.83	$1 409.50	$685.89	$16 751.71	$29 358.98
Food	USA	CA		$20 026.18		$1 960.53	$47 226.11	$69 212.82
		OR	$37 778.35				$23 818.87	$61 597.22
		WA	$32 497.76		$10 392.19	$4 149.19	$67 915.69	$114 954.83
	USA Total		$70 276.11	$20 026.18	$10 392.19	$6 109.72	$138 960.67	$245 764.87
Food Total			$70 276.11	$20 026.18	$10 392.19	$6 109.72	$138 960.67	$245 764.87
Nonconsumable	USA	CA		$5 064.79		$474.35	$12 344.49	$17 883.63
		OR	$10 177.89				$6 428.53	$16 606.41
		WA	$8 706.36		$2 813.73	$1 060.54	$17 416.38	$29 997.01
	USA Total		$18 884.24	$5 064.79	$2 813.73	$1 534.90	$36 189.40	$64 487.05
Nonconsumable Total			$18 884.24	$5 064.79	$2 813.73	$1 534.90	$36 189.40	$64 487.05
Grand Total			$97 279.40	$27 483.80	$14 615.42	$8 330.51	$191 901.77	$339 610.90

Figure 8-4

OLAP Product Family and Store Location by Store Type

Source: Microsoft Excel

In Figure 8-5, for example, the user has drilled down into the stores located in California; the OLAP report now shows sales data for the four cities in California that have stores.

Look at another difference between Figures 8-4 and 8-5. The user has not only drilled down but has also changed the order of the dimensions. Figure 8-4 shows Product Family and then store location within Product Family. Figure 8-5 shows store location and then Product Family within store location.

Store Sales Net				Store Type					
Store Country	Store Sta	Store City	Product Family	Deluxe Super	Gourmet Supermarket	Mid-Size Grocery	Small Grocery	Supermarket	Grand Total
USA	CA	Beverly Hills	Drink		$2 392.83				$2 392.83
			Food		$20 026.18				$20 026.18
			Nonconsumable		$5 064.79				$5 064.79
		Beverly Hills Total			$27 483.80				$27 483.80
		Los Angeles	Drink					$2 870.33	$2 870.33
			Food					$23 598.28	$23 598.28
			Nonconsumable					$6 305.14	$6 305.14
		Los Angeles Total						$32 773.74	$32 773.74
		San Diego	Drink					$3 050.43	$3 050.43
			Food					$23 627.83	$23 627.83
			Nonconsumable					$6 039.34	$6 039.34
		San Diego Total						$32 717.61	$32 717.61
		San Francisco	Drink				$227.38		$227.38
			Food				$1 960.53		$1 960.53
			Nonconsumable				$474.35		$474.35
		San Francisco Total					$2 662.26		$2 662.26
	CA Total				$27 483.80		$2 662.26	$65 491.35	$95 637.41
	OR		Drink	$4 438.49				$2 862.45	$7 300.94
			Food	$37 778.35				$23 818.87	$61 597.22
			Nonconsumable	$10 177.89				$6 428.53	$16 606.41
	OR Total			$52 394.72				$33 109.85	$85 504.57
	WA		Drink	$3 680.56		$1 409.50	$458.51	$7 968.50	$13 517.07
			Food	$32 497.76		$10 392.19	$4 149.19	$67 915.69	$114 954.83
			Nonconsumable	$8 706.36		$2 813.73	$1 060.54	$17 416.38	$29 997.01
	WA Total			$44 884.68		$14 615.42	$5 668.24	$93 300.57	$158 468.91
USA Total				$97 279.40	$27 483.80	$14 615.42	$8 330.51	$191 901.77	$339 610.90
Grand Total				$97 279.40	$27 483.80	$14 615.42	$8 330.51	$191 901.77	$339 610.90

Figure 8-5

OLAP Product Family and Store Location by Store Type

Source: Microsoft Excel

Both displays are valid and useful, depending on the user's perspective. A product manager might like to see product families first and then store location data. A sales manager might like to see store locations first and then product data. OLAP reports provide both perspectives, and the user can switch between them while viewing the report. Unfortunately, all this flexibility comes at a cost. If the database is large, doing the necessary calculating, grouping, and sorting of such dynamic displays will require substantial computing power. Although standard, commercial database management system (DBMS) products do have the features and functions required to create OLAP reports, they are not designed for such work. They are designed instead to provide rapid response to transaction-processing applications, such as order entry or manufacturing operations. Accordingly, special-purpose products called *OLAP servers* have been developed to perform OLAP analysis.

OLAP tools have become the primary tools used in the area of business intelligence (BI). "MIS in Use" (below) provides an example of how BI can be used to support decisions in pro-hockey. We will learn more about BI in the section that follows.

Q4 What Are BI Systems, and How Do They Provide Competitive Advantage?

A **business intelligence (BI) system** is a system that provides information for improving decision making. BI systems vary in their characteristics and capabilities, and in the way they foster competitive advantage.

Figure 8-6 summarizes the characteristics and competitive advantage of five categories of BI systems. **Group decision support systems (GDSSs)** allow multiple parties to participate in decision making and improve outcomes by reducing often inherent

Sports Decisions Go High Tech

How sports teams choose athletes has changed a lot in the past 10 years. Although how fast an athlete can run or how many pushups he or she can do are still important,

fewer and fewer general managers make multimillion-dollar decisions with regard to players on the basis of a scout's qualitative assessment. Instead of gut instinct and intuition, managers are increasingly turning to scientific and statistical techniques that capture more data and reduce biases.

First introduced in professional baseball, this approach is often credited to Oakland Athletics general manager Billy Beane, who used unconventional measures to select his athletes. Described in Michael Lewis's bestselling book *Moneyball* (and later the movie starring Brad Pitt), decision making in professional sports now includes objective data that are often statistically analyzed to provide insight and reduce flaws. Although there has been some resistance from managers who claim that the *Moneyball* approach does not work in true team sports, technology, computation, and statistics are essential and accepted aspects of

Business Intelligence System	Characteristics	Competitive Advantage
Group Decision Support Systems (GDSS)	Allow multiple decision makers to collaborate, often anonymously and at different times and in different locations.	Improve decision outcomes by reducing many of the biases inherent in group discussion and option evaluation.
Reporting Systems	Integrate and process data by sorting, grouping, summing, and formatting. Produce, administer, and deliver reports.	Improve decisions by providing relevant, accurate, and timely information to the right person.
Data-Mining Systems	Use sophisticated statistical techniques to find patterns and relationships.	Improve decisions by discovering patterns and relationships in data to predict future outcomes.
Knowledge Management Systems	Share knowledge of products, product uses, best practices, etc., among employees, managers, customers, and others.	Improve decisions by publishing employee and others' knowledge. Create value from existing intellectual capital. Foster innovation, improve customer service, increase organizational responsiveness, and reduce costs.
Expert Systems	Encode human knowledge in the form of If/Then rules and process those rules to make a diagnosis or recommendation.	Improve decision making by non-experts by encoding, saving, and processing expert knowledge.

Figure 8-6

Characteristics and Competitive Advantage of BI Systems

decision making, and adoption of the technique has been extended not only to basketball but to hockey as well.

The stakes are high, and mistakes can be expensive. The lowest National Hockey League rookie's salary in 2012 was $525 000, and yet research has found that less than 40 percent of drafted athletes will ever play in a single NHL game, and of those who do, 20 percent will play in fewer than 10 games. Even if a team can afford it, the salary cap (a fixed amount that a team can spend on its payroll) limits the ability of the team to buy up all the available talent.

Teams are reluctant, of course, to discuss the specifics of how they apply technology to decision making, but numerous sources have noted an increase in technology spending by professional teams. And the number of managers with advanced degrees in statistics or analytics is increasing as well.

Watch the MIT sports analytics video "Better off Guessing" available at http://video.mit.edu/watch/better-off-guessing-measuring-the-quality-of-draft-decisions-peter-tingling-7270/.

Questions

1. What process would you use to identify your choice of a first round athletic draft?
2. Is choosing athletes any different from hiring any other kind of employee?
3. Why do you think these techniques first appeared in baseball, rather than hockey or basketball?
4. Why would teams be reluctant to discuss how they use technology?
5. Is this increased sophistication in decision making inevitable? How do you make decisions, and how has this changed over time?

biases. GDSSs, for example, allow participants across different geographical locations and times to provide anonymous input that is automatically summed or communicated to the group and contributes to a decision. **Reporting systems** integrate data from multiple sources and process those data by sorting, grouping, summing, averaging, and comparing. Such systems format the results into reports and deliver those reports to users. Reporting systems improve decision making by providing the right information to the right user at the right time.

Data-mining systems process data by using sophisticated statistical techniques, such as regression analysis and decision tree analysis. Data-mining systems might find patterns and relationships that cannot be found by simpler reporting operations such as sorting, grouping, and averaging. Data-mining systems improve decision making by using the discovered patterns and relationships to *anticipate* events or to *predict* future outcomes. An example of a data-mining system is one that predicts the likelihood that a prospect will donate to a cause or political campaign on the basis of the prospect's characteristics, such as age, gender, and home postal code. **Market-basket analysis** is one of the data-mining systems; it computes correlations of items on past orders to determine items that are frequently purchased together. We will discuss data mining in more detail later in this chapter.

Knowledge management (KM) systems create value from intellectual capital by collecting and sharing human knowledge—of products, product uses, best practices, and other critical information—with employees, managers, customers, suppliers, and others who need it. Knowledge management is a process supported by the five components of an information system. By sharing knowledge, KM systems foster innovation, improve customer service, increase organizational responsiveness by getting products and services to market faster, and reduce costs.

Expert systems are the fifth category of BI systems shown in Figure 8-6. Expert systems encapsulate the knowledge of human experts in the form of *If/Then* rules. In a medical diagnosis system, for example, an expert system might have a rule such as the following:

If Patient_Temperature > 103, *Then* Initiate High_Fever_Procedure

Operational expert systems can have hundreds or even thousands of such rules. Although few expert systems have demonstrated a capability equivalent to that of a human expert, some are good enough to considerably improve the diagnosis and decision making of non-experts.

As with all information systems, it is important to distinguish between BI *tools* and BI *systems*. Business Objects licenses the reporting tool Crystal Reports. SPSS licenses the data-mining suite Clementine, and Microsoft offers SharePoint Server as, in part, a KM system. All these products are, however, just software. They represent only one of the five components.

To reap the benefits of improved decision making, organizations must incorporate data-mining products into complete information systems. A reporting tool can generate a report showing that a customer has cancelled an important order. It takes a reporting *system*, however, to alert the customer's salesperson to this unwanted news in time for the salesperson to attempt to reverse the decision. Similarly, a data-mining tool can create an equation that computes the probability that a customer will default on a loan. A data-mining *system*, however, uses that equation to enable banking personnel to approve or reject a loan on the spot.

A relatively simple example of this is provided by RFM analysis. An **RFM analysis** is a way of analyzing and ranking customers according to their purchasing patterns.[5]

[5] A. M. Hughes, "Boosting Response with RFM," *Marketing Tools*, May 1996. See also www.dbmarketing.com.

It is a simple technique that considers how recently (R) a customer has ordered, how frequently (F) a customer orders, and how much money (M) the customer spends per order. We consider this technique here because it is a useful analysis that can be readily implemented.

To produce an RFM score, the application first sorts customer purchase records by the date of most recent (R) purchase. In a common form of this analysis, the program then divides the customers into five groups and gives customers in each group a score of 1 to 5. Thus, the 20 percent who have the most recent orders are given an R score of 1, the 20 percent who have the next most recent orders are given an R score of 2, and so on, down to the last 20 percent who are given an R score of 5.

The program then re-sorts the customers on the basis of how frequently they order. The 20 percent of customers who order most frequently are given an F score of 1, the next 20 percent are given a score of 2, and so on, down to the least frequently ordering customers, who are given an F score of 5.

Finally, the program sorts the customers again according to the amount spent on their orders. The 20 percent who have ordered the most expensive items are given an M score of 1, the next 20 percent are given an M score of 2, and so forth, down to the 20 percent who spend the least, who are given an M score of 5. A reporting system can generate the RFM data and deliver it in many ways. For example, a report with RFM scores for all customers can be given to the vice-president of sales; reports with scores for particular regions can be given to regional sales managers; and reports with scores for particular accounts can be given to the account salespeople. And all of this reporting can be automated.

Q5   What Are the Purpose and Components of a Data Warehouse?

Watch

Go to MyMISLab to watch a video about the purpose and components of a data warehouse.

The purpose of a **data warehouse** is to extract and clean data from operational systems and other sources and to store and catalogue that data for processing by BI tools. Figure 8-7 shows the basic components of a data warehouse. Programs read operational data and extract, clean, and prepare that data for BI processing. The prepared data are stored in a data warehouse database using a data warehouse DBMS, which can be different from the organization's operational DBMS. For example, an organization might use Oracle for its operational processing, but SQL Server for its

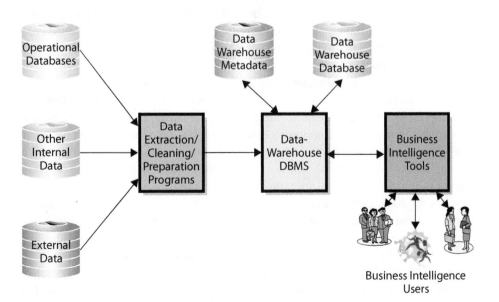

Figure 8-7

Components of a Data Warehouse

Figure 8-8

Consumer Data Available for Purchase from Data Vendors

- Name, address, phone
- Age
- Gender
- Ethnicity
- Religion
- Income
- Education
- Voter registration
- Home ownership
- Vehicles
- Magazine subscriptions
- Hobbies
- Catalogue orders
- Marital status, life stage
- Height, weight, hair and eye colour
- Spouse name, birth date
- Children's names and birth dates

data warehouse. Other organizations use SQL Server for operational processing, but DBMSs from statistical package vendors, such as SAS or SPSS, in the data warehouse.

Data warehouses include data that are purchased from outside sources. A typical example is customer credit data. Figure 8-8 lists some of the consumer data that can be purchased from commercial vendors today. An amazing (and, from a privacy standpoint, frightening) amount of data is available.

Metadata are data about data. For example, a database might store not only data but also data about the source of the data, the format of the data, and other facts about the data. This type of data is stored as metadata in the data warehouse. The DBMS that runs the data warehouse can be used to extract information and provides data to BI tools, such as data-mining programs.

By the way, do not interpret the term *warehouse* literally. It is a warehouse only in the sense that it is a facility for storing data for use by others. It is *not* a large building with shelves and forklifts buzzing through aisles loaded with pallets. Physically, a data warehouse consists of a few fast computers with very large storage devices. The data warehouse is usually staffed by a small department consisting of both technical personnel and business analysts. The technical personnel work to develop the best ways of storing and cataloguing the data warehouse's contents. The business analysts work to ensure that the contents are relevant and sufficient for the business needs of BI system users.

👁 Watch

Go to MyMISLab to watch a video about data marts and data warehouses.

Q6 What Is a Data Mart, and How Does It Differ from a Data Warehouse?

A **data mart** is a data collection that is created to address the needs of a particular business function, problem, or opportunity. An electronic commerce (e-commerce) company, for example, might create a data mart storing clickstream data that are pre-sampled and summarized so as to enable the analysis of webpage design features.

That same company might have a second data mart for market-basket analysis. This second data mart would contain records of past sales data organized to facilitate the computation of item–purchase correlations. A third data mart could contain inventory data and may be organized to support a BI system used to plan the layout of inventory.

So, how is a data warehouse different from a data mart? In a way, you can think of a *data warehouse* as a distributor in a supply chain. The data warehouse takes data from the data manufacturers (operational systems and purchased data), cleans and processes the data, and locates the data on its shelves, so to speak—that is, on the disks of the data warehouse computers. The people who work with a data warehouse are experts at data management, data cleaning, data transformation, and the like. However, they are not usually experts in a given business function.

As stated, a *data mart* is a data collection, smaller than the data warehouse, that addresses a particular component or functional area of the business. If the data

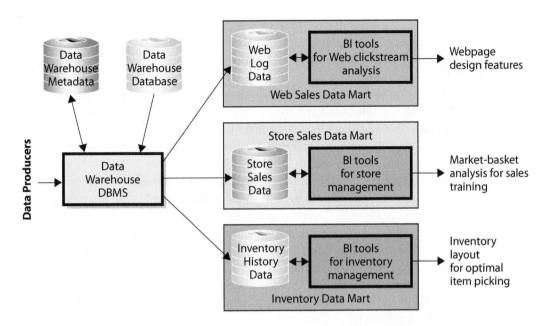

Figure 8-9

Data Mart Examples

warehouse is the distributor in a supply chain, then a data mart is a retail store in a supply chain. Users in the data mart obtain data from the data warehouse that pertain to a particular business function. Such users do not have the data management expertise that data warehouse employees have, but they are knowledgeable analysts for a given business function. Figure 8-9 illustrates these relationships.

As you can imagine, it is expensive to create, staff, and operate data warehouses and data marts. Only large organizations with considerable resources can afford to operate a system like the one shown in Figure 8-9. Smaller organizations operate subsets of such a system; they may have just a simple data mart for analyzing promotion data, for example.

Q7 What Are Typical Data-Mining Applications?

We now return to the concept of data mining. **Data mining** is the application of statistical techniques to find patterns and relationships among data and to make classifications and predictions. As shown in Figure 8-10, data mining represents a convergence

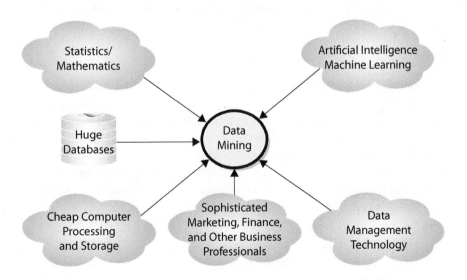

Figure 8-10

Convergence Disciplines for Data Mining

of disciplines. Data-mining techniques emerged from statistics and mathematics and from artificial intelligence and machine-learning fields in computer science. As a result, data-mining terminology is an odd blend of terms from these different disciplines.

Data-mining techniques take advantage of developments in data management for processing the enormous databases that have emerged in the last decade. Of course, these data would not have been generated were it not for fast and cheap computers and low-cost storage—and without these components, the new techniques would be impossible to compute.

Most data-mining techniques are sophisticated, and many are difficult to use. Such techniques are valuable to organizations, however, and some business professionals, especially those in finance and marketing, have become expert in their use. Today, in fact, there are many interesting and rewarding careers for business professionals who are knowledgeable about data-mining techniques. It is important, however, to recognize that data mining has limitations, which we discuss in the exercise "Data Mining in the Real World" at the end of this chapter on pages 278–279.

Data-mining techniques fall into two broad categories: *unsupervised* and *supervised*. We look at both types here.

Unsupervised Data Mining

With **unsupervised data mining**, analysts do not create a model or hypothesis before running the analysis. Instead, they apply the data-mining technique to the data and observe the results. With this method, analysts create hypotheses after the analysis to explain the patterns found.

One common unsupervised technique is **cluster analysis**, in which statistical techniques identify groups of entities that have similar characteristics. A common use for cluster analysis is to find groups of similar customers from customer order and demographic data.

For example, suppose a cluster analysis finds two very different customer groups—one group has an average age of 33 years, and each member owns at least one laptop and at least one smartphone, drives an expensive sport utility vehicle (SUV), and tends to buy expensive children's toys. The second group has an average age of 64 years, and each member owns a vacation property, plays golf, and buys expensive wines. Suppose the analysis also finds that both groups buy designer children's clothing.

These findings are obtained solely by data analysis. There is no prior model of the patterns and relationships that exist. It is up to the analyst to form hypotheses, after the fact, to explain why two such different groups are both buying designer children's clothes.

Supervised Data Mining

With **supervised data mining**, data miners develop a model prior to the analysis and apply statistical techniques to data to estimate the parameters of the model. For example, suppose marketing experts in a communications company believe that cellphone usage on weekends is determined by the age of the customer and the number of months he or she has had the cell phone account. A data-mining analyst would then run an analysis that estimates the impact of customer and account age. One such analysis, which measures the impact of a set of variables on another variable, is called a **regression analysis**. A sample result for the cellphone example is as follows:

```
CellPhoneWeekendMinutes =
12 + (17.5 * CustomerAge) + (23.7 * NumberMonthsOfAccount)
```

Using this equation, analysts can predict the number of minutes of weekend cellphone use by summing 12 plus 17.5 times the customer's age, plus 23.7 times the number of months of the account.

As you will learn in your statistics course, considerable skill is required to interpret the quality of such a model. The regression tool will create an equation such as the one above. Whether that equation is a good predictor of future cellphone usage depends on statistical factors, such as *t*-values, confidence intervals, and related statistical techniques.

Neural networks are another popular supervised data-mining technique used to predict values and make classifications, such as good prospect or poor prospect customers. The term *neural networks* is deceiving, however, because it connotes a biological process similar to that in brains. In fact, although the original *idea* of neural nets may have come from the anatomy and physiology of neurons, a neural net is nothing more than a complex set of possibly nonlinear equations. Explaining the techniques used for neural networks is beyond the scope of this text. If you want to learn more, search www.kdnuggets.com for the term *neural network*.

Another technique is *market-basket analysis*. Suppose you run a dive shop, and one day you realize that one of your sales associates is much better than anyone else at upselling to your customers. Any of your sales associates can fill a customer's order, but this one person is especially good at upselling, that is, selling other items in addition to those customers ask for. One day, you ask her how she does it.

"It's simple," she says. "I just ask myself what the next product a customer would want to buy might be. If someone buys a dive computer, I don't try to sell her fins. If she's buying a dive computer, she's already a diver and she already has fins. But dive computer displays are hard to read. So, a better mask makes it easier to read the display and get the computer's full benefit."

Without knowing it, your sales associate is using a market-basket analysis, which is a data-mining technique for determining sales patterns. A market-basket analysis shows the products that customers tend to buy together. In marketing transactions, the fact that customers who buy product X also buy product Y creates a cross-selling opportunity. That is, "If they're buying X, sell them Y," or, "If they're buying Y, sell them X."

Figure 8-11 shows hypothetical sales data of 1000 items at a dive shop. The first row of numbers under each column is the total number of times an item was sold. For

1000 Items	Mask	Tank	Fins	Weights	Dive Computer
	270	200	280	130	120
Mask	20	20	150	20	50
Tank	20	80	40	30	30
Fins	150	40	10	60	20
Weights	20	30	60	10	10
Dive computer	50	30	20	10	5
No additional product	10	—	—	—	5

Figure 8-11
Market-Basket Example

Support = P (A & B)   Example: P (Fins & Mask) = 150/1000 = 0.15

Confidence = P (A | B)   Example: P (Fins | Mask) = 150/270 = 0.5556

Lift = P (A | B)/P (A)   Example: P (Fins | Mask)/P (Fins) = 0.5556/0.28 = 1.98

Note: P(Mask | Fins)/P(Mask) = (150/280)/0.27 = 1.98

example, 270 in the first row of Mask means that 270 of the 1000 purchased items were masks. The number 120 under Dive Computer means that 120 of the 1000 purchased items were dive computers.

We can use the numbers in the first row to estimate the probability that a customer will purchase an item. Because 270 of the 1000 items were masks, we can estimate the probability that a customer will buy a mask to be 270/1000, or 0.27.

In market-basket terminology, *support* is the probability that two items will be purchased together. To estimate that probability, we examine sales transactions and count the number of times that two items occurred in the same transaction. For the data in Figure 8-11, fins and masks appeared together 150 times, and, thus, the support for fins and a mask is 150/1000, or 0.15. Similarly, the support for fins and weights is 60/1000, or 0.06, and the support for fins along with a second pair of fins is 10/1000, or 0.01.

The Market-Basket Example

These data are interesting in themselves, but we can refine the analysis by taking another step and considering additional probabilities. For example, what proportion of the customers who bought a mask also bought fins? Masks were purchased 270 times, and of those individuals who bought masks, 150 also bought fins. Thus, given that a customer bought a mask, we can estimate the probability that he or she will buy fins to be 150/270, or 0.5556. In market-basket terminology, such a conditional probability estimate is called *confidence*.

Reflect on the meaning of this confidence value. The likelihood of someone walking in the door and buying fins is 280/1000, or 0.28. But the likelihood of someone buying fins, given that he or she bought a mask, is 0.5556. Thus, if someone buys a mask, the likelihood that he or she will also buy fins almost doubles, from 0.28 to 0.5556. Thus, all sales personnel should be trained to try to sell fins to anyone buying a mask.

Now, consider dive computers and fins. Of the 1000 items sold, fins were sold 280 times, so the probability that someone walks into the store and buys fins is 0.28. But of the 120 purchases of dive computers, only 20 also bought fins. So, the likelihood of someone buying fins, given he or she bought a dive computer, is 20/120, or 0.1666. Thus, when someone buys a dive computer, the likelihood that she will also buy fins falls from 0.28 to 0.1666.

The ratio of confidence to the base probability of buying an item is called *lift*. Lift shows how much the base probability increases or decreases when other products are purchased. The lift of fins and a mask is the confidence of fins given a mask, divided by the base probability of fins. In Figure 8-11, the lift of fins and a mask is 0.5556/0.28, or 1.98. Thus, the likelihood that people buy fins when they buy a mask almost doubles. Surprisingly, it turns out that the lift of fins and a mask is the same as the lift of a mask and fins. Both are 1.98.

We need to be careful, however, because this analysis only shows shopping carts with two items. We cannot say from these data what the likelihood is that customers, given that they bought a mask, will buy both weights and fins. To assess that probability, we need to analyze shopping carts with three items. This statement illustrates, once again, that we need to know what problem we are solving before we start to build the information system to mine the data. The problem definition will help us decide whether we need to analyze three-item, four-item, or some other sized shopping carts.

Many organizations are benefiting from market-basket analysis today. You can expect that this technique will become a standard CRM analysis during your career.

Big Data

No MIS text today could ignore the relatively new but poorly defined term, **Big Data**. Although this term is poorly defined and its usage varies, almost all definitions and uses involve or reference the core concept that large amounts of varied data from a variety of sources over a period of time could be used to make better decisions. In 2008, for example, then-Senator Barack Obama's election project, Project Narwhal, used mail addresses, ZIP codes, and a variety of other data to customize email messages to appeal to voters most likely to support his election rather than send out a generic email message to everyone.

As might be expected, big data is controversial for a number of reasons. Beyond the lack of precision in its definition (when does data become big data), it is also criticized because it adds to excessive data collection, is expensive, and occasionally results in predictions that do not stand the test of time, are overly vague or general (left turns result in lower fuel economy), or confuse correlation with causality. While suntan lotion sales may go up in warm weather, no amount of suntan purchases will stop the rain. Nevertheless, while imprecise, big data is not likely to disappear soon.

Active Review

Use this Active Review to verify that you have understood the material in the chapter. You can read the entire chapter and then perform the tasks in this review, or you can read the material for just one question and perform the tasks for that question before moving on to the next one.

Q1 What challenges do managers face when making decisions?

Describe the factors, including information overload, uncertainty, and poor data quality, that make management decision making challenging. Explain how information systems have the potential to meet some of these challenges.

Q2 What is OLTP, and how does it support decision making?

Explain why information systems are a critical component for capturing details about transactions. Explain how online transaction processing (OLTP) can be used to support decision making.

Q3 What are OLAP and the data resource challenge?

Explain what is meant by the term *OLAP*. What is the data resource challenge? Do you believe that information is a company asset? What does this have to do with viewing data as an asset?

Q4 What are BI systems, and how do they provide competitive advantage?

Define *business intelligence system*. Name five categories of BI systems, and describe the basic characteristics of each.

Explain how systems in each category contribute to competitive advantage.

Q5 What are the purpose and components of a data warehouse?

State the purpose of a data warehouse. Explain the role of each component in Figure 8-7. Of the many different types of data that can be purchased, name five that you think are the most problematic from a privacy standpoint. State reasons why some businesses might want to purchase these data. Explain why the term *warehouse* is misleading.

Q6 What is a data mart, and how does it differ from a data warehouse?

Define *data mart*, and give an example of one that is not described in this chapter. Explain how data warehouses and data marts are like components of a supply chain. Under what conditions does an organization staff a data warehouse with several data marts?

Q7 What are typical data-mining applications?

What is the purpose of data-mining systems? Explain how data mining emerged from the convergence of different disciplines. Explain the characteristics and uses of unsupervised data mining. Explain the characteristics and uses of supervised data mining. Explain what is meant by market-basket analysis.

MyMISLab MyMISLab is an online learning and testing environment that features the perfect study tools to help you master the concepts covered in this chapter. Log in to MyMISLab to test your knowledge of key chapter concepts and explore additional practice tools, including videos, flashcards, annotated text figures, and more!

Key Terms and Concepts

Big Data 272

Business intelligence (BI) system 264

Clickstream data 259

Cluster analysis 270

Data mart 268

Data mining 269

Data-mining system 266

Data resource challenge 260

Data warehouse 267

Decision support systems (DSSs) 261

Dirty data 258

Drill down 261

Exabytes 257

Expert systems 266

Granularity 259

Group decision support systems (GDSSs) 264

Information overload 257

Knowledge management (KM) systems 266

Market-basket analysis 266

Metadata 268

Neural networks 271

Online analytic processing (OLAP) 261

Online transaction processing (OLTP) 259

Petabytes 257

Regression analysis 270

Reporting systems 266

RFM analysis 266

Supervised data mining 270

Unsupervised data mining 270

Using Your Knowledge

1. How does the data storage trend affect your university? What types of data are growing the fastest? Of these, what amount is generated by students? by classroom activities? by administration? by research?

2. OLTP systems are focused on providing three things: (a) efficient data input, (b) reliability, and (c) effective processing of a single transaction at a time. Use the knowledge you have gained to contrast these OLTP design principles with the design of OLAP systems. Do you see why the two types of systems require different designs?

3. Suppose you work for the university and have access to student, class, professor, department, and grade data. Now suppose you want to determine whether grade inflation exists, and, if so, where it seems to be the greatest. Describe a reporting system that would produce evidence of grade inflation. How would you structure the reports to determine where it is the greatest?

4. Suppose you work for the university and have access to student, class, professor, department, and grade data. Assume the student data include students' home address, high school, and prior post-secondary performance (if any). Describe an unsupervised data-mining technique that could be used to predict which applicants are likely to succeed academically. Is it a responsible or irresponsible thing to use an unsupervised technique for such a problem?

5. Explain how a set of If/Then rules could be used to select a supplier. Give an example of five rules that would be pertinent to this problem. Given the nature of a dive shop's product, and the size and culture of the organization, do you think it is likely that the shop would embrace an expert system? What about Carrie's Custom Clothing business? Why or why not?

6. What do you think is the minimum size or the basic attributes that a company would need to consider a data warehouse? Figure 8-9 implies that data marts require the existence of a data warehouse, but this is not always the case. Some companies could construct a data mart containing inbound logistic and manufacturing data without a data warehouse. In this case, the data mart would need to clean and prep its own operational data. List seven decisions that such a data mart might support, and describe the BI system that would support each decision. Explain how such BI systems contribute to competitive strategy.

7. The list below shows a set of customers that a company has and their RFM scores. Answer the following questions using information from the list.

Customer	RFM Score
Ajax	1 1 5
Bistro	3 3 3
Carpenter	2 5 4
Dog Walker	1 5 1
Elephant Trainer	4 2 5

a. On which of the customers should the company focus its marketing efforts? Justify your answer.
b. Which of the customers brings the most money to the organization? How can you tell?
c. If the organization had to drop one of the customers from the list, which customer would you choose to drop? Justify your answer.

Collaborative Exercises

Many grocery stores sponsor card programs, in which customers use special cards to receive purchase discounts. Shoppers Drug Mart, for example, sponsors the Optimum Card. The customer provides personal data, including his or her name, phone number, and address, and in return receives an identification card with a magnetic strip. When checking out, the customer gives the card to the cashier and points are added that can be redeemed for future purchases. The potential discount encourages people to use the card.

Card programs are popular; many grocery and retail chains have them, so they must provide value. The question is, what is that value?

1. Consider this question from a BI perspective:
   a. What might Shoppers Drug Mart or a grocery chain do with data that can correlate a particular customer to that customer's purchases over time?
   b. What information can such data provide? Assume that the data include not only the customer's identity, purchases, and purchase items, but the store location and the date and time of sale. The cards are valid at any store in the chain, so purchases at different stores can be associated with the same customer at a centralized data warehouse.

2. Describe market-basket analysis, and explain how a grocery store could perform such an analysis using its club card data. Suppose the lift of high-quality dog food

and premium cheese is 3.4. Explain what this means. Describe four possible ways that Shoppers Drug Mart could use this information. As a team, rank the four possibilities from best to worst. Justify your ranking.

3. Mary Keeling owns and operates Carbon Creek Gardens, a retailer of trees and garden plants, including perennials, annuals, and bulbs. "The Gardens," as her customers call it, also sells bags of soil, fertilizer, small garden tools, and garden sculptures. Mary started the business 14 years ago, and it has grown steadily.

"The problem is, however," Mary says, "I have grown so large that I've lost track of my customers. The other day I ran into Tootsie Swan at the grocery store, and I realized I had not seen her in ages. I said hello and asked how she was doing, and that statement unleashed an angry torrent from her. It turns out she wanted to return a plant and one of my part-time employees apparently insulted her, and she has not been back since. She was one of my best customers, and I didn't even know she had decided not to shop at The Gardens."

Given this information, answer the following questions:
a. Describe the best possible application of an OLAP tool for Carbon Creek Gardens. Can it be used to solve the lost-customer problem? Why, or why not?
b. Describe the best possible application of market-basket analysis that could occur at Carbon Creek Gardens. Can it be used to solve the lost-customer problem? Why, or why not?
c. Which BI application would provide Mary with the best value? If you owned Carbon Creek Gardens, which application would you choose?

Case Study 8

Building Data for Decision Making at Home Depot

Home Depot is a major retail chain specializing in the sale of construction, home repair, and maintenance products. The company has more than 2240 retail stores in North America and employs over 340 000 people worldwide.

Suppose you are a buyer for the clothes washer and dryer product line at Home Depot. You work with seven different brands and numerous models within each brand. One of your goals is to turn your inventory as many times a year as you can, and to do so you want to identify poorly selling models (and even brands) as quickly as you can. This identification is not as easy as you might think because competition is intense among washer and dryer manufacturers, and a new model can quickly capture a substantial portion of another model's market share. Thus, a big seller this year can be a dog (a poor seller) next year.

Another problem is that while some sales trends are national, others pertain to specific regions. A strong seller on the East Coast may not sell as well on the West Coast. In other words, a brand can be a big seller in one region and a dog in another.

In answering the following questions, assume that you have total sales data for each brand and model, for each store, for each month. Also assume that you know the store's city and province.

Questions

1. Explain how reporting systems could be helpful to you.
2. Show the structure of one or two reports you could use to identify poorly selling models. How would you structure the reports to identify different sales trends in different regions?

3. For one of these reports, write a description of your requirements that would be suitable for communication to an IT professional. Be as complete and thorough as you can in describing your needs.
4. Explain how data-mining systems could be helpful to you.
5. How could cluster analysis help you identify poorly selling brands? How could it help you determine differences in sales for different geographical regions? Is the unsupervised nature of cluster analysis an advantage or a disadvantage for you?
6. Do you believe there is an application for a KM system for identifying poorly selling brands? Why, or why not?
7. Do you believe there is an application for an expert system for identifying poorly selling brands? Why, or why not?

Data Mining in the Real World

"I'm not really a contrarian about data mining. I believe in it. After all, it's my career. But data mining in the real world is a lot different from the way it's described in textbooks.

"There are many reasons it's different. One is that the data are always dirty, with missing values, values way out of the range of possibility, and time values that make no sense. Here's an example: Somebody sets the server system clock incorrectly and runs the server for a while with the wrong time. When he notices the mistake, he sets the clock to the correct time. But all the transactions that were running during that interval have an ending time that's before the starting time. When we run the data analysis and compute elapsed time, the results are negative for those transactions.

"Missing values are a similar problem. Consider the records of just 10 purchases. Suppose that two of the records are missing the customer number and one is missing the year part of the transaction date.

So, you throw out three records, which is 30 percent of the data. You then notice that two more records have dirty data, and so you throw them out, too. Now you've lost half your data.

"Another problem is that you know very little when you start the study. So, you work for a few months and learn that if you had another variable—say, the customer's postal code, or age, or something else—you could do a much better analysis. But those other data just aren't available. Or maybe they are available, but to get them you have to reprocess millions of transactions, and you just don't have the time or budget to do that.

"Overfitting is another problem, a huge one. I can build a model to fit any set of data you have. Give me 100 data points, and in a few minutes I can give you 100 different equations that will predict those 100 data points. With neural networks, you can create a model of any level of complexity you want, except that none of those equations will predict new cases with any accuracy at all. When using neural networks, you have to be very careful not to overfit the data.

"Then, too, data mining is about probabilities, not certainty. Bad luck happens. Say, I build a model that predicts the probability that a customer will make a purchase. Using the model on new-customer data, I find three customers who have a 0.7 probability of buying something. That's a good number, well over a 50/50 chance, but it's still possible that none of them will buy. In fact, the probability that none of them will buy is $0.3 \times 0.3 \times 0.3$, or 0.027, which is 2.7 percent.

"Now suppose I give the names of the three customers to a salesperson. He calls on them, and sure enough, we have a stream of bad luck and none of them buys. This bad result doesn't mean the model is wrong. But what does the salesperson think? He thinks the model is worthless and that he can do better on his own. He tells his manager, who tells her associate, who tells the northeast region, and soon the model has a bad reputation all across the company.

"Another problem is seasonality. Say, all your training data are from the summer. Will your model be valid for the winter? Maybe, but maybe not. You might even know that it won't be valid for predicting winter sales, but if you don't have winter data, what do you do?

"When you start a data-mining project, you never know how it will turn out. I worked on one project for six months, and when we finished, I didn't think our model was any good. We had too many problems with data: wrong, dirty, and missing. There was no way we could know ahead of time that it would happen, but it did.

"When the time came to present the results to senior management, what could we do? How could we say we took six months of our time and substantial computer resources to create a bad model? We had a model, but I just didn't think it would make accurate predictions. I was a junior member of the team, and it wasn't for me to decide. I kept my mouth shut, but I never felt good about it."

Discussion Questions

1. Did this employee have an ethical responsibility to speak up regarding his belief about the quality of the data-mining model? Why, or why not?

2. If you were this employee, what would you have done?

3. This case does not indicate how the data-mining model was to be used. Suppose it was to be used at a hospital emergency room to predict the criticality of emergency cases. In this case, would you change your answers to questions 1 and 2? Why, or why not?

4. Suppose the data-mining model was to be used to predict the likelihood of sales prospects responding to a promotional postal mailing. Say, the cost of the mailing is $10 000 and will be paid by a marketing department with an annual budget of $25 million. Do your answers to questions 1 and 2 change for this situation? Why, or why not?

5. If your answers are different for questions 3 and 4, explain why. If they are not different, explain why.

6. Suppose you were this employee and you spoke to your direct boss about your misgivings. Your boss said, "Forget about it, Junior." How would you respond?

7. Suppose your boss told you to forget about it, but in a meeting with your boss and your boss's boss, the senior manager asks what you think of the predictive ability of this model. How do you respond?

9 Ecommerce, Social Networking, and Web 2.0

Running Case

Carrie's personality and professional nature have helped her create a good customer base for her business. She gets her fair share of one-of-a-kind events but has focused her efforts on customers who provide her with repeat business, such as schools, sports clubs, and annual charity events.

To grow her company further, Carrie realizes that she must find ways to expand beyond her traditional customer base. To do this, she is turning her attention toward ecommerce, social media, and the internet. She has already developed a company website, which has some basic information about her company. She is able to show off a range of her designs and has found the website to be a useful tool for discussing options with clients. Although it has been useful, the website has not created much customer interest. Carrie often has to point people to the website, and some people have had a hard time finding the site.

Carrie recognizes that search engines could do more work for her if she were able to get closer to the top of the most frequent searches. She is not sure how to do that. She has thought about using targeted content directories, such as T-ShirtCountdown.com and americantshirtnetwork.com, to attract more attention to some of her own designs. However, she is worried that moving in a direction that caters to selling to a larger consumer market might dilute her repeat customers strategy.

Carrie is often on Facebook and Twitter and enjoys using these sites. She has been frustrated trying to find out how to use these sites to the advantage of her company. She does see the power of social networking, but it seems like there is already too much traffic and that it is hard to get heard above all the noise.

One place for Carrie to start would be to investigate Web 2.0. Carrie should realize that more and more of her work for the company can be done through her website. For example, she could integrate her invoicing, customer relationship, supplier relationship, and order status data on her website. This would allow her to have all the information she needs at her fingertips and enable her to focus more attention on selling (rather than on administration). In this chapter, we will look at how Web 2.0 and social media are changing the way small and large organizations are doing business.

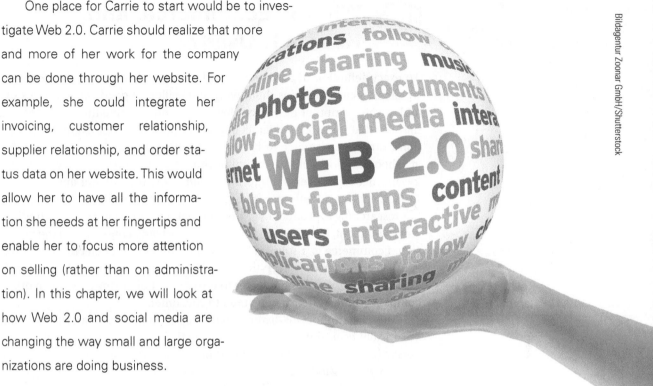

Study Questions

Q1 What is ecommerce, and how is it used?

Q2 What is social networking, and how is it enabled and affected by IS/IT?

Q3 What is Web 2.0?

Q4 Is there a Web 3.0?

Watch

Go to MyMISLab to watch a video about ecommerce and Web 2.0.

Q1 What Is Ecommerce, and How Is It Used?

An exact definition of *ecommerce* is a lot harder than you might think. In this text, we define **ecommerce** as the buying and selling of goods and services over public and private computer networks. However, if you examine this definition closely, you may see that it is not as clear as it might appear. Note, for example, that this definition restricts ecommerce to buying and selling transactions. Checking the weather at yahoo.ca is not ecommerce, but buying a weather service subscription that is paid for and delivered over the internet is. Similarly, researching and buying a good or service, such as a computer from Dell or OnStar from GM, qualifies as ecommerce, but researching a product over the internet and purchasing it in a traditional retail store would not, even though these activities clearly contribute to the purchase decision. Ecommerce is a subset of the broader definition of electronic business, which is usually described as everything having to do with the application of information and communication technologies to the conduct of business between organizations, company to consumer, or consumer to consumer.

This is an important distinction to keep in mind. The majority of commerce has historically been done in-person. Information was gathered directly from the sales person (e.g., the way that your parents may have purchased a new car). In ecommerce, this is not true. Modern consumers are less and less likely to use a single information channel to make buying decisions. A customer might search for the item online, look for prices in several stores offering the product, and read the manufacturer's website. A customer might also look at a few reviews and talk to people who have tried the product. All of this makes the customer quite knowledgeable. In fact, ecommerce customers can know more about a product or service than the salesperson who is actually facilitating the sale.

The emergence of ecommerce has provided much more information for consumers. Think about a recent large purchase that you may have made, for example, a new computer. It is possible that you simply walked into Future Shop or Best Buy to buy it or bought it online from Dell.ca, but it is much more likely that you first researched your options online and talked to your friends. You may even have gone into one store to familiarize yourself with the physical device, although you intended to buy it elsewhere. Depending on the specific purchase, it is also possible that you used a referral website, such as Yelp (or, when choosing classes, ratemyprofessor). Customers are now potentially more knowledgeable than ever before about products and services they purchase.

Ecommerce has other implications. From a technology perspective, additional infrastructure (more technology) for organizations will be required. The technological issues are not usually the biggest consideration for large organizations. Large organizations, such as Wal-Mart or Target, often provide and support many of these required technological capabilities. However, smaller organizations may have difficulty keeping up with this technological change. So how might a smaller company keep up? One option is to purchase the technologies as business services. Goods or services offered by a smaller company may be listed on larger sites, such as eBay, Craigslist, Amazon, or the Apple store; payment processing may be handled by PayPal or a local bank; and hosting may be done by internet service providers (ISPs), such as GoDaddy or Amazon.

A further implication of ecommerce is the increased coordination between organizations and systems. In the case of large companies, the linkages required by ecommerce could be extensive, especially when partners are involved. Inventory, for example, will need to be updated and require communications among the supply

Merchant Companies	Nonmerchant Companies
– Business-to-consumer (B2C) – Business-to-business (B2B) – Business-to-government (B2G)	– Auctions – Clearinghouses – Exchanges

Figure 9-1

Ecommerce Categories

chain management (SCM) system, the customer relationship management (CRM) system, and the accounting system. In short, ecommerce may require interconnectedness of the entire enterprise resource planning (ERP) process.

Beyond the technology issues (which are significant, as we will discuss in this chapter), ecommerce has large implications for management and governments. Before the enterprise management systems are securely connected, organizations need to ensure that all aspects of the business operate smoothly and do not operate at cross purposes. Externally, companies need to ensure that end-to-end customer security is enabled and that the information is only shared appropriately and with customer permission.

Although the definition of *ecommerce* is not as broad as the definition of *ebusiness*, there are many varieties. These are listed in Figure 9-1.

Merchant companies are defined as those that take title to the goods they sell—they buy goods and resell them. **Nonmerchant companies** are those that arrange for the purchase and sale of goods without ever owning or taking title to those goods. Merchant companies sell services that they provide; nonmerchant companies sell services provided by others. We will consider merchants and nonmerchants separately in the following sections.

Ecommerce Merchant Companies

There are three main types of merchant companies: (1) those that sell directly to consumers, (2) those that sell to companies, and (3) those that sell to government. Each uses slightly different information systems in the course of doing business. **Business-to-consumer (B2C)** ecommerce concerns sales between a supplier and a retail customer (the consumer). A typical information system for B2C provides a web-based application or **web storefront** by which customers enter and manage their orders.

The term **business-to-business (B2B)** ecommerce refers to sales between companies. As Figure 9-2 shows, raw materials suppliers use B2B systems to sell to manufacturers, manufacturers use B2B systems to sell to distributors, and distributors use B2B systems to sell to retailers.

Business-to-government (B2G) ecommerce refers to sales between companies and governmental organizations. As Figure 9-2 shows, a manufacturer that uses an ecommerce site to sell computer hardware to a government ministry is engaging in B2G commerce. Suppliers, distributors, and retailers can sell to government as well.

B2C applications first captured the attention of mail-order and related businesses. However, companies in all sectors of the economy soon realized the enormous

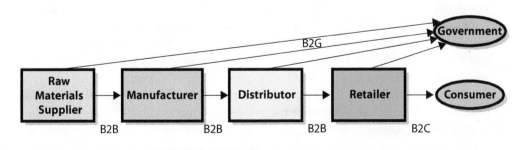

Figure 9-2

Examples of B2B, B2G, and B2C

potential of B2B and B2G ecommerce. The number of companies engaged in B2B and B2G commerce now far exceeds those engaging in B2C commerce. For example, consider Dell Computer. Although the basis for buying computers has changed and other competitors have replicated aspects, Dell has structured its website in such a way that almost anyone can configure and order a computer online. The site guides home users, novice business users, and expert users (from business and government) into different parts of the site that provide different experiences. Home users, for example, may be offered computer packages with easy-to-understand options. Business or government experts, who are more likely to be buying high-performance server computers, could be offered a larger and more complex array of options and choices. Dell's site offers extensive support, with definitions and explanations, all online. In this way, Dell has almost completely automated ordering and has dramatically reduced the cost of processing an order. The system is consistent with Dell's competitive strategy, which is to provide the computers to its customers at the lowest possible cost.

Today's B2B and B2G ecommerce applications implement just a small portion of their potential capabilities. Their full utilization is some years away. Although most experts agree that these applications involve some sort of integration of CRM and supplier relationship management (SRM) systems, the nature of that integration is not well understood, as it is still being developed. Consequently, you can expect further progress and development in B2B and B2G applications during your career.

Nonmerchant Ecommerce

The most common nonmerchant ecommerce companies are auctions (such as eBay) and clearinghouses. **Ecommerce auctions** match buyers and sellers by using an ecommerce version of a standard auction. This ecommerce application enables the auction company to offer goods for sale and to support a competitive-bidding process. The best-known auction company is eBay, but many other auction companies exist; many serve particular industries. One of the world's largest industrial auctioneers, Ritchie Bros. (www.rbauction.com), based in Richmond, B.C., uses the web to hold virtual auctions that allow bidders from across the world to take part in industrial equipment auctions without having to physically attend an event.

Clearinghouses provide goods and services at a stated price and arrange for the delivery of the goods, but they never take title. One division of Amazon.ca, for example, operates as a nonmerchant clearinghouse and sells books owned by others. As a clearinghouse, Amazon.ca matches the seller and the buyer and then takes payment from the buyer and transfers the payment to the seller, minus a commission.

Other examples of clearinghouse businesses are **electronic exchanges** that match buyers and sellers; the business process is similar to that of a stock exchange. Sellers offer goods at a given price through the electronic exchange, and buyers make offers to purchase over the same exchange. Price matches result in transactions from which the exchange takes a commission. Priceline.com is an example of an electronic exchange used by consumers.

Benefits of Ecommerce

The debate continues among business observers as to whether ecommerce is something new or just a technology extension of existing business practice. During the dot-com heydays of 1999–2000, some claimed that ecommerce was ushering in a new era and a new economy. Although experts differ as to whether a new economy was created, all agree that ecommerce does lead to greater market efficiency.

One effect frequently associated with ecommerce is **disintermediation**—the removal of intermediaries between parties. As ecommerce first started to become popular, it was widely believed that some of the agents in the distribution process

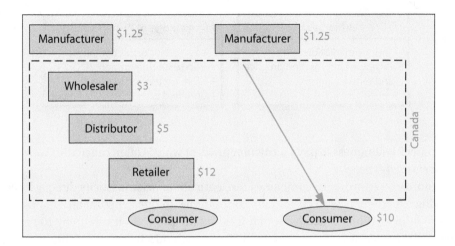

Figure 9-3

Disintermediation–Manufacturer to Consumer.

would be eliminated. This is illustrated by the hypothetical transactions on the left side of Figure 9-3. In this example, a manufacturer produces a good for $1.25, and it sells it to the wholesaler for $3. The wholesaler then sells it to the distributor for $5, who, in turn, sells it to the retailer for $12. The retailer is free to set the final price that is paid by the end consumer. The right side of Figure 9-3 shows the elimination of the intervening layers between manufacturers and end consumers facilitated by direct website sales.

The general results of disintermediation are higher revenues for manufacturers and lower consumer prices, but the broader implications are more significant. Canada is a very large country and much of the Canadian economy involves distribution. Some consultants estimate that 80% of the goods being sold are not actually in stores, but moving through the supply chain in transport or stored in warehouses and distribution centres. If Canadian consumers buy from Amazon.com rather than from local retailers, large amounts of the Canadian economy could be disrupted.

The good news is that consumers have generally benefited from ecommerce, and the net effect has not been quite as negative as initially imagined. In many cases, manufacturers have found it much more difficult to eliminate intermediaries, and although distribution channels have become more efficient, new players have inserted themselves into the sales and distribution processes (not surprisingly, this process is called *intermediation* or sometimes *re-intermediation*). Apple, for example, has become a significant actor in the retail of music and media. Often, rather than buying directly from airlines and hotels, many consumers prefer to use websites, such as Trivago.com, Travelocity.ca, Expedia.ca, and Priceline.com, to find low-cost airline tickets and accommodation.

Ecommerce also improves the flow of price information. As a consumer, you can go to any number of websites that offer product price comparisons. You can search for information on the high-definition television (HDTV) you want and sort the results by price and vendor reputation. You can find vendors that waive or reduce shipping charges. The improved distribution of information about price and terms enables you to pay the lowest possible price and serves ultimately to remove inefficient vendors. The market, as a whole, becomes more efficient.

From the seller's side, ecommerce produces information about price elasticity that has not been available before. **Price elasticity** measures how much demand rises or falls with changes in price. Using an auction as an example, a company can learn not only what the top price for an item is but also the second, third, and other prices of the losing bids. In this way, the company can understand more about various

Figure 9-4

Ecommerce Market Consequences

Greater Market Efficiency	Knowledge of Price Elasticity
– Disintermediation – Increased information on price and terms	– Losing-bidder auction prices – Price experimentation – More accurate information obtained directly from customer

customers' willingness to pay a particular price, or what is often called the *shape of the price elasticity curve.*

Similarly, ecommerce companies can learn about price elasticity directly by conducting experiments with customers. For example, in one experiment, Amazon.com created three groups of similar books. It raised the price of one group by 10 percent, lowered the price of the second group by 10 percent, and left the price of the third group unchanged. Customers provided feedback on these changes by deciding whether to buy books at the offered prices. Amazon.com measured the total revenue (quantity times price) of each group and took the action (raise, lower, or maintain prices) on all books that maximized revenue. Amazon.com repeated the process until it reached the point at which the indicated action was to maintain current prices.

Managing prices by direct interaction with the customer yields better information compared with managing prices by watching competitors' pricing. By experimenting with customers, companies learn how customers have internalized competitors' pricing, advertising, and messaging. Customers may not know about a competitor's lower prices, in which case there is no need for a price reduction. Or the competitor may be using a price that, if lowered, would increase demand sufficiently to increase total revenue. Figure 9-4 summarizes ecommerce market consequences.

The Challenges of Ecommerce

Although there are tremendous advantages and opportunities for many organizations to engage in ecommerce, the economics of some industries may disfavour ecommerce activity. Companies need to consider the following economic factors:

- Channel conflict
- Price conflict
- Logistics expense
- Customer service expense
- Showrooming
- Taxation

Figure 9-3 shows a manufacturer selling directly to a government agency. Before engaging in this B2G ecommerce, the manufacturer must consider each of the economic factors listed above. First, what **channel conflict** will develop? Suppose the manufacturer is a computer maker that is selling directly (B2G) to a government agency. When the manufacturer begins to sell goods B2G that employees of the agency had previously purchased from a computer retailer down the street, that retailer will resent the competition and may drop the manufacturer. This creates channel conflict. If the value of the lost sales is greater than the value of the B2G sales, ecommerce is not a good solution, at least not on that basis.

Furthermore, when a business engages in ecommerce, it may also cause **price conflict** with its traditional channels. Because of disintermediation, the manufacturer may be able to offer a lower price and still make a profit. However, as soon as the manufacturer offers the lower price, existing channels will object. Even if the manufacturer and the retailer are not competing for the same customers, the retailer still will not want a lower price to be readily known via the web.

Furthermore, the existing distribution and retailing partners do provide value; they are not just a cost. Without them, the manufacturer will have the increased **logistic expense** of entering and processing orders in small quantities. If the expense of processing a single-unit order is the same as that for processing a 12-unit order (which is possible), the average logistic expense per item will be much higher for goods sold via ecommerce.

Similarly, **customer service expenses** are likely to increase for manufacturers that use ecommerce to sell directly to consumers (B2C). The manufacturer will be required to provide service to less-sophisticated users and on a one-by-one basis. For example, instead of explaining to a single sales professional that the recent shipment of 100 Gizmo 3.0s requires a new bracket, the manufacturer will need to explain that 100 times to less knowledgeable and more frustrated customers. Such service requires additional training and expense.

A growing issue for merchants with traditional stores is that of showrooming. **Showrooming** occurs when a customer learns about or tries a product or service in the high cost bricks-and-mortar retail store while completing the sales transaction at the low-cost internet sales channel of another retailer. The ethics of showrooming and the impact on profitability have been widely debated, but there is little doubt that it occurs.

Shopping has been considered a social activity, and many people still want to see and touch goods before purchasing them. In May 2012, Target stopped selling Amazon's Kindle in their stores after realizing that consumers were using their stores to examine the Kindle but were actually buying the eReader from Amazon.com—a practice that they claimed Amazon encouraged by giving customers a 5 percent discount if they uploaded a copy of the UPC barcode (typically, this is only accessible in a traditional store). Online purchases are often (but not always) price sensitive, particularly when the product is interchangeable and there are limited expectations for service. Some students, for example, may visit their university bookstore (the showroom) to identify the book needed for a particular course, inspect it, and decide if they are going to buy it (a practice that, as authors and professors, we highly recommend) before purchasing a copy at an online retailer (or photocopying one, a process we do not recommend). Of course, not all aspects of showrooming are unanticipated or counter-strategic. Future Shop, for example, considers its combination of both retail stores and ecommerce websites to be part of their strategic advantage, and customers are encouraged to browse the physical store and buy online or to browse online and then buy in the store.

For governments, a large problem is determining how to tax ecommerce. Normally, taxes are based on the location of the creation or consumption of the particular good and service, but this is complicated with regard to ecommerce. If, for example, Canadian consumers download an antivirus service from a website based in a U.S. state that does not have sales tax (as one of your authors has done), what taxes are due, and who is responsible for collecting and remitting them? This problem, of course, is not completely new. Consumers located near Alberta, which does not have a sales tax, have long been able to cross the provincial border for large (or small, depending on the distance) purchases. However, this is made worse through ecommerce and is a major concern for all levels of government. Online and predominantly service-based businesses that have more location flexibility compared with retail operations are often able to pay much lower taxes. Apple, for example, has an overall U.S. tax rate of 24.2 percent, whereas Wal-Mart's average U.S. tax rate is 32.5 percent.

Beyond these economic factors, another consideration for organizations that are contemplating ecommerce is reduced profitability and margin squeeze. Because information is so freely available to consumers, it is harder to raise prices. Customers often know more about competitive pricing than salespeople do, and prices can be driven below the point at which companies can earn a reasonable profit. This scenario, of course, is not just related to ecommerce. Even if a particular company does not participate in selling directly to consumers, more and more information is freely available on the web and accessible via smartphones. This can increase consumers' ability to negotiate lower prices.

Q2 What Is Social Networking, and How Is It Enabled and Affected by IS/IT?

It is likely that you do not need this book to learn how to use Facebook or Twitter. You already know how to do that. But when you use such sites, there is more going on than you realize. If you are using such sites solely for entertainment or self-expression, then a deeper understanding of them is not too important. But if, like many professionals, you use such sites for both self-expression and for professional purposes, then understanding how such sites contribute to your social capital and how such capital influences and benefits organizations is important.

Social capital is earned through social networking. A *social network* is a structure of individuals and organizations that are related to each other in some way. *Social networking* is the process by which individuals use relationships to communicate with others in a social network.

What Is Social Capital?

Business literature defines three types of capital: physical capital, human capital, and social capital.

Karl Marx defined *physical capital* as the investment of resources for future profit. This traditional definition refers to investments in physical resources, such as factories, machines, manufacturing equipment, and the like.

Human capital is the investment in human knowledge and skills for future profit. By taking this class, you are investing in your own human capital. You are investing your money and time to obtain knowledge that you hope will differentiate you from other workers and ultimately give you a wage premium in the workforce.

According to Nan Lin,[1] *social capital* is investment in social relations with the expectation of returns in the marketplace. When you attend a business function for the purpose of meeting people and reinforcing relationships, you are investing in your social capital. Similarly, when you join LinkedIn or contribute to Facebook, you are (or can be) investing in your social capital.

According to Lin, social capital adds value in four ways:

1. Information
2. Influence
3. Social credentials
4. Personal reinforcement

First, relationships in social networks can provide information about opportunities, alternatives, problems, and other factors important to business professionals.

---

[1] N. Lin, *Social Capital: The Theory of Social Structure and Action* (Cambridge, UK: Cambridge University Press, 2001), Location 310 of the Kindle Edition.

Second, they can provide an opportunity to influence decision makers in one's employer or in other organizations who are critical to your success. Such influence cuts across formal organizational structures, such as reporting relationships. Third, being linked to a network of highly regarded contacts is a form of *social credential*. You can bask in the glory of those with whom you are related. Others will be more inclined to work with you if they believe critical personnel are standing with you and may provide resources to support you. Fourth, being linked to social networks reinforces your professional image and position in an organization or industry. It reinforces the way you define yourself to the world (and to yourself).

Social networks differ in value. The social network you maintain with your high school friends probably has less value than the network you have with your business associates, but not necessarily so. According to Henk Flap,[2] the value of social capital is determined by the number of relationships in a social network, by the strength of those relationships, and by the resources controlled by those related. If your high school friends happen to be Bill Gates or Mark Zuckerberg, and if you maintain strong relations with them via your high school network, then the value of that social network likely far exceeds any you will have at work. For most of us, however, it is the network of our current professional contacts that provides social capital.

So, when you use social networking professionally, consider the four factors mentioned above. You gain social capital by adding more friends and by strengthening the relationships you have with existing friends. Further, you gain more social capital by adding friends and strengthening relationships with people who control resources that are important to you. Such calculations may seem cold, impersonal, and possibly even phony. When applied to the recreational use of social networking, they may be. But when you use social networking for professional purposes, consider them important. The popular term *frenemy*, a combination of the words *friend* and *enemy*, is sometimes used to discuss ambiguous or complex social relationships. In the context of all of the new things that technology has made possible, it is interesting to note that this word was, in fact, first used in 1953.[3]

The Importance of Weak Relationships

Strong relationships create the most social capital in a social network, but, ironically, it is weak relationships that contribute the most to the growth of social networks. To understand why, consider the network diagram in Figure 9-5. Assume that each line

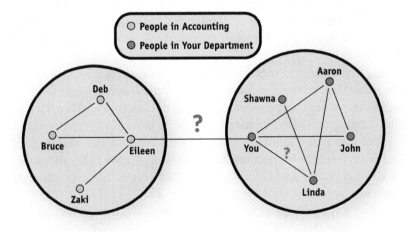

Figure 9-5

A Network Diagram

[2] H. D. Flap, "Social Capital in the Reproduction of Inequality," *Comparative Sociology of Family, Health, and Education* 20 (1991): 6179–202, quoted in N. Lin, *Social Capital* (Cambridge, UK: Cambridge University Press, 2002), Kindle location 345.
[3] W. Winchell, W., "How About Calling the Russians Our Frenemies?" *Nevada State Journal* (May 19, 1953).

represents a relationship between two people. Note that the people in your department tend to know each other, and that the people in the accounting department also tend to know each other. That is typical.

Now, suppose you are at the weekly employee after-hours party and you have an opportunity to introduce yourself to Linda or Eileen. Setting aside personal considerations and thinking just about network building, which person should you meet?

If you introduce yourself to Linda, you shorten your pathway to her from two steps to one and your pathway to Shawna from three to two. You do not open up any new channels because you already have them to the people in your department.

However, if you introduce yourself to Eileen, you open up an entirely new network of acquaintances. So, considering just network building, you use your time better by meeting Eileen and other people who are not part of your current circle. It opens up many more possibilities. The connection from you to Eileen is called a *weak tie* in social network theory,[4] and such links are crucial in increasing the number of relationships in your network. In general, the people you know the least contribute the most to your network.

This concept is simple, but you might be surprised to learn how few people pay attention to it. At most company events, everyone talks with the people they already know. If the purpose of the occasion is to have fun, then that behaviour makes sense. In truth, however, no business social function exists just for having fun, regardless of what people say. Business functions exist for business reasons, and you can use them to create and expand networks. Given that time is always limited, you may as well use such functions efficiently.

The same comments apply to online social networking: Weak links add the greatest number of new connections to your social network.

How Do Social Networks Add Value to Business?

Organizations have social capital just as humans do. Their social capital is measured in the same way: number of relationships, strength of relationships, and resources controlled by friends. Historically, organizations have created social capital via salespeople, customer support, and public relations. Endorsements by high-profile people are a traditional way of increasing social capital, but there are tigers in those woods.

Today, progressive organizations maintain a presence on Facebook, LinkedIn, Twitter, Foursquare, Pinterest and often other sites. They include links to their social networking presence on their websites and make it easy for customers and interested parties to leave comments. In most cases, such connections are positive, but they can backfire or occasionally result in unintended consequences; for example, when a large number of strangers or friends of friends show up at what was supposed to be a small house party.

Consider organizational social networking from the standpoint of social capital. Copyright restrictions prevent us from showing you our actual pages (which is interesting given that we actually provided or created the information) but if we were able to include a photograph of our status page (as of October 2014) you might notice that one of us had just added a few new connections, bringing his total up to 274. The total number of people in his network had increased to 4 904 744. You would also see that LinkedIn has posted a few links to stories that were of interest to the author and invited people to comment on these stories.

The author has just a basic account on LinkedIn, but even with just this level of access, links can be posted, endorsements provided for known people, and

---

recommendations or comments made on a variety of things. Of course, all of this also brings scrutiny as well, since much of it is public. In May 2012, for example, the CEO of Yahoo! joined a long list of people who were found to have added fake credentials to their résumés when he claimed to have earned a degree in computer science.

Looking at the other side of this exchange, the author can also keep in touch with all of the contacts attached to his account, and can choose to share a variety of information and links. He can, for example, see if he has colleagues in common or how far away a particular person is. If the relationship is close and the parties are often in touch anyway, this connection may not reveal a lot of new information, but it is easy to see how useful this profile can be. Of course, sometimes we make assumptions about the person based on what we read on their profile. In this specific case, for example, the author knows that the co-author has been using LinkedIn as he has updated his profile to include an accounting designation that he received in 2013.

How Is Social Networking Enabled by IS/IT?

Human beings, by definition, are social creatures, and many people claim that social networking has existed since the Stone Age. Indeed, some suggest that social networks are really just an extension of the networking concepts developed in clubs and universities (Facebook was started at Harvard University) and that these relationships are often used to facilitate introductions. A question, therefore, is how social networking has been enabled by technology. Besides the ubiquity of computers and their relatively low cost, three other considerations are (1) improved search capabilities, (2) reduction in the trade-off of richness and reach, and (3) network effects.

Search capabilities are important to social networking because they enable us to quickly sort through large amounts of data and find the specific person or relationship that we are interested in. Even those with an uncommon name, in many cases, may find that they have internet doppelgängers, or people with the same name. Sometimes, if you have the same name as a celebrity, this can be useful for getting reservations at a popular restaurant. Conversely, if you share a name with a criminal or person on a do not fly list, it can be troublesome. To deal with this type of event, large organizations, such as airlines and CSIS (the Canadian Security Intelligence Service), maintain lists and processes to reduce the impact and confusion. In managing your digital persona, one thing to be aware of is what happens when people search for you on the internet by ego surfing (searching one's own name to see the results).

The second advantage of technology is the ability to keep track of many more people and enhance personalization. For example, the more people that we connect with, the lower the level of interaction that can exist with each connection. Although finite limits exist—there are only so many things that we can keep track of, and each day only has 24 hours—we can use databases and systems to store information and remind us of friends' birthdays, wedding anniversary dates, and other key pieces of information.

The final technological consideration is that of network effects. As we have described earlier, a network of 10 people is five times more valuable than a network of two people. As a network grows, the benefit or utility that each person adds tends to increase. This can accelerate the speed at which networks grow and how useful they become.

Q3 What Is Web 2.0?

There is no universally accepted definition for the term *Web 2.0*. **Web 2.0** was first popularized in 2005 by Tim O'Reilly to refer to the integration and interaction of products and services, such as smartphones, user-created content, social networking, location

Figure 9-6

Comparison of Web 2.0 with
Traditional Processing

Web 2.0 Processing	Traditional Processing
Major winners: Google, Amazon.com, eBay	Major winners: Microsoft, Oracle, SAP
Software as a (free) service	Software as a product
Frequent releases of thin-client applications	Infrequent, controlled releases
Business model relies on advertising or other revenue-from-use	Business model relies on sale of software licences
Viral marketing	Extensive advertising
Product value increases with use and users	Product value fixed
Organic interfaces, mashups encouraged	Controlled, fixed interface
Participation	Publishing
Some rights reserved	All rights reserved

and context-based services, and dynamic marketplaces, not as a specific technology. Figure 9-6 compares Web 2.0 with traditional processing.

Software as a (Free) Service

Google, Amazon.com, and eBay exemplify Web 2.0. These companies do not sell software licences because software is not their product. Instead, they provide software as a service (SAAS). You can search Google, run Google Docs, use Google Earth, process Gmail, and access Google Maps, all from a thin-client browser, with the bulk of the processing occurring in the cloud (somewhere on the internet). Instead of software licence fees, the Web 2.0 business model relies on advertising or other revenue that results as users employ the software as a service.

Web 2.0 applications are thin clients. As such, they do not require installation on users' computers. Web servers download Web 2.0 programs as code within HTML, as Flash, or as Silverlight code. Because of this, they are readily (and frequently) updated. New features are added with little notice or fanfare. Web 2.0 users are accustomed to, and even expect, frequent updates to their licence-free software.

Software as a service clashes with the software model used by traditional software vendors, such as Microsoft, Oracle, and SAP. Software is their product. They release new versions and new products infrequently. For example, three years separated the release of Microsoft Office 2007 from 2010, and yet another 3 years until Office 2013. Releases are made in a very controlled fashion, and extensive testing and true beta programs precede every release.

Traditional software vendors depend on software licence fees. If a large number of Office users switched to free word-processing and spreadsheet applications, the effect on Microsoft's revenue would be catastrophic. Because of the importance of software licensing revenue, substantial marketing efforts are made to convert users to new releases.

In the Web 2.0 world, little such marketing is done; new features are released, and vendors wait for users to spread the news to one another—one friend sending a message to many friends, most of whom send that message, in turn, to their friends, and so forth—in a process called *viral marketing*. Google has never announced any software in a formal marketing campaign. Users carry the message to one another. In fact, if a product requires advertising to be successful, then it is likely not a Web 2.0 product.

By the way, traditional software companies do use the term *software as a service*. However, they use it only to mean that they will provide their software products via the cloud rather than having customers install that software on their computers. Software licences for their products still carry a sometimes significant licence fee. So, to be accurate, we should say that in the Web 2.0 world, software is provided as a free service.

Use Increases Value

Another characteristic of Web 2.0 is the extent of network effects. The value of the site increases with number of users and their use of the site. Amazon.com gains more value as more users write more reviews. Amazon.com becomes the place to go for information about books or other products. Similarly, the more people who buy or sell on eBay, the more eBay gains value as a site.

The term *user-generated content* (UGC) refers to website content that is contributed by users. Although reviews are still the bulk of such content (and their objectivity is often questionable), some companies have created websites and tools that encourage users to contribute in other ways. On some sites, users can provide customer support to one another or even participate in the creation of product specifications, designs, and complete products in a process called *crowdsourcing*. The startup company Kickstarter (www.kickstarter.com) allows nascent companies to post descriptions of their ideas for new products and services that the public can pre-order and, in doing so, contribute to their initial funding or suggest design improvements.

Crowdsourcing combines social networking, viral marketing, and open-source design, saving considerable cost while cultivating customers. With crowdsourcing, the crowd performs classic in-house market research and development and does so in such a way that customers are being set up to buy.

Another particular form of crowdsourcing, where a start-up raises money from a relatively large group of people who invest directly or prepay for a new good or service, is called *crowdfunding*. This is an area that is popular but relatively unregulated.

Organic User Interfaces and Mashups

The traditional software model carefully controls users' experience. All Office programs share a common user interface; the ribbon (toolbar) in Word is similar to the ribbon in PowerPoint and in Excel. In contrast, Web 2.0 interfaces are organic. Users find their way around eBay and PayPal, and if the user interface changes from day to day, well, that is just the nature of Web 2.0. Further, Web 2.0 encourages *mashups*, which result when the output from two or more websites is combined into a single user experience.

Google's My Maps is an excellent mashup example. Google publishes Google Maps and provides tools for users to make custom modifications to those maps. Thus, users mash the Google Maps product with their own knowledge. One user demonstrated the growth of gang activity to the local police by mapping new graffiti sites on Google Maps. Other users share their experiences or photos of hiking trips and other travel.

In Web 2.0 fashion, Google provides users a means for sharing their mashed-up map over the internet and then indexes that map for Google Search. If you publish a mashup of a Google map with your knowledge of a hiking trip on Mt. Pugh, anyone who performs a Google search for Mt. Pugh will find your map. Again, the more users who create My Maps, the greater the value of the My Maps site.

Participation and Ownership Differences

Mashups lead to another key difference. Traditional sites are about publishing; Web 2.0 is about participation. Users provide reviews, map content, discussion responses, blog entries, and so forth.

A final difference concerns ownership. Traditional vendors and websites tend to lock down all the legal rights they can. For example, Oracle publishes content and demands that others obtain written permission before reusing it. Web 2.0 locks down only some rights. Google publishes maps and says, "Do what you want with them. We'll help you share them."

How Can Businesses Benefit from Web 2.0?

Amazon.com, Google, eBay, and other Web 2.0 companies have pioneered Web 2.0 technology and techniques to their benefit. A good question today, however, is how these techniques might be used by non-internet companies. How might 3M, Alaska Airlines, Procter & Gamble, or the bicycle shop down the street use Web 2.0?

Advertising

Consider again the Oracle CRM ad in the print version of *the Globe and Mail*. Oracle has no control over who reads that ad, nor does it know much about the people who do (just that they fit the general demographic of *Globe and Mail* readers). On any particular day, 10 000 qualified buyers for Oracle products might read the ad or, then again, perhaps only 1000 qualified buyers might read it. Neither Oracle nor *The Globe and Mail* knows the number, but Oracle pays the same amount for the ad, regardless of the number of readers or who they are.

In the Web 2.0 world, advertising can be specific to user interests. Someone who searches online for "customer relationship management" is likely an information technology (IT) person (or a student) who has a strong interest in Oracle and its competing products. Oracle would like to advertise to that person.

As stated earlier, Google pioneered Web 2.0 advertising. Through its AdWords software, vendors pay Google a certain amount for particular search words. For example, The 1881 (the bed and breakfast hotel featured in Part 2) might agree to pay $2 for the words *bed* and *breakfast* and *Lunenburg*. When someone Googles that term, Google will display a link to The 1881 website. If the user clicks on that link (and only if the user clicks on that link), Google charges $2 to The 1881's account, but charges nothing if the user does not click on the link. This is targeted advertising because The 1881 can specifically tailor its ads.

The amount that a company pays per word can be changed from day to day and even from hour to hour. If The 1881 is having a promotion around Thanksgiving, it may be willing to pay more for the word *Thanksgiving* or *getaway* before the hotel is fully booked than when it has no vacancies. The value of a click on *getaway* is low when the hotel is full compared with other times of the year.

Google AdSense is another advertising alternative. Google searches an organization's website and inserts ads that match the content on that site. When users click on those ads, Google pays the organization a fee. Other Web 2.0 vendors offer services similar to AdWords and AdSense.

With Web 2.0, the cost of reaching a particular, qualified buyer is much smaller than in the traditional advertising model. As a consequence, many companies are switching to the new lower-cost medium, and, consequently, newspapers and magazines are struggling with a sharp reduction in advertising revenue.

Mashups

How can two non-internet companies mash up the contents of their websites? Suppose you are watching a hit movie and you would like to buy copies of the jewellery, dress, and watch worn by the leading actress. Suppose that Target sells all of those items. With Web 2.0 technology, the movie's producer and Target can mash up their contents together so that you, watching the movie on a computer at home, can click on the item you like and be directed to Target's ecommerce site, which will sell it to you. Or, perhaps, Target is disintermediated out of the transaction, and you are taken to the ecommerce site of the item's manufacturer.

Not for All Applications

Before you get too carried away with the potential for Web 2.0, you should note that not all business information systems benefit from flexibility and organic growth. Any information system that deals with assets, whether financial or material, requires some level of control. You probably do not want to mash up your credit card transactions on My Maps and share that mashup with the world. As a chief financial officer (CFO), you probably do not want your accounts payable or general ledger system to have an organic user interface; in fact, Canadian Bill 198 (and the U.S. Sarbanes-Oxley Act) prescribes much of the information that you can provide and how it is to be displayed.

Q4 Is There a Web 3.0?

When you hear the term *Web 2.0*, it would seem almost self-evident that it was preceded by Web 1.0 and that it will be followed by Web 3.0. However, explaining the past and predicting the future of this technology are a lot more difficult than one might imagine. As Marshall McLuhan suggested, the first use of a new technology nearly always mirrors how we used the old technology. Early televised news, for example, focused on a reporter speaking directly to the camera, unlike current newscasts, in which advanced cinematic photography, interviews, and live information are used. In short, we cannot predict what Web 3.0 will look like (or even if it will be called "Web 3.0") because we do not know what will be imagined by the next generation of inventors and entrepreneurs—some of whom may be in your class (this might be a good time to add them to your network).

Henry Ford famously said that had he asked his customers what they wanted, they would have replied "faster horses." Until we are presented with a technology, our mental models—how we see the world—often prevent us from imagining radically different ideas. Think, for example, of the last time that you ordered a pizza for delivery and were told how long it would take. Did you think that you could click on a webpage and track the delivery as it actually happened? Technically, of course, cellular devices, other mobile devices, and the global positioning system (GPS) have long enabled this capability, but it is only recently that Track My Pizza has actually deployed it. Domino's, which uses this service in the United States, updates street-by-street progress of the delivery person every 15 seconds, and this has had a substantial impact on Domino's business. In areas where this service is available, more than 18 percent of its customers have used it, and online orders have increased by more than 100 percent. Online orders, of course, are not only cheaper to process, as there are fewer humans involved, but Domino's has also found that customers using the online service spend, on average, $2 more per order.

MIS in Use

Computing Your Social Capital

Social capital is not an abstract concept that applies only to organizations; it applies to you as well. You and your classmates are accumulating social capital now. What is the value of that capital? To see, form a group and answer the following questions:

1. Define *physical capital*, *human capital*, and *social capital*. Explain how these terms differ.

2. How does the expression "It's not *what* you know but *who* you know that matters" pertain to the terms you defined in Question 1?

3. Do you agree with the statement in Question 2? Form your own opinion before discussing it with your fellow group members.

4. As a group, discuss the relative value of human capital and social capital. In what ways is social capital more valuable than human capital? Formulate a group consensus view on the validity of the statement in Question 2.

5. Visit the Facebook, LinkedIn, Twitter, or another social networking site of each group member.
   a. Review the four ways in which social capital adds value (on page 288), and assess the value of each group member's social networking presence.
   b. Recommend at least one way to add social capital value to each group member's site.

Figure 9-7
Are All Connections the Same, and How Should They Be Measured?

6. Suppose you each decide to feature your Facebook or other social networking page on your professional résumé.
   a. Explain how you would change your presence, evaluated in Question 5, to make it more appropriate for that purpose.
   b. Describe three or four types of professionals you could add to your social network to facilitate your job search.

7. Imagine that you are the CEO of a company that has just one product to sell.
   a. Explain how you could use your social networking presence to facilitate social CRM selling of your product.
   b. Devise a creative and interesting way to use this exercise as part of your social CRM offering.

8. Present your answers to Questions 4 and 7 to the rest of the class.

By the time that this book is published, we can be certain that more existing business models and ideas will have been disrupted. At the time of writing, for example, startups such as NowPublic (www.nowpublic.com/) are changing the way news is collected and distributed by allowing anyone with a cell phone to gather and share videos (as we have seen from reports by local people in the Middle East), and services such as ShopSavvy (http://shopsavvy.mobi/) are allowing anyone with a cellphone to scan a barcode to find the lowest price within the local area. Such services challenge the efficiency and effectiveness of retail supply chains. The fundamental drivers of ecommerce—low-cost computing and storage, ubiquitous networking, and collaborative services—are not likely to lose momentum any time soon.

Active Review

Use this Active Review to verify that you have understood the material in the chapter. You can read the entire chapter and then perform the tasks in this review, or you can read the material for just one question and perform the tasks for that question before moving on to the next one.

Q1 What is ecommerce and how is it used?

Define *ecommerce*. Explain the difference between ecommerce and ebusiness. Describe why the distinction is important. Differentiate each of the types of merchant sites and discuss the benefits and liabilities of ecommerce from the perspective of business, consumers, and society (government).

Q2 What is social networking, and how is it enabled and affected by IS/IT?

Define *social capital* and the four ways in which it is valuable. Explain how its creation has been affected by technology. Explain network effects and how the amount of value that a member receives varies, depending on when they join a network.

Q3 What is Web 2.0?

Explain the essence of Web 2.0 and why it lacks a common definition. Discuss how each of the main elements (e.g., UGC) contributes to some of the more well-known examples of Web 2.0.

Q4 Is there a Web 3.0?

Discuss why it is hard to predict the impact of technological change. Explain Henry Ford's famous statement about "faster horses."

MyMISLab MyMISLab is an online learning and testing environment that features the perfect study tools to help you master the concepts covered in this chapter. Log in to MyMISLab to test your knowledge of key chapter concepts and explore additional practice tools, including videos, flashcards, annotated text figures, and more!

Key Terms

Business-to-business (B2B) 283

Business-to-consumer (B2C) 283

Business-to-government (B2G) 283

Channel conflict 286

Clearinghouses 284

Crowdsourcing 293

Customer service expense 287

Disintermediation 284

Ecommerce 282

Ecommerce auctions 284

Electronic exchanges 284

Logistic expense 287

Merchant companies 283

Nonmerchant companies 283

Price Conflict 286

Price elasticity 285

Showrooming 287

Web 2.0 291

Web storefront 283

Using Your Knowledge

1. Use a search engine to identify crowdfunding sites. Browse some of the opportunities to invest or pre-purchase the good or service being offered. Be prepared to discuss why some more are more likely than others to be successful.

2. Except for the occasional use of PowerPoint and computers to take notes, education has not yet been radically reformed by technology—most courses still involve a professor lecturing at the front of a class and distance education is only slowly starting to change. While it may seem odd to label students as customers (some universities argue that employers are their real customers and students are the product that they produce), if they are customers identify how ecommerce, social media, and Web 2.0 are affecting higher education.
   a. Draw a process diagram of a regular, non-distance learning class. Label the activities and the flows among the activities.
   b. Draw a second process diagram of a distance learning class. In what ways are the two diagrams similar? In what ways are they different?
   c. What is the competitive strategy of your university? How do distance learning classes contribute to that competitive strategy?
   d. Assuming that no face-to-face meeting is required to successfully teach a distance learning class, neither students nor professors need live near campus. In fact, they do not even need to reside on the same continent. What opportunities does that fact present to your university? What new educational products might your university develop?
   e. Considering your answer to (d), what opportunities does distance learning provide your professor? Is there any reason a professor should not teach for more than one university? Do you think there is a realistic opportunity for a group of professors from different universities to band together to form a virtual college? What competitive advantage might they accrue by doing so?

3. Google the "ice bucket challenge." Discuss how and why this has been a successful use of social media. Discuss why this many not work for other organizations.

Collaborative Exercises

This chapter provides several examples of companies that use information systems to gain a competitive advantage. This collaborative exercise asks your group to take a more critical and in-depth look at the companies and the offerings they provide. Using the web as a resource, collaborate with your team to answer the following questions:

1. Create a maximum two-page information sheet that summarizes the company, the idea, and the system it uses. The summary should include the following:
   a. An introduction to the company (example companies are listed below, but you are welcome to use another company).
   b. Outline the basis of the idea.
   c. Identify, to the best of your ability, the strategy of the company (*Note:* You can use Porter's five forces to understand the company's industry.)
   d. Identify the information systems you think will be most critical to support the strategy.
   e. Provide suggestions on how the company should consider investing in information systems to support its business. Justify your suggestions.

2. Choose one of the following companies (or ask your professor if you can choose a different company):
   a. Priceline (www.priceline.com)
   b. Trivago (www.trivago.com)
   c. Trip Advisor (www.tripadvisor.com)
   d. Epinions (www.epinions.ca)
   e. Doodle (www.doodle.com).
   f. Hotwire (www.hotwire.com)
   g. Hootsuite (www.hootsuite.com)

3. Now create a presentation (using PowerPoint, Keynote, or another presentation software), and present the topic to the students in your class. Be sure to include a title page.

Case Study 9

Let Me Get That: Buyatab and Where Good Ideas Come From

Matias Marquez could be forgiven if his mind drifted off in his entrepreneurism class as the professor talked about the millions of people who must have pulled burrs off their clothes long before someone thought of Velcro. Matias was still in university, but working with fellow students he had already founded a customer-oriented company that continued to smash its revenue targets and had received national attention.

Buyatab (www.buyatab.com) first took shape when one of Matias's friends tried to give his father a surprise gift. Calling the Chicago restaurant where he knew his father was dining, he asked if he could "buy the tab" or pay the bill by putting it on his credit card. The problem, as he found out, was that although the restaurant had the policies and processes in place to sell him a physical gift card over the telephone (that they would later mail), the only way that he could pay the bill by telephone was if he faxed them a letter with a copy of the front and back of his credit card—something that would be very hard to do, since he was calling from his cellphone.

Matias' friend described the problem to Matias, and they tried to figure out how this could be solved. When they both realized that gift cards were really not about the tangible plastic but more about what they represented, their frustration only grew. The 16 to 24 digits that made up each gift card validated its authenticity and the restaurant could then trust that it was legitimate. There was no reason why this validation could not be done on the internet, thought Matias. Customers should be able to go online, sign up at his website, and instantaneously be able to pick up the tab, or pay for meals at participating restaurants.

Of course, if things were really easy, very few of us would be sitting in this classroom. Getting the first restaurants signed up was immensely difficult, and Matias found that there were many technical and security problems to be addressed. Still, he was persistent, refined the process, and slowly managed to build his network. Parts of the business model evolved, and Matias soon realized that working with the gift card infrastructure was important; specifically, integrating the Buyatab technology with that of his customers' websites and working with credit card companies were crucial to his success.

The future for Buyatab is bright. Its customers include some of North America's most famous restaurant brands, and the company has added professional management, secured external financing, and won national innovation and entrepreneurial awards.

Questions

1. How hard would it be for Buyatab to sign its first customer?
2. Many others might have had this same problem, but why didn't they think of developing a solution?
3. Why wouldn't the credit card companies have solved this problem?
4. Could Buyatab have been formed in the 1980s? (*Hint:* What enabling technologies were required to form such a company?)

Running Case Assignment Part 3

1. Carrie has decided to understand more about her printing situation. She collected information about clients and their orders in the last two years in an Excel spreadsheet labelled "Carrie Creations Order Information.xls." You can find this spreadsheet on the MyMISLab for Chapter 7. Use the data in the spreadsheet to answer the following questions:
   a. How many different customers did Carrie's Creations have over the past two years?
   b. What was the overall average number of t-shirts printed per order?
   c. What was the average number of t-shirts Carrie sold per month?
   d. On average, how long did it take to complete an order (end date – start date)
   e. What was the average time between the end date of production and the delivery date (delivery date – end date).
   f. Were there any orders that were not delivered on time (delivery date > required by)? List the order numbers along with the number of days late for each late order.
2. Carrie is considering buying a new drop-on-demand inkjet printer. She has one printer that has already been paid off. The new printer's retail price is $16 500. But Carrie has chosen to lease over five years at $250 per month. She then has the option to buy the five-year-old printer for $2500.

   a. Assume that Carrie has a margin of $1.75 for each shirt that she sells (in total, she makes $1.75 more than she pays for making the shirt). If Carrie increases her monthly sales by 10 percent, will this increase in sales cover the increased cost associated with leasing the printer?
   b. Given the assumption in (a), how many additional t-shirts does Carrie have to sell in a month to break even on the lease on the printing machine?
   c. What is the total cost of the five-year lease excluding the purchase at the end of five years? If Carrie decides to buy the printer after five years, what will be the total cost of using and obtaining the printer?

Collaborative Questions

1. In your opinion, is the decision to acquire a new garment printer justified? List the advantages and disadvantages associated with this decision and create a recommendation for Carrie.
2. Do you think that having this printer (either through a lease or a purchase) will create a competitive advantage for Carrie's Creations? Justify your answer.

MyMISLab Visit MyMISLab to access the data files to complete these questions.

Hiding the Truth?

No one is going to publish their ugliest picture on their Facebook page, but how far should you go to create a positive impression? If your hips and legs are not your best features, is it unethical to stand behind your sexy car in your photo? If you have been to one event with someone very popular in your crowd, is it unethical to publish photos that imply you meet on a daily basis? Surely, there is no obligation to publish pictures of yourself at boring events with unpopular people just to balance the scale after posting photos in which you appear unrealistically attractive and overly popular.

As long as all of this occurs on a Facebook or Twitter account that you use for personal relationships, it may not have any significant consequences. (Remember, though, that what goes around comes around.) However, consider social networking in the business arena.

a. Suppose a river-rafting company starts a group on a social networking site to promote rafting trips. Graham, a 15-year-old high school student who has no relationship with the company but wants to appear more grown up than he is, posts a picture of a handsome 22-year-old male as a picture of himself. He also writes witty and clever comments on the site photos and claims to play the guitar and be an accomplished masseur. Are his actions unethical? Suppose someone decided to go on the rafting trip, partly influenced by Graham's postings, and was disappointed when he learned the truth about Graham. Would the rafting company have any responsibility to refund that person's fees? Bonus question: Would it make a difference if Graham was related to one of the company owners?

b. Suppose you own and manage that same rafting company. Is it unethical for you to encourage your employees to write positive reviews about your company? Does your assessment change if you ask your employees to use an email address other than the one they have at work?

c. Again, suppose you own and manage the rafting company and that you pay your employees a bonus for every client they bring to a rafting trip. Without specifying any particular technique, you encourage your employees to be creative in how they obtain clients. One employee invites his Facebook friends to a party at which he shows photos of prior rafting trips. On the way back from the party, one of the friends is involved in an automobile accident and dies. His spouse sues your company. Should it be held accountable? Would it matter if you had known about the employee's party? Would it matter if you had not encouraged your employees to be creative?

d. Suppose your rafting company has a website for customer reviews. In spite of your best efforts at camp cleanliness, on one trip (out of dozens) one of your staff members accidentally serves contaminated food, and everyone becomes ill with food poisoning. One of those clients writes a poor review because of that experience. Is it ethical for you to delete that review from your site?

e. Assume that you have a professor who has written a popular textbook. You are upset with the grade you received in his class, so you write an extremely harsh review of that professor's book on Amazon.com. Are your actions ethical?

f. Suppose you were at one time employed by the river rafting company and you were, you think undeservedly, terminated by the company. To get even, you use Facebook to spread rumours among your friends (many of whom are river guides) about the safety of the company's trips. Are your actions unethical? Are they illegal? Do you see any ethical distinctions between this situation and that in item (d)?

g. Again, suppose that you were at one time employed by the rafting company and were undeservedly terminated. You notice that the company's owner does not have a Facebook account, so you create one for her. You have known her for many years and have dozens of photos of her, some of which were taken at parties and are unflattering and quite scandalous. You post those photos along with critical comments that she had made about clients or employees. Most of the comments were made when she was tired or frustrated, and they are hurtful, but they are also witty and humorous. You send friend invitations to people she knows, many of whom are the target of her biting and critical remarks. Are your actions unethical?

Discussion Questions

1. Read the situations in items (a) through (g), and answer the questions contained in each.
2. On the basis of your answers for Question 1, formulate ethical principles for creating or using social networks for business purposes.
3. On the basis of your answers for Question 1, formulate ethical principles for creating or using user-generated content for business purposes.
4. Summarize the risks that a business assumes when it chooses to sponsor user-generated content.
5. Summarize the risks that a business assumes when it uses social networks for business purposes.

PART 4 Information Systems Management

"We are a social generation. Even so, I think that we tend to underestimate the power of networking."

In Octavian's Words

Consulting is a dream job. The travel is occasionally hectic but the projects can be exciting and allow the development of diverse skills across a wide range of industries. Perhaps because of this, I am often asked, "How did you get in?" I definitely think you have to be proactive about recruitment—putting yourself in the right place, at the right time, with the right skills is key.

Octavian Petrescu graduated from the University of Ottawa in 2008 with a commerce degree, specializing in Management Information Systems. Today, he is a technology architect at Accenture. He specializes in integration architecture in the communications, media, and high technology (CMT) industry group. His clients include Canada Post, TD Bank, Fidelity Investments, and, most recently, what he calls the "Happiest Place on Earth"—Disney World.

My strategy was three-pronged. First, I have always been interested in IT and never shied away for working with it, no matter the role. Second, I have tried to have a variety of work experiences. Although I have worked at a startup, I also worked as a gondolier in Ottawa and a teaching assistant at university. Third, I tried to really take advantage of all that the school has to offer by joining clubs, such as the Management Information Systems Association (MISA), and competing in business case competitions. Even when we didn't win we still learned a lot. It is really an advantage to be able to tell an interviewer, "I was chosen to represent my school." Your own path might be different, but planning will help.

We are a social generation. Even so, I think that we tend to underestimate the power of networking. No matter where you are in the world, being able to connect with someone that you know is often just as important as what you know. I try to have a range of connections and follow up with them on a regular basis. Some mentors talk to me about my career, and others offer broader life or work balance advice. Above all, I continually ask myself, "Am I part of an organization that allows me to interact with people who can help me move forward and be successful?"

As nerdy as it may sound, I chose IS as a career because it is my passion. Whether I am helping my grandmother (who is a youthful 81) read Romanian newspapers and listen to radio online or I am solving client problems, I view every business challenge as something that technology can improve. All disciplines, accounting, finance, marketing, and human resources, are, of course, important, but in my opinion, MIS is particularly important because all disciplines use some kind of

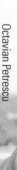

Octavian Petrescu

technology to do their work. Accountants need accounting software to keep track of the myriads of documents they create. Financiers use chart analysis software to perform technical analysis. Marketing mavens use CRM software to manage customer relationships, and HR systems are often used to manage talent. I am not sure what the future may bring, but I do know that technology is not going away anytime soon and people with skills like mine are needed to understand, design, configure, implement, and support them.

Our final "funning case" is concerned directly with the IT industry. Like many of you, Akbar Saied is a sophomore and has used computers for as far back as he can remember. Unlike many of you, he has already managed to turn this interest into a successful business.

The computer industry, however, continues to change significantly, and Akbar's business is facing growing pains. Although the need for personalized computer services seems to be growing, computers are also becoming more complicated. Less and less of his business is hardware based, and the problems that he and his staff are solving are often very complicated. The next three chapters offer the opportunity for you to integrate many of the concepts and ideas discussed in the course and to help Akbar prepare for the future.

Running Case Introduction

Just 21 years old and a commerce sophomore at Ryerson University, Akbar Saied runs a successful computer support company and has big plans for its future.

A long-time geek, Akbar cannot remember when computers were not a big part of his life. Early family photographs of him as a toddler playing simple games on an oversized desktop computer blend into more recent images of him working on an ultra-slim notebook and with an assortment of computer hardware, software, and networking technology. Of course, growing up with technology was not unique to Akbar; it is likely true of everyone reading this book. The difference, however, may be that Akbar was interested in more than just using technology. When he was unable to do something on his computer or ran into a problem, he tended to try to solve it on his own. His parents initially humoured him by leaving him to tinker with his computer; however, over time, they began asking him for advice. Whether it was his dad asking how to link information from a spreadsheet to a document or his mom asking how to connect a scanner to their network, Akbar was the go-to-guy when friends and family needed technical help.

Things really started to get busy for him in August 2009, when his mom asked him if he could look at an urgent problem her boss was having. On the evening before leaving for a major presentation, his mom's boss was unable to finalize her PowerPoint slides because her computer would not start up. Since he lived just 15 minutes away, Akbar rode his bicycle over and not only fixed the problem in just half an hour but also copied a backup version of the PowerPoint slides onto a memory stick just in case. What looked like a complex problem turned out to be a quick fix (he described it as "restoring a missing DLL that must have been accidentally deleted"). His mom's boss was so happy that she gave Akbar $100. What had started out as a hobby had just earned him more money than many of his friends had ever earned.

Akbar continued to offer free advice to friends and family but started to develop a business. He kept his website updated with advice and technical information but, more importantly, began to provide more and more personal service. Akbar (or, increasingly, one of his associates) could provide on-site service at a flat fee of $50 to solve simple problems. By the start of last year, Akbar's Computer Technology Service (ACTS) employed six full-time and part-time technicians (students mostly) and earned service revenue of more than $10 000 a month.

Akbar successfully moved from solving technical problems to actively running his own business. As he made this transition, he encountered issues with managing the information systems related to his business.

In this chapter, when we meet Akbar, he is thinking about the implementation of a new software system. We meet him again in Chapter 11 as he thinks about business strategy. How should he respond to competition from such companies as Geek Squad, and does he need advice from more experienced people on such things as franchising? Finally, in Chapter 12, he confronts contingency planning and disaster issues—things he has often talked about to customers but has had little time to address in his own business.

Akbar is a fictitious character, but when thinking about this case, it might be useful to consider that Michael Dell started his company while he was a student at the University of Texas. You or the person sitting next to you might be the founder of the next Instagram.

👁 Watch

This case will run throughout Part 4. Read more at the beginning of each chapter, and then visit MyMISLab to access the data files to complete the running case questions at the end of Part 4.

MyMISLab

10 Acquiring Information Systems Through Projects

Running Case

"How did I get into this mess?" Akbar said to himself. He was usually the one giving advice to his clients about how to solve technical challenges. But today, Akbar realized that he had a major problem on his hands, and he was not sure what to do next on his information systems project.

It started six months ago, when Akbar decided it was time to upgrade his customer relationship management (CRM) system. At that time, Akbar was too busy to build a full CRM system himself, so he decided to license one from a vendor. He spent an entire evening scouring the Web for CRM software that would fit his budget. Late in the evening, he hit upon what he thought was a winner. Akbar phoned the CRM vendor the next day, and the vendor agreed to send a licence within a week. "It was the first time I had ever licensed an information system for my company," he said. "In hindsight, I should have done more due diligence."

Akbar, like many of his clients, had not recognized some of the most common mistakes people make when acquiring software and information systems. First, he spent only a single night thinking about the requirements for the system. "It turned out that the system I purchased was not really a good fit for my company. There were better products on the market," he noted, "but I was in a hurry to get something up and running."

Akbar realized that there was a need to convert current data into a format that could be accurately read by the new system. He had originally estimated that this data conversion would take a week of his time. Six months later, it had still not been completed, and, without all of the data, the CRM system could not be fully functional.

Finally, Akbar did not fully realize the extent to which the new CRM system would change his business practices. Collecting data suddenly became much more important with the new system. His employees were not prepared to collect and enter accurate information about each customer. Without the processes to collect this information, there was little ability to generate invoices and check for accounts receivables from all clients. Moreover, Akbar had already lost jobs from reliable clients because the new information system had no accurate way of tracking customer work orders.

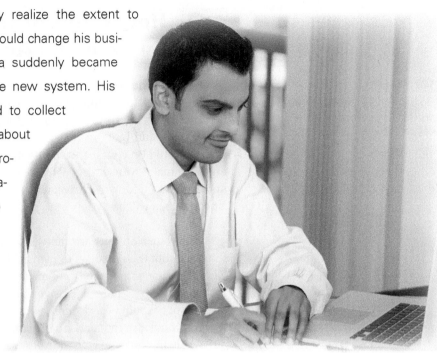

PathDoc/Shutterstock

Akbar looked at his project that was already over budget, past schedule, and providing less than half of the functionality he originally desired. "Information systems projects are even more challenging than I'd thought. It made me recognize what some of my clients must go through on a daily basis."

Study Questions

Q1 How can information systems be acquired?

Q2 What are IT projects, and what does PMBOK mean?

Q3 What should you know about IT operations and IT projects?

Q4 Why are IT projects so risky?

Q5 What is an SDLC?

Q6 How are information systems designed, implemented, and maintained?

Q7 What is outsourcing, and what are application service providers?

Watch

Go to MyMISLab to watch a video about systems development.

Watch

Go to MyMISLab to watch a video about information systems development.

Q1 How Can Information Systems Be Acquired?

In some ways, information systems are like any other product or service we want to acquire. For example, think about buying a car. Perhaps you are looking for a convertible with lots of horsepower and a great sound system. What options do you have? You could buy the car from a dealer. That would initially be expensive, but the car would be yours, and the dealer would usually offer you a warranty in case anything major went wrong with the car. You could see the car before you bought it and even take it for a test drive, which reduces the risk. Although the car may not be a perfect fit, it will likely serve its purpose and provide you with many of the benefits you desire.

What other options are there in acquiring the car? What if you bought it from the dealer but then made your own customizations? You could repaint it, change the wheels, upgrade the stereo, and make it fit you the way you like it. This is called *customizing*, and it is more expensive than just using the car the way it comes from the dealer. But it would be a closer fit with your needs.

You could also rent or lease the car. When you rent or lease a car, you do not actually own it. Instead, you own the right to use the car for a specific period. The car rental or dealer retains ownership, and you pay for the use of the car. Similarly, you can buy some software outright, but most applications are licensed, which is similar to renting. Some licences have a fixed term, while others have none.

Alternatively, if you were really good with your hands and had the proper tools, you might be able to build the car yourself. Of course, if you have never done this before, it is a risky undertaking, but if you (or your organization) know what you are doing, then this might be a realistic option. When you build a car yourself, you can make it fit your needs perfectly. You can choose the colour, the stereo, and every other feature. You custom-build it for yourself. And if you ever need to make changes or adapt it at some point in the future, you know exactly how to do it. Will it cost less? Will it work better than the dealer's car? That depends on how good you are at building cars. When an organization builds software, we call that software development (or application development).

There is one final method for acquisition. What if you do not have the expertise to build your customized car. You could hire another company to build it and maintain it for you. We might refer to this as outsourcing. When you outsource, you rely on another company to provide you with products or services that you are either unable or unwilling to develop yourself. For example, many companies outsource their office cleaning. Rather than hiring full-time cleaners, a company hires another company to do the cleaning for them. Many services, such as food services, building maintenance, and window washing, are outsourced.

Acquiring a new software application is similar to buying a car. And if we apply this idea to organizations, we can identify five basic ways to acquire a software application:

1. Buy it and use it as is.
2. Buy it and customize it.
3. Rent or lease it.
4. Build it yourself.
5. Outsource it.

Organizations use all of these methods; however, option 2, in which companies purchase prebuilt software and then customize it to some degree, is the most common method for acquiring software applications.

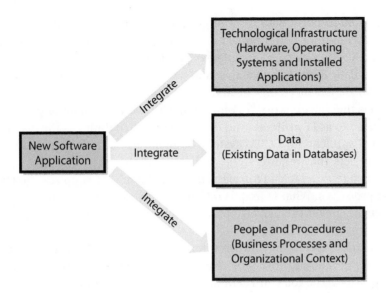

Figure 10-1

New Software Must Be Integrated into Existing Systems

Before we end this section, it is important to reiterate a point made in Chapter 1: Acquiring *software applications* is *not* the same as acquiring *information systems*. If you read the advertisements in trade magazines, you might believe that substantial business process improvements are just around the corner, if only you could find a way to acquire the latest and greatest software applications.

The model of information systems we introduced in Chapter 1 suggested that systems combine hardware, software, data, procedures, and people. Acquiring an information system, therefore, involves more than just obtaining and installing software. It involves incorporating the software into the current technological infrastructure and integrating the software into the data and procedures people use to make things happen in an organization. This process is shown in Figure 10-1. Acquiring new software is *not* the same as acquiring new information systems, because there is a lot more to think about in systems than just software.

As a future business manager, it is important for you to realize that even if the software is free, or what is often referred to as *open source*, the organization will always face the cost of integrating the software with its current hardware, data, and procedures. These costs are often substantial—they can exceed the cost of the software itself. Organizations that understand these costs before acquiring applications are more likely to be successful in eventually integrating software compared with organizations that think software equals systems. Now you know better!

Q2 What Are IT Projects, and What Does PMBOK Mean?

When an organization acquires an information system, it has embarked on a project. But what exactly is a project? To answer that question, we refer to the **project management body of knowledge (PMBOK)**, which was developed by the Project Management Institute (www.pmi.org). The guide to the PMBOK was first published in 1996, and the most recent (fourth) edition was published in 2008. The guide to the PMBOK notes that a project "consists of a temporary endeavor undertaken to create a unique product, service or result."[1]

---

[1] Project Management Institute, *A Guide to the Project Management Body of Knowledge (PMBOK Guide)*, 4th ed. (Newtown Square, PA: Author, 2008).

Projects often begin with a set of goals or objectives. From these, a scope for the project is developed, and project managers are given resources, such as people, money, and working space, to complete the project. Projects usually have a start date and an end date. Since the objective is to accomplish something new and unique, projects often represent change in an organization.

Projects that have a large IT component (in terms of budget or personnel) are often referred to as **IT projects**, and these include such things as the installation of a new email application, a CRM system, or an enterprise resource planning (ERP) system. Projects that require some fundamental changes to business processes are often also referred to as *IT projects* because the new IT supports the change in business processes. What is important for a business student to recognize is that IT projects are never exclusively about technology: They affect data, people, and processes.

Information technology project management (ITPM) is the collection of techniques and methods that project managers use to plan, coordinate, and complete IT projects. The tools of ITPM are basically the same tools used in any project management process. The tools include work breakdown structures; budgeting methods; graphical scheduling methods, such as PERT (Program Evaluation Review Technique) and Gantt charts; risk management techniques; communication planning; and high-tech team development. Application Extension 10a, "Introduction to Microsoft Project" (which follows Chapter 10), provides you with some introductory information about some of these tools.

A full description of project management techniques is beyond the scope of this book; however, project management skills are relevant to any student considering a career in business. The guide to the PMBOK suggests that there are five process groups in any project: (1) initiating, (2) planning, (3) executing, (4) controlling and monitoring, and (5) closing. These process groups should not be viewed as independent entities but, rather, as a collection of activities that often overlap and occur throughout the project. Later in this chapter, you will see that these process groups are related to the notion of a systems development life cycle (SDLC), which is often used to describe IT projects. Each of these process groups can be related to one of the nine project knowledge areas: (1) integration management, (2) scope management, (3) time management, (4) cost management, (5) quality management, (6) human resources management, (7) communications management, (8) risk management, and (9) procurement management. Inside each of these knowledge areas are techniques that project managers use to manage their projects.

The increasing importance of projects, in particular IT projects, has led to a rapid increase in the number of people seeking certification of project management skills. For example, the PMI is a global institute that has certified over 620 000 **project management professionals (PMPs)**. The PMI also offers a Certified Associate in Project Management (CAPM) program, which includes an introduction to PM. It requires 36 hours of study in project management, after which one must pass a 150-question, three-hour examination.[2] Completing this program can be an effective way for you to differentiate yourself. The International Project Management Association (www.ipma.ch) also offers a Certified Project Manager certification, and the Project Management Association of Canada (www.pmac-ampc.ca) has recently joined the IPMA and offers a certification for Agile Project Managers.

These institutions have clearly indicated that a crucial skill for a successful project manager, in IT and other industries, is communication. As the Canadian Coalition for Tomorrow's ICT Skills (www.ccict.ca) suggests, organizations are looking for *business professionals* who have the knowledge, skills, and personal qualities to lead and

---

[2] You can read more about CAPM at www.pmi.org/certification/~/media/pdf/certifications/pdc_capmhandbook.ashx.

support the effective, competitive use of information technologies.[3] Although technical knowledge is an asset for an IT project manager, the ability to communicate with technical and business-oriented people about project objectives and challenges is the key skill for a successful manager.

The business environment continues to change rapidly. As a business student, you should realize that this rapid pace of change suggests that organizations must improve their ability to adapt to changing conditions. As we noted earlier and will discuss further below, organizations adapt to change through projects. Project management skills are, therefore, likely to become even more important for any manager in the future. Students should also recognize that most significant projects have some technology component. So, ITPM is central to the skills needed for organizations to adapt appropriately to an increasingly complex business environment.

Q3 What Should You Know About IT Operations and IT Projects?

The IT department is generally responsible for providing IT services to an organization. There are two basic activities required to provide these services. The first is maintaining the current IT infrastructure, while the second is renewing and adapting the infrastructure to keep IT working effectively in the future.

The delivery of service, maintenance, protection, and management of IT infrastructure are often accomplished as part of **IT Operations** or **IT Services**. These services demand a large portion of the IT department's operational budget. Industry professionals often refer to this as keeping the lights on, or KTLO.

The renewal and adaptation of IT infrastructure is normally accomplished through projects. IT projects come in all shapes and sizes. Large IT projects are often high-profile, high-cost changes to the status quo of the organization and can often be funded outside of the IT operations budget.

The distinction between operations and projects is important for several reasons. For one, operational work and project work tend to attract two different types of IT professionals. IT people who prefer to work in operations often want to specialize in particular technologies. Networking specialists, operating systems specialists, database administrators, and hardware technicians are examples of these types of positions. These workers continually seek ways to improve the efficiency and security of the entire set of systems that support operations. These active systems are often referred to as **production systems**. *Stability, predictability, accountability, reliability,* and *security* are keywords in IT operations.

Other people in the IT department are responsible for changing the production systems, rather than maintaining them. These professionals work on IT projects. Because projects are temporary and often change existing infrastructure, they generally require broad skills, and they challenge project team members to learn new technologies. Since different projects often operate at the same time, team members may work on several projects simultaneously. This makes for an exciting (and, some would argue, hectic and chaotic) workday for many project team members. Since large IT projects are often funded from outside of the IT department, IT projects can provide more opportunities for contact with project stakeholders (such as users, managers, and sponsors) in other departments.

Beyond the people involved, there are also differences in the core practices of IT professionals. Within IT operations, **Information Technology Infrastructure Library (ITIL)** is a well-recognized collection of books that provide a framework

---

[3] See http://ccict.ca/challenge for more information.

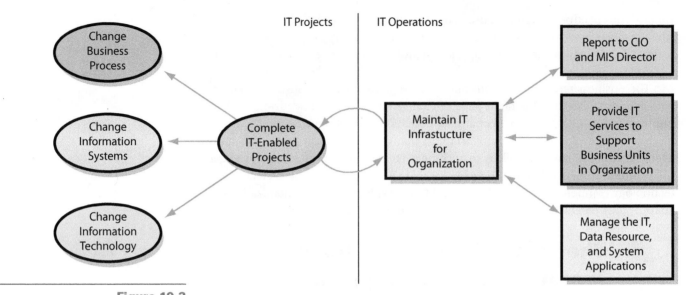

Figure 10-2

What the IT Department Does

of best-practice approaches to IT operations. ITIL offers a large set of management procedures that are designed to help businesses achieve value from IT operations. Developed during the 1980s, ITIL has gone through several revisions; core books from the latest refresh (ITIL V4) were published in June 2011. As business students, it is not important for you to understand the details of ITIL. What *is* important is that you recognize that a well-developed set of best practices that can support IT operations has been established.

It is important to note that while operations and IT projects are separate fields, they rely on each other for success. Projects come to an end and must be maintained, and infrastructure must eventually be replaced. So, there is always a natural balance between projects and operations within any IT department. This balance is shown in Figure 10-2.

What About the Web?

In Chapter 9, we discussed how the web has become an important avenue for delivering IT services to both internal employees and external customers. Large and small IT departments use the web as a first step in many internal service requests. For example, when a new employee joins a company, many IT services need to be provided. The new employee may require a computer, which needs to be set up with software the company uses. He or she will need network access, which requires an identification (ID) and password, as well as an email account. The employee may travel with a laptop computer, which requires a virtual private network (VPN) connection provided by the IT department. The IT department also determines where the employee can print documents and sometimes provides an access card so that the person can get into the building. Where can all these services be accessed?

In many companies, the IT department has developed an intranet website with frequently asked questions (FAQ), web-based forms for requesting services, and some web-based applications that help support tasks, such as adding a new employee. Your school likely has a site like this. The people working at the IT help desk, which is normally the frontline of IT department services, often rely heavily on the intranet site to help support customer issues and requests.

Support for external customers, such as FAQ, customer support information, and company director and contact information, are likely to be available on the company's website. The IT department is normally responsible for maintaining information about IT services on the site. In addition, the IT department supports the company website, making sure the servers and applications that provide the website are up and running. The web, therefore, plays a critical role in the delivery of IT services in many organizations.

Q4 Why Are IT Projects So Risky?

Any project manager will tell you that all projects, no matter how small or how well defined, face risks. There is some dispute over the level of **IT project risk**. For example, the oft-quoted *CHAOS Report*, created by The Standish Group (www.standish-group.com), suggests that only 16 percent of IT projects were delivered on time, on budget, and on scope, whereas more than 30 percent of IT projects were cancelled before delivering any benefits. In a later study, Sauer, Gemino, and Horner-Reich (www.pmperspectives.org)[4] indicated that the success rate of IT projects was roughly two out of three, or 66 percent, with only 9 percent of projects cancelled. They also indicated, however, that IT projects underperformed at a rate of 25 percent, regardless of their size. Whatever the actual numbers are, it is clear that IT projects face significant risks.

So, what makes IT projects so risky? Consider a construction project, such as building a bridge. The project begins with an architect, who creates a model of the bridge. People involved in the project can look at the model and quickly understand what will be built.

Now, consider an IT project—for example, installing a new web-based CRM. What does a model for an IT project look like? Have you ever seen one? What would the picture look like? How would you draw the hardware, software, data, procedures, and people? Most IT project definitions are not that easy to represent graphically. This makes it difficult for people to understand what the system will "look like," and how it will behave when it is finished. The lack of a good model is, therefore, an important risk to recognize in IT projects.

What about estimating costs for a project? Besides labour, a bridge is built by using steel, concrete, and other industrial products. These components are stable, well known, and have been used for hundreds of years. In an IT project, however, the tools for building the project are constantly changing. Computers get cheaper and faster; programming languages, operating systems, and databases get more complex; and the web makes projects even more difficult to estimate. So, precise estimates for IT projects are difficult to develop because the technology is continually changing.

Assuming that you can make some relatively accurate estimates, the next step in the bridge-building project is to actually start building the bridge. How can you tell how far the project has gone? Well, you just look at the bridge—if it is halfway across the river, then the bridge is about half complete. But what about an IT project? What does a half-complete IT project look like? It is hard to tell. It gets even more difficult because systems development often means aiming at a moving target. System requirements change as the system is developed, and the bigger the system and the longer the project, the more those requirements change. It is difficult to estimate how far an IT project has come and how far it needs to go. So, being able to monitor progress is another challenge for IT projects.

Clearly, there are some risks inherent in IT projects. But how many risks should we consider, and what are these risks? The first thing to recognize is that the primary

---

[4] C. Sauer, A. Gemino, and B. Horner-Reich, "Managing Projects for Success: The Impact of Size and Volatility on IT Project Performance," *Communications of ACM* 50, no. 11 (November 2007): 79–84.

risks do not necessarily emerge from the technology. A comprehensive list of the risks—52 in total—is provided in an article by Wallace and Keil.[5] These risks include lack of experience in the team, lack of support from top management, lack of participation from system users, unclear and uncertain project requirements, a high level of technical complexity, and changes in the project environment. Real IT projects are subject to many different effects.

Q5 What Is an SDLC?

The **systems development life cycle (SDLC)** is the classic process used to acquire information systems. The IT industry developed the SDLC through the school of hard knocks—many early projects met with disaster, and companies and systems developers sifted through the ashes of those disasters to determine what went wrong. By the 1970s, many professionals began to recognize the basic tasks to successfully acquire and maintain information systems. These basic tasks are combined into phases of **systems development**.

The number of phases in the SDLC varies by organization and author. To keep it simple, we will look at a five-phase process:

1. System definition
2. Requirements analysis
3. Component design
4. Implementation
5. System maintenance

Figure 10-3 shows how these phases are related. Acquisition begins when a business-planning process identifies a need for a new system. For now, suppose that

Figure 10-3

Phases in the SDLC

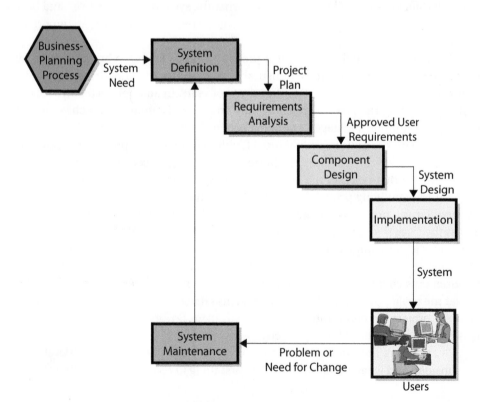

[5] L. Wallace and M. Keil, "Software Project Risks and Their Effect on Outcomes," *Communications of the ACM*, April 2004, 68–73.

management has determined in some way that the organization can best accomplish its goals and objectives by acquiring a new information system.

As a future business manager, you will likely play a key role in the SDLC at your organization. Employers are looking for individuals who have the knowledge and skills to innovate through IT. Although you might refer hardware, software, or data problems to the IT department, you cannot hand-off procedural or personnel problems: These are your problems. The single most important criterion for information systems success is for users to take ownership of their systems.

The IT industry has more than 50 years of experience acquiring and developing information systems, and, over those years, methodologies that successfully deal with many of these problems have emerged. In this section, we will consider SDLC, the classic process for systems development. Many other development methods exist, including rapid application development (RAD) and object-oriented systems development (OOD). In recent years, SCRUM and extreme programming (XP) have emerged from a movement toward **agile methods**. You can read about the principles underlying agile methods in the Manifesto for Agile Software Development (http://agilemanifesto.org).

You might be wondering why there are so many methodologies. There are several reasons. No single process can work for all organizational situations. The scale of information systems also varies widely. Personal systems support one person with a limited set of requirements. Workgroup systems support a group of people, normally with a single application. Enterprise systems support many workgroups with many different applications. Given the variety of possible systems, it is not surprising that there are different acquisition methodologies. Different methodologies are appropriate for different types of systems.

In this section, we will focus on the first two phases of the SDLC. These are the phases that you as a business manager will most likely be involved in. These phases are often called **systems analysis**.

Phase 1: Defining Systems

In response to the need for the new system, the organization will assign a few employees, possibly on a part-time basis, to define the requirements for the new system, assess its feasibility, and plan the project. Typically, someone from the IS department leads the initial team, but the members of that initial team are both users and IS professionals.

Define System Goals and Scope

As Figure 10-4 shows, the first step in the **system definition phase** is to define the goals and scope of the new information system. As you learned in Part 3, information systems exist to facilitate an organization's competitive strategy by supporting business processes or by improving decision making. At this step, the development team defines the goals and purpose of the new system in terms of these purposes.

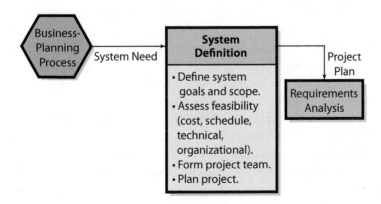

Figure 10-4

SDLC: System Definition Phase

A clear definition of project scope greatly simplifies requirements determination and other subsequent development work.

Assess Feasibility

Once the project's goals and scope have been defined, the next step is to assess feasibility. This step answers the question, "Does this project make sense?" The aim here is to eliminate obviously inappropriate projects before forming a project development team and investing significant labour. This step is sometimes referred to as *creating the business case for the project*.

Feasibility has four dimensions: **cost feasibility**, **schedule feasibility**, **technical feasibility**, and **organizational feasibility**. Because IS development projects are difficult to budget and schedule, *cost* and *schedule feasibility* can be only an approximate, back-of-the-envelope analysis. The purpose is to eliminate any obviously infeasible ideas as soon as possible. Cost and schedule feasibility are relatively straightforward, since they consider whether the organization has the money and time to complete the project. *Technical feasibility* refers to whether existing information technology is likely to be able to meet the needs of the new system. Finally, *organizational feasibility* concerns whether the new system fits within the organization's customs, culture, charter, or legal requirements.

Phase 2: Requirements Analysis

If the defined project is determined to be feasible, the next step is the **requirements analysis phase**, in which the project team is formed and requirements are developed. Developing requirements is a process that might be considered somewhat unique to the area of management information systems. This is why any student interested in a career in management information systems (MIS) will take a course in systems analysis and design. The development of project requirements is essentially the management of scope in an IT project. The accounting department can teach us about maintaining budgets, and the operations research department can focus on minimizing project schedules, but only the MIS area focuses on how to define and manage project scope. This is why systems analysis and design is a core skill in MIS. The reason why MIS professionals are focused on defining requirements and scope centres around the difficulty of conceptualizing just what an information system looks like and what it should do.

When developing requirements, the team normally consists of both IT personnel and user representatives. The project manager and IT personnel can be internal personnel or outside contractors. Typical personnel on a development team are a manager (or managers, for larger projects), **systems analysts**, programmers, software testers, and users.

The work of analysis and design is often completed by **business analysts** and systems analysts. Business analysts tend to focus on the analysis of the current system and procedures, and they interact with the stakeholders of the system. Systems analysts tend to be more technically focused IT professionals who understand both business and technology. Both of these analysts are active throughout the systems development process and play a key role in moving the project through the process. Depending on the nature of the project, the team may also include hardware and communications specialists, database designers and administrators, and other IT specialists.

The team composition changes over time. During requirements definition, the team will mainly consist of business analysts and systems analysts. During design and implementation, the emphasis will shift to programmers, testers, and database designers. During integrated testing and conversion, the team will be augmented with testers and business users.

User involvement is critical throughout the system development process. Users are involved in many different ways. *The important point is for users to have active involvement and to take ownership of the project through the entire development process.*

If the new system involves a new database or substantial changes to an existing database, then the development team will create a data model. As you learned in Chapter 5, that model must reflect the users' perspective on their business and business activities. Thus, the data model is constructed on the basis of user interviews and must be validated by those users.

Once the requirements have been specified, the users must review and approve them before the project continues. The easiest and cheapest time to alter the information system is in the requirements phase. Changing a requirement at this stage is simply a matter of changing a description. Changing a requirement in the implementation phase may require weeks of reworking applications components and the database. Before going further, you might want to read about how estimates of budget and schedule are often created in the real world in the What Do YOU Think? exercise "The Real Estimation Process," at the end of this chapter on page 330. This exercise will help you understand how difficult it can be to develop accurate estimates for IT projects.

Q6 How Are Information Systems Designed, Implemented, and Maintained?

While managers and system users are not often asked to implement and maintain systems, it is important to understand the choices made during these phases. Before we consider component design, we need to discuss the options we have for developing the system. Our previous discussion in this chapter suggested five ways to acquire an information system: (1) buy it, (2) buy it and customize it, (3) rent or lease it, (4) build it yourself, or (5) outsource it. For the first three of these methods, the information system is already built, so the organization does not have to do major development. This type of acquisition requires the organization to match its requirements with the capabilities of the software application that has already been built. Figure 10-5 summarizes this matching process.

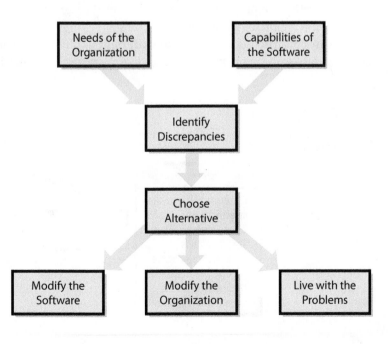

Figure 10-5

Matching Organizational Needs and COTS Software Capabilities

When an organization works through the matching process, it will almost always find discrepancies between the requirements of the business and the capabilities of the software application. No application fits perfectly. When these discrepancies are identified, the organization faces one of three choices, as shown in Figure 10-5. These choices are to (1) modify the software, (2) modify the organizational procedures and data, or (3) live with the problems. In reality, the final solution for the organization is likely a combination of these three choices.

As a future business manager, it is important for you to realize that **commercial-off-the-shelf (COTS)** software will never fit your organizational requirements exactly. So, it is reasonable to expect and budget for some cost and some time before the software is successfully implemented in the organization. How long would that be? For a large implementation, like that of an ERP system, it is reasonable to consider a span of 18 months before things settle down. For smaller systems, this time will be a significantly shorter period.

In the rest of the chapter, we will discuss the steps in the SDLC, assuming that the organization will be building the system itself. What you should realize now is that regardless of whether you buy, rent/lease, or build the information system, the basic steps for acquiring it are the same. First, you have to understand your objectives and analyze your requirements. Next, you design the system using either COTS or a custom design. Then, you implement it and maintain it.

Phase 3: Component Design

Each of the five components of an information system must be designed. Typically, the team designs each component by developing alternatives, evaluating each of those alternatives against the requirements, and then selecting among those alternatives. Accurate requirements are critical here; if they are incomplete or wrong, then they will be poor guides for evaluation. Figure 10-6 illustrates design tasks that pertain to each of the five IS components.

For hardware, the team determines specifications for the hardware it wants to acquire. The team needs to specify the computers, operating systems, networks, and network connections that will process the data. The software design depends on the source of the programs. For off-the-shelf software, the team must determine candidate products and evaluate them against the requirements. For off-the-shelf-with-alterations software, the team identifies products to be acquired off the shelf and then determines the alterations required. For custom-developed programs, the team produces design documentation for writing program code.

If developers are constructing a database, then, during this phase, they convert the data model to a database design using techniques like those described in Chapter 5.

Figure 10-6

SDLC: Component Design Phase

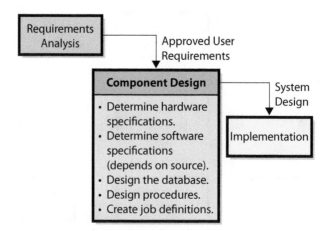

	Users	Operations Personnel
Normal processing	• Procedures for using the system to accomplish business tasks	• Procedures for starting, stopping, and operating the system
Backup	• User procedures for backing up data and other resources	• Operations procedures for backing up data and other resources
Failure recovery	• Procedures to continue operations when the system fails • Procedures to convert back to the system after recovery	• Procedures to identify the source of failure and get it fixed • Procedures to recover and restart the system

Figure 10-7
Procedures to Be Designed

If developers are using off-the-shelf programs, then little database design needs to be done; the programs handle their own database processing. For a business information system, the system developers and the organization must also design procedures for both users and operations personnel. Procedures need to be developed for normal processing, backup, and failure recovery operations, as summarized in Figure 10-7. Usually, teams of systems analysts and key users design the procedures.

Design also involves developing job descriptions for both users and operations personnel. Sometimes, new information systems require new jobs. If so, the duties and responsibilities for the new jobs need to be defined in accordance with the organization's human resources policies. More often, organizations add new duties and responsibilities to existing jobs. As with procedures, teams of systems analysts and users determine job descriptions and functions.

Phase 4: Implementation

Once the design is complete, the next phase is implementation. Tasks in this phase include building, testing, and converting the users to the new system (Figure 10-8). Developers construct each of the components independently. They obtain, install, and test hardware. They license and install off-the-shelf programs and write adaptations

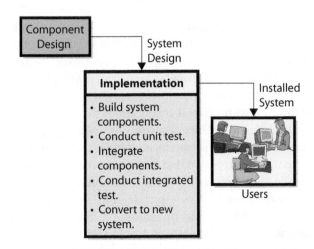

Figure 10-8
SDLC: Implementation Phase

and custom programs, as necessary. They construct a database and fill it with data. They document, review, and test procedures, and they create training programs. Finally, the organization hires and trains needed personnel.

System Testing

Once developers have constructed and tested all the components, they integrate the individual components and test the system. So far, we have glossed over testing, as if there was nothing to it. In fact, however, software and system testing are difficult, time-consuming, and complex tasks. Developers need to design and develop test plans and record the results of tests. They need to devise a system to assign fixes to people and to verify that fixes are correct and complete.

A **test plan** consists of sequences of actions that users take when using the new system. Test plans include not only the normal actions that users will take but also the incorrect actions. Today, many IT professionals work as testing specialists. Testing, or **product quality assurance (PQA)**, as it is often called, consists of constructing the test plan with the advice and assistance of users. PQA test engineers perform testing and supervise users' test activity.

Users can also be part of the test team. If you are invited to participate as a user tester, you should take the responsibility seriously. It will become much more difficult to fix problems after you have begun using the system in production.

Beta testing is the process of allowing future system users to try out the new system on their own. Software vendors, such as Microsoft, often release beta versions of their products for users to try and to test. These users then report problems back to the vendor. Beta testing is the last stage of testing. Usually, products in the beta test phase are complete and fully functioning; they typically have few serious errors.

System Conversion

Once the system has passed integrated testing, the organization will install it. The term **system conversion** is often used to refer to this activity because it implies the process of *converting* business activity from the old system to the new.

Organizations can implement a system conversion in one of four ways:

1. Pilot
2. Phased
3. Parallel
4. Plunge

IS professionals recommend any of the first three phases, depending on the circumstances. In all but the most extreme cases, companies generally avoid taking the plunge.

With **pilot installation**, the organization implements the entire system in a limited portion of the business. The advantage of pilot implementation is that if the system fails, the failure is contained within a limited boundary. This reduces the business's exposure and also protects the new system from developing a negative reputation throughout the organization.

As the name implies, with **phased installation**, the new system is installed in phases across the organization. Once a given piece works, the organization then installs and tests another piece of the system, until the entire system has been installed. Some systems are so tightly integrated that they cannot be installed in phased pieces. These must be installed using one of the other techniques.

With **parallel installation**, the new system runs in parallel with the old one until the new system is tested and fully operational. Parallel installation is expensive because the organization incurs the costs of running both systems. Users must work

	Hardware	**Software**	**Data**	**Procedures**	**People**
Design	Determine hardware specifications.	Select off-the-shelf programs. Design alterations and custom programs, as necessary.	Design database and related structures.	Design user and operations procedures.	Develop user and operations job descriptions.
Implementation	Obtain, install, and test hardware.	License and install off-the-shelf programs. Write alterations and custom programs. Test programs.	Create database. Fill with data. Test data.	Document procedures. Create training programs. Review and test procedures.	Hire and train personnel.
	Integrated Test and Conversion				

Unit test each component (bracket spanning Implementation row)

Figure 10-9

Design and Implementation for the Five Components

double time, if you will, to run both systems. Then, considerable work is needed to determine whether the results of the new system are consistent with those of the old system.

However, some organizations consider the cost of parallel installation a form of insurance. It is the slowest and most expensive style of installation, but it does provide an easy fallback position if the new system fails.

The final style of conversion is **plunge installation** (sometimes called *direct* or *cutover installation*). The organization shuts the old system down and starts the new system. If the new system fails, the organization is in trouble: Nothing can be done until either the new system is fixed or the old system is reinstalled. Because of this risk, organizations should avoid this conversion style, if possible. The one exception to this is when the new system is providing a service that is not vital to the day-to-day operation of the organization.

Figure 10-9 summarizes the tasks for each of the five components during the design and implementation phases. Use this figure to test your knowledge of the tasks in each phase.

Phase 5: Maintenance

The last phase of the SDLC is maintenance. The term *maintenance* is, however, somewhat of a misnomer: The work done during this phase is either to *fix* the system so that it works correctly or to *adapt* it to changes in requirements.

Figure 10-10 shows the tasks that must be completed during the **maintenance phase**. First, there needs to be a way to track both failures[6] and requests for enhancements to meet new requirements. For small systems, organizations can track failures and enhancements using word-processing documents. As systems become larger, however, and as the number of failure and enhancement requests increases, many organizations find it necessary to develop a failure tracking database. Such a database contains a description of each failure or enhancement.

---

[6] A *failure* is the difference between what the system actually does and what it is supposed to do. Sometimes, you will hear the term *bug* used instead of *failure*. As a future user, you should call failures *failures*, for that is what they are: Do not have a *bugs list*, have a *failures list*. Do not have an *unresolved bug*, have an *unresolved failure*. A few months of managing an organization that is coping with a serious failure will show you the importance of this difference in terms.

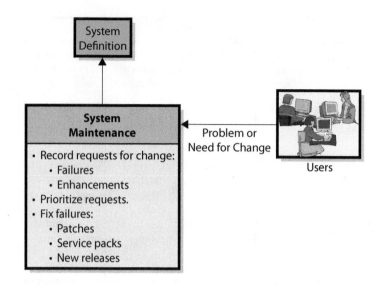

Typically, IS personnel prioritize system problems according to their severity: They fix high-priority items as soon as possible, and they fix low-priority items as time and resources become available.

With regard to the software component, software developers group fixes for high-priority failures into a **patch** that can be applied to all copies of a given product. As described in Chapter 4, software vendors supply patches to fix security and other critical problems. They usually bundle fixes of low-priority problems into larger groups called **service packs**. Users apply service packs in much the same way that they apply patches, except that service packs typically involve fixes to hundreds or thousands of problems.

Keep in mind that although we usually think of failures and enhancements as applying to software, they can apply to the other components as well. There can be hardware or database failures or enhancements. There can also be failures and enhancements in procedures and people, though the latter is usually expressed in more humane terms, rather than as *failure* or *enhancement*. The underlying idea is the same, however.

Problems with the SDLC

Although the industry has experienced notable successes with the SDLC process, there have been many problems with it as well. One of the reasons for these problems is the **waterfall method** of the SDLC. Like a series of waterfalls, the process is often described as a sequence of nonrepetitive phases. For example, the team completes the requirements phase and goes over the waterfall into the design phase, and on through the process (look again at Figure 10-3). Unfortunately, systems development seldom works so smoothly. Often, there is a need to crawl back up the waterfall, so to speak, and repeat the work done in a prior phase.

Another problem, especially with complicated systems, is the difficulty of documenting requirements in a usable way. One of the authors of this book once managed the database portion of a software project at Boeing, in which he and his team invested more than 70 labour-years into a requirements statement. The document comprised 20-some volumes that stood more than 2 metres tall when stacked. When the team entered the design phase, no one really knew all the requirements that concerned a particular feature. The team members would begin to design a feature only to find that they had not considered a requirement buried somewhere in the documentation. In short, the requirements were so unwieldy as to be nearly useless. Projects in which people spend so much time documenting requirements are sometimes said to be in **analysis paralysis**. These difficulties with the SDLC have led some companies to leave the job of designing, implementing, and maintaining systems to another organization. This option is explored in the next section.

Q7 What Is Outsourcing, and What Are Application Service Providers?

👁—Watch

Go to MyMISLab to watch a video about outsourcing.

Outsourcing is the process of hiring another organization to perform a service. Just about any business activity in the value chain can be outsourced, from marketing and sales to logistics, manufacturing, or customer service. The outsourced vendor can be domestic or international. When a vendor is overseas, outsourcing is referred to as *offshoring*. Offshoring has become an important consideration for IT services because of cost advantages. Offshoring experience has shown that establishing clear requirements is the key to providing success in an offshoring agreement.

Many companies today have chosen to outsource portions of their information systems activities. Why? First, outsourcing can be an easy way to gain expertise. Suppose, for example, that an organization wants to upgrade its thousands of user computers on a cost-effective basis. To do so, the organization would need to develop expertise in automated software installation, unattended installations, remote support, and other measures that can be used to improve the efficiency of software management. Developing such expertise is expensive, and is not part of the company's strategic direction. Consequently, the organization might choose to hire a specialist company to perform this service.

Other common reasons for choosing to outsource include cost reductions. Skilled programmers in other countries, such as China, India, and Russia, make as little as one-sixth the wage of an experienced programmer in North America. Even without this wage difference, organizations can obtain part-time services with outsourcing. An office of 25 lawyers does not need a full-time network administrator. It does need network administration, but only in small amounts. By outsourcing that function, the office can obtain network administration services only when it needs them.

Another reason for outsourcing might be to reduce development risk. Outsourcing can cap financial risk by setting specific prices on components of the system. In addition, outsourcing can reduce risk by ensuring a certain level of quality or avoiding the risk of having substandard quality. Organizations also choose to outsource IS activities to reduce implementation risk. Hiring an outside vendor can reduce the risk of picking the wrong hardware or the wrong software, using the wrong network protocol, or implementing incorrectly.

With so many advantages and with so many different outsourcing alternatives, you may wonder why any company has any in-house IS/IT functions. In fact, outsourcing presents significant risks, as listed in Figure 10-11.

The first risk of outsourcing is the ensuing loss of control over the service. Outsourcing puts the vendor in the driver's seat. Each outsource vendor has methods and procedures for its service, and an organization and its employees will have to conform to those procedures. For example, a hardware infrastructure vendor will have standard forms and procedures for requesting a computer, for recording and processing a computer problem, and for providing routine maintenance on computers. Once the vendor is in charge, the organization's employees must conform to the vendor's procedures.

In addition, the outsource vendor may change its pricing strategy over time. Initially, an organization obtains a competitive bid from several outsource vendors. However, as the winning vendor learns more about the business and as relationships develop between the organization's employees and those of the vendor, it becomes

Figure 10-11

Outsourcing Risks

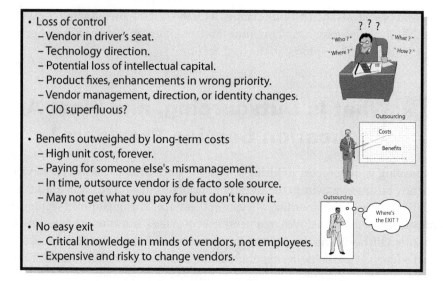

- Loss of control
  - Vendor in driver's seat.
  - Technology direction.
  - Potential loss of intellectual capital.
  - Product fixes, enhancements in wrong priority.
  - Vendor management, direction, or identity changes.
  - CIO superfluous?

- Benefits outweighed by long-term costs
  - High unit cost, forever.
  - Paying for someone else's mismanagement.
  - In time, outsource vendor is de facto sole source.
  - May not get what you pay for but don't know it.

- No easy exit
  - Critical knowledge in minds of vendors, not employees.
  - Expensive and risky to change vendors.

difficult for other firms to compete for subsequent contracts. The vendor becomes the de facto sole source and, with little competitive pressure, may increase its prices.

Another problem is that an organization can find itself paying for another organization's mismanagement, with little recourse. Over time, if the outsource vendor is mismanaged or suffers setbacks in other arenas, costs will increase.

The final category of outsourcing risk concerns ending the agreement. There is no easy exit. For example, the outsource vendor's employees have gained significant knowledge of the company. Only they may know the server requirements in customer support, the patterns of usage, and the best procedures for downloading operational data into the data warehouse. Consequently, lack of knowledge within the company will make it difficult to bring the outsourced service back in-house.

MIS in Use

From Lemons to Lemonade

"Why would you want to leave our company? You have such a promising career here in research."

That was the last thing that Chantelle Jones[7] remembered her boss telling her as she resigned from her position at the local office of a national market research firm. For Chantelle, the question was certainly difficult and one that she had pondered for a long time.

At her first job since graduating with a business degree and an MIS concentration, Chantelle was the sole employee on the company help desk, and, by any definition, it was not what she had expected. Working from 6:00 a.m. to 2:00 p.m. (the early start allowed her to support offices in the Eastern Time zone) at a peanut-shaped desk, she was frequently alone, and her day was spent almost entirely on the telephone talking to people throughout the company. She felt underutilized and unmotivated. She remembered thinking, "Is this MIS? I thought I was going to be a liaison between business and technology, a part of great system builds, and at the very forefront of communication!"

Fortunately, despair did not set in. Realizing that all of the support calls had given her extensive knowledge of the entire organization and what each system could do,

[7] The subject of this "MIS in Use" (a former student of one of the authors), asked that we not use her real name, but this case reflects her actual experience.

Application Service Providers

Application service providers (ASPs) are a particular form of outsourcing. In an ASP agreement, an organization contracts with a vendor to "rent" applications from the vendor company on a fee-for-service basis. In traditional outsourcing, the vendor often maintains the systems at the organization's location. But that is not the case for an ASP. In an ASP, the vendor maintains the system at its own web location, and the client organization accesses the application on the vendor's website. The application software, therefore, does not have to be located with the client. The vendor can then offer standardized software to many companies while maintaining only a single site (where the actual application resides). This reduces the costs of supporting the application and theoretically reduces the costs associated with outsourcing. The payments are made either monthly or yearly and are often based on the number of employees or on the number of users of the software.

The ASP model has some significant risks. The client company loses physical control over some corporate data that are stored in the vendor's machines. In addition, any failure of the internet means that the client company cannot operate, even internally. Finally, there is the potential for lock in of the ASP, which may not allow corporate data to be easily ported to competing vendor's sites. Ownership of the data has to be very clearly stated in the ASP contract. The potential benefits of ASP must be weighed against these significant risks.

ASPs are just one type of outsourcing alternative. There are many other alternatives, and each type carries with it benefits and risks. Business managers need to be aware of the alternatives and be able to balance the benefits and risks associated with them. What is clear is that what works for one company may not work for another. It is very important to consider the fit between the client and the vendor and to carefully develop the relationship between the two companies. Outsourcing deals are very similar to partnership agreements. Companies that are successful with outsourcing have recognized the importance of establishing the relationship first before engaging in significant outsourcing arrangements.

Chantelle began to track and analyze the calls. Quickly realizing that she was often being asked the same questions over and over, she knew that if she could automate that part of her job she would be well positioned to move somewhere else in the company. So, using the knowledge gained from the MIS classes at university, she wrote a knowledge base that allowed people to solve many of their own problems. This improved productivity brought her to the attention of senior managers, who allowed her to focus on more interesting things. Her initiative and the knowledge of what the systems could do resulted in her becoming very valued within the company, and she was frequently asked to participate in new and more interesting assignments.

Now, one year later, Chantelle reflected on her boss's question and admitted that she was nervous. Her most recent project had brought her to the attention of a new company, and she had been offered a much more senior position with a 50 percent increase in salary. After she had accepted the new position, she said, "I felt uneasy about that at first, and then realized I'm not in just one position, I'm in MIS. I fit into EVERY business model. I have skills that I can mould and make relevant for all businesses, if I so choose—MIS has opened a lot of doors for me."

Questions

1. **What do you think is Chantelle's biggest asset for an employer?**

2. **How would you decide how and when to change jobs?**

3. **How have jobs and careers changed in the past 20 years? (*Hint:* How many employers have your parents worked for? How many do you anticipate working for?)**

4. **Do you think Chantelle's job allowed her to see more of the company compared with jobs in other functional areas?**

5. **Would Chantelle's situation have been any different if she worked for a much larger company?**

Active ? Review

Use this Active Review to verify that you have understood the material in the chapter. You can read the entire chapter and then perform the tasks in this review, or you can read the material for just one question and perform the tasks for that question before moving on to the next one.

Q1 How can information systems be acquired?

Explain the four ways that systems can be acquired. What is the most popular method for acquiring systems? Explain why buying software is different from acquiring information systems.

Q2 What are IT projects, and what does PMBOK mean?

What is a project? What does PMBOK mean? What is an IT project? What is ITPM? What are the five process groups in project management? What is the most important skill in IT project management?

Q3 What should you know about IT operations and IT projects?

What is the difference between IT operations and IT projects? What is ITIL? How is it related to the PMBOK? What are some of the ways the web has altered IT operations?

Q4 Why are IT projects so risky?

Explain why IT projects tend to be risky. List some of the major risks associated with IT projects.

Q5 What is an SDLC?

What are the five phases of the SDLC? Explain each of these phases. Why are systems analysis and design unique to management information systems? Explain why requirements development is not just for technical experts. What activities can a nontechnical business manager be expected to do in an IT project? Explain why developing a clear list of requirements is important for IT project success.

Q6 How are information systems designed, implemented, and maintained?

Summarize design activities for each of the five components of an information system. Name the two major tasks in systems implementation. Summarize the system testing process. Describe the difference between system testing and software testing. Name four ways to implement system conversion. Describe each way, and give an example of when each would be effective.

Q7 What is outsourcing, and what are application service providers?

Define *outsourcing*. Explain why some companies choose to outsource their projects. Explain what risks can be associated with outsourcing. Define what an application service provider is. Explain the benefits and risks of the ASP model.

MyMISLab MyMISLab is an online learning and testing environment that features the perfect study tools to help you master the concepts covered in this chapter. Log in to MyMISLab to test your knowledge of key chapter concepts and explore additional practice tools, including videos, flashcards, annotated text figures, and more!

Key Terms and Concepts

Using Your Knowledge

1. Using the knowledge you have gained from this chapter, summarize the roles that you think users should take during an information systems development project. What responsibilities do users have? How closely should they work with the IS team? Who is responsible for stating requirements and constraints? Who is responsible for managing requirements?

2. When you ask users why they did not participate in requirements specification, some of the common responses include the following:
   a. "I wasn't asked."
   b. "I didn't have time."
   c. "They were talking about a system that would be here in 18 months, and I'm just worried about getting the order out the door today."
   d. "I didn't know what they wanted."
   e. "I didn't know what they were talking about."
   f. "I didn't work here when they started the project."
   g. "The whole situation has changed since they were here; that was 18 months ago!"

   Comment on each of these statements. What strategies do they suggest to you as a future user and as a future manager of users?

3. Consider outsourcing the following business functions:
   - Employee cafeteria
   - General ledger accounting
   - Corporate IT infrastructure (networks, servers, and infrastructure applications such as email)
   a. Compare the benefits of outsourcing for each business function.
   b. Compare the risks of outsourcing for each business function.
   c. Do you believe that the decision to outsource is easier for some of these functions than for others? Why, or why not?

4. Assume that you are a project manager charged with developing the implementation plan to switch an entire country from driving on the right side of the road to the left. Which conversion approach would you use and why?

Collaborative Exercises

1. Take a look at the report written by David Ticoll for the Canadian Information and Communications Technology Council, "Jobs ICTS 2.0: How Canada can win in the 21st century global marketplace for Information and Communications Technologies and Services (ICTS)." (Go to http://ccict.ca/reports/jobs-2-0). The report suggests that changes in the demands for skills have created new

opportunities for students, companies, and educators in the ICT sector. Discuss the findings in this report, and answer the following questions:

    a. What skills are employers looking for in ICTS 2.0? How do these skills differ from the skills in ICTS 1.0?

    b. What will the changes in ICTS as outlined in this report mean to the members of your group? How will traditional business jobs change? Create a list of at least five ways that you, as a business professional, can take advantage of the changes that are coming to the industry.

    c. Where could a student best begin to develop the skills that are noted in ICTS 2.0? Develop a list of opportunities that people who are interested in developing these skills can be a part of.

2. Visit sites that offer certification for project managers and business analysts (for example, www.pmi.org, www.iiba.org, www.businessanalystworld.com, and www.pmac-ampc.ca). Use the information you find to answer the following questions:

    a. Compare and contrast the roles of a project manager and a business analyst. Identify the most important skills for each of these roles. Are there skills that are common to both roles?

    b. Identify five different types of certification that a person could collect in project management and/or business analysis. Provide at least three reasons why certification is important for those who are interested in project management or business analysis.

    c. Provide three reasons why the roles of project manager and business analysis are getting so much attention in the workplace.

Case Study 10

Email or Freemail?

Everybody knows that email is important, but should each company develop, own, support, and maintain its own email infrastructure, or should it instead use lower-cost or free services? That is the question that Michael Jagger, CEO of Provident Security, faced as he contemplated a costly upgrade of the company's internal email infrastructure.

Founded in 1996 by Michael Jagger as a way to pay his undergraduate tuition, Provident (www.providentsecurity.ca) started out as a company that provided special event security. Today, it has grown to become a full-service security company with more than 4500 customers and 200 employees. Offering a wide range of services for residential, commercial, and industrial clients, Provident is organized into three divisions: guard services, alarm services, and special event/personal protection. Guard services offers uniformed security guards and specializes in high-tech and pharmaceutical markets; it also offers community and mobile patrol services that guarantee a five-minute response to burglar alarms and client emergencies. The alarm services division installs, services, and monitors alarm systems for residential and industrial clients, including sophisticated closed circuit television (CCTV) and access control systems for the high-risk buildings of clients such as the federal government. The special event/personal protection division provides security for many important public figures, including elected officials and business leaders.

The company's email system was based on Microsoft Exchange/Outlook and completely managed by the company's small but effective internal information systems staff. After an increase in volume, however, the system was beginning to show signs of strain. In addition, recent analysis indicated that to cope with projected growth, Provident would have to invest a further $60 000 in a combination of hardware and software upgrades and operating expenses.

To combat this expense, one employee suggested that Provident convert its internal email to Google's $50-per-user corporate Gmail service (www.google.com/apps/intl/en/business/messaging.html#mail). This service was very similar to Google's popular consumer email system and could be accessed from any web browser, which meant that it required no hardware or software and was available anywhere. And not only was the service comparatively inexpensive, but it allowed Provident to maintain its existing email IDs and it integrated easily into other popular and useful Google applications, such as Google Docs and Google Calendar.

A few other organizations had already converted to Gmail, and as he considered whether to authorize the increased expenditure or not, Michael wondered whether it was time for Provident to get out of the email business.

Questions

1. What are the benefits and risks that Provident faces when considering maintaining its own email system or moving to another service, such as Gmail? (*Hint:* How much control do *you* have when you use free web services, and how are those services funded?)
2. How is email different, if at all, from other technology or nontechnology services, such as telephone systems or regular mail? (*Hint:* How differentiated are these services, and are there various levels of service?)
3. How should a company decide which functions should be provided internally and which ones should be obtained externally? Is there a difference between the cafeteria or health services and an information system?
4. How does the industry in which a firm operates or the actions of its competitors affect your recommendation? (*Hint:* Would your recommendation differ if Provident was a health services organization)?
5. Are there any other options that Provident should consider? (*Hint:* Is there a mid-point between self-service options and using free services?)

Source: Courtesy of Michael Jagger, Provident Security Corp.

The Real Estimation Process

"I'm a software developer. I write programs in an object-oriented language called C++. I'm a skilled object-oriented designer, too. I should be—I've been at it for 12 years and have worked on major projects for several software companies. For the last four years I've been a team leader. I lived through the heyday of the dot-com era and now work in the IT department of a giant pharmaceutical company.

"All this estimating theory is just that—theory. It's not really the way things work. Sure, I've been on projects in which we tried different estimation techniques. But here's what really happens: You develop an estimate using whatever technique you want. Your estimate goes in with the estimates of all the other team leaders. The project manager sums all those estimates together and produces an overall estimate for the project.

"By the way, in my projects, time has been a much bigger factor than money. At one software company I worked for, you could be 300 percent over your dollar budget and get no more than a slap on the wrist. Be two weeks late, however, and you were finished.

"Anyway, the project managers take the project schedule to senior management for approval, and what happens? Senior management thinks they are negotiating.

"'Oh, no,' they say, 'that's way too long. You can surely take a month off that schedule. We'll approve the project, but we want it done by February 1 instead of March 1.

"Now, what's their justification? They think that tight schedules make for efficient work. You know that everyone will work extra hard to meet the tighter time frame. They know Parkinson's Law—'The time required to perform a task expands to the time available to do it.' So, fearing the possibility of wasting time because of too-lenient schedules, they lop a month off our estimate.

"Estimates are what they are; you can't knock off a month or two without some problem, somewhere. What does happen is that projects get behind, and then management expects us to work longer and longer hours. Like they said in the early years at Microsoft, 'We have flexible working hours. You can work any 65 hours per week you want.'

"Not that our estimation techniques are all that great, either. Most software developers are optimists. They schedule things as if everything will go as planned, but things seldom do. Also, schedulers usually don't allow for vacations, sick days, trips to the dentist, training on new technology, peer reviews, and all the other things we do in addition to writing software.

"So, we start with optimistic schedules on our end, then management negotiates a month or two off, and, voilà, we have a late project. After a while, management has been burned by late projects so often that they mentally add a month or even more back to the official schedule. Then both sides work in a fantasy world, where no one believes the schedule, but everyone pretends they do.

"I like my job. I like software development. Management here is no better or worse than in other places. As long as I have interesting work to do, I'll stay here. But I'm not working myself silly to meet these fantasy deadlines."

Discussion Questions

1. What do you think of this developer's attitude? Do you think he is unduly pessimistic, or do you think there is merit in what he says?

2. What do you think of his idea that management thinks they are negotiating? Should management negotiate schedules? Why, or why not?

3. Suppose a project actually requires 12 months to complete. Which do you think is likely to cost more: (a) having an official schedule of 11 months with at least a 1-month overrun, or (b) having an official schedule of 13 months and, following Parkinson's Law, having the project take 13 months?

4. Suppose you are a business manager and an information system is being developed for your use. You review the scheduling documents and see that little time has been allowed for vacations, sick leave, miscellaneous other work, and so forth. What do you do?

5. Describe the intangible costs of having an organizational belief that schedules are always unreasonable.

6. If this developer worked for you, how would you deal with his attitude about scheduling?

7. Do you think there is a difference between scheduling information systems development projects and scheduling other types of projects? What characteristics might make such projects unique? In what ways are they the same as other projects?

8. What do you think managers should do in light of your answer to Question 7?

Ksrisanga/Shutterstock

Application Extension 10a

Study Questions

Q1 What is project management software?

Q2 How do I create and manage tasks?

Q3 How do I manage resources?

Introduction to Microsoft Project

This application extension teaches basic skills with Microsoft Project 2007, a product designed to help organize and manage projects. If you already know how to use MS Project, use this application extension as a review. Otherwise, use it to gain essential knowledge that every business manager needs.

Q1 What Is Project Management Software?

There are many types of project management software. Some software focuses on organizing tasks. Other software helps you manage resources or schedules. Still other software tracks employee work hours on different projects, or provides repositories for storing and providing access to project documentation. What is important to understand is that no one piece of project management software does it all. So, the choice as to which software to use in an organization is something that takes careful analysis.

Although no one product does it all, there are many products that provide strong support for the project management process. MS Project is an example of this type of full-service product. The program has the largest number of installed users in project management software and provides an excellent entry point into how project management software differs from other applications, such as spreadsheets and databases.

Though MS Project often looks like a spreadsheet, it is best described as a database product. Underlying MS Project is a sophisticated relational database that stores information about tasks, resources, schedule, baselines, and budgets. MS Project allows you to enter information into the database through specifically designed forms and then presents the project data through specially designed views that often focus on one or two aspects of the project. Since projects are often complex, it is difficult to present all of the information about them on one screen. So, MS Project provides a variety of screens to capture the full picture of the project. The interface for MS Project is illustrated in Figure AE10a-1.

Figure AE10a-1
The Gantt Chart View in MS Project

Source: Microsoft Project Software

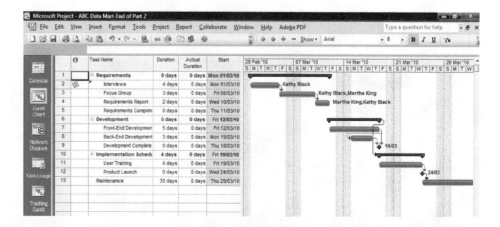

Figure AE10a-2

The MS Project Resource Sheet

Source: Microsoft Project Software

The default view for MS Project is the Gantt Chart view. In the Gantt Chart view, all of the tasks (or work packages) associated with the project are listed on the left side of the screen. On the right side, a bar indicates when the activity is estimated to begin and how long that activity is expected to last. A **Gantt chart** is a quick way to see which activities are happening and how much further the project has to go before completion. Note that the Gantt Chart view shown in Figure AE10a-1 also lists the people who are working on the project. The arrows that point toward bars indicate a dependency between two activities, which means that one activity must be completed before the other one can begin. These **dependencies** are important when scheduling a project.

The Gantt Chart is one view provided by MS Project. **Resource Sheet view** is another, as shown in Figure AE10a-2. In this view, we see the people who are available to work as well as their available work hours. Resource Sheet view provides a place to enter project team member roles, chargeout rate, expected hours of work, and other items.

A related view is the Resource Usage view, as shown in Figure AE10a-3. This view shows the date and number of hours that each employee is expected to work on a project. This view lets you quickly see whether an employee is over-allocated (has too many hours) and whether to expect overtime or to find someone who can fill in for the employee.

There are a number of other views in MS Project, including Tracking Gantt (where project progress is measured against a baseline), Network Diagram, Calendar, and Resource Graph views. We will not look at these views in detail in this introduction.

Now that you have been introduced to what MS Project can do, you can start adding tasks to a project.

Figure AE10a-3

The Resource Usage Sheet

Source: Microsoft Project Software

Q2 How Do I Create and Manage Tasks?

In this application extension, we will use the example of a systems development project where requirements are created, some development is undertaken, and then the system is implemented. Regardless of what project you may be working on, all project management begins with an understanding of the tasks that need to be accomplished. Let us begin with a brand-new file. To do this, open MS Project, select New File, and create a blank project. Then, save this project as "Intro to MSProject." If you are successful, your screen should look like the screen in Figure AE10a-4.

You are now ready to add a task. Start at the top of the Task Name column and complete the following:

1. Click in the first row of Task Name column.
2. Type "Requirements."
3. Press Enter.

You will see the word "Requirements" at the top of the list, followed by some information about duration, and start and end dates. Don't worry about adding the duration right now. This is shown in Figure AE10a-5. Note how a one-day-long task has been added on the Gantt Chart on the right of the screen.

Let us add more tasks. Take a minute or two and add the tasks provided below in Table 1 (in the same order) and their durations into your project. Note that the tasks Requirements, Development, Implementation Schedule, and Product Launch are examples of high-level tasks. We will calculate the duration of these tasks based on the time needed for subtasks.

Figure AE10a-4
Blank Project in MS Project

Source: Microsoft Project Software

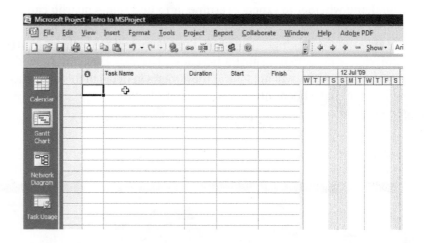

Figure AE10a-5
Adding a Task to a New Project

Source: Microsoft Project Software

Task Name	Duration
Requirements	1 day
Interviews	3 days
Focus Group	4 days
Requirements Report	2 days
Development	1 day
Front-End Development	5 days
Back-End Development	3 days
Implementation Schedule	1 day
User Training	4 days
Product Launch	0 days

Table 1

Tasks and Durations

Creating Subtasks

We are now going to organize our tasks a little more, by creating tasks and **subtasks**. To create a subtask, select one or more tasks and then click the right tab button, as shown in Figure AE10a-6. The three selected tasks then become subtasks. The opposite happens when you select a task and click on the left tab button. Note as well what happens to the Gantt Chart, where tasks and subtasks are created. The higher-level tasks are given a different icon, which envelops all the subtasks within it. You will also notice that the duration time for the tasks is now also equal to the largest subtask duration. This happens automatically when you create tasks and subtasks. Figure AE10a-7 shows the arrangement of tasks and subtasks we will use in our project. Spend a little time creating the appropriate tasks and subtasks as shown in Figure AE10a-7.

Creating Dependencies

We noted earlier that some tasks cannot be completed until other tasks are completed. When this is the case, we say that there is a dependency between the two tasks. One task therefore becomes the **predecessor** (must happen before) and the other task is the successor (occurs after the predecessor is completed). These dependencies are crucial for creating a meaningful schedule.

To assign predecessors, we use the task window in MS Project. In this example, we will make Task 2, Interviews, the predecessor of Task 3, Focus Group. To get to the task window, double-click on the Focus Group tasks (which has Task ID 3). The task

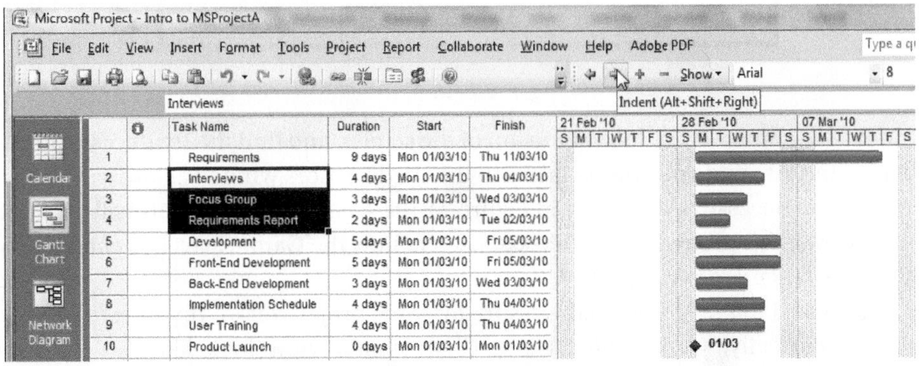

Figure AE10a-6

Preparing to Create Subtasks

Source: Microsoft Project Software

Figure AE10a-7

Project Tasks and Subtasks Created

Source: Microsoft Project Software

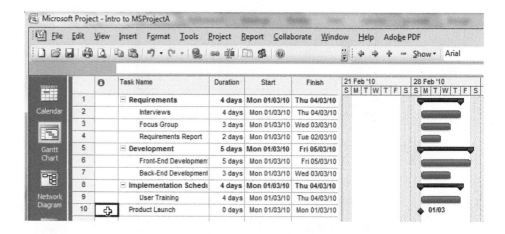

Figure AE10a-8

Assigning a Predecessor to Task 3—Focus Group

Source: Microsoft Project Software

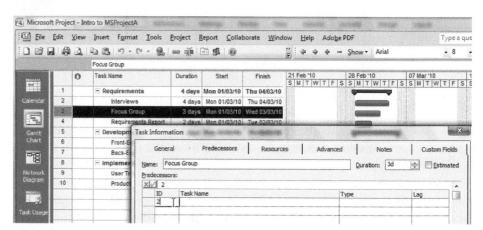

Table 2

Tasks and Predecessors

Task Name	Predecessors
1. Requirements	
2. Interviews	
3. Focus Group	2
4. Requirements Report	3
5. Development	
6. Front-End Development	4
7. Back-End Development	4
8. Implementation Schedule	
9. User Training	7
10. Product Launch	8

window will pop up. Next, look at the top of the screen, and find the Predecessors tab. Click on the tab, and you will be taken to the Predecessors window. Now type "2" in the list of predecessors, as shown in Figure AE10a-8, and hit Enter. This will set Task 2, Interviews, as a predecessor to Task 3. Look at how the Gantt Chart has changed to reflect the dependency.

Now use Table 2 to set predecessors for your project tasks. If you set the predecessor correctly, your project Gantt Chart should now look like the chart in

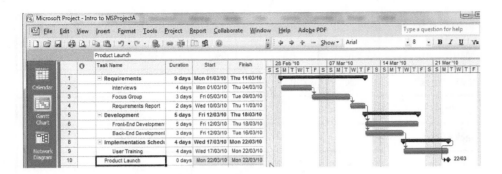

Figure AE10a-9. There is more we can do with tasks, but what we have learned is enough for this introduction. Our next question will look at resources.

Q3   How Do I Manage Resources?

Let us now turn our attention to resources. We will work with the Resource Sheet view in MS Project. The view can be selected by clicking on the View menu and highlighting the Resource Sheet view, as shown in Figure AE10a-10. You can also select the Resource Sheet icon that is provided on the quick navigator, located on the far left side of the screen.

Once Resource Sheet is selected, a blank Resource Sheet pops up. The Resource Sheet is empty because no one has filled in the information about the people who may be working on your project. Table 3 provides you with some information about the people working on this project. Enter this information into the Resource Sheet. The data entry in the Resource Sheet is the same as that for the Gantt Chart. Click in the appropriate cell, and type the information in.

Figure AE10a-10
Selecting the Resource Sheet View

Source: Microsoft Project Software

Resource Name	Initial	Group	Max Units	Std Rate	Ovr Rate
Martha King	M	BA	100%	$30.00/hr	$50.00/hr
Kathy Black	K	BA	100%	$40.00/hr	$60.00/hr
Tim Pape	T	PM	100%	$100,000.00/yr	$0.00/hr
Jack Booth	J	FD	100%	$50.00/hr	$75.00/hr
Edward Healy	E	FD	100%	$50.00/hr	$75.00/hr
Peter Draude	P	BD	100%	$50.00/hr	$75.00/hr
Harry Dion	H	BD	100%	$50.00/hr	$75.00/hr
Kim Trent	K	UT	100%	$90.00/hr	$115.00/hr

If you are successful, your Resource Sheet should look like the one in
Figure AE10a-11.

We are now ready to use the Resource Sheet and assign people to the tasks that
need to be accomplished. To do this, let us return to the Gantt Chart view.

Adding Resources to Tasks

Next, we will assign people on our Resource Sheet to the tasks we defined earlier. Let
us start in the Gantt Chart view. This view can be selected by clicking on the View
menu and highlighting the Gantt Chart view, or by selecting the Gantt Chart view icon
that is provided on the quick navigator on the far left-hand side of the screen.

Start by assigning resources to Task 2, Interviews. To add a resource, double-click
on the Task 2, Interviews row. This will bring up the Task Window. Look to the top of
that window, and you will find the Resources tab. Click on this tab, and you will get a
form that allows you to add resources to this task. Click in the top box in the resource
table, and you will see a drop-down box appear. This is a list of all of the resources
that can work on this task. Select Kathy Black as a resource for this task, as shown in
Figure AE10a-12.

To add more than one resource to a task, use another row in the resource form.
Now that you are able to add resources, use Table 4 as a guide to adding the appropri-
ate resources to each of the subtasks in your project. If you are successful, your Gantt
Chart should resemble Figure AE10a-13.

Once you have allocated resources to the tasks, you can look at the **Resource
Usage view** of the project. This view shows you how active each of your project

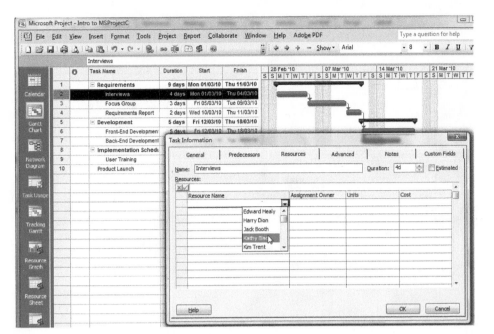

Figure AE10a-12

Assigning a Resource to a Task

Source: Microsoft Project Software

Task Name	Predecessors
1. Requirements	
2. Interviews	Kathy Black
3. Focus Group	Kathy Black, Martha King
4. Requirements Report	Kathy Black, Martha King
5. Development	
6. Front-End Development	Jack Booth, Edward Healy
7. Back-End Development	Harry Dion, Peter Draude
8. Implementation Schedule	
9. User Training	Kim Trent
10. Product Launch	

Table 4

Resource Allocations for Tasks

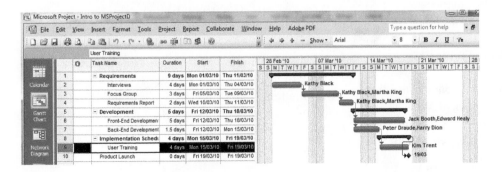

Figure AE10a-13

Resources Allocated to Tasks

Source: Microsoft Project Software

Figure AE10a-14
The Resource Usage View of the Project

Source: Microsoft Project Software

members will be over the course of the project. One important thing you are looking for as a manager is to make sure that people are not working overtime (unless it is necessary) and that no one is overburdened with work.

The Resource Usage view (Figure AE10a-14) can be selected by clicking on the View menu and highlighting the Resource Usage view or by selecting the Resource Usage view icon that is provided on the quick navigator on the far left side of the screen.

This application extension has introduced you to MS Project and some of its basic features. You have learned how to create and manage tasks, define predecessors, enter resources, and assign those resources to tasks. Although there are many other features in MS Project, the features we have described in this extension are critical to planning and executing a successful project. You should keep using MS Project and developing your project management skills.

Active Review

Use this Active Review to verify that you have understood the material in the application extension. You can read the entire extension and then perform the tasks in this review, or you can read the material for just one question and perform the tasks for that question before moving on to the next one.

Q1 What is project management software?

Is MS Project more like a spreadsheet or a database? What is a Gantt chart? What are dependencies? What is the Resource Sheet view of a project? How does the Resource Sheet view differ from the Resource Usage view? Can you show a Network Diagram for a project?

Q2 How do I create and manage tasks?

Can you open a new MS Project file? Can you add tasks to a new project? Can you create subtasks within a task list? Can you create a dependency between two tasks? Can you enter resources into the resource page?

Q3 How do I manage resources?

Can you select the Resource Sheet view? Can you add information about resources (std. rate, ovt. rate, etc.)? Can you add resources to tasks? How does adding resources change the Gantt Chart? Can you select the Resource Usage view?

MyMISLab MyMISLab is an online learning and testing environment that features the perfect study tools to help you master the concepts covered in this chapter. Log in to MyMISLab to test your knowledge of key chapter concepts and explore additional practice tools, including videos, flashcards, annotated text figures, and more!

Key Terms and Concepts

Dependencies 333

Gantt chart 333

Predecessor 335

Resource Sheet view 333

Resource Usage view 338

Subtask 335

Using Your Knowledge

1. Open MS Project, and duplicate each of the actions in this application extension.

2. This exercise is best done as a group exercise. Your group is planning an end-of-term party to celebrate the completion of your course. You have decided to organize the party as a project. You will use MS Project to organize the party.
    a. Name and save a new MS Project file.
    b. Brainstorm a set of tasks that you will need to accomplish to successfully hold your party (e.g., finding a venue, writing invitations, booking entertainment, deciding on food and beverages, organizing setup and take down, etc.). It is often best to think of the end of the process—holding a successful party—and then think about the tasks you have to accomplish to achieve this result. Enter these tasks into the MS Project file you created.
    c. Add estimates of the duration of each task.
    d. Find the dependencies that exist between the different tasks. Create these dependencies in the MS Project file.
    e. Add your group members as resources in the Resource Sheet view.
    f. Assign resources to each task. You can add more than one resource to each task.
    g. Print the Gantt Chart for the party project that you have designed.

3. This exercise is best done as a group exercise. Your group is planning a project that will send extremely rich tourists on trips to the International Space Station. You have decided to organize this project using MS Project.
    a. Name and save a new MS Project file.
    b. Brainstorm a set of tasks that you will need to accomplish to successfully offer your tour (for example, finding/negotiating space on the shuttle for the trip, marketing, insurance, transportation logistics, etc.). If you are having trouble, think of the end of the process—successfully returning the tourists to Earth—and then think about the tasks you have to accomplish to get them back. Enter these tasks into the MS Project file you created.
    c. Add estimates of the duration of each task.
    d. Find the dependencies that exist between the different tasks. Create these dependencies in the MS Project file. Identify any subtasks.
    e. Add your group members as resources in the Resource Sheet view.
    f. Assign resources to each task. You can add more than one resource to each task.
    g. Print the Gantt Chart for the International Space Station tour that you have designed.

11 Structure, Governance, and Ethics

Running Case

When Akbar started his company, there were very few competitors in his industry. His customers sought him out directly, and Akbar went above and beyond to provide a high level of business service. It was a model that worked very well. But lately, Akbar has noticed that he is receiving fewer customer referrals, and he has had to work harder to find new customers. Many of his potential customers are getting their advice from larger retail chains offering their very own versions of the Geek Squad. Akbar is considering how to respond to these new competitive challenges.

Akbar knows, from his course on business strategy, that he could take one of two approaches to this competition. He could try to take the competition on directly and become the low-cost solution for his clients. By being more efficient and charging less than the retail stores, his business would have a competitive advantage it could cling to.

The second path would be to differentiate the services that his company supplies. He could focus on delivering more value and offer niche services that the Geek Squads of larger chain stores would have difficulty delivering. He could then charge more for his services and be able to compete on the niche services he can provide.

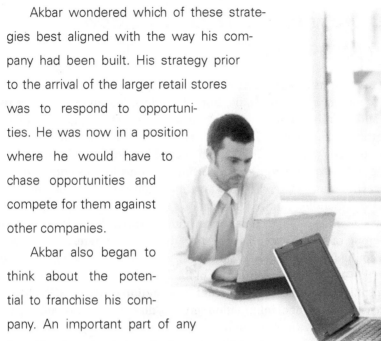

StockLite/Shutterstock

Akbar wondered which of these strategies best aligned with the way his company had been built. His strategy prior to the arrival of the larger retail stores was to respond to opportunities. He was now in a position where he would have to chase opportunities and compete for them against other companies.

Akbar also began to think about the potential to franchise his company. An important part of any franchise is to have standard processes in place to allow the franchisee to create successful new business partners. Had he invested enough into his business processes to successfully franchise his company? Was he ready to take the next step with his company?

Study Questions

Q1 How is the IT department organized?

Q2 What jobs exist in IT services?

Q3 What is IT architecture?

Q4 What is alignment, why is it important, and why is it difficult?

Q5 What is information systems governance?

Q6 What is an information systems audit, and why should you care about it?

Q7 What is information systems ethics?

Q8 What is Green IT, and why should you care about it?

Q1 How Is the IT Department Organized?

Most organizations rely on information technology (IT) services. All of the email systems, accounting applications, desktop computers, and mobile devices used in an organization require some form of technical support. The department of people who provide this support is often referred to as *IT Services* or *Information Systems Services*. This group needs to be organized and managed like any other business department. Figure 11-1 shows typical top-level reporting relationships in an organization that has IT services. As you will learn in your future management classes, organizational structure varies, depending on the organization's size, culture, competitive environment, industry, and other factors. Larger organizations with independent departments will have a group of senior executives, such as those shown here, for each department. Smaller companies may combine some of these departments under a single executive.

The title of the principal manager of the IT department varies from organization to organization. A common title is **chief information officer (CIO)**. Other common titles are vice-president of information services, director of information services, and, less commonly, director of computer services.

In Figure 11-1, the CIO, like other senior executives, reports to the chief executive officer (CEO), though sometimes these executives report to the chief operating officer (COO), who, in turn, reports to the CEO. In some companies, the CIO reports to the chief financial officer (CFO). That reporting arrangement may make sense if the primary information systems support accounting and finance activities. In some organizations, such as manufacturers, which operate significant non-accounting information systems, the arrangement shown in Figure 11-1 is more common and effective. It shows a typical IT department with four subgroups and a data administration staff function.

Most IT departments include a *technology office* that investigates new information systems technologies and determines how the organization can benefit from them. For example, many organizations are using web services technology and planning how they can best use that technology to accomplish their goals and objectives. A **chief technology officer (CTO)** often heads the technology group. The CTO sorts

Figure 11-1

Typical Senior-Level Reporting Relationships

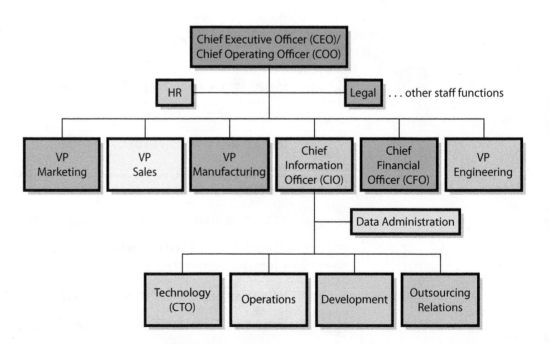

through new ideas and products to identify those that are most relevant to the organization. The CTO's job requires deep knowledge of information technology and the ability to envision how new IT will affect the organization over time.

The next group in Figure 11-1, *operations*, manages the computing infrastructure, including individual computers, computer centres, networks, and communications media. This group includes system and network administrators. As you will learn, an important function of this group is to monitor user experience and respond to user concerns or problems.

The third group in the IT department in Figure 11-1 is *development*. This group manages projects that acquire new information systems and maintains existing information systems. The size and structure of the development group depends on whether programs are developed in-house. If they are not, this department will be staffed primarily by **business analysts** and/or **systems analysts** who work with users, operations, and vendors to acquire and install licensed software and to set up the system components around that software. Business analysts are normally involved in developing the business case for a newly proposed system as well as the requirements for that system. Systems analysts are normally involved in designing and implementing the new system. If the organization develops programs in-house, then this department will also include programmers, project managers, test engineers, technical writers, and other development personnel.

The last IT department group shown in Figure 11-1 is *outsourcing relations*. This group exists in organizations that have negotiated outsourcing agreements with other companies to provide equipment, applications, or other services. These relationships require constant attention, so this department monitors service levels and focuses on developing good relations with outsourcing vendors. Figure 11-1 also includes a *data administration* staff function. The purpose of this group is to protect data and information assets by establishing data standards and data management practices and policies.

There are many variations on the structure of the IT department shown in Figure 11-1. In larger organizations, the operations group may itself consist of several different departments. In smaller organizations, one person might serve as an entire department. Sometimes, there is a separate group for data warehousing and data marts.

What About the Web?

The web has had a significant impact on the organization of IT departments. In its early years, the responsibility for technology supporting the web, as well as for the content and design of a company's website, was exclusively within the IT services department. But as companies recognized the impact that the web could have on its brand and its customers, control of the content and the look and feel of the website were moved to marketing departments, while IT maintained the technical responsibilities.

Of course, creating a well-designed company website requires knowledge of branding and marketing. But it also requires knowledge of such things as TCP/IP (Transmission Control Protocol/Internet Protocol) networks, HTML (Hypertext Markup Language), XML (eXtensible Markup Language), content management systems, and web design applications, such as Adobe Flash. Recognition of the importance of website design created a whole new set of related jobs. These jobs combine traditional business skills (like branding and marketing) with technical skills.

Many companies have faced difficulties attracting and retaining employees who have the combination of web design skills and business skills necessary to create excellent websites. (Perhaps this is a competitive advantage you could use when you graduate. It is certainly a good reason to include some IS courses, or even an IS major, in your marketing degree.)

As a result, a whole new industry, the web design consulting industry, was born. There are many small and large web design firms. One large Canadian firm is Blast Radius (www.blastradius.com). Created in 1997, the company has grown to more than 350 employees while serving international clients, such as Nike, BMW, Converse, Nintendo, and Virgin.

One important point you should learn in this chapter is that it can take a lot of people to make a great website because a number of skills are involved. For example, a web design project of any size will require the following people:

- *Project manager:* Responsible for interacting with the client and moving the project successfully toward completion
- *Lead designer/analyst:* Responsible for understanding client needs and developing the overall look and feel of the site and all the design elements (colours, navigation, graphics, buttons, animation, etc.)
- *Developer:* Responsible for taking the design and creating the functioning site; usually specializes in static content (i.e., information that is not automatically updated)
- *Technical architect:* Responsible for making decisions about technical issues related to the site, including server/browser support, database integration, administrator access, and any scripting issues

There is a misperception among many business people that putting together a website is relatively easy. Actually, it is harder than most people think. While it might be easy to get a site on the web, ensuring that the site is properly designed, easy to maintain, and provides an enjoyable customer experience is work for professionals. This has made the job of the IT department not only more important but also more challenging. Web design has changed the skill set of many IT workers and created both challenges and opportunities for employees who can combine the right types of business design and technical skills.

Q2 What Jobs Exist in IT Services?

We noted in Chapter 1 that the Information and Communications Technology sector has a wide range of interesting and well-paying jobs. Many students enter an introductory MIS class thinking that the industry consists only of programmers and computer technicians who have great technical skills. If you reflect on the five components (hardware, software, data, procedures, and people) of an information system, you can understand why this cannot be true. The *data, procedures,* and *people* components of an information system require professionals with highly developed interpersonal communication skills. The reality is that most jobs that are in the highest demand in the ICT sector require a mix of interpersonal and technical skills. The most effective MIS personnel are often people who are thoughtful communicators, have basic technology skills, and are comfortable leading significant projects that change business practices. The entire sector is looking for people who can bridge the knowledge gap between computer technicians and business system users. Your training in business is an excellent foundation for doing this type of work.

Figure 11-2 lists the major job positions in the IS industry. With the exception of computer technicians and possibly professional quality assurance (PQA) test engineers, all of these positions require a four-year degree. Furthermore, with the exception of programmers and PQA test engineers, all of these positions require business knowledge. In most cases, successful professionals have a degree in business. Note, too, that most positions require excellent verbal and written communication skills. Business, including information systems, is a social activity.

Title	Responsibilities	Knowledge, Skills, and Characteristics Requirements	2006 Cdn. Salary Range ($CDN)
Computer technician	Install software, repair computer equipment and networks	Associate degree, diagnostic skills	$30 000–$60 000
Quality Assurance (QA) test engineer	Develop test plans, design and write automated test scripts, perform testing	Logical thinking, basic programming, superb organizational skills, detail oriented	$40 000–$75 000
User support representative	Help users solve problems, provide training	Communications and people skills, product knowledge, patience	$35 000–$60 000
Technical writer	Write program documentation, help-text, procedures, job descriptions, training materials	Quick learner, clear writing skills, high verbal and communications skills	$35 000–$60 000
Programmer/ Developer	Design and write computer programs	Logical thinking and development, skills, programming	$45 000–$110 000
Website Designer	Work with clients to develop designs for websites, work with developers to finalize designs	Excellent interpersonal skills, design skills, detail oriented, good technical skills, flexible business/marketing skills	$45 000–$110 000
Network administrator	Monitor, maintain, fix, and tune computer networks	Diagnostic skills, in-depth knowledge of communications, technologies, and products	$65 000–$120 000+
Database administrator	Manage and protect database (see Chapter 12)	Diplomatic skills, database technology knowledge	$65 000–$120 000
Systems analyst, Business analyst	Work with users to determine system requirements, design procedure	Strong interpersonal and communications skills, business and technology knowledge	$50 000–$110 000
Consultant	Wide range of activities: programming, testing, database design, communications and networks, project management, strategic planning	Quick learner, entrepreneurial attitude, communications and people skills, respond well to pressure, particular knowledge depends on work	From $35 per hour for a contract tester to more than $400 per hour for strategic consulting to executive group
Salesperson	Sell software, network, communications, and consulting services	Quick learner, knowledge of product, superb professional sales skills	$65 000–$200 000+
Project manager (PM)	Initiate, plan, manage, monitor, and close down projects	Management and people skills, technology knowledge, highly organized	$75 000–$150 000
Enterprise Architect (EA)	Manage and document the technological infrastructure of the firm	Diplomatic skills, database technology knowledge, strategic planning	$100 000–$200 000
Chief technology officer (CTO)	Advise CIO, executive group, and project managers on emerging technologies	Quick learner, good communications skills, deep knowledge of IT	$100 000–$250 000+
Chief information officer (CIO)	Manage IT department, communicate with executive staff on IT- and IS-related matters, member of the executive group	Superb management skills, deep knowledge of business, and good business judgment; good communicator, balanced and unflappable	$150 000–$300 000, plus executive benefits and privileges

Figure 11-2

Job Positions in the Information Systems Industry

Many of the positions in Figure 11-2 have a wide salary range. Lower salaries are paid to professionals with limited experience or to those who work in smaller companies or on small projects. Larger salaries are paid to those with deep knowledge and experience who work for large companies on large projects. Do not expect to begin your career at the high end of these ranges.

The authors of this book, who have nearly 80 years of combined experience, have worked as systems analysts, programmers, small- and large-scale project managers, consultants, business unit managers, and chief technology officers (CTO). They have enjoyed their experience in the field, as the industry becomes more and more interesting each year. Give these IT careers some thought while you are in school. Keep in mind that the changing nature of technology—and of business generally—will demand that you incorporate technology into the way you work.

By the way, for most technical positions, knowledge of a business specialty can really add to marketability. Note that the high-paying jobs toward the bottom of the list all require communication, leadership, and business skills. If you have the time, a dual major can be an excellent choice that can open up opportunities for you. Popular and successful dual majors include accounting and information systems, marketing and information systems, and management strategy and information systems.

JUMPING ABOARD THE BULLDOZER

A recent popular theme in the media is how overseas outsourcing is destroying the North American labour market: "Jobless recovery" is how it is headlined. However, a closer look reveals that overseas outsourcing is not the culprit. The culprit—if *culprit* is the right word—is productivity. Because of information technology (IT), Moore's Law, and all of the information systems that you have learned about in this book, worker productivity continues to increase, and it is possible to have an economic recovery without a binge of new hiring.

Austrian economist Joseph Schumpeter called processes such as outsourcing and technological innovation "creative destruction" and said that these processes are the cleansers of the free market.[1] Economic processes operate to remove unneeded jobs, companies, and even industries, thereby keeping the economy growing and prospering. In fact, the lack of such processes hindered the growth of Japan and some European nations in the 1990s.

So, what do you do? How do you respond to the dynamics of shifting work and job movements? As you have learned, management information systems (MIS) are about the development and use of information systems that enable organizations to achieve their goals and objectives. When you work with information systems, you are more than a professional in any one particular system of technology; rather, you are a developer or user of systems that help your organization achieve its goals and objectives.

From this perspective, the technology you learned in this class can help you start your career. If information systems based productivity is the bulldozer that is mowing down traditional jobs, then use what you have learned here to jump aboard that bulldozer—not as a technologist, but as a business professional who can determine how best to use that bulldozer to enhance your career. Your long-term success depends not on your knowledge of specific technologies but, rather, on your ability to think, communicate, solve problems, and use technology and information systems to help your organization achieve its goals and objectives.

[1] J. Schumpeter, *Capitalism, Socialism, and Democracy* (New York: Harper, 1975), pp. 82–85.

Q3 What Is IT Architecture?

We learned in Chapter 3 that an organization's goals and objectives help determine its competitive strategy. We used Porter's five forces model to consider the structure of the industry under which a company operates. Given that structure, we could develop a **competitive strategy** for the organization. This strategy is supported by activities in the value chain, which consist of a collection of business processes supported by information systems. This idea is illustrated in Figure 11-3.

In Chapter 2, we learned that information systems exist to help organizations achieve their goals and objectives. Thus, in an ideal world, the information systems that a company chooses to use should support the company's competitive strategy.

We will learn in this section that effectively managing information systems so that they support business objectives is a difficult process. The challenge in developing these plans is that it requires an understanding of both organizational strategy and the technological architecture underlying information systems. And because it is so challenging, organizations sometimes get it wrong, resulting in a misalignment between information systems and business strategy.

Take a moment and think about what it means to understand the technology that supports an organization. How many computers are there in the company? Are they all the same brand? When were they bought? What operating system are they using? What applications are being run by the company? What software, official and unofficial, is installed on the computing devices? Who purchased the software? What company is supporting the software if there are bugs or other problems? What networks are the computers connected to? Does the company limit internet addresses to and from computers within the company? If so, who is monitoring this? Which email package is the company using? What is the company's policy regarding spam? What are its privacy and security policies? When is the company upgrading machines, software licences, network protocols, etc.? Does the company support wireless access? If so, what levels of access and where? The questions can go on and on.

An **IT architecture** is like a city plan that lays out the street network, water system, sewer system, emergency services, and power grids. An IT architecture is the basic framework for all the computers, systems, and information management that support organizational services. Like a city plan, an IT architecture is complex, and that complexity is increasing as more services are supported and different technologies are used.

In response to this complexity, some organizations have created a new job description—the **enterprise architect**—to describe the person who does this work. One organization that supports enterprise architects is Enterprise-Wide IT Architecture (EWITA; www.ewita.com); there are others as well. The enterprise architect's job is to create a blueprint of an organization's information systems and the management of these systems. The blueprint should provide an overview that helps people in the organization better understand current investments in technology and plan for

Figure 11-3

Organizational Strategy and Information Systems

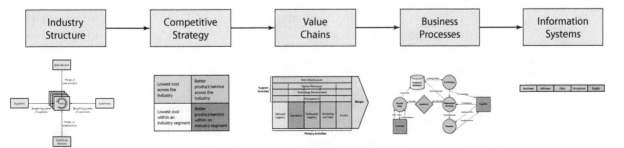

Layer	What? Data	How? Function	Where? Network	Who? People	When? Time	Why? Motivation
Planner	List of important things for business	List of business processes	List of where enterprise operates	List of business functional units	List of business events and cycle	List of business goals and strategies
Owner	Entity Relationship Model	Moving down provides higher levels of detail	Moving across shows different perspectives on systems			
Builder	Normalized data model					
Implementer	Relational data model					
Worker	Input screens					

Figure 11-4

A Framework of Enterprise Architecture

changes. In developing the architecture, the enterprise architect usually considers organizational objectives, business processes, databases, information flows, operating systems, applications and software, and supporting technology.

So, what does an IT architecture look like?[2] The first thing to note is that there are few standards because companies and systems are so diverse that it is hard to develop an architecture. An architecture is usually a long document with many sections that include quite complicated diagrams (see footnote 2) as well as management policies (such as privacy, sourcing, and security) and discussion of future changes to the architecture.

Since the development of an IT architecture is so complex, it is often helpful to use a method that organizes the development. One of the most popular of these is the **Zachman framework**, conceived by John Zachman at IBM in the 1980s. The framework divides systems into two dimensions: One is based on six reasons for communication (*what*—data, *how*—function, *where*—network, *who*—people, *when*—time, *why*—motivation), and the other is based on stakeholder groups (planner, owner, designer, builder, implementer, and worker). The intersection of these two dimensions helps provide a relatively holistic view of the enterprise. An example from Zachman International (zachmaninternational.com) is provided in Figure 11-4.

While it may sound boring to some people, the development of an enterprise architecture can be critically important when organizations are considering significant changes, such as mergers, acquisitions, divestiture, or rapid growth. Like a city, information systems are continually in use and often involved in change. Having a single planning office where all of the different systems are viewed from the big perspective can often have advantages.

Defining the architecture is the first step in understanding how information systems support business objectives. You should carefully consider getting involved in

[2] A number of graphic models of enterprise architectures can be viewed on the web. Examples include an enterprise modelling process (www.enterpriseunifiedprocess.com/essays/enterpriseArchitecture.html), an enterprise model for a laboratory (commons.lbl.gov/display/cio/Architecture); and an architecture developed using the Zachman framework (zachmaninternational.com).

discussions about enterprise architecture at your company. These discussions are a great opportunity to better understand how the company currently works and how it will have to change to work even more effectively. This knowledge is often very valuable regardless of where you work, so try not to run too fast when you hear the architects coming your way.

Q4 What Is Alignment, Why Is It Important, and Why Is It Difficult?

The process of matching organizational objectives with IT architecture is often referred to as **alignment**, but the term has been somewhat difficult to define. MIS researchers have suggested that alignment should be viewed as an ongoing process—that fitting IT architecture to business objectives is continually evolving. The alignment process takes advantage of IT capabilities as they develop, at the same time maintaining a balance between business objectives and IT architecture. What works for one organization as a balance may not work for another, since alignment depends on business goals, the organizational context, and the state of IT architecture in an organization.

Matching investments in IT with organizational strategy is not as straightforward as it may seem. Take the example of Wal-Mart, the largest retailer in the world. Customers know that when they shop at Wal-Mart they are getting the goods they buy at low prices. Wal-Mart has been very successful in maintaining a competitive strategy based on being a low-price retailer, which means maintaining costs that are lower than industry average. So, if Wal-Mart is focused on maintaining low costs, one might think that aligning IT objectives with this strategy would see Wal-Mart spending less on IT than the industry average.

In fact, just the opposite is true. Wal-Mart spends more than the industry average on IT. Why? Because, over several decades, the company has developed a sophisticated network of IT applications that allows it to collect and share vast amounts of enterprise information throughout the organization. Access to these data allows Wal-Mart employees and suppliers to make more effective decisions and to operate more efficiently. Wal-Mart is very much a high-technology company that has found success as a low-cost retailer.

It is clear that supporting business objectives with appropriate IT investments remains a critical part of IT management. In their study of IS alignment, Chan, Sabherwal, and Thatcher[3] considered both the factors affecting alignment and the impact of alignment on perceived business performance. Results showed improvements in perceived performance when technology was aligned with some strategic objectives.

If alignment is recognized as important, then what makes it so difficult to achieve? Canadian researchers Reich and Benbasat[4] first measured alignment as the degree to which the IT department's missions, objectives, and plans overlapped with the overall business missions, objectives, and plans. In a later paper, the authors[5] recognized the importance of the social dimension of alignment. Effective alignment occurred in organizations that had developed a climate supporting the sharing of domain

---

[3] Y. Chan, R. Sabherwal, and J.B. Thatcher, "Antecedents and Outcomes of Strategic IS Alignment: An Empirical Investigation," *IEEE Transactions on Engineering Management* 53, no. 1 (February 2006): 27–47.

[4] B. H. Reich and I. Benbasat, "Measuring the Linkage between Business and Information Technology Objectives," *MIS Quarterly* 20, no. 1 (March 1996): 55–81.

[5] B. H. Reich and I. Benbasat, "Factors That Influence the Social Dimension of Alignment between Business and Information Technology Objectives," *MIS Quarterly* 24, no. 1 (March 2000): 81–111.

knowledge and common business practices. The importance of the social dimension was confirmed by Chan.[6]

Communication between business and IT executives is the most important indicator of alignment. Successful companies find ways to help share knowledge and frustrations between the IT department and the business functions. This shared knowledge can become a source of competitive advantage for firms because the firms are better able to align their IT investments with the overall business objectives.

Alignment remains a difficult issue for many firms, but it can help provide competitive advantage for those who are willing to make the investment in developing communication and sharing knowledge.

Q5 What Is Information Systems Governance?

Governance has become a popular word in the field of information systems. The term suggests that some committee or group has the ability to govern or decide on expectations for performance, to authorize appropriate resources, and perhaps eventually to verify whether expectations have been met. In publicly traded organizations, one purpose of governance is to ensure that an organization is working on behalf of its shareholders to produce good results and avoid bad ones.

For business organizations, **governance** is the development of consistent, cohesive management policies and verifiable internal processes for information technology and related services. Managing at a corporate level often involves establishing the way in which governing boards oversee a corporation and developing the rules that apply to such issues as sourcing, privacy, security, and internal investments. The goal of information systems governance is to improve the benefits of an organization's IT investment over time. Figure 11-5 shows how stakeholder value can be increased, for example, by better aligning with business objectives, improving service quality, and controlling IT risks. Reporting structures and review processes can be established and can work over a period to improve quality, reduce service costs and delivery time,

Figure 11-5

Creating Benefits from IT Governance

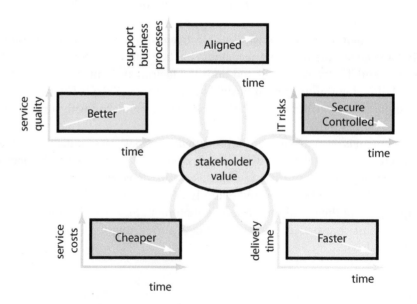

[6] Chan, Y.E., "Why haven't we mastered alignment? The importance of the informal organization structure," *MIS Quarterly Executive* 1, no. 2 (June 2002): 97–112.

reduce IT risks, and better support business processes. It is the responsibility of those charged with information systems governance to make sure that these benefits are realized over time.

Information systems governance is a piece of organizational governance that is associated with IT architecture. The increasing interest in information systems governance is the result of laws, such as the **Sarbanes-Oxley Act (SOX)** in the United States and **Bill 198**, commonly known as the **Budget Measures Act**, in Ontario. These laws force companies to comply with governance standards for collecting, reporting, and disclosing information.

The Sarbanes-Oxley Act and the Budget Measures Act

In recent years, the Sarbanes-Oxley Act (SOX) in the United States and the Budget Measures Act (or Bill 198) in Ontario have affected many information systems, particularly accounting information systems. The SOX of 2002 governs the reporting requirements of publicly held companies. SOX was enacted to prevent corporate frauds, such as those perpetrated by WorldCom, Enron, and others. Ontario introduced similar legislation in the form of Bill 198, commonly known as the Budget Measures Act. Its regulations increase the level of responsibility and accountability of executive management of publicly held Canadian companies traded on the Toronto Stock Exchange in a fashion similar to that described in SOX.

Both pieces of legislation require management to create internal controls sufficient to produce reliable financial statements and to protect the organization's assets. As well, management is required to issue a statement indicating it has done so. The organization's external auditor must also issue an opinion on the quality of the internal controls and the credibility of management's statement. Bill 198 and SOX expose both management and the external auditor to financial and potential criminal liability if subsequent events show that internal controls were defective.

One example of an internal control is the separation of duties and authorities. In an accounts payable system, for example, three separate individuals are required: one to authorize the expense, one to issue the cheque, and a third to account for the transaction. No one person should perform two or more of these actions. You will learn about other such controls in your accounting classes.

If management is relying on computer-based accounting information systems for the preparation of financial statements—and all large organizations do—then those computer-based systems must have appropriate controls, and management must assert that those controls are reliable. This places a greater burden on the development and use of information systems than was prevalent prior to this act.

Additionally, information systems can produce valuable assets that are subject to liability. For example, the database of an order-processing information system that stores customer identities and credit card data represents an organizational asset. If the design of the information systems is ineffective in preventing unauthorized persons from accessing data, then a contingent (possible) liability exists. Without effective controls, someone could steal a customer's name and credit card data and cause harm to the customer. The customer could then sue the organization. Even if no one has yet sued, if the results could be considered significant, management is required to report the liability in its financial statements and to take action to remedy the situation by eliminating the contingent liability.

Summary

A consistent message surrounding information systems governance is that the IT department can no longer appear as a black box or an unknown process to the organization or to external stakeholders. In years past, corporate boards have tended to leave key IT decisions to IT professionals. This often occurred because board members lacked expertise in the IT area. Information systems governance in the future will require that all stakeholders, including corporate board members, have input into important information systems decisions. This may be a silver lining for some IT departments, since they may no longer be blamed exclusively for poor decisions, and users will have fewer grounds to complain that systems did not perform as predicted.

Q6 What Is an Information Systems Audit, and Why Should You Care About It?

A financial audit can be defined as an examination and verification of a company's financial and accounting records and supporting documents by an accredited professional. In Canada, that is a Chartered Professional accountant (CPA). A financial audit is closely related to the processes involved in financial governance of an organization.

The concept of an **information systems audit** is analogous to a financial audit. However, instead of financial and accounting records, the focus is placed on information resources that are used to collect, store, process, and retrieve information. Standards for information systems audits were first developed in the early 1970s and have been evolving with changes in technology. The recent increase in attention on information systems governance has meant a greater focus on the information systems audit and the establishment of methods for examining and verifying organizations' information systems policies and procedures.

Many firms offer information systems audit services. The **Information Systems Audit and Control Association** (ISACA; www.isaca.org) is an organization that was formed in 1969 by a group of individuals who were in charge of auditing controls for newly developed computer systems. The group has grown to more than 115 000 members (in 2014) and has become a leader in developing knowledge and standards relating to IT audit and IT governance. The **Certified Information Systems Auditor (CISA)** certification is recognized globally and has been earned by more than 100 000 professionals. Members have job titles such as information systems auditor, consultant, information systems security professional, regulator, chief information officer, and internal auditor.[7]

In Canada, the Canadian Institute of Chartered Accountants (CICA) has an agreement with ISACA that recognizes the Certified Information Systems Auditor (CISA) designation developed by ISACA as the only designation that leads to recognition as a CA-designated specialist in information systems audit, control, and security. One of the developments provided by ISACA along with the IT Governance Institute (ITGI) is the **Control Objectives for Information and Related Technology (COBIT)**. COBIT is a framework of best practices designed for IT management.[8] This framework provides board members, managers, auditors, and IT users with a set of generally accepted measures, indicators, processes, and best practices to assist them in getting the best from their organizational IT investments.

The latest edition, COBIT 5, was released in June 2012 and provides a set of tools and guidelines for establishing IT management practices. The COBIT control

---

[7] If you are interested, ISACA offers an inexpensive ($25 annual fee) student membership. You can find more details at the ISACA site (www.isaca.org) under the Membership > Student Membership.

[8] For those interested in understanding more about COBIT, an executive summary can be found at the ISACA site (www.isaca.org).

framework establishes links between strategic objectives and business requirements, organizes IT activities into a generally accepted process model, identifies the major IT resources in the organization, and defines the management control objectives to be considered. In establishing these foundations, COBIT can help link business goals to IT goals, providing metrics and maturity models to measure their achievement and identifying the associated responsibilities of business and IT process owners.

The simple translation is that COBIT provides a process through which alignment between IT and business objectives is developed. As noted earlier, processes such as COBIT are not likely to guarantee alignment on their own; researchers have found that the ability to communicate and share knowledge across organizational boundaries remains an important determinant for successful alignment. IT auditing frameworks such as COBIT enable the organization to move in the right direction.

Why Should You Care About Information Systems Governance and Information Systems Audits?

Our discussion of information systems governance and information systems audits has demonstrated the growing importance of information systems issues and operations across all business functions. The increased need to report and disclose information systems operational information will require employees at all levels of an organization to become more familiar with the issues facing IT management. Although this familiarity comes at a cost, the increased exposure to IT issues should improve the ability of organizations to use IT more effectively and efficiently. An argument can be made that the result of increased reporting compliance should be improved alignment between organizational strategy and business objectives. Since compliance issues will remain for the foreseeable future, business students across all functions will gain from increased knowledge of IT issues.

This chapter's Case Study, "Governance at Pacific Blue Cross" on pages 361–362, provides a glimpse of the importance of information systems governance. If you are not yet convinced that you, as a general business major, need the knowledge that this MIS class will give, the advent of such legislation as SOX should convince you. As a senior manager, you will be required to make assertions about the controls on your information systems that will expose you to both financial and criminal penalties. When that day arrives, it will be well worth knowing the fundamentals of information systems. For a more critical review of SOX, see this chapter's "MIS in Use" on pages 356–357.

Q7 What Is Information Systems Ethics?

In Part 3 of this book, we discussed how organizations gain a competitive advantage by achieving objectives with the effective use of IT. We understand that cross-functional systems help realize advantages by more efficiently or effectively handling business processes. We learned in Chapter 8 that the information we collect in business intelligence systems can be used to improve decision making and, ultimately, performance. In Chapter 9, we have shown that utilizing social media and Web 2.0 can create new opportunities for developing competitive advantage.

It may seem as though there are few limits to the use of IT and information systems in developing competitive advantage—but there are. For example, some use of IT may be against the law, and illegal behaviour has legal consequences. Another important limit for business students to recognize is that of ethical behaviour. Actions may not be illegal, but they could be unethical. It is important to understand the difference. The questions provided at the end of What Do You Think? in Chapters 1, 8, 9, and this chapter help make this difference clear.

In previous chapters, some of our exercises have focused on specific ethical issues. These exercises help you establish the ethical boundaries that are comfortable for you. In this section, we address the issue of **information systems ethics** more generally.

It is important to note that information systems ethics is not about hardware or software but, rather, about the people involved in the system. Computers do not threaten our privacy; it is the people who will use our private information who create threats. Computers are great at manipulating logic, but a machine does not understand what it is doing. Machines are not people, so they have no sense of decency, nor have they established character, which is an important part of being human.

Advances in IT bring new opportunities as well as new risks to individuals and organizations. As humans, we can choose to take advantage of technological innovation; however, we should be sensitive to the risk of abusing these advances. Our concern should be placed on the people whose lives can be affected by our actions and not on the computers that complete the actions.

Information systems ethics is not about detailing appropriate rules for our behaviour. The legal system develops rules of law and their enforcement. If we could put ethics into rule-based behaviour, then computers could control ethics. Instead, information systems ethics is about understanding our own behaviour—the way we think and act in situations in which our choices affect others. We face choices in situations, and these choices should be guided by principles. There are many examples of ethical principles: the United Nations Declaration of Human Rights, the Canadian Charter of Rights and Freedoms, and the Association for Computing Machinery's code of ethics (www.acm.org/about/code-of-ethics) are three good examples.

MIS in Use

Sarbanes-Oxley: Boon or Bane?

In 2002, in response to the corporate crimes committed by Enron, WorldCom, and others, the U.S. Congress passed the Sarbanes-Oxley Act (SOX). The goal of this act was to strengthen and upgrade financial reporting and, thus, maintain and improve trust in public companies' financial reports. Such trust is crucial; without it,

the investment community and the entire U.S. economy would come to a standstill.

CIO Magazine publishes articles of interest and importance to chief information officers (CIOs, discussed on page 344). If you search for topics on SOX at www.cio.com, you will find a series of revealing articles. The initial articles reported confusion and concern among CIOs. These were followed by other articles that explained how to comply.

Most recently, *CIO Magazine*'s editor, Gary Beach, published an editorial entitled "Repeal Sarbanes-Oxley." What happened? Surely no one is opposed to accurate financial reporting. Mr. Beach stated, "While foreign companies are free to grab market share, U.S. executives are instead grabbing their Sarbanes-Oxley manuals" to learn how to comply with the Act.

According to a poll conducted by *CIO Magazine*, large companies expect to divert more than 15 percent of their information systems budgets to compliance with SOX. That represents a huge investment, but, given the importance of a favourable audit report, it is an expense that organizations view as mandatory, whether or not it is sensible.

It is not our intention in this chapter to establish any set of principles for ethical behaviour relating to information systems. Rather, our intention is to raise your awareness of the need to understand your own principles related to your use of information systems. When your actions can cause harm to others, you need to be aware of that potential harm and to understand the principles you are working under in making your choice.

Whistleblowers have shown us that it is no longer acceptable to do what your boss says or do what the system tells you when it comes to ethical situations. It is up to you to establish the boundaries within which you are comfortable working. Understanding your own personal principles is an important part of establishing your ethical behaviour.

The best way to understand your ethical principles is to place yourself in ethical situations and to think about what you would do. The exercise at the end of this chapter on pages 364–365 provides an opportunity to try this. We invite you to test your principles using this exercise or similar exercises at the end of Chapters 3, 8, 9, and 10.

Q8 What Is Green IT, and Why Should You Care About It?

So far, we have talked about aligning organizational objectives with IT architecture. We have explored the concepts of information systems governance and information systems audits and considered what is meant by information systems ethics. The

---

Part of the problem is that no one knows exactly what is necessary to comply with SOX. The act requires external auditors to become even more independent than they have been in the past, and, thus, many will not issue opinions on the specific controls that information systems need. The attitude seems to be, "Show us what you have, and we'll tell you if it's enough." IT managers are understandably frustrated. Further, the wording of the act is so vague that auditors have taken the broadest possible interpretation to protect themselves. Consider, for example, Section 409, which requires disclosure of significant financial events within 48 hours. But what characterizes an event as significant? If a customer cancels a large order, is that significant? If so, how large must an order be before it is considered large? If a supplier is devastated by a hurricane, is that significant? Many CIOs ask, "How can we determine from our information systems that a significant event has occurred within 48 hours? Are we supposed to reprogram our applications to include alerts on all such events? What other events should we look for? And who's paying for all this?"

One thing is certain—SOX will provide full employment for internal auditors in general and for IT auditors in particular. Organizations will have to sponsor a flurry of activity, however uneconomical, to show that they are doing something to comply. No company can afford to ignore the act.

Senators Sarbanes and Oxley are both attorneys, neither of whom has ever worked in a publicly traded company. In light of the financial disasters at Enron and WorldCom, their law was highly praised by the public. But is it worth its cost?

Questions

1. In your opinion, are the millions, perhaps billions, of dollars spent on compliance with SOX and the Budget Measures Act unnecessary waste?

2. In the long run, will these acts hamper North American corporations in their competition with international corporations that are not burdened by them? Will they ultimately work to reduce investor choices?

3. Given the requirements of SOX, do you believe that a privately owned company still has an incentive to choose to become a public company?

concepts of IT architecture, information systems governance, information systems audits, and information systems ethics all surround the idea of choices. In making choices about the systems we build and use, we are often guided by ethics, audit and control principles, or alignment principles. Green IT provides a good example of the importance of understanding the choices an organization makes and the impact of those choices.

Green IT, or green computing, means using IT resources to better support the **triple bottom line** for organizations. The triple bottom line includes measures of traditional profit along with ecological and social performance. There are many elements of Green IT, but its primary goals are to improve energy efficiency, promote recyclability, and reduce the use of materials that are hazardous to the environment. Green IT, therefore, represents a choice to consider not only the financial implications of adopting and using IT but also the effects of those choices on people and the environment.

In many cases, Green IT is simply a common-sense approach to computing. An example of this approach is the **ENERGY STAR** program, which is an international government–industry partnership that is intended to produce equipment that meets high-energy efficiency specifications or promotes the use of such equipment. For example, simple ideas, such as using the sleep mode on your computer, can provide energy savings with little impact on performance. Laptops also use less power (maximum of 15 watts) compared with desktop computers (80 to 160 watts). As well, laptops often automatically power down after several minutes of inactivity. The U.S. Environmental Protection Agency (EPA) notes that if all computers sold in the United States met ENERGY STAR requirements, the savings in energy costs would be more than $2 billion every year. This is the equivalent of removing nearly 3 million vehicles and their greenhouse gas emitting engines from the road every year.[9]

Many agencies promote and support Green IT. For example, the Green Computing Impact Organization—now the Object Management Group (OMG; www.omg.org)—is a nonprofit organization that suggests ways in which end-users can be more environmentally responsible. You will find some helpful ideas here to make your own computing more green. For vendors, the Electronics Product Recycling Association (EPRA; www.recyclemyelectronics.ca) offers a directory of Canadian services for recycling electronic products.

One of the most important issues in Green IT is **e-cycling**, or the recycling of electronic computing devices. The **e-waste** industry has only recently developed and is expanding quickly. An example of a company in this industry is Electronics Product Recycling Association (EPRA; www.recyclemyelectronics.ca). Companies in this industry benefit from stricter government controls on e-waste by helping other companies comply with e-waste guidelines.

The fact that the e-waste industry faces significant regulatory restrictions suggests that e-cycling will be an important consideration for any significant user of IT. It will affect information systems governance and information systems audit procedures. You may or may not agree with the focus of Green IT, but it is clear that any business professional will need to understand how he or she can support its development. We started this section with the idea that we need to understand the choices that we make and the impact of these choices. Understanding more about green IT gives us more information about the choices we are making in responsibly using IT.

[9] See www.energystar.gov/index.cfm?fuseaction=find_a_product.showProductGroup&pgw_code=CO.

Active Review

Use this Active Review to verify that you have understood the material in the chapter. You can read the entire chapter and then perform the tasks in this review, or you can read the material for just one question and perform the tasks for that question before moving on to the next one.

Q1 How is the IT department organized?

Draw an organization chart for a typical IT department. Explain the functions of the CIO and the CTO. Describe typical reporting relationships of the IT department and the CIO. What positions require mostly technical skills? What positions require mostly business skills?

Q2 What jobs exist in IT services?

Identify the different types of IS and IT positions available in mid-sized organizations and contrast the education and skill requirements. Which appeal most to you? How can you prepare yourself for these positions? Explain why a joint major of IS and another functional discipline may make sense.

Q3 What is IT architecture?

Why do organizations need an IT architecture? What is an enterprise architect? What does an IT architectural document look like? How can a method such as the Zachman framework support the development of an IT architecture?

Q4 What is alignment, why is it important, and why is it difficult?

Why do organizations have a difficult time aligning IT planning and organizational objectives? In what ways can you measure alignment? What factors make for improved alignment? When should organizations care about alignment, and what can they do to improve it?

Q5 What is information systems governance?

What is governance? Why do organizations need governance? How does information systems governance differ from financial governance? Why has information systems governance increased in prominence only recently?

Q6 What is an information systems audit, and why should you care about it?

Why do companies need auditors? What do information systems auditors do? What organization supports information systems auditors? What is the designation for an information systems auditor in Canada? What is the relationship between information systems audits and information systems governance? Do you believe that information systems governance is an issue that will affect many business people? Justify your answer.

Q7 What is information systems ethics?

Do you believe ethics is an important consideration in information systems? Can computers act unethically? Explain your answer. What is the difference between illegal behaviour and unethical behaviour? Why is it important to understand your own ethical behaviour?

Q8 What is Green IT, and why should you care about it?

What is Green IT? What is meant by the triple bottom line? Provide two examples of agencies that are focused on supporting efforts in Green IT. What is e-cycling, and why should you, as a business professional, care about e-waste?

MyMISLab MyMISLab is an online learning and testing environment that features the perfect study tools to help you master the concepts covered in this chapter. Log in to MyMISLab to test your knowledge of key chapter concepts and explore additional practice tools, including videos, flashcards, annotated text figures, and more!

Key Terms and Concepts

Alignment 351

Bill 198 or Budget Measures Act 353

Business analysts 345

Certified Information Systems Auditor (CISA) 354

Chief information officer (CIO) 344

Chief technology officer (CTO) 344

Competitive strategy 349

Control Objectives for Information and Related Technology (COBIT) 354

E-cycling 358

ENERGY STAR 358

Enterprise architect 349

E-waste 358

Governance 352

Using Your Knowledge

1. Figure 11-3 illustrates the links between industry structure, competitive strategy, value chains, business processes, and information systems. As we have learned in this chapter, there can be misalignment between strategy and information systems. In your opinion, where do things go wrong, and how does misalignment occur? How do organizations get out of alignment?

2. Research the IT architecture at your university or college. Is an IT architecture available, and do you have enterprise architects? What IT architectural issues can you see developing, and how would you manage them?

3. Consider two car repair shops. One is newly renovated and has a bright, clean reception/office area at the front of the shop and standard company overalls for all employees. It has just invested in a new computer application that integrates its parts ordering, repair, and service cost estimates and accounting. Next door, the other repair shop has a small, dimly lit office at the rear of the shop, crammed with notes and papers. The office looks as though it was last painted in the early 1960s. It has no computer and still runs on a paper-based system. When you ask the owners of the two repair shops, they both state that their company's strategic objectives are well aligned with their IT planning and that each maintains a competitive advantage. How can this be true?

4. The goal of information systems governance is to improve the benefits of an organization's IT investment over time. However, people who are accountable for governance usually do not manage directly but sit on a corporate board that oversees the company's operations. What mechanisms can the board use to improve the benefits a company realizes from its IT investment? Use the web or other resources to provide some specific examples of board techniques to improve IT performance.

5. Explain how information systems governance and information systems audits are related. Can a firm complete an information systems audit without having information systems governance in place? Can information systems governance exist without an information systems audit?

6. The Zachman framework is explained in detail at www.zachmaninternational.com. Use this information and the Zachman framework to develop a diagram of your personal IT architecture. Remember to include all the technical support you would use (including resources and school as well as mobile devices).

7. COBIT is just one method for developing a document to support information systems governance. Identify reasons why companies would choose not to use COBIT for an information systems audit. Search the web for at least one other method, and develop a comparison between this method and COBIT. What are the benefits of using the new method? Can you suggest ways to improve COBIT?

Collaborative Exercises

1. This chapter introduced the concept of Green IT. Do some research into methods that will help make your personal computing more green. To complete the assignment, your team should do the following:
   a. Identify at least three things that you can do to reduce the energy consumption of your everyday computing resources.
   b. Estimate the savings that your group could achieve from the above recommendations.
   c. Combine what you have learned in parts (a) and (b) and create a one-page description of your proposal to reduce energy consumption. Your description should be aimed at people who are not familiar with green computing. Be prepared to share your document with the class.

2. Read the "What Do YOU Think?" titled "The Ethics of Misdirected Information" on pages 364–365.
   a. Discuss your answers to the questions, and talk about any differences you may have. Try to form a consensus, and come up with a set of group answers to the questions. Did your group find this to be a difficult task? Why, or why not?
   b. What did you learn about ethics from this exercise? Be prepared to share your thoughts with the class.

Case Study 11

Governance at Pacific Blue Cross

The data on information systems projects almost speaks for itself. Although better than its 1994 survey results, the 2004 Standish Group (www.standishgroup.com) survey on IT projects found that only 34 percent of these projects could be considered successes (on time, on budget, and delivering the desired benefits), 51 percent were challenged (delivered late, exceeded their budget, or lacked critical features and requirements), and a full 15 percent were out-and-out failures.

For Dr. Catherine Boivie, a large part of the solution begins with governance. Before joining Pacific Blue Cross (PBC)—British Columbia's leading provider of extended health and dental benefits—as chief information officer and senior vice-president, her impression of IT projects was that although all of them were important to some aspect of the business, most IT departments were kept busy constantly putting out fires.

Governance, says Dr. Boivie, simply deals with who makes which decisions and does not have to be complex; it consists of four iterative steps:

1. Identify the areas that require formal decision-making processes.

2. Document how decisions are currently made, the people involved, and their role (i.e., do they recommend, approve, or concur with the decision, or do they provide input or need to be notified?).

3. Use this information as input into a discussion of how decision processes could be improved.

4. Develop a plan for implementing the new processes—including communication and buy-in with all affected parties.

Building on these ideas, Dr. Boivie's first action at PBC was to make certain that her two foundational principles—that technology has no value by itself and that the technology management department must switch its focus from operations to business enablement—were shared by the chief executive officer. Once this was done and after working through the governance stages, PBC implemented a process to ensure that all projects under consideration were evaluated using the same mechanism and criteria. Using the Balanced Scorecard approach,[10] the strategic alignment, architecture, business process impact, direct payback, and risk of each project were measured against qualitative and quantitative perspectives and infrastructure, clients, people, and community-related goals.

The project approval process consists of five decision stages or gates. The first gate, sometimes called the "Thumbs Up/Down" stage, requires sponsorship by a vice-president who presents the idea to the executive committee. If approved, the project proceeds to gate two, which requires a business case outlining the costs and benefits. Gates three and four are similar, but have minimum price floors of $500 000 and $1 000 000 or include projects that are considered much more organizationally or technologically complex. Projects at these gates require comprehensive definition and analysis. Gate five is the post implementation review, which verifies and validates the costs and attainment of the benefits previously described in the business case.

Ongoing project reports are provided to the executive committee and board of directors using an aptly named "Traffic-Light Report." This report visually identifies, with red, yellow, or green symbols, whether a project is on time, on budget, and on scope.

Dr. Boivie does plan further enhancements, but so far, the process seems to be working. Business leaders have welcomed the new process and noted that it gives them enhanced visibility, a much better view of all projects, and greater control and accountability.

Questions

1. What are the various roles of decision-making participants at PBC?
2. How important is communication and buy-in to implementing the new system?
3. Can you think of reasons why an organization would resist governance processes?
4. What challenges may exist in the system?
5. Are the foundational principles valid or reasonable? Why did Dr. Boivie make sure these principles were shared by the CEO?

[10] R. S. Kaplan and D. P. Norton, *The Balanced Scorecard: Translating Strategy into Action* (Boston, MA: Harvard Business School Press, 1996).

The Ethics of Misdirected Information

Consider the following situations:

Situation A: Suppose you are buying a condominium and you know that at least one other party is bidding against you. While agonizing over your best strategy, you stop at a local Starbucks. As you sip your latte, you overhear a conversation at the table next to yours. Three people are talking so loudly that it is difficult to ignore them, and you soon realize that they are the real estate agent and the couple who is competing for the condo you want to buy. They are preparing their offer. Should you listen to their conversation? If you do, do you use the information you hear to your advantage?

Situation B: Consider the same situation from a different perspective—instead of overhearing the conversation, suppose you receive that same information in an email. Perhaps an administrative assistant at the agent's office confuses you and the other customer and mistakenly sends you the terms of the other party's offer. Do you read the email? If so, do you use the information you now have to your advantage?

Situation C: Suppose you sell computer software. In the midst of a sensitive price negotiation, your customer accidentally sends you an internal email that contains the maximum amount the customer can pay for your software. Do you read that email? Do you use the information it contains to guide your negotiating strategy? What do you do if your customer discovers that the email may have reached you and asks, "Did you read my email?" How do you answer?

Situation D: Suppose a friend mistakenly sends you an email that contains sensitive personal medical data. You read the email before you realize what you were reading, and you are embarrassed to learn something very personal about your friend that truly is none of your business. Your friend asks, "Did you read that email?" How do you respond?

Situation E: Suppose you work as a network administrator and that your position allows you unrestricted access to your company's mailing lists. Assume that you have the skill to insert your email address into any company mailing list without anyone knowing about it. You insert your address into several lists and, consequently, begin to receive confidential email that no one intended for you to see. One of those emails indicates that your best friend's department is about to be eliminated and all of its personnel fired. Do you warn your friend?

Discussion Questions

1. Do your answers to the questions in situations A and B differ? Does the medium through which the information is obtained make a difference? Is it easier to avoid reading an email than it is to avoid overhearing a conversation? If so, does that difference matter?

2. Do your answers to the questions in situations B and C differ? In situation B, the information is for your personal gain; in C, the information is for both your personal gain and your organization's gain. Does this difference matter? How do you respond when asked if you have read the email?

3. Do your answers to the questions in situations C and D differ? Would you lie in one case and not in the other? Why, or why not?

4. Answer the question in situation E. What is the essential difference between situations A through D and situation E? Suppose you had to justify your behaviour in situation E. How would you argue? Do you believe your own argument?

5. In situations A through D, if you access the information, you have done nothing illegal. You were the passive recipient. Even in situation E, although you undoubtedly violated your company's employment policies, you most likely did not break the law. So, for this discussion, assume that all of these actions are legal.

   a. What is the difference between *legal* and *ethical*? Look up both terms in a dictionary, and explain how they differ.

   b. Make the argument that business is inherently competitive, and that if something is legal, then it is acceptable to do it if it helps to further your goals.

   c. Make the argument that it is never appropriate to do something unethical.

6. Summarize your beliefs about proper conduct when you receive misdirected information.

12 Managing Information Security and Privacy

Running Case

It was Sunday and Akbar was looking forward to some well-deserved rest and relaxation. He was just about to leave for his trip to the Bahamas when he received a call from one of his workers. "Did you leave the water on last night?" his employee said, "because the floor is flooded. Our servers are all under three inches of water." Akbar froze in his tracks.

Those servers were his company's lifeblood. Everything ran on them. Having had some previous experience with disasters, Akbar had backed up each of his servers, but all of the backups were in the same room. It looked like Akbar's Sunday was not going to be as relaxing as he had hoped it would be.

When Akbar got to his office, he realized two things. First, the water had come from a leak upstairs in a part of the building Akbar did not have access to. He was happy that the flooding was not his fault, but it really did not change the outcome. Second, he immediately called a disaster recovery company that specialized in fire and water restorations. He had used them once before, and they had been able to get back almost all of his data. They had four pieces of advice for him:

1. Never assume that data are lost for good. You would be surprised what can be salvaged even from a damaged hard drive.
2. Do not shake a damaged hard drive or server. Let the professionals move it.
3. Do not dry a wet hard drive by opening it and using a hairdryer.
4. Do not freeze or refrigerate IT equipment.

Akbar's experience enabled him to react quickly and appropriately, and he was able to restore more than 98 percent of the data that he had prior to the accident. The accident had slowed his business down for more than two weeks, and it was two days before he was able to get some systems to support his day-to-day work.

Having lived through another scare, Akbar was determined to never let it happen again. He decided to invest in a disaster recovery plan for his company. He had suggested and even completed some disaster plans for other companies. Now he was going to take his own advice.

Rawpixel/Shutterstock

Study Questions

Q1 **What is identity theft?**

Q2 **What is PIPEDA?**

Q3 **What types of security threats do organizations face?**

Q4 **How can technical safeguards protect against security threats?**

Q5 **How can data safeguards protect against security threats?**

Q6 **How can human safeguards protect against security threats?**

Q7 **What is disaster preparedness?**

Q8 **How should organizations respond to security incidents?**

Q1 What Is Identity Theft?

We begin this chapter by considering your personal security and one of the fastest growing threats to it—identity theft. It is very important to be aware of security issues. Once you are aware of threats to your own security, it is often easier to consider security threats to the organizations you work for. The focus of this chapter is on understanding and managing security threats to organizations, but understanding threats to your own privacy will help make you more sensitive to the importance of security and privacy.

Consider all of the things you do in a day and how many of those things revolve around electronic information. If someone else had your personal information, what could they do with it? In **identity theft**, vital information, such as a person's name, address, date of birth, social insurance number, and mother's maiden name, are often all that is needed to facilitate impersonation. With this information, the identity thief can take over a victim's financial accounts; open new bank accounts; transfer bank balances; apply for loans, credit cards, and other services; purchase vehicles; take luxury vacations; and so on.

Identity theft is one of the fastest-growing crimes in Canada because it is relatively easy to do. This kind of theft involves stealing, misrepresenting, or hijacking the identity of another person or business and provides an effective way to commit other crimes. The Public Safety Canada website (www.publicsafety.gc.ca/prg/le/bs/identhft-eng.aspx) provides useful information about what identify theft is and who to contact if it happens to you. You can read about protecting yourself from identify theft in the box on page 369.

Q2 What Is PIPEDA?

We all do business with many companies. Every time we buy or ask for something, we create a transaction. When you interact with organizations, you often leave behind personal information about yourself. Your name, address, debit card number, and other behaviours are information, and they can be of great value to an organization. The **Personal Information Protection and Electronic Documents Act (PIPEDA)** is intended to balance an individual's right to the privacy of his or her personal information with an organization's need to collect, use, and share that personal information for business purposes. To oversee this Act, the Privacy Commissioner of Canada was created as the ombudsman for privacy complaints in Canada.

Every Canadian business professional needs to be aware of PIPEDA because it governs how data are collected and used. One of the most critical elements in PIPEDA is the principle that individuals have the right to know what type of information an organization collects about them and also how that information is going to be used. PIPEDA suggests that organizations should not use the information collected for any purpose other than what the organization agreed to use it for. For example, if an organization collects information about a customer, it cannot sell or move that information to another company unless it initially told the customer that the organization may share personal information with others. PIPEDA, therefore, creates some protection of personal privacy.

A second responsibility that an organization takes on when it collects personal information is securing that information. PIPEDA suggests that it is the duty of an organization to protect the information it collects. To ensure this, PIPEDA provides an individual with the right to know who in the organization is responsible for securing the information. PIPEDA also requires that this information be complete, up to date, and accurate.

When organizations collect information, PIPEDA ensures that they do so only by fair means and that their terms and policies are clearly expressed so that people

---

PROTECTING YOURSELF FROM IDENTITY THEFT

According to www.safecanada.ca, you can do many simple things to lower your risk of identity theft:

- When someone asks for information, especially identification, ask why they need it and what they will use it for before agreeing to provide it.
- Buy a shredder, and *use* it. Shred all personal or financial information.
- Carry only the identification and credit card(s) you will need that day. You rarely need to carry your birth certificate, Social Insurance Number (SIN) card, health card, or passport every day.
- Cut up expired and unused credit cards. The numbers on these cards could still be used by an identity thief.
- Do not fill in forms for contests, rebates, or draws that ask for more information than you are prepared to give.
- Use the best available passwords and authentication methods (see the box on pages 381–382) on your credit card, financial, and other accounts, rather than easily available information, such as your mother's maiden name, your birthdate, parts of your phone number, or a series of consecutive numbers.
- Do not give personal information to anyone who phones or emails you unless you know who they are. Identity thieves may pose as representatives of financial institutions, internet service providers, or government agencies to get you to reveal identifying information.
- Wipe or erase (not just delete) personal data and information on electronic devices that you may resell or give away.

Be very careful with the identification you provide, especially if it is one of the main identity documents, such as a birth certificate, driver's licence, or Social Insurance Number (SIN). These source documents can be used to produce other identification (ID) and gain access to more of your personal and financial information.

Source: Based on Safe Canada, www.safecanada.ca.

---

understand them before using the services of the organizations. PIPEDA does not, however, facilitate individuals suing organizations. If issues arise that cannot be resolved between an individual and an organization, they should file a complaint with the Office of the Privacy Commissioner of Canada. The Privacy Commissioner then reviews the case and produces a report stating its conclusions. This report cannot be used directly to obtain compensation but can be used in a federal court when and if a lawsuit is filed.

PIPEDA has helped establish some confidence in the collection of digital information to support e-commerce. It does not completely establish personal privacy and cannot eliminate the problems of information theft. PIPEDA has, however, been used to reduce risk and safeguard the rights of individuals. PIPEDA has also helped assure other countries, such as those of the European Union, that Canadian laws on personal information privacy are sufficient to protect the rights of their citizens.

Q3 What Types of Security Threats Do Organizations Face?

It is not just individuals who face threats to their security. Organizations face the same threats. There are three sources of **security threats**: (1) human error and mistakes, (2) malicious human activity, and (3) natural events and disasters.

Figure 12-1

Security Threats

		Source		
		Human Error	**Malicious Human Activity**	**Natural Events and Disasters**
Problem	**Unauthorized data disclosure**	Procedural mistakes	Pretexting Phishing Spoofing Sniffing Computer crime	Disclosure during recovery
	Incorrect data modification	Procedural mistakes Incorrect procedures Ineffective accounting controls System errors	Hacking Computer crime	Incorrect data recovery
	Faulty service	Procedural mistakes Development and installation errors	Computer crime Usurpation	Service improperly restored
	Denial of service	Accidents	DOS attacks	Service interruption
	Loss of infrastructure	Accidents	Theft Terrorist activity	Property loss

Human errors and mistakes include accidental problems caused by both employees and others outside the organization. An example is an employee who misunderstands operating procedures and accidentally deletes customer records; another example is a physical accident, such as an employee driving a forklift through the wall of a computer room.

The second source is *malicious human activity*. This category includes employees and others who intentionally destroy data or other system components. It also includes hackers who break into a system, virus and worm writers who infect computer systems, and people who send millions of unwanted emails (referred to as **spam**).

Natural events and disasters are the third source of security problems. This category includes fires, floods, hurricanes, earthquakes, tsunamis, avalanches, and other acts of nature or accidents. Problems in this category include not only the initial loss of capability and service but also losses stemming from actions to recover from the initial problem.

Figure 12-1 summarizes threats by type of problem and source. Five types of security problems are listed: (1) *unauthorized data disclosure*, (2) *incorrect data modification*, (3) *faulty service*, (4) *denial of service*, and (5) *loss of infrastructure*. We will consider each type below.

Unauthorized Data Disclosure

Unauthorized data disclosure can occur by human error when someone inadvertently releases data in violation of policy. An example at a university would be a new department administrator who posts student names, numbers, and grades in a public place, when the releasing of names and grades violates provincial law. In Canada, this type of disclosure is covered by PIPEDA. Personal information is defined under this act as information about an identifiable individual but does not include the name, title, business address, or telephone number of an employee of an organization. The Act gives individuals the right to know why an organization collects, uses, or discloses personal information. So, organizations are required to identify why they are collecting information and how they will use it. As we noted earlier, PIPEDA also requires organizations to identify anyone in the organization responsible for keeping personal information private and secure and who allows other individuals to have access to this information, as necessary, to check its accuracy.[1]

The popularity and efficacy of search engines have created another source of inadvertent disclosure. Employees who place restricted data on websites that can be uncovered by search engines may mistakenly publish proprietary or restricted data over the web.

Of course, proprietary and personal data can also be released maliciously. **Pretexting** occurs when someone deceives by pretending to be someone else. A common scam involves a telephone caller who pretends to be from a credit card company and claims to be checking the validity of credit card numbers: "I'm checking your MasterCard number; it begins with 5181. Can you verify the rest of the number?" The first four digits of most credit cards can be easily identified from the internet (Wikipedia, for example) and it is likely that the caller is attempting to obtain a complete and valid number.

Phishing is a similar technique for obtaining unauthorized data, and it uses pretexting via email. The *phisher* pretends to be a legitimate company and sends an email requesting confidential data, such as account numbers, social insurance numbers, account passwords, and so on. Phishing compromises legitimate brands and trademarks. Case Study 12, on pages 389–391, looks in more detail at some examples of phishing.

Spoofing is another term for someone pretending to be someone or somewhere else. If you pretend to be your professor, you are spoofing your professor. **IP spoofing** occurs when an intruder uses another site's IP (Internet Protocol) address as if it were that other site. An example of this is using an American IP address in place of a Canadian IP address in order to access the U.S. version of Netflix. **Email spoofing** is a synonym for phishing.

Sniffing is a technique for intercepting computer communications. With wired networks, sniffing requires a physical connection to the network. With wireless networks, no such connection is required—**drive-by sniffers** simply take computers with wireless connections through an area and search for unprotected wireless networks. They can monitor and intercept wireless traffic at will. Even protected wireless networks are vulnerable, as you will learn. Spyware and adware are two other sniffing techniques discussed later in this chapter.

Incorrect Data Modification

The second problem category in Figure 12-1 is *incorrect data modification*. Examples include incorrectly increasing a customer's discount or incorrectly modifying an employee's salary, earned days of vacation, or annual bonus. Other examples include placing incorrect information, such as incorrect price changes, on the company's website or portal or accidently giving a student the wrong grade. This happened to one of the authors of this textbook and interestingly enough only students who got lower grades advised the author. All students who got higher grades kept quiet.

Incorrect data modification can occur through human error when employees follow procedures incorrectly or when procedures have been incorrectly designed. For proper internal control on systems that process financial data or that control inventories of assets, such as products and equipment, companies should ensure separation of duties and authorities and have multiple checks and balances in place.

A final type of incorrect data modification caused by human error is *system errors*. An example is the lost-update problem discussed in Chapter 5.

---

[1]You can learn more about PIPEDA at www.priv.gc.ca/leg_c/leg_c_p_e.asp.

Hacking occurs when a person gains unauthorized access to a computer system. Although some people hack for the sheer joy of doing it, other hackers invade systems for the malicious purpose of stealing or modifying data. One major difference between computer crime and other types is that when data are stolen the original data are still there and there may be no trace of the crime. Computer criminals invade computer networks to obtain critical data or to manipulate the system for financial gain. Examples are reducing account balances or directing a shipment of goods to unauthorized locations and customers.

Faulty Service

The third problem category, *faulty service*, includes problems that result because of incorrect system operation. Faulty service could include incorrect data modification, as described above. It could also include systems that work incorrectly by sending the wrong goods to the customer or ordered goods to the wrong customer, incorrectly billing customers, or sending the wrong information to employees. Humans can inadvertently cause faulty service by making procedural mistakes. System developers can write programs incorrectly or make errors during the installation of hardware, software programs, and data.

Denial of Service

Human error in following procedures or a lack of procedures can result in **denial of service (DOS)**. For example, employees can inadvertently shut down a web server or corporate gateway router by starting a computationally intensive application. An online analytic processing (OLAP) application that uses the operational database management system (DBMS) can consume so many DBMS resources that order-entry transactions cannot get through.

Denial-of-service attacks are often launched maliciously. A malicious hacker can flood a web server, for example, with millions of bogus or fraudulent service requests that so occupy the server that it cannot service legitimate requests. Computer worms can infiltrate a network with so much artificial traffic that legitimate traffic cannot get through. Finally, natural disasters may cause systems to fail, resulting in denial of service.

Loss of Infrastructure

Human accidents can cause *loss of infrastructure*. Examples are a bulldozer cutting fibre-optic cables, or the maintenance staff unplugging an important device in order to plug in a vacuum cleaner.

Theft and terrorist events also cause loss of infrastructure. A disgruntled former employee or contractor (such as Eric Snowden) can walk off with corporate data servers, routers, or other crucial equipment. Terrorist events can also cause the loss of physical plants and equipment. Natural disasters present a large risk for infrastructure loss. A fire, flood, earthquake, or similar event can destroy data centres and all they contain. You may be wondering why Figure 12-1 does not include viruses, worms, and zombies. The answer is that viruses and worms are *techniques* for causing some of the problems in the figure. They can cause a denial-of-service attack, or they can be used to cause malicious, unauthorized data access or data loss.

Elements of a Security Program

All the problems listed in Figure 12-1 are as real and as serious as they sound. Accordingly, organizations must address security in a systematic way. A security program[2] has three components: (1) senior management involvement, (2) safeguards of various kinds, and (3) incident response.

---

[2]Note that the word *program* is used here in the sense of a management program that includes objectives, policies, procedures, directives, and so forth. Do not confuse this term with *computer program*.

Hardware	Software	Data	Procedures	People

Technical Safeguards	Data Safeguards	Human Safeguards
Identification and authentication	Data rights and responsibilities	Hiring
Encryption	Passwords	Training
Firewalls	Encryption	Education
Malware protection	Backup and recovery	Procedure design
Application design	Physical security	Administration
		Assessment
		Compliance
		Accountability

Effective security requires balanced attention to all five components!

Figure 12-2

Security Safeguards as They Relate to the Five Components

The first component, senior management, has two critical security functions. First, senior management must establish the security policy. This policy sets the stage for the organization's response to security threats. However, because no security program is perfect, there is always risk. Senior management's second function, therefore, is to manage risk by balancing the costs and benefits of the security program.

Safeguards are protections against security threats. An effective way to view safeguards is in terms of the five components of an information system, as shown in Figure 12-2. Some of the safeguards involve computer hardware and software; some involve data; and others involve procedures and people. In addition to these safeguards, organizations must also consider disaster-recovery safeguards.

The final component of a security program consists of the organization's planned response to security incidents. Clearly, the time to think about what to do is not when computers are crashing throughout the organization. We will discuss incident response in the last section of this chapter.

Q4 How Can Technical Safeguards Protect Against Security Threats?

Technical safeguards involve the hardware and software components of an information system. Figure 12-3 lists primary technical safeguards. We have discussed all of these safeguards in prior chapters. In this chapter, we will supplement those prior discussions.

👁 Watch

Go to MyMISLab to watch a video about information security management.

👁 Watch

Go to MyMISLab to watch a video about technical safeguards.

Figure 12-3

Technical Safeguards

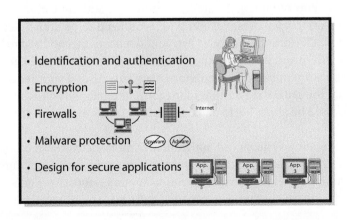

- Identification and authentication
- Encryption
- Firewalls
- Malware protection
- Design for secure applications

Identification and Authentication

Every non-trivial information system should require some form of authentication. Users should sign on with a user name and password, for example. The user name *identifies* the user (the process of **identification**), and the password *authenticates* that user (the process of **authentication**). See the box "How Can You Create a Strong Password?" on page 381 for more on this topic. Note that authentication methods fall into three categories: (1) what you know (password or PIN), (2) what you have (smart card), and (3) what you are (biometric).

Passwords have many weaknesses. First, users tend to be careless in their use. Despite repeated warnings to the contrary, yellow sticky notes holding written passwords adorn many computers. In addition, users tend to be free in sharing their passwords with others. Finally, many users choose ineffective, simple passwords or use the same password for many systems. Intrusion systems can very effectively guess these easy passwords.

These deficiencies can be reduced by using smart cards and biometric authentication.

Smart Cards

A **smart card** is a plastic card that is similar to a credit card. Unlike credit, debit, and ATM (automatic teller machine) cards, which have a magnetic strip; smart cards have a microchip. The microchip, which holds far more data than a magnetic strip, is loaded with identifying data or algorithms. Users of smart cards are required to enter a **personal identification number (PIN)** to be authenticated. Alternatively, smart cards can enable **challenge-response** authentication, in which a new password is generated at each login by an algorithm accessed by or stored on the chip. In a simple example (the real algorithms are highly sophisticated), the chip uses a 'multiply by 2 and subtract 1' formula to validate the correct user. When challenged with '8', the correct response would be '15', and, since the challenge varies each time, responding '15' (rather than '5') to a challenge of '3' would be invalid.

Biometric Authentication

Biometric authentication uses personal physical characteristics, such as fingerprints, facial features, and retinal scans, to authenticate users. Biometric authentication can provide strong authentication, but the required equipment is expensive. Often, too, users resist biometric identification because they feel it is invasive and sometimes simple work-arounds, such as using a photograph to bypass facial recognition, are quickly discovered and publicized.

Single Sign-On for Multiple Systems

Information systems often require multiple sources of authentication. For example, when you sign on to your personal computer, you need to be authenticated. When you access the LAN (local area network) in your department, you need to be authenticated again. When you traverse your organization's WAN (wide area network), you will need to be authenticated to even more networks. Also, if your request requires database data, the DBMS server that manages that database will authenticate you yet again. It would be annoying to enter a name and password for every one of these resources.

Today's operating systems can authenticate you to networks and other servers. You sign on to your local computer and provide authentication data; from that point on, your operating system authenticates you to another network or server, which can authenticate you to yet another network and server, and so on.

Encryption and Firewalls

The next two categories of technical safeguards, as shown in Figure 12-3, are encryption and firewalls. In Chapter 6, firewalls were discussed briefly and encryption was noted in the discussion of VPNs (virtual private networks). We will not repeat that discussion here. You should just understand that they are very important technical safeguards.

Malware Protection

The next technical safeguard in our list in Figure 12-3 is malware. The term **malware** has several definitions. Here we use the broadest one: *malware* includes viruses, worms, Trojan horses, spyware, and adware. We discussed viruses, worms, and zombies in Chapter 4; you should review that material now if you have forgotten the definitions.

Spyware and Adware

Spyware programs are installed on the user's computer without the user's knowledge or permission. Spyware resides in the background and, without the user's knowledge, observes the user's actions and keystrokes, monitors computer activity, and reports that activity to sponsoring organizations. Some malicious spyware captures keystrokes to obtain user names, passwords, account numbers, and other sensitive information. Other spyware supports marketing analyses, observing what users do, the websites they visit, the products they examine and purchase, and so on.

Adware is similar to spyware in that it is installed without the user's permission and resides in the background to observe user behaviour. Most adware is benign in that it does not perform malicious acts or steal data. It does, however, watch user activity and produce pop-up ads. Adware can also change the user's default window or modify search results and switch the user's search engine. For the most part, it is simply annoying, but users should be concerned any time they discover unknown programs on their computers that perform unrequested functions.

Figure 12-4 lists some of the symptoms of adware and spyware. Sometimes, these symptoms develop slowly over time as more malware components are installed. Should these symptoms occur on your computer, you can remove the spyware or adware using anti-malware programs.

Malware Safeguards

Unfortunately, viruses and malware are a growing problem. Most safeguards require that the virus first be identified, so antivirus systems are predominantly reactive rather than proactive. However, many of the existing or known problems can be avoided by adhering to the following safeguards:

1. *Install antivirus and anti-spyware programs.* Your IT department will have a list of recommended (perhaps required) programs for this purpose. If you choose a

- Slow system start-up
- Sluggish system performance
- Many pop-up advertisements
- Suspicious browser homepage changes
- Suspicious changes to the taskbar and other system interfaces
- Unusual hard-disk activity

Figure 12-4

Spyware and Adware Symptoms

program yourself, make sure it is from a reputable vendor. Check reviews of anti-malware software on the Web before purchasing.

2. *Set up your anti-malware programs to scan your computer frequently.* You should scan your computer at least once a week, possibly more often. When you detect malware code, use the anti-malware software to remove it. If the code cannot be removed, contact your IT department or anti-malware vendor.

3. *Update malware definitions.* **Malware definitions**—patterns that exist in malware code—should be downloaded frequently. Anti-malware vendors update these definitions continually, and you should install these updates as they become available.

4. *Open email attachments only from known sources.* As well, even when opening attachments from known sources, do so with great care. According to professor and security expert Ray Panko, about 90 percent of all viruses are spread through email attachments.[3] This statistic is not surprising because most organizations are protected by firewalls. With a properly configured firewall, email is the only outside-initiated traffic that can reach user computers.

   Most anti-malware programs check email attachments for malware code. However, all users should form the habit of *never* opening an email attachment from an unknown source. Also, if you receive an unexpected email from a known source or an email from a known source that has a suspicious subject, odd spelling, or poor grammar, do not open the attachment without first verifying with the source that the attachment is legitimate.

5. *Promptly install software updates from legitimate sources.* Unfortunately, all programs are chock full of security holes; vendors are fixing them as rapidly as they are discovered, but the practice is inexact. Install patches to the operating system and application programs promptly.

6. *Browse only in reputable internet neighbourhoods.* It is possible for some malware to install itself when you do nothing more than open a webpage. Do not go there!

Q5 How Can Data Safeguards Protect Against Security Threats?

Data safeguards protect databases and other organizational data. Two organizational units are responsible for data safeguards. **Data administration** refers to an organization-wide function that is in charge of developing data policies and enforcing data standards. As discussed in Chapter 11, data administration is typically a staff function reporting to the chief information officer (CIO).

Database administration refers to a function that pertains to a particular database. The enterprise resource planning (ERP), customer relationship management (CRM), and supply chain management (SCM) databases each have a database administration function. Database administration ensures that procedures exist to facilitate orderly multiuser processing of the database, to control changes to the database structure, and to protect the database.

Both data and database administration are involved in establishing the data safeguards shown in Figure 12-5. First, data administration should define data policies that govern how customer data will be used and shared—for example, "We will not share identifying customer data with any other organization." Then, data administration and database administration(s) work together to specify user data rights and

[3]R. Panko, *Corporate Computer and Network Security* (Upper Saddle River, NJ: Prentice Hall, 2004), p. 165.

- Defined data policies
- Data rights and responsibilities
- Rights enforced by user accounts authenticated by passwords
- Data encryption
- Backup and recovery procedures
- Physical security

Figure 12-5

Data Safeguards

responsibilities. Third, those rights should be enforced by user accounts that are authenticated by, at the minimum, passwords.

An organization should protect sensitive data by storing them in encrypted form. Such encryption uses one or more keys in ways similar to that described for data communication encryption. One potential problem with stored data, however, is that the key might be lost or that disgruntled or terminated employees might destroy it. Because of this possibility, when data are encrypted, a trusted party should have a copy of the encryption key. This safety procedure is sometimes called **key escrow**.

Another data safeguard is to periodically create backup copies of database contents. The organization should store at least some of these backups off the premises, possibly in a remote location. Additionally, IT personnel should periodically practise recovery, to ensure that the backups are valid and that effective recovery procedures exist. Do not assume that just because a backup is made, the database is protected.

Physical security is another data safeguard. The computers that run the DBMS and all devices that store database data should reside in secure, controlled-access facilities. If not, they are subject not only to theft but also to damage. For better security, the organization should keep a log showing who entered the facility, when, and for what purpose.

In some cases, organizations contract with other companies to manage their databases. If so, all the safeguards in Figure 12-5 should be part of the service contract. As well, the contract should give the owners of the data permission to inspect the premises of the database operator and to interview its personnel on a reasonable schedule.

Q6 How Can Human Safeguards Protect Against Security Threats?

Human safeguards involve the people and procedures components of information systems. In general, human safeguards result when authorized users follow appropriate procedures for system use and recovery. Restricting access to authorized users requires effective authentication methods and careful user account management. In addition, appropriate security procedures must be designed as part of every information system, and users should be trained in the importance and use of those procedures. In this section, we will consider the development of human safeguards, first for employees and then for non-employees.

Human Safeguards for Employees

Figure 12-6 lists security considerations for employees. We discuss these considerations below.

Figure 12-6

Security Policy for In-House Staff

- Position definition
  - Separate duties and authorities.
  - Determine least privilege.
  - Document position sensitivity.

"OK to pay this"

- Hiring and screening

"Where did you last work?"

- Dissemination and enforcement (responsibility, accountability, compliance)

"Lets talk security..."

- Termination
  - Friendly

"Congratulations on your new job."

  - Unfriendly

"We've closed your accounts. Goodbye."

Position Definitions

Effective human safeguards begin with creating definitions of job tasks and responsibilities. In general, job descriptions should provide a separation of duties and authorities. For example, no single individual should be allowed both to approve expenses and to write cheques. Instead, one person should approve expenses, another should pay them, and a third should account for the payment. Similarly, in inventory, no single person should be allowed to authorize an inventory withdrawal and also to remove the items from inventory.

Given appropriate job descriptions, user accounts should be defined to give users the *least possible privilege* needed to perform their jobs. For example, users whose job description does not include modifying data should be given accounts with read-only privileges. Similarly, user accounts should prohibit users from accessing data that their job description does not require. Because of the problem of security, even access to seemingly innocuous data may need to be limited.

Finally, the security sensitivity should be documented for each position. Some jobs involve highly sensitive data (e.g., employee compensation, salesperson quotas, and proprietary marketing or technical data). Other positions involve no sensitive data. Documenting *position sensitivity* enables security personnel to prioritize their activities in accordance with the possible risk and loss. The "MIS in Use" on pages 384–385 provides an example of the need for position sensitivity.

Hiring and Screening

Security considerations should be part of the hiring process. Of course, if a position involves no sensitive data and no access to information systems, then screening for information systems security purposes will be minimal. When hiring for high-sensitivity positions, however, extensive interviews, references, and background investigations are appropriate. Note, too, that security screening applies not only to new employees but also to employees who are promoted to sensitive positions.

Dissemination and Enforcement

Employees cannot be expected to follow security policies and procedures that they are not aware of. Therefore, employees need to be made aware of the security policies and procedures and of their responsibilities. Employee security training begins during new-employee orientation. This general training must increase in accordance with the position's sensitivity and responsibilities. When employees are promoted, they should receive the security training that their new position requires. As well, the company should not provide user accounts and passwords until employees have completed required security training.

Enforcement consists of three interdependent factors: (1) responsibility, (2) accountability, and (3) compliance. First, the company should clearly define the security *responsibilities* of each position. The design of the security program should be such that employees can be held *accountable* for security violations. Second, procedures should exist so that when critical data are lost, it is possible to determine how the loss occurred and who is accountable. Finally, the security program should encourage security *compliance*. Employee activities should be regularly monitored for compliance, and management should specify action to be taken in the event of noncompliance.

MIS in Use

What Is My True Name?

Howard Roark, a professor at a large Canadian university, would often log on to the websites of various textbook publishers to review or order copies of textbooks he was considering for his courses or to obtain access to restricted instructor materials, such as test banks and sample examinations.

Registering with a publisher was usually a relatively simple process of completing an online request form on the website with information, such as name, university, and contact details. Once verified by the publisher (usually by email or telephone), log-in information (an ID and password) would then be emailed back to the professor.

One day, as he was reading an email message from a publisher, Roark wondered whether the existing processes were adequate.

The publisher had noticed that the email address used in a recent request for access did not match the email address on file for Roark, and so the publisher asked him to confirm that it was valid. Rather than the standard university address of Howard.Roark@universitydomain.com, a new account had been set up at a generic email service (such as Yahoo! or Hotmail) with the same name (i.e., Howard.Roark@emailservice.com). All other details in the request, such as address, title, and so on, were correct.

Roark was alarmed—was someone trying to impersonate him? What could he do about it?

Questions

1. Why do you think this situation has occurred? (*Hint:* Who could benefit from this?)

2. Who has been harmed (if anyone), or is this a victimless situation?

3. Are the registration procedures adequate? What changes, if any, would you recommend?

4. What action should be taken by Roark, the university, or the publisher? Does it matter where the request came from (e.g., what if it was a student at Roark's university)?

5. Is this a case of identity theft?

6. Assuming that the individual is identified, what would be an appropriate penalty?

Management attitude is crucial: If managers write passwords on staff bulletin boards, shout passwords down hallways, or ignore physical security procedures, then employee security attitudes and employee security compliance will suffer.

Termination

Companies also must establish security policies and procedures for the termination of employees. Most employee terminations are friendly and occur as the result of promotion, retirement, or when the employee resigns to take another position. Standard human resources policies should ensure that system administrators receive notification in advance of the employee's last day so that they can remove accounts and passwords. The need to recover keys for encrypted data and any other special security requirements should be part of the employee's out-processing.

Unfriendly termination is more difficult because employees may be tempted to take malicious or harmful actions in retaliation for the termination. If such a possibility exists, system administrators may need to remove user accounts and passwords prior to notifying the employee of his or her termination. Other actions may also be needed to protect the company's information assets. A terminated sales employee, for example, may attempt to take the company's confidential customer and sales-prospect data for future use at another company.

As the line between personal and professional time becomes more blurred and more companies employ a "Bring Your Own Device" (BYOD) strategy, data protection has become more complicated. In one case, for example, an employee found that their personal telephone was reset back to the original condition (erasing many personal photographs) within hours of resigning from their position.

The human resources department should be aware of the importance of giving information systems administrators early notification of employee termination. No blanket policy exists; the information systems department must assess each case on an individual basis.

Human Safeguards for Non-employees

Business requirements may necessitate opening information systems to non-employees—temporary personnel, vendors, partner personnel (employees of business partners), volunteers, and the public. Although temporary personnel can be screened, to reduce costs the screening process is often reduced compared with that for employees. In most cases, companies cannot screen vendor or partner personnel and public users cannot be screened at all. Similar limitations apply to security training and compliance testing.

In the case of temporary, vendor, and partner personnel, the contracts that govern the activity should call for security measures appropriate to the sensitivity of the data and the information systems resources involved. The situation differs for public users of websites. In general, the best safeguard from threats from public users is to *harden* the website or other facility against attack as much as possible. **Hardening** a site means to take extraordinary measures to reduce a system's vulnerability. Hardened sites use special versions of the operating system and lock down or eliminate operating system features and functions that are not required by the application. Hardening is actually a technical safeguard, but we mention it here as the most important safeguard against public users.

Finally, note that the business relationship with the public, and with some partners, differs from that with temporary personnel and vendors. The public and some partners use the information system to receive a benefit. Consequently, safeguards need to protect such users from internal company security problems. A disgruntled employee who maliciously changes prices on a website potentially damages both public users and business partners. As one experienced IT manager put it, "Rather than protecting ourselves from them, we need to protect them from us."

I hereby acknowledge personal receipt of the system password(s) associated with the user IDs listed below. I understand that I am responsible for protecting the password(s), will comply with all applicable system security standards, and will not divulge my password(s) to any person. I further understand that I must report to the Information Systems Security Officer any problem I encounter in the use of the password(s) or when I have reason to believe that the private nature of my password(s) has been compromised.

Figure 12-7

Sample Account Acknowledgment Form

Source: National Institute of Standards and Technology, *Introduction to Computer Security: The NIST Handbook,* Special Publication 800–812, p. 114.

Account Administration

The third human safeguard is account administration. The administration of user accounts, passwords, and help-desk policies and procedures is an important component of the security system.

Account Management

Account management concerns the creation of new user accounts, the modification of existing account permissions, and the removal of unneeded accounts. Information system administrators perform all these tasks, but account users are responsible for notifying the administrators of the need for these actions. The IT department should create standard procedures for this purpose. As a future user, you can improve your relationship with information systems personnel by providing early and timely notification of the need for account changes.

The existence of accounts that are no longer required or in use is a serious security threat. It can be difficult for information systems administrators to know if an account should be removed; so it is up to users and managers to provide this notification.

Password Management

Passwords are the primary means of authentication. They are important not just for access to the user's computer, but also for authentication to other networks and servers. Because of the importance of passwords, the National Institute of Standards and Technology (NIST) recommends that employees be required to sign statements similar to the one shown in Figure 12-7.

HOW CAN YOU CREATE A STRONG PASSWORD?

Whatever opportunities you find for using information systems in your career—and your life—one issue that will remain constant is the security of those systems. Security is vitally important. As a user of information systems in a business organization, you will be given a user name and password. You will be instructed to create a strong password, and it is vitally important for you to do so. (In fact, you should now be using such passwords at your university.) So, what is a strong password, and how do you create one?

Strong Passwords

Microsoft, a company that has many reasons to promote effective security, defines a strong password as one that has the following characteristics:

- Contains seven or more characters
- Does not contain your user name, real name, or company name

(continued)

- Does not contain a complete dictionary word in any language
- Is different from previous passwords you have used
- Contains both upper- and lowercase letters, numbers, and special characters (such as ~ ! @; # $ % ^ &; * () _ +; − =; { } | [ ] \ : "; ' <; >; ?,. /)

  Examples of good passwords are the following:
  - Qw37^T1bb?at
  - 3B47qq<3>5!7b

The problem with such passwords is that they are nearly impossible to remember. And the last thing you want to do is write your password on a piece of paper and keep it near your workstation. Never do that!

One technique for creating memorable, strong passwords is to base them on the first letter of the words in a phrase. The phrase could be the title of a song or the first line of a poem, or one based on some fact about your life. For example, you might take the phrase, "I was born in Calgary, Alberta, before 1990." Using the first letters from that phrase and substituting the character < for the word before, you create the password IwbiC,AB<1990. That is an acceptable password, but it would be better if all the numbers were not placed at the end. So, you might try the phrase, "I was born at 3:00 a.m. in Calgary, Alberta." That phrase yields the password Iwba3:00AMiC, AB—a strong password that is easily remembered.

Password Etiquette

Once you have created a strong password, you need to protect it. Proper password etiquette is one of the marks of a business professional. Never write down your password, and do not share it with others. Never ask others for their passwords, and never give your password to anyone else.

But what if you need someone else's password? Suppose, for example, you ask someone to help you with a problem on your computer. You sign on to an information system, and for some reason, you need to enter that other person's password. In this case, say to the other person, "We need your password," and then get out of your chair, offer your keyboard to the other person, and look away while he or she enters the password. Among professionals working in organizations that take security seriously, this little do-si-do move—one person getting out of the way so that another person can enter a password—is common and accepted.

If someone asks for your password, do not give it out. Instead, get up, go over to that person's machine, and enter your own password yourself. Be around while your password is in use, and ensure that your account is logged out at the end of the activity. No one should mind or be offended in any way when you do this. It is the mark of a professional.

When an account is created, users should immediately change the password they are given to a password of their own. In fact, well-constructed systems require the user to change the password on first use.

Additionally, users should change passwords frequently thereafter. Some systems require a password change every three months or even more frequently. Users grumble at the nuisance of making such changes, but frequent password changes reduce not only the risk of password loss but also the extent of damage if an existing password is compromised.

Some users create two passwords and switch back and forth between them. This strategy results in poor security, and some password systems do not allow the user to reuse recently used passwords. Again, users may view this policy as a nuisance, but it is important.

Help-Desk Policies

In the past, help desks have been a serious security risk. A user who had forgotten his password would call the help desk and plead for the help-desk representative to tell him his password or to reset the password to something else. "I can't get this report out without it!" was (and is) a common lament.

The problem for help-desk representatives is, of course, that they have no way of determining that they are talking to the true user. But they are in a difficult situation: If they do not help in some way, the help desk is perceived to be the unhelpful desk.

To resolve such problems, many systems give the help-desk representative a way of authenticating the user. Typically, the help-desk information system has answers to questions that only the true user would know, such as the user's birthplace, mother's maiden name, or last four digits of an important account number. Usually, when a password is changed, notification of that change is sent to the user in an email. Email, as you learned, is sent as plain text, however, so the new password itself ought not to be emailed. If you ever receive notification that your password was reset when you did not request it, immediately contact IT security. Someone has likely compromised your account.

System Procedures

Figure 12-8 shows a grid of procedure types—normal operation, backup, and recovery. Procedures of each type should exist for each information system. For example, the order-entry system will have procedures of each of these types, as will the web storefront, the inventory system, and so forth. The definition and use of standardized procedures reduces the likelihood of computer crime and other malicious activity by insiders. It also ensures that the system's security policy is enforced.

Procedures exist for both users and operations personnel. For each type of user, the company should develop procedures for normal, backup, and recovery operations. As a future user, you will be primarily concerned with user procedures. Normal-use procedures should provide safeguards appropriate to the sensitivity of the information system.

Backup procedures concern the creation of backup data to be used in the event of failure. Whereas operations personnel have the responsibility for backing up system databases and other systems data, departmental personnel need to back up data on their own computers. Good questions to ponder are, "What would happen if I lost my computer (tablet or phone) tomorrow?" "What would happen if someone dropped my device during an airport security inspection?" "What would happen if it was stolen?" Employees should ensure that they back up critical data on their computers. The IT department may help in this effort by designing backup procedures and making backup facilities available.

	System Users	Operations Personnel
Normal Operation	Use the system to perform job tasks, with security appropriate to sensitivity.	Operate data centre equipment, manage networks, run web servers, and do related operational tasks.
Backup	Prepare for loss of system functionality.	Back up website resources, databases, administrative data, account and password data, and other data.
Recovery	Accomplish job tasks during failure. Know tasks to do during system recovery.	Recover systems from backed-up data. Perform role of help desk during recovery.

Figure 12-8
System Procedures

Finally, systems analysts should develop procedures for system recovery. First, how will the department manage its affairs when a critical system is unavailable? Customers will want to order, and manufacturing will want to remove items from inventory even though a critical information system is unavailable. How will the department respond? Once the system is returned to service, how will records of business activities during the outage be entered into the system? How will service be resumed? The system developers should ask and answer these questions and others like them and develop procedures accordingly.

Security Monitoring

Security monitoring is the last of the human safeguards we will consider. Important monitoring functions are analysis of activity logs, security testing, and investigating and learning from security incidents.

Many information system programs produce *activity logs*. Firewalls produce logs of their activities, including lists of all dropped packets, infiltration attempts, and unauthorized access attempts from within the firewall. DBMS products produce logs of successful and failed log-ins. Web servers produce voluminous logs of web activities. The operating systems in personal computers can produce logs of log-ins and firewall activities.

Privacy and the Federal Government

Social networking sites, such as Facebook, LinkedIn, Pinterest, and Twitter, are cultural phenomena that have attracted billions of people. These sites let users easily communicate with existing friends, gather new ones, and re-establish contact with others who may have moved away or become temporarily forgotten. However, while there is no doubt of their popularity, some serious concerns have been raised about their impact on productivity and personal privacy.

Acting on a complaint from the Canadian Internet Policy and Public Interest Clinic (CIPPIC), the Office of the Privacy Commissioner of Canada (www.priv.gc.ca) filed a multifaceted complaint against Facebook Inc. in 12 areas, ranging from the collection of members'

birthdates during registration to the sharing of users' personal information with third-party application developers. After a series of meetings with Facebook and a cooperative investigation in June 2009, the Privacy Commissioner found that four of the concerns were unfounded and could be dismissed and that four others, although reasonable, had been addressed by Facebook or could be controlled by the individual settings made by each user (e.g., changing the default privacy options).

On the remaining subjects of third-party applications, account deactivation and deletion, accounts of deceased users, and nonusers' personal information, the Privacy Commissioner found Facebook to be in contravention of the Privacy Act. Most notably, regarding third-party applications, the Privacy Commissioner determined that Facebook did not have adequate safeguards in place to prevent unauthorized access to users' personal information and was not doing enough to ensure that meaningful consent had been obtained.

Questions

1. **How important are such agencies as the Office of the Privacy Commissioner of Canada?**

2. **What tools does the Privacy Commissioner have, and how can they be used? (*Hint:* Does it matter if the organization in question resides outside of Canada?)**

3. **How might Facebook respond to the Privacy Commissioner?**

4. **How does an organization respond to conflicting privacy issues (e.g., PIPEDA and the U.S. Patriot Act)?**

None of these logs adds any value to an organization unless they are used. Accordingly, an important security function is to analyze these logs for threat patterns, successful and unsuccessful attacks, and evidence of security vulnerabilities.

Additionally, companies should test their security programs. Both in-house personnel and outside security consultants should conduct such testing.

Another important monitoring function is to investigate security incidents. How did the problem occur? Have safeguards been created to prevent a recurrence of such problems? Does the incident indicate vulnerabilities in other portions of the security system? What else can be learned from the incident?

Security systems reside in a dynamic environment. Organizational structures change: Companies are acquired or sold; mergers occur. New systems require new security measures. New technology changes the security landscape, and new threats arise. Security personnel must constantly monitor the situation and determine whether the existing security policy and safeguards are adequate. If changes are needed, security personnel need to take appropriate action.

Security, like quality, is an ongoing process. There is no final state that represents a secure system or company. Instead, companies must monitor security on a continuing basis.

Q7 **What Is Disaster Preparedness?**

A substantial loss of computing infrastructure caused by acts of nature, crime, or terrorist activity can be disastrous for an organization. Of course, the best way to solve a problem is to prevent it. The best safeguard against a disaster is appropriate location. If possible, place computing centres, web farms, and other computer facilities in locations not prone to floods, earthquakes, hurricanes, tornados, or avalanches. Even in those locations, place infrastructure in unobtrusive buildings, basements, back rooms, and similar locations well within the physical perimeter of the organization. As well, locate computing infrastructure in fire-resistant buildings designed to house expensive and critical equipment.

Sometimes, however, business requirements necessitate locating the computing infrastructure in undesirable locations. And, even at a seemingly ideal location, disasters do occur. Therefore, some businesses prepare backup processing centres in locations geographically removed from the primary processing site.

Figure 12-9 lists major disaster preparedness tasks. After choosing a safe location for the computing infrastructure, the organization should identify all mission-critical systems. These are systems without which the organization cannot carry on and which, if lost for any period, could cause the organization's failure. The next step is to identify all resources necessary to run those systems. Such resources include computers, operating systems, application programs, databases, administrative data, procedure documentation, and trained personnel.

Next, the organization creates backups for the critical resources at the remote processing centre. So-called **hot sites** are remote processing centres and may be run by commercial disaster-recovery services. For a monthly fee, they provide all the equipment needed to continue operations following a disaster and there may be minimal

- Locate infrastructure in safe location.
- Identify mission-critical systems.
- Identify resources needed to run those systems.
- Prepare remote backup facilities.
- Train and rehearse.

Figure 12-9
Disaster Preparedness Guidelines

downtime or unavailability following a disaster. **Cold sites**, in contrast, provide space and limited technology and customers provide and install the equipment needed to continue operations following a disaster. Recovery time is considerably longer. **Warm sites** are somewhere in the middle of the two extremes.

Once the organization has backups in place, it must train and rehearse cutover of operations from the primary centre to the backup. Periodic refresher rehearsals are mandatory.

Preparing a backup facility is very expensive; however, the costs of establishing and maintaining that facility are a form of insurance. Senior management must decide whether to prepare such a facility by balancing the risks, benefits, and costs. In some cases where the service is considered essential, for example banking, backup sites and disaster plans are required by law.

Q8 How Should Organizations Respond to Security Incidents?

The last component of a security plan we will consider is incident response. Figure 12-10 lists its major factors. Every organization should have an incident-response plan as part of the security program. No organization should wait until some asset has been lost or compromised before deciding what to do. The plan should include how employees are to respond to security problems, whom they should contact, the reports they should make, and steps they can take to reduce further loss.

Consider, for example, a virus. An incident-response plan will stipulate what action is to be taken in the event of a virus. It should specify whom to contact and what to do. It may stipulate that the employee should turn off his or her computer and physically disconnect from the network or shut down the server. The plan should also indicate what users with wireless computers should do.

The plan should provide centralized reporting of all security incidents. Such reporting will enable an organization to determine whether it is under systemic attack or whether an incident is isolated. Centralized reporting also allows the organization to learn about security threats, take consistent actions in response, and apply specialized expertise to all security problems.

When an incident does occur, speed is of the essence. Viruses and worms can spread very quickly across an organization's networks, and a fast response will help mitigate the consequences. Because of the need for speed, preparation pays. The incident-response plan should identify critical personnel and their off-hours contact information. These personnel should be trained in where to go and what to do when they get there. Without adequate preparation, there is substantial risk that the actions of well-meaning people will make the problem worse. Also, there may be many rumours and incorrect or inappropriate ideas about what to do. A team of well-informed, trained personnel will serve to dampen such rumours.

Finally, organizations should periodically practise incident response. Without such practice, personnel will be poorly informed on the response plan, and the plan itself may have flaws that become apparent only during a drill.

Figure 12-10

Factors in Incident Response

- Have plan in place
- Centralized reporting
- Specific responses
  - Speed
  - Preparation pays
  - Don't make problem worse
- Practise!

Active Review

Use this Active Review to verify that you have understood the material in the chapter. You can read the entire chapter and then perform the tasks in this review, or you can read the material for just one question and perform the tasks for that question before moving on to the next one.

Q1 What is identity theft?

What is identity theft? List five ways you can protect yourself from identity theft.

Q2 What is PIPEDA?

What is PIPEDA? How does PIPEDA restrict the use of personal information by organizations? Can an individual sue an organization because of PIPEDA? What role does the privacy commissioner have with PIPEDA?

Q3 What types of security threats do organizations face?

Explain the differences among security threats, threat sources, and threat types. Give one example of a security threat for each cell in the grid in Figure 12-1. Describe a phishing attack. Explain the threat of phishing to individuals. Explain the threat of phishing to company and product brands.

Q4 How can technical safeguards protect against security threats?

List five technical safeguards. Define *identification* and *authentication*. Describe three types of authentication.

Define *malware*, and name five types of malware. Describe six ways to protect against malware. Summarize why malware is a serious problem.

Q5 How can data safeguards protect against security threats?

Define *data administration* and *database administration*, and explain their differences. List data safeguards.

Q6 How can human safeguards protect against security threats?

How do you create a strong password? Summarize human safeguards for each activity in Figure 12-6. Summarize safeguards that pertain to non-employees. Describe three dimensions of safeguards for account administration. Explain how system procedures can serve as human safeguards. Describe security monitoring techniques.

Q7 What is disaster preparedness?

Define *disaster*. List major considerations for disaster preparedness. Explain the difference between a hot site and a cold site.

Q8 How should organizations respond to security incidents?

Summarize the actions that an organization should take when dealing with a security incident.

MyMISLab MyMISLab is an online learning and testing environment that features the perfect study tools to help you master the concepts covered in this chapter. Log in to MyMISLab to test your knowledge of key chapter concepts and explore additional practice tools, including videos, flashcards, annotated text figures, and more!

Key Terms and Concepts

Adware 375

Authentication 374

Biometric authentication 374

Cold sites 386

Data administration 376

Data safeguards 376

Database administration 376

Denial of service (DOS) 372

Drive-by sniffers 371

Email spoofing 371

Hacking 372

Hardening 380

Hot sites 385

Human safeguard 377

Identification 374

Identity theft 368

Using Your Knowledge

1. Find the cheapest way possible to purchase your own credit report. Two sources to check are www.equifax.com and www.transunion.com.
   a. Search for guidance on how best to review your credit records. Summarize what you learn.
   b. What actions should you take if you find errors in your credit report?
   c. Define *identity theft*. Search the web, and determine the best course of action for someone who has been the victim of identity theft.

2. Suppose you lose your company laptop at an airport. What is more valuable, the laptop or the data? Under what circumstances should you now focus on updating your résumé?

3. Suppose Akbar's company, discussed in the chapter introduction, is located in a hurricane zone and that it has been given 36 hours' warning that a serious, category 4 hurricane is headed its way.
   a. List all the information systems assets that are in danger.
   b. For each asset in your list in (a), describe an appropriate safeguard.
   c. Suppose Akbar has done little disaster preparedness planning. Summarize what you would do in that 36-hour period.
   d. Suppose Akabar does have a disaster preparedness plan. Summarize what you would do in that 36-hour period.
   e. Compare your answers to (c) and (d). In your own words, state the advantages of a disaster preparedness plan.

Collaborative Exercises

1. Your group has been given the task of finding ways to enjoy a free pancake breakfast at a restaurant. Do not feel limited by any ethical or legal issues related to getting the breakfast. In a brainstorming session, come up with as many ideas as you can for getting a free breakfast.
   a. List the ideas that you created, and prioritize them in the order that your group thinks would be the most successful.
   b. Try the exercise again, but this time, ask your group to come up with as many ideas as you can for gathering someone else's personal information so that it could be used for identity theft. You can use whatever mechanisms you think might be successful. Again, do not consider only ethical or legal means.
   c. Recognize that there are groups of people, with lots of resources, thinking about exactly what your group has just thought about. Now that you have your list, create a list of things you can do to protect your personal

information. Be ready to share the information you have learned with others in your class.

Case Study 12

Phishing for Credit Card Accounts

Before you read further, you need to know that the graphics in this case are fake. They were not produced by a legitimate business but were generated by a phisher. A *phisher* is an operation that spoofs legitimate companies in an attempt to illegally capture credit card numbers, email accounts, driver's licence numbers, and other data. Some phishers even install malicious program code on users' computers.

Phishing is usually initiated via an email. Go to www.fraudwatchinternational.com/phishing to view several examples that appear to be email messages from legitimate senders but that are, in fact, fake. The most common phishing attack is initiated with a bogus email. For example, you might receive the email shown in Figure 12-11.

This bogus email is designed to cause you to click on the "See more details here" link. When you do so, you will be connected to a site that will ask you for personal data, such as credit card numbers, card expiration dates, driver's licence number, social insurance number, or other data. In this particular case, you will be taken to a screen that asks for your credit card number (see Figure 12-12).

> Your Order ID: "17152492"
> Order Date: "09/07/12"
> Product Purchased: "Two First Class Tickets to Cozumel"
> Your card type: "CREDIT"
> Total Price: "$349.00"
>
> Hello, when you purchased your tickets, you provided an incorrect mailing address.
> See more details here
> Please follow the link and modify your mailing address or cancel your order. If you have questions, feel free to cortact with us account@usefulbill.com

Figure 12-11
Phishing Email

Figure 12-12
Phishing Screen

Source: Chachas /Dreamstime/ GetStock.com

This webpage is produced by a non-existent company and is entirely fake, including the link "Inform us about fraud." The only purpose of this site is to illegally capture your card number. It might also install spyware, adware, or other malware on your computer. If you were to get this far, you should immediately close your browser and restart your computer. You should also run anti-malware scans on your computer to determine if the phisher has installed program code on your computer. If so, use the anti-malware software to remove that code.

How can you defend yourself from such attacks? First, you know you did not purchase two first-class tickets to Cozumel. (If, by odd circumstance, you *have* just purchased airline tickets to Cozumel, you should contact the legitimate vendor's site *directly* to determine whether there has been some mixup.) Because you have not purchased such tickets, suspect a phisher.

Second, note the implausibility of the email. It is exceedingly unlikely that you can buy two first-class tickets to any foreign country for $349. Additionally, note the misspelled word and the poor grammar ("cortact with us"). All these facts should alert you to the bogus nature of this email although you should be aware that these types of email are growing in sophistication.

Third, do not be misled by legitimate-looking graphics. Phishers are criminals; they do not bother to respect international agreements on the legitimate use of trademarks. The phisher might use names of legitimate companies, such as Visa, MasterCard, Discover, and American Express, on the webpage, and the presence of those names might lull you into thinking this is legitimate. The phisher is illegally using those names, however. In other instances, the phisher will copy the entire look and feel of a legitimate company's website.

Phishing is a serious problem. To protect yourself, be wary of unsolicited email, even if the email appears to be from a legitimate business. If you have questions about an email, contact the company directly (*not* using the addresses provided by the phisher!) and ask about the email. And above all, never give confidential data, such as account numbers, social insurance numbers, driver's licence numbers, or credit card numbers, in response to *any* unsolicited email.

Running Case Assignment Part 4

1. Akbar Saied has decided to invest in a new CRM system. The system will enable his company to collect information about customers and the services that his company provides. He has outlined the goals for the system and completed a requirements analysis. He created a document outlining his requirements and had it approved in a meeting with his staff of six. His next step is to choose CRM software for the system.

   He has narrowed his choices to three options. The first option is a company that sells proprietary software requiring a Microsoft SQL server and software for each of the desktops running at the company. Akbar already has a Microsoft SQL server at his company. The server license costs $8000 and each desktop costs $1000. Akbar estimates he can get by with four desktop licences. There is a yearly maintenance cost of $1500 that provides updates and bug fixes for the server and desktop during the year. Akbar knows he will need help integrating the software, migrating the data, and training his people to use the system. He estimates these costs as $4000 (integration), $10 000 (migration), and $2000 (training). He is confident that this product is comprehensive as it has been installed in thousands of companies. So, he should get all the functions he needs.

   a. Estimate the total cost of ownership for this desktop system assuming that the system will operate for seven years. (*Hint:* Total cost of ownership includes software purchase, implementation, and maintenance costs)

   The second option is a web-based software that uses the application service provider model. There is no server or desktop software to install. Instead, each person using the software pays a yearly fee of $500 (corporate rate), which includes guaranteed service levels and 10 gigabytes (GB) of storage. Akbar estimates he will need seven accounts on the web-based system. Akbar will again need help integrating the software, migrating the data, and training his people to use the system. He estimates these costs as $5000 (integration) and $10 000 (migration). The web-based vendor supplies training videos as part of the corporate rate, so Akbar feels that these should be adequate for training.

   b. Estimate the total cost of ownership for this web-based system assuming that the system will operate for seven years.

   The third option is an open source software application. The software is free to download and uses a Linux server to centralize the data. Akbar already maintains a Linux server, so it is no additional cost. Akbar's company does not have any programmers who could update and upgrade the open source software, so he has found a company that can support the open source software. This company can install and integrate the software for $5000 and then could support the software and provide updates and bug fixes for $5000 per year. Data migration will still be required, and the consultants suggest that it will cost approximately $8000 (migration). No online training is available, but a training workshop is conducted in San Diego, and one of his employees will attend it. The workshop and travel will cost $3000.

   c. Estimate the total cost of ownership for this open source system, assuming that the system will operate for seven years.

   d. Given your answers to parts a, b, and c, above, which one of the three options would you suggest for Akbar? Justify your answer.

Collaborative Question (could be done in class or in discussion/wiki area)

2. Akbar is expecting his company to grow over the next seven years. The Excel spreadsheet "Akbar Growth Estimates.xls" provides estimates of the growth in terms of the number of employees.

   a. Use the information in Question 1 above and the growth estimates in the spreadsheet "Akbar Growth Estimates.xls" to re-estimate the total cost of ownership for each of the three options.

   b. Given the new growth information, which of the three options would you now suggest for Akbar? Justify your answer.

   c. List three risks that Akbar might face in his implementation project.

   d. What advice would you give to Akbar to make his implementation project as successful as possible.

MyMISLab Visit MyMISLab to access the data files to complete these questions.

The Final, Final Word

Congratulations! You have made it through the entire book. With this knowledge, you are well prepared to be an effective user of information systems. And with hard work and imagination, you can be much more than that. Many interesting opportunities are available to those who can apply information in innovative ways. Your professor has done what she or he can do, and the rest, as they say, is up to you.

We believe that today, computer communications and data storage are free—or so close to free that the cost is not worth mentioning. What are the consequences? Our experience in the IT business makes us wary of predictions that extend beyond next year. But we know that free communication and data storage will cause fundamental changes in the business environment. When a company, such as Getty Images, can create its products at zero marginal cost, something is fundamentally different. Further, Getty Images is not the only such business; consider YouTube.

We suspect that the rate of technology development will slow in the next five years. Businesses are still digesting the technology that already exists. According to Harry Dent, technology waves always

occur in pairs.* The first phase is wild exuberance, in which new technology is invented, its capabilities flushed out, and its characteristics understood. That first phase always results in overbuilding, but it sets the stage for the second phase, in which surviving companies and entrepreneurs purchase the overbuilt infrastructure for pennies on the dollar and use it for new business purposes.

The automotive industry, for example, proceeded in two stages. The irrational exuberance phase culminated in a technology crash; General Motors' stock fell 75 percent from 1919 to 1921. However, that exuberance led to the development of the highway system, the development of the petroleum industry, and a complete change in the conduct of commerce in the United States. Every one of those consequences created opportunities for business people alert to the changing business environment. We believe that we are poised today to see a similar second stage in the adoption of information technology. Businesses are configuring themselves to take advantage of the new opportunities. Dell builds computers to order and pays for the components days after the customer has paid Dell for the equipment. A customer begins using his or her new computer before Dell pays the supplier for the monitor.

Fibre-optic cable has come to many homes and created new services previously unavailable. Companies such as Netflix have taken advantage of this new bandwidth, and this has signalled an end to the traditional video store rental. This is another example of how technological changes can drive changes in industries.

Bloggers and social media sites, such as YouTube, Twitter, and Facebook, have changed mainstream media with their commentary and access to real-time information. A new age has emerged as media, journalism, and mass communication have been altered by social media. The readership of newspapers has fallen consistently for more than a decade; newsprint cannot last in an era of free data communications.

So, as you finish your business degree, stay alert for new technology-based opportunities. Watch for the second wave and catch it. If you found this course interesting, take more information systems (IS) classes. Enroll in a database class, a project management class, or a systems analysis and design class, even if you do not want to be an IS major. If you are

*H. Dent, *The Next Great Bubble Boom* (New York: The Free Press, 2004).

technically oriented, take a data communications class or a security class. If you enjoy this material, become an IS major. If you want to program a computer, that is great, but if you don't, then don't. There are tremendous opportunities for nonprogrammers in the information systems industry. Look for novel applications of information systems technology to the emerging business environment. Hundreds of them abound! Find them, and have fun!

Discussion Question

1. How will you further your career with what you have learned in this class? Give this question serious thought, and write a memo to yourself to read from time to time as your career progresses.

Rawpixel/Shutterstock

Glossary

10/100/1000 Ethernet A type of *Ethernet* that conforms to the IEEE 802.3 protocol and allows for transmission at a rate of 10, 100, or 1000 Mbps (megabits per second). 200

Access A popular personal and small workgroup DBMS product from Microsoft. 141

Access control list (ACL) A list that encodes the rules stating which packets are to be allowed through a firewall and which are to be prohibited. 211

Access points (APs) Points in a wireless network that facilitate communication among wireless devices and serve as points of interconnection between wireless and wired networks. APs must be able to process messages according to both the 802.3 and 802.11 standards because they send and receive wireless traffic using the 802.11 protocol and communicate with wired networks using the 802.3 protocol. 200

Accurate information Information that is factual and verifiable. 29

Activities Parts of a business process that transform resources and information of one type into resources and information of another type; can be manual or automated. 28

Advanced Research Projects Agency Network (ARPANET) The world's first operational packet switching network, which provided access to many research investigators who were geographically separated from the small number of large, powerful research computers available at the time. 210

Adware Programs installed on the user's computer without the user's knowledge or permission that reside in the background and, unknown to the user, observe the user's actions and keystrokes, modify computer activity, and report the user's activities to sponsoring organizations. Most adware is benign in that it does not perform malicious acts or steal data. It does, however, watch user activity and produce pop-up ads. 375

Agile methods Development methods, such as rapid application development (RAD), object-oriented systems development (OOD), and extreme programming (XP). 315

Alignment The ongoing, continually evolving challenge of fitting IT architecture to business objectives. 351

Alternatives formulation A step in the decision-making process in which decision makers lay out various alternatives. 37

Analog A continuously variable electronic signal. 205

Analysis paralysis When too much time is spent documenting project requirements. 323

Antivirus program Software that detects and possibly eliminates viruses. 124

Application service provider (ASP) A special form of outsourcing, in which an organization contracts with a vendor to rent applications from the vendor company on a fee-for-service basis. 325

Application software Programs that perform a business function. Some application programs are general purpose, such as Excel or Word. Other application programs are specific to a business function, such as accounts payable. 118

Applications Computer programs. 6

Asymmetric digital subscriber line (ADSL) ADSL line that has different upload and download speeds. 206

Attribute (1) A variable that provides a property for an HTML tag. Each attribute has a standard name. For example, the attribute for a hyperlink is *href*, and its value indicates which webpage is to be displayed when the user clicks the link. (2) Characteristic of an entity. Examples of attributes of *Order* would be *OrderNumber, OrderDate, SubTotal, Tax, Total*, and so forth. Examples of attributes of *Salesperson* would be *SalespersonName, Email, Phone*, and so forth. 159

Authentication The process whereby an information system approves (authenticates) a user by checking the user's password. 374

Automated system An information system in which the hardware and software components do most of the work. 32

Basic Input/Output System (BIOS) An important piece of firmware used when a computer is initially booted up. The first thing a computer does is to load BIOS from ROM and run through the commands provided by the firmware. BIOS checks to make sure the memory and input devices are functional. Once these are working, the operating system will be loaded. 121

Beta testing The process of allowing future system users to try out the new system on their own. Used to locate program failures just prior to program shipment. 320

Big Data An imprecise term that generally refers to large volumes of a variety of data over a long period of time that are used to draw general and specific inferences and analysis—for example the spread of disease, customer preferences, or individual behaviors. 272

Bill 198 or Budget Measures Act Law enforcing compliance with standards for collecting, reporting, and disclosing information. 353

Binary digits The means by which computers represent data; also called *bits*. A binary digit is either a zero or a one. 111

Biometric authentication The use of personal physical characteristics, such as fingerprints, facial features, and retinal scans, to authenticate users. 374

Bit The means by which computers represent data; also called *binary digit*. A bit is either a zero or a one. 111

Botnet A set of computers or applications that are coordinated through a network and used to perform malicious tasks. 124

Bring Your Own Device (BYOD) A policy in which employees are encouraged to simply use their own devices for work rather than being provided with additional company-issued devices. 203

Browser A program that processes the HTTP protocol; receives, displays, and processes HTML documents; and transmits responses. 204

Bus Means by which the CPU reads instructions and data from main memory and writes data to main memory. 112

Business analysts Analysts who develop the business case for a newly proposed system and develop the requirements for the system. 316, 345

Business intelligence (BI) system A system that provides the right information, to the right user, at the right time. A tool produces the information, but the system ensures that the right information is delivered to the right user at the right time. 264

Business process A network of activities, resources, facilities, and information that interact to achieve some business function; sometimes called a *business system*. 26

Business process design The creation of new, usually cross-departmental business practices during information systems development. With process design, organizations do not create new information systems to automate existing business practices. Rather, they use technology to enable new, more efficient business processes. 235

Business process management (BPM) The process of generating information that will be useful for management and strategy decisions. 31

Business Process Modelling Notation (BPMN) A standard set of terms and graphical notations for documenting business processes. 28

Business system Another term for *business process*. 26

Business Technology Management (BTM) A category of skills focused on the ability to effectively innovate using information technology in organizations. 62

Business value Tangible benefits for organizations through either more efficient use of resources or more effective delivery of their services to customers. 60

Business-to-business (B2B) Ecommerce sales between companies. 283

Business-to-consumer (B2C) Ecommerce sales between a supplier and a retail customer (the consumer). 283

Business-to-government (B2G) Ecommerce sales between companies and governmental organizations. 283

Byte (1) A character of data. (2) An 8-bit chunk. 112, 137

Cable modem A type of modem that provides high-speed data transmission using cable television lines. The cable company installs a fast, high-capacity optical fibre cable to a distribution centre in each neighbourhood that it serves. At the distribution centre, the optical fibre cable connects to regular cable-television cables that run to subscribers' homes or businesses. Cable modems modulate in such a way that their signals do not interfere with TV signals. Like DSL lines, they are always on. 207

Cache A file on a domain name resolver that stores domain names and IP addresses that have been resolved. Then, when someone else needs to resolve that same domain name, there is no need to go through the entire resolution process. Instead, the resolver can supply the IP address from the local file. 112

Canadian Coalition for Tomorrow's ICT Skills (CCICT) A nonprofit organization created to support the development of skills for the information and computing technology industry. 62

Cell The intersection of a column and row in a Microsoft Excel spreadsheet. 81

Central processing unit (CPU) The CPU selects instructions, processes them, performs arithmetic and logical comparisons, and stores results of operations in memory. 110

Certified Information Systems Auditor (CISA) A globally recognized certification earned by more than 50 000 professionals; members have job titles like information systems auditor, consultant, information systems security professional, regulator, chief information officer, and internal auditor. 354

Challenge/Response A form of authentication that uses a varying form of numeric question and algorithmic response (usually involving sophisticated computerized tokens) to validate users. 374

Channel Conflict Differences in the way that products or services are delivered or supported by different sales channels. For example, if products sold online are priced lower than those sold in traditional stores or if they have a different level of after sales support. 286

See also *Showrooming* and *Price Conflict.*

Chief information officer (CIO) The title of the principal manager of the IT department. Other common titles are *vice-president of information services, director of information services*, and, less commonly, *director of computer services*. 344

Chief technology officer (CTO) The head of the technology group. The CTO sorts through new ideas and products to identify those that are most relevant to the organization. The CTO's job requires deep knowledge of information technology and the ability to envision how new IT will affect the organization over time. 344

Choice A step in the decision-making process in which decision makers analyze their alternatives and select one. 37

Clearinghouses Entities that provide goods and services at a stated price and arrange for the delivery of the goods, but never take title to the goods. 284

Clickstream data E-commerce data that describe a customer's clicking behaviour. Such data include everything the customer does at the website. 259

Client A computer that provides word processing, spreadsheets, database access, and usually a network connection. 114

Cloud computing Customers do not necessarily own the computer they use. Instead, hardware, software, and applications are provided as a service, usually through a web browser. The cloud is a metaphor for the internet, which makes software and data services available from any location at any time. 115

Cluster analysis An unsupervised data-mining technique whereby statistical techniques are used to identify groups of entities that have similar characteristics. A common use for cluster analysis is to find groups of similar customers in data about customer orders and customer demographics. 270

Cold sites Remote processing centres that provide office space and limited computer equipment for use by companies that need to continue operations after a loss of their primary computing site (see *Warm* and *Hot sites*). 386

Collaboration Occurs when two or more people work together to achieve a common goal, result, or product. 195

Columns Also called *fields*, or groups of bytes. A database table has multiple columns that are used to represent the attributes of an entity. Examples are *PartNumber, EmployeeName*, and *SalesDate*. 137

Commercial-off-the-shelf (COTS) Software that is purchased as-is and is not customized. 318

Communication systems Email, virtual private networks, instant messaging, and more sophisticated communications systems, dependent on the network technology available in an organization. 195

Competitive strategy The strategy an organization chooses as the way it will succeed in its industry. According to Michael Porter, there are four fundamental competitive strategies: cost leadership across an industry or within a particular industry segment, and product differentiation across an industry or within a particular industry segment. 67, 349

Computer hardware One of the five fundamental components of an information system. 6

Content management systems (CMSs) An information system that tracks organizational documents, webpages, graphics, and related materials. 135

Control Objectives for Information and Related Technology (COBIT) A framework of best practices designed for IT management; provides board members, managers, auditors, and IT users with a set of generally accepted measures, indicators, processes, and best practices to assist in getting the best from organizational IT investments. 354

Cost feasibility One of four dimensions of feasibility. 316

Cross-departmental systems The third type of computing systems. In this type, systems are designed not to facilitate the work of a single department or function but, rather, to integrate the activities of a complete business process. 232

Cross-functional systems Synonym for *cross-departmental systems*. 232

Crow's foot A line on an entity-relationship diagram that indicates a 1:N relationship between two entities. 160

Crow's-foot diagram A type of entity-relationship diagram that uses a crow's foot symbol to designate a 1:N relationship. 161

Crowdsourcing A process through which users can provide customer support to one another or even participate in the creation of product specifications, designs, and complete products. 293

Custom-developed software Software that is tailor-made for a company or organization. 120

Customer life cycle Taken as a whole, the processes of marketing, customer acquisition, relationship management, and loss/churn that must be managed by CRM systems. 241

Customer relationship management (CRM) system An information system that maintains data about customers and all their interactions with the organization. 241

Customer service expense The costs involved in supporting a customer's purchase or use of a product or service. 287

Data Recorded facts or figures. One of the five fundamental components of an information system. 6

Data administration A staff function that pertains to *all* of an organization's data assets. Typical data administration tasks are setting data standards, developing data policies, and providing for data security. 376

Data channel Means by which the CPU reads instructions and data from main memory and writes data to main memory. 112

Data flow An element in a data flow diagram that depicts the movement of data. 47

Data flow diagram (DFD) A diagram focused on information processes that is composed of four basic elements (data flow, data store, external entity, and process). 49

Data integrity problem In a database, the situation that exists when data items disagree with one another. An example is two different names for the same customer. 162

Data mart A database that prepares, stores, and manages data for reporting and data mining for specific business functions. 268

Data mining The application of statistical techniques to find patterns and relationships among data and to classify and predict. 269

Data model A logical representation of the data in a database that describes the data and relationships that will be stored in the database. Similar to a blueprint. 158

Data resource challenge Occurs when data are collected in OLTP but are not used to improve decision making. 260

Data safeguards Steps taken to protect databases and other organizational data by means of data administration and database administration. 376

Data store A diagram element in a data flow diagram depicting a database. 51

Data warehouse A facility that prepares, stores, and manages data specifically for reporting and data mining. 267

Database A self-describing collection of integrated records. 137

Database administration The management, development, operation, and maintenance of the database so as to achieve the organization's objectives. This staff function requires balancing conflicting goals—protecting the database while maximizing its availability for authorized use. In smaller organizations, this function is usually served by a single person. Larger organizations assign several people to an office of database administration. 376

Database application A collection of forms, reports, queries, and application programs that process a database. 143

Database application system Applications with the standard five components that make database data more accessible and useful. Users employ a database application that consists of forms, formatted reports, queries, and application programs. Each of these, in turn, calls on the database management system (DBMS) to process the database tables. 141

Database management system (DBMS) A program used to create, process, and administer a database. 141

Data-mining system Information system that processes data using sophisticated statistical techniques, such as regression analysis and decision-tree analysis, to find patterns and relationships that cannot be found by simpler operations, such as sorting, grouping, and averaging. 266

DB2 A popular, enterprise-class DBMS product from IBM. 141

Decision support systems (DSSs) Systems that focus on making data collected in OLTP useful for decision making. 261

Denial of service (DOS) Security problem in which users are not able to access an information system; can be caused by human errors, natural disaster, or malicious activity. 372

Dependencies When one activity must be completed before the other one can begin. 333

Dial-up modem A modem that performs the conversion between analog and digital in such a way that the signal can be carried on a regular telephone line. 217

Diffusion of innovation The process by which an innovation is communicated through certain channels over time among the members of a social system. 69

Digital subscriber line (DSL) modem A special telephone line that connects home and small-business computers to an ISP. 206

Dirty data Problematic data. Examples are a value of *B* for customer gender and a value of *213* for customer age. Other examples are a value of *999-999-9999* for a North American phone number, a part colour of *green*, and an email address of WhyMe@GuessWhoIAM.org. All these values are problematic when data mining. 258

Disintermediation Elimination of one or more middle layers in the supply chain. 243, 284

Disruptive technology A product that introduces a very new package of attributes from the accepted mainstream products. 68

Domain name system (DNS) A system that converts user-friendly names into their IP addresses. Any registered, valid name is called a *domain name*. 205

Drill down With an OLAP report, to further divide the data into more detail. 261

Drive-by sniffers People who take computers with wireless connections through an area and search for unprotected wireless networks in an attempt to gain free internet access or to gather unauthorized data. 371

Ecommerce The buying and selling of goods and services over public and private computer networks. 282

Ecommerce auctions Applications that match buyers and sellers by using an ecommerce version of a standard auction. This ecommerce application enables the auction company to offer goods for sale and to support a competitive bidding process. 284

E-cycling The recycling of electronic materials. 358

Effectiveness Doing the right things. 63

Efficiency A measure of productiveness also refers to accomplishing a business process either more quickly with the same resources or as quickly with fewer resources. 63

Electronic exchanges Sites that facilitate the matching of buyers and sellers; the business process is similar to that of a stock exchange. Sellers offer goods at a given price through the electronic exchange, and buyers make offers to purchase over the same exchange. Price matches result in transactions from which the exchange takes a commission. 284

Email spoofing A synonym for *phishing*. A technique for obtaining unauthorized data that uses pretexting via email. The *phisher* pretends to be a legitimate company and sends email requests for confidential data, such as account numbers, social insurance numbers, account passwords, and so forth. Phishers direct traffic to their sites under the guise of a legitimate business. 371

Encryption The process of transforming clear text into coded, unintelligible text for secure storage or communication. 212

ENERGY STAR An international government–industry partnership that is intended to produce equipment that meets high-energy efficiency specifications or promotes the use of such equipment. 358

Enterprise application integration (EAI) An approach to combining functional systems that uses layers of software as a bridge to connect different functional systems together. 235

Enterprise architect Manages the company's complex information systems. 349

Enterprise DBMS A product that processes large organizational and workgroup databases. These products support many users, perhaps thousands, and many different database applications. Such DBMS products support 24/7 operations and can manage databases that span dozens of different magnetic disks with hundreds of gigabytes or more of data. IBM's DB2, Microsoft's SQL Server, and Oracle's Oracle are examples of enterprise DBMS products. 147

Enterprise resource planning (ERP) system The integration of all the organization's principal processes. ERP is an outgrowth of MRP II manufacturing systems, and most ERP users are manufacturing companies. 239

Entity In the E-R data model, a representation of something that users want to track. Some entities represent a physical object; others represent a logical construct or transaction. 159

Entity-relationship (E-R) data model Popular technique for creating a data model, in which developers define the things that will be stored and the relationships among them. 158

Entity-relationship (E-R) diagram A type of diagram used by database designers to document entities and their relationships to one another. 160

Ethernet Another name for the IEEE 802.3 protocol, Ethernet is a network protocol that operates at Layers 1 and 2 of the TCP/IP–OSI architecture. Ethernet, the world's most popular LAN protocol, is used on WANs as well. 200

E-waste Electronic garbage. 358

Exabytes 10^{18} bytes. 257

Expert systems Knowledge-sharing systems that are created by interviewing experts in a given business domain and codifying the rules used by those experts. 266

External entity (Interface) An element in a data flow diagram that signifies a component that is outside of the internal system being considered. 51

Facilities Structures used within a business process. 28

Fields Also called *columns*, groups of bytes in a database table. A database table has multiple columns that are used to represent the attributes of an entity. Examples are *PartNumber*, *EmployeeName*, and *SalesDate*. 137

File A group of similar rows or records. In a database, sometimes called a *table*. 137

Firewall A computing device located between a firm's internal and external networks that prevents unauthorized access to or from the internal network. A firewall can be a special-purpose computer or it can be a program on a general-purpose computer or a router. 211

Firmware Computer software that is installed on devices, such as printers, print services, and various types of communication devices. The software is coded just like other software, but it is installed on special, programmable memory of the printer or other device. 121

Five forces model A model proposed by Michael Porter that assesses industry characteristics and profitability by means of five competitive forces—bargaining power of suppliers, threat of substitutions, bargaining power of customers, rivalry among firms, and threat of new entrants. 65

Five-component framework The five fundamental components of an information system—computer hardware, software, data, procedures, and people—that are present in every information system, from the simplest to the most complex. 6

Foreign keys A column or group of columns used to represent relationships. Values of the foreign key match values of the primary key in a different (foreign) table. 139

Form Data entry forms are used to read, insert, modify, and delete database data. 144

Functional silos An organizational area (such as marketing or finance) that operates without considering other organizational areas. 231

Functional systems The second era of information systems. The goal of such systems was to facilitate the work of a single department or function. Over time, in each functional area, companies added features and functions to encompass more activities and to provide more value and assistance. 231

Gantt chart A project management diagram that depicts a project schedule and task relationships. 333

Gigabyte (GB) 1024 megabytes. 112

Global Positioning System (GPS) A collection of dozens of satellites orbiting the earth that transmit precise microwave signals. A GPS receiver can calculate its position by measuring the distance between itself and several of the satellites. 197

Governance Using a committee to decide on expectations for performance, to authorize appropriate resources and power to meet expectations, and perhaps eventually to verify whether expectations have been met. 352

Granularity The level of detail in data. Customer name and account balance are large granularity data. Customer name, balance, and the order details and payment history of every customer order are smaller granularity. 259

Green IT Using information technology resources to better support the triple bottom line for organizations. 358

Group decision support systems (GDSSs) An application that enables more than one individual to undertake a decision. Often includes voting and brainstorming functions. 264

Hacking Occurs when a person gains unauthorized access to a computer system. Although some people hack for the sheer joy of doing it, other hackers invade systems for the malicious purpose of stealing or modifying data. 372

Hardening The process of taking extraordinary measures to reduce a system's vulnerability. Hardened sites use special versions of the operating system, and they lock down or eliminate operating systems features and functions that are not required by the application. Hardening is a technical safeguard. 380

Hardware Electronic components and related gadgetry that input, process, output, store, and communicate data according to instructions encoded in computer programs or software. 109

Hertz Cycles of CPU speed. 110

Horizontal market application Software that provides capabilities common across all organizations and industries; examples include word processors, graphics programs, spreadsheets, and presentation programs. 119

Hot sites Remote processing centres in an advanced state of readiness that have equipment companies need to continue operations in the event of a loss of their main computing sites (see *Cold* and *Warm sites*). 385

Human safeguard Steps taken to protect against security threats by establishing appropriate procedures for users to follow for system use. 377

Hypertext transfer protocol (HTTP) A Layer-5 protocol used to process webpages. 204

Identification The process whereby an information system identifies a user by requiring the user to sign on with a user name and password. 374

Identifier An attribute (or group of attributes) whose value is associated with one and only one entity instance. 159

Identity theft Stealing, misrepresenting, or hijacking the identity of another person or business. 368

IEEE 802.3 protocol This standard, also called *Ethernet*, is a network protocol that operates at Layers 1 and 2 of the TCP/IP-OSI architecture. Ethernet, the world's most popular LAN protocol, is used on WANs as well. 200

Implementation A step in the decision-making process in which decision makers implement the alternative they have selected. 37

Industry standard processes Processes built into business applications from companies such as Oracle or SAP. 237

Information (1) Knowledge derived from data, where the term *data* is defined as recorded facts or figures. (2) Data presented in a meaningful context. (3) Data processed by summing, ordering, averaging, grouping, comparing, or other similar operations. (4) A difference that makes a difference. 28

Information and Communications Technology (ICT) Industry Provides products and services that other industries rely on to get their work done. 11, 60

Information overload An overabundance of irrelevant data. 257

Information system (IS) A group of components that interact to produce information. 6

Information systems audit An audit focusing on information resources that are used to collect, store, process, and retrieve information. 354

Information Systems Audit and Control Association (ISACA) A key organization in developing knowledge and standards relating to information systems audits and information systems governance. 354

Information systems ethics Concern for the people whose lives can be affected by our actions. 356

Information technology (IT) The products, methods, inventions, and standards that are used for the purpose of producing information. 10

Information Technology Infrastructure Library (ITIL) A well-recognized collection of books providing a framework of best practice approaches to IT operations. ITIL provides a large set of management procedures that are designed to support businesses in achieving value from IT operations. 311

Information technology project management (ITPM) The collection of techniques and methods that project managers use to plan, coordinate, and complete IT projects. 310

Innovation Rogers' five characteristics: relative advantage, compatibility, complexity, trialability, and observability. 62

Input devices Hardware devices that attach to a computer; for example, keyboards, mouse, document scanners, and barcode (Universal Product Code) scanners. 110

Instruction set The collection of instructions that a computer can process. 116

Intellectual property A form of creative endeavour that can be protected through a trademark, patent, copyright, industrial design, or integrated circuit topography. 134

Intelligence gathering The first step in the decision-making process in which decision makers determine what is to be decided, what the criteria for selection will be, and what data are available. 37

Internet Either a private network of networks or, more commonly, the public network known as the internet. 197

Internet service provider (ISP) An ISP provides a user with a legitimate internet address, it serves as the user's gateway to the internet, and it passes communications back and forth between the user and the internet. ISPs also pay for the internet. They collect money from their customers and pay access fees and other charges on the users' behalf. 204

Interorganizational systems Information systems processing of routine transactions between two or more organizations. 232

IP address A series of dotted decimals in a format, such as 192.168.2.28, which identifies a unique device on a network or internet. With the IPv4 standard, IP addresses have 32 bits. With the IPv6 standard, IP addresses have 128 bits. Today, IPv4 is more common but will likely be supplanted by IPv6 in the future. With IPv4, the decimal between the dots can never exceed 255. 205

IP spoofing A type of spoofing whereby an intruder uses another site's IP address as if it were that other site. 371

IT architecture The basic framework for all the computers, systems, and information management that support organizational services. 349

IT operations Service, maintenance, protection, and management of IT infrastructure. 311

IT project risk Structural risk, volatility risk, and project process; performance, knowledge resources, organizational support, project management practices, and both process and product performance. 313

IT projects Projects of all shapes and sizes that renew and adapt IT infrastructure. 310

Just barely so (information) Information that meets the purpose for which it is generated, but just barely so. 30

Key (1) A column or group of columns that identifies a unique row in a table. (2) A number used to encrypt data. The encryption algorithm applies the key to the original message to produce the coded message. Decoding (decrypting) a message is similar; a key is applied to the coded message to recover the original text. 138

Key escrow A control procedure whereby a trusted party is given a copy of a key used to encrypt database data. 377

Kilobyte (KB) 1024 bytes. 112

Knowledge management (KM) systems Information systems for storing and retrieving organizational knowledge, whether that knowledge is in the form of data, documents, or employee know-how. 266

Lean production A manufacturing method focused on using resources as efficiently as possible. 32

Level-0 diagram The most basic level of data flow diagram. 51

Level-1 diagram A data flow diagram that shows basic processes contained within a system. 52

Levelling Creating a series of data flow diagrams that incrementally show more levels of detail within a system. 51

Licence An agreement that stipulates how a program can be used. Most specify the number of computers on which the program can be installed and sometimes the number of users that can connect to and use the program remotely. Such agreements also stipulate limitations on the liability of the software vendor for the consequences of errors in the software. 117

Linux A version of Unix that was developed by the open-source community. The open-source community owns Linux, and there is no fee to use it. Linux is a popular operating system for web servers. 117

Local area network (LAN) A network that connects computers that reside in a single geographical location on the premises of the company that operates the LAN. The number of connected computers can range from two to several hundred. 197

Logistic expense The costs associated with the coordination or movement, transportation, and storage of goods or services, particularly if the supply chain involves multiple parties or remote locations. 287

Lost-update problem An issue in multiuser database processing, in which two or more users try to make changes to the data but the database cannot make all the changes because it was not designed to process changes from multiple users. 147

MAC (media access control) address Also called *physical address*. A permanent address given to each network interface card (NIC) at the factory. This address enables the device to access the network via a Level-2 protocol. By agreement among computer manufacturers, MAC addresses are assigned in such a way that no two NIC devices will ever have the same MAC address. 198

Mac OS An operating system developed by Apple Computer, Inc., for the Macintosh. The current version is Mac OS X. Mac OS was developed for the PowerPC but, as of 2006, runs on Intel processors as well. 117

Macro-viruses Viruses that attach themselves to Word, Excel, PowerPoint, or other types of documents. When the infected document is opened, the virus places itself in the startup files of the application. After that, the virus infects every file that the application creates or processes. 124

Main memory A set of cells in which each cell holds a byte of data or instruction; each cell has an address, and the CPU uses the addresses to identify particular data items. 110

Mainframe The first digital computing machine used in business and government. 105

Maintenance phase Last part of the SDLC, which starts the process all over again. 321

Malware Viruses, worms, spyware, and adware. 375

Malware definitions Patterns that exist in malware code. Anti-malware vendors update these definitions continuously and incorporate them in their products in order to better fight against malware. 376

Management information systems (MIS) Information systems that help businesses achieve their goals and objectives. 7, 35

Managerial decisions Decisions that concern the allocation and use of resources. 35

Manual system An information system in which the activity of processing information is done by people, without the use of automated processing. 34

Many-to-many (N:M) relationship A relationship involving two entity types in which an instance of one type can relate to many instances of the second type, and an instance of the second type can relate to many instances of the first. For example, the relationship between Student and Class is N:M. One student may enroll in many classes and one class may have many students. Contrast with *one-to-many (1:N) relationship*. 160

Margin The difference between value and cost. 64

Market-basket analysis A data-mining technique for determining sales patterns. A market-basket analysis shows the products that customers tend to buy together. 266

Maximum cardinality The maximum number of entities that can be involved in a relationship. Common examples of maximum cardinality are 1:N, N:M, and 1:1. 161

M-commerce Short for *mobile commerce*, its applications allow mobile phones to conduct certain kinds of transactions, such as mobile banking and mobile ticket purchases at movie theatres and sporting events. 202

Megabyte (MB) 1024 kilobytes. 112

Memory swapping The movement of programs and data into and out of memory. If a computer has insufficient memory for its workload, such swapping will degrade system performance. 113

Merchant companies In ecommerce, companies that take title to the goods they sell. They buy goods and resell them. 283

Metadata Data that describe data. 140, 268

Microcomputer Smaller than mainframes, the precursor to personal computers. 106

Minimum cardinality The minimum number of entities that must be involved in a relationship. 161

Modem Short for *modulator/demodulator*, a modem converts the computer's digital data into signals that can be transmitted over telephone or cable lines. 205

Moore's Law A law, created by Gordon Moore, stating that the number of transistors per square inch on an integrated chip doubles every 18 months. Moore's prediction has proved generally accurate in the 40 years since it was made. Sometimes, this law is stated as the speed of a computer chip doubles every 18 months. While not strictly true, this version gives the gist of the idea. 14

Multiuser processing When multiple users process the database at the same time. 147

MySQL A popular open-source DBMS product that is licence-free for most applications. 141

Network A collection of computers that communicate with one another over transmission lines. 197

Network externality The larger the number of people using a network, the more valuable that network becomes. 196

Network interface card (NIC) A hardware component on each device on a network (computer, printer, etc.) that connects the device's circuitry to the communications line. The NIC works together with programs in each device to implement Layers 1 and 2 of the TCP/IP-OSI hybrid protocol. 198

Neural networks A popular supervised data-mining technique used to predict values and make classifications, such as good prospect or poor prospect. 271

Nonmerchant companies Ecommerce companies that arrange for the purchase and sale of goods without ever owning or taking title to those goods. 283

Nonvolatile (memory) Memory that preserves data contents even when not powered (e.g., magnetic and optical disks). With such devices, you can turn the computer off and back on, and the contents will be unchanged. 113

Normal form A classification of tables according to their characteristics and the kinds of problems they have. 163

Normalization The process of converting poorly structured tables into two or more well-structured tables. 162

Off-the-shelf software Commercial software. 120

Off-the-shelf with alterations Commercial software that has been modified for a particular organization. 120

Onboard NIC A built-in NIC. 200

One-of-a-kind application Software that is developed for a specific, unique need, usually for a particular company's operations. 120

One-to-many (1:N) relationship A relationship involving two entity types in which an instance of one type can relate to many instances of the second type, but an instance of the second type can relate to at most one instance of the first. For example, the relationship between Department and Employee is 1:N. A department may relate to many employees, but an employee relates to at most one department. 160

Online analytic processing (OLAP) A dynamic type of reporting system that provides the ability to sum, count, average, and perform other simple arithmetic operations on groups of data. Such reports are dynamic because users can change the format of the reports while viewing them. 261

Online transaction processing (OLTP) Collecting data electronically and processing transactions online. 259

Open-source community A loosely coupled group of programmers who mostly volunteer their time to contribute code to develop and maintain common software. Linux and MySQL are two prominent products developed by such a community. 117

Operating system (OS) A computer program that controls the computer's resources: It manages the contents of main memory, processes keystrokes and mouse movements, sends signals to the display monitor, reads and writes disk files, and controls the processing of other programs. 112

Operational decisions Decisions that concern the day-to-day activities of an organization. 35

Optical fibre cable A type of cable used to connect the computers, printers, switches, and other devices on a LAN. The signals on such cables are light rays, and they are reflected inside the glass core of the optical fibre cable. The core is surrounded by a *cladding* to contain the light signals, and the cladding, in turn, is wrapped with an outer layer to protect it. 199

Oracle A popular, enterprise-class DBMS product from Oracle Corporation. 141

Organizational feasibility One of four dimensions of feasibility. 316

Output hardware Hardware that displays the results of the computer's processing. It consists of video displays, printers, audio speakers, overhead projectors, and other special-purpose devices, such as large flatbed plotters. 110

Outsourcing The process of hiring another organization to perform a service. Outsourcing is done to save costs, to gain expertise, and to free up management time. 323

Packet switching network A system in which messages are first disassembled into small packets, then sent through the network and reassembled at the destination. 210

Packet-filtering firewall A firewall that examines each packet and determines whether to let the packet pass. To make this decision, it examines the source address, the destination addresses, and other data. 211

Parallel installation A type of system conversion in which the new system runs in parallel with the old one for a while. Parallel installation is expensive because the organization incurs the costs of running both systems. 320

Patches A group of fixes for high-priority failures that can be applied to existing copies of a particular product. Software vendors supply patches to fix security and other critical problems. 124, 322

Payload The program code of a virus that causes harmful or hurtful actions, such as deleting programs or data or, even worse, modifying data in ways that are undetected by the user. 124

People As part of the five-component framework, one of the five fundamental components of an information system; this component includes those who operate and service the computers, those who maintain the data, those who support the networks, and those who use the system. 6

Personal DBMS DBMS products designed for smaller, simpler database applications. Such products are used for personal or small workgroup applications that involve fewer than 100 users and normally fewer than 15. Today, Microsoft Access is the only prominent personal DBMS. 148

Personal identification number (PIN) A form of authentication whereby the user supplies a number that only he or she knows. 374

Personal Information Protection and Electronic Documents Act (PIPEDA) In Canada, PIPEDA gives individuals the right to know why an organization collects, uses, or discloses their personal information. 368

Petabytes 10^{15} bytes. 257

Phased installation A type of system conversion in which the new system is installed in pieces across the organization(s). Once a given piece works, then the organization installs and tests another piece of the system, until the entire system has been installed. 320

Phishing A technique for obtaining unauthorized data that uses pretexting via email. The *phisher* pretends to be a legitimate company and sends an email requesting confidential data, such as account numbers, social insurance numbers, account passwords, and so forth. 371

Pilot installation A type of system conversion in which the organization implements the entire system on a limited portion of the business. The advantage of pilot implementation is that if the system fails, the failure is contained within a limited boundary. This reduces exposure of the business and also protects the new system from developing a negative reputation throughout the organization(s). 320

Plunge installation Sometimes called *direct installation*, a type of system conversion in which the organization shuts off the old system and starts the new system. If the new system fails, the organization is in trouble: Nothing can be done until either the new system is fixed or the old system is reinstalled. Because of the risk, organizations should avoid this conversion style if possible. 321

Port A number used to uniquely identify a transaction over a network. 211

Predecessor In project management, it is a work package that must come before another work package can be completed. 335

Pretexting A technique for gathering unauthorized information in which someone pretends to be someone else. A common scam involves a telephone caller who pretends to be from a credit card company and claims to be checking the validity of credit card numbers. *Phishing* is also a form of pretexting. 371

Price conflict Differences in the price of a good or service based on the way that it is obtained or delivered. For example, U.S. prices may be lower than Canadian prices even after adjusting for currency exchange rate, or online products may cost less than those sold in traditional stores. 286 See also *Channel conflict* and *Showrooming*.

Price elasticity A measure of the sensitivity in demand to changes in price. It is the ratio of the percentage change in quantity divided by the percentage change in price. 285

Primary activities In Michael Porter's value chain model, the fundamental activities that create value—inbound logistics, operations, outbound logistics, marketing/sales, and service. 64, 231

Procedures Instructions for humans. One of the five fundamental components of an information system. 6

Process Symbolizes a set of related activities. 51

Process aware When people view their actions in the light of the larger business process and think about ways to improve the processes they are involved in. 48

Process blueprint In an ERP product, a comprehensive set of inherent processes for organizational activities. 239

Process modelling applications Computer programs that enable the drawing of models of business processes. 49

Process modelling techniques Collections of diagrams and instructions for creating process models of information systems. 49

Processing devices Computing technology that allow for the modification, storage, or deletion of data. 110

Product quality assurance (PQA) The testing of a system. PQA personnel usually construct a test plan with the advice and assistance of users. PQA test engineers perform testing, and they also supervise user-test activity. Many PQA professionals are programmers who write automated test programs. 320

Production systems The entire set of systems that support operations. 311

Productivity The creation of business value. 60, 311

Productivity paradox The lack of evidence of an increase in worker productivity associated with the massive increase in investment in information technology. 60

Project management body of knowledge (PMBOK) Provides project managers, sponsors, and team leaders with a large array of accepted project management techniques and practices. 309

Product management professionals (PMPs) Individuals certified by the Product Management Institute as having product management skills. 310

Protocol A standardized means for coordinating an activity between two or more entities. 198

Query A request for data from a database. 145

Random access memory (RAM) Memory that is external to the processing unit that is used for primary working memory in a computing system. 110

Records Also called *rows*, groups of columns in a database table. 137

Regression analysis A type of supervised data mining that estimates the values of parameters in a linear equation. Used to determine the relative influence of variables on an outcome and also to predict future values of that outcome. 270

Relation The more formal name for a database table. 139

Relational databases Databases that carry their data in the form of tables and that represent relationships using foreign keys. 139

Relationship Association among entities or entity instances in an E-R model or an association among rows of a table in a relational database. 159

Relevant (information) Information that is appropriate to both the context and the subject. 30

Report A presentation of data in a structured, or meaningful, context. 144

Reporting systems Systems that create information from disparate data sources and deliver that information to the proper users on a timely basis. 266

Requirements analysis phase The second phase in the SDLC, in which developers conduct user interviews, evaluate existing systems, determine new forms/reports/queries, identify new features and functions, including security, and create the data model. 316

Resource Sheet view The view of employees available to work on a project in Microsoft Project. 333

Resource Usage view The view of how much a particular employee is being used on a project in Microsoft Project. 338

Resources Items of value, such as inventory or funds, that are part of a business process. 28

Review The final step in the decision-making process, in which decision makers evaluate results of their decision and, if necessary, repeat the process to correct or adapt the decision. 37

RFM analysis A way of analyzing and ranking customers according to their purchasing patterns. 266

Ribbon The wide bar of tools and selections that appears just under the tabs in Microsoft Office programs. 83

Router A special-purpose computer that moves network traffic from one node on a network to another. 204

Rows Also called *records*, groups of columns in a database table. 137

SAP R/3 A software product licensed by German company SAP that integrates business activities into *inherent processes* across an organization. 237

Sarbanes-Oxley Act (SOX) Law passed by the U.S. Congress in 2002 that governs the reporting requirements of publicly held companies. Among other things, it strengthened requirements for internal controls and management's responsibility for accurate financial reporting. 353

Schedule feasibility One of four dimensions of feasibility. 316

Security threats A problem with the security of information or the data therein, caused by human error, malicious activity, or natural disasters. 369

Server farm A large collection of server computers that coordinates the activities of the servers, usually for commercial purposes. 115

Servers Computers that provide certain types of service, such as hosting a database, running a blog, publishing a website, or selling goods. Server computers are faster, larger, and more powerful than client computers. 115

Service packs A large group of fixes that solve low-priority software problems. Users apply service packs in much the same way that they apply patches, except that service packs typically involve fixes to hundreds or thousands of problems. 322

Showrooming A customer visits a store to examine or gain information about a product but then purchases the product online. 287

Six sigma A business process improvement method developed by Motorola that focuses on developing quality. 32

Skills Framework for the Information Age (SFIA) A set of skills thought to be useful for those employees focused on developing and maintaining information technology. 62

Smart card A plastic card similar to a credit card that has a microchip. The microchip, which holds much more data than a magnetic strip, is loaded with identifying data. Normally, it requires a PIN. 374

Smartphone Phones that combine a powerful processor with sophisticated operating systems and cellular network technology to provide a host of applications to their users including voice, text, email, web browsing, and much more. 200

Sniffing A technique for intercepting computer communications. With wired networks, sniffing requires a physical connection to the network. With wireless networks, no such connection is required. 371

Software Instructions for computers. One of the five fundamental components of an information system. 6

Spam Unwanted email messages. 370

Special function devices Devices that can be added to the computer to augment the computer's basic capabilities. 111

Spoofing When someone pretends to be someone else with the intent of obtaining unauthorized data. If you pretend to be your professor, you are spoofing your professor. 371

Spreadsheet A table of data having rows and columns. 81

Spyware Programs installed on the user's computer without the user's knowledge or permission that reside in the background and, unknown to the user, observe the user's actions and keystrokes, modify computer activity, and report the user's activities to sponsoring organizations. Malicious spyware captures keystrokes to obtain user names, passwords, account numbers, and other sensitive information. Other spyware is used for marketing analyses, observing what users do, websites visited, products examined and purchased, and so forth. 375

SQL Server A popular enterprise-class DBMS product from Microsoft. 141

Storage hardware Hardware that saves data and programs. Magnetic disk is by far the most common storage device, although optical disks, such as CDs and DVDs, also are popular, and semiconductor-based storage (also called solid-state drives) are gaining marketshare. 110

Strategic decisions Decisions that concern broader-scope, organizational issues. 36

Structured decision A type of decision for which there is a formalized and accepted method for making the decision. 36

Structured Query Language (SQL) An international standard language for processing database data. 142

Subtask The hierarchy of tasks within a project in Microsoft Project. 335

Sufficient (information) Adequate information to perform the task. 30

SUM A shorthand way of summing the values in a set of Excel cells using a function built in to the program. 94

Supervised data mining A form of data mining in which data miners develop a model prior to the analysis and apply statistical techniques to data to estimate values of the parameters of the model. 270

Supplier relationship management (SRM) A business process for managing all contacts between an organization and its suppliers. 244

Supply chain A network of organizations and facilities that transforms raw materials into products delivered to customers. 243

Supply chain management An information system that integrates the primary inbound logistics business activity. 244

Support activities In Michael Porter's value chain model, the activities that contribute indirectly to value creation—procurement, technology, human resources, and the firm's infrastructure. 64, 231

Sustained competitive advantage The development of people and procedures that are well supported by the underlying technology. 72

Sustaining technologies Changes in technology that maintain the rate of improvement in customer value. 68

Switch A special-purpose computer that receives and transmits data across a network. 198

Switching costs The process of locking in customers by making it difficult or expensive for them to switch to another product. 70

Symmetric digital subscriber lines (SDSL) DSL lines that have the same upload and download speeds. 207

System conversion The process of *converting* a business activity from the old system to the new. 320

System definition phase The first phase in the SDLC, in which developers, with the help of eventual users, define the new system's goals and scope, assess its feasibility, form a project team, and plan the project. 315

Systems analysis The process of creating and maintaining information systems, sometimes called *systems development.* 315

Systems analysts Information systems professionals who understand both business and technology. They are active throughout the systems development process and play a key role in moving the project from conception to conversion and, ultimately, maintenance. Systems analysts integrate the work of the programmers, testers, and users. 316, 345

Systems development The process of creating and maintaining information systems. It is sometimes called *systems analysis and design.* 314

Systems development life cycle (SDLC) The classic process used to develop information systems. These basic tasks of systems development are combined into the following phases: system definition, requirements analysis, component design, implementation, and system maintenance (fix or enhance). 314

Table Also called a *file*, a group of similar rows or records in a database. 137

Tailor made (software) Software adapted to a particular organization's needs. 120

Technical feasibility One of four dimensions of feasibility. 316

Technical safeguards Safeguards that involve the hardware and software components of an information system. 373

Terabyte (TB) 1024 gigabytes. 112

Test plan Groups of sequences of actions that users will take when using the new system. 320

Thick client A software application that requires programs other than just the browser on a user's computer—that is, that requires code on both a client and server computers. 122

Thin client A software application that requires nothing more than a browser and can be run on only the user's computer. 122

Timely information Information that is produced in time for its intended use. 30

Total quality management (TQM) A business process improvement method focused on improving quality. 32

Transaction processing system (TPS) An information system that supports operational decision making. 35

Transmission control program/Internet protocol (TCP/IP) Provides definition and specification of the network layers. 208

Transmission media Physical media, such as copper cable and optical fibre (glass fibre) cable, or wireless media transmitting light or radio frequencies (including cellular and satellite systems) which transmit electronic signals. 197

Triple bottom line A concept that expands the notion of traditional financial reports, which are based solely on financial performance, to take into account ecological and social performance. 358

Tunnel A virtual, private pathway over a public or shared network from the VPN client to the VPN server. 213

Unauthorized data disclosure Can occur because of human error when someone inadvertently releases data in violation of policy, or when employees unknowingly or carelessly release proprietary data to competitors or the media. 370

Unified Modelling Language (UML) A series of diagramming techniques that facilitates OOP development. UML has dozens of different diagrams for all phases of system development. UML does not require or promote any particular development process. 158

Uniform resource locator (URL) A document's address on the web. URLs begin on the right with a top-level domain, and, moving left, include a domain name and then are followed by optional data that locates a document within that domain. 204

Unix An operating system developed at Bell Labs in the 1970s. It has been the workhorse of the scientific and engineering communities since then. 117

Unshielded twisted pair (UTP) cable A type of cable used to connect the computers, printers, switches, and other devices on a LAN. A UTP cable has four pairs of twisted wire. A device called an *RJ-45 connector* is used to connect the UTP cable into NIC devices. 198

Unstructured decision A type of decision for which there is no agreed-on decision-making method. 36

Unsupervised data mining A form of data mining whereby the analysts do not create a model or hypothesis before running the analysis. Instead, they apply the data-mining technique to the data and observe the results. With this method, analysts create hypotheses after the analysis to explain the patterns found. 270

Value chain A network of value-creating activities. 63

Vertical market application Software that serves the needs of a specific industry. Examples of such programs are those used by dental offices to schedule appointments and bill patients, those used by auto mechanics to keep track of customer data and customers' automobile repairs, and those used by parts warehouses to track inventory, purchases, and sales. 119

Virtual private network (VPN) A WAN connection alternative that uses the internet or a private internet to create the appearance of private point-to-point connections. In the IT world, the term *virtual* means something that appears to exist that does not exist in fact. A VPN usually uses the public internet to create the appearance of a private connection. 213

Virus A computer program that replicates itself; unchecked replication is like computer cancer, by which ultimately the virus consumes the computer's resources. Many viruses also take unwanted and harmful actions. 124

Volatile (memory) Data that will be lost when the computer or device is not powered. 113

Warm sites Remote processing centres that have some equipment that may be used in the event that an organization loses its primary computing facility. Readiness is somewhere between a *Cold site* and a *Hot site.* 386

Waterfall method A sequence of nonrepetitive phases. 322

Web 2.0 The term used to describe applications and platforms on the web. 291

Web crawler A software program that browses the web in a very methodical way. 214, 291

Web storefront In ecommerce, a web-based application that enables customers to enter and manage their orders. 283

Wide area network (WAN) A network that connects computers located at different geographical locations. 197

Windows An operating system designed and sold by Microsoft. It is the most widely used operating system. 117

Wireless NIC (WNIC) Devices that enable wireless networks by communicating with wireless *access points.* Such devices can be cards that slide into the PCMA slot or they can be built-in, onboard devices. WNICs operate according to the 802.11 protocol. 200

Workbook A collection of worksheets in Microsoft Excel. 81

Workflow A process or procedure by which content is created, edited, used, and disposed. 196

Worksheet The basic structure of a spreadsheet in Microsoft Excel. 81

Worm A virus that propagates itself using the internet or some other computer network. Worm code is written specifically to infect another computer as quickly as possible. 124

Worth its cost (information) When an appropriate relationship exists between the cost of information and its value. 30

Zachman framework Conceived by John Zachman at IBM in the 1980s, it divides systems into two dimensions, one based on six reasons for communication (*what*—data, *how*—function, *where*—network, *who*—people, *when*—time, *why*—motivation), and the other based on stakeholder groups (planner, owner, designer, builder, implementer, and worker). The intersection of these two dimensions helps to provide a relatively holistic view of the enterprise. 350

Zombies Subsequent computers infected with the worm or virus that infected an initial computer. 124

Index